PEOPLE OF INDIA

WEST BENGAL

Volume XXXXIII

Part Two

PEOPLE OF INDIA

NATIONAL SERIES

VOL. I	PEOPLE OF INDIA	AN INTRODUCTION
VOL. II	PEOPLE OF INDIA	THE SCHEDULED CASTES
VOL. III	PEOPLE OF INDIA	THE SCHEDULED TRIBES
VOL. IV	PEOPLE OF INDIA	ALL COMMUNITIES
VOL. V	PEOPLE OF INDIA	ALL COMMUNITIES
VOL. VI	PEOPLE OF INDIA	ALL COMMUNITIES
VOL. VII	PEOPLE OF INDIA	IDENTITY, ECOLOGY, SOCIAL ORGANIZATION ECONOMY, DEVELOPMENT PROCESS AND LINKAGES : A QUANTITATIVE PROFILE
VOL. VIII	PEOPLE OF INDIA	COMMUNITIES. SEGMENTS. SYNONYMS. SURNAMES AND TITLES
VOL. IX	PEOPLE OF INDIA	LANGUAGES AND SCRIPTS
VOL. X	PEOPLE OF INDIA	THE BIOLOGICAL VARIATIONS IN INDIAN POPULATIONS
VOL. XI	PEOPLE OF INDIA	AN ANTHROPOLOGICAL ATLAS

STATES SERIES

VOL. XII	ANDAMAN AND NICOBAR ISLANDS
VOL. XIII	ANDHRA PRADESH
VOL. XIV	ARUNACHAL PRADESH
VOL. XV	ASSAM
VOL. XVI	BIHAR
VOL. XVII	CHANDIGARH
VOL. XVIII	DADRA AND NAGAR HAVELI
VOL. XIX	DAMAN AND DIU
VOL. XX	DELHI
VOL. XXI	GOA
VOL. XXII	GUJARAT
VOL. XXIII	HARYANA
VOL. XXIV	HIMACHAL PRADESH
VOL. XXV	JAMMU AND KASHMIR
VOL. XXVI	KARNATAKA
VOL. XXVII	KERALA
VOL. XXVIII	LAKSHADWEEP
VOL. XXIX	MADHYA PRADESH
VOL. XXX	MAHARASHTRA
VOL. XXXI	MANIPUR
VOL. XXXII	MEGHALAYA
VOL. XXXIII	MIZORAM
VOL. XXXIV	NAGALAND
VOL. XXXV	ORISSA
VOL. XXXVI	PONDICHERY
VOL. XXXVII	PUNJAB
VOL. XXXVIII	RAJASTHAN
VOL. XXXIX	SIKKIM
VOL. XXXX	TAMIL NADU
VOL. XXXXI	TRIPURA
VOL. XXXXII	UTTAR PRADESH
VOL. XXXXIII	WEST BENGAL

PEOPLE OF INDIA

WEST BENGAL

Volume XXXXIII

Part Two

General Editor

K. S. SINGH

Editors

SHEKHAR BANDOPADHYAY

TILAK BAGCHI

R. K. BHATTACHARYA

सत्यमेव जयते

ANTHROPOLOGICAL SURVEY OF INDIA

SEAGULL BOOKS

CALCUTTA 2008

Cover design: Naveen Kishore

ISBN 81 7046 300 9

Published on behalf of ASI by Naveen Kishore
Seagull Books, 26 Circus Avenue
Kolkata 700017

Laserset and printed by Helios Designworks at
EC-32 Salt Lake, Calcutta 700 064

Contents

Contents

A NOTE ON THE SERIES

There exists an information gap on a very large number of communities in India, and whatever information exists on them is scanty or needs to be updated. The Anthropological Survey of India (ASI) launched a project on the People of India on 2 October 1985. The objective of the project was to generate a brief, descriptive anthropological profile of all the communities of India, the impact on them of change and development processes and the links that bring them together. This was on accordance with the objectives of the ASI, established forty-five years ago in December 1945. The ASI has been pursuing bio-cultural research among different population groups from its eighty regional centres, Its objectives gave been redefined in the policy resolution, adopted in 1985, which commits this organisation to a survey of the human surface of India.

The identification of communities and their listing began at an early period of our history, with Manu. Regional lists of communities figured in Sanskrit works. Medieval chronicles contained a description of communities located in various parts of the country. Listings in the colonial period were undertaken on an extensive scale, after 106. The process gathered momentum in course of the censuses from 1881 to 1941. In our compilation of the lists of the communities of India under the People of India project, we drew upon ethnographic surveys, the lists of Scheduled Castes and Scheduled Tribes drawn up by the Government of India, the lists of backward classes prepared by Backward Classes Commissions set up by various state governments, and the list that exists in the Mondal Commission Report, We were able to put together about 6748 communities at the start. This list was taken to the field, tested and checked, and finally 4635 communities were identified and studied.

Unlike surveys in the colonial period, which covered British India and a few princely states, our project covers the whole country, bringing within its ambit also those parts that had not been ethnographically surveyed earlier or where the survey had been done in a perfunctory way, Each state and union territory was treated as an unit of study. It was decided to start with the investigation of the least-known com-

munities, and then move on to a field study of the lesser-known and better-known ones. Investigators for the survey were identified for each area on the basis of their experience and expertise. Teams of investigators of the Survey, as well as local scholars, were set up for each state and union territory to plan the surveys, seek the co-operation of local scholars, generate and evaluate findings, etc., etc. Later, editorial boards consisting of local scholars—one or more of these were nominated as co-editor/s for each local volume—were set up for each state and union territory. We sought the co-operation of the state governments in implementing the project, and this we received in ample measure, particularly from the welfare and backward classes departments of the state governments, local officers of the Census of India, tribal research institutes, university departments of anthropology, the departments of local universities, etc. Local scholars participated enthusiastically in our project as well as in the seminars held by us.

The progress in the investigation and coverage of communities from 2 October 1985 to 31 March 1992 was steady and impressive. We were able to identify, locate and study 4635 communities in all the states and union territories of India, out of the 6748 listed initially. As many as 600 scholars participated in this project, including 197 from 26 institutions. About 100 workshops and rounds of discussions were held in all the states and union territories, and in these about 3000 scholars participated. The investigators spent 26, 510 days in the field, which works out to 5.5 days per community studied in the various states and union territories of India. Our scholars interviewed a large number of people, out of whom we have recorded only the key informants, i.e. 24,951. This works out to about 5 'informed' informants per community. Of the informants, 4,981 were women. Our instruction to the investigators was to study a community at two or three places, and in at least two or three cultural regions into which the larger states of India are divided. Interviews were conducted in connection with the study of the communities in 3581 villages, mostly multi-community villages, and in 1011 towns and cities spread over almost all the districts of India, i.e. 421 districts and 91 cultural regions, We were able, thus, to study on an average a community at about two places. It should be noted that most of the smaller communities could be studied at only one place since they are not located in more than one area.

A major achievement of this project was the preparation of cartographic maps showing the distribution of the communities and the

location where they were studied. About 4000 maps were prepared. Yet another achievement was the visual documentation of the people of India as part of the field operations. About 21,362 photographs were generated, most of them in black and white, and a substantial number in colour, by amateur photographers.

At an early stage of our project in March 1985, we decided to transfer the data to a computer. We were subsequently able to develop probably the first software in the country—and one of the first in the world—in ethnography, in close collaboration with the National Informatics Centre. From 28 May 1988 we started transferring the quantitative data collected in computer format to floppies. Simultaneously, the transfer of descriptive data (abstracts etc.) on to the computer also started at almost all the regional centres. We succeeded in computerising an enormous mass of data, and also in producing the first results of univariate analysis, by March 1990.

The descriptive material, running into 120 manuscript volumes, and the quantified data contained in 257 diskettes, were released on 1 October 1990 by Sri Chimanbhai Mehta, Minister of State for Human Resources Development, in the presence of a distinguished audience in Delhi, for use by scholars at the Nehru Memorial Museum and Library, and at eight regional centres of the ASI.

The phase of more elaborate analysis started in July 1991, in collaboration with the Centre for Ecological Sciences, Indian Institute of Science, Bangalore. This resulted in a voluminous output of analysed data, which have been presented in a comprehensive matrix consisting of the four categories of populations, the constitutional, religious, occupational and locational. These sets of data, together with a map, were released by Shri Arjun Singh, Minister of Human Resources Development, on 24 December 1991. The last workshop on the People of India project was held at the Indian Institute of Social and Economic Change in Bangalore, where the preliminary results of the analysis presented by the ASI were discussed by distinguished scholars.

It should by noted that the study of the communities has been conducted in 3581 villages and 1011 towns situated in 421 districts of the States and Union Territories of India. The information was collected from about 25,000 of the 'learned' informants by our scholars, 500 of them, over the period 1985 to 1992. Therefore, the observations to this limited time frame and to the universe of the ethnographic project titled People of India. The percentages relate strictly to the responses made by the informants to the questionnaire contained in

munities, and then move on to a field study of the lesser-known and better-known ones. Investigators for the survey were identified for each area on the basis of their experience and expertise. Teams of investigators of the Survey, as well as local scholars, were set up for each state and union territory to plan the surveys, seek the co-operation of local scholars, generate and evaluate findings, etc., etc. Later, editorial boards consisting of local scholars—one or more of these were nominated as co-editor/s for each local volume—were set up for each state and union territory. We sought the co-operation of the state governments in implementing the project, and this we received in ample measure, particularly from the welfare and backward classes departments of the state governments, local officers of the Census of India, tribal research institutes, university departments of anthropology, the departments of local universities, etc. Local scholars participated enthusiastically in our project as well as in the seminars held by us.

The progress in the investigation and coverage of communities from 2 October 1985 to 31 March 1992 was steady and impressive. We were able to identify, locate and study 4635 communities in all the states and union territories of India, out of the 6748 listed initially. As many as 600 scholars participated in this project, including 197 from 26 institutions. About 100 workshops and rounds of discussions were held in all the states and union territories, and in these about 3000 scholars participated. The investigators spent 26, 510 days in the field, which works out to 5.5 days per community studied in the various states and union territories of India. Our scholars interviewed a large number of people, out of whom we have recorded only the key informants, i.e. 24,951. This works out to about 5 'informed' informants per community. Of the informants, 4,981 were women. Our instruction to the investigators was to study a community at two or three places, and in at least two or three cultural regions into which the larger states of India are divided. Interviews were conducted in connection with the study of the communities in 3581 villages, mostly multi-community villages, and in 1011 towns and cities spread over almost all the districts of India, i.e. 421 districts and 91 cultural regions, We were able, thus, to study on an average a community at about two places. It should be noted that most of the smaller communities could be studied at only one place since they are not located in more than one area.

A major achievement of this project was the preparation of cartographic maps showing the distribution of the communities and the

location where they were studied. About 4000 maps were prepared. Yet another achievement was the visual documentation of the people of India as part of the field operations. About 21,362 photographs were generated, most of them in black and white, and a substantial number in colour, by amateur photographers.

At an early stage of our project in March 1985, we decided to transfer the data to a computer. We were subsequently able to develop probably the first software in the country—and one of the first in the world—in ethnography, in close collaboration with the National Informatics Centre. From 28 May 1988 we started transferring the quantitative data collected in computer format to floppies. Simultaneously, the transfer of descriptive data (abstracts etc.) on to the computer also started at almost all the regional centres. We succeeded in computerising an enormous mass of data, and also in producing the first results of univariate analysis, by March 1990.

The descriptive material, running into 120 manuscript volumes, and the quantified data contained in 257 diskettes, were released on 1 October 1990 by Sri Chimanbhai Mehta, Minister of State for Human Resources Development, in the presence of a distinguished audience in Delhi, for use by scholars at the Nehru Memorial Museum and Library, and at eight regional centres of the ASI.

The phase of more elaborate analysis started in July 1991, in collaboration with the Centre for Ecological Sciences, Indian Institute of Science, Bangalore. This resulted in a voluminous output of analysed data, which have been presented in a comprehensive matrix consisting of the four categories of populations, the constitutional, religious, occupational and locational. These sets of data, together with a map, were released by Shri Arjun Singh, Minister of Human Resources Development, on 24 December 1991. The last workshop on the People of India project was held at the Indian Institute of Social and Economic Change in Bangalore, where the preliminary results of the analysis presented by the ASI were discussed by distinguished scholars.

It should by noted that the study of the communities has been conducted in 3581 villages and 1011 towns situated in 421 districts of the States and Union Territories of India. The information was collected from about 25,000 of the 'learned' informants by our scholars, 500 of them, over the period 1985 to 1992. Therefore, the observations to this limited time frame and to the universe of the ethnographic project titled People of India. The percentages relate strictly to the responses made by the informants to the questionnaire contained in

munities, and then move on to a field study of the lesser-known and better-known ones. Investigators for the survey were identified for each area on the basis of their experience and expertise. Teams of investigators of the Survey, as well as local scholars, were set up for each state and union territory to plan the surveys, seek the co-operation of local scholars, generate and evaluate findings, etc., etc. Later, editorial boards consisting of local scholars—one or more of these were nominated as co-editor/s for each local volume—were set up for each state and union territory. We sought the co-operation of the state governments in implementing the project, and this we received in ample measure, particularly from the welfare and backward classes departments of the state governments, local officers of the Census of India, tribal research institutes, university departments of anthropology, the departments of local universities, etc. Local scholars participated enthusiastically in our project as well as in the seminars held by us.

The progress in the investigation and coverage of communities from 2 October 1985 to 31 March 1992 was steady and impressive. We were able to identify, locate and study 4635 communities in all the states and union territories of India, out of the 6748 listed initially. As many as 600 scholars participated in this project, including 197 from 26 institutions. About 100 workshops and rounds of discussions were held in all the states and union territories, and in these about 3000 scholars participated. The investigators spent 26, 510 days in the field, which works out to 5.5 days per community studied in the various states and union territories of India. Our scholars interviewed a large number of people, out of whom we have recorded only the key informants, i.e. 24,951. This works out to about 5 'informed' informants per community. Of the informants, 4,981 were women. Our instruction to the investigators was to study a community at two or three places, and in at least two or three cultural regions into which the larger states of India are divided. Interviews were conducted in connection with the study of the communities in 3581 villages, mostly multi-community villages, and in 1011 towns and cities spread over almost all the districts of India, i.e. 421 districts and 91 cultural regions, We were able, thus, to study on an average a community at about two places. It should be noted that most of the smaller communities could be studied at only one place since they are not located in more than one area.

A major achievement of this project was the preparation of cartographic maps showing the distribution of the communities and the

location where they were studied. About 4000 maps were prepared. Yet another achievement was the visual documentation of the people of India as part of the field operations. About 21,362 photographs were generated, most of them in black and white, and a substantial number in colour, by amateur photographers.

At an early stage of our project in March 1985, we decided to transfer the data to a computer. We were subsequently able to develop probably the first software in the country—and one of the first in the world—in ethnography, in close collaboration with the National Informatics Centre. From 28 May 1988 we started transferring the quantitative data collected in computer format to floppies. Simultaneously, the transfer of descriptive data (abstracts etc.) on to the computer also started at almost all the regional centres. We succeeded in computerising an enormous mass of data, and also in producing the first results of univariate analysis, by March 1990.

The descriptive material, running into 120 manuscript volumes, and the quantified data contained in 257 diskettes, were released on 1 October 1990 by Sri Chimanbhai Mehta, Minister of State for Human Resources Development, in the presence of a distinguished audience in Delhi, for use by scholars at the Nehru Memorial Museum and Library, and at eight regional centres of the ASI.

The phase of more elaborate analysis started in July 1991, in collaboration with the Centre for Ecological Sciences, Indian Institute of Science, Bangalore. This resulted in a voluminous output of analysed data, which have been presented in a comprehensive matrix consisting of the four categories of populations, the constitutional, religious, occupational and locational. These sets of data, together with a map, were released by Shri Arjun Singh, Minister of Human Resources Development, on 24 December 1991. The last workshop on the People of India project was held at the Indian Institute of Social and Economic Change in Bangalore, where the preliminary results of the analysis presented by the ASI were discussed by distinguished scholars.

It should by noted that the study of the communities has been conducted in 3581 villages and 1011 towns situated in 421 districts of the States and Union Territories of India. The information was collected from about 25,000 of the 'learned' informants by our scholars, 500 of them, over the period 1985 to 1992. Therefore, the observations to this limited time frame and to the universe of the ethnographic project titled People of India. The percentages relate strictly to the responses made by the informants to the questionnaire contained in

the schedule guideline and computer format, and to the queries made by the investigators at the places of investigation. The responses have been supplemented with observations of the investigators. The secondary material from the census, ethnographic records etc. The material has been checked and cross-checked by scholars, particularly local scholars, at many levels with other sources of information.

We are presenting the material assembled under the People of India project in two parts which are interrelated. The first consists of the ten-volume national series, five of which contain an abstract on all communities across the length and breadth of the country. The data generated in this respect has been supported with the addition of information from census and other secondary sources. These volumes include two of the Scheduled Castes and Scheduled Tribes, prepared as part of the celebration of Dr B R Ambedkar's birth centenary; three on all the communities of India, and two containing data on the languages and biological structure of Indian populations. The remaining volumes contain description of the quantitative profile, an annotated list of communities and their segments, community-specific languages and the biological structure of the Indian populations.

The second part comprises the State/union territory volumes, with detailed descriptive accounts of each community of India. The contributors to the national volumes on the SC, ST and all communities are listed in the last volume, Volume 6. The Glossary given in Volume 6 is common to all the national volumes. At the end of each account we have given references to the texts from which we have quoted, or references for further reading. This is only illustrative. An exhaustive bibliography appears at the end of the national volumes, in Volume 6.

A consortium of publishers has been set up to publish the material on states and union territories. Seven volumes each for the northern states,, southern states and the islands, the central and western states are being published respectively by M/s Manohar Publishers and Distributors (New Delhi), M/s Affiliated East-West Press Private Limited (Madras) and M/s Popular Prakashan Pvt. Ltd. (Bombay). The eleven volumes on the north-eastern and eastern states are being published by Seagull Books Private Limited (Calcutta), which has already published the introductory national volume, which in its turn is followed by the other national volumes being published by the Oxford University Press.

I trust this series on the People of India which is based on a comprehensive anthropological survey of the country, will be found useful by all sections of our people, including students, researchers, teachers, social activists, administrators and political leaders. I hope we have laid the groundwork for a comprehensive ethnography of the people of India which needs to be continually updated and built upon by successive generations of researchers and scholars.

K. S. SINGH

FOREWORD

I

The peopling of West Bengal in pre-history is still to be reconstructed. The archaeologists have associated the Mundari speaking people with the use of copper hordes, rice cultivation, domestication of plants and animals. A DNA-based study establishes the speakers of the Austro-Asiatic languages as the oldest settlers in this region. It is speculated that the ancient peoples of Vanga and Pundra were Australoid (Chattopadhyay, 2002). The linguists have used place names to reconstruct the pattern of early settlements. In Bengal there are place names of Aryan, non-Aryan (Kol and Dravidian) and Tibeto-Burman origin. In the old Bengal inscriptions dating back from 5th century AD We have several Bengali words like *jola*, *joli*, *jota* etc., which are of Dravidian or Kol origin. The words *kunda* and *kundi* are connected with the Telugu word, *konda* which means hill, rock etc., and are used as suffix in many place names. The words *daba* or *da* are common second part or suffix to many place names which are Austric in origin (cf. Munda, *da* water); place names ending in *ra* are found plentiful all over Bengal, having some connection with the Dravidian word *vada* or Kol word *orak*. The place name *camunda* or *gomunda* preserve the word *munda* which is an Austric word. There are other Austric words like *kol* or *kola* , *bira*, a Santali word meaning forest. The word *co* or *cu* meaning water, are of Tibeto-Burman origin. Some place names show duplication of the same word like Bajbaj, Dumdum etc., which are obviously non-Aryan in origin. Recently Calcutta has been de-anglicised and renamed Kolkata, after one of the three villages which formed the nucleus of the city. It is not certain whether Calcutta or Kolkata as a place name is anyway related to the tribal Munda word *kol*. There are place names like Baranda and Rarh in Munda Jharkhand; Baranda is associated with a *bonga*.

In the early Sanskrit texts dating back to the sixth century BC, there is a reference to a territory called Banga, which means a riverine, low-lying, flood-prone terrain (personal correspondence with Prof. S. K. Sen).

According to some scholars the word Bengal which is not known by this name before the Muslim conquest, emerged during the medieval period. The English name, Bengal, and its Portuguese form Bengala, were both derived, not from Vanga, as is generally supposed, but from Vangala which the Muslim rulers adopted as the name of the province.

Vangala in the form of Bangalah was the name adopted by the Muslim rulers from the 12th century. Abul-i-Fazl says that the original name of Bangalah was Bang. Its former rulers raised mounds ten yards in length and twenty yards in breadth throughout the province which were called *al* (embankment) from this suffix the name Bangalah took its rise. Some modern writers derive Vangala from Vangalaya, i.e. Vangallay or home of the Vanga appear probable or reasonable. The name Vangala might have been derived from *vanga* as Upavanga undoubtedly was, perhaps to denote a separate unit of Vanga. In fact the word Vangala never disappeared; it figures in the Nesari plates (805 A.D.) of Rashtrakuta Govinda III which speaks of Dharma and Dharmapala as a king of Vangala.

A later Tirumalai inscription (1025 A. D.) of Rajendra Chola speaks of Govindchandra as the lord of Vangala-desh. From Vanga to Vangala and to Bengal in the anglicised form, it was a natural course of development of the nomenclature. The Pala rulers also called themselves lord of Gauda which has a threefold connotation. Gauda is the name of the capital city, the name of Bengal or North Bengal and the name of the whole of north India.

The word Gauda is not derived from the word *gud* or jaggery found in Haryana in North India, but probably from the *gaur* which means a bison which was native to and roamed about the terrain. The place Gauda became sufficiently important to determine the twofold classification of Brahmans into Panch Gaud and Panch Dravid, the dividing line being food habit. The Panch Gaud are supposed to be non-vegetarian. However the People of India (POI) project shows that except the hill Brahmans and eastern Brahmans who are non-vegetarians, most of the Brahman groups of north India are vegetarian; the Dravidian Brahmans are strictly non-vegetarian.

From the earliest historical times till the sixth-seventh century AD ancient Bengal was divided into a number of tribal formations (*janapadas*) such as Pundrabardhana, Radh, Suhma, Bajra or Brahman, Tamralipti, Samatat, Banga and so on, the main ones being Bango (now Bangladesh), Radh i.e. western part and Barendra or northern part of modern West Bengal. These regions have been in a flux, their boundaries constantly shifting.

It was in the early seventh century under king Sasanka (AD 595-621) of Gauda that western Bengal up to Orissa (or Utkal of olden times) established the political unity of the territory. The process of unification across tribal formations of Bengal under Gauda continued under the Pala and Sena kings (8-13 Century AD). And Bengal emerged as a 'ethnic territory'. The process was fully accomplished after Akbar's conquest of Bengal (1574-75) and the creation of the Bengal *subah* which continually grew in size through the incorporation of the adjoining parts of Bihar and Orissa. The process of territorial expansion of Bengal also continued under the British who had between 1757-1790 gained complete control over its administration. In 1905 the controversial first Partition of Bengal took place when the eastern districts of Chittagong, Dacca and Rajshahi divisions along with the districts of Malda and hill Tippera were separated constituting a new province together with Assam which had been detached from Bengal Presidency. However, this territorial arrangement had to be revoked in 1911 under nationalist pressure. The eastern Bengal districts were again reunited with Bengal proper while linguistically distinct Orissa and Bihar were separated. This continued till the next important change in political geography came with the transfer of power and the second Partition of 1947 with the creation of East Pakistan, with India's independence and with the reorganisation of state in 1956 with the transfer of the Bengali speaking areas from Bihar to West Bengal and which emerged West Bengal in its present shape as a distinct state within the Union of India with the three regions, North Bengal, Radh Bengal, and South and Lower Bengal.

Bengal was a multi-ethnic region in the ancient period. There are references to many communities such as Vangas, Pundras, Suhmas and Radhas, Gaudas and Gaudiyas, all named after the territories, There were two typical Bengali castes: Ambashta or Kayastha and Vaidya. The Pala army consisted of local people and also of foreigners such as Odras, Hunas, Khasas, Kulikas, Karnatas, Malavas and Latas. The *Brihadharampuran* gives us the ethnic profile of Bengal before the Muslim conquest. This *puran* speaks of three groups of people, viz., (i) group of twenty good mixed castes (*uttam sankarah*), (ii) twelve *madhyama* or intermediate mixed castes and (iii) eight *antyajas* or outcastes. The interesting point noted that all the castes are referred to as mixed castes because of the prevalence of *anuloma* and *pratiloma* forms of marital union. Most of the castes mentioned in the Puran are like modern castes. *Kalika Puran* of the tenth century speaks of various practices of worship and propitiation of the deities adopted by various castes.

In fact Bengal presents an interesting example of establishment of Brahminical system in a somewhat non-Brahminical milieu which has been discussed by Nihar Ranjan Ray and others. The *varna* system of Bengal which could be described as a frontier region during the period was more flexible than in other parts of India till at least the period or

Sena-Barman hegemony began. During the Sena-Barman period Bengal witnessed a formalization of *varna-jati* social organisation. Albeit, some marriages are recorded along *varna* lines emerged, *sankara-jatis* and sizable sections of tribal population and original derivatives still remained outside the *varna-jati* social order. The picture of early medieval Bengal that we derived mainly form the *Mangalkavyas* indicated the existence of a segmented society, but not of a rigidly segregated conservative society. *Varna Ratnakara* of Mithila speaks of *bhadra* and *mand jatis* among Hindus. There were no Kshatriyas or substantial Rajput castes. Even after the Muslim conquest, the Kayasthas as semi independent chiefs called *bhuinyas* ruled twelve kingdoms. Even now there has been greater social flexibility in Bengal, as suggested by POI study, which will be discussed later.

In the medieval period Bengal became a separate Mughal Subah as mentioned above and the Muslim emerged as a dominant community largely as a result of conversion from the Hindus. The old theory of conversion stressed the oppression and unequality of Hindu system. The various old theories of conversion are now being reconsidered. Religious equality apart, social equality is a modern concept. Focus is shifting to patronage of all classes extended as a result of conversion and other opportunities for advancement. The latter included making land available for cultivation as a result of clearing of forests mediated by Mollas and Maulavis. The availability of land and extension of cultivation directly affected peasants who converted to Islam in larger numbers in parts of Bengal.

Like in other parts of India, Bengal too witnessed rise of syncretism or of blending *sufi* and *bhakti* traditions. Medieval period is marked by rising of neo-Vaishnavism, popular sects like Baul, blending of *vaishnavism*, *shakti* and *sufi* traditions. There was an influx of population groups from the north and the west. Apart from the four-fold divisions of the Muslim, viz., Sayed, Mughal, Pathan and local inhabitants; there were new occupational groups such as the Pithari (cake-seller), Kabari (fish-seller), Rangrej (cloth-dyers). An example of syncretism is the Bengali *san* or Bengali calendar is influenced by Akbar's Tarikh-Ilahi which *inter alia* was influenced by Hijri calendar (Sen, Amartya, 2001) Islam and Muslim rule influenced language, culture, cuisine, couture. The camp is exile set up by Wajid Ali Shah, deposed Nawab of Oudh in Calcutta acted as another centre of diffusion of North Indian music, cuisine and couture. Introduction of *bullion* is another feature of the period which makes the rich class richer.

Minor related developments could be noted during this period. Following the creation of Bengal *subah* Raja Man Singh was appointed Governor. He was instrumental in bringing traders, businessmen, and artisans from Rajasthan to Bengal and carried back the image of Kali from Jessore to Jaipur and established a colony of Bengali Brahman priests in the city of Jaipur.

The second development is about the Marathas called Bargi who plundered Bengal till they were defeated and thrown out by Aliwardi Khan. According to folklore they were also defeated by local chief such as the Raja of Panchkot. The Maratha soldiers were disbanded and the stragglers got mixed up with many castes of Bengal. A Maratha community, Baishya/ Bassi is a least known agricultural and trading community of Purulia. Some Maratha Brahmins also settled in Bardhaman and bear the surname Layek. The local communities bear surnames like Desmukh, Senapati, Tendulkar, Bassi, Adhikari, Sarvadhikari or other names with the suffix Kar, which are still used as a Bengali surname. A second generation Maharashtrian scholar, Sakharam, Ganesh Deshkar (1869-1910) wrote a classic in Bengali *Desher Katha* (1904) which is the story of the freedom struggle.

During the colonial period, pluralism in Bengali society was enhanced by various factors, immigration being the most important of them. Increased trading activities in the seventeenth-eighteenth centuries brought in the European traders. They introduced Christianity in Bengal, mainly among the tribal communities and the lower orders Hindus. With the rise of Calcutta as a capital, a commercial and industrial centre spread along the side of the river Hooghly as well as in the Durgapur-Asansol regions where mining started in big way. This brought in the immigrant labour force from the adjoining areas and different parts of India. Besides labour other communities such as traders, artisans, professionals, poured in.

The colonial period witnessed a social upheaval in the ranks of the *bhadralok* category of the Bengali society with the abolition of *sati*, widow remarriage, education for women and upgradation of the status as far as the *bhadralok* category is concerned. So far as the lower order is concerned widow remarriage and *sati* was a not a problem. Our data also shows that widow remarriage is allowed in 80% of communities.

A major dichotomy among the Muslim communities in Bengal had developed by the nineteenth century between the Urdu speaking *ashraf*, the immigrants divided into ethno stocks such as the Pathan, Afgan, Mughal, etc. and the *atrap* mainly converted Bengali speaking Muslims.

This differentiation both at social, behavioural as well as interactional levels still persists. Dichotomy also developed between Bengali Hindu and Bengali Muslim over politics, economic and agrarian issues, as a result of which cultural distance between the two communities grew and was rationalised in various ways.

The Partition of India in 1947 brought about a major shift in the ethnographic scenario of West Bengal, with the influx of mainly Hindu populations of all classes and castes including the Vaidyas from East Pakistan, now Bangladesh. The Anthropological Survey of India conducted a study of the refugees, in 1957, who occupied Sealdah and Howrah railway station areas, after deserting Bettiah and Mana Camps on the pretext of lack of proper amenities in those camps. These refugees mostly belonged to the Namasudra caste (who were sharecroppers or agricultural labourers), Chhutor (carpenter), Kamar (blacksmith), Kumbhakar (potter), Keot/Kaibarta (fisherman), etc, the lowest rung of the erstwhile East Pakistan society. Many members of the landed aristocracy and service holders belonging to the Brahman, Kayastha, Vaidya etc., castes had crossed over to India in the post-1950 period. The Muslim groups in Bangladesh moved in to fill the vacancies created due to the exodus of the specialised craftsmen and occupational castes. But certain occupations viz. making of Bengali sweets, ayurvedic treatment, weaving of cloth, making of stone pots / plates, pot making etc. The Namasudras emerged in a new role during the partition, as the sword and the shield of the Hindus (personal correspondence with S. K. Mukherjee). In a recent publication (1996) : *Setubandhan (Bridging the Gap*) Annada Sankar Roy describes how the gradual exodus continued from 1948 till date and the Hindu population of Bangladesh dwindled from around 30% in 1947- 48 to around 10% in 2000 and 2001 AD.

West Bengal absorbed the refugees, survived the crises and became socially cohesive. A continuous process of acculturation among all these diverse elements created a composite culture, in which every community retains its distinctive identity as well as borrows the behavioural traits from others and thus effectively supplements and enriches each other.

II

Sir H.H. Risley has been regarded as the architect of colonial ethnography and its chief theorist. Though there was diversity within this ethnographic tradition and other ethnographers like Denizel Ibbetson tried to blaze their own trail. Risley started with the race theory of caste, divided castes into neat racial types—the Aryan, the Dravidian and the

Mongoloid—the higher castes belonging to the Aryan—the intermediate caste ranks of mixed origin and the lower groups mostly consisting of tribal and lower castes. Risley's theo of nasal index stands at the centre of his anthropometry : a man's social status varies in inverse ratio to the width of his nose; the finest nose shall be at the top of the hierarchy and the coarsest at the bottom (Risley, xxxiv). This is not accepted now. As D. D. Kosambi pointed out to the general editor, physical anthropometry gives less reliable result, because nasal index, height and change. Nor is Risley's related view about Aryan or Dravidian as a race acceptable. However his work is still important for ethnographic information on castes and tribes that he collected. Risley focused on hypergamy, female infanticide, child marriage, etc., and linked Indian ethnography with western ethnography, its methodology and the main trends.

In 1896 Jogendra Nath Bhattacharya published his book on *Hindu Castes and Sects*. Prof. Nirmal Kumar Bose who generally frowned upon the survey of castes commended it as a piece of authentic research in a fond foreword to the second edition (1968). Bhattacharya's work was however both Bengal specific and pan-Indian based largely on secondary source materials and his own observations.

Scholars in Bengal recognised from the beginning the fact that Bengal was the meeting place of Aryan, non-Aryan, and Mongolian races Kshitimohan Sen in *Bengali Sadhana* (1352 B.S.) argued that Bengal had many striking resemblance with the Dravidian culture. He particularly mentioned similarities in house types, concept of *mangal* (the auspicious), *amangal* (the inauspicious), *mritachar* (death rite), *desachar* (country rite), *lokachar* (folk rite), puberty rites, sending of marital gifts to bride's house and maternal uncle's role in birth and marriage ceremonies between Bengal and Kerala (to which we might add Karnataka).

Nagendra Nath Vasu produced eight volumes of ethnography in Bengali on castes and sects of Bengal under the title *Banger Jatio Itihas* in 1936. According to the scholars who have read the book, it is based on the genealogies (*panjis*) maintained by the genealogists (*panjikar*) and Vasu's own considerable field work. The description of the castes and sects are said to be more extensive than those available in colonial ethnography.

The publication of what may be described as a trilogy, Kshitimohan Sen's *Bangali Hindur Barnabhed*, Nihar Ranjan Ray's *Bangalir Itihas : Adi Parva* and N. K. Bose's *Hindu Samajer Garan*, around 1949, was an event of considerable significance in reconstructing the social history of Bengal. All these three works concerned essentially with historical themes, used in varying manner, the anthropological material and techniques, bringing together ethnology and indology. Ray's work has been admirably translated into English by John. W. Hood (1994). Ray analyses the land, economic life, caste patterns, village and towns, terracotta temples, religious thoughts and practices as well as the class pattern of the Bengali people from the social historical point of view in the ancient period. It was a history of the people from below. The chapter 'every day life' has discussed the history of the ordinary people. Ray also shows that Brahmanism in Bengal existed from the fifth century onwards and Brahman and Sudra were the only two *varnas* that existed in Bengal. He came to the conclusion that even in the day of Buddhist influence in Bengal it was the code set by Brahmanism that had deep and pervasive influence on the life of the Bengali people. However the small cultures maintained a degree of autonomy and still survive. Ray discusses at length the influence of Buddhism and non-Brahminical system in Bengali surnames, humanism, relative weakness of caste, gender equality (in *tantra*), *Dayabhag* school of jurisprudence which regulates right of wife's right in property. etc. Ray's analysis of Hindu society ends with ancient period.

Bose brings together a number of perspectives in the formation of Hindu society based on the materials taken from the writings of Sarat Chandra Ray, his own investigation and the classical literature on caste. The prologue contains probably the first social literary account of the Jharkhand taken from *Srisrichaitanyacharitamrita*. The book incorporated Boses' own study of the Telis, family history of the Sinha's of Raipur and the excellent account of the social movements among the Jogis, Namsudras and Muslims. Bose has shown the power and influence of the Aryan Brahmanical system including the *varna* sub-system to mould the societies lying away from the main castes of Sanskritic culture. He also emphasized the role of economic factor in the cultural integration of tribes into the larger society. The translation of Chhimohan Sen work was not available, but another important book, Dinesh Chandra Sen's *Brihat Banga* published in 1935, was an exercise in reconstructing history from below.

III

Bengal was extensively surveyed in physical anthropology. Mujumdar and Rao (1960) in their well known treatise entitled 'Race Elements in Bengal' carried forward the work on ethnic typology and suggested that Bengal does have a brachycephalic element although there are more mesocephalis than brachycephals. The bulk of the population which is constituted of lower castes is long headed, particularly the tribal and the semi-tribal elements, belonging to the Proto-Australoid or Australoid race elements. The high castes who have been derived from the migrants from the north west and the Uttar Pradesh are also long headed. The Mongoloid elements of Bengal are both long headed and round headed. The original population of Bengal was akin to the Khasi of Assam as far as cephalic index is concerned. The Maratha element has made a dent in the Bengalee racial type during the predatory and organised raids into Bengal popularly known as the 'intrusion of the Bargees'. The same view could apply to the hoe cultivating people. The higher castes in Bengal (undivided) are composed of the Mediterranean people. The lower castes and tribes represented by the Bagdi, the Bauri and the Santal are definitely of the Proto-Austroloid racial origin. The Koch and the Rajbanshi represent a mixed population between the Proto–Austroloids and the Mongoloids types. A strong Mediterranean influence is noticed, among the Tibetan and Burmese in the south of Bengal in the deltaic region which could be traced to Portuguese infiltration. The Negrito element will remain a myth unless more definite evidence is available. The social history of Bengal, replete with accounts of race consciousness, hypergamy and ***kulinism,*** has secured some semblance of racial purity in the higher rank of Bengali caste structure. The bulk of the population of Bengal is of mixed origin. Yet they constitute a homogeneity and a type today which distinguishes them from the people of other states. In short excluding the few foreign elements, the race elements in Bengal are (i) the Mediterranean, (ii) the Proto-Austroloid and (iii) the Mongoloid both of Tibetan and Burmese type, with occasional pockets of brachycephals who do not form the mass of the population even among the higher castes.

We decided to introduce the All India Anthropometric Survey under the auspices of the People of India Project in West Bengal in order to maintain uniformity in our findings and fill some gaps left uncovered by earlier surveys. Our survey revealed that people of West Bengal are below medium in stature, have round head and face with medium nose. However when data from published literature are scanned, lot of variations are noticed. The non-tribals vary from short statured to above medium, have long to round head, long to medium nose and broad to long facial profile. The tribes, speaking Tibeto–Burman languages are short statured, have round head and medium nose. On other hand Austro-Asiatic speaking tribes are short statured, have long to medium head, medium to broad nose and broad face, Muslim communities are below medium in stature, have round head and long nose. Loops (40-66 per cent) preponderate over whorls (39-57 per cent) in all groups except tribes speaking Tibeto-Burman languages where incidence of whorl (52 per cent) is high than loops (46 per cent). Incidence of colour blindness is relatively high in Muslim groups (6 per cent) and tribes speaking Austro-Asiatic languages (5-8 per cent). In other populations it ranges from complete absence to 7 per cent. The frequency of non-taster gene is high in non – tribals (50-70 per cent) than tribal groups (33-64 per cent), whereas incidence of B gene (12-47 per cent) seems to be more common than A gene (11-33 per cent). Likewise r haplotype varies from complete absence in Tibeto-Burman speaking tribes to as high as 15 per cent in Muslim population. Hp shows low incidence in Austro-Asiatic language speaking tribes to as high as 24.36 per cent in tribes speaking Indo-Aryan languages. Other Biochemical traits studied are : Go (69-79 per cent). P^a (16 – 32 per cent). PGM (59-93 per cent), ESD (21-48 per cent), GLD (19-35 per cent)., Ak (90-100 per cent), and PGD^A (82-94 per cent).

IV

The concept of Aryanisation of Bengal has been discussed primarily in terms of spread of the languages of the Indo-Aryan languages family particularly Sanskrit and Bengali, the efflorescence of Bengali language and literature which had an all pervasive impact and which emerged as a marker of Bengali identity. However there were variants of Bengali language and there were other languages which interacted. According to the Prof. Suniti Kumar Chattopadhyay (1926) Bengal is a meeting ground of Indo-Aryan languages (Bengali), Austro-Asiatic branch of Austic family of languages (Mundari, Santali, Ho), Dravidian family of languages (Malto, Oraon) and Tibeto-Burman family of languages and its six different languages. the Indo-Aryan languages are most widely spread. They influenced and they were influenced the languages of other families. It is said that degendering of the Indo-Aryan languages in the east occurred under the influence of Austro-Asiatic family of languages during the sixth to the twelfth century AD.

In all, forty one languages are spoken in West Bengal. The languages are: Arabic, Armenian, Asuri, Bengali, Bhojpuri, Bhotia, Birhor, Birjia, Bodo/Boro, Chinese, Dhimal, English, Garo, Gujarati, Halam, Hindi, Ho, Khotta, Kudmali, Kurukh/Oraon, Lepcha, Lodha, Magali, Maithili, Malhar,

Malto, Marathi, Marwari, Mundari, Nepali, Oriya, Panchpargania, Paschima, Punjabi, Rajasthani, Sadri, Santali, Sherpa, Telugu, Toto, Urdu.

Bengali is spoken by the largest number of communities (118), followed by Nepali (10), Hindi (9), Oriya (6) Sadri (6), Urdu (5) and Khotta (5). The following seven languages : Asuri, Birhor, Birjia, Ho, Lodha, Mundari and Santali are Austro-Asiatic languages and are spoken by eight communities. Bhotia, Bodo/Boro, Dhimal, Garo, Halam, Lepcha, Sherpa and Toto are the Tibeto-Burman languages and are spoken by nine communities. The Dravidian languages Kurukh, Malhar, Malto and Telugu are spoken by five communities. The Arabic, Armenian, Chinese and English are foreign languages. All other languages belong to the Indo-Aryan family of languages.

According to 1981 census, Bengali is spoken by the largest number of persons (46, 347,935) followed by Hindi (3,627,298), Urdu (1,331,022), Oriya (157,182), Telugu (105,527) Punjabi (75,626) and Gujarati (39,247). There are 747,699 persons who speak Gorkhali/Nepali language. The English language is spoken by 21,232 persons. The other languages spoken are : Arabic (2,446), Bhotia (3,828), Bodo/Boro (22,566), Garo (2,178), Koda/Kora (18,633) Kurukh/Oraon (190,027), Lepcha (4,523), Malto (4,803), Munda (62,845), Mundari (18,235), Rabha (7,620), Santali (1,632,440), Sherpa (1,533), Tamang (2,487), ad Tibetan (3,735).

Bengali speakers are bilingual in Sanskrit (64,263), Hindi (1,471,956), Arabic (22,300), Urdu (44,614), Santali (14,326), Oriya (13,268), English (7, 571), Assamese (2,789), Gujarati (1,022), and Nepali (1,498). Hindi speaker are bilingual in Bengali (521,422), Urdu (16,782), Punjabi (2,405), English (1,913), and Sanskrit (1,267). Urdu speakers are bilingual in Bengali (8,911), Arabic (4,698), Gujarati (26,176) and Hindi (16,616). Telugu speakers are bilingual in Hindi (32,392) and Bengali (4,766). Punjabi speakers are bilingual in Hindi (24,292), Bengali (6,519) and Urdu (526).

Gorkhali/Nepali speakers are bilingual in Hindi (128,172), Bengali (20,472), Tamang (588), Tibetan (537) and Bhotia (510). Arabic speakers are bilingual in Bengali (514). Urdu (164) and Hindi (129). English speakers are bilingual in Hindi (7,161), Bengali (2,808) and Urdu (168). Bhotia speakers are bilingual in Hindi (843), English (248) and Nepali (80). Sherpa speakers are mostly bilingual in Hindi (179). Tibetan speakers are bilingual in Hindi (913) and Nepali (71). Tamang speakers are mostly bilingual in Hindi (289).

The tribes are more bilingual than non-tribals. Santali speakers are bilingual in Bengali (652,086), Hindi (9,211), Urdu (490) and Oriya (483).

Munda speakers are bilingual in Bengali (14,210), Hindi (8,891) and Santali (236). Mundari speakers are bilingual in Bengali (5,086) and Hindi (2,652). Koda/Kora speakers are bilingual in Bengali (8,053) and Santali (101). Kharia speakers are bilingual in Hindi (2,015) and Bengali (822). Ho speakers are mostly bilingual in Bengali (526). Kurukh/Oraon speakers are bilingual in Hindi (33,385) and Bengali (28,602). Malto speakers are mostly bilingual in Bengali (1,365).

Gauda or proto Bengali script which was prevalent from 10th to 14th century AD was derived from Siddhmatrika script. The Bengali script emerged around 15 century. Now Bengali script is most widely used in the state. Apart from the Bengali and Perso-Arabic scripts, minor scripts like Olchiki, Tibetan and U-Med are also in use in West Bengal.

V

Ecology *inter alia* explains the extraordinary range of heterogeneity of traditional social formations including communities, segments, titles, surnames which at one level are derived from the territory. The main communities, Brahman, Kayastha and others have their divisions on a territorial basis and also other components of identity such as segments, surnames and titles. The Brahmans are divided into territorial groups with distinct titles and surnames so as the Kayastha, who are not only divided into broad territorial divisions but also sub-divided into Uttar Radhi and Dakshin Radhi. The sub-groups are further sub-divided into hypergamous units, unequally placed. Our data reports that Bengal has the higher number of social division with hierarchy among 77 communities. Most of the communities see differentiation within themselves at social level (123/60.59 as against national average of 48.39%) followed by differentiation at territorial (44/21.67 as against national average of 11.68%), and occupational (37/18.23% as against national average of 12.60%). Less differentiation is seen at religious level (14/6.90% as against national average of 9.99%), followed by economic (4/1.97% as against national average of 7.49%) and educational levels (1/0.49% as against national average of 3.45%).

The total number of communities studied West Bengal under POI project are 203 communities. One linguistic community (Assamese) has been added and one community (Sikh of Calcutta) has been deleted. However for the purpose of analysis the old data set of 203 communities has been kept intact.

Forty nine communities belong to scheduled caste category (24.14% as against national average of 16.20%) and 28 communities (13.79% as against national average of 13.72%) belong to scheduled tribe category. Rest are other communities.

Most of communities have identified themselves regionally or locally. As many as 58 communities (28.57% as against national average of 14.69%) are identified at national level with Bengali communities settled elsewhere and 10 communities (4.93 per cent as against national average of 2.93%) at transnational level in Bangladesh and other countries. With tradition of strong ethnography in Bengali life in maintaining genealogy and *panji* for family, most of the communities 142 (69.95% as against national average of 62.05%) have ethnographic, accounts, 48 communities have been mentioned in *jati purana* (23.65% as against national average of 16.89%) and 81 communities of them have historical references (39.90% as against national average of 38.42%).

The state is divided into three cultural zones. North Bengal (or old Barendra) includes the districts of Darjeeling, Jalpaiguri, Malda, Cooch Behar and West Dinajpur. The Radh Bengal includes the plateau regions of Bankura, Purulia, Birbhum parts of Midnapur, Burdwan, Hooghly and Murshidabad districts. Southern Radh now includes the South and Lower Bengal includes the Gangetic plains of Howrah, Calcutta, 24 Parganas (North & South), Nadia parts of Hooghly, Barddhaman, Medinipur and Murshidabad districts.

We may now discuss regionwise distribution of communities. In North Bengal, as tea plantation is a major industry, it has attracted immigrants as well as brought in population from outside on persuasion. The tea plantation areas in the mountains have Nepali as the predominant immigrant groups besides the Lepcha, Bhutia and Sherpa as local inhabitants. The tea estates of the Terai region have relatively heterogenous population coming from Madhya Pradesh, Bihar and Orissa and are often known by a single term 'Modesia'. A part of this immigrant group comprises tribes such as the Munda, Oraon, Santal, Kisan, Nagasia, Asur, Birjia and Ho. The Rabha, Mech, Toto, Garo and Rajbanshi are also found exclusively in North Bengal.

The Radh region has Mundari speaking population which includes the Munda, Santal, Kora, Birhor and Mahali. Communities like the Lodha, Pahariya, Kharia (hill), Savara are also present in the plateau region. The Sarak who once professed Jainism, the Baishya, Let, Bhalla, Kunui and Bauri are mainly concentrated in this region.

The Southern and Lower Bengal has larger population of the Pod, Keora, Namasudra, Kotal, Bahelia, Pasi, Bagdi, Jhalo Malo, Barujibi and Tambuli. Kapali, Byadha and Hela are found only in this region. Subarna

Banik, one of the traditional business communities have their largest concentration in this region. The Kalwar Karan, Raju, Khandait, Kela, Kakmara (semi-nomadic migrated from Andhra Pradesh) and a small community of Portuguese are concentrated in this region. Calcutta, the only metropolis of eastern India, has attracted communities like the Gujarati, Punjabi, Bihari, Maharastrians, Marwari, South Indians and also Anglo Indians, Armenian and Chinese.

There has been a clear pattern in the migration of communities in the post-Partition West Bengal. As many as 131 communities (64.53% as against national average of 59.98%) recall having migrated to their present habitat; 87 communities (42.86% as against national average of 40.93%) recall their migration in their oral tradition and as many as 15 communities (7.39% as against national average of 8.76%) claim to have migrated in recent years. The tempo of migration has slowed down.

All climatic zones of the state are inhabited, the most prominent being the warm and temperate zone (90/48.77% as against national average of 47.70%) followed by moderate (89/43.84% as against national average of 39.98%) and cold zones (19/9.36%). The plains account for the largest concentration of communities (161/79.31% as against national average of 61.38%) followed by plateau (38/18.72% as against national average of 17.35%) hilly terrain (21/10.34%), valley (12/5.91% as against national average of 5.09%) high altitude (7/3.45% as against national average of 2.20%) and coastal regions (5/2.46%).

Of the 203 communities in West Bengal under the project POI, as many as 140 communities constituting 70.0% live in rural areas; 18 communities (8.9%) live in urban areas and about 38 communities (18.7%) inhabit rural / urban settings.

The major general communities of West Bengal and their approximate population according to the 1931 Census are as follows: Mahishya 20,75,840; Brahman 14,47,691; Kayastha / Karan / Prabhu 6,76,654; Sadgop 5,50,813; Tanti 3,10,805. However the census figure of the major scheduled castes as per 1981 census are Rajbanshi 22,58,760; Namasudra 16,92,233; Pod/Poundra 15,36,197; Bagdi 18,31,565; Chamar, Mochi etc. 7,11,024; Bauri 7,32,205; Jalia Kaibartta 3,18,344; Dhoba/Dhobi 2,51,737; Dom/Dhangad 2,31,595. The scheduled tribes are Santal 16,66,610; Oraon 4,37,574; Bhumij/Bhumiji 2,33,906; Munda 2,30,016.

Some of the indigenous communities of West Bengal include the Brahman, Kayastha/ Karan /Prabhu, Mahishya, Bagdi, Rajbanshi and Namasudra, while the immigrant communities include the Bihari, Chinese Gujarati, and Jew/ Bene Israel. The minorities in the state are Anglo-

Indian, Bihari, Jew/ Bene Israel and Sikhs. The Lodha is a denotified community while Anglo-Indian is a typical example of a miscegenated group. The service castes/ communities which extend specialised service are Baidya, Brahman, Nai/ Napit, Bhat, and Jogi/ Jugi to mention a few. The non-pastoral nomadic communities in the state are Kakmara and Nat.

Let us now discuss communities according to their occupations—traditional and modern. The Birhor, Chik Barak, Chirimar, Kharia, and Birjia are some of the examples of the communities whose traditional occupation centred around hunting, gathering, trapping/catching of birds and animals. The Gurung and the Limbu are the traditional terrace-cultivators while the Mech have nowadays discontinued their traditional occupation of shifting cultivation. The peasant communities of West Bengal are the Aguri (Ugra Kshatriya), Angarosk, Bhuimali, Chasa Dhoba, Khen, Mahishya, Paliya, Sadgop, Kisan, Chasot and so on, the communities engaged in fishing are Bagdi, Jalia Kaibarta, Jhalo Malo, Kondara/Kandara/ Kandra, Keora/Kewra, Kewat/Keyot/ Keot, and Namasudra. The Ahir and Goala are the example of the communities whose traditional occupation is pastoralism. The communities engaged in business and trade include Bohra, Gujarati, Subarna Banik, Jew/ Bene Israel, Sikh and Parsi. The communities like the Bauri, Ghasi, Kalal, Keora, Kharia and so on by and large are unskilled labourers. The communities like the Chero, Hela, Lalbegi, Patni are involved in unorganised services.

West Bengal has an indigenous category of artisans called *nabasankh*, which comprises Gandha Banik, Napit, Tambuli, a section of Kumhar and such other castes that are considered ritually clean (that is from whom the Brahman can accept water). These *nabasankh* castes are ritually superior to the artisan castes such as the Kamar (blacksmith), Chhutor (carpenter), Tanti (weaver) and others. In the Western part of West Bengal (in Purulia and the neighbouring districts) these *nabasankhs* are called by the term 'Lob Sena' giving a mythological touch to the ritual status. However, in the rural areas (of the above region) the related positions in the local caste hierarchy and the exact ritual status of the *nabasankh* groups remains controversial. The major artisan communities in the state include the Dom (basket maker), Kamar (black-smith and metal worker), Kansari (bell metal worker), Kumbhar/Kumhar (potter), Mahali (basket-maker), Malakar (manufacturer of exquisite ornament and decoration of *sola*), Malhar (*dokra* art and tattooing), Mali (garland maker), Muchi/ Chamar (footwear maker and leather worker), Sutradhar (carpenter),

Swarnakar (goldsmith) etc. The occupation of Kunni, Pan, Tanti is textile weaving.

Territorial endogamy is a unique feature of Old Bengal. In West Bengal many of the Hindu communities have territorial segments viz. Radhi, Barendra, Panchakoti, Banga and so on. Many segments have been subsegmented. For example, Kulin has been further subdivided into Kulin, Banga Kulin and so on, while Radhi have been divided into Uttar and Dakshin Radhi. The root of this practice lay in the inaccessibility of the territories divided by rivers and hills. Now with the improvement of communication this practice is breaking down.

Similarly a unique feature of the eastern part of the Indian subcontinent including Bangladesh and Assam is the proliferation of endogamous units within the large occupation group with sub-occupational differentiation. For example the artisans are broadly divided into two endogamous groups of those who manufacture and those who sell. This may probably be due to the fact that land is now available for reclamation and cultivation, and agrarian castes and artisan groups dependent on them took advantage of this opportunity to expand, evolve and involve.

Name and surname is an indication of identity and status. In ancient Bengal according to *Manusanghita* and *Brihadharmpuran* the Brahmans used the surname Sharma or Dev Sharma; Kshatriyas used Burman or Roy Burman; Vaishyas used Bhuti while Sudras used the surname of Das. In Bengal before the advent of Chaitanya Dev, the Brahmanical surnames became the symbol of social aristocracy. According to *Bangalir Samajik Itihaser Bhumika* (1974) by Prof. S. Chattopadhyay before the 5th century we have come across surnames like Mitra, Dutta, Dhara etc., which exhibit the influence of Buddhist era. The various forms of Upadhyay like Mukhopadhyay, Bandyopadhyay etc. come in much later period and the name is by and large derived from the name of the villages. The family surnames was seriously changed when the British Government passed Affidavit Act., 1875. In West Bengal many peoples use titles as surnames. Sarkar, Majhi, Mandal, Singhas, Samanta, Chakraborty, Roy, Majumdar, Choudhury, Pandit, Shastri etc., are some of the titles used as surname. The surnames which are commonly in vogue in West Bengal includes Ghosh, Bose, Dey, Mitra, Das, Dutta, Bandopadhyay, Maity, Dhar, Bagchi, Lahiri. In West Bengal most interesting feature is the presence of composite surnames like Sengupta, Dasgupta, Duttagupta, Roy Choudhury, Sinha Ray, Mitra Majumdar, Dutta Majumdar, Ghosh Moulik, Das Sharma and so on.

In West Bengal a number of communities take synonyms either to sanskritise their name or to link up their name with traditional occupations or in order to raise their status in regional social hierarchy simply by adopting synonyms with or without formulation of any myth. Thus we have Ugra Kshatriya, Malla Kshatriya, Byagra Kshatriya and Poundra Kshatriya are the synonym of Aguri, Mal, Bagdi and Pod respectively. Similarly Bhat Brahman is the synonym of the Bhat, Baisya Behara is the synonym of Daoi. Some synonyms denotes the traditional occupation of the communities. For example, Goala is the synonym of Ahir. The Nuniya, Sat Chasi, Jamadar, Patua, Putli, Bara Tantubai, Jele, Teli, Sabjhiphor, Hele Kaibarta, Phulmali, Chasa, Gandha Banik, Genesh, Jalia Kaibarta, Kalu, Kujra, Mahishya, Mali, Sadgop and Malhar have occupation based synonyms or community names. Some of the synonyms are the sanskritised form of the community name. For example, Barujibi, Kansari and Sankhakara. Some synonyms tell us about their larger affiliation and. Thus we see that Chai Mandal, Kol, Kudmi Mahato, Malla Bagdi, Bagar Nabdak, Chamar are the synonyms of the Chain, Ho, Kudmi, Mete, Nagar and Muchi respectively.

Social divisions exist in 167 communities (82.27% as against the national average of 81.51%) . The exogamous divisions are locally called *bamsha*, *got*, *gotra*, *gusthi*, *kul*, *khunt*, *ru*, and *thar*. Clan organisation is present in as many as 136 communities (67% as against national average of 64.75%). The social divisions mainly regulate marriages (149/73.40%), indicate status (76/37.44%) and descent (72/35.47%).

VI

We may now discuss the cultural traits. As a whole, markers of community identification are less marked in West Bengal in comparison with the national average. Some people however identify themselves by all sorts of markers such as dress, including shawl and turbans; ornaments—body marking and tattooing. Prominent markers of community identification include female dress (13/6.40% as against national average of 13.27%), male dress (9/4.43% as against national average of 12.25%), turban (7/3.45% as against national average of 4.44%), female ornaments (7/3.45% as against national average 6.86%), and female tattooing (4/1.97% as against national average of 1.60%). However *dhoti* or *lungi* and *punjabi* for male and handloom *sari* for women are the traditional dress of most of the Bengali people.

Rice is the staple cereal (202/99.51% as against national average of 88.18%) followed by wheat, a recent entrant (111/54.68% as against national average of 56.70%). Rice is consumed by most communities in West Bengal as it falls in the south east Asian rice eating zone and in the state, rice is mostly taken as of a parboiled variety. Wheat has been introduced in recent years in the diet of average Bengali communities as it is available in fare price (ration) shop and as West Bengal has now become a major wheat producer. Of the pulses *moong* is consumed (191/ 94.09% as against national average of 67.66%) followed by *masur* (190/ 93.60% as against national average of 47.14%), *urad* (159/78.33% as against national average of 68.04%), gram (140/68.97% as against national average of 48.89%). Mustard oil (188/92.61%) is used as cooking by a majority of the communities. Rapeseed oil is also consumed by 30.54% of communities (as against the national average of 6.49%). Like wheat, rapeseed is also consumed by a large segment of communities mainly due to easy availability at fair price (ration) shops.

In spite of a higher value attached to vegetarianism, only nine communities (4.43%) are pure vegetarian. Of them, four (1.97%) abstain from onion and garlic. Incidentally fish is not considered vegetarian in Bengal except among four communities (2.0 against the national average of 2.8 communities). In fact fish is widely considered a non-vegetarian food and in this sense it is a great leveller. Thus in West Bengal most of the communities including the Brahman consume fish. Women are specially vegetarian in only nine communities (4.43 percent as against national average of 12.21%). Most of the communities are regular non vegetarian (175 / 86.21% as against national average of 49.77%) and 25 communities (12.32%) are occasional non-vegetarian. Existence of numerous rivers and other water bodies where the fish are easily available account for the easy availability of fish food. In fact West Bengal now ranks first in the production of fish.

There is little in access to non-vegetarian food are in 119 communities (93.60 percent against the national average of 72.55 per cent), women vegetarian in Bengal are lower than the national average.

Food habit in Bengal have remain stable and there is no marked movement from vegetarianism to non-vegetarianism or vice-versa, as in other parts of the country.

In spite of economic disparities, the consumption of milk and milk products is high (198 / 97.54% as against the national average of 86.47%). In West Bengal sweets made of *chhana* (posset) and sweetened curd are very popular. The world famous sweet *rasogolla* first appeared in Calcutta in 1878, the then capital of British Empire in India, made by Navin Chandra Das. Rabindranath Tagore named a variety of sweetened curd *poyodhi* . The milk culture of Bengal drawn from both soft and dense milk, of cows and buffaloes respectively was once related to the availability of cattle population, particularly the population of cows. Now West Bengal is one of the primary centres of Operation Flood and White Revolution.

Most of the communities consume non-alcoholic drinks like tea, sherbet. (165/81.28% as against national average of 33.79%). Tea culture with milk is later introduced in West Bengal. Many tribals and poor people consume with salt only. Nowadays tea without adding milk and lemon tea is also consumed by many. Alcoholic beverages are occasionally consumed by men in 108 communities (53.20% as against national average of 53.27%) whereas only in 62 communities (30.54% as against national average of 23.86%) alcohol is consumed by men regularly. Alcoholic drinks are occasionally consumed by the women in 93 communities (30.49% as against national average of 22.37%) and regularly consumed by women in 11 communities (3.61% as against national average of 5.01%). In most cases the alcoholic drinks are procured from the market by 163 communities (80.30% as against national average of 66.49%). Smoking of *bidi* (181/89.16%), cigarette (148/72.91%), chewing of tobacco in the form of *khaini*, *gutkha* etc (103/50.74%) and the habit of chewing betel i.e. *pan* (158/ 78.83%) are common in West Bengal. However, use of snuff is limited to members in 44 communities (21.67%). The district of Murshidabad is famous for *bidi* making while Midnapur and Hooghly are particularly famous for the growing of betel leaf.

About other sources of nutrition in Bengali diet consumption of pulses does not show an increase but vegetables are taken on a larger scale, because of the higher production of vegetables. Similarly consumption of fruits shows a rise

Community endogamy is the rule. However intercommunity marriages are reported among members of 33 communities (16.26% as against national average of 23.80%), though it is more extensive in qualitative material. Clan endogamy is generally prohibited but is reportedly practised, sanctioned by *Smiritis*, among members in 18 communities (8.87%), which is higher than national average of 2.31%,. Of various types of exogamy, surname exogamy is very prominent. In West Bengal practice of junior levirate is lower (50/24.63% as against national average of 30.33%) and so is junior sororate (87/42.86% as against national average of 52.04%).

West Bengal reports a high incidence of hypogamy and hypergamy across communities, their segments and varna order which suggests a higher degree of mobility. The incidence of hypergamy is 6.4% (as against national average of 4.44%) while the incidence of hypogamy is 5.91% (as against national average of 2.03%). The general trend is towards equality of hypergamous units and breakdown of sub-group endogamy.

The incidence of consanguinity is very low. Cross-cousin marriages with mother's brother's daughter are reported to be practiced among 36 communities (17.7%), comprising two (4.1%) of scheduled caste, one (3.6%) scheduled tribe and 30 other communities (23.8%) are reported to practice cross cousin marriages with father's sister's daughter. Uncle–niece marriages are reported among four communities (2.0%) i.e. one scheduled tribe and three other communities. A majority of them follow adult marriage (190/93.60% as against national average of 89.06%) and monogamy is the rule. Payment of bride price in cash and kind is generally found among the scheduled tribe and other backward communities. In West-Bengal among 11 scheduled tribes/ communities the practice of payment in bride price in both cash and kind is reported. Payment of dowry in cash and kind is higher than the national average.

Child marriage is allowed in 15 communities (7.39% as against national average of 7.10%) following *goona* among 3 communities (1.48%).

We have been able to identify nine symbols indicating marital status for women. Of them use of vermilion (164/80.79%) is most prominent followed by the wearing of bangles (142/69.95%) of *pala* (lac), *loha* (iron) and *sankha* (conch shell), finger ring (6/2.96%), toe ring (5/2.46%), *mangalsutra*–the popularity of which in Bengal is phenomenal–and *bindi* (4/1.97%). Bengali typical married women can easily be identified by putting of vermilion mark and wearing of *sankha* (conch shell), *pala* (shellac), and *loha* (iron) bangles. Many married women paint their foot with *alta* (red lac dye) particularly during auspicious time or rituals or religious observances. Vermilion is a symbol of marriage. Nowhere it is as long, deep, visible and demonstrative as in Bengal. On Vijaya Dashami Hindu married women put vermilion to the forehead of Devi Durga before She leaves to join Shiva on Kailash and play with *sindur* (vermilion) among themselves in a ritual known as *sindur khela*.

The primary mode of acquiring mate is through negotiation (190/93.60%) followed by mutual consent (56/27.59%). Little less than half (97/47.78%) of the communities marry daughters in a ritual known as *kanyadan*.

The communities are generally monogamous. There are 57 communities (28.08% as against national average of 24.70%) who practises non sororal polygyny and 23 communities (11.33% as against national average of 14.67%) practising sororal polygyny. Fraternal polyandry is present in one community (0.49 as against national average of 0.60%).

Most of the communities pay dowry either in cash or in kind. Junior sororate, divorce, remarriage of widowed and divorced persons are allowed. Most of the communities are typically patrilineal. Junior sororate, divorce, remarriage of widowed and divorced persons are allowed. Most of the communities normatively live in nuclear families though various forms of joint living are not unknown. Succession of eldest son is a common practice. Principle of equigeniture is gaining ground and is recognized among 43 communities (21.80 per cent as against national average of 10.94 percent) but male equigeniture still predominant among 133 communities (65.22 per cent as against the national average of 29.40 per cent). Women's rights in property are still to be widely recognized and enforced.

The common life cycle rituals includes pre-delivery restrictions on food and on activities, pre-delivery ritual namely *sadhbhakshan*, post delivery pollution, post natal restrictions and rituals like *narta*, *shasthi puja*, *ekushia* and so on, naming ceremony and first rice-feeding ceremony, namely, *anaprashan* (rice feeding ceremony), *kanyadan* (giving the daughter ceremonially), *boubhat* (serving of rice to the relatively by the newly married bride at her in law's house), *phulsajya* (spending night by newly married couple in floral bed) are the common marriage rituals. Important death rituals includes *ghat*, *pindadan*, *shraddha* and so on. However, many tribal people and other religious and linguistic minorities and immigrant communities have been their own rituals associated with life cycle events. In West Bengal *mama* (maternal uncle) has some specific and important role in some life cycle rituals. Hindu and Hindulsed tribal communities who form the bulk of the communities of West Bengal cremate the corpse and dispose of bones in any sacred river.

Change is reflected in many aspects such as increase in the age at marriage (172/84.73%), bride price giving way to dowry (78/38.42%), liberalization of rules for marriage (31/15.27%) and so on.

Divorce is permissible in 169 communities (83.25%), the main reasons being maladjustment (151/74.38%), adultery (132/65.02%), cruelty (58/38.57%), barrenness (55/27.09%) and insanity (43/21.18%). Changes in divorce rule are observed in 17 communities (8.37%).

The nuclear family is the predominant type (196/96.55% as against national average of 88.93%) followed by vertically extended family (102/50.25%), mixed extended family (97/47.78% as against national average of 33.57%) and horizontally extended family (38/18.72% as against national average of 11.56%). Nuclearization of family is the main trend but extended family is not losing ground.

The main rule of residence is patrilocal (201/99.01% as against national average of 97.45%). Only among two communities (0.99% as against national average of 0.91%) observance of matrilocal residence is found. In about 31 communities (15.27% as against national average of 10.20%) along with patrilocal residence, neolocal is practised. Despite law, male equigeniture is the dominant principle. Property is inherited equally by the sons in 133 communities (65.52% as against national average of 29.40 per cent) and only 43 communities (21.18% as against national average of 10.94%) allow equal share in property among both sons and daughters. Succession goes to the eldest son in as many as 200 communities (98.52% as against national average of 95.56%) .

Most of the communities are aware of *varna* order. More than half of the communities (107/52.71%) recognize their place in *varna* order. In West Bengal nine communities are recognized as Brahman (4.43% as against national average of 7.81%) and seven as Kshatriya (8.37% as against national average of 15.90%), lower than national average while 23 communities belong to Vaishyȧs (11.33% as against national average of 9.36%) and 71 to Sudra (34.98% as against national average of 29.08%) , higher than national average. Most of the communities place themselves in low (93/45.81%) and middle (81/39.90%) order.

Bengal has had a long record of struggle against gender discriminatory practices. Abolition of Sati, widow remarriage, female education, were some of the high points of the gender struggle involving women of the higher category. An observer from outside cannot fail to notice the respect, even reverence shown to women, which he generally links with shakti tradition. However gender discrimination and matter of property representation of women in institutions continues. According to POI data women in all parts of the state and in most communities take part in social functions (196/96.55%), rituals (194/95.57%), religious spheres (158/77.83%). They take part in economic activities (176/86.70%), agricultural operations (81/39.90%), animal husbandry (97/47.78%), collection of fuel (129/63.55%) and fishing (41/20.20% as against national average of 12.45%). Women generally have a low status (141/69.46%), however, they have equal status in 60 communities (29.56% as against national average of 25.74%) and in only 1 community (0.49%), their status is considered high.

In West Bengal due to several feminist movements, the status of women has gone up to an extent. Widow remarriage has also become a common phenomenon even to the upper caste peoples. Many elites now raise their voice against the dowry. Previously widows—particularly upper caste widows did not take any food of animal origin and maintained a simple style of life as is reflected from their dress, food habits etc. and not allowed to participate in many auspicious socio-religious observances. However, such restrictions have not been strictly followed during the recent years. Atrocities towards women have also been checked to an extent due to the interventions of the *mahila samity* and women commission. The reservation of seat for women in various local bodies also enable them to put their voice not only in welfare and development affairs but also in mechanism of social control.

The bipolar concept of purity and pollution is an integral part of our social system and is abundantly revealed from the findings of our project. The observance of post child-delivery pollution (192/92.61 percent as against national average of 90.38%) and death pollution (183/90.15% as against national average of 84.68%) are most common. The common rites of passage are pre-delivery rituals (159/78.33 per cent as against national average of 51.63%), the naming ceremony (132/65.02% as against national average of 73.92%), *mundan* for boys (40/19.70% as against national average of 61.34%) and for girls (16/7.88%). Besides circumcision (21/10.34%), rice feeding ceremony (159/78.33% as against national average of 30.77%), *aqiqa* ceremony (15/7.39) and thread wearing ceremony (15/7.39%) are also important rituals of West Bengal. Main modes of disposal of corpse are cremation (164/80.79% as against national average of 66%) and burial (84/42.36% as against national average of 51.41%). There are a number of communities who practice both. Rituals connected with life cycles are curtailed in about half of the communities (100/49.26 per cent) because the rituals have become increasingly expensive as reported with reference to 142 communities (69.95%).

We found caste council (*jati sabha*) in a vestigial form, yet fairly active in West Bengal. Traditional caste council exists among 110 communities (54.19%) and village council in a smaller number of communities, 35 (17.24%). Among three tribal communities (1.48%) chieftainship exists and exercises social control and supervises welfare measures. They enforce norms, settle disputes and dispense justice in civil matters. The statutory panchayats have come up as a major institution in the state and their function largely pertains to developmental and welfare activities.

VII

Land is the main resource for 136 communities (67% as against national average of 64.10%) which is mainly controlled by the individuals. Next to land comes water on which 17 communities mainly fisher folk subsist. A welcome development in recent years has focused on the relatively obscure role of fishers and fisheries. Geomorphologically Bengal with its water reservoirs is the riches repository of fish resources. As mentioned earlier, Bengal has already emerged as the largest breeder of fish. And yet while fisher and pisciculture are celebrated in literature, very few anthropological studies outside Anthropological Survey of India have been conducted in this area.

Next to water forest is the most important resource on which 19 communities, mainly tribals depend for subsistence.

An important finding of our project relates to the diversification of occupations. We have been able to identify 60 odd occupations. Of the 28 scheduled tribes/communities studied under the project in West Bengal, 15 communities have reported to have been engaged in hunting and gathering activities and only two communities engaged in shifting cultivation. Further analysis of occupation among scheduled tribes shows three communities (11.5%) are engaged in fishing and nine communities (19.6%) in animal husbandry. One community each is pastoral nomad and non-pastoral nomad. About 23 communities are pursuing agriculture, and as many as 28 communities are engaged in unskilled labour. Nine communities have reported to pursue artisan work and eight communities each in unorganised services and in business, trade and industry. As many as 24 communities reported to have engaged in organised services. There has been a sharp decline in traditional occupations like hunting and gathering which has gone down by 50 per cent, trapping of birds and animals by 36 per cent and shifting cultivation by 50 per cent. There has been a rise in relatively new and enlarged modern occupations like settled cultivation, wage labour, animal husbandry, business, trade, fishing, industrial labour. etc. Occupational diversity across the communities have shattered caste / community based occupational compartmentalization to a large extent. There has been substantial rise in number of daily wage casual labourer, agricultural labourer, plantation labourer etc. Child labour has been reported from as many as 75 communities (36.95% as against national average of 43.32%) In West Bengal traditional scavenging communities are not much visible in rural areas as people defecate in the open far away from their habitat.

VIII

According to the POI data out of the 203 communities studied in West Bengal 161 communities profess Hinduism (79.31% as against national average of 76.35%) followed by tribal/folk religion (38/18.72% as against national average of 8.31%); 21 communities are Muslims (10.34%) 10 communities Christian, (4.93%) 7 communities Buddhist, (3.45%) 2 communities Sikh (0.99%) and one Jain community (0.49%) and a Jewish community (0.49%). According to 1991 census 74.72% of the rural populations of West Bengal are Hindus, 23.6% Muslims, 0.76% Christians, 0.08% Sikhs, 0.30% Buddhists, 0.05% Jains and 0.67% follow other religions. Traditional forms of shamanism are surviving in the state with almost 16 percent of the communities seeking protection from evil spirits and for curing of diseases through the medium of shamans.

In the mountainous of North Bengal influence of Buddhist religion and tradition and of Christianity are strong. In the plains most of the communities profess Hinduism, Islam and tribal religion. There is evidence of Buddhist and Jain influence folk cults practised by the communities having a relatively low social status in Radh Bengal. Radh has the maximum number of pilgrim centres associated with Sati which grew up at places where it is believed a part of her body fell. There is also a preponderance of cults in lower Bengal associated with Manasa, Sitala, Olaichandi etc. *Banbibi*, a typical *puja* of Sunderban area, is performed with a view to safeguarding oneself from the Royal Bengal Tigers, by those who enter deep forests of this area in search of honey.

Feminization of the Divine principle in the concept of *Shakti* is a dominant feature of Hinduism of Bengal. The Naga cult associated with fertility, production, prosperity and protection is feminized with Mansadevi worshipped as a Naga goddess. Durga *puja*, Lakshmi *puja*, Kali *puja*, and Saraswati *puja* are very common observances. People participate in various folk festivals like Manasa *puja*, Makar sankranti and so on. Various immigrant communities and religious groups however have their own religious observances. Bengal has more than a share of what is known as the folk component of Hinduism. It consists of deities at family, village, regional and national level which are propitiated on a larger scale than elsewhere in the country. Only clan deities are fewer; they might have been replaced by family *(kula)* deity. Similarly, given the impact of sufism the network of affliation of Muslim families to *pir* and *silsila* is quite extensive.

Another interesting feature is that the sacred specialists are more from other communities than one's own, suggesting the role of Brahman priests on all kinds of occupations and for all kinds of rites for all classes.

Bengal is the land of artistic creativity. *Pala gan*, *Kirtan*, Kali *gan*, or Kali *kirtan*, *Boul gan* etc are the important oral narratives prevalent in West Bengal. *Yatra* is a popular mode of folk entertainment.

The mountainous region is rich in its traditions such as songs, ballads, dances and folktales. Festivals such as Gambhira, Jalpesh siber *puja*, Mashan *puja* are observed in West Bengal. Tusu, Bhadu, Sharul, Karam, Sohorai and Chhata *parab* are well known folk festivals of Radh area. Chhau is a very well known folk dance of the area. Syncretism manifest in many facets of religious of beliefs and practices. For example the same deity is worshipped as Satyanarayan and Satya Pir by Hindu and the Muslim communities respectively. Another example of syncretism in Bengali calendar which is based on Akbar's calendar which in term was *inter alia* influence by Hijri calendar, as mentioned above.

According to the POI different forms of oral traditions exist in vibrant forms in 173 communities (85.22%). Different forms of arts and crafts are practised by a number of communities. The most popular form is floor painting (46/22.66%) followed by wall painting (38/18.72%), weaving (25/12.32%), embroidery on cloth (23/11.33%), basketry (20/9.85%) and so on. Bankura horse is a symbol of craftsmanship.

Popular Hinduism was transformed and became more human equal and modern in West Bengal owning to many religious movements which included. Mahaprabhu Sri Chaitanya Dev's *bhakti* movement, Brahma Samaj Movement led by Raja Rammohan Roy, Keshav Chandra Sen, Devendra Nath Thakur, Ramakrishna's teaching of *sarba-dharma-samanwaya* (doctrine advocated synchronisation of all religions) . Socio-religious mobility in West Bengal was largely a gift of *bhakti* and *sufi* traditions, which influenced people of low status in social hierarchy. The modern movements inspired the middle classes and popular movements.

Bengal has been at the centre of popular movements and struggles led by tribes, peasant, middle classes, for their rights, national freedom and social emancipation. Our POI data reports caste based solidarity and mobility movements led by caste associations, etc. among 21 communities.

It is a tribute to social stability promoted by various religious movements that change of religion is reported in 22 communities, which has been lower than the national average (10.84 against national average of 15.8 per cent)

Because of its humanistic traditions and people's mobilisation West Bengal reports operation of linkages, traditional and modern on a higher scale than the national average. Thus we find exchange of food and water, sharing and participation in each others social religious festivals, putative kinship, sharing of water resources and cremation/burial ground on a larger scale. We also find the rise of professionals, political leaders, village leaders, business men and entrepreneurs as members in new middle class across communities.

However, untouchability though weak remains a blind spot. We will discuss it at some length. Like Assam, Tripura and other parts of North-East India, Bengal did not have any indigenous scavenging communities. The scavengers came with toilets probably in the medieval period. They multiplied in the colonial period with urbanisation. These castes came from Bihar and other parts of north India. According to 1931 census scavenging communities of Bengal included the Bhuinmali, Dom, Halalkhor, Hari, Kaora, Kichak, Lalbegi and Mehtor. A study shows that the Helas work as service-privy Mehtor (i.e. who removes night soil from the service privies) in the conservancy department of Calcutta Corporation (Sengupta 1982). Another recent study (Bandyopadhyay, 2001) reports that in Kolkata and Howrah five communities viz. the Hela, Hadi, Valmiki, Dhanuk, and Rawat are primarily working as *safai karmees* or scavengers and sweepers. The communities who are involved in 'degraded' vocation are referred to as *jalachal* or *chotolok* cluster of castes in rural Bengal. The Muchi, Hari, Dom, Bhangi etc. are placed under the category stated above.

Our data shows that about 80% of the communities are involved in the exchange of water and food, a much wider coverage than is generally believed. The right of agricultural serfs, marginal farmers and rural poors have been protected to a considerable extent because of *barga* operation, successful implementation of three tier statutory panchayati raj system and land reforms. Atrocities committed against this people have comedown due to intervention by the state.

IX

West Bengal is a frontline state in development and poverty alleviation. It has implemented some aspects of land reforms effectively and executed developmental programme through the statutory panchayats which are now becoming very powerful. Participatory model of development and planning from below, i.e. village and block level planning now became very much popular in rural Bengal. We undertook the evaluation of the people's perception of development programmes when *Operation Barga* was on and completed it factoring its impact.

According to the POI 69.0 per cent communities prefer education for boys and 45.3 per cent for girls. Religion wise break up shows that 67.7 per cent Hindus, 67.2 per cent Muslims, 90.0 per cent Christians, cent per cent Sikhs, 85.7 per cent, Buddhists and 43.9 per cent communities following 'other religions' prefer education for boys. Similarly 44.7 per cent Hindus, 42.9 per cent Muslims, 90.0 per cent Christians, 42.9 per cent Buddhists and 22.0 per cent communities following' other religions' prefer education for girls.

Female literary rate in West Bengal according to 1991 census is 46.6 per cent and is higher when compared to 39.3 per cent at all India level. The infant mortality rate in West Bengal is 65 per 1000 births compared to 79 at all India level.

Family welfare programmes are accepted by 76.4 per cent communities, Religion wise break up shows that 84.5 per cent Hindus, 28.6 per cent Muslims, 60.0 per cent Christians, cent per cent Sikhs, 57.1 per cent Buddhists and 65.9 per cent communities following' other religions' accept the family welfare programmes. The modern methods of family welfare programmes are adopted by 100 communities (49.3 per cent) and the indigenous methods by 31 communities (15.3 per cent) . Sterilisation for men is reported among 15 communities (7.4 per cent) and sterilisation for women among 71 (3.50 communities per cent).

According to the POI data collected in the 1980s those benefited by employment through IRDP programmes covered 112 communities (55.2 per cent). Members in as many as 196 communities (96.6 per cent) reported coverage by radio, 105 communities (51.7 per cent) by television and 186 communities (91.6 per cent) by cinema. With the impact of modernisation people of most of the communities now prefer to send their children in school, receive health care services from health centre/ hospitals, use both modern medicine and indigenous system, use tubewell for safe drinking water (77.83 per cent against national average of 29.36 per cent) in rural areas and tap water in urban areas . Peoples also avail the benefit of fair price shop.

However, child labour in West Bengal has been estimated at 6,05,263 (1981) which increased to 7,11,691 (1991). According to POI this child labour is drawn from 94 communities including 31 scheduled caste, 17 scheduled tribe and 46 other communities.

We generated information on fuel resources and the consumption pattern for its implication for environmental and general issues. The communities in West Bengal are more dependent on electricity, cowdung cakes, coal, saw dust, kerosene and now *gobar* gas. Its dependents on fir wood is substantial (86.89%). *Census of 1991 (Housing and Amenities)* supplements the set of information but put wood (32.13%) in the first place followed by coal and coke (23.27%), cowdung cake (18.04%), cooking gas (4.87%), kerosene (3.69%) and others (15.3%)

As a result of these measures poverty levels have plunged. The poverty incidence at rural and urban by head count index stand at 27.3 and 22.5 respectively. *The National Human Development Report 2001* places West Bengal 20th place in terms of Human Poverty Index 1991. By 2000 A.D. West Bengal has reduced the poverty ratio by nearly half (25%). This report also ranks West Bengal eighth in terms of Human Development Report. Earlier in 1997 a World Bank Report placed Bengal in the first place with the highest rate of reduction in poverty level (4.2 per cent), along with social indicators of literacy of 72 per cent, female literacy of 63 percent, birth rate of 23 per cent and infant mortality of 55 percent. (*India Reducing Poverty, Accelerating Development, A World Bank Country Study*, Oxford, 2000).

K. S. SINGH

ACKNOWLEDGEMENTS

In preparing this volume help and cooperation has been received from many quarters which is appreciated with a deep sense of gratitude. We received full cooperation from the local authorities in generating the maternal which was analyzed, discussed and evaluated at a number of seminars organized in Kolkata and at North Bengal University. Our thanks are due to team members for the People of India, West Bengal Volume and scholars who had contributed to this volume. The scholar from West Bengal who had helped us in report writing and for editing the volume was Dr. Shekhar Bandopadhyay, Professor of History, University of Calcutta. Outside scholars who had contributed papers to this volume were Late Professor P. K. Bhowmick of the University of Calcutta, Professor Kumkum Bhattacharya and Professor D. Sinha of Visva Bharati University, Santiniketan, Sri Ugen Lama of North Bengal University, Dr. Jyoti Sen, Mr. Paul Mantose, Dr. K. Basu, Sri H. C. Narjinari, Dr. P. K. Gupta and Smt. Rita Gangopadhyay. Scholars from the Anthropological Survey of India who had contributed to this volume were Dr. Ranjit Kumar Bhattacharya (coordinator of the People of India, West Bengal State), Dr. Archana Datta, Sri A. Mitra, (assistant coordinators), Dr. Swaran Singh, Dr. A. V. Arakeri, Dr. P. P. Mahato, Dr. Tilak Bagchi, Sri Badal Bose, Dr. S. Maiti, Smt. Chandrima Chaudhuri, Sri A. K. Mukhopadhyay and Sri Gautam Kumar Bera. Besides a few research scholars of the Anthropological Survey of India namely Dr. Madhumala Chattopadhyay, Dr. Smita Sengupta and Dr. Snigdha Chakraborty also contributed to this volume.

Dr. B. N. Sarkar wrote a paper on bio-anthropological information. Dr. (Smt) Bharati Debi, Smt. Bela Moulik, Dr. Sikha Chatterjee and Sri S. C. Mandal provided library support. Photographs were taken by Sri A. K. Giri, Sri Abhik Kumar Dey and others. Dr Archana Datta, Sri A. Mitra and Sri Swapan Kumar Saha prepared the maps.

Last but not the least, we are indebted to all the informants and above all to all people of West Bengal who shared their information with our investigators.

KHARWAR

The Kharwars are a small tribal community of West Bengal. An ethnographic account on them is available in Risleys book, though he refers to the Kharwars of Bihar. They are inhabitants of Blocks I and II of Ratua and Chanchol block of Maldah district, in West Bengal, earlier attached to Bhagalpur division, along with Purnea and Katihar districts of Bihar. The Kharwar population by the 1981 census was 11,727. They speak Bengali and Hindi at home and write in the Bengali and Devanagari script both at home and with outsiders. They are a scheduled tribe community of West Bengal.

The Kharwars are non-vegetarian and eat fish, eggs, mutton and pork, but not beef. Their staple food is rice and wheat. They have such pulses as ***kesari***, ***moong***, ***masur***, ***tuar***, ***urad*** and gram and all locally available vegetables. They normally do not take fruits. They use mustard and rapeseed oil as cooking mediums. They have tea, milk and milk products. They are very fond of home brewed *panchai* and *tari*. Alcohol is a must on such festive occasions as Gambhira puja and Dhapri puja (tree-worship). They smoke *bidis* and *cheroots* (cigars) and chew *khaini*.

They have no social divisions and have only one *gotra*, Kashyap. They use Mondal as a surname. They consider themselves equal to Mahars, Kahars and Dhobas. They believe that the Brahmans, Kayasthas and Kshatriyas are of higher rank. They are not aware of the *varna* system.

The Kharwars are endogamous at the community and *gotra* levels, but avoid marriage within a few ascending generations in their fathers lineage, including that of the person concerned. They marry when they become adult. Marriages are negotiated, but mates can also be acquired by mutual consent. Marriages are mostly monogamous, though polygamy is permitted. *Sindur*, and in some cases, *sankha* are symbols of a married woman. Bride price is paid in cash, but is now giving way to dowry in cash and kind. The wife lives with her husband after marriage. *Chhara-chhari* (divorce) is not a legal practice, but remarriage after divorce is possible. *Beoa-biya* (widow and widower remarriage) is also permissible, though rare. Junior levirate and sororate are permissible.

The Kharwars prefer nuclear families, though a few mixed extended families exist. A husband-wife relationship is one of love and cooperation in daily life. A woman has a relationship of distance with her father-in-law. Jocular relations exist between grandparents and grandchildren, as well as between a man and his elder brothers wife. Sons equally share their parents property. The eldest son succeeds to his fathers position. Conflict centres on property. Inter-family links are apparent on festive occasions and at social or religious ceremonies.

The Kharwar women have a specific economic role. They gather firewood and collect drinking water, as well as help their husbands in agriculture, often by working as agricultural labourers. They contribute to the family income, though their status is lower than that of men. They do not take part in political activities.

There are certain rituals associated with childbirth. Pollution lasts seven days after a child is born. The naming ceremony and *annaprashan* are held when the baby is six months old. The wedding rituals take place at the brides house. A senior member of the community officiates as priest. The brides parents hold a feast. Consummation takes place on the third day after the wedding at the grooms house.

The Kharwars cremate their dead. Pollution lasts ten days. On the eleventh day, sradh is held and a feast is held for relatives.

The Kharwars are both landowners and landless. Their traditional occupation is cultivation. The main occupations now are *bhag-chas* (share cropping) and daily wage labour. The Kharwar children prefer to work as daily wage labourers, instead of going to school. A few Kharwars take up jobs in the government and private sectors. Their link with the market is either direct, or through middlemen and wages are paid in cash.

The Kharwars have a traditional caste council, headed by the *mondal*, a hereditary post. He wields the power of social control and is also an ex-officio member of the *chhatrisi* (heterogeneous village panchayat). The statutory panchayat looks after village development.

The Kharwars are Hindus and worship Goddess Parameswari as a home deity. Dhapri is a village deity, in which a tree is worshipped as God Dhapri. They also worship such Hindu gods and goddess as Shiva, Kali and Lakshmi. The *mondal* acts as a priest. Charak is a major festival. Kharsanna, held in April-May, is a popular fair. Kashi is their major centre of pilgrimage.

Their only handicraft is making *chatais* (mats) from palm leaves. They have a rich tradition in folk songs and folk tales.

Brahmans do not accept water or food from them. Inter-community marriage is not permissible, though a few cases do exist. Such putative kinship as *dharam-bhai* and *dharam-bahin* exist with other communities. They share water sources, roads and schools with others. The community has teachers and government employees in its fold.

Their attitude towards education and literacy is poor. They generally use indigenous medicines, but are favourably disposed towards family planning. They draw their drinking water from wells and tube wells. Some get loans under the Integrated Rural Development Project. Transistor radio sets are their only media of mass communication. Their villages do not have electricity. Wood, cowdung cakes and kerosene are used as fuel. They get their irrigation water from canals and use chemical fertilizers. Nutrition programmes exist at their childrens schools. Rationing facilities though very poor, are they availed of them, as well as banking facilities, though they do not have a favourable attitude towards savings and many depend on moneylenders.

AMITABHA MITRA

KHATIK

The Khatiks are a very small community of West Bengal without any synonym. According to existing literature, they are a caste of Behars (Risley, 1981:477) who migrated from Ayodhya, Varanasi, Sultanpur and Faizabad districts of Uttar Pradesh. They now live in Howrah, Midnapore, Burdwaṇ and Hooghly districts of West Bengal. The climate of the area, which has laterite soil, is warm and temperate, with medium rainfall and high humidity. By the 1981 census, Khatiks numbered 4862 in the state, with a maximum concentration of 961 in Midnapore district. They speak Hindi at home and with kin and Bengali with their Bengali-speaking neighbours. They write in the Devanagari script at home and with kin and Bengali with others. They are a scheduled caste by the Constitution.

The Khatiks are non-vegetarian and eat fish, eggs and mutton, but do not eat pork or beef. Their staple food is rice and wheat. They have such pulses as *moong*, *masur* and *urad* and locally available vegetables. Mustard oil is their cooking medium. They have seasonal fruits occasionally. Tea is a common drink. Those who can afford give their children and old people milk and milk products. *Ksheer*, or *payesh* is a special food on an auspicious *tithi*, such as the day of the full moon, when they do Satyanarayan puja. They do not drink alcohol. They smoke *bidis* and cigarettes and chew betel.

The Khatiks are territorially divided into two sub-groups: a) Khatiks; and b) Sonakars. The first migrated from Ayodhya and Varanasi districts of Uttar Pradesh and ranks higher than the Sonakars, who migrated from Faizabad and Sultanpur districts of Uttar Pradesh. The Khatiks are an endogamous community and all belong to the Kashyap *gotra*. They use Khatik as a surname. They rank themselves higher than the Doms, Muchis, Methores and Bhangis, but lower than the Brahmans, Kayasthas and Kamars. They say they are Sudras in the *varna* order.

The Khatiks have endogamous subgroups. Marrying within five generations in the fathers lineage is avoided. Marriages are negotiated and monogamous. Though polygamy is not encouraged, a man may take a second wife if the first is infertile. The marriageable age for boys is between eighteen and twenty years, and for girls sixteen to twenty. *Sindur* is the symbol of a married womaṇ. Dowry is given in kind. After marriage, the bride lives with her husband. Either partner may initiate divorce, granted with social approval on grounds of adultery, maladjustment, or infertility. Compensation is paid to the aggrieved partner. Children are the liability of either parent. Divorced men and women, widowers and young childless widows may remarry. Recently, child marriage (between five and twelve years) has gone out of vogue and there has been a rise in age at marriage. Married women now strictly observe the marriage symbol.

The Khatik families are nuclear, though a few are mixed extended. The eldest man is regarded as head of a family. The husband-wife relationship is close-knit, and based on love and respect. Children are affectionate and treated with love. A man has a jocular relationship with his elder brothers wife. A grandchild-grandparent relationship is one of love and joking. A man usually, has a relationship of distance with his daughter-in-law. Conflict centres on property. Sons equally inherit property. The eldest son succeeds to his fathers position. Inter-family links are in evidence at the life-cycle rituals. Members of other families attending family occasions help and cooperate with the host family. The only change is that the number of nuclear families is increasing.

Women do not get a share of property. Their economic role is limited to domestic chores. They do no work outdoors, except fetching water. Women take part in various life-cycle rituals. They do not control family finances, or take part in political activities. They have a lower status than the men.

In pregnancy, the Khatik women do not take part in any ritual. A Barui *dai* helps during the delivery. After the child is born, pollution lasts six days. *Annaprashan* and *namkaran* are held in the sixth month if the child born is a boy and in the seventh if the child is a girl.

A wedding is held on an auspicious day, after *ghar-dekhi* (mutual visit of inspection) by parents. The wedding rituals, conducted by a Brahman *purohit*, take place at the brides house. *Gaye-haldi*, *malabadal*, *kanyadan* and *home-yogna* are important rites. The brides parents hold a feast. Consummation takes place at the grooms house on the third day after marriage.

The Khatiks cremate their dead. Mourning lasts twelve days. *Ghatkaj* is held on the twelfth day on the bank of a river, conducted by an Agradani Brahman. *Sradh* is held on the thirteenth day, when rice, sweets and curd are offered to the departed soul. A feast is held for friends, relatives and neighbours.

The Khatiks major economic activity is selling fruits and vegetables, also mentioned by Risley (1981: 477). They are, mainly, a landless community. They have no subsidiary occupation. Only a few work as non skilled labourers under contractors. They are totally dependent upon the local daily market. The community has no bonded or child labour. Wages are paid in cash.

The Khatiks have no caste or *jati panchayat*. Only the modern statutory panchayat functions, and implements government welfare and development programmes in the villages.

The Khatiks are Hindus and worship Satyanarayan and Lakshmi as their family deities. They also worship Shiva, Durga, Sitala and Kali. The *purohit*, or *bamun*, is their religious expert, who worships the deities and conducts life-cycle rituals. Varanasi, or Kashi, Prayag, Ayodhya and Hardwar are the major pilgrimages. Janmashtami, Charak, Rathayatra and Holi are the main festivals. Risley (1981: 477) says the community has "minor gods, Bandi and Mira", though they do not worship them now.

The Khatiks have no tradition in the arts or craft, nor do they have any oral tradition. They have no traditional music or dance forms.

They have traditional inter-community links by virtue of their occupation and rituals. They have *jajmani* relations with the Brahmans, Napits, Bauris and Dhobas. The community has no scholars, doctors, engineers or teachers. Only one person holds a white collar job in Midnapore Collectorate. They are a *jal-achal* community. The Brahmans, Kshatriyas, Kayasthas and Baidyas do not accept water from them, though the Kamars, Napits, Dhobas and Kumbhars do. The Khatiks, on their part, do not accept water and food from the Haris, Muchis, Bhangis and Doms, but they share *siddha* food with all other neighbouring communities. There are no inter-community marriages. They have no problems in sharing water sources, crematoriums, schools and roads with others.

The Khatiks are educationally backward. Only 22.4 per cent of school students attended school in 1962. Children now attend school regularly and continue up to the secondary level. They use modern and traditional medicare. They use modern family planning methods and prefer two to three children. They draw drinking water from tube wells and taps. Their villages are connected by road and rail. Many own transistor radios. Their villages do not have electricity. They use coal, firewood and cowdung cakes as fuel. They go to post offices and banks and pick up their rations from fair price shops. There are midday meal programmes at their childrens schools. They do not depend on moneylenders and their attitude towards small savings is favourable.

AMITABHA MITRA

KHEN

The Khens are also known as Sens in and around Koch Behar district in North Bengal. They are always mentioned as Khens in available literature. They think that because of wrong pronunciation, the name, Sen, has become Khen in the course of time. They do not have any Jati-Purana. The Khens have been living in these areas from time immemorial. They are peculiar to Koch Behar and its neighbourhood and have a social status close to that of the *navasakhas* of Bengal. The line of kings who preceded the ruling family of Koch Behar belonged to the Khen community. They are originally low caste Hindus who later got raised to the level of pure Hindus. They also are said to be a branch of the Kalitas of Assam. Colonel Dalton (1872) mentioned that the Khens are decidedly superior to the Rajbanshis.

According to the history of Rangpur, this region was ruled by three dynasties of the Naraks, Pals and Khens. Nildhwaja was the first Khen King, with his capital at Kamtapur on the western bank of the Dharela river. The Khen dynasty had come to the end with the defeat of Nilambar, grandson of Niladhwaja, by the Pathan Sultan Alauddin Hussain Shah of Bengal in 1498. From the present distribution of the Khens in Koch Behar, Jalpaiguri and Assam and on the basis of the existing literature it can be said that the Khens might have migrated to North Bengal as rulers from Assam. The use of the synonym, Sen, appears to be a recent phenomenon, indicating their aspirations of being treated at par to the Kayasthas of Bengal.

In Koch Behar, the Khens are mainly found in such areas as Dhalakopa, Maradanga, Jhaljhali (Deosarai), Deonhat, Koch Behar town, Dinahata, Chakchaka, Kaljani, Beneswar, Nazirhat, Seoraguri, Bamunhat, Lanchapara, Tufanganj, Shalbari, Mathabhanga, Mekhligunj, Haldibari, Dewanganj, Gitaldaha, Falimari, Patla, Gosanimari, Agamani, Satkachal, Pabchora, Pratapganj, Harinchara, Gouripur, Rupasi, Dabhangi, Khudimari and Kolarhat. They are also found in such places as Khalpara, Saptibari, Jalpesh, Shibpur and Jalpaiguri town in Jalpaiguri district.

Koch Behar district is surrounded by Jalpaiguri on the northwest, Rangpur (Bangladesh) on the south and Goalpara, Assam, on the east. Koch Behar is an extension of the Himalayan Terai region, comprising 3,386 square kilometres. The climate is temperate and humid, and has an average rainfall of 3021.3 mm (126.3"). After Independence, the Maharaja of Koch Behar, Jagadurpendranarayan Bhup Bahadur, joined the Indian Union through the agreement signed on August 28, 1949.

According to Clause 29(A) of the Government of India Act, 1935, Koch Behar was declared a district of West Bengal state on January 1, 1950. A large population has migrated from Dhaka, Faridpur, Pabna, Rajshahi and Mymensingh districts of Bangladesh and settled in Koch Behar. The villages comprise mostly Koch, Paliya, Khen, Rajbanshi and Muslim communities and Brahmans from Kanauj. Several low caste Hindus are reported to have been converted to Islam during the reign of Muslim dynasties in the region, thereby creating a synthesis of cultural traits and religions to some extent.

According to the Land Revenue Settlement of Koch Behar, there were 4,755 Khens in 1903, while 8,830 Khen were returned as Sen Kayasthas in 1941. There is no up to date information on the Khen population. They speak the Koch Behar dialect of Bengali with their own people and with people of other communities. They can also speak the normal Bengali language. Bengali is the only script they generally use. There is no identification mark that distinguishes the Khens.

Their staple food is rice. They are non-vegetarian, but do not eat beef, pork or chicken. Neither do they drink alcohol. The Khens still recall the days when they had plenty of milk and fish in their houses. *Dai* (curd) and *chira* (pressed rice) was once their favourite dish. Most families stored dry fish. Mere scarcity over time has compelled them to change their food habits to some extent. Now *dai-chira* constitutes only an occasional dish for a few. They do not prefer dry fish anymore. The Khens have nicely explained their present condition through the following proverb: "Domok dharen kudin, Sukar kobae barun" (The Doms too, drive away their pigs with broomsticks when bad days befall them).

The only recognized social groups among the Khens are *gotras*, though it has been mentioned that they have five sections, the Mahendris, Telis, Barois, Salooyas and Patiyars (Harendra Narayan Chowdhury, 1903). They recognize the following gotras: a) Modgolya; b) Aladhirishi; c) Alemman; d) Modhugolya Rishi; and e) Mrigarishi. Inter-*gotra* marriage is prohibited. Members of different *gotras* often help and render services to each other. Earlier, Khen was used as their *jati* name, but later they began to describe themselves simply as Hindus. They used Das and Sarkar as surnames in the past, but now they use Sen, Sarkar, Baxi, Deb, Basunia and Das. In the local hierarchy, the Khens claim they are higher than the Rajbanshis, Doms, Muchis and Daois, but lower than Brahmans and Kshatriyas.

The Khens perceive that human society is divided into four *varnas*. *Dalbhag* (pollution after death) is considered an important factor of the *varna* order. The Brahman, by virtue of having *dalbhag* for only eleven days, occupies the highest position in the *varna* order, followed by Kshatriyas, with *dalbhag* for thirteen days and Vaishyas, with *dalbhag* for thirty days. It is more on other considerations that Sudras rank last. Since thirty days is the longest period of *dalbhag*, Sudras also observe it like the Vaishyas. But, apart from *dalbhag*, *paita* (sacred thread) is also considered an important feature of hierarchical status in the *varna* order. Brahmans occupy the highest rank by virtue of wearing the *paita*.

The Khens do not have any document, nor can they otherwise ascertain their place in the *varna* order, though the fact remains that they observe *dalbhag* for thirty days like the Vaishyas or Sudras. But locally they have a good reputation among other communities for their clean habits and practice of Hindu cultural practices. They are perceived to be on the same level as the Kayasthas and have marriages with the Kayastha community.

Normally, Khens do not marry outside their own community, or in the same village. Persons observing death pollution for a common relative are mutually avoided for marriage. Consanguineous marriage is forbidden. A man can marry his dead wifes younger sister. Khen girls generally marry at age fourteen to eighteen years, and boys at age twenty to thirty. Marriages are usually negotiated and monogamous. However, one can remarry only with the approval of the first wife. *Sindur*, *sankha* and *ghomta* (part of the sari used as a veil) are the symbols of married women. Earlier, bride price varied from 50 to 200 rupees, but this has given way to dowry, varying between 5,000 to 10,000 rupees, depending upon the educational qualifications and earnings of the prospective groom, beside the familys socio-economic status. The travelling expenses of the *bar-yatri* (group accompanying the groom) are paid by the brides parents.

Apart from these, the estimated expenses of the feast to be held at the grooms house are also claimed from the brides parents. The problem of space in the grooms house, if any, is also, generally resolved in advance at the negotiations. After marriage, the bride lives with her husband. Divorce is not generally permitted. One who divorces is looked down upon. Children are the mothers responsibility, while the expenses for their upbringing is borne by the father. Remarriage was prohibited earlier, but now they do take place, though rarely. Widow remarriage strictly forbidden in the past is possible with only a widower or a divorced man, without ritual, as also of a divorced man. Age at marriage has increased with education and exposure to urban lifestyles through improved communication, and the Khens show permissiveness towards remarriage.

They still recall the extended families of the past, where grandparents, parents and their children lived together. The only common source of earning was land. Extended families, dependent upon agriculture, have gradually disintegrated with the enacting of various land Acts and laws by the government.

A man has a relationship of distance with his *bou* (daughter-in-law) and a woman with her husbands elder brother. A grandparent-grandchild and *deor-boudi* relationship is jocular and friendly, as that with ones *nandai* (husband of ones husbands sister). Sons, daughters, son-in-law, daughter-in-law and grandchildren are subjects of love, affection and care, who, in turn, show reverence and friendliness towards their elders. A childless widow earlier used to get only maintenance from her husbands property, but now a widow with or without children gets half her husbands property, with the remaining half equally divided among all the married, and unmarried, sons and daughters. Khen families often help and cooperate with each other on socio-religious occasions. Extended families have of late been disintegrating, and the number of nuclear families is on the rise. There has been a shift in sources of income and provision of a share of property for the widow and married daughter.

Generally, Khen women do not work as daily wage labourers, or even on their own agricultural land. Apart from houschold chores, they perform most socio-religious functions in the family. They do not have any political role, but caste their votes as advised by the head of the family.

Panchamrita is observed in the fifth month of pregnancy. The expectant mother is offered five of her favourite dishes. The seventh month is *sadh-mas*. During *sadh*, apart from being offered the choicest items of food, the pregnant woman is gifted *sindur*, *saris* and *sankha* by her parents. At least five married women neighbours and the sons-in-law are invited. A *kure-ghar* (delivery hut) is set up outside the living room. An elderly Dom, Muchi, or Doai midwife helps with the delivery, after which the mother is given rice, ghee and milk for a month. *Khour* is performed on the seventh day, when a barber cuts the nails of the mother and newborn before having a bath. The new mother may not enter the kitchen, or take part in any religious performance for a month.

After a month, *shanti-santan* is performed; The Brahman *purohit* performs Shiva puja and sprinkles *shantir-jal* on mother and child for their well being. In the sixth month, *annaprashan* is held. When the child is 18 months old, *chura-karan*, or *mundan*, is performed and a Napit tonsures the child. A small family feast generally follows.

On wedding day, the groom along with a few relatives and friends reaches the brides house with *niriksban* articles. The grooms parents, finally, give their approval by gifting the bride *goyna* (gold ornaments), *sindur*, *sankha*, *sari*, *machh* and *mishti*. The grooms parents do not accompany the *barjatri*. A *purohit* performs the wedding rituals at the brides house. A *rayobairati* (group of five married women, other than the brides mother, or aunts) is entrusted with the responsibility of supervising all wedding rituals. The following morning, *basi-biya* is held and the groom puts *sindur* on the bride's forehead. The newly married couple may not sleep together till *boubhat*, or *paksparsha* takes place.

On the afternoon of *basi-biya*, the groom takes his wife home. They may not enter his house before sunset. The next day, *boubhat* is celebrated at the grooms house and a feast held for friends and relatives of both families. The bride serves cooked food to the family in her new role. That night, *phulsajjya* (ritual consummation) takes place on a bed bedecked with flowers.

Khens cremate the dead. The eldest or youngest son of the deceased performs *mukhagni*. He is known as *mukhanali*. The thirty-day pollution period is called *dalbhag*, or *purna-asouch*, when the *mukhanali* and the rest of the family abstain from eating non-vegetarian food, or mustard oil and *masur-dal*. The *mukhanali* has just milk and fruits. Every day, the person boils rice and one vegetable in a new earthen pot and eats it with ghee and *saindhab-laban* (mineral salt) by dusk before the jackals howl. The pot of rice is boiled over a slow fire from four branches of the *jiga* tree. The *mukhanali* wears the same dhoti, called *uttariya*, throughout pollution.

On the thirtieth day, the Napit performs *khoura-karma* on the men and pares the nails of all women. *Sradh* is held on the thirty-first day. An *Agradani purohit* popularly known as a *paschima* Brahman, with surname Tiwari performs the death rites outside the house. He is gifted various items to appease the departed soul. The following day, *sapindakaran* is held inside the house by the *kul-purohit* (family priest), who offers *pinda* to unite the spirit of the deceased with those of his ancestors. The following day (not a Thursday or a Sunday), *matsa-mukhi* (ritual of eating fish) takes place and a feast is held for friends and relatives. A small quantity of all items cooked on this occasion is offered in a *patil* (earthen pot) to the departed soul by the *mukhanali*. The family is considered *patit* (polluted) till this day, when the *mukhanali* formally asks his *bhaigna* (sister's son) whether they can resume eating fish from this day. Married daughters of the deceased complete the death rites on *teratri* (day after the third night), by offering *pinda* through the *purohit*.

The Khens major economic resource is land. Most Khens are owner-cultivators, though a few are *adhiars* (share croppers), with no land of their own. All agricultural inputs, such a seeds and manure, are provided by the landowner, for which he gets half the produce. Agriculture is also a secondary occupation for those engaged in other main occupations. They sell whatever meagre amounts of agricultural produce they can save, such as *dhan* (paddy), *pat* (jute), or *aloo* (potato), in the local daily and weekly markets for cash. There are no bonded or child labourers among them. *Kamlas* (daily-wage labourers) are paid in cash and kind. They get one breakfast, one meal and eight rupees in cash. Certain government laws enacted on share croppers have resulted in eviction of share croppers by landowners, and landlessness, as well as the number of agricultural labourers, has increased. Landlessness has induced many to change over to government and private jobs and petty businesses.

They have no traditional caste council, or regional association. The *gram panchayat* comprising, mainly, Rajbanshis is the only modern statutory council in operation. There are no Khens in the panchayat. Overall village development is the main function of the *gram panchayat*, but its main role is executing through the Block Development Offices government public benefit schemes. The role of the informal council of elders in the village to deal with minor problems has become marginal. The Khens are now more inclined to approach a court of law for redressal of problems.

The Khens are Hindus. Lakshmi and the *tulsi* plant (representing Narayan) are family deities, the latter worshipped every Thursday for peace and prosperity. Most families generally have a *tulsi* plant or *bael* tree, or both in the courtyard. Elderly members water and worship the plant after a bath. Durga is the village deity and Durga mandir her abode. The Kali-sthan (abode of the regional deity, Kali) is also a major sacred centre. Gaya, Kashi, Vrindaban, Prayag, Hardwar and Lakshmanjhola are major pilgrimages. The Brahman *purohit* worships at the Durga mandir and Kali-sthan, besides performing life-cycle rituals.

All religious experts are paid in cash and kind. Several fairs are organised in the locality on the occasion of Durga puja, the major festival. Dol (Holi) is the next major festival, in which all village communities take part. No change in religion, nor change in religious behaviour is reported. They have not organized any religious movement.

Making fish traps from bamboo poles, knitting and drawing *alpana* on Lakshmi puja are some traditional craft known to them, but they normally do not take part in any singing or dancing. The Khens have no folk songs or folklore of their own.

The Khens establish links with the Brahman and Napit through interaction at life-cycle rituals, with the Kamar and Kumbhar from whom they buy agricultural implements and earthen pots, and with the Dom, Muchi and Doai who serve them as midwives and musicians. A kind of economic link is established with wholesale buyers to whom they sell agricultural produce at the local weekly market.

The Khens do not accept water and *kacha* food from Doms, Mehtors and Muslims. All communities, including Brahmans, accept water from them, but the Brahmans do not accept *pucca* food from them. There is no inter-community marriage. The putative relationship of *dharma bhai* and *dharma bon* is established ritually, or verbally, with people from other communities, since Khens believe in having a stranger as friend. They have no problems in sharing wells and other water sources, roads, schools, or crematoriums, or in entering temples, or panchayat offices.

They have not taken part in any political, or ethnic, movement at the *taluka* or district level. Apart from the economic dealings between share cropper and landowner, cordial social links are maintained. Certain other kinds of links are established with other communities through Khens who are in different jobs, teaching, or small businesses.

About one-fourth of the Khens are educated; of these, about three-fifths are men. The opening of primary schools is considered the main reason for their interest in education. They do not have any indigenous medicare. With the establishment of primary health centres, Khens have become acquainted with modern health and medicare methods. Most have a favourable attitude towards government family planning schemes. The women, mostly, have undergone tubectomy operations. They generally prefer two to three children. Their only source of drinking water is tube wells. Though the area comes under the government s CODI project, they are not supplied pure drinking water. The Khens have not benefited from the IRDP project.

They have a post office in their village, and regular bus services to Koch Behar town. Some own transistor radios. They go to the cinema once in awhile. Most Khens cannot afford electricity. They use firewood, dry leaves and cowdung cakes as fuel. Though shallow tube wells have been sunk under the CRDP scheme, most Khens do not get its benefit to irrigate land. Cowdung is used as manure. They can get only kerosene and sugar under the rationing system. Banking facilities exist, but investment and savings are beyond their means.

BADAL KUMAR BASU

KISAN

Etymologically the name Kisan seems to have come from the profession of agriculture. Risley (1891:122) says they are "a small Dravidian tribe of Chhotanagpur, described by Colonel Dalton as dark complexioned and of a short stature, with very ugly features". Some say they were originally inhabitants of Sarguja district of Madhya Pradesh, brought by the British to tea plantation areas as labourers, who, ultimately settled permanently by getting land as *bakshees* (reward). The land was popularly known as *bakshees-khet* (donated tax-free land).

They are primarily distributed in Jalpaiguri and Darjeeling districts, especially in the Dooars and Terai regions of West Bengal. They do not have a large concentration in any one village. To negotiate a marriage, they travel out of their own district. The climate varies from moderate to cold. Forests are close by, and so the areas abound in wild animals such as elephants, leopards, bison, rhinoceroses and deer. Many varieties of birds also flock to the area. The rainfall varies from medium to high. The total population was 716 by the 1981 census.

They speak a local form of language, called Sadri, and use either the Devanagari, or Bengali, script at home, as well as outside. They speak to others — especially non-tribals — in Bengali. The men sometimes wear a *dhoti* like a *kupni*, and a turban and women wear a petticoat, blouse and a piece of coloured cloth tied round their head. They are a scheduled tribe community.

The Kisans are non-vegetarian and eat all kinds of meat, including pork, *googli* (water snail), rat and bat, but not beef. Their staple food is rice and *kalai* and *masur*. They have mustard seed, and roots, tubers and bark of different vegetables in curries. Mustard oil is used as a medium of cooking. *Jungli-sak* (a wild leafy vegetable) is a regular food item. They do not buy locally available fruits — such as mango, jackfruit, dates, papaya and banana — from the market, except when there is an illness in the family. They drink milk regularly, and some have tea, without milk sweetened with molasses, instead of sugar. Both men and women drink *haria* and *daru*, usually home-brewed, but also bought from the market. The women sometimes prepare special food, such as *pithe*, *payesh* and sweets. There are no seasonal restrictions of food. Many now have *roti*s for dinner since rice is costlier.

The major sub divisions hierarchically are: a) Telia-Kisans (ones who use oil in the wedding ritual); b) Sindria-Kisans (ones who put *sindur*, instead of oil); c) Dhulia-Kisans (ones who make handicraft items with bamboo-sticks); and d) Agaria-Kisans (ones who are in business). The basis of differentiation among the last two is occupational. Now, group delineation is not strictly followed. Kisan is a surname, as well as *gotra*. Some use Nagasia-Kisan as a surname. They think both groups have come from the same racial stock. Some say 'Kisan' has come from the occupation of agriculture, since, in rural West Bengal, the term is used for agricultural labourers, especially tillers of land.

The community believes that all tribal communities are equal and there is no difference in terms of subordination or superiority. They say they are not treated as equals by Hindu communities. The Kisans have no idea of the *varna* order, nor do Hindu communities place them in the *varna* system since they are of tribal origin.

The Kisans are endogamous and marry when adult. Marriages are negotiated and monogamous. Junior levirate and sororate are permissible. Sororal and non-sororal polygyny is not taboo, especially when the first wife is childless. The symbol of a married woman is *sindur*, though not regularly worn. Bride price is a custom, and a wife lives with her husband after marriage. Divorce is sought, and granted, on grounds of maladjustment, cruelty and impotence. The village headman and elders, usually, arbitrate. The husband pays compensation. Remarriage is permitted, but without elaborate ceremony. There has been an increase in age at marriage, dowry has been introduced and exogamous marriages take place with the Nagesias.

The Kisans have nuclear families. Relations within a family revolve round love, respect, mutual obligation and cooperation. A man may not come in contact with his younger brother's wife. A woman does not utter the names of her husband, his elder brother, or father- and mother-in-law. A woman has a jocular relationship with her husband's younger brother. Conflicts arise if someone is lazy in carrying out his social, or economic, duties, or over property. Property is inherited equally by sons and the eldest son succeeds to his father's position. Solidarity creates close inter-family links.

Women do not normally inherit property. Their economic role is limited to domestic chores — gathering fodder and fuel, fetching water, rearing children and looking after the family. They also have roles in rituals. They perform *upas* on certain *pujas*. They do not take part in political activities. They work in agriculture and tea plantations as labourers and contribute whatever they earn to the family budget. Women have no prescribed rights, but many obligations.

After a child is born, pollution lasts fifteen days. An old, experienced woman cuts the umbilical cord. The Napit conducts purification rites on the fifteenth day. In summer, the child is bathed. Used kitchen earthenware is thrown away after delivery. Mother and child are kept warm by applying dry compress. For three to five days after the delivery, the mother has boiled rice, fried plantain and potatoes. Family elders name the child on the basis of the birthday. For instance, a boy born on a *Sombar* (Monday) is named 'Somra'. For a girl, this will be 'Somri'. There is no special ceremony at which the child formally tastes rice. When the child is five or six months old, the mother chews the rice to make it soft and feeds it to the child. In this manner, the child learns to eat rice and curries. Boys and girls go about naked till the age of four or five.

Men and women do not marry in the month of their birth. Wedding involves several rituals — applying turmeric paste on the bodies of bride and groom, welcoming the groom and his companions, the actual wedding rites, a wedding feast at the bride's house (where *handia* and meat are compulsory items), the new couple going to the groom's house after marriage and a feast at the groom's house. The bride and groom's parents or elders — and, sometimes, the *mukhia*, and not a priest conduct the wedding rites. There is no formal day for consummation.

The Kisans mostly cremate their dead, though some bury the corpse. After cremation, fragments of bone are collected, placed in a pot and buried outside the house and a bamboo is placed over this place. Some keep them in an urn, before throwing them into the river after a few months. Mourning lasts fifteen days. The bereaved family does not drink liquor, or eat meat, for fifteen days. A Napit tonsures the sons and lineage members of the deceased and pares their nails. The chief mourner offers rice, bananas and vegetables to the departed soul on the fifteenth day. From then onwards, the mourners may resume normal food. Recently, life-cycle rituals have been curtailed due to rising costs and mourning lasts only a day.

Land — owned individually — is a major economic resource for Kisans, who are both landowners and landless. Landlessness among the community is high, and so also the number working in agriculture or plantations. Their traditional occupation is agriculture. Sharecropping, daily wage labour and tea plantation labour are subsidiary means of livelihood. They depend upon markets where transactions are in cash. There are no bonded labourers. Children help their parents in agriculture. Wages are paid in cash and kind to agricultural labourers, always in cash to tea plantation workers. After Independence, a few have got government help in their economic activities through schemes such the Integrated Tribal Development Project. There is one educated Kisan clerk in the Land Reforms Department of the Government of West Bengal, posted in the Kharibari police station area of Darjeeling district.

The Kisans have no regional association. There is only an amorphous council, the Kisan Samaj, headed by a *mukhia*, or *mahato*, who, generally settles petty family and matrimonial disputes. The post of *mukhia* is hereditary, but may be transferred to another person if the *mukhia's* son is considered incompetent. In this case, a *mukhia* is elected publicly. The Samaj may admonish an offender, or sometimes ostracize him for drunken behaviour, or theft. There is no system of reward for good work. The role of modern statutory councils, such as the *gram-panchayat*, or *panchayat samity*, is important. No agency can undertake development work without its consent. Since Independence, the Samaj has been losing its grip and the Adivasi Mahasabha has been set up, in which they have taken membership as one of the scheduled tribes.

The Kisans are Hindus but believe in tribal religion as well. They have no family deity. Their religious faith is expressed through ancestor worship. They believe in *pitri-kul* (ancestors on the father's side). Risley (1891: 122) says their "chief God is Moihidhumia, to whom fowls are sacrificed every year and a buffalo every three years. They also recognize *Darha*, the village god of the Mundas", and Kali, Shiva, Parvati and Ganesh are major village and regional deities. All Hindu sacred centres are their centres of pilgrimages. Charak mela, Poush mela and Rashutsab are major local fairs. Karam puja, Dausi puja and Tusu puja are considered tribal festivals. Durga puja, Saraswati puja and Basanti puja are general community festivals. Recently, many women have begun worshipping Ganesh and Santoshi Ma because of sustained proximity with neighbouring Hindus.

The community has no tradition in the arts or craft. Mats made from date-palm leaves — woven for domestic purposes — are their only handicraft. Both men and women sing several traditional tribal songs at social and religious rituals, accompanied by music and dance.

Because of their tribal origin, they are considered a *jal-achal* community by Hindus, who however accept *siddha* from them. Other tribals have no restrictions on accepting food or water from them. They have ceremonial relationship, such as *dharam*-friend, or *dharam*-brother with neighbouring tribal communities. They have no problems in sharing wells and other water sources, roads, schools, or crematoriums, or in entering temples and houses. They have a patron-client relationship with the Napit, but hardly establish any modern inter-community links with others. The community is not interested in political activities or public functions. However, in 1967, they were actively involved in an armed revolution, the Naxalbari political movement. They have good relations with landowners, cultivators and employees of estates, as also panchayat members.

Education has made very little impact on them. They consult doctors at health centres, and get medicine from there, though many use indigenous medicines too. Family planning programmes have made no impact on them. They get drinking water from wells. Very few Kisans have got employment under government schemes or self-employment through government loans. They avail of buses and the railway. A few own radio sets. Electricity has not reached their villages.

Wood and cowdung cakes are used as fuel. Environmental conservation does not interest them. No irrigation system has been developed. They do not use chemical fertilizers or insecticides. School children get bread occasionally. They avail of the rationing facilities in the area. Kisans do not save in banks, nor invest.

SUBHRENDU MAITI

KOERI

The name of the community is Koeri. Its synonyms are Mehta, Kuiri and Prasold. The surnames of the community are Mahato, known to many key informants and even ordinary people. Some said, etymologically, *ku* means earth and *iri* means cultivation; so, they are cultivators and vegetable growers.

On the origin of the community, Risley (1891: 500) observed that Koiri-Muraos are a large cultivating caste of Behar and Chhotanagpur, whom Dr Wise believed to be "closely allied to the Kurmis, with whom they drink, but do not eat". According to their own tradition, that they were created "by Shiva to tend to *murai* (radishes) and to look after the sacred gardens of Benares, is of the common mythological type and gives no clue to their descent" (*ibid*: 501).

The community has got different subgroups. Risley (*ibid*: 501) mentioned thirteen subcastes — Barki-Dangi, Chhotki-Dangi, Banapor, Jaruhar-Kananjia, Maghira-Tirhutia, Chirmait, Kumarh, Goita, Dhar, Reutia, Pauria, Barakar and Palmoha.

In Purulia district of West Bengal, the fieldwork was carried out in Chhota-Balarampur and Puarha villages, where we find the Koeris divided into four subgroups or subcastes (*char-thak*s) such as the Baradangin, Chhotadangin, Banaphorh and Maghaya.

The Koeris were one of the earliest settlers in the Manbhum, Singbhum, Ranchi and Hazaribagh regions of the Chhotanagpur Plateau. They migrated to this region from Hazaribagh and from neighbouring Ranchi district to the erstwhile Manbhum district on the invitation of local tribal chiefs, to settle around their *garh*. Later, because of famine in the region, they migrated to the Sunderbans area and Assam tea gardens in large numbers along with other tribals.

The Koeris are distributed mainly in such villages as Chhoto-Balarampur, Ketika, Bhut-Satar, Kukurgaria and Dimdiha in the Purulia police station area, in Hensla, Jhughaka, Kiruta, Sirkubad and Aharrha in the Arsha police station area and in Puyarha, Chakaltor, Panchara, Kamla, Turang and Biyadih villages. There are a few prominent Koeri villages in the Bagmura and Jhalda police station areas too. The community has such titles as Mahato or Majhi (headman of a Koeri village) and Paramanik and Pargonait, conferred by the tribal chiefs of the area on certain families. By the 1881 census, the Koeri population in Manbhum was 2,404, while, in 1872, it was 4,528. Key informants say that their present number is within 10,000.

They live in the Chhotanagpur Plateau region, where the climate is warm and temperate, with medium rainfall, and the area has laterite and red soil. They speak Jharkhandi Bangla or the Kudmali dialect with kin, and Bengali and Hindi with outsiders. They write in Bengali. They are an educationally backward community as identified in the Kakakalalkar Report and B. P. Mandal Commission Report.

Koeris are purely non-vegetarian, and eat mutton, chicken and duck meat, but not beef or pork. They eat eggs and all kinds of freshwater fishes. Their staple food is rice. They eat different kinds of pulses, such as gram, *kurthi*, *arhar* and *masur*. They eat a sufficient amount of vegetables and all kinds of seasonal fruits. They drink tea and milk. Very few of this community are addicted to alcohol since alcoholism is looked down upon. They do not drink *haria*, either, though some Koeris have, of late started drinking alcohol bought from the market. Some now eat *chapati*s or *roti*s. They have onion and garlic. Koeris smoke *bidi*s and chew betel leaves with tobacco, besides *khaini*.

Koeris have five major social divisions or subcastes: Baradangin, Chhotadangin, Banaphor, Maghaya and Bagmuria (or Jalowar). The subdivisions are differentiated in terms of hierarchy. Informants failed to explain how and why these social divisions — or even the differentiations — came into being. These groups, at a later stage, became endogamous and assumed the form of *thak*s, or subsections. The differentiations existed at the territorial level. The current study has been conducted among the Banaphors. Key informants speak of only two Sanskritized clan names — Nag (Nagrishi) and Kachchim (Kashyap) — which regulate marriages and indicate ancestry. Recent changes in surname are Mehta and Prasad.

Purulia Koeris consider themselves at the middle of the Hindu *jati-varna* hierarchy. Brahmans, Baidyas, Rajputs, Kshatriyas, Vaishnavas, Tambulis and Benes are at the top of the hierarchy, and look upon them as on the middle rungs of the hierarchy, too, namely Sudras, because of their occupation. Koeris recognize the Kudmi-Mahaṭos as their social equals, but claim superiority over the Lohars, Bauris, Doms and Ghasis.

Koeri marriages are monogamous and negotiated. They are endogamous at the community level, but exogamous at the clan level. Since they are a very small community, they arrange marriages after four ascending generations. They have *badal-biha*, *sali-biha* and *bhaj-rakha*. The other modes of marriage are *tane-biha*, *raji-khusi biha*, *dekha-suna biha*, *dukhu biha* and *palai biha*. About twenty years ago, child marriage was in vogue, but now they marry when adult. The marriageable age for girls in between sixteen and eighteen years. The groom's family initiates the search for a suitable bride. Earlier a bride-price of Rs 51 was essential, along with 400 to 500 *pitha*s (cakes), ornaments and four *sari*s as *aji-sari* and *ma-sari*. But now, an educated and employed groom fetches Rs. 500 to Rs. 5,000 in dowry. After marriage, the bride lives with her husband.

The symbols of a married woman are *sindur* and *loha-kharu*. *Chhara-chhari* takes place on grounds of adultery, infertility, maladjustment, insanity, chronic sickness, impotence, cruelty or insanity. It begins with the wife living separately at her parents' house. Sometimes, the woman's parents may take her back because of her husband's poverty. A woman may demand divorce compensation before the *jati-sabha*. Young children of divorced parents live with their mother and her parents, but grownup children live with the father. *Sangha* is permissible, where a divorcee or widow puts the *sindur* on her own head. Widowers and male divorcees may marry another divorcee or widow. Nowadays, *sangha* and *bhaj-rakha* are looked down upon. The incidence of dowry is on the rise. Since the Koeris are a very small community, all lineages are linked by marital ties.

Koeri families are mostly nuclear, but joint families are not uncommon. The eldest male is head of the family. Elder members are respected, feared and loved by younger ones, who in turn are cared for by elders in a family. All members try to avoid confrontation and relate to each other out of a sense of obligation.

There is a jocular relationship between a woman and her husband's younger brother, a man and the brothers and younger sisters of his wife, and between grandparents and grandchildren. A woman has a relationship of distance with her son-in-law, or her father-in-law. Sons inherit their parents' property, with the eldest getting *boro-bhag* (a little extra as his share). The eldest son, usually, succeeds to his father's official position in the community, as that of *mahato* or *majhi*). Inter-family links are maintained through sharing of labour and money, exchanging cattle, building houses and rendering free service.

Changes noticed after Independence are that the unified behaviour of the community has lost its strength and the members are becoming increasingly more self-centred. Earlier, the opinion of women in the family was taken on all major issues, but not any longer. Women do not inherit property. Only through sale deeds can Koeris transfer property to their daughters. The sons of an only daughter get *dahattar* (his maternal grandparents' property).

Women do not have status equal to that of men, but play a crucial role in a family's economic activities. They help the men in vegetable cultivation and selling. The latter responsibility is shouldered entirely by the women. They gather fuel and fodder for domestic animals and birds. They have a certain amount of freedom at different social activities, such as welcoming guests, or visiting neighbours and kin. They observe some exclusively feminine rituals, such as gathering at the Ma Shasthi-than. Women join the men in performing religious rituals wherever necessary. They, however, do not take part in political activities, other than in the exercise of adult franchise — as advised by the men.

In the ninth month of pregnancy, a woman is offered *na-mashi* (special food and sweets), prepared by her parents. After the child is born, the *larh* (umbilical cord) is cut by a Hari *dai*. On the ninth day, *larat* (purification) is held. The Napit and Dhopa serve in the ritual. After *larat*, naming takes place and the baby is accepted as a member of the clan, as well as the family and ethnic group. *Ekusha* takes place on the twenty-first day and, after women lineage members bathe the child and return from the Shashthi-tala, *chiri* is performed on the baby. *Mu-jutha* takes place in the sixth month, when the maternal uncle or either grandfather feeds the baby.

On coming of age, girls do not observe any ritual after the first menstruation.

At the wedding, the groom first marries a mango tree in *am-biha* and the bride marries a *mahua* tree. A wedding has elaborate rituals, such as *neg* and *amla-khaawa*, besides *pacha-khela*, at which a Brahman priest officiates. Consummation, usually, takes place six months after the wedding, when *dira-gaman* is held and the bride's father gifts the groom *chhata-dhuti* and groom's father *karam-sari* to the wife.

Pollution lasts ten days after death. On the tenth day, *ghate-utla* is performed with the help of the barber and Vaishnavas. The *sradh* feast is held on the eleventh day, when all relatives are invited. The fathers-in-law of the respective members share the costs. This gesture is later reciprocated when the need arises.

Though not compulsory, young Koeri men take part in the *disum-sendra* (hunting festival of the region). Of late, the *chiri* system and *disum-sendra* are being abolished. At wedding and death rituals, the

Brahman priest has been getting more importance than earlier and *sangha* marriages are becoming rare.

The Koeri's major economic resource is land. By their craftsmanship and skill combined with hard labour, they never let *bari* (vegetable) fields to lie fallow. They are good cultivators even otherwise and grow paddy, wheat, sugarcane and various seasonal vegetables. Men, women and children work hard. They are, mainly, individual owners of land. Some are marginal, landless farmers. They are experts in the vegetable trade, and, for this, they fully depend upon the local markets. The *paikars*, or *pharia*s (middlemen) buy their products at a cheap rate and sell the goods in Jamshedpur, Calcutta, Rourkela and Purulia.

Landless Koeris work as *bagal*s and *munishe*s in other people's houses on annual contract or as daily wage labourers. Landlessness among Koeris is increasing with rising population. Even children below fifteen years work as labourers on their own land or in other people's houses. A child *bagal* gets 10 *maunds* of paddy a year and an adult *munish*, Rs. 8 to Rs. 10 a day. They also work at government construction sites or road repair schemes and get Rs. 8 to Rs. 10 a day.

The Purulia Koeris who migrated to the Sunderbans are called *bunos* by locals. They were brought there for land reclamation. Now, Purulia Koeris are taking up jobs in businessmen's houses as *muhri*s and as salesmen in Purulia town. Some hold government jobs or are primary and high school teachers. Increasing landlessness has been forcing them to migrate to coalfields and industrial areas.

The Koeris have their own *jati-samaj*, divided into six *barhs*. The *majhi* is the headman of the village and *mahato* head of the caste council of a particular *barh*. *Choddar* is the assistant to the *majhi* and *mahato* of a community. The mechanism of social control rests on them. Inter-community marriages are forbidden, as also marriage with close kin. Men and women who break social laws are punished by the caste council and made *ek-ghore* (outcaste). Cow slaughter is another punishable offence. Only through the elaborate rituals of *prayaschitta* is a *go-badhya* (man or woman who has killed a cow) accepted back in society.

The offender has to hold a community feast at which the *choddar* first eats. The modern *gram panchayats* are very powerful and intervene in every social issue. The power of the Koeri caste panchayats has been diminishing every day and rebellious youths have been increasingly questioning the decisions of the caste panchayats. Their decree is respected only in cases of marriage and death and other social rituals.

Koeris are mostly Hindus, and also believe in folk religion and worship of nature. They worship the Gosain-Rai, Jitam-Dharam and Tusu deities, besides Durga, Lakshmi and Saraswati as gods and goddesses. Their family gods are Manasa and Sitala, and village deities Shiva, Kali, Gour-Garam and Mahadana. Koeri shrines and sacred centres are Gourimath Dham, Telkupi, Para and Kalyaneswari and pilgrimages Gaya, Kashi, Srikshatra, or Puri, Vrindaban and Mathura.

They have both local sacred specialists and outsiders. The local ones are the *ojha*, *jan-guru* and *kanphuka-guru* and outside specialists are *pardas*, who come annually to arrange pilgrimages to sacred places, the Kathak Thakur, who sings songs from the Ramayana and Mahabharata and the Vaishnava, who chants the names of Hari or Vishnu. Their major fairs and festivals are all related to the economic production system — either appeals for fertility or rain. Tusu, Bhadu, Jita-Jawa, Karam, Ind, Chata, Ayodhya Sikar and Bandna are the local festivals. They hold Durga puja, Kali puja and Saraswati puja, besides. The Koeris have been converting themselves fast from pure believers of folk religion to Hinduism, but they still worship their traditional local deities, such as *Kudra*, *Rangahari* and *Gossayanrai*. Their highest family deity is *Dharam*, worshipped with a gap of one generation.

The Purulia Koeris' social movement was led by Manmath Kuiri of Kukurgoria village, in the Joypur police station area. They claimed they were Kuswaha Kshatriyas and joined the All India Kuswaha Kshatriya movement, started in 1928-'29. As a community, they accepted the Brahman Pandey Guru as *guru*, as also the Gossain Vaishnavas. The Pandey Vaishnava Brahmans of Satar village have acted as priest from that time onwards. They are now more vigorously practising Hindu rituals and worshipping Satyanarayan.

The Koeris sing such regional folk songs as Jhumur, Tusu and Karam. They do not have a group dance for women; only for very young girls who dance with the Karam and Jawa songs. They decorate their walls with colourful flowers and paintings. They dance the Chou and Nachni. Some young artists do clay modelling.

Traditional inter-community links are maintained through different life-cycle rituals, as also different festivals and religious worship. Brahmans and Vaishnavas, often, take part in Koeri family rituals. Koeris take the advice of headmen of other communities at social gatherings, especially that of the local Mahato, Kumbhar and Napit. Koeris have ceremonial friendship with the Kudmi-Mahatos, Gunnyas, Bouri-Tambulis and Bhumijs, locally known as *phool* and *saiba*. In selecting a *phool* or *saiba* Koeris do not discriminate among castes. Now the *guru-bashi* (disciples of the same religious priest) system of religious brotherhood is propagated from the Satsangh and Ram Narayan Ram group.

Inter-community bonds are very strong in the field of occupation. Since they are vegetable growers and sellers, they interact with all groups in a village, market or town. Those who are job holders among them interact with others too. Politically, they work for different groups and attend village, regional and state level meetings. Brahmans of any subgroup consider Koeris *jal-achal* and accept only *siddha* or *kachcha* food from them. They do not have commensal relations with Bengalis — of the Brahman, Kayastha, Bene, Tambuli, Suri and Utkalsreni-Brahman castes — who do not sit in the same row as they at social feasts. But they do accept food from the Kudmi-Mahatos. Similarly, they do not accept food or water from the Santals, Mundas, Bhumijs, Bauris and Haris. They do not endorse inter-community marriages, either. They share wells, ponds, roads, schools, crematoriums, temples and *panchayat ghar*s with the other communities. But Bengali upper castes maintain a distance while bathing in the same pond.

The Pandeys (Kathak Brahmans of Purulia) are Vaishnavas by faith, and so are the *kanphuka-guru*s. The Pandas of Gaya and Puri have an annual *jajmani* and occasional *jajmani* relationship with Koeris. With the Napit, Lohar, Kumbhar and Dhopa, they have a *gau-ghar* system. They work for them and supply the necessary items, thereby annually collecting their remuneration from each family on the basis of a unit of *hal* (plough). On buses and trains, in schools, colleges and markets and at festivals they interact with different communities. Their ethnic organization is known as the Manbhum Kuiri Samaj, which spearheads ethnic movements. They maintain production relations with the Bhumijs, Bauris, Bagdis and Hari, since young men and women of these communities work in well-to-do Koeri houses as *bagal*s and *munishe*s.

Koeris are educationally backward. The literacy rate is very low. Only of late have Koeri boys and girls been studying in schools and colleges. For health and medicare, most depend on traditional, indigenous medicine and *Ojhas*. But recently, they have become interested in family planning and adopting measures recommended by different health centres. They collect drinking water from their own wells, tube wells and ponds. They have not got enough opportunities under the Integrated Rural Development Project schemes. Most are self employed in vegetable cultivation.

A radio-set is a very common household item. The more educated among them read newspapers. Some Koeri villages have electricity. Coal, wood, cowdung cakes and dry leaves are their fuel resources. They irrigate their own fields from wells, since government effort is lacking in this direction. They use chemical fertilizers, insecticides and other kinds of manure. In the Arsha and Bagmundi areas, schools where Koeri children study have nutrition programmes, but very few get the benefit. Every village has ration shops, but only kerosene and sugar are available at these. Koeris save in banks and get investment facilities.

They have opened a few high schools and small shops on their own initiative. A few Koeri families of Balampur are experts in classical music, and one even edits a journal of poems. There are expert Chou dancers and Jhumur singers in the community, too.

PASHUPATI PRASAD MAHATO

KONAI

The Konais are referred to as Chasi Konai meaning cultivator Konai. The majority of them, however, are not cultivators; but work as agricultural labourers. As regards the etymology of the name Konai, only one old respondent from the village Karkaria of Rampurhat, Birbhum states that they are the progenies of the Brahman, but were born of a *ku-udar* (i.e., a polluted womb) and thus known as Konai. By *ku-udar*, he means, a menstruating womb. When it was pointed out that it is not possible for a woman to give birth during menstruation, he further states that this account is written in the *Brahmavaivarta Puran*. There exists hardly any written history of the Konais. The Konais maintain that they are found in a few districts of West Bengal. Their present concentration is in the Murshidabad district. The areas inhabited by them have laterite soil. Their total population in West Bengal is 71,423 as per the 1981 Census. They speak the local form of Bengali dialect both among themselves and with the neighbouring communities, and use the Bengali script both at home and outside. They belong to the scheduled caste community in West Bengal.

The Konais are non-vegetarian, but do not eat beef, pork or meat of buffalo. Their staple food consists of boiled rice, pulses (most common is *biuli*) and when they can afford it they eat either seasonal vegetables or fish. Mustard oil is the most common cooking medium. At times, they also use *til* (sesame) oil. When they can afford it, they provide their children with milk. They occasionally consume brewed as well as distilled liquor. They do not eat radish in the Bengali month of *Magh*, *lau* (gourd) in the month of *Bhadra* and *sim* (a kind of bean) in *Chaitra*. In the past, consumption of liquor had social acceptance, but nowadays they do not drink publicly.

The Konais use either Konai or Mondal as their surname. In terms of caste hierarchy, they consider themselves as a low caste, but rank themselves above the Muchi and the Dom. They claim themselves as Sudra. The neighbouring Hindu communities corroborate their view regarding caste position and position in the *Varna* order.

The Konais avoid marital relations between persons belonging to the same *pitrikul* (father's lineage) up to a minimum of seven generations. They do not marry their mother's immediate kin and their children. Since the community has a single clan or *gotra*, there is no scope for clan exogamy. Village endogamy is practised, i.e., two persons of the same village who are not of the same *pitrikul* or are not related on their mother's side, can marry. Besides these rules, there are no elaborate or exclusive marriage rules. Age at marriage varies from eighteen to twenty-three years for boys and for girls it is between thirteen to eighteen years. Negotiated marriages are practised as a rule. There are few love matches and these are usually within the community. The father or the guardian of the girl takes the initiative to contact the father/guardian of a suitable marriageable boy. In fact the boy's parents and guardians do not visit the house of the girl's parents till the girl's parents and guardians pay a visit to their house. The Konais practice endogamy. The symbols of marriage for women are use of vermilion on the forehead and in the parting of the hair, conch-shell and iron bangles. Dowry in both cash and kind is demanded and is often exorbitant. Consequently the parents and guardians of marriageable girls find it very pressing for them to marry their daughters/wards to suitable boys. After marriage, the wife goes to live in the husband's house. Since divorce has become obsolete, there are hardly any rules regarding this custom. Remarriage is practised after the death of one of the spouses and there is no social stigma attached to it. Junior levirate is allowed. There are quite a few observable changes in their marriage customs. i) Child marriage is no longer practised; ii) The parents and guardians of the girl initiate the search for a suitable boy; iii) After marriage, women used to tattoo a small circle on their chin, forehead and hand. This practice was common among those women who were mothers of one or two children and was done at their husband's house. This practise has been discontinued; iv) Earlier, an incipient system of bride-price was in existence, which has been replaced by the dowry system; v) After marriage the bride would stay with her own family for at least a year. She used to come to live at the house of her in-laws or husband permanently in the month of *Agrahayan* and used to bring her trousseau and gifts for her husband and his family. Nowadays, out of greed for trousseau and gifts, the newly wed wife, even if she has arrived earlier, is sent back to her parents in *Agrahayan* so that she is sent back with gifts. vi) Divorce was practised and infidelity and barrenness on the part of the woman used to be the major reasons for it; vii) Remarriage used to be done without elaborate rituals. Nowadays there is hardly any difference between marriage and remarriage.

The Konais live in nuclear families. A few joint and/or extended families are found among the richer sections. Within the nuclear family, the head is the husband. Grownup children are timid in presence of their father or elder brother(s). Parents are affectionate towards their sons and daughters during their childhood. Adolescent children share economic responsibilities by way of assisting their parents in the maintenance of the family or by taking up employment as servants or labourers. When sons grow up, they stand on equal footing with their parents, in terms of mutual dependence, and obligation in their efforts to contribute to the family's budget. The relation between husband and wife is one of mutual dependence and obligation, though the husband dominates the wife. The wife looks after the domestic side and she is helped by her daughters in carrying out the domestic chores. Siblings are playmates, and an elderly sibling takes the responsibility of looking after the younger ones lovingly. In a joint family, relationship between the husband's elder brother and younger brother's wife is that of avoidance. Even slightest physical contact between them is avoided. The relation between husband's younger brother and elder brother's wife is that of joking. The grandchildren and the grandparents are on joking terms. The major interfamily linkages are either consanguineous or affinal. Interfamily linkages are observed through mutual exchange of labour (*gaontar*) and reciprocal help in kind and/ or cash. Property is equally shared among the sons after the death of the father. Succession is through the father's line. Nowadays, in some exceptional cases, property is being equally divided among sons and daughters. The major change from past customs and practices is the introduction of the Hindu Code Bill sanctioning equal shares to the daughters along with the sons in their inheritance of parental properties.

As stated above, women and men are entitled to equal shares on their parental properties; but, in actual cases, women are denied their shares. There are concepts regarding division of labour between men and women. Men are supposed to be the breadwinners, while women take care of the domestic chores such as cleaning, fetching water and rearing the children. In practice, women are often earning members too. Still women are subservient to men. They are never given the position of the head of the family. The decisions taken by them in family management are not considered final till these are accepted and approved by the male head of the family.

In the seventh month of conception, a ceremony known as *sadhbhakshan* is observed in the husband's house. A ceremony known as *annaprashan* or first rice eating is observed at the age of six months for a male child and seven months for female child. The maternal uncle of the child is invited to perform the duty of feeding it with the first morsel of rice. This occasion is also observed as a name giving ceremony, as on this day the baby is formally given a name.

Marriage is the most elaborate of all the life-cycle ceremonies. It is a three day ceremony. A few major rites during marriage are *gayehalud* or smearing of body of groom and bride with a turmeric paste; *nandimukh* or worship and propitiation of forefathers through male line and immediate dead kin of bride and groom; *satpake ghora,* literally going round seven times and *phulsajjya,* i.e., the first night after marriage, that the spouses share the same bed. A Brahman priest is engaged for performing the marriage. Services of the barber are not necessary during the ceremony.

They prefer to cremate their dead; but as cremation entails more expenditure, they often bury their dead. The head of the dead is kept towards the north at the time of burying. Death brings a period of pollution for eleven or rather ten days. During this period the family members as well as members of the lineage of the dead do not use oil (on the body) or soap and do not shave or pare nails. On the eleventh day after death, the period of pollution is considered to be over and mourners both of the family and lineage shave and pare nails before a bath. As no barber serves them, they shave on their own.

The Konais are predominantly a landless class of agricultural labourers. They claim that they are occupationally cultivators, as they are known as Chasi Konai. The neighbouring communities are aware of their *chasi* (agriculturist) status. However, both men and women among them work in the field as agricultural labourers. A few of them possess cultivable land (of insignificant size), and use it for producing vegetables, for consumption as well as for sale. They depend on markets for buying necessities as well as for selling their produce, if any. There is an incipient barter system in the rural areas of Birbhum, where paddy is often bartered for items of daily necessity. This is done at grocers' shops in the village, or outside it, at weekly markets. However, this barter is rather seasonal; it functions only for a few months after the paddy harvest. The Konais like many other communities have been affected by extra-traditional demographic factors, such as population pressure on land, due to which there is a slow but steady growth in the number of landless among them. Consequently, there is a rise in the number of agricultural labourers among them. Adolescent children work as labourers in cultivation – girls from the age of fourteen to fifteen years begin working as *kamin* (agricultural day-labourer) and boys from the age of ten years are employed as *mahendar* (cowherd-cum-agricultural helping hand). These child labourers receive their wages in cash and kind. The younger generation who have secured education, aspire for jobs in the tertiary sector and a few of them are employed in government offices, banks and schools

A male member of the village functions as leader or *modal*, a hereditary post of the Konai community. His main function is to preside over any panchayat (council) convened within his village community for the purpose of settling disputes between members, or for taking any major decision such as, welfare scheme concerning his community. In reality, he has little specific function. Whatever role he plays in arbitration or in taking decisions he always does it in conjunction with village elders of his community. Statutory panchayat control is a universal post-Independence phenomenon in our country and these people are aware of responsibilities of the panchayat. *Panchayats* in areas where the Konais are in large numbers have elected representatives from their community.

The Konais profess Hinduism. Dharmaraj, the popular village deity of the central and western parts of Bengal is worshipped by them jointly with other communities (mostly low castes). Besides, they organise themselves along with other low castes of their villages to worship sundry Hindu gods and goddesses, like Kartik in the Bengali month of *Kartik*, Shib (Shiva) and so on. On those occasions Brahman priests are employed. Tarapith, a well-known local/regional pilgrim centre attracts the Konais and a large number of Hindus. Besides, they consider Gaya, Vrindaban and Kashi as centres pilgrimage. They regard Durga Puja, the main festival of Bengal, as their major festive occasion. They wear new clothes during this occasion. A major fair known as Baruni is held at Tarapith. Another fair in the month of *Ashwin* is also held at Tarapith.

Being a class of agricultural dependents, the Konais have worked for generations for the neighbouring peasantry and the landed gentry. They traditionally share a kind of religious linkage with the other Hindu low castes, especially when they organise themselves for worshipping the popular deity, Dharmaraj. They secure the services of midwives from the Dom. The Patni or Gangaputra provide them with their services at the time of burying the dead. The high and the clean castes (*i.e.* popularly known as *varna* Hindus) do not accept water from the Konai and consider them *jalachal*. However, they accept *sidha* from them. Putative kinship such as *gangajal* (established during a ceremonial dip in the Ganga), *shibjal* (established on the occasion of worship of Shiva), *tarajal*, *rathjal*, *barunijal* etc. is quite common. This kind of kinship established with a Muslim is known as *sai*, (*i.e. sakhi*). The only persistent patron-client relationship of *jajmani* is between the Brahman priest and this Konai client. The respective Brahman priests visit their clients at least once a year to collect their yearly dues either in cash or in kind or both. A handful of Konais of the younger generation who can afford to continue their education are coming closer, through their schools and colleges, to the youngsters of various communities. Adult franchise has provided the community with opportunities to have a pan-Indian linkage. They have succeeded in sending their elected members to statutory panchayats of both villages and regional levels from areas where they are in large numbers. A very small fraction of the community is involved in share cropping and they have taken it mostly as a subsidiary occupation, as primarily they remain agricultural labourers. Cultivator-labour relationship is exploitive in nature, because those who form the major workforce have no control over what they produce. However, it is often not a very strained relationship. The agricultural labourers consider their occupation as a sure source of livelihood and are aware of their dependence and their underprivileged position in life.

Literacy and education among the Konais is slowly increasing. In almost all villages where they live, a handful of educated persons are found among their younger generation. The facilities for health services are still very poor. However, only in certain areas, they get health and medical care through the Primary Health Centres established in the various rural areas of West Bengal. They have a positive attitude to family planning. Vasectomy is a common measure taken to control birth. Contraceptives are not used. Drinking water is generally fetched from wells and tube wells constructed in villages in recent years. Employment and self-employment opportunities are still not within the easy reach. However, a few educated persons of the community are in white colour jobs and still fewer persons are self-employed after securing loans from banks. All weather roads and a number of private buses and minibuses facilitate communication. The economically well off Konais buy transistors sets. Due to poor economic conditions the Konais find it difficult to install electricity in their homes, even if available in their villages. Electricity is not available in a large number of villages in rural areas of Birbhum. They use cowdung cakes and *gul*, made of coal dust, cowdung and earth as fuel. The better off Konais manure their fields with both chemical and organic fertilizers and also use insecticides to protect their crops. There are irregular nutrition programmes for children in their schools.

R. K. BHATTACHARYA

KORA

The Koras are a little-known community of West Bengal. Das (1964: 20-21) says, "Kora seems a generic name, signifying the occupation of digging earth. It is not unlikely that the common generic name, Kora, has come to be associated with sections of different tribes in different areas, upon their taking up the occupation of earth-digging as a means of livelihood". Risley (1891: 506) refers to "Kora, Kaora, Khaira, or Khayra, a Dravidian caste of earth-workers and cultivators in Chhotanagpur and western and central Bengal, probably an offshoot of the Munda tribe". But the Koras, or the Khairas, of the area under study do not agree. The four Kora subgroups identified are the a) Mudi-Koras; b) Kudmi-Koras; c) Nagbanshi-Murali-Koras; and d) Dhangar, or Orang-Koras.

All claim to have migrated from Chhotanagpur and its adjacent areas, except the Nagbanshi-Muralis, who say they have come from Nagpur. They are distributed in the entire region. The area under study in Burdwan district is characterized by a warm and temperate climate, high humidity and medium rainfall. Their total population in West Bengal was 96,835 in 1981 census. They speak the Kora dialect at home and Bengali with others. They write in Bengali. The Koras are a scheduled tribe under the Constitution.

The Koras are non-vegetarian and eat fish, mutton, chicken and pork. Their staple food is rice and wheat. *Masur dal* is a favourite. Their cooking medium are mustard oil and sesame oil. Now, they have more of such vegetables as *lau-sak*, *lau* (bottle gourd) and *jhinga* (ridge gourd). They eat fruits occasionally. Both men and women drink home brewed *haria*, or *badeh* at festivals. They have milk and milk products, smoke *bidi*s, cigarettes and cheroots, and chew tobacco and betel. They do not eat mangoes till the Charak festival on the last day of *Chaitra*.

Subgroups, or sub-castes and clans are social divisions to regulate marriages and indicate ancestry. Kachhap, Sapu (snake) and Maram (goat) are clan names and Kora and Rajput are their surnames. They have a low social status.

The subgroups are strictly endogamous, but Koras are clan-exogamous. Both child and adult marriages are in vogue. Marriages are monogamous. Vermilion and iron-bangles are symbols of married women. Bride price is paid in cash. A wife lives with her husband after marriage. Divorce is permissible on grounds of adultery and maladjustment. Both partners may seek divorce, and compensation is paid to the aggrieved party. In case of a divorce, the *mondal*, *chharidar*, or *layek* and the husband's father visit the wife's family and take back the iron-bangles given by the husband's family. This applies also to the bride price if the wife is at fault. Children are the liability of either parent. Remarriage of widows (*sanga*), widowers and male and female divorcees is permissible. Junior levirate, or junior sororate, is permissible only after the first husband or wife dies. The number of divorce cases is on the rise.

Kora families are nuclear, but vertically extended ones also exist. A woman has a relationship of distance with her daughter's husband, father-in-law and husband's elder brother. There is a jocular relationship between a woman and her husband's younger brother, a man and his wife's younger siblings and between grandchildren and grandparents. Conflict arises from poverty. Sons equally inherit their father's property. The eldest son succeeds to his father's position. Nuclear families are increasing in number with the decline of vertically extended families.

Kora women have various socio-economic roles. They work in agriculture, look after domestic animals and poultry birds, gather fuel, fetch water and do various other domestic chores. They have roles in rituals and some take part in politics. Kora women shoulder the family's economic burden along with the men. Many control family expenses, but still women have a low status.

After a child is born, they perform Shashthi *puja*, or Satyanarayan puja, on the fifth, seventh, ninth, or eleventh day. The *layek* offers *rasi* (alcohol) under a *sheora* tree (the abode of Gram Bonga) and pares the nails of the parents and baby. Pollution lasts till Shashthi *puja*, or Satyanarayan puja. After a month, the mother has a bath in the Ganga. She may not enter the kitchen till the *pujas* are held, nor take part in any worship until she has a bath in the Ganga. All members of the family drink alcohol on the *puja* day. *Bhujno* is held in the seventh month if the newborn is a girl and ninth if a boy. The *mama* (mother's brother) feeds the child *prasad* of Duardhara Thakur (family deity).

Relatives usually negotiate marriage. After negotiations a date is fixed. The boy's father blesses the girl with new clothes and ornaments, followed by the girl's father, who blesses the boy with a few rupees, and sometimes with a ring. *Gayehalud*, *aiburobhat* and *mandoa* (place where the wedding is held) *puja* are the common wedding rituals, held in both the bride's and groom's houses. On the wedding day, the members of the family plant four sticks outside the house to form a *mandoa*. The man's father, or sometimes, the *layek*, or *bamre*, sacrifices a red cock and ties threads round the man's wrist. The woman's father, or the priest, sacrifices a red hen and ties threads round the man's wrist and it is known as *mandoa puja*. The wedding rituals take place in the bride's house. *Satpak*, *malabadal* and *sindurdan* are essential rites. The bride's father holds a feast on this day; and the groom's father arranges another feast on the third day after the wedding, known as *bou-bhoje*. Consummation takes place on this day at the groom's house.

The Koras usually cremate their dead, though some may bury the corpse also. Pollution lasts ten, fifteen, or twenty-one days and *omrakababo* (purification) takes place on any of these days and a feast, with alcohol, is held. *Uturtungi* (ancestor worship) is held on the eleventh, sixteenth, or twenty-second day. The priest sacrifices a red cock on the occasion. There has been an increase in expenses on rituals.

The Koras are mainly engaged as agricultural labourers, share croppers, and woodcutters, or in constructing roads, tanks and wells — their traditional occupation. Pig-rearing is a secondary occupation. They have direct links with the weekly market, where transactions are in cash. Child labour exists and labourers are paid in cash and kind. They have a hereditary traditional caste council comprising two members, the *mondal*, who is the leader, and the *chharidar*. Both of them jointly solve social problems.

The main duty of the *chharidar* is to gather members of the community together in a place to solve any social problem. Persons guilty of theft are punished physically and fined. In case of adultery or elopement too, the offender is punished physically and fined. The amount of money thus collected is used to treat all members to a drinking binge. Those who do not pay the fine are ostracized. The *gram-panchayat* is the statutory council, where members plan and implement welfare programmes for the entire village.

The Koras believe in tribal religion. *Gram-bonga* is the village deity, though Manasa and Kali are also worshipped. The *layek*, or *deora*, serves them at pujas and life-cycle rituals, while a Brahman priest, who serves the Bagdi, serves them in Kali worship.

The community sings folk songs at weddings and the Karam festival. Both men and women dance to the beat of the *madal*. One such folk song for weddings runs:

"Samtake in chakuli baharam,/ Horare namkin munda kuri/ Ato do kainsanai bandha kami" (I started with two baskets on a yoke and a spade. But I met a maiden on the way. So, I will not go to work today). This folk song also indicates their way of life.

The Koras accept cooked food from the higher castes, but do not share food or water with other communities. They have no restriction on sharing *siddha* food with them. Different communities join in their worship of *Gram-bonga* and Kali, which helps foster inter-community links. The community priest worships *Gram-bonga*. A patron-client relationship exists with the Brahman priest and the Napit. A landlord-tenant, or cultivator-labourer, relationship is established with other neighbouring higher castes. Some rear pigs and sell them in the market. According to informants, there is one member in the defence services.

The Koras are still educationally backward. Most boys and girls study up to the primary level, though a few boys have studied up to the secondary level. They go to hospitals when ill, but also depend upon traditional indigenous medicare. Their attitude towards family planning is not favourable. They fetch drinking water from local tube wells. Some have taken loans under the IRDP to buy hogs, or for cultivation. The radio and cinema are the most common communication media. News is also disseminated through extension agencies and political parties.

Their villages are connected by road and rail. Post offices are nearby. Firewood and cowdung cakes are used as fuel, and water from shallow tube wells for irrigation. They use organic manure, chemical fertilizers and insecticides for a better crop yield. Their children do not get any midday meal. They pick up their rations from fair price shops. They cannot save money in banks since they are very poor.

ARCHANA DATTA

KOTAL

The Kotals are a small community of West Bengal, with synonym Kotwal. Their titles are Mondal and Roy. The term, Kotal, has come from their occupation of being *kotwal*, meaning guard, or watchman. They say they are Namasudras and have the following subgroups: a) Kotal; b) Nune; c) Ghune; and d) Sangal, or Chandal. According to informants, they have other subdivisions — Fotosing, Manusing, Engineer Pargana and Dhenyen Pargana though not everyone recognizes these. On the contrary, Risley (1891: 514) mentions the following subgroups: Atpara, Dhukursani, Kutabpur and Manoharsahi. They believe that they are descendants of Guhak, the traditional ancestor of the Chandals *(ibid)*. But none of the present informants could identify the divisions stated by Risley and claim they are descendants of Namashmuni.

It was said that the Hindu feudals had *kotals* (watchmen) in the Nawabi period. They were given *chakran* (rent-free land), instead of a salary. Some became *chowkidar*s after British rule in India. The Kotals lost the right of rent-free land with the abolition of the previous Kotwali system. So, many left their allotted land in fear of having to pay rent.

This community is found mainly in Burdwan district, though they say they have relatives in Birbhum, Murshidabad and Hooghly districts. Their total population in West Bengal was 19,310 in the 1981 census. They live in the plains, characterized by a warm and temperate climate, high humidity and medium rainfall. They speak and write in Bengali. They have no identification mark and are a scheduled caste by the Constitution.

The Kotals are non-vegetarian. Their staple food is rice. They have *masur dal* and curries of locally available vegetables. Mustard oil and rapeseed oil are their cooking mediums. They have vegetables and fruits occasionally. Tea is a common drink. Men sometimes drink alcohol bought from the market. They have milk and milk products when they can afford them. Men smoke *bidi*s, and sometimes, indigenous cheroots, and chew tobacco. They do not eat radish in *Magh*. There have been no recent changes in their food habits, except that they now have meat and eggs.

Sub-castes and *gotra*s are the major social divisions. A person does not marry into five generations on either the father's or mother's side.

No hierarchy exists among the subgroups and *gotras*. The first regulates marriages and the second indicates ancestry. They can remember only three — Kashyap, Madhukulya and Nagrishi. They think they are socially lower than the Brahmans, Kayasthas, Aguris, Vaishnavas, Napits and Telis, but higher than the Bagdis, Santals, Haris and Bauris. They believe they are Sudras in the *varna* order, and so do others.

The Kotals are endogamous at the community level and subgroup, or sub-caste, level, but exogamous at the *gotra* level. Exogamy at the subgroup level and endogamy at the *gotra* level are also accepted now. The marriageable age for girls is between fifteen and sixteen years and for boys about twenty-two. Marriages are negotiated and monogamous. A man may remarry if his wife dies, or is infertile, but this rarely happens. Vermilion and iron and conch shell bangles are the symbols of a married woman. Dowry — a recent introduction — is given in cash and kind. The groom's parents, usually, demand a ring, a wristwatch, a bicycle and a radio for their son.

The wife lives with her husband after marriage. Divorce is rare, so there are no strict rules on divorce. Very rarely do they go to court, though such cases are rising. When there is an adjustment problem between a couple, the wife goes back to her father's house — a rather common phenomenon. Both partners may seek divorce on grounds of adultery and maladjustment, and children are the liability of either parent. Neither widow remarriage, nor that of a divorcee, is acceptable. Junior sororate is permissible only after the wife dies. *Gotra* endogamy and subgroup, or sub-caste, exogamy has now been accepted and age at marriage has increased.

The Kotal families are mostly nuclear. Young ones obey the head of the family and elders have affection for the young. A woman has a relationship of distance with her *bhasur* (now slightly relaxed) and her *shvashur*. A husband and wife have a relationship of mutual obligation, as also parents and grownup children. A man has jocular relations with his *boudi*, *shala* and *shali*. Relations with one's *thakurda* and *thakurma* are also jocular. Poverty is the main cause of conflict between husband and wife. Adolescents are not as obedient as before, leading to conflicts between elders and youngsters. Only the sons inherit property equally after a man dies, though this rule has now been relaxed and equigeniture is followed. But, in spite of the Kotals being aware of the Hindu Code Bill on inheritance, women do not stake their claim. The eldest son used to succeed his father as head of family, though, nowadays, any eligible son may do so.

They live in a *para* (locality) of the village, where the major link between families is based on community. Inter-family links are seen at life-cycle rituals and at different festivals, and are based on reciprocity. They borrow money or goods from their neighbours in times of need. There is also a mutual exchange of labour between families. The joint family structure has of late been breaking up.

The Kotal women work as agricultural labourers or as maids in the houses of rich neighbouring communities. Women are not barred from going to the cinema, theatre or *jatras*, in or outside the village. They have an important role in the life-cycle rituals. The Kotal women arrange religious worship, though they do not perform *pujas* themselves. They attend political meetings in their village or in the urban areas. Though a Kotal woman never becomes head of the family, she shares the family's economic burden with her husband. Daughters are considered liabilities, since their marriages entail substantial dowries.

The Kotals observe several life-cycle rituals. *Panchal* in the fifth, *sat-vaja* in the seventh and *sadhbhakshan* in the ninth month are predelivery rituals. A Hari *daima* conducts the delivery and Shasthi puja is held at the Shasthi-*tala* seven days later. The *daima* gets *siddha* (uncooked food) and about five rupees for her services. No barber serves them. A Kotal functions as barber on the ninth, thirteenth and twenty-first days after the child is born and pares the nails of newborn and mother, who later have a bath (with soap and water) on the thirteenth day. The floors of rooms get a fresh coat of cowdung on these occasions. Pollution lasts twenty-one days. After thirty days, the mother may enter the kitchen. The mother of the newborn, and those of the family who nursed the mother have a bath in the Ganga for ritual purification on the thirtieth day, or else they may not perform a *puja*.

They have no naming ceremony. *Annaprashan* or *bhujno* is held in the sixth month if the newborn is a boy, and in the seventh month, if a girl. The child is tonsured on the day, and the hair and a *puja* are offered at the *Smashan-tala*, where the family prays for their children, and from where *prasad* is brought to be fed to the child by the *mama*. After that, he also feeds the child a morsel of rice. They invite their kin and neighbours to a feast. The *dai* offers Shasthi puja at the Shasthi-*tala* on the occasion.

There is no ritual on the occasion of the first menstruation of a girl. The girl has a bath only after four days. She does not touch any jar of seeds and *gur* (molasses) on these days.

After a marriage is negotiated, a Brahman fixes a date, though marriage is not performed in *Bhadra*, *Ashwin*, *Kartik*, *Poush* or *Chaitra*. The wedding takes place in the bride's house. *Ashirbad* is held at the groom's house and the bride's father blesses him with a gift, before the same ceremony is held at the bride's house on the eve of the wedding. On wedding day, *gayehalud*, *nandimukh*, *satpakghora*, *shuvadrishti, malabadal* and *kusumdinga* are observed. *Gayehalud* is held in the groom's house before the *halud-tel*, a new *sari*, cosmetics and sweets are sent over to the bride's house where *gayehalud* is repeated. The bride's father holds a feast for the *bar-jatri*, neighbours and kin on wedding day. The next day is *kal-sajjya* and the one after *phulsajjya*, when *boubhat* is held and a feast hosted by the groom's father in his house in the evening.

The Kotals cremate their dead and the eldest or youngest, son performs *mukhagni*. Pollution lasts ten days after death on the day of *ghat*, when the sons of the deceased are tonsured and shaved and have their nails pared by a barber from the community, since the Napits do not serve them, before having a bath. *Sradh* is held on the eleventh day. A feast is held for relatives, neighbours and *kendo* (those who have carried the corpse) on the twelfth day. No significant change is noted in their life-cycle rituals, though expenses have increased.

The Kotals are mostly landless agricultural labourers. Some are share croppers. Very few own land and even fewer hold jobs in different industries. Their traditional occupation was *chowkidary*, or *kotwali*, though now they have, by and large, shifted from this occupation. Animal husbandry or poultry farming are subsidiary occupations. Some men have recently started pulling cycle rickshaws and vans. They have direct links with the daily and weekly markets, where transactions are in cash. The Kotal children, generally, start working as cowherds between eight and ten years of age. The Kotals work as *mahindar*s or *nagare*s, who work on an annual contract and are paid in cash and kind; they may work on others' agricultural lands when their employer does not require their services. *Mahindar*s get four to five *maunds* of rice, two pieces of cloth and two *gamchha*s and Rs 400-500 as wages. A *nagare* gets three to four *maunds* of rice, including *muri* and cash, according to the seasonal rate, and two square meals a day. They also work as *kishan*s (daily-wage agricultural labourers) and are paid in cash according to the local rate, besides breakfast.

The number of agricultural labourers has increased. Earlier, they depended upon the landlord to a large extent, for money. If a person defaulted in repayment, he was physically punished. With the development of agriculture and an increase in the wage rate, they are not much dependent upon landlords now. The landlord, too, cannot torture them as before because they can ask the *panchayat* for protection. The shift of agriculture from the tertiary sector to the primary sector is a significant change.

There is one *mondal* (leader), elected by a village community from among elders. The post is not hereditary. He arranges Graha puja (worship of nabagraha) with their help. They take his advice on matters relating to family or property disputes. Only if he fails do they go to the *gram panchayat*, their statutory council. The *gram panchayat* members look after their welfare. Earlier, they had a caste council, known as the *samaj*. In those days, they themselves took care of the community's problems and welfare schemes. But now the statutory council has taken up such responsibilities.

The Kotals are Hindus, and several are Vaishnavas. Lakshmi, Narayan and Gour-Nitai are family deities. Nabagraha is a community deity, while Kali, Kuluichandi and Kshetrapal are village deities. The Kali Temple is a sacred centre, and Kshetrapal, Nabagraha and Kuluichandi their sacred shrines. They visit Kashi, Gaya and Vrindavan on pilgrimage, though rarely. Degraded Brahmans perform their *pujas*. Graha puja (worship of *nabagraha*) in *Poush* is an important socio-religious festival. They worship Nabagraha to ward off evil planetary influences. Important fairs are held during Kshetrapal and Dharmaraj worship. Earlier, they were followers of folk religion, but now, they are more inclined to worship Durga and Saraswati, the younger generation has of late started organizing these pujas.

They have no tradition in arts and culture. However, before Durga puja, walls are decorated with colourful paintings, usually of different flowers. This practice of drawing designs on plastered walls is a regional characteristic. Their women draw *alpana* on different religious occasions. Some folk tales about them also exist.

Traditional inter-community links are maintained through different social and religious rituals and activities. They live in multi-ethnic villages, and so form part of a composite rural society. Being agricultural labourers, they have depended for generations upon the neighbouring landed gentry of various castes and communities. The Brahman priest and Hari *dai* have served them — at *pujas* and life-cycle rituals — for generations together, and wages are now paid in cash and kind. The Bagdis sell them fish and the Santals dig the earth when they construct houses. The Aguris give them loans in the lean season, while the Vaishnavs perform *namkirtan* in the villages in the month of *Kartik*. They are however, not paid immediately. They visit the villages after *nabanna* (a harvest festival) and get one kilogram of rice from each Kotal family.

Though Porter (1933: 498) writes that the Kotal is 'untouchable', it has been noticed that the Haris and Bagdis accept food from them on different occasions as their guests, though the Kotals do not reciprocate, since they consider these two as lower castes. Other higher caste communities accept sweets and *luchi*s from them — albeit sitting separately — but avoid eating other food cooked by them, especially rice. The younger generation, however, share cooked food and water with the other neighbouring communities. There are instances of putative kinship and friendship — *dharma-ma* and *sai* — within their own community. This has strengthened inter-community links. The Kotals offer *puja* through their own priest — to Kuluichandi outside the main village shrine of Kuluichandi, common to all high caste communities. The other communities come to Kotal-para during Graha festival and offer *puja* to *nabagraha*.

The Kotal share croppers bear the total expenses of cultivation of land owned by other communities, and the produce is shared equally between share croppers and landlords. The Kotal villagers are members of the Krishak Samity and women are active members of the Mahila Samity. Both men and women attend political meetings, locally or outside. These activities have fostered political and socio-economic inter-community links. The Kotals take advantage of the improved transport facilities and go to nearby towns for shopping or to the cinema, which has helped to establish modern inter-community links. The community has businessmen (grocers and vegetable vendors), job holders, primary school teachers and defence services personnel. These people have helped broaden modern inter-community links. Their link with other communities has also been strengthened by jointly sharing the benefits of various development programmes in the area.

Most Kotals are illiterate, though some boys study up to the secondary level and a few up to the college level, while some girls study up to the primary level. Das and Raha (1966: 68-69) mentions that 16.8 per cent of the secondary students attended school in 1962. Most

Kotals avail of health centre facilities, especially during delivery and illness, though traditional, indigenous medicare is not unknown. They still depend upon the *ojha* to cure them of snakebite and *bhute-dhara* (influence of evil spirits). Most Kotals prefer two to three children. Many women have got sterilized after having their third child.

They fetch drinking water from tube wells sunk by the *gram panchayat*. The Kotals have got employment under government schemes, such as the IRDP and NREGS. They take loans from the government to buy goats, cows, and bullocks for ploughing, rickshaw vans, and setting up poultry. The Kotal share croppers take loans for cultivation from the Block Development Office and from the Gramin Bank. Most Kotal families own radio sets. Some occasionally watch television, at their neighbours' houses. They take the advice of agricultural extension officers for cultivation. They get different kinds of information through political leaders whose meetings they attend. Post offices are located in their villages, but they hardly make use of them.

The Kotals cannot afford electricity for domestic purposes. Firewood and cowdung cakes are used as fuel. Very few can afford coal. The Kotal share croppers and cultivators use canal water if available for irrigation. Or else, they depend upon the traditional irrigation system of lifting water from ponds with *donga*s (canoe-like buckets). The Kotals use chemical fertilizer and insecticides for bettering crop yields.

Though the ICDS runs Anganwadi centres, Kotal children get no benefit of mid-day meals as it is irregular. Every Kotal household avails of rationing facilities from nearby fair price shops. Most Kotals cannot avail of banking facilities, as they are very poor and spend whatever they earn. They have not yet developed the habit of saving. Sometimes, they take loans from moneylenders to buy groceries.

The current study shows the popular myth on their origin and subgroups differ from what Risley (1891) wrote on this aspect about a century ago. However, on their distribution, status and other social rituals, the present study finds similarities with those described by Risley. But Risley does not refer to their section or mention *Graha* puja (worship of planets) which seems to be by far their most important religious aspect. It is, of course, likely that *Graha* puja is a major festival for only the Kotals under study.

ARCHANA DATTA

KUDMI

The name of the community is Kudmi. Its synonyms are Kudmi-Mahato, or Kurmi-Mahato, and Mahato. Since they have been living with tribals for centuries, others call them Kol-Kurmi. The term, Kudmi, comes from the word, *kurum*, meaning tortoise. They are people who settled in this part of the country along with tribals as *khutkathidar*s and have been instrumental in spreading agricultural technology and craft among fellow tribals in the Chhotanagpur plateau region. Risley (1981: 529) observed "the Kurmis of Behar, who are, on the whole, a fine-looking race, though, perhaps, hardly so Aryan in appearance, as Colonel Dalton seeks to make out". The caste, bearing the same name in Chhotanagpur and Orissa, belongs to an entirely different type.

"Short, sturdy and of very dark complexion, these Kurmis closely resemble in feature the Dravidian tribes around them. In Manbhum and the north of Orissa, it is difficult to distinguish a Kurmi from a Bhumij or a Santal, and the latter tribe, who are more particular about food than is commonly supposed, will eat boiled rice prepared by Kurmis. And, according to one tradition, regard them as half-brethren of their own, sprung from the same father, who begot the Kurmis on the elder and the Santals on the younger of two sisters".

Singh and Mahato (1982) observed that: "The Mahatos' homeland consists of parts of Chhotanagpur, and the adjoining regions of West Bengal and Orissa and its heart lies in erstwhile Manbhum district. A well-defined territory washed by the four rivers — Damodar, Kangsabati, Subarnarekha and Vaitarani — it has been a part of lower Jharkhand, where the Mahatos have coexisted with the tribal communities." They further observed that ethnographic accounts of the Mahatos have differed in description of their origin and migration, but most ethnographers agreed on the close relationship which have existed between the Mahatos and the tribals, and have described the processes which have led to the emergence of the Mahatos as a sturdy peasantry.

The Kudmis are found in the Chhotanagpur North and South divisions, in the Santhal Parganas divisions of Bihar, in Mayurbhanj, Keonjhar, Sundargarh, Balasore and Cuttack districts of Orissa and in Purulia, Bankura, Midnapore, Burdwan, Birbhum, Nadia and the 24-Parganas districts of West Bengal as also in North Bengal. Risley observed a few endogamous subgroups among them live in Manbhum and Orissa, such as Kurum, Adh-Kurmi or Madhyam Kurmi, Sikharia or Chhota-Kurmi and Nich-Kurmi Gaysari, Maisasari, Bagsari and Oadasari. Though the terms, Adh-Kurmi, Sikharia, or Bagri are levelled at some of the Kudmis for identifying their last place of settlement and migration, all subgroups inter-marry among themselves.

The Bedia-Kudmis or Chhoto-Kudmi/San-Kudmis are the *patit* (ostracized) groups of Kudmis. They were once not treated as equals, but now, marriage with them is accepted. Mahato (1975) observed that a remarkable thing was that the Kudmis of Chhotanagpur had no ethnic subdivisions, sub-castes, or even subgroups. This singleness of the community's unity totally differentiates it from the Kudmis of Bihar, who are divided into different sub-castes, for instance the Awadhias, Ghamalias, Kochaisas, Joshowars, or Dhanuks. This lack of division singularly confirms that the Kudmis of Chhotanagpur have migrated somewhere from the central part of India, where they have their original kinsman, Kunbis. For a Santal of Chhotanagpur, the Kudmi is not a Kudmi, but a Kurbi. They have surnames such as Mahato, Maato, Chowdhury, or Sing. They have titles such as Mahato, Laya, Mahanta, Pargonait, Rout, Paramanik, Deshmandal, Gonju, Munda, or Majhi.

They speak the Kudmali language at home and Bengali, Hindi, Oriya, Bhanjabhumia, Manbhuinya, Dhalbhumia, Panchpargonia, Khortha and Sadri with outsiders. In some parts, they can speak the Santali, Ho and Mundari dialects. In West Bengal, they use mostly the Bengali and Roman scripts and speak Bengali. In Bihar, they use the Devanagari script and use Hindi language with others. In Orissa, they use the Oriya, Roman and Devanagari scripts and speak in the Bhanjbhumia and Oriya languages. The Kudmi-Mahatos are scheduled as another backward class, though in the 1921 census, they were reported as a scheduled tribe. They were dropped from the tribal category in 1931. They live in areas having a hard laterite soil, with moderate temperature in the plateau region. They live in close proximity of forests and hills.

They are non-vegetarian and eat pork, but not beef. They eat different kinds of fishes and also chicken and mutton. Their staple food is rice and pulses. They eat such leafy vegetables as *munga*, *khapra*, *khari* and *laita*, besides other vegetables. Their cooking mediums are mustard oil and *mahua* oil. They eat roots, tubers and locally available seasonal fruits and drink milk, tea and *mahua* liquor, besides *badia*. On special occasions, both men and women drink liquor, both *badia* (home brewed), and bought from the market. Both men and women chew tobacco and betel leaves and smoke *bidis* and *sal-chutas* (indigenous cheroot). They eat *kado*, *gundli*, *marua* and *jonar* (maize) at times of scarcity.

They have got eighty-one, or more, totemistic lineages or clans (*bangshas*), such as Nag (serpent), Sankhowar (conch), Bara Nag (King cobra), Hindowar (a kind of wild grass), Keshria (*kesar* grass), Kaidowar (buffalo), Katiar (silk cocoon), Banowar (monkey), Baghowar (tiger), Hansda (duck), Phecha (owl), Chirrha (squirrel), Kurum (tortoise), Murmu (*nilgai*), Musa (rat), Chanch Mutra (spider), Tiruar, Birhor Banowar, Rajmour, Shiar (fox), Dumria (fig), Jal Banowar, Chiloar (kite), Goisari, Gadhasari, Karowar Bilar (wild cat), Banshiar (wild bamboo), Bagh Banowar, Hathi Banowar, Mangriar, Hembram and Hembramia.

The *jati-varna* concept is still not very clear to the ordinary Kudmi-Mahatos. *Gotras* or *bangshas* regulate marriage and also indicate ancestry. The settlement pattern of each *bangsha* in the village, known as *Baghal*, is well demarcated. There have been practically no changes in the surname. Mahato, or Mahto, or Mahanta are the most popular surnames. But some have changed their surname to Mehta, Sing, or Chowdhury. They believe that they are a low caste in the *jati-varna* order. Even women do not accept cooked food from the Brahmans of the area. The Brahmans, Vaishnavas, Rajputs, Karnas, Telis, Tambulis, Benes, Khandayets, Oriyas, Bathudis, Bhuinyas and Napits also consider them a *jalachal* community and accept only *kachcha* and *siddha* food from them.

Local tribals such as the Santals, Bhumijs, Mundas and Hos drink with them and form an emotion based social group. They even drink with the Bauris in the Manbhum region, but they consider the Doms and Ghasis as the lowest among communities. They consider the Santals, Bhumijs, Koras, Mundas and Lohars their social equals and the Lodhas, Kharias, Ghasis and Doms as inferior. The Utkal Brahmans, Benes, Tambulis, Vaishnavas and Rajputs are considered superior in the caste hierarchy and are placed at the top.

The Kudmis are endogamous at the community level, but exogamous at the lineage or clan level. The marriageable age for girls is between fourteen and eighteen years and, for men between eighteen and twenty-four. Adult marriage is in vogue and marriage takes place through negotiations, mutual consent, *raji-khusi* (love), or *dukhu* (intrusion). Marriage by service, *badal-biha* (marriage by exchange) and marriage by elopement are also allowed. Most marriages are monogamous, though polygyny is also permitted in special cases. *Salibiha*, or junior sororate, and *bhajrakha*, or junior levirate, arc permissible. The symbols of a married woman are vermilion and iron bangles.

Dowry is rarely reported, but if an unmarried girl becomes pregnant, her parents are required to buy a groom by paying a heavy dowry. The husband so bought is considered the father of the child. In case of an illegitimate child, the *deshpradhan* of the traditional panchayat declares himself the father of the child to protect the social norms of the community. The marriage is performed by the community elders by giving a feast in both the bride's and groom's houses. They do not have the custom of *kanyadan*, though weddings do involve different rituals. The minimum bride price is Rs. 21 to Rs. 51, ornaments and clothes. After marriage the wife lives at her husband's house.

Either spouse can divorce (*chharachhari*) on grounds of adultery, barrenness, chronic sickness, cruelty, or insanity. The husband does not pay compensation to the *chhari* (divorced wife). Grownup children of divorced parents live with their father and younger ones with their mother. *Sangha* is permissible. The Kudmi families are nuclear, with the men dominating women. Elderly women are consulted on every family issue and help in production, maintenance, distribution and marketing.

There is mutual understanding and reciprocity between men and women in everyday family life. A man has a jocular relationship with his elder brother's wife and grandparents, and a relationship of distance with his younger brother's wife and wife's elder sisters. Property disputes and laziness spark conflict in a family. All the sons inherit property equally. Women have no right of inheritance. The eldest son succeeds to his father's position. Extended families have been giving way to nuclear families. Women enjoy much freedom, but not equality with men. They have economic and social roles, contribute to family income and control family expenditure.

Among the life-cycle rituals, *saad-khaawa* takes place nine months of pregnancy. After a child is born, the umbilical cord is cut by a Hari midwife. *Narta* takes place on the seventh or ninth day. Oil and *haldi* are distributed among lineage members within the village and the newborn is accepted into the clan. *Ekusa* is held on the twenty-first day when *chiri* is performed on the baby. The other rituals are done at the Shasthi-than or Garam-than. The naming ceremony is held on this day. Before this, the baby is called after the grandfather or grandmother. In the sixth or seventh month, the *mu-juthani* (first rice eating) ritual is held.

Before the wedding, the groom must perform Dharam puja. Negotiations for the marriage are carried out by a *raibar* (middleman) representing both sides. The groom's family initiates the negotiation proceedings with the bride's parents. The *bar-dekha* or *kanya-dekha* ceremonies are held by the respective families with the *ashirbad* or *darkhanda* rituals. The *lagna* is then fixed. *Marua* puja is performed first. At the start of the wedding, the groom begins with the *amla-khaawa* ritual by marrying a mango tree with the help of his would-be brother-in-law. The bride sits on her *marua* at her own house, and is smeared in a paste of oil and turmeric by her sisters-in-law.

When the groom arrives with his companions, new clothes and other items are gifted to the bride. A Dom orchestra, accompanying the groom, go with the bride for the *mahul-biha* ritual (marrying a *mahua* tree). The *sala-dhuti* and *behai-bajar* rituals are performed between the brothers of the bride and the groom, and the fathers or uncles of both. Then the *sindurdan* ritual is held with the help of elders and close kin of both families. The Kudmi-Mahato weddings have *solo-saguner bihar* (sixteen rituals).

The Kudmi-Mahatos cremate their dead, and pollution lasts ten days. The *ghate-utla* ritual is performed by elderly persons and the Vaishnavas (Baishtams). Ancestor worship is held on the third day of the pollution period, is known as *tita-bhat*. The ashes of the dead are poured into the Damodar River from the Telkupi *ghat*, or in Baitarani or Kangsabati. Sometimes, monoliths are erected at the burial ground in certain cases, where the body has been buried.

Regarding their personal hygiene and habits they have regular baths after massage of oil. They wash their mouth with *neem* twigs.

The Kudmi-Mahatos are mainly an agrarian community. Most of them are marginal farmers and landless share croppers. There are only a few rich farmers among them. In West Bengal most of the Kudmi-Mahatos are marginal farmers. In the Gopiballavpur, Nayagram, Jamboni and Rohini areas of Jhargram, they make and sell *sabui*-grass ropes. In Purulia, Bankura and Midnapore, they are mostly casual labourers working in road construction, forestry programmes and canal projects.

Though the Kudmi-Mahatos are a very close-knit and large community, very few are government officers, lecturers, lawyers, engineers or doctors. They prefer teaching in primary and high schools. Many work in the Railways as *khalasis* (load-bearers). Forests are an important economic resource. They gather *mahua* and *sal* (teak) flowers and fruits along with other tribals. They have not yet picked up the art of business.

Many Kudmi-Mahatos have been displaced along with other tribals because of land acquired for project implementation by the Damodar Valley Corporation, the Kangsabati and Subarnarekha river valley projects, or the Chittaranjan, Bokaro, Rourkela and Jamshedpur industrial complexes, but very few have been given jobs, and compensatory payments are pending. Since they are very hardworking, skilful and thrifty, they manage to survive. The Kudmi-Mahatos have direct links with the local daily and weekly markets. Wages are paid in cash and kind. In the regional economy, they are subsistence peasants and very good cultivators.

They have got their own cast councils, for instance, the *baisi* or *jati panchayat* headed, traditionally, by a *deshmondal* at the regional level, a *parganait* at the *pargana* level, and a *mahato* at the village level. The *baisi*, or village *soloana*, of the Kudmi-Mahatos decrees on issues of *chharachhari*, cow slaughter, or any violation of social norms or taboos. Social offenders or sometimes their entire families, are made *ek-gharia* (ostracized) and barred from feasts, or even drinking water from the source of potable water of the village. Only after hosting a feast and eating *panta-bhoj* are they readmitted to the community fold. A statutory panchayat too functions in the village and many Kudmi-Mahatos are elected to the panchayat and *zilla parishad* posts in West Bengal.

The Kudmi-Mahatos are inclined to folk religion and worship Garam (Sarna), Kudra, Baram, Rankini, Sitala, Manasa and Mahadev. They believe in the evil spirits of *dakin* and *jugin* and there are many *ojhas* and *sakhas* among them, who do *jharphoonk* (exorcism). They take part in the Shiva, Nawakhiya, Gajan, Bandna, Tusu, Rajja, Jitua, Karam, Jawa, Akkyan Jatra and Sarul festivals. Both men and women dance the Chou, Paik, Danr, Kathi, Karam and Jhumur and sing Jhumur, *bihageet*, Tusu *geet* and Karam *geet*. The Kudmi-Mahatos have a rich cultural heritage and their women are very creative.

They have a rich tradition in proverbs, riddles, rhymes and indoor games. They often teach their young through riddles:

"Ek thal supari, / Gunte lare byapari" (There are betel nuts in a metal pot and no business man is able to count. What are they?) The answer the youngster gives is "Stars".

The Kudmi Mahatos are experts in different styles of Chou dance, namely the Mayurbhanj, Seraikela and Manbhum schools of Chou dance.

Their creative abilities are reflected in the Jhumur songs. Different ragas, such as *Patiamedha*, *aar-khemta*, *khemta*, *domkoch, bhadria* and *chaiti* are used in Jhumur, which, through continuous influence of Visnamism, was transformed into another dance form, Nachni, patronized by local chieftains and landed peasantry. Once, keeping *nachni*s (dancing girls) was a status symbol. The rhythm and *tala*s of Jhumur are also the main constituents of the Chou. The dancers of Mayurbhanj, Seraikela and Manbhum schools of Chou, dance, mostly, without masks. Chou dance is a collective form of the unique regional choreographic imagination and aesthetic beauty based on stories from the Ramayana, Mahabharata and Puranas. The Chou dance form of Purulia starts with Ganesh Bandana, the singer sings the Jhumur:

"Prathame bandana kari, / Ganesh charan, namo namo Narayan"

The Radha-Krishna, Savartaka, or Nishith Milan stories are used with Jhumur tunes and songs.

The Kudmi Mahatos also dance the Paika, or Paik, in Jhargram. In Purulia district, they also dance the Natua.

Apart from these songs and dances, they have other folk forms of such dance dramas. Kap-Jhap is performed during the Shiva Gajan festival and Machchani folk drama of Purulia district, is performed during the Dharamer Gajan festival. Another kind of dance drama is performed at the annual hunting festival in the Ayodhya Hills of Purulia at the time of Baisakhi Purnima (full-moon night in Baisakh) is Sikaria, or Singrai, comprising sexual songs, known as Udaya Jhumur. They also perform the annual Bhan Sing festival on Akkyan Jatra day (first day of *Magh*), or first day of the annual agricultural season of the region. At this time, in some village festivals, they have *bheja-binda* (archery displays).

At the Jatra Buri festival, they have wrestling bouts and the *murgi-ura* and *bhera-ura* rituals, in which all young and grownup boys take part. The *naya*, or priest, flies a hen tied to a string in the sky and when it comes down, the youngsters jump on it and catch it. One may be happy with just a handful of flesh, or simply, with a part of the bloodstained intestines. Through this "game" they learn that the spoils of a hunt must be shared by all; otherwise some people will snatch a larger part. The *lok-dharma*, or folk religion, is passed on from generation to generation through this ritual.

They have their own indoor and outdoor games. *Bagh-chhagal*, *guti-khela*, *kari-khela* and *tentul-bichi khela* are examples of the first kind; outdoor games are *hadu-du-du*, *kabadi*, *Sita-churi*, *jharal-jhap*, *chur*, *tir-dang*, *ghuchi* and *kait*. Swimming and football are very popular too, while children love playing *buri-dhara*, *jhim-jhima*, *araiadega* and *chil-murgi*. Nowadays however, a popular pastime of the Kudmi youngsters is practising the Chou dance and story-telling.

The Kudmi Mahatos have a traditional inter-community relationship with local artisans and the functional and agricultural communities. They are treated by tribals as *mitan*. The Kudmi women never accept food from the upper castes. But the men share food and drinks with the Santals and Mundas. It is reported that in the past they treated some communities, such as the Ghasis and Doms as untouchables. However now, the concept is not in vogue. They do not prefer a commensal relationship with Brahmans, Karans, Khandayets and Rajputs. They have the *gou-ghar*, or *bartani* system with Bariks (Napits), Kamars, Doms and Kumbhars and *jajmani* with the Vaishnava *kanphuka guru*. The number of such families is not very high. Poor and marginal farmers do not keep such relationships. They have a ceremonial friendship of *sangat*, *phool* and *saiba* — a strong emotional bondage with members of the other communities.

The level of literacy of the Kudmi is low and the dropout rate among both girls and boys is extremely high, because of their poverty and remoteness. More students, however, are now going to schools, colleges and universities. A few are employed in banks, the Customs, post offices, state transport companies and private offices. They, sometimes, work in the IRDP. NREP and the ICDS have been implemented in some Kudmi areas. They often visit nearby primary health centres and are favourably disposed towards family planning. Kudmi villages have drinking water facilities. They gather firewood from nearby forests for fuel. Post offices, fair price shops and banks exist in their localities. They travel in trains and buses.

The Kudmis have taken part in socio-political movements at different times in history. During the time of colonial rule, they took part in the Chuar revolt of 1785-1800 along with the Bhumijs, Mundas and other tribal communities of West Bengal, Bihar and Orissa. Sri Raghunath Singh Mahato was their main leader, and Gopal Majhi was a famous leader in the Manbhum area. During the Kol insurrection and Bhumij revolt under the leadership of Ganga Narayan Sing and Buli Mahato of Barabhum, they waged an historic struggle against the British and the Bengali *mahajan*s and *thikadar*s (contractors) under them.

During the Santal rebellion in the Santhal Parganas and Manbhum, the Kudmis fought under the leadership of Chanku Mahato, later hanged in Godda, in 1856. In the Sepoy Mutiny of 1857, the Kudmis joined the Hos and Mundas under the leadership of Maharaja Nilmoni Singdeo and Maharaja Arjun Singh of Porahat, Chakradharpur and Chaibasa; and, in the Birsa Revolt, they joined hands with the Mundas in the Tamar and Bundu areas and drove out the *mahajan*s, or moneylenders and wine traders. Later, when a famine occurred, they migrated with the Santals, Mundas, Hos and Oraons to the Assam tea gardens as *coolies*. They also reclaimed land in the Sunderbans and worked in Nadia as indigo planters and as *basil* labourers in erstwhile East Bengal (presently Bangladesh). Later on at different times, they came as seasonal *namal* labourers to Hooghly, Burdwan, Howrah and coastal Midnapore districts. The Kudmis of Mayurbhanj joined the Medi movement under the leadership of Kanka Mahanta and Kalia Majhi.

The Kudmis of Manbhum joined *en masse* in the freedom movement led by Mahatma Gandhi. In 1930 five aboriginal Kudmis were shot dead by the British. They were Gokul Mahato, Mohan Mahato, Sital Mahato, Sahadev Mahato and Ganesh Mahato. Many were arrested, convicted and sent to prisons for long terms by the authorities. In 1942, two other Kudmi-Mahato youths were shot dead — Chunaram Mahato and Gobinda Mahato. In the entire Manbhum, Hazaribagh, Singbhum and Jhargram areas, the Kudmi-Mahatos joined the 'Quit India Movement' under the leadership of Maheswar Mahato, Brindaban Mahato, Bhajahari Mahato, Bhim Chandra Mahato, Rajkishore Mahato, Satyakinkar Mahato and Jhyotindra Nath Mahato.

An important social movement where the Kudmi-Mahato elite took part was the Kurmi-Kshatriya movement, demanding that they be accepted into the Hindu fold and to find out a respectable position for themselves in the Hindu *varna* hierarchy. They took part in different Kudmi-Kshatriya Mahasavas at different places in Bihar and Uttar Pradesh and tried to establish themselves as Kshatriyas. Shivaji was their hero and they practically banned group dancing and singing and restricted *sangha* marriages.

Some landowning and literate Kudmi families tried to engage Brahmans for Kudmi weddings. In 1918, Niranjan Mahato (Nirvayananda Maharaj) of Bhanjakiya village, in Panchpirh subdivision of Mayurbhanj, organized the Kudmis with the help of Dinabandhu Bed Shastri of the Arya Samaj and Digendra Nath Bhattacharya of the Hindu Mahasabha, who supplied necessary myths to the Kudmi elites. In 1927, Kudmi Mahatos organized a large rally at Ghagharjwari village, in which Maharaj Kumar Jyothi Prasad Singdeo was the president. The sacred thread ceremony was held in different areas.

At this time, the Hindu Muslim controversy between the Arya Samaj, Hindu Mahasabha and Hindu Mission on one side, and the Muslim League on the other, had sensitized the issue. The Bengali-Bihari-Oriya upper castes became their spokesmen and, since the Kudmi-Mahato elites joined the freedom struggle *en masse*, the Government of India, under pressure from the Hindu upper castes, de-scheduled them in 1931 from the list of tribals and withdrew administrative and legal protection to the Kudmis of Chhotanagpur and the Santhal Parganas. From Purulia constituency, Upendra Nath Dasgupta and, from Jamshedpur, Bhattasali, a Bengali upper caste Brahman were elected. Tikaram Majhi was elected from the Dhanbad seat reserved for tribals. The Kudmi elites denied and disowned the cultural commonness and tolerance of the Chhotanagpur tribals.

In 1946, Atul Chandra Ghose, a local lawyer and president of the Manbhum District Congress Committee, at a meeting in Jitan village, moved a resolution saying that, since a majority in Manbhum spoke Bengali, Manbhum should be merged with Bengal. The motion was defeated and Ghose resigned form the Lok Sevak Sangha. Later, Maheswar Mahato became district president of the Congress. The movement for merger of Manbhum on the basis of language was then gaining strength. The Kudmi Mahatos were practically divided into three groups: the pro-Biharis; pro-Bengalis; and pro-Jharkhand state.

Finally, on November 1, 1956, Manbhum was divided on the recommendation of the State Reorganization Committee. Dhanbad remained with Bihar. At this time, the pro-Jharkhand Kudmis were also given nominations in the Jharkhand Party under the leadership of Jaipal Sing. Jagannath Mahato was elected from the Tamar constituency and V.C. Mahato and Padmalochan Mahato were defeated by Congress candidates in Silli, Ranchi district, and in Baripada Sadar, Mayurbhanj district, constituencies. Later, Sisir Mahato of the Jharkhand Party was elected from the Chakulia-Ghatsila constituency.

After Ranchi University was established, the Kudmi Mahatos got better opportunities for higher education. Before that, they had felt discriminated against, compared with Santals, Mundas and Oraons, who were scheduled tribes. Up to 1967, the Kudmi Mahato students were divided into two factions: since they were listed as other backward class under Annexure I, they enjoyed some benefits in schools and colleges, although there was no job reservation. The Kudmis of Bihar meanwhile, had been managing to get benefits from the Patna administration.

So, they decided to have a common platform in the form of the Jharkhand Students' Association, in which Kudmis, Mundas, Bhumijs, Santals, Hos and Muslim university students joined. The Kudmi elites felt that a Jharkhand state was the only solution and, for this they would have to launch a movement to demand rescheduling of the Kudmi Mahatos as a scheduled tribe. A resolution to this effect was accepted at the thirtieth annual conference of the All India Kudmi Mahasava held on May 1971 in Patna. The Silli conference took place in 1987; the Purulia conference in 1987; the All-India Indigenous and Tribal People's Conference at Rourkela in 1988; and the Adivasi Kudmi Conference in Jashipur in 1989 were some of the notable conferences in this direction.

Everywhere the common working class and intellectuals of the Kudmi-Mahatos attended the meetings in large numbers. The leaders of the Santals and other tribal groups — Chaitan Majhi (Janata Party), Kuaria Majhi (Congress), Birbhadra Sing (Congress) and Chandra Mohan Sing in Mayurbhanj, Salkhan Murmu (Jharkhand Liberation Front), Shibu Soren (Jharkhand Mukti Morcha), Surya Sing Besra and Prabhakar Tirkey (AJSU), Nirmal Horo (Jharkhand Party), Ramdayal Munda (Jharkhand Coordination Committee), Amiya Kumar Kisku and Nirmal Minz openly advocated in favour of granting the tribal status to the Kudmi Mahatos of Jharkhand. The biggest rallies for the legitimate demand of the Kudmis was held in Jhajka village, in Purulia district, on December 27, 1987, where Thakurdas Mahato (Retd. IAS) was president and Ram Ratan (M.P.) the chairman of the parliamentary committee on the welfare of the scheduled castes and tribes was chief guest.

The same resolution was also passed at the following conferences: Jhargram (West Bengal) in 1971; Ranchi (Bihar) in 1972; Rangarh (Bihar) in 1975; Chitorda (Mayurbhanj district, Orissa), in 1977; Ranchi in 1978; Jamshedpur in 1979; Pukhuria (Jhargram) in 1980; Raipur

(Bankura) in 1981; Jhalda in 1982; Krantikari Yuva Chhatra Morcha (Dighi Chandil) in 1983; Bhanjakia (Mayurbhanj) in 1984; Nayagram (West Bengal) in 1985; Bispuria (Purulia district) in 1986; All Jharkhand Students' and Intellectuals' Conference in 1986; JCC Conference (Ramgarh) in 1987; All India Indigenous and Tribal People's Affairs Conference (Ranchi) in 1987.

PASHUPATI PRASAD MAHATO

KUMHAR

The Kumhars are a potter caste of West Bengal with synonyms Kumar, Kumbhakar, Rudra Pal and Kumore. They have such titles as Kavi, Bhaskar and Dikpal. The etymology of the word, Kumhar, shows it has come from making *pot*s (*kumbha* – pot; *kara*s – makers). It means those who are makers of *pot*s. Locals consider themselves as potters and clay modellers. According to Risley (1891: 84), West Bengal Kumhars are of four kinds: Rarhi; Barendra; Daspari; and Chaurasi. Present day Kumhars are aware of the abovementioned groups, but say Rarhi Kumhars have been divided into two groups — Uttar Rarhi; and Dakshin Rarhi. Midnapore Kumhars claim they have only three groups — Uttar Rarhi; Dakshin Rahri; Barendra.

The story on the origin of the Kumhars has been mentioned by Risley who quotes the *Brahmavaivartta Purana*: "The Kumbhakar, or maker of water jars (*kumbha*), is born of a Vaishya woman and a Brahman father; the Parasara Sanhita makes the father a Malakar (gardener) and the mother a Chamar, while the Parasara Padhati holds that the ancestor of the caste was begotten of a Tilli woman by a Pattikar, or weaver of silk cloth" (1891: 517-518). Sir Monier Williams describes them as "the offspring of a Kshatriya woman by a Brahman" *(ibid)*.

Risley also mentions that "the Kumhar says that, at the marriage of Shiva, a *ghot* (water jar) was wanted, but no one knew how to make one. The God therefore, took a bead from his necklace and, with it, created a potter, while with a second, he made a woman, who became the potter's wife. This man was the father of all those who work in pottery, and, in the memory of their Creator, all potters bear the title Rudra Pal" *(ibid)*. It is said, "The divine association and origin of the caste indicate 'discovery', or 'introduction' of a new craft by primitive talent in a remote period, when primitive society had recourse to magic which could produce strange things for the benefit of their household operations" (Mitra: 1953: 318).

This was continued as caste functions of craftsmen and traditionally maintained to execute cult instruments to invoke boons and *mangala*. Mitra also says, "A potter's work began with the creation of the Mangala-*har*s, intimately connected with the magic formula of the Barna and invocation of the souls of departed ancestors, and he is still associated in present Bengali society with the same function" (1953:318).

The Kumhars are found in almost all districts of the state. They are not concentrated in large numbers in any one village. They are aware of their widespread distribution in different parts of the state. The climate of the areas they live in is warm and temperate. The inhabited areas are mainly the eastern plains of our country. Humidity is high during summer and rainfall is medium to high during the rainy season. Their total population in the state was 2,89,810 by the 1931 census, out of which 27,277 belonged to Midnapore district, where the study was conducted. Their written and spoken language, both at home and outside, is Bengali. Their constitutional status is that of another backward class.

The Kumhars are, basically, non-vegetarian but cannot afford fish, eggs or meat regularly. They do not have *boal* fish, beef or pork. Their staple food is rice, but, now, most have *roti*s at night. They eat all locally available pulses, vegetables, roots and tubers, besides bark, such as *thore* and flowers, such as *mocha*, *bak* and *sajne*. They, occasionally, have seasonal fruits, but oranges, apples and grapes only when ill. They can afford milk only for children and the old. They have tea, and smoking is quite common. Many chew *pan*. Though some adults drink frequently, alcoholism in any form is looked down upon by them. Drinking, especially at cremations, or festive occasions, is quite common nowadays.

There are certain restrictions on food items in certain seasons or occasions. Besides, they have numerous common beliefs regarding food items to be eaten on certain days or *tithi*s. On the seventh day of *Ashar*, they observe *ambubachi* as a measure to prevent snakebite. On this day, each one in the family has milk and mangoes.

West Bengal Kumhars have been divided into the four major subgroups mentioned. Besides they have several *srenis*, or *thaks*, or *ghars*, based primarily on the territory where they live. Among the Rarhis, Uttar Rarhi Kumhars are in a higher position than Dakshin Rarhi Kumhars, since the former make large sized earthenware. The basis of differentiation among these groups is territorial, as well as occupational.

Mitra writes (1953: 319): "The Kumharkars, distributed all over Bengal, at present, denote no sharp occupational, ritual or ethical differences. And the methods, techniques or processes also do not classify them into such caste groups". Dakshin Rarhis and Chourashis enjoy equal status since they produce and supply items of local religious and household demand. Mitra *(ibid)* mentions three categories of potters: Kuchols (those who produce small items); Hammors (those who produce large vessels for storing fodder or cattle feed); and Deoras (those who specialize in making clay images).

It is clear that the *sreni* is not so important outside their own caste hierarchy; in fact, people are more interested about the centres or *ghar*s that produce items of a special quality, use and interest. For instance, some are specialists in *pot*-making, tile-making or image-making. No changes have been noticed in surname or clan name. The following surnames are common in thè state: Pal, Jana, Das, Chowdhury or Mandal. The clans/*gotras* of the Kumhars are: Kashyap, Modhugolla (Maudhalya), Sandilya or Ilish. Kashyaps do not eat tortoise. They have mainly animistic and totemistic *gotra*s.

Kumhars are considered a part of the *nabasakha* group of West Bengal. They have a lower social status than upper castes, such as Brahmans, Vaidyas and Kayasthas. The Kumhars are numerically superior to the other low caste people. The community believes they are clean Sudras, belonging to the service community. The role and function of the community are explicit in terms of their traditional caste occupation, since they play an important role in rituals and religious ceremonies.

The Kumhars are exogamous at the clan level. The marriageable age for men varies between twenty-one and twenty-five years, and, for women between eighteen and twenty-one. Kumhar marriages are only negotiated and monogamous, and arranged through a *ghatak* (matchmaker) or a community elder. The symbols of a married woman are *sindur* and *sankha*. Dowry is paid in both cash and kind, but it depends on the financial condition of the bride's parents. After marriage, the bride lives in her husband's house. A husband or wife may initiate divorce proceedings, under the guidance of an educated community elder.

Remarriage is also permitted. A man may remarry if his first wife is infertile. Remarriage of young widows or divorced women is socially approved. In general, divorced women are looked down upon, though allowed to remarry, though no elaborate ceremony takes place. Recent changes have been noticed in the marriageable age. The younger generations now marry after the age of twenty-five.

The Kumhars live in both nuclear and joint families. Relations within a family are cordial. A husband-wife relationship depends upon love, respect, reciprocal duties and mutual obligation. Children are made to fear punishment if not attentive to studies. Generally, the *jethamoshai* (father's elder brother) looks after this. A man has a relationship of distance with his younger brother's wife and a woman with her father-in-law and mother-in-law. Parents' relationship with their adult children is one of mutual affection and responsibility. A woman has jocular relations with her husband's younger brothers.

Conflict and confrontation are common in joint families and sparked by maladjustment between a woman and her mother-in-law or sister-in-law, resulting in tension between father and son, and so leading to breaking up of a joint family. Confrontation may also arise out of property issues. Sons inherit their father's property and the eldest son succeeds to his father's position. A widow gets ownership of property if she does not have any male child. Inter-family links are cordial and families may exchange essential commodities of daily use in times of sudden need.

Families also exchange firewood, required to burn the clay models. In times of emergency, these links become even stronger and a network of relationships and social solidarity is maintained.

Women play several roles. They do not, normally, get a share of their parents' property, though they are aware of their legal right of inheritance. With the enactment of the Hindu law of inheritance, a few women get a small share of their father's property. But, under normal circumstances, they do not claim their share. Their economic role is limited to gathering fuel and fodder, fetching water and to perform other domestic chores. Their social role encompasses looking after the children and the well-being of the family. They also have a role in the life-cycle rituals. Their religious role is one of observing *bratas* and *upas* and cooking certain kinds of food. Women are not politically active, but do cast their votes. They do not have the scope to earn and so, do not contribute to the family budget. Women do not play any role in family management, but have many responsibilities and duties.

There are no pre-delivery rituals for pregnant women. A *dai* helps with the delivery and cuts the umbilical cord. It is buried under the door for a first-born and, for others, thrown away far from the locality. *Janma-asouch* (pollution) lasts a month after a child is born, for the family and those related by blood. Used kitchen earthenware is discarded by the family and neighbouring lineage families. *Ekusia* takes place on the twenty-first day, when a barber pares the nails of mother and newborn. They have a bath in lukewarm water added to turmeric paste with the help of a *dai*. A Dhoba washes the used clothes. On this day, Goddess Shashthi is worshipped for the baby's welfare.

On the third or fourth day, a *jyotish* prepares the child's horoscope and names the child. *Annaprashan* takes place in the sixth month if the child born is a girl and, in the ninth, if a boy. The *mama* feeds the child its first morsel of solid food and a Brahman priest and a Napit conduct the rituals. The child is reared with care and affection by the grandmother and other elderly women. An adolescent girl lives in the family under strict discipline and is not allowed to move out alone, or even meet relatives alone.

Rituals for the first menstruation are held for seven days and the girl is not allowed either to venture out, or enter a kitchen or rooms where the family deity is housed. After seven days, she has a bath and worships Goddess Shashthi, Lakshmi or any other family deity.

A Kumhar wedding is an elaborate ceremony of rituals comprising *gayehalud*, *biya* and *boubhat*. On the wedding day, both bride and groom have a ceremonial bath with oil and turmeric paste. The groom goes to the bride's house for the wedding rites. A booth is erected where the bride and groom sit and five *eyos* (married women) go round them seven times, carrying twenty-seven sticks of *chitta-khara* (a kind of tree). The wedding is of the orthodox type and the most essential rite is *sindurdan*. The groom does this while he chants passages from the sacred scriptures. A Brahman priest solemnizes the marriage before a *hom*. The services of a barber are required for part of the ceremony.

The wedding rites take place in an atmosphere of great merriment, accompanied by *sankha-dhwani* (blowing of conch-shells) and *ulu-dhwani* (a loud ululating sound, usually made by a group of women). The day after the wedding, the bride goes to her husband's house, where she spends eight days, and later, the couple visit the house of the bride's father. On the second day after the wedding, the couple observe *kaal-ratri* (traditionally an inauspicious night when the couple are not supposed to sleep together, or even to meet. This has its roots in the mythical story of *Manasa-Mangal*, where Lakhindar died from snakebite when he slept with his wife, Behula, in the *basarghar* on the second day after the marriage). On the third day after the wedding, a feast is held and consummation takes place on this day.

The Kumhars cremate their dead and mourning lasts a month. Neighbours help to carry the body on a bier made of bamboo poles.

Either the eldest, or youngest, son lights the funeral pyre. The bereaved family does not cook for three days and bathes for a whole month without oil or soap. The sons of the deceased eat *habishyi* (*atap-chal* and boiled vegetables with *ghee* and salt) for thirty days. *Ghat* rituals take place on the thirtieth day. *Sradh* is held on this day with the help of a Brahman priest. The day after, a feast is held for neighbours, friends and relatives to mark the day when the family resumes eating normal food.

Various changes may be observed in the life-cycle rituals of Kumhars. Many now observe fifteen days as pollution period after a baby is born. Pregnant women earlier followed many folk-beliefs and taboos, but no longer do so. Earlier, too, there were two feasts at the groom's house, but now only one on the day of *boubhat*. Mourning after death has been cut down to only fifteen days instead of the earlier thirty days. These changes have been influenced by the lack of manpower, high prices and modern lifestyles.

Manufacture of pottery and clay modelling are the major traditional economic activities of the Midnapore Kumhars. Individual families control resources. There are both landowning and landless Kumhars. Now, their primary occupations are cultivation and working as daily wage labourers. Most have no subsidiary source of income. They are wholly dependent on markets. There is neither any bonded labour, nor child labour, in their society. Those who are landless, work as sharecroppers and daily wage labourers, for landowning neighbours, for wages in cash and kind. The children often, help with tools and raw material associated of their traditional craft.

Risley says, "A potter never cultivates the soil, or serves as a domestic servant, a writer, or a servant to a shopkeeper. The village potter, occasionally, holds *chakran* land, on the condition that he supply the vessels required at all festivals observed by the *zamindar*, or the village community. Hindu households generally contract for their annual supply of earthenware; while a few pay the market rate for what is wanted" (1891: 525).

The Kumhars have no traditional caste-council or regional association. There is no traditional village *panchayat* either, for settling disputes among various communities. Those who live in Medinipur town take economic assistance from the municipality members and settle serious disputes through them. Those in rural areas get such help from members of the modern statutory councils. Adultery, rape or disrespect towards traditional norms are considered serious offences, for which social boycott, physical punishment and a cash fine are imposed.

The Kumhars are Hindus. Risley states: "Vaishnavism seems the favourite religion of the caste" (1891: 522). Kumhars worship Shasthi, Lakshmi and Itu as their family deities and the ancient Vedic deities, Agni, Brahma, Indra and Pavana. On the first day of *Jaistha*, special services are held in their honour, at the same time as the festival of Vishwakarma is celebrated *(ibid)*. Besides, they worship Shiva and Manasa and organize Khamar puja in *Poush* (when new paddy is harvested and brought into the house) and *Chaitra*-Sankranti puja. On the first day of *Baisakh*, they put an image of Lord Shiva on their wheel and leave it upturned for the whole month. On the thirteenth day, Shiva is formally worshipped, and his image thrown into a river or tank. The wheel is then brought into use.

Radhaballav, Kali and Sitala are considered village and regional deities. All major Hindu sacred centres and shrines are considered potential centres of pilgrimage. They also visit several Muslim shrines, situated near their areas for fulfilment of their worldly desires. Brahman priests are employed as religious specialists. The major fairs are Pous mela, Janda mela and Charak mela. The Kumhars observe Saraswati puja, Durga puja and Kali puja as general community festivals. They never had any success with socio-religious movements to claim a higher status.

The Kumhars are specialised in pottery and clay modelling. Pottery is one of the most ancient of crafts and is still extensively practised. It is interesting that the art of pottery is still a living tradition in Bengal. A particular shape and size cater to a specific demand and standard devices and shapes are patented by particular families. Terracotta pottery (incised and without colours or unglazed usually brownish red earthenware), *kucho* (small) pottery, basket-mould potteries (large pots for cattle and storage, *chong* (tiles for cottages), household pottery, rings for wells, reinforced images, models, shells for musical instruments, flowerpots and tubs, dolls and toys are some of the important specialized potteries of the West Bengal Kumhars.

The potter's wheel in use is a circular table of baked clay weighted along the rim, revolving rapidly on a pivot cut from the heart of a tamarind tree. The neck and shoulders of globular vessels are made with the *chak* (wheel), but the body is fashioned by hand, often by women. A round ball of hardened clay is held inside, while, with a wooden mallet, the material is beaten from the outside into the requisite shape and thinness. Painting is done on the vessel after it has been baked. Red paint is prepared with red lead; yellow with arsenic; green by mixing yellow arsenic with indigo; and black with lamp-black, charred rice. "Idols, toys and tobacco bowls are also painted with these colours, and images of deities are further embellished, by having powdered mica sprinkled over them, while the paint is still wet" (Risley: 1891: 525).

The oral traditions observed among them are taken from their inhabited regions. Sometimes, these are taken from the religious texts and recited at rituals and other religious ceremonies. Kumhars are not expert in any music or dance form.

They are considered one of the *nabasakha* communities of West Bengal and, so, regarded as *jalchal*. They refrain from sharing *pucca* food with the scheduled castes and other low caste communities. Marriages are not allowed with other communities. Ritual-based friendship is, however, permitted. They do not have any problem in sharing wells and other water sources, roads, schools, crematoriums, temples, or the *panchayat-ghar*. They maintain a patron-client relationship with Brahmans, Napits and *dais*. The Kumhars show an interest in political discussions though they do not take part actively in politics except in exercising their voting rights at elections.

The sharecroppers and daily wage labourers among them maintain good relations with their landowning neighbours. Besides, they engage labourers for manufacturing different items from among the neighbouring communities which helps to foster closer ties. They also have good relations with the Muslims, since clay for making pots is supplied them.

The Kumhars are not very advanced educationally, though the percentage of literacy is more or less high. They have a progressive outlook on health, medicare and family planning matters. They do not have any problem in getting drinking water from municipality taps and tube wells. They do not get adequate self-employment facilities or help from other government sponsored employment guarantee schemes.

Many households have radios, but only a few well off families in towns own television sets. The Kumhars avail of all modern systems of communication. Though electricity has reached their areas, most cannot afford it. Wood, *gul*, cowdung cakes and coal are used as fuel. The irrigation system has not developed in their areas and they have to depend solely upon rain water. Chemical fertilizer, organic manure and insecticides are used by landowning families and sharecroppers.

Nutritional programmes at schools are irregular and perfunctory. The Kumhars collect essentials from the ration shops under the public distribution system. A few avail of banking, savings and investment facilities.

The Kumhars are a functional caste of West Bengal. Though they manufacture a large variety of potteries, they face a great deal of problems in maintaining their livelihood. Most are poor and landless and educationally backward. They say they buy firewood for baking their clay material at a lower cost. Sometimes, due to lack of fuel, they cannot stick to their delivery schedule for supply of pots. Hence, they want electric ovens for baking household potteries. They also say they do not get a fair price for the work they do.

SUBHRENDU MAITI

KUNJRA

The Kunjras of West Bengal are a Muslim community; its synonyms are Subzifrosh and Rai. The legend on the etymology of the word runs as follows: The people who used to live at Kunj — a place in Arabia — and grow vegetables and fruits to sell according to the Prophet's instruction were known as Kunjra. Risley (1891: 527) referred to the Kunjra as "a greengrocer who sells *tarkari* and *sabji*, an occupation usually, but not exclusively, followed by Mahomedans in Behar". They came from Arabia and settled first in Kanpur, Uttar Pradesh. They came to West Bengal from Gaya or Patna, Bihar, and settled down mostly in the urban areas of Hooghly and the 24-Parganas to avail of market facilities.

The areas under study are dominated by a monsoon climate. The Kunjras speak in Hindi with kin groups and in Bengali and Hindi with others. They write in the Arabic and Devanagari scripts.

The Kunjras are a non-vegetarian community. They eat beef, mutton and chicken. They eat rice for lunch and *roti*s for dinner. *Arhar*, *moong* and *masur* are their favourite pulses. They use mustard oil and rapeseed oil as cooking mediums. They eat all available seasonal vegetables, such as potato and radish and fruits, such as mango and guava. Most drink tea and milk regularly. A few men drink alcohol bought from the market. The men and some old women smoke *bidi*s and chew tobacco. Some also chew betel. The Kunjras do not eat crabs.

The Kunjras have no social divisions. Siddiqui (1974: 100) refers to Kunjras or Rais as occupying an intermediate position within the third block among four blocks of the Muslim hierarchical order. The Kunjras are lower in social status than the Mansooris, Ansaris or Momins — their neighbouring communities.

Kunjras are endogamous, and follow rules of consanguineous marriages at the community level. Junior sororate and junior levirate are permissible only after the first wife or husband dies. The marriageable age for boys is about twenty years and, for girls, about fifteen. Marriages are, usually, negotiated and monogamous, though polygyny is permissible. Vermilion and *nak-chabi* (nose-stud) are symbols of a married woman. Dowry is paid in cash and kind. *Denmohar* is promised for future payment. The husband has to pay this amount back at the time of divorce. After marriage, the wife lives with her husband.

Only a man can divorce his wife on grounds of maladjustment or infertility, while a wife may leave her husband because of adultery, cruelty or maladjustment. But she has no right to give *talak* (divorce) to her husband as long as he does not take the initiative. A man has only to utter the word, *talak*, thrice before witnesses of both sides. He has also to return all the articles given to him by his wife's father at the time of the wedding. Neither can marry again before three months and thirteen days. Widow and widower remarriage are also permissible. Introduction of *dahej* (dowry), an increase in the incidence of divorce and of second marriages for girls are significant changes.

Kunjra families are mostly nuclear, though vertically extended ones also exist. Of late, the trend has been towards the former. The father is head of the family and the younger ones obey him. There is a relationship of distance between a woman and her son-in-law, father-in-law, or husband's elder brother. There is a jocular relationship between a man and his wife's younger brothers and sisters. Poverty creates the ground for conflict between husband and wife, or between adolescent children and parents. They follow Muslim rules of inheritance for distribution of a dead man's property, and the women get less than the men. The eldest son succeeds his father as head of family. Inter-family links are maintained through life-cycle rituals, and during religious festivals.

Kunjra women go to the market to sell vegetables. Some work as agricultural labourers. They also take care of their poultry birds. A few Kunjra women earn by doing embroidery. Women engaged in economic activities, share the financial burden with the men. Kunjra women have a significant role in the life-cycle rituals, but do not get involved in politics. They do not have any decision making power, though family expenditures are generally controlled by women.

The Kunjras observe *sadhoury*, a predelivery ritual in the ninth month of pregnancy, when some married women — either relatives or neighbours — are invited to lunch. The pregnant woman wears new clothes and is offered *khir* and different curries. *Chhatti* is observed on the sixth day after the child is born. A barber (either Hindu or Muslim) tonsures the baby and pares the nails of mother and newborn. They name the child on this day. The *aqiqa* ceremony is not strictly observed by them, but a man who wants to perform this ceremony may do so at any time in life. Pollution after a child is born gets over on the sixth day after mother and baby have a bath. After *saoamahina* (forty days), the mother may perform *namaz*. *Milad* is performed on the fortieth day, when friends and relatives are invited. The invitees give gifts to the baby. Well-off people hold the *kshir-khaoano* ceremony (offering the baby a sweet preparation of milk and rice) in the fifth month. Circumcision is performed on boys within eight years of age.

When Kunjra boys and girls reach a marriageable age, parents launch the search for a suitable partner. After preliminary negotiations are over, both families visit each other. The marriage is finalized after new clothes and some money are given to the boy and the girl in a ceremony called *mangni*. The *manja* (smearing of turmeric on the body) ceremony is held in both the houses. *Nikah* — the main wedding ceremony — is performed in the bride's house. *Suhagrat* (consummation) takes place on the same day in the groom's house.

The Kunjras bury their dead, and do not eat fish for three days, while the women do not use vermilion for thirty-nine days. The Kunjras observe *chaharam*, *dashma*, *bishma* and *challisha*, according to Muslim rules. The barber pares the nails of the men. Earlier, all the sons of the deceased had to shave their heads, but now they only pare their nails. This is the only change in their life-cycle rituals.

The Kunjras are mainly vegetable and fruit sellers. In West Bengal they are mostly landless. Now, some are in the business of selling utensils and fish, or hold jobs. The Kunjras generally live in towns or cities, so that they are close to daily markets where they can sell their vegetables, fruits and fish. They also enter into contracts with different hotels for supplying vegetables. Kunjra boys help their fathers in business from the age of thirteen to fourteen years.

The Kunjras have a *malat* (caste-council) of their own. It consists of forty to sixty members in its executive body. *Sardar, nayeb sardar*, secretary and *khajanchi* are the main office bearers. They also have a regional association in Calcutta, known as the "All Bengal Jamiat-ul-Racen". Such an association exists in Bihar too. All the caste-council or regional association members are elected by voice vote. If anybody disobeys traditional norms, for instance if a man does not attend *milad*, he has to pay a cash fine to the caste-council. If anybody marries within the Hindu caste or even into another Muslim community, or disobeys the council's order, he is ostracized. He has to pray and donate some utensils to the council for salvation and re-entry into society.

The Kunjras hire tarpaulin sheets and utensils for a wedding from the council at subsidized rates, by paying cash. Since the Kunjras live in municipal towns, they are controlled mainly by the rules and regulations of the municipality of that area and share the benefit of the welfare activities of the municipality with other communities.

The Kunjras are followers of Islam. The *majar*, mosque and *pirtala* are their sacred centres. None of them goes on pilgrimage. The *maulavi* is their sacred specialist who attends to them during the life-cycle rituals. Id-ul-Fitr and Id-uz-Zoha are their major festivals.

The Kunjra women are skilled in embroidery and knitting sweaters. The women sing songs on the occasions of *sadhoury*, *chhatti* and *manja* to the accompaniment *dholki* beats.

The Kunjras maintain inter-community links at different levels. A barber belonging to another community attends to them on the occasions of *chhatti* (post-natal ceremony) and *challisha*. The *moulavi* — not necessarily from their own community — attends to them during religious rituals. Married women of other Muslim communities visit them on the occasion of *sadhoury*. The Hajams, another Muslim community, perform circumcision of Kunjra boys. People from other Muslim communities attend the circumcision and wedding ceremonies, as also *milad*. Besides, the Kunjras have business transactions with different Hindu communities, such as the Khatiks and Marwaris, who are their wholesale suppliers of commodities. The Kunjras, in turn, attend the occasion where their suppliers open *naya khata* (new books of accounts).

They share water and cooked food with other Muslim communities, but the Hindus do not accept these from them. However, the younger generations do not strictly follow this practice. Some Kunjra men take part in the activities of different political parties. They have teachers, engineers and white collar job-holders among the community, though few. Inter-community links are established through educated persons holding jobs and posts in the municipal corporations.

The Kunjra literacy rate is quite insignificant. Boys and girls, usually, study up to the primary level, and most girls drop out after that. Some boys do go up to high school and only a few up to college. The Kunjras are not averse to modern medicine, but their belief in primitive methods of treatment, such as *jalpara* and *jharphunk* is quite deep rooted. The Kunjra women are either sent to hospital or kept at home during delivery. They are not interested in any family planning methods. Since the Kunjras live in urban areas, they fetch drinking water either from municipal corporation taps or tube wells.

They avail of all media and communication facilities available in the urban areas. Those who can afford use electricity. Coal, sawdust and cowdung cakes are used as fuel. They are covered by the statutory rationing system of the urban area. Since they are poor, the Kunjras cannot save money in banks. They sometimes buy commodities from shops on credit.

ARCHANA DATTA

KUNUI

The Kunuis are a small community in terms of population. In the Rajnagar areas of Birbhum district, near Sadar Suri, the rajas of Rajnagar patronized and helped them to settle as *tantis*, or weavers, while, in general, they have a role to play while a pond is being dug. There is a general belief, or a local convention, which dictates that, after a pond is dug, a Kunui must dig the bottom of the pond thrice. Otherwise underground water will not be available. Besides this special role, the community traditionally practises weaving, while some families in almost all villages, work on a handloom. These two roles have complicated the communitys position in the local caste hierarchy.

Because of their profession of weaving in certain areas, they have been assigned the status of *tanti*, though they have neither any commensal, nor connubial, relations with the artisan Tanti caste (Hindu weaver caste). Their role at the time of digging ponds has, substantially, brought their social position down in the eyes of their neighbours, especially those from the upper castes, to that of the Konras, or Koras, a Mundari speaking Hindu caste of low social status, having a low rank in society. In the circumstances, the Kunuis should have preferred the *tanti* status. In recent years the situation has become very complex. There is a scheduled caste of Konai living almost as neighbours to these people. This has prompted the Kunuis to claim they are Konais in recent years, in order to get benefits given to the scheduled castes.

The spatial distribution in of the Kunuis in West Bengal is limited to the two districts of Murshidabad and Birbhum. The natural environment of their habitat is the undulating plains of these districts, criss-crossed by such major rivers as the Bhagirathi, or the Ganga in Murshidabad, and the Mayurakshi in Birbhum. The two minor rivers, the Dwarka and the Brahmani, flow through Birbhum and Murshidabad, respectively. The climate is warm and humid. The vast, arable, undulating plains of these districts are dotted by villages with fruit bearing trees, trees of medicinal value and old and large trees with a socio-religious importance.

The thatched and corrugated tin roofs of the mud houses of these villages may be seen through a tangle of these trees from a distance. The area abounds in birds and snakes of different local varieties and in rodents. They speak the local form of Bengali at home and outside in dialects peculiar to the district to which they belong. The literate ones write only in the Bengali script. As stated, Kunuis are very keen on changing their community name and surname from Kunui to Konai in order to obtain the benefits and advantages bestowed by the government on the Konais, who are a scheduled caste.

The Kunuis are non-vegetarian and eat fish, meat and eggs, though beef and pork are taboo. Their staple food is parboiled rice. Puffed rice, in a way, forms a part of their staple food, since, without a considerable amount of this, a person's *jal-khabar* (breakfast) remains incomplete. Puffed rice, when eaten in large quantities, is soaked in water and then taken with either molasses or with cooked vegetables. *Kala-kalai* and *moong-kalai* are the two varieties of pulses used to make *dal*. *Moong* is considered an expensive variety and *kalai* as a nutritious one. Their cooking medium is the oil extracted from mustard seeds.

Roots (ginger and turmeric) and tubers constitute different items of food. Potato and yam of different varieties are commonly eaten tubers and vegetables are brinjal, *parval*, cabbage, gourd, *karela*, *uchhe* and *jhinge*. Milk is expensive and not freely available, so, mostly unaffordable. There is a taboo on drinking alcohol. A few who have embraced Vaishnavism avoid meat, garlic and onions.

There are no major social divisions and groupings among the Kunuis. Earlier, they used Das and Mondal as surname. The recent change in their surname from Kunui to Konai has thrown up several administrative problems for the scheduled tribe and scheduled caste welfare officer at the Sadar district headquarters in Suri. The office has not agreed to treat Kunuis garbed in their new surname, Konai as equivalent to the latter, a constitutionally declared scheduled caste community and, hence, has not extended much assistance or special constitutional facilities earmarked for the scheduled castes to the Kunuis.

In the documents of the recent past deeds on land transfer, purchase and sale it has been found that the Kunuis were always referred to as Kunuis, and never Konais. Besides this documentary evidence, there are certain social institutions that indicate a difference between the two communities. For instance, the Kunuis have several clans, while the Konais are a community of only one clan; the former community does not have widow remarriage, while the latter does; pollution following a death in either community lasts for different periods;

the Kunuis require the services of both the Brahman priest and barber in their life-cycle rituals, while the Konais are not served by barbers.

The following clans, to name a few, are observed among the Kunuis: Madhurashi, Nag, Shandilya, Kashyap and Almasi. Some of these clans observe certain restrictions. For instance, a person from the Madhurashi clan (*madhu* - honey) does not collect honey from a honeycomb; a person from the Nag clan (*nag* - snake) does not kill a snake; and a person from the Kashyap clan (*kashyap* - tortoise) does not kill or eat a tortoise. The members of this community claim they are socially inferior to the Brahman, Kayastha and *nabasakha* group of castes and superior to the Mal, Hari and Muchi. The older members of the community consider they are one of the *thaks* (or ranks) of the Tanti caste.

However, this claim is not strongly emphasised in the backdrop of the younger generations earnest endeavour to secure the constitutional status of scheduled caste. The communitys perception of the *varna* order is not clear. Neighbouring communities often consider them outright as a low caste, but, in certain areas where their involvement in weaving is conspicuous, neighbours feel hesitant in ascribing to them such a status. However, those in the high echelons of the caste structure the Brahman or the Kayastha show no hesitation in ascribing to them a low social status and, consequently, the status of Sudra, and expect them to serve as labourers too. Since they are poor, some work as agricultural labourers.

The Kunuis are clan-endogamous, but do not marry their *bhayad*. The marriageable age for girls is between sixteen and eighteen years, and, for men, between twenty-two and twenty-eight. Marriages are negotiated and monogamous. Polygyny is allowed when the first wife is infertile. *Ayuti* (conch-shell bangle), *sankha* and *sindur* are symbols of a married woman. Nowadays there is often a delay in girls getting married because of *pan*, since it frequently requires a long time for people of this poverty stricken community to procure enough money to meet the demands of *pan*, which is given in cash and kind. A woman lives with her husband after marriage, except in the case of a *ghar-jamai*, when the groom goes to live with his in-laws. Neither divorce, nor remarriage, is in vogue, though there is no customary bar on widower remarriage.

The changes in the light of past practices are: a gradual decline in the institution of child marriage; and *pan* replacing the custom of the groom's family sending gifts to the bride's family.

Joint families outnumber nuclear ones. A father-and-son relationship is one of control and respect. There is a relationship of distance between a man and his younger brothers wife and a jocular relationship between a man and his elder brothers wife, as between grandchildren and grandparents; relations of conflict and confrontation exist between brothers wives, or between daughters-in-law and their mother-in-law. There is a relationship of love and affection between young children and parents. Grownup children and their parents as also husbands and wives have relations of mutual obligation, dependence, cooperation and understanding.

According to customary rules of inheritance, sons equally share their parents property. Nowadays, the daughters husbands also stake their claim to a share of the property on behalf of their wives, since daughters have an equal right of inheritance by law. The eldest son succeeds to his fathers position as head of family. Inter-family links are many sided. Different families occupy a hamlet within a village, and thus, are close-set residentially. The feeling of being members of the same community adds an element of closeness, besides having a close spatial distribution. Coupled with these, they have ties with relatives across families. This tangled mass of families maintains relations of cooperation, obligation, reciprocity, mutual dependence and exchange of ideas, commodities, assistance and money when in need. At times, the families come into conflict with each other, but this is resolved through a combined effort of all families. A significant change is the peoples awareness of the introduction of the Hindu Code Bill stipulating womens right to parental property.

But women's right of inheritance is largely inoperative. Pressure of habits and social and family opinion act in subtle ways and, in many a case, the right conferred by law, is voluntarily given up by the women. Womens role in the family constitutes doing household chores, gathering fuel, such as dried leaves and twigs, or making cowdung cakes; fetching water; cooking; cleaning; washing and serving food. A major social role is that of rearing children and observing *bratas* and *upas*. Poor Kunui women work as agricultural daily wage labourers during transplantation and harvest. They also work on contracts for binding *bidi*s. The money so earned is contributed to the family kitty.

Antur (pollution) lasts a month after a child is born with the help of a Hari *dai*. The first childbirth customarily takes place in the natal house of the mother. This custom is prevalent among all communities, irrespective of caste or creed, except in the case of the local tribes. Within a month or two, the child is named. However, no naming ceremony is held. The name is given by an Acharya Brahman. *Annaprashan* takes place in the sixth month if the child born is a boy, and seventh, if a girl. *Prasad* of a god or a deity is brought and offered to the child by the maternal uncle or paternal grandfather.

A wedding is a three day affair the first day known as *adhibas*, when the *gayehalud* ritual is held at the homes of both the bride and groom. The second is wedding day, when the groom goes to the brides house accompanied by a party known as *barjatri*, comprising relatives, friends and villagers. The actual ceremony is held in the evening, according to the time of *lagan* (auspicious time) fixed from an almanac. On the third and final day, a feast is held at the grooms house in *boubhat*, where kin, friends, villagers and newly formed affinal kin are invited.

Kunuis now cremate their dead over a wood fire, while, earlier, they used to bury their dead. *Asouch* (pollution for family and *bhayad* after a person dies) lasts thirty days. On the twenty-ninth day after the death, *ghat* is held and the sons of the deceased shave their heads and beards. On the thirtieth day, *sradh* is held and a feast is hosted. There is a system of eating *kanika* (left-over crumbs) from the plates of community elders, collected and eaten by members of the family of the deceased.

The community is mainly landless, with hardly anyone having control over land, considered a major economic resource by the people in pre-eminently agricultural areas where the Kunuis live. Very few are individual proprietors of land. This landless community, however, claims *chasbas* (cultivation) is its traditional occupation. Primarily, they are a class of agricultural dependants. A few have small land holdings, while still fewer are sharecroppers. The bulk of them work as labourers. Weaving may be considered a subsidiary occupation, though it is slowly becoming obsolete because of the following reasons: i) the trade has become very competitive and Kunui weavers who, nowadays, weave only *gamchas*, find it unprofitable; ii) younger generations have no interest in learning the trade; iii) weaving as a traditional occupation of the Kunuis is, often, considered an identifying mark to distinguish them from the Konais with whom they want to merge. So, those who are still involved in this craft do not find the atmosphere congenial to pursuing this art, at all.

Kunuis are totally dependent upon markets. There are no bonded labourers in this community. Because of their landlessness, there is a slow and steady rise in the number of agricultural labourers and *bidi*-binders. Child labour in the form of *mahendari* and *bagali* exists. In agriculture, wages are paid in cash and kind, but, in industry, only in cash. Post Independence changes in their economic activities are: i) a rise in the incidence of landlessness. This has become conspicuous since they are slowly giving up their traditional craft of weaving and are forcing their way into the potential agricultural labour force, already overburdened with a lack of sufficient opportunities; ii) there is no migration of labour; iii) there is almost an unnoticeable shift from the primary and secondary to the tertiary sectors.

Their *jati* (traditional) council, as well as regional associations are now defunct. There is no traditional village panchayat for settling disputes among various communities. The modern statutory councils are at the helm of all affairs. They monopolise all formal, and informal, sources of power and influence in the villages. They generally have a hold on the channels of communication between their villages and outside organizations, such as the block development offices, irrigation department and other government offices. The following are the post-Independence changes: i) earlier, there was a *jati* council; each Kunui hamlet had a *mondal* and, under his chairmanship, the *murubbis* (village community elders) used to sit to settle disputes and discuss issues concerning the village community; ii) there were regional councils, called *panchagramis* (literally meaning concerning five villages), which used to sit under the chairmanship of an elected *matabbar*. The functions of these councils were limited among the members of this community; and iii) the *jati* and regional councils imposed fines on wrong doers.

Kunuis profess Hinduism and do not belong to any particular sect. There is no evidence of the existence of any family or clan deity. Their village and regional deity is often one and the same Dharamaraj. The major sacred centres or shrines, or pilgrimages are Vrindavan and Gaya; and, closer home, Phullara, Tarapith and Kankalitala. The role of sacred specialists is vested in *purohits* (Brahman priests). The local major fairs are held at Tarapith and Kankalitala. The major local festival is *Nabanna*. The fair at Kankalitala is held on *Sankranti* (the last day) of the last month of the Bengali year. People go there to take a dip in the river Kopai, which flows near the temple of Kankali. *Nabanna* is a post harvest ritual, held in *Agrahayan*. On this day, the villagers offer preparations of rice from newly harvested *aman* paddy and their obeisance to Goddess Lakshmi.

A few old Kunuis have embraced Vaishnavism. It is locally called *malanewa* (taking a necklace), since these people wear a small necklace made of beads of *tulsi* plant seeds, wound twice round their necks.

The Kunuis do not have any tradition in the plastic or graphic arts. The craft of weaving they practise gives them hardly any scope of pursuing aesthetics. They do not know the art of making a loom and depend upon carpenters for this service.

The Kunuis claim that the *nabasakha* group of castes accepts water from them, but not cooked food. There are no restrictions on sending *siddha* to any community of a high social status. Inter-community marriage is taboo and there is hardly any breach of this rule. Putative kinship based and ritual based friendship is common, such as *gangajal*. Namesakes often form a friendship formally. In multi-community village situations, the Kunuis do not face any problem in sharing wells and other water sources and roads, or entry into schools, crematoriums, houses or *panchayat-ghars*. *Jajmani* is still prevalent between Kunuis and their *purohits*, or *bamuns* (Brahman priests).

The other form of close socio-economic inter-dependence is that between members of the community and Hari midwives. With barbers, the traditional relationship is not always maintained. Instead, the Kunuis secure the services of any barber and is free to make payments in cash or in both cash and kind. No active political participation other than the exercise of adult franchise is reported. The present conscious effort to merge their identity with that of Konais can be termed a combined political and ethnic movement in order to have an equal edge with the latter in sharing opportunities that lie open for the scheduled castes. The extent of efforts on the part of Kunuis is intense and it appears that, after a decade or so, there will be no trace of this community.

A landlord-tenant relationship, or rather owner-sharecropper relationship, exists between the various rich landowning neighbours and Kunuis. A cultivator-labourer relationship constitutes the main economic relationship that rich members of different neighbouring communities maintain with poor Kunuis. The women employed during paddy transplantation are known as *putuni-munish*, or *putunis*. An employer-worker relationship is maintained by those who are in the *bidi*-making industry. To bind a thousand *bidis*, which takes almost a whole working day for an individual (8 a.m. - 6 p.m.) with a few breaks for breakfast and lunch, and for doing a few household chores, a person gets only Rs. 7 to Rs. 8 a day.

Literacy is not very low among the modern day Kunuis, though the dropout rate at schools is high. The main reason is that they are poor. Health and medicare awareness is poor, the reason once again, being their poverty. The concept of family welfare is non-existent, though their attitude towards family planning is positive. This small community seems to have failed in making local administrative bodies aware of their acute drinking water problems, or of their need for government employment and self-employment schemes. Except for roads and public transport and a few transistor radio-sets owned by some families in each hamlet, there is no significant improvement in use of communication media.

Electricity is beyond their means. A positive attitude towards irrigation and use of chemical fertilizer, insecticides and organic manure is observed. There is still a lack of a proper irrigation network in most areas inhabited by this community. A public distribution system operates in the region and people take advantage of this to buy kerosene and sugar at subsidised rates. Nutritional programmes at schools are irregular. The Kunuis, in their present economic position, find banking facilities of no consequence.

The role of a Brahman priest is purely a perfunctory one. Often, an adolescent Brahman boy (helped, sometimes, by his widowed mother) comes to perform his duties. The Brahmans serving low castes are, at times, called Sudra Brahmans. They are a category in themselves, but, to an outsider, their identity remains concealed, since they use such surnames as Bhattacharya or Chakraborty, used by Brahmans belonging to the highest caste of the Hindu social hierarchy. These Brahmans who serve the low castes do not disclose their identity under normal circumstances, especially to an outsider. Besides, they feel it an affront to be asked a straight question on their identity. However, their identity is always known to those who live nearby.

The Kunuis refer to a place known as Kumirkhala across the West Bengal border in the Santhal Parganas district of Bihar, where they have a major concentration and where they think several of their traditional *jati* councils are still in existence. The Kunuis have a traditional role to play there – at Rajput weddings. Rajput women employ the Kunuis to give them two and a half hoeful of earth to be carried to the *chharala* (or *chhandna-tala*, the wedding marquee) to raise a *bedi* (mud platform).

R. K. BHATTACHARYA

KUROL

The Kurols, or Kurals, are a less-known community of West Bengal, who also claim to be known as Rishis, or Jogis. The community has been named after the Bengali word, *kural*, or *kurol*, meaning 'axe'. Since they have been using an axe as a traditional woodcutter, the name, Kurol, has come to stay. There are two sub-groups: i) Bar-Kurol; and ii) Chhot-Kurol. They do not have any title. The community is identified, mainly, in certain localities. There is neither any historical, nor ethnographic, account on them. They claim they are one of the original settlers of the region, where they have been living since time immemorial.

According to them, members of this community may be found in the districts of Maldah and West Dinajpur in West Bengal and also in the adjoining districts of Katihar and Purnea in Bihar. The region they inhabit has a moderate climate, medium rainfall, high humidity, thin forests, and a plain land surface. Their population figure is not available. They use the local Bengali dialect and use Bengali script. They do not belong to any special constitutional category. There is no bio-anthropological information available on them.

The Kurols are non-vegetarian, but do not eat beef, pork or chicken. Their non-vegetarian dishes comprise *samuk* (snails, mussels or molluscs), *jhinuk* (oysters), *kachim* (turtle), *paira* (pigeon) and *khasi* (he-goat). They have different roots and tubers as vegetables. Their staple food is rice. Tea and milk are common beverages. Some men occasionally drink alcohol bought from the market. Most smoke *bidi*s and chew betel.

The two subgroups mentioned above are, in fact, sub-castes of the community. Hierarchical differentiation between the two sub-castes is made at the occupational and social levels. Bar-Kurols do lighter jobs and are engaged as *din-majur* or *jan-khata* (daily wage labourer). Chhot-Kurols subsist mainly on their traditional occupation of cutting trees and *bans-jhar* (bamboo shoots) — uprooting *bhutta* (roots of bamboo), splitting them as firewood and selling them in the market. Besides, Chhot-Kurol women are experts in collecting snails and oysters from marshy land, and ponds in and around the locality, and making lime by burning them in small indigenous *bhatti*s (kilns) for selling in the market.

Earlier, marrying outside the sub-caste was prohibited, but now as there is no such restriction; marriages often take place both outside and within the sub-caste. There are three recognized *gotras* among them: i) Alsdi; ii) Kashyap; and iii) Angari. Earlier, they used Kurol, Rishi and Chunari as surnames, but now, most use Rishi, Chunari and Jugi, or Jog. They believe they have a middling status in the regional social hierarchy. They are neither aware of the *varna* system, nor do they recognize their position in the system. They are reported to be of a lower status in the regional social hierarchy according to the point of view of other neighbouring communities.

They generally do not marry outside their own community. Marriage within a *gotra* is, traditionally, prohibited. Both hypergamy (marriage with women of a lower social status) and hypogamy (marriage with women of a higher social status) prevail. Marriage alliances among relatives who observe death pollution for one another are prohibited. Adult marriage has now become a common practice. Most marriages are either negotiated or by mutual consent, and monogamous. But marrying either the younger sister-in-law, or any other girl for that matter, while the first wife is alive, is not altogether unknown. *Sindur* and *sankha* are symbols of a married woman.

Earlier, the custom of paying bride price was prevalent, but now, dowry in both cash and kind has become a common practice. After marriage, the couple either lives with the husband's parents, or may set up home on their own. Both husband and wife may initiate divorce, which was easier in the past, compared to now. Earlier, mutual consent of the partners was sufficient for divorce and social approval was not important. Nowadays getting a divorce has become difficult and rare, since obtaining the social approval of the council of community elders, or sometimes, a court of law has become difficult.

Bhat-khabona (refusal to accept food, from the partner) is the ultimate word in obtaining divorce. Adultery, maladjustment, impotence, barrenness and cruelty are common grounds for divorce. No divorce compensation is paid. The liability of children of divorced parents may be borne by both father and mother or either. Widows, widowers and divorcees are free to remarry as they wish. Junior levirate and junior sororate are preferred in remarriage. The changes in the institution of marriage are changes in marriage rules, an increase in age at marriage, a shift from bride price to dowry, and rules of residence after marriage.

Nuclear families — with the husband, wife and unmarried children — are quite common now, compared to the number of extended families. Respect and reverence for parents, grandparents and elders, in general, and love and affection for the young are common principles that bind a family. A man has a relationship of distance with his *bhai-bou*, as also his *bhagin-bou* (nephew's wife). A man has a jocular and friendly relationship with his elder brother's wife, wife's and husband's younger siblings and grandparents, as also with his *beyan-bihai*. Sometimes, conflicts arise over property.

Traditionally, a man's property was equally inherited only by the sons. But of late, because of government legislation, all sons and daughters inherit property equally. Even married daughters have begun to claim an equal share of parental property. The maintenance of a widowed mother is, usually, the common responsibility of all sons, but, if she claims a share of her dead husband's property, she cannot demand maintenance. The eldest son succeeds his father as head of family.

Apart from performing household chores, women look after domestic animals, gather fuel and fetch water. They also play an important role in most socio-religious rituals. Women not only contribute to family income, but also exercise control over expenditure and take part in the decision making process on an equal footing with men. They do not have any direct role either in the political sphere, or in the mechanism of social control.

The *sadh-khawai* ritual is held in the seventh month of pregnancy, when the woman's mother offers her the choicest food and gifts her new clothes. A child is generally born at home with the help of a Hari *daima*. Pollution lasts seven days, during which the mother is given a meal in the morning and some *sukha* (dry and light) food at night. *Mundan* of the child takes place after a month. *Chumai* (blessing with blades of grass and corn) and *bhat-choa*, or *swad* (first feeding of rice mixed with milk and sugar), by the grandfather at seven to nine months of age, are important rituals associated with child birth.

Wedding rituals are held at the bride's house and wedding feasts are held by both the bride's and groom's families. *Biddhi* (propitiating ancestors) is also observed by both families along with wedding rituals at the bride's house performed by a Pandey Brahman priest. The *sindurdan* ritual is performed to the accompaniment of *mantra*s chanted by a priest and *basarghar* (night of abstinence before consummation) is held before the *bidai* ritual (farewell to the bride the following morning) and *boubhat* at the groom's house, *phulsajjya* and *ashtamangala* (return of the bride with her husband to her parental home after a couple of a days for *kapad-dhowa* — washing clothes).

Kurols cremate their dead, but bury the body of a minor. The *mukhagni* ritual is performed by the eldest son for a father and youngest for a mother. Pollution lasts thirteen days, during which the *agnikarta* has only one meal a day after seeing the first star come out in the evening sky and making *utsarga* (offering of food to ancestors). The men are tonsured and shaved on the eleventh day and *pinda* is offered to ancestors by a Kantha Brahman (degraded Brahman) outside the home, *bile kria* (mortuary rites) are conducted by a Maithili Brahman or Pandey Brahman priest.

Forest, water and, to some extent, land are the main natural resources on which a Kurol depends. They are basically, a landless community, subsisting mainly on individual labour. Except a few who individually own land, they do not have any control over natural resources. Cutting trees, *bansjhar*, digging for *bhutta*, *cherai* (splitting them into pieces as firewood), *chowkidari* (job of a village watchman) and *din-majuri*, or *jan-khata* (daily wage labour) are traditional and primary occupations. Women and children are also engaged in the traditional occupation of making *chun* (lime) by burning *samuk*s and *jhinuks*.

The women sell *chun* (lime), *chal* (rice), *chira* and *muri* (puffed rice). They have direct links with the daily and weekly markets and the medium of exchange is cash. Bonded labour does not exist; but children contribute directly, or indirectly, to family income. Landlessness is the main reason they have become more and more dependent on earning wages.

An informal council of elders exists at the community and village levels. Adultery, theft and quarrels at the community and inter-community levels are dealt with by the council of community and village elders. Sometimes, community level disputes are dealt with by village elders through imposition of cash fines and social boycotts. The members of the informal council of elders are elected by a voice vote. There is no system of chieftainship among them. They are aware of the existence of the modern statutory panchayat that implements welfare and development programmes for the public of the region, in general. No change or development has taken place in their condition of existence in recent times. They still languish in deprivation and poverty as in the past.

They profess Hindusim. Lakshmi, Gossain and Gram-Thakur are deities at the family, *gotra* and village levels. Besides, Durga, Kali and Manasa are deities of the wider Hindu pantheon that they recognize. The Pandey and Maithili Brahmans serve them as their religious experts who perform life-cycle rituals. Durga puja, Kali puja, Rash, Holi, *Chirua*, or *Chait Sankranti* and *Tilua Sankranti* are the major festivals. A few girls have married into Muslim families, either after elopement, or courtship. All of them have embraced Islam and follow the Shariat. They do not follow the practices of their religion before the change. Their relationship with their families is limited only to occasional visits. *Radharani* and Durga temples are the religious centres commonly visited. Gaya, Kashi, Vrindaban and Ramkeli Gour, near Malda town, are recognized pilgrimages.

Tattooing on different parts of the body is an art only the women indulge in. The walls and floors of their houses are painted with floral designs by the women on different socio-religious occasions. *Makha-ranga* is a typical wall or floor design painted with rice flour paste by women as decorations for a wedding. They do not, however, have any specific craft of their own. The women sing folk songs on the occasion of birth or marriage. They do not, play any musical instruments, but hire musicians from the Hari or Muchi communities on socio-religious occasions. They do not have any traditional dance form.

Traditionally, they do not accept food from the Doms, Mathors or Muchis. Except Brahmans, all other neighbourhood communities accept food from them. Acceptance of food, or otherwise, by Brahmans is a matter of individual choice rather than a community norm. The putative kinship of *bandhu* may be established by men and women with all communities through sharing food, clothes and, sometimes, garlands of flowers. The parents of putative friends are called *mit-baba* and *mit-ma*, or *sangra*. Marriages outside the community rarely take place. Nowadays they have no problems in sharing water sources, religious shrines, crematoriums and other public amenities with the other communities of the region. Earlier however, they did face problems in this regard.

Traditional links have been established with various communities through a patron-client or landlord-tenant relationship. Though the traditional *jajmani* with Brahmans, Napits and Dhopas continues, many have begun to hire their services only when required.

A few tea stall and betel shop owners, primary school teachers and defence service holders, from among the community, have established modern links with other communities, with whom they interact in their spheres of work. No leadership is however reported to have emerged from among them at any level.

Though they realize the need for education and want at least their children to study, they lag far behind the others in this regard. A few boys have studied up to the lower primary level and a few others are continuing their studies. Girls, generally do not study at all. Though most make full use of modern medicare facilities, they have not yet altogether discarded their indigenous medicare system. They are favourably disposed towards family planning and prefer two to three children per family. They adopt both indigenous and modern methods of family planning. Men prefer to get sterilized, rather than women. Drinking water is available in their localities from tube wells. No provision of employment has been made available to them through any government scheme. Some have benefited under the IRDP loan scheme at a thirty-three per cent subsidy. With the loan, they have either set up small tea-stalls and betel shops or sell rice and puffed rice in the market.

Though electricity is available in their localities, most cannot afford it. They are exposed to the modern mass media and communication facilities — the radio, cinema, roads, railways and newspapers. Dry leaves and branches, *ghusi* (cowdung cakes) and firewood are their main fuel. Children have nutritious food at school, but the schemes are, mostly, irregular. Only kerosene and sugar are provided by the local fair price shops, but that supply is irregular, too. Though they are favourably disposed towards the banking system, most cannot afford to save in banks. Most of them take *dhar* (credit) from shops and moneylenders upon keeping sufficient temporary *bandhak* (mortgage).

Kotua-biye (symbolic marriage) is a unique custom among them. Men and women who are either extremely poor, or are vagabonds, ugly, or physically handicapped — without any scope of getting married — generally have marriages of this kind. In other words, when a man faces the prospect of remaining an *akuar* (bachelor) for his whole life, or a woman an *akuari* (spinster), *kotua-biye* with the vermilion box is a way out. In the presence of a few community elders, a Brahman priest gives a small box of vermilion to the man concerned after chanting *mantras*. The man accepts this box as his wife by applying vermilion on the lid of the box in exactly the same way that a groom applies vermilion on the forehead of the bride. The container is then kept carefully hidden at some place in the house.

Meanwhile, a few women of the village and community first put vermilion on the forehead of the woman concerned and then wash it off. She is then made to wear *sankha* bangles and a *thethi* (coarse *sari*) and given a fresh vermilion mark by the women who escort her to the house of the man concerned. Symbolizing the vermilion container, with which the man has actually got married, the woman starts living with the man and performs all the roles and duties as his wife. She is, for all practical purposes, socially accepted as his wife.

A similar kind of a symbolic marriage, *path-biye* (marriage with a path) also exists among the community. Here, the man concerned puts a little vermilion at the base of a *binnar-jhad* (a clump of elongated grass found along the boundaries of crop-fields). By doing so, the man symbolically accepts as his wife the portion of the path where the *binnar-jhad* is located. Now, there may be women who are supposed to, or are likely to, go in for a similar kind of a symbolic marriage. But the one who first passes down the path is accepted as the symbolic wife of the man. Once the partners are chosen, the rest of the procedures follow the same pattern as in *kotua-biye*.

BADAL KUMAR BASU

LALBEGI

Some written documents published on the Lalbegis, as described by Russell and Hiralal (1916), say: "Mr Greeven gives seven main subdivisions (about the Mathores or sweepers), of which Lalbegi — the patron saint of sweepers — are the most important. The Rawatis appear to be an aristocratic sub-division of the Lalbegis, though there has been a corruption of the Sanskrit 'Rajputra', meaning a 'prince'... Though the Lalbegis worship an usual 'man-saint' they remain Hindus. The Lalbegis are, often, considered Mohammedans here rather than Hindus, and bury their dead. The religion of the sweepers has been described at length by Greeven and Crook and centres on the worship of two saints, Lalbegi, or Bale Shah, and Balnek, or Balmik, who is really Valmiki, author of the Ramayana.

Some members of this sweeper community, who live in the Jhalda police station area of Purulia district, have the surnames of Begi and Valmiki. They describe themselves as immigrants from Rajasthan, where they were known as Lalbegi Marwari. Originally, they were called Balmiki-*jati*, but after taking a *mantra*, or becoming disciples of Kabir, they took the title of Kabir, or Lalbegi. Now, all their cultural and religious rituals reveal that they are totally 'Hindu-ised' people. The community in the area under study is not aware of any subgroup.

The natural environment, in which the Lalbegi Mathore community lives, is generally that of the urban centres in the municipal areas where they mostly work. They say they are distributed in Hazaribagh, Jharia, Ranchi, Raniganj and Giridih, and in different pockets of Calcutta. They speak among themselves in Rajasthani and write in Devanagari, but a few do speak in Bengali and Hindi. The Lalbegis have no mark of identification, and are constitutionally a scheduled caste community.

They are non-vegetarians, but do not eat beef. Their staple food is rice and wheat, with all kinds of locally available vegetables and pulses. Their cooking medium is mustard oil. They eat all kinds of fruits and have milk and milk products. Very few drink alcohol. The men smoke cigarettes and *bidis* and both men and women chew betel leaves. A day before Sitala puja, the women cook special dishes with gram, pulses, curd and *pakari* and have it the following morning. There have been no significant changes in their food habits.

The Lalbegis are unaware of their sub-divisions, or stratifications. Their only clan is Balmiki and the only change in their surname is from Lalbegi to Begi. They — and other locals — believe they are of a lower social order and are Sudras in the *varna* order.

They are endogamous in marriage at the community and clan levels, though marriages do not take place within a locality. The marriageable age for girls is between fifteen and sixteen years and, for men, between twenty and twenty-five. Marriages are negotiated and monogamous. Polygyny is allowed if the first wife is infertile. *Pola* and *nath* (nose-ring) are symbols of a married woman. There is no system of paying bride price, or dowry, in their society, but a groom has to be paid Rs. 21, or Rs. 51, or Rs. 101 as *tilak*. If a divorce is sought, a meeting is called in the presence of the *mukhia* or *sarpanch*, who decides on it and the cash is given to the aggrieved party. *Sanga* (remarriage of widows) is rare, but permissible, as is junior levirate. Even men may remarry, but have to pay Rs. 305 as penalty to the family in which the bride has been living as widow or wife. There have been no significant changes in these aspects.

The Lalbegis have both vertically extended and nuclear families. Inter-personal relations are extremely cordial and close knit. The eldest man is head of the family. Children are brought up with affection and care by parents. Younger members respect elders. There is a relationship of distance between a woman and her husband's elder brother, between a man and his nephew's wife as between a man and the wife of his brother's son. Inter-family links are very much in evidence, especially at different life-cycle rituals and religious ceremonies, where relatives gather and women sing songs together. Property is inherited equally by the sons, and the eldest son succeeds his father as head of the family. There have been no recent changes in family pattern.

Women do not inherit property. They work under municipalities and are paid wages equal to men's. Women contribute equally to the family, besides doing their household chores of cooking, cleaning, child-rearing and fetching water. Women are very particular about rituals and have special songs for every ceremony.

The Lalbegis do not have such pre-delivery rituals as *sadhbhakshan*, and pregnant women do not go to graveyards or houses where death has occurred. Pollution lasts nine days after a child is born and, on the fifth day, they have a bath. The new mother does not wear vermilion, *sankha* or glass bangles, does not cook and does not touch drinking water meant for the family for these nine days. The delivery room is called *japa*. On the ninth day, after having a bath, they offer puja at a well and the mother anoints her body, as well as the newborn's, with turmeric paste and *mehendi* for purification, whereupon she is allowed to enter the kitchen. If they fail to perform the ritual on the ninth day because of the baby's, or mother's, illness, it is held on the twenty-first day.

If a boy child is born, they beat a brass gong, though not for a girl child. There in no naming ceremony. Instead, they go to the Brahman priest of a temple and tell him the baby's time of birth, whereupon the priest selects a name on the basis of the position of the stars at the time of birth. A Ghasi midwife helps with the delivery. The services of a Napit or Dhopa are not required for birth rites. *Annaprashan* is held only if the child born is a boy when he is six months old. The ritual is called *mujhuti*, in which the *dadi* (grandmother) feeds the baby some rice. There is a childhood rite for both boys and girls, in which the ear-lobes are pierced in a ritual called *kan-chhed*. Lalbegis have no adolescence rites for women.

Lalbegi weddings are not held in the *Shravan* and *Kuer* months of the Bangali calendar. A wedding is preceded by the *lagan* ceremony, performed nine, seven, or five days earlier, in which the groom's father pays one Rupee to the bride's father and gifts glass bangles, vermilion, *alta* and soap to the bride. The *tilak* ritual follows, in which the groom is given Rs. 21, or Rs. 51, or Rs. 101 and a *nariel* (coconut) by the bride's family. These rituals are held as a sign of formal recognition between the two families, after which the marriage cannot be dismissed.

On the night before the wedding, women in both houses do not sleep the entire night and keep both the groom and bride awake in their respective homes singing religious songs and anointing the bride's body with *mehendi*. *Manda*s are constructed in both the houses. This is done by erecting a bamboo pole and placing an earthen pot covered with a red piece of cloth and a *kansar-lota* (brass pitcher) containing a five paisa coin, turmeric and salt. This is believed to be a good omen. A Brahman priest from Ranchi conducts the wedding rituals. Marriage also takes place in the presence of the *mukhia* and is solemnized the day after. The party accompanying the groom then returns to his house and a feast follows. Consummation takes place on *sohagrat*.

Lalbegis cremate their dead, with the eldest son lighting the funeral pyre. All the sons and grandsons of the deceased shave their heads. Pollution lasts twelve days. The *asthi* (bones) are preserved at the crematorium for three days and then carried to Gaya for immersion. On the twelfth day, *sradh* is held and, on the thirteenth, a *barohi* (non-vegetarian feast for relatives), in which meat and fish are served. There have been no significant changes in their life-cycle rituals.

Their only occupation is that of sweepers at different municipality offices, where men, women and grown-up children work for a monthly salary. They have no subsidiary occupation. Children below fifteen years do not work.

The Lalbegis have their traditional *jati-panchayat*, which functions for the entire region, from Ranchi to Purulia. The panchayat headman is the *mukhia* or *sarpanch*, who has to be present at weddings and divorce proceedings. There is no other member of the council. There is no traditional village panchayat. Nor are they, in any way, associated with the modern *gram panchayat*. There have been no significant changes in the mechanism of social control of the Lalbegis.

Lalbegis are Hindus and say that their religious rituals are similar to those of the Marwaris of Rajasthan. Lakshmi is a family deity worshipped every day. The major religious festivals are Valmiki Jayanti on full moon day in *Kartik*, Ramdeo on Bhadra Dasami, Janmashtami in *Bhadra*, Ramnavami in *Chaitra* — in which they offer puja at the nearby Mahabir Temple — Manasa puja in Shravan and Sitala puja in *Chaitra*. Besides these, they observe Shivaratri and Holi. On such occasions as Holi, they have *Holi-jalano*, or *Mataji-jalano*, or *Hiranyakuser Mata-jalano*. They make small cowdung cakes, with which they prepare garlands, and burn them. They wear new clothes on Durga puja and Diwali days and have a bath on *Poush*-Sankranti — the day of Makar. At Diwali, they worship Lakshmi and Ganesh. Tijsindhara and Rakhi-bandhan are the other festivals. Their major sacred centres are Gaya, Vrindaban, Allahabad, Kashi and Mathura.

Their religious expert is a priest whom they call Brahman and who belongs to their own caste. The major fairs they visit every year are the Rash mela, Rather mela, Annapurna mela and the *mela* on the occasion of Kali puja. No change of religion has been reported and neither any socio-religious movement is reported. There have been no significant changes in their religious behaviour.

The Lalbegis have no tradition in the plastic or graphic arts, but they do have an oral tradition in music and dance forms. The women sing songs at ceremonies and rituals.

Lalbegis do not have any bar on accepting *kachcha*, *pucca*, or *siddha* food from anyone, though others do not always reciprocate. No inter-community marriage has taken place in their society. Sometimes, they establish ceremonial friendship within or outside the community. They do have socio-economic inter-dependence on other communities whose houses and toilets they clean. Modern inter-community links are limited. Their political activity is restricted to casting votes.

Their children go to school, but the general standard of education is very poor. There was only one matriculate among the group studied. Girls study only up to Class III. They do visit dispensaries and hospitals, and, sometimes, health workers visit them to advise them on family planning and childcare methods. Some men and women have got sterilized. They get their drinking water from municipal taps. Some have got jobs through employment exchanges. No one is self employed.

Lalbegi localities are well connected with the outside world by buses and trains. They listen to the radio and go to the cinema. They have electricity in their areas. They use wood, cowdung cakes and coal as fuel. Their children have no midday meal scheme at school. They get their rations from fair price shops. They have no savings, but some do have bank accounts.

CHANDRIMA CHOWDHURY

LEPCHA

The Lepchas are a scheduled tribe of West Bengal, and generally, call themselves "Rong", meaning "dwellers of rocky land". Risley says the Lepchas, Rongs, Khambas and Mons were a Mongolian tribe of Sikkim, western Bhutan, eastern Nepal and Darjeeling. They are divided into two branches — the Rongs and Khambas. The former claim to be original inhabitants of Sikkim, while the Khambas are believed to have migrated about 250 years ago from China's Kham Province, where a deputation of Lamas had been sent to choose a ruler for Sikkim (Risley, 1891: II 6-14).

However, West Bengal Lepchas have migrated from the neighbouring state of Sikkim. Their main concentration is in the three sub-divisions — Kalimpong, Kurseong and Darjeeling Sadar of Darjeeling district. The Lepcha population in Darjeeling district is 22,749 and in the State 23,409 as per 1981 Census. The Lepcha language is known as "Rong". They speak Nepali with neighbours and write in the Devanagari script, both at home and with outsiders. They hold the constitutional status of a scheduled tribe. Bio-anthropological information on somatometry on the Darjeeling Lepchas is available. The average stature of Lepcha is 1,570 mm. The cephalic index is 79.9 (mesocephalic) and the nasal index is 67.2 (mesorrhine) (Gupta & Dutta: 1966: 79).

The Lepchas are non-vegetarians. They have *utan sa-ojaong* (breakfast) and *namung sa-ajang* (dinner). Their staple food is rice and they also have maize, eaten in the form of bread. They eat meat and fish. The meat is kept for four days in summer and up to a fortnight in winter. They also have pork and beef. *Punjak-bak* (yak) meat is considered the best beef. They have almost all kinds of pulses, vegetables, roots and tubers. Of late, they have started using small quantities of iodized salt, mustard oil and other common spices. Lard is a traditional cooking medium. They are very fond of alcohol and have homemade *chi* liquor, prepared from *kodo* (millet). They believe *chi* has medicinal properties and protects against chills. It is compulsory on social and religious occasions. Another kind of alcoholic beverage is the *dyo*, prepared from roots and herbs. They have milk, tea and milk products, and smoke cigarettes.

Their major social division is the *agit*, the residential kin group and social unit based on blood. In most areas of Darjeeling district, members of an *agit* acknowledge a traditional bond of common descent in the paternal line. The *agit* name is handed down from father to sons and daughters. *Agit* plays an important role in regulating marriage. The legends refer to the *agits* being named after various mountains (a common belief). The *agit*s found in the field studies are: Chongmu, Kengmu, Songmu, Songdiamu, Namodamu, Mongmingmu, Nongsongmu, Namchingmu, Sungutmu, Monlumu, Simikmu, Tamsangmu and Gormu.

They use Lama, Lepcha or their *agit* names as surname. The Lepchas consider such neighbouring communities as the Rais, Limbus and Tamangs of the same rank. Their neighbours also believe the Lepchas have a status equal to that of the communities mentioned. The Rais, Limbus, Tamangs and Bhutias regard the Lepchas as a casteless and classless society.

The Darjeeling Lepchas are endogamous at the community level and exogamous at the *agit* level. They cannot marry within their own *agit* and marriage is generally forbidden with parallel or cross cousins. Marriages are usually monogamous and negotiated. Sometimes, service is rendered to the future father-in-law in the hope of getting his consent for the marriage. They prefer adult marriages. Junior levirate is permissible, but rare, unlike in the past, when it was customary for a widow to marry the younger brother of her dead husband whatever his age. This was also applicable to a widower. He could remarry, but the bride had to be a younger sister-in-law (junior sororate) or a younger member of his wife's family. These customs are not strictly observed now.

There is no rigidity regarding marriage symbols. Normally, a *potemala* (bead necklace) is the symbol of a married woman. Earlier, a groom had to pay a bride-price — cash, domestic animals, utensils and clothing — besides rendering service to the bride's family as conditions of marriage. After marriage, the bride lives with her husband. Divorce is still very rare. By the 1961 census, 0.88% of the Lepchas are either divorced or separated. The main cause for this is, usually, incompatibility, or refusal by the wife to work properly. If a woman is childless, the husband may marry again (usually his wife's younger sister). Widow and widower remarriage is permissible.

Most Lepcha *tiyan*s (families) are nuclear, though extended ones also exist. Lepcha families in Darjeeling district are patriarchal. Husband and wife regard each other as helpmates and partners in different spheres of activity. The father is head of the family. There is a relationship of distance between a woman and her son-in-law and a jocular relationship exists between a man and his elder brother's wife. Property issues spark conflict. In matters of inheritance, they follow their own customs. "On a man's death, his property is supposed to be divided equally among his sons, but the rule of equal division is liable, in practice, to be modified by other considerations. Thus, the widow and daughters of the dead person usually live with the eldest son. In this case, he gets an extra share..." (Risley: *op. cit: 9*). The eldest son succeeds to his father's position.

Women do not inherit parental property. They have various roles in their daily life. They gather firewood, fetch drinking water, look after domestic animals, do household chores and take part in economic activities outside the home. They have roles in social and religious rituals, too. They contribute whatever they earn to the family. They do not take part in politics and neither do they control the social mechanism. Women have a definite say in domestic affairs, though they have a lower status than men.

Inter-family links are kept up at various social and religious rituals, when different families get a chance to meet and interact.

Pregnant Lepcha women have no restrictions on movement or diet. Pollution after a child is born ranges from three to seven days, during which the new mother is barred from entering the kitchen. When pollution ends, the *bongthing*, or *mun*, or *lama* performs a rite known as *tumbu-fat*, signifying the end of pollution. After this, the *abreyang thom-gacho* (naming ceremony) is held along with the ceremony at which the child has its first taste of rice.

Most Lepcha weddings take place in autumn. Preliminary selection for their sons' and daughters' marriage is made by the respective parents. The wedding date is fixed by a *lama*. On wedding day, the groom, accompanied by relatives, friends and a group of musicians, goes to the bride's house. The party gifts a pig to the bride's parents, besides other things, such as *fila* (bullock's leg), *serbum-komkat* (a one rupee coin), *chirung-yak* (a basketful of *chi*), *jer-lup* (clothes) and *pamby-lade* (a bowl and plates). A wedding is held in the daytime with the sun as witness. A wedding has five essential parts — *lagto*, *chhamu*, *tung-gung*, *ashek* and *nomchum*. The *lama* and the *bongthing*, or *mun*, are in attendance as priests. The *bonthing*, or *mun*, usually, conducts all the functions, while the *lama* chants hymns and prays for the couple's well being. Afterwards, a feast with pork, rice, beef and *chi* is held.

After a person dies, the *lama* and the *bonthing* are called in. The *lama* prays to God for the soul and the *bongthing* chants *mantras*. Generally, Lepchas bury their dead near the house. They carry with them a *tibu* (bell), *damu* (conch shell) and a *tangdar* (musical instrument) and play music. After the grave is dug, the coffin is lowered into it, with the head of the dead pointing towards the Kanchenjunga. After the grave is filled up, a fowl's egg is broken on the grave and some rice, meat, sweets and *chi* are placed over it and offered to the soul. There is no rigid rule on pollution, or purification thereafter, connected with death among the Lepchas of this area. However, some restrictions on food, such as meat, and sexual cohabitation are observed for only a week. *Chi* is a compulsory drink during this period. Twenty-one, or forty-nine, days after the death, a rite, *sanglion matgachio*, is held in which a cow is sacrificed and a feast held for assembled persons. The beef is served with *chi*.

Lepchas practise settled 'terrace cultivation' at altitudes of 2,500 feet to 8,000 feet. This is their principal means of subsistence. Traditionally, they were a hunting and gathering tribe. But, now, they cultivate *zoman* (paddy) in *pani-khet* (wetlands) and *kodo* (millet), *phaphar* (buck-wheat) and maize in *sunkha-khet* (dry land). They also grow cardamom, potato, orange and vegetables as cash crops. They are both a landowning and landless community. Apart from cultivation, they are involved in such other occupations as government or private sector service, business or animal husbandry, forestry, mining or plantation, or work as agricultural labourers.

By the 1981 census, 42.23% were workers. Of them 73.22% were in agriculture, 7.12% worked as agricultural labour, 5.37% worked in animal husbandry, forestry, etc., and the remaining 14.29% followed various other vocations. Wages are paid in cash. They depend directly on the market, where transactions are in cash. Child labour or bonded labour does not exist.

The Lepchas have their own traditional *jati-panchayat*. The eldest man in the Lepcha society does the job of a chief, or *mondal*. Every Lepcha village has a *mondal* and a *muktiyar* acts as chief of the *mondals*, liaising between several villages. The post of *muktiyar* was created by the Maharaja of Sikkim, but the post is not as prestigious now in Darjeeling district as in the past. A statutory panchayat exists and looks after the villagers' welfare.

The Lepchas are generally Buddhists. By the 1981 census, 57.12% were avowed Buddhists, followed by 35.70% as Christians. Their indigenous religion is tribal religion, or *bonthing*. Lepchas have mainly two classes of *lamas* — the *pembay* and the *bongthingpa*. The first calls and drives away evil spirits and the second simply worships. *Lirum*, the household deity, and Lord Buddha are worshipped at individual homes. God is known among the Lepchas as *rum*, meaning a benevolent spirit. *Ta-she-thing* is another god and Lepchas believe he lives everywhere. A Lepcha *lama* functions as both priest and doctor. Darjeeling Lepchas observe such festivals as *Nambun*, in January, *Losar*, in March, and *Chechu*, on a full-moon day, since Lord Buddha was born on such a day. They also celebrate the Buddha's birth anniversary. A *gompha* (monastery) is the sacred centre where they go every morning.

The traditional Lepcha handicraft is weaving on a handloom. They are very proficient in mural art. Their monasteries are well decorated with mural paintings, which depict the life and teachings of Lord Buddha. Darjeeling Lepchas have retained a fairly good stock of myths connected with demons and the creation of god and other folk tales connected with the creation of man and god. They have folk love songs, such as *go-ung sa vam*, as also *then-ung sa vam* (comic songs) and *femere-sa vam* (ceremonial songs).

They are very fond of chatting in groups and playing for hours on end a long bamboo flute, known as *puntong palit*, and a joint flute, known as *nabryok palit*. Dancing is a part of life. The *zo-mal lok* (agricultural dance) and *pasyai-lyon guru-tak* (historical dance) are common forms.

The Lepchas are allowed to share meals from the plates of the Rais, Limbus and Tamangs, while the Rais, Limbus, Tamangs and Gurungs can share food with them. A few cases of inter-community marriages have been reported among them. They share drinking water sources, roads and schools with others. They have a landlord-tenant or cultivator-labourer relationship with others. The community comprises businessmen, teachers and government employees.

The literacy rate is poor. But they are now aware of the need for education. They use both modern and folk medicine. They are not aware of family welfare measures. Small rivulets and waterfalls in the hills are their main water sources. The transistor radio is the most common mass media. They use electricity. Firewood and kerosene are their main fuels. They use organic manure. They avail of rationing and banking facilities, and are favourably disposed towards savings.

AMITABHA MITRA

LET

The Lets are a community often confused with the Bagdis. The word Bagdi is often suffixed to the word Let, and Let-Bagdi is used in common local parlance to refer to the Lets. But the Lets, themselves, are confident in that they claim a separate identity for their community as Lets.

The etymology of the name Let is not traceable. They have a subgroup Chhoto-Let (small Let). They have no recorded or oral history of any kind. They are distributed in Murshidabad district, and parts of Birbhum district adjacent to Murshidabad. The area they live in has laterite soil. They speak the local Bengali dialect, both among themselves and with neighbouring communities. They write, both at home and outside in Bengali. They have no special identification marks.

Though the community is not listed under the scheduled castes and scheduled tribes, they enjoy the constitutional status of a scheduled caste. Certificates on their status are issued by the Block Development Office, mentioning their community name, Let, as a sub-caste under the larger scheduled castes category. This is the general practice followed in issuing such certificates, wherein the name of the scheduled caste and the scheduled tribe is shown as a sub-caste, or a sub-tribe, as the case may be, under the larger respective categories of the scheduled castes and scheduled tribes.

The Lets are non-vegetarian, but do not eat beef or pork. Their staple food is parboiled rice, boiled potato or *dal*, or any seasonal vegetable, and fish. Their cooking medium is mustard oil. Children have milk if their parents can afford it; otherwise, children are mostly breastfed. They drink *mod* (brewed and distilled liquor) bought from markets. They have the brewed variety, *pochai*, more often than the other variety, *paki*. The latter is more expensive and they drink it in the company of distinguished relatives, guests and friends. There is a government ban on the brewing and distilling of liquor at home.

In *Phalgun* and *Chaitra*, they include *neem-begun* — made by frying newly sprouted *neem* leaves (locally known as *neem shak*), mixed with small pieces of brinjal — as an item on their menu. The taste is bitter and they believe it purifies the blood. They do not eat radish in *Magh*, *lau* in *Bhadra* and *seem* and *puin* from *Chaitra* to *Jaistha*. They begin eating *seem* and *puin* from *Ashar*.

The two social divisions are Let and Chhoto-Let. The latter group is considered a lower social group compared to the former. The main difference is occupational. Chhoto-Lets are, traditionally, palanquin-bearers, while Lets are agricultural labourers. The Lets, like quite a few low castes of the area, for instance the Mal-Konais, have a single clan, Kashyap. They use either Let or Das as a surname. Those who are literate or live in towns prefer Das. They believe they are hierarchically below the *nabasakhas* (literally nine artisan castes — Kamars, Kumors, or Kumbhakars, Patalis, Gops, Napits, Gochhalis, Tilis, Malis and Tamalis, or Tambulis) as also below such other castes as Brahmans and Kayasthas, who are ranked socially above the *nabasakhas*. They consider the Mals, Bagdis and Gonds (or Gonrs) as their social equals and rank them above the Konais, Doms and Muchis.

However, anxiety about the social status is a universal phenomenon among the low castes of the area, who compete among themselves for a higher status in the eyes of the upper castes. There is no clear concept of *varna*. The neighbouring communities consider the Lets a low caste, equivalent to the Bagdis. However, Bagdis claim there is a difference, since the Lets use Das as a surname, while they do not.

Lets do not marry their *daida*s (lineage members or consanguineous kin). Marrying within the village is not taboo. The marriageable age for girls is between thirteen and eighteen years, and for men, between twenty and twenty-five. Marriages are negotiated and monogamous. The girl's family initiates the search for a suitable match, often with the help of a *ghatak* (match maker) from within the kin group. The symbols of a married woman are *sindur*, *sankha*, *noa* and a tattoo on the left hand (considered lucky for a woman). Tattooing is done at the husband's home, the belief being that the mythical *Yama* does not allow a married woman through the doors of the celestial world after death if she has no tattoo on her hand.

Dowry is paid in both cash and kind. The bride lives at her husband's house after marriage. There is no specific rule on divorce, which is rare now. In fact, it has become obsolete since dowry was introduced, since husbands are required to return the amount paid in dowry if they seek a divorce. There is no provision for post divorce maintenance either. *Sanga* (*senga*) is permitted, though without ceremony. In the past few decades, the following changes have occurred: the age at marriage for both men and women has increased; negotiations depend mainly on the amount of *pan* (dowry) involved; divorce and remarriage have both shown a decline.

Let families are predominantly nuclear. The husband is head of the family. There is usually very little expression of emotions among members of a family. There is no overt show of love or affection between husband and wife, or between parents and children. However, small children get a great deal of affection. Husband, wife and grownup children demonstrate concerted efforts towards the upkeep of the family. Thus, inter-personal relations within a nuclear family depend upon mutual obligation and cooperation. Older children are at times given the job of looking after their younger brothers and sisters. Siblings, in childhood, are playmates and interact with each other with love, affection and, sometimes, jealousy, especially if parents are partial to one or the other. As they grow up, the sexes maintain a distance with each other.

In a joint, or extended, family, inter-personal relations of a few other kinds are noticeable: a man has a relationship of distance with his younger brother's wife, and there are jocular relations between a woman and her husband's younger brother, or between grandparents and grandchildren. Constrained relations between brothers' wives are common and are the main reason why extended families often break down. The major inter-family links are based on the feeling that they all belong to the same community — the members of different families are socio-ritually similar, especially in the context of a multi-community milieu. The families share common *para*s (residential areas or zones) in a village. Besides, some families are *daida*s (related by blood or are affinal kin). Cooperation among families is observed. Women from different families go out together to fish in nearby ponds, or rivulets. Men from various families discuss issues of minor and major importance and children are friends and playmates.

Sons and daughters are now supposed to inherit parents' property equally, but in reality daughters are persuaded to not claim their shares. In their poverty stricken condition, there is very little justification for disputes over property. The Lets rationalize that the expenditure incurred on paying suitable dowries for their daughter's marriage compensates for the loss suffered in foregoing their share of property. Succession follows the male line and the hereditary post of *Mondal* goes to the eldest son after the father's death.

Women are on an equal footing with men as breadwinners in a family. They work as *kamin*s, or agricultural daily wage labourers, or as *ek-dupur* (working for half a day) in their master's house to support their families. There is a discrepancy in the wage rates for men and women labourers and men, usually, get more. By tradition, women are not given very heavy work, for instance agricultural operations, such as ploughing and levelling. However, the total working hours of women is more than that of men. Women cook, fetch water, collect dried leaves and twigs for fuel, rear children and fish with the help of *jali*s (a net, wound round a large bamboo ring, with four bamboo supports, for catching small fish). They are, however, not politically active. They have an active role in life-cycle rituals, besides other traditions and customs. Let women have many obligations, but hardly any rights.

Antur (pollution) lasts twenty-one days for the immediate family and next of kin after a child is born. On *ekusia* (the twenty-first day), the new mother has a dip in the Ganga to end *antur*. Several rites are observed during *antur* — *sanjlara* on the second day after the birth, when the mother may eat for the first time after the delivery; *panchuti* on the fifth day, when a barber is in attendance; *seter-in* (seventh day); *shuddhur-din* (day of purification) on the ninth day, when both the barber and midwife attend. The *mama*, a special invitee, feeds the baby its first morsel of food at a ceremony in the sixth month if the child born is a boy, and in the seventh, if a girl. If the child's parents can afford it, they gift new clothes to the *mama*, who has to wear them for the occasion. But, if they are poor, the *mama*, himself, might buy the new clothes. The child is tonsured on the day and a formal name chosen.

A wedding is a three-day ceremony, comprising *gayehalud*, *adhibas* and *basibiye*. Before this, a day is observed as *bara-malar din*, or *ashirbad*, when the wedding day is fixed. *Gayehalud* is the usual ritual with turmeric a day before the wedding. *Adhibas* is the day of the wedding, when the bride and her parents are on fast till she is ritually handed over to the groom. Since boys and girls marry only after they attain adolescence nowadays, consummation takes place after the marriage.

After a person dies, *asouch* (pollution) lasts eleven days for the *daida* when mourners avoid eating non-vegetarian food or cooking with oil and turmeric. The eldest or youngest son performs the *mukhagni*. The sons of the dead wear new clothes sent by their maternal uncle or parents-in-law, after disposal of the body. Let's, often bury their dead because of poverty. On the eleventh day, *sradh* is performed by a Brahman, and the sons of the deceased get their heads shaved by a barber.

The Lcts are mainly a landless people — a class of agricultural labourers — though few own land. Traditionally, their subsidiary occupation is fishing. They are dependent upon markets. For a few months after paddy is harvested, they barter paddy for seasonal vegetables and such tuberous roots as *sank-alu* (considered a fruit) with itinerant Chain community sellers of Murshidabad district. Nowadays a very few, have acquired the right to cultivate small plots through *barga*, a system introduced by the state government to hand over land belonging to absentee landlords, to the tiller. A rise in their population has led to an increase in the number of landless labourers, a potential labour force for cultivation. Boys of fourteen years upwards work as *bagal*s, *mahendra*s, or *munish*. Agricultural labourers and *bagal*s are paid in cash and kind.

The traditional mechanism of social control through the offices of the *mondal* or *murubbi* is now almost defunct. The modern statutory panchayat has a greater influence. The members and office bearers elected from within the community to the panchayat mediate between parties involved in disputes. They also deliberate on major decisions for the community. Their influence is not restricted to the community, but extends to the members of neighbouring communities.

The Lets are Hindus. Their village and regional deity is Dharmaraj. They have a strong faith in all gods and goddesses of the Hindu pantheon, such as Manasa, Sitala, Kali, Durga and Shiva. The major local shrine is Tarapith. Gaya is the most popular pilgrimage where they offer *pinda*s to the memory of their ancestors. Brahman priests are the only religious experts who perform rites and rituals for them. The local major fairs are held at Tarapith — *Baruni*, in *Chaitra*, and *Troiyodashir* mela, in *Ashwin* after Durga puja. Their major festival is Durga puja. Before this *puja* is held, they clean their huts; plaster the mud walls and balconies and paint motifs or designs on the walls.

Let's, in their fight against poverty, hardly get time to develop the finer aspects of arts and culture. Some knit fishing-nets. Youths in some villages have their own bands for playing music at weddings.

The Lets have no commensal restrictions with regard to Bagdis, Chhoto-Lets, Gonrs or Mals. They do not accept cooked food from the Doms, Muchis and Haris. Upper and clean castes do not accept cooked food from them, but do accept *siddha*. Inter-community marriages between Lets and the neighbouring communities are not the norm, though there are a few stray cases. *Bandhu-patano* (putative kinship) with different communities is common. *Sai*, or *sakhi*, is common among women. The *bandhu* and *sai* are invited to life-cycle ceremonies. Lets and other low castes are not allowed to enter temples belonging to upper castes. They face no problems in using any public facilities, such as roads, schools, crematoriums or the panchayat office.

They have *jajmani* relations with their Brahman priest and barbers, the one with the former being more stable. Adult franchise has helped the community graduate from village level politics to national politics. The relationship between cultivators and their labourers is formal and stiff. Often, such relations are maintained for generations. The local variants of such relations are: the *mahendra* and *munish*, the latter being of two kinds — *bandha* (where part payment is made before actual employment, so that the labourer is obliged to work for his master) and *alga* (literally 'free', where no such arrangements are made beforehand).

Literacy or the level of education among the Lets is very poor. There are no special arrangements to provide health and medicare services to these people. They try to avail of such facilities through primary health centres. But it is, usually, quite difficult to spare the amount of time one requires to take advantage of these facilities. Let's prefer small families and family planning (both vasectomy and tubectomy) has become quite popular with the community, which is quite aware of its advantages. Tube wells have been sunk by the government in all villages and drinking water poses no problem. Rural employment programmes — such as the IRDP and EGS — have given the community no benefits. A small number are self employed in petty businesses — setting up tea stalls or dealing in fish.

Though there are metalled roads and different kinds of transport, they have no use for these. Electricity is unaffordable for most. Cowdung cakes and *gul* are their fuel. The community comprises mainly landless people and makes very little use of irrigation, chemical fertilizers, insecticides or organic manure. There are, in certain areas, very irregular nutrition programmes in which only a piece of bread is given to every student. There is no public distribution system in their areas. Savings through banking facilities are still not within their means.

R. K. BHATTACHARYA

LIMBU

The Limbus, or Limboos, trace their descent from Kiranti, or Kirati, or Kirat. The communities of eastern Nepal are known collectively as Kiranti. To this group belong the Limbus, or Yakthumbas (synonym for Limbu), and the Rais, known also as Khambus, or Yakkas. The Limbus use Subba as a title. "The Limbus, or Yakthumbas, have a tradition that they came originally from Benares and, although often mentioned in early Hindu writings, no history of the Kirantis is obtainable on which any dependence can be placed" (Morris: 1933: 85). The name, Limbu, writes Risley, is used only by outsiders. Tibetans have no special name for Limbus; they call all Nepalese communities by the general name, Monpa (dwellers of the ravine). The Bhutias speak of Limbus as Tsongs and Lepchas call them Changs, which may be a corruption of Tsong. By other members of the Kiranti group, they are addressed by the honorific title of Subbah, or Suffah, a chief (Risley: 1981: II: 15).

The Limbus migrated to Darjeeling from east Nepal (west of Darjeeling district). The Limbus, themselves, claim to have come from the Tamba-Khola Valley on the upper stream of the Tamba-Kosi river. The main concentration of Limbus is found in the hills of Darjeeling Sadar, Kurseong and Kalimpong sub-divisions of Darjeeling district. By the 1931 census, their population in West Bengal was 17,506, of which 16,238 lived in Darjeeling District alone. They live in hilly terrain, with medium rainfall, low humidity and cold weather.

They speak Nepali at home, though their own dialect is Limbukura. They write in the Devanagari script at home and to outsiders. They speak Nepali, Hindi and a mixture of both with neighbours.

The Limbus are non-vegetarian and eat fish, meat, eggs, pork and beef. Their staple food is rice, wheat and maize. They have all vegetables and such pulses as *urad*, *moong* and *masur*. They eat roots and tubers. Mustard oil is their cooking medium. Men have *nighar-jnar* (beer), brewed at home, as well as bought from the market. Women have *nighar-jnar* only occasionally, especially during festivals and weddings. They have milk and milk products. They eat fruits in moderation. Men smoke *bidi*s and cigarettes.

They are divided into several non-hierarchical exogamous *thar*s, differentiated on a social basis to regulate marriages. The *thar*s are Panch-thar, Che-thar, Tero-thar, Yakten, Yakpangten, Yakshoma,

Pheodan, Phejom, Phyapa, Thekim, Meongpa and Manglagpa. They rank themselves below the *babuns*, (Brahmans), Mangers, Gurungs and Chhetris in the local social hierarchy, but higher than the Kamis, Damais and Sarkis. They are aware of the *varna* order and believe they are Sudras.

The Limbus are endogamous at the community level and exogamous at the *thar* level. They prefer adult marriages, which take the *mangni-biya* (negotiated) form and are monogamous. *Choriya-biya* (marriage by elopement) — a symbolic form — is non-existent today. Junior levirate and sororate marriages are permissible. Vermilion and *potemala* are the symbols of a married woman. *Rith* (bride price) is a custom and paid in both cash and kind. It is, however, giving way to dowry in kind. After marriage the wife lives with her husband. Divorce is permitted with social approval on grounds of maladjustment. Either partner can seek divorce. Children of divorced parents are the liability of either mother or father. Compensation is paid to the aggrieved party. Men and women divorcees can marry again, as well as widows and widowers. The recent changes are a rise in the incidence of divorce and a liberalization of the rules of remarriage.

Limbu families are mostly nuclear. A few mixed-extended families can also be seen, but are giving way to nuclear ones. A woman has a relationship of distance with her father-in-law and a jocular relationship with her husband's younger brother. A grandparent-grandchild relationship is also of the latter kind. Property issues spark conflict. Parents' property is shared equally by the sons. The eldest son succeeds to his father's position. Inter-family links are in evidence at various rituals and during festivals.

Limbu women do not inherit parents' property. The women gather fuel and fetch drinking water. They also work in local tea gardens. They have a role in religious and social rituals, but none in the political sphere. (One exception was a woman of this community who was a popular leader of West Bengal a few years ago). Women have decision making powers at home, though they have a lower status than that of men. They contribute whatever they earn to the family.

Limbus observe post-delivery restrictions and pollution after a child is born. The naming ceremony, and another one, when it has its first taste of cereals, take place in the sixth or seventh month.

Wedding rituals are held at the bride's house. *Home-jognya*, wearing of *potemala* and *sindurdan* are the main wedding rituals. The *babun* (Nepali Brahman) performs the wedding rites. The bride's parents hold a feast after the wedding.

The Limbus bury their dead. Pollution lasts ten days after a person dies and *sradh* is held on the eleventh day. A Brahman helps to perform the *sradh* rites.

They depend on agricultural land. They are both a landowning and landless community. Terrace cultivation is a traditional occupation, as well as a current one. They also work as labourers in tea gardens and as porters in Darjeeling and Mirik, besides doing jobs in the government and private sectors and in the army. They have direct links with the daily market, where transactions are in cash. Of late, there has been a marked increase in the number of tea plantation labourers in the community.

They have a traditional caste-*panchayat*, comprising ten members and headed by a *pradhan* — a hereditary post. The statutory panchayat also exists for development activities.

The Limbus profess Hinduism and worship *kuldevata* as a home deity. They worship all Hindu gods and goddesses, such as Saraswati, Kali and Shiva. Their main festivals are Shivaratri, Holi and Dassehra. The Mahakal Baba Temple in Darjeeling town is their sacred centre. The Nepali Brahman does the job of a priest and performs the life-cycle rituals.

They have a rich oral tradition of folk tales on their native place and on their origin. They are very fond of music and play such instruments as the *kay*, *nagara* and *banshi*.

They accept water from the Nepali Brahmans and Chhetris. They share food and drinks with the Rais, Gurungs, Tamangs and Newars, but not with the Sarkis and Damais. A few instances of inter-community marriages are reported, though such marriages are not recognized by the society. They share water sources, roads and burial grounds with the neighbouring communities, and take part in festivals with them. They have a cultivator-labourer relationship with the neighbouring people. The community has in its fold teachers, army men and political leaders.

All, except a few, show rank ignorance about the necessity for education. They use both modern, and traditional, medicare. They do not have a favourable attitude towards family planning. Waterfalls and rivulets in the hills are their main sources of water. They irrigate their fields with water from waterfalls and small streams. They use chemical fertilizers, if available. Public distribution system facilities are not available in their areas. They do not avail of banking facilities and depend upon moneylenders and shopkeepers for credit.

AMITABHA MITRA

LODHA

The Lodhas were, earlier, accredited with criminal propensities and known as a "criminal tribe" till the revocation of the Criminal Tribes Act. A reference about them in the epic literature, Savara, has pitch forked them to their traditional glory. They now assert themselves as scions of the Savara and, to justity the epic reference, they point out their gathering-hunting, or fowl-trapping, economy. The Lodhas have been notified with Kherias in West Bengal and their combined population is 53,718 (1981 census). The total number of the Lodhas alone is about 26,000 in West Midnapore district of West Bengal, and, in other bordering regions of Mayurbhanj district of Orissa, or Singhbhum district in Bihar — in the jungle-covered, rugged terrain — a contiguous tract. Deforestation compelled them to move out to the furthest eastern tract of their habitat in search of food and shelter.

They speak a distorted Bengali, with a smattering of some Mundari dialects. Under the Constitution, they are now treated as a Primitive Tribal Group (PTG) and are included in the scheduled tribes list since 1956, and, before that, as a scheduled caste. Lodhas are of medium height, with prominent cheek bones and not much facial hair, dark brown to dark in complexion and with a dolichocephalic head.

They have all kinds of locally available food, but do not eat beef. Their staple food is rice. They are very fond of molluscs, tortoise, *godhis* (the Bengal monitor) and all kinds of fish. Most drink *toddy* from the local market. Agricultural development around them has given them vegetables to which they have adjusted their food habits.

Territorial affiliations with those who live in the jungle tracts on the southern bank of the Subarnarekha River are, sometimes, termed *junglees*, but this does not indicate any special social status. They have such exogamous totemic clans as the Bhaktas, Digars, Dandapats and Kotals. Certain kinds of food are banned for members of certain clans. Lodhas in the jungle areas use Sabbar as a surname, while, in other areas, their clan names serve as surname. They consider themselves Hindus — yet the regional caste-groups are known as 'Bangali Babus' (Bengali gentlemen) and all tribal groups as 'Adivasis', indicating their distinct ethnic position somewhere in the middle.

Lodhas, generally, marry outside the clan, but, of late, a few isolated incidents of inter-community, or inter-group, marriage — even marriage within a clan — have taken place. The marriageable age for girls is before puberty, and, for boys, below twenty years. Paying a bride-price — some amount in cash and a new clothes — is customary. Marriage by mutual consent is not unheard of. After marriage, the wife wears iron bangles, given ceremonially by the groom, and vermilion, too. The bridegroom's parents want the bride to live in their house along with her husband, but the husband mostly prefers to build his own hut.

Divorce is easy. It is nothing but a simple refusal by the wife to live with her husband in symbolic divorce. Remarriage is possible on a token payment of Rs. 1.50 to the headman of the wife's village and two pieces of cloth gifted to the wife's parents. No ceremony takes place in this case.

Lodha families are nuclear. A married man sets up home with his wife, either in his father's village, or in the village of his wife's father. Parents, or elderly persons, in a family have status and privilege. They show love and affection towards the younger ones. A man has a jocular relationship with his wife's younger sister and a woman with her husband's younger brother.

Lodha society is patrilineal and parents' property is equally divided among the sons, though, in reality, they have very little to be divided as far as land and other immovable property is concerned. Women play an equally important role in family management, especially if the husbands are alcoholics, and so hold a strong position in society. A pregnant woman has rules, taboos and restrictions on food and movement. These are in fact imposed upon her. Birth rituals exist and the umbilical cord is cut by a midwife — either an elderly woman from the community or a Hari. The placenta is interred near the hut to avoid the evil effects of witchery. There are such rituals as a purification ceremony and a naming ceremony.

Girls, sometimes, marry before puberty, so a second nuptial ceremony is held, at which the bride and groom show each other red flowers. There is a series of rituals in both houses in this connection. Marrying a tree is customary, and the ceremonial tying of a thread dyed yellow with *sambar* signifies consummation. In case of child marriage, a second wedding ritual is held, at which the bride after attaining puberty, shares a bed with her husband.

The Lodhas have mortuary rites, as also a pollution period following death in the family. The Lodhas both bury and cremate their dead. *Sradh* is held to end the pollution.

The Lodhas, a community of forest dwellers, earlier had access to forests. But, now, with the enactment of newer laws, this privilege has been curtailed. Yet, most surreptitiously enter forests and make use of water reservoir and other facilities. After a few criminal cases were instituted against them and the land colonization scheme was passed, some have taken up agriculture. They have no means to supplement their income by working as daily wage labourers and the opportunities of hunting game or fishing have become scarce. They sell firewood, honey, *godhi* or snakeskins and *tusser* (cocoons) at the local markets. Children also gather edible roots and tubers and catch rats, contributing to the economic process, except in certain areas where there are schools or hostels. The Lodhas also work as domestic help for wages paid in both cash and kind.

Village elders, including the *mukhia*, *kotal* (messenger, bailiff or *dakua*) and *deheri* (priest) take care of village or community problems. Earlier, the punishment for violating social rules was a fine. Now, *gram panchayat*s are there, and in some villages, Lodhas are representatives in the democratic setup, though influenced by local political parties.

There are such village tutelary deities as Baram, Garam, Sitala, Chandi and Yugini — propitiated with animal sacrifices, by a special person who helps the priest in performing rituals. The Lodhas have their own music and dance, along with folklore and riddles. Lodhas attend local fairs and festivals and have ceremonial or ritual kinsmen and friends among them.

Lodhas have access to water sources and schools in their localities. A new feeling of solidarity through political movement has been reinforced among the varied ethnic groups.

Science, technology and modern education have brought about an awakening in them. Though earlier traditional methods of treatment were followed, modern medicare systems are not unknown. Quite a few Lodhas have got employment under the IRDP through project loans. A certain section aspires for higher education, indicating that winds of change have started blowing. Many villages have electricity. Lodhas use fertilisers in agriculture, and get the facilities of ration shops, banks, railways and roads.

P. K. BHOWMICK

LOHAR

The community, Lohar (meaning blacksmiths), has the synonym, Nar. Majhi is, sometimes, used as a title in Burdwan district. Blacksmiths consider themselves Karmakars, and, so, Lohars feel inclined to claim the status of Karmakar. They claim they were originally Karmakars, but were ostracized because of their over indulgence in *mod*. Now, they are very particular in introducing themselves as Lohars, since they are aware of their constitutional status of scheduled caste and its incumbent benefits.

Lohars have no sub-groups. They are quite parochial in their statements concerning their distribution. They can only talk about their distribution in their immediate environment, or in terms of the district they inhabit, or at best, in terms of the adjoining districts. The major concentration of Lohars by the 1961 Census is in Bankura district, though they are found in all West Bengal districts except Purulia.

The area they inhabit is the plains of eastern India, with a warm and temperate climate, high humidity and medium rainfall. They prefer to live in areas that are comparatively dry and like plateaus. The major river in this state is the Ganga. A few others are Mayurakshi, Kangsabati and Kopai. Their total population in West Bengal is 151,609 by the 1981 Census. They speak and write in Bengali, both at home and outside. They do not have any identification mark. Constitutionally, they belong to the scheduled castes.

The Lohars are non-vegetarian and their concept of non-vegetarianism is fairly wide. They do not eat beef or pork, but do have the meat of field rats, *godak* (squirrels), a variety of birds, amphibians (mostly large size toads and tortoises), all kinds of fish, molluscs, *situ*s (snails) and *gugli*s (small water snails). Their staple food is parboiled rice. Among pulses, they prefer *kalai* most. In summer, pulses are substituted by such green vegetables as *pater-shak*, or *lalte-shak* (a variety of greens with a reddish tinge). Their cooking medium is mustard oil. Among the roots and tubers that they eat, the ones worth naming are yam, turnips, sweet potato, potato, turmeric and ginger. Other vegetables are brinjal, bean, gourd and in winter cauliflower and cabbage. They have seasonal fruits, such as mango, jackfruit and melon, occasionally, in certain seasons when they are available in plenty.

They do not drink milk, since it is expensive, or any other non-alcoholic drink. Alcohol — brewed at home as *pachoio* (beer), or bought from shops — however, is very popular. Beer is brewed publicly — with permission from the Excise Department — at weddings and *sradhs*, or Dharmaraj puja and other festivals and ceremonies. In summer, they drink *toddy* in large quantities in areas where palm trees grow in plenty. They do not eat certain vegetables in certain seasons or months, nor grow them at those times. A few are: radish in *Magh* and a particular variety of gourd in *Bhadra* and *Chaitra*. This taboo however, is not strictly followed. A change in food habits depends upon one's financial condition.

The Lohars have no major divisions, or groups, and the community is neither hierarchically divided, nor socially stratified. The community comprises a single clan, Shalshi, or Shaldashi. They use the surname, Lohar (one who forges iron). However, by profession they are not blacksmiths. The surname, Lohar, is used by those who live in Birbhum district, while those in adjoining Burdwan district use Majhi. The community believes they are hierarchically low in the *varna* order, as do the neighbouring communities. Among the lower groups, they consider themselves equal to the Bagdis and, at times, claim to be one of the four mythical *thaks* of Bagdis.

The basis on which the Lohars claim they are a *thak* of the Bagdis may have some connection with the general usage of the word, Bagdi, in the local context. The Lohars are frequently referred to as Lohar Bagdis, or Nar Bagdis. Similarly, the Mals are called Mal Bagdis. Here, the suffix, Bagdi, with a long-standing, distinctive hierarchical position, seems to be indicative of the community's hierarchical status in society, in relation to other social communities. However, neighbouring communities rank the Lohars below the Bagdis, but above such other low caste communities as the Muchis (or Bayans), Haris and Doms. The Lohars regard themselves as Sudras, as do their neighbours. As a community of a lower social position, the Lohars' role and function are defined as that of dependent labour.

The Lohars do not marry members of their *gusthi*, or *bhayad*. The marriageable age for men is between twenty and twenty-five years, and for girls, between fifteen and sixteen. They feel girls should marry early, or else be discredited for not being virgins. Marriages are negotiated and monogamous.

During the negotiations, the man's family invites the *mondal* to accompany them to the woman's house, as a kind of precaution for the future, since he is the person who would have to deal with the differences between the spouses later, if any. The groom's family considers the present act of taking the groom along would, at a later date, give them an advantage. The symbols of a married woman are *sindur*, *loha* and *sankha*. Dowry is paid in cash and kind. The wife lives with her husband after marriage, though in rare cases, the husband is a *ghar-jamai*.

There are no specific rules on divorce, which is sanctioned by the *mondal*, in consultation with other community elders. A fine of Rs. 150 – Rs. 200 is levied on the husband and the money is spent on a drinking binge. The husband has to return the amount taken in dowry, or a part of it, to his divorced wife. No post-divorce maintenance has to be paid. There are no specific rules on *senga*, or *sanga* (remarriage). A widow avoids marrying her husband's elder brother, while her husband's younger brothers are looked upon as sons; so, junior, or senior, sororate does not exist.

The following customs were earlier in vogue: i) age at marriage was lower for both men and women and child marriage was a custom; ii) no dowry was paid; instead, the groom's family provided the bride's family with a *sali* of rice (roughly 20 seers, or 18 kilograms), firewood, *sal*-leaf plates, clothes and, if needed, money; iii) out of modesty, remarriage was termed *biye*, instead of *senga*.

Lohar families are, predominantly, *bhinna* (nuclear). Inter-personal relations within the family are not of a primordial, emotive nature. These relations are need based and largely dependent on mutual cooperation and obligation. Under the circumstances, certain abstract normative concepts, such as respect, remains imprecise as an aspect of inter-personal relations. A parent-child relation is one of love and affection. As the child grows up, he or she is made to obey elders, and so, develops a relation of fear with the disciplinarians. Inter-personal relations of mutual cooperation, obligation and complementary role performances are observed between parents and grownup boys or girls, and husband and wife in a nuclear family. Relations sour when conflict arises.

A grandchild-grandparent relation is built on love, affection and joking. A man has a relationship of distance with his younger brother's wife. By the rules of inheritance, the wife gets half of her dead husband's property, the other half being equally distributed among the sons. After the widow dies, however, her sons share her wealth equally. Succession is patrilineal. Inter-family links are mainly, kin-based relations of agnates and affinity, village-based, community-based, putative kinship-based or ritual-based relations, besides landlord-tenant and cultivator-labourer relationships. All these are direct and personal relationships, providing a scope for a relationship of dependence and assistance. Individual and corporate help is reciprocated between families.

Due to poverty, the system of *gaon-tar* (mutual assistance between families within the community) has given way to a system of buying (employing labourers from within the community). The only change is related to the rules of inheritance, where women's share in property has been statutorily defined, and, since the Hindu Code Bill, women have a right of inheritance. But this is not put to practice unless one takes legal steps.

Women's role in a family is restricted to cooking, cleaning, fetching water, washing, gathering firewood, or making cowdung cakes, besides rearing children. They undertake several *brata*s and ritual fasts for the well being of their husbands, children and families. Their political activity runs only to casting their votes in favour of candidates of their husbands' choice. Lohar women fish regularly with a *jali* (round net). A portion of the catch is eaten at home, and the rest sold at the market.

After a child is born in a Lohar family, *antur* (pollution) lasts a month, when the mother is not allowed to perform *pujas*. The fifth day after the birth is *panchute*, when a barber's services are required. There is no naming ceremony, though *annaprashan* is quite popular, especially if the first-born is a boy. The ceremony is held in the sixth month if the child born is a boy, and seventh, if a girl. The child's maternal uncle or grandfather feeds the baby its first morsel of solid food. A plate, bowl and a tumbler are gifted to the child by the maternal uncle.

There is no ritual observed in connection with a boy or girl attaining puberty.

A wedding has several rituals. A few are: *gayehalud*, *nandimukh* and *ashtamangala*. There is no ritual associated with consummation.

Lohars cremate their dead and *asouch* (pollution) lasts a month for family and *bhayad*. The eldest, or the youngest, son performs *mukhagni*; when there are no sons, the widow does it. In pollution, the bereaved family and *bhayad* turn vegetarian; neither do they use turmeric, oil or salt in their food. However, *sindur-nun* (rock-salt) is permitted.

The Lohars are a predominantly landless class of agricultural labourers. An insignificant number owns land and can claim land to be their major economic resource. This community of mainly landless people claims no particular occupation as a traditional vocation, except that they have been labourers for generations. The community's subsidiary occupations are assorted odd jobs of labour, such as earth-moving, roof-thatching or building mud houses. Women have fishing as a subsidiary occupation. The Lohars are dependent upon markets for buying essential commodities. There are no bonded-labourers among them.

With rising population, there has been a steady increase in landlessness, and so, a rise in the number of labourers working in agriculture and in odd jobs. Child labour is common among the poor. Young boys, from the age of ten, work for their rich neighbours — within the community and outside — as *mahendar*s or *bagal*s. As these boys grow up, and especially, after marriage, *mahendari* no longer suits them, since a *mahendar* has to spend most of his time at his master's house. *Bagali* is very lowly paid, and so, suits only very young boys. Wages are paid in cash and kind and, often, it includes breakfast, one meal and some *bidi*s.

For the past three decades, the government has been trying steadily for a planned transformation — initially through community development programmes, and later through block-offices — by introducing such agricultural innovations as high yielding varieties of rice and other crops, more effective agricultural implements and irrigation facilities. This has brought about a sea change in the country's agricultural sector and substantially increased the number of man-hours, so giving an opportunity to the landless Lohars to have employment for more days a year. No migration of labour from among the Lohars is reported and they have shown no sign of any shift from the primary to the secondary or tertiary sectors.

The Lohars of a village have a hereditary post of a *mondal*, handed down from father to the eldest son. Another hereditary post is that of *paramanik* (the village messenger). The traditional *jati* council comprises a *mondal*, a *paramanik* and *murubbi*s (village community elders). But its role is now limited. There is no evidence of any *sabha* (regional association). There is no traditional village panchayat now for settling disputes among communities. The caste-council imposes fines on wrong-doers, but there is no form of reward. The role of the modern statutory councils — the *gram panchayat*, *anchal samiti* and *zilla parishad* — is widespread, especially in village development, providing employment opportunities under different government schemes, issuing certificates stating the constitutional status of the members of various scheduled castes and tribes, distributing funds and doling out ration cards. Changes since Independence are: i) a weakening of the caste-council's control over the community; ii) introduction of modern statutory councils; and iii) politicization of the electorate for election of representatives to the statutory councils.

The Lohars are Hindus, though there is no particular family, clan or village deity. A few Lohar families in a village may worship family deities — Kali, Manasa or Sitala — but this is an exception, rather than the rule. The family holds *nityaseva* (daily propitiation) of the deities. There are no clan deities, however. In certain parts, for instance Birbhum, Dharmaraj is a recognized village deity. Several others, such as Kalorai, or Kelorai, Chandrai, Katarai, Maghrai, Bandorai and Fatikrai, may accompany Dharamraj. Baneswar (a form of Shiva) — represented by a piece of wood embedded with nails and smeared with vermilion — is a close companion of Dharmaraj.

Dharmaraj and his companions are represented by black granite smeared with vermilion. The function of these deities is to strengthen faith and confidence, among the devotees, in a world beyond the earthly one and in miracles. Lohars respect all major Hindu sacred centres and shrines. The following Hindu pilgrimages are popular among the Lohars: Gaya, Varanasi, Vrindaban, Calcutta, Tarapith and Kankalitala. The last three places are closer home for them. Brahmans are their religious experts.

Their major fairs and festivals are the ones locally organized, either in the village or nearby. Relatives from all over flow into the villages during these festivities. Married daughters, with children, visit their parents, or, in their absence, their brothers' families, on an excuse of visiting the fairs or taking part in the festivals. Sons-in-law are specially invited to these occasions. Some of the festivals — Dharmaraj and Charak — bring a kind of an atmosphere of castelessness in this caste-ridden, multi-ethnic society and help villagers interact across caste borders, disregarding obligations and duties concerning the festivals. There is, however, no instance of any change of religion — only a few who have taken *diksha* from Vaishnava *gurus*. The Lohars have not taken part in any socio-religious movement. There has been no significant change in the pattern of religious behaviour and organization in recent years.

The Lohars do not have any tradition in the plastic or graphic arts, or in any other craft, except handicraft (weaving and mending *jalis*). The women sew *kanthas* (quilts) from torn *saris* and *dhotis* sewn together in layers. But this has only a utilitarian aspect and no attempt at aesthetics. The community has no indigenous forms of music or dance.

Commensal norms among the Lohars are fast changing. People talk in terms of *ruchi* (taste). For instance, if a person of a high caste is served food in a clean manner in a low-caste household, the person would eat it. This is no doubt true in individual cases. But, by societal norms, the Lohars are a *jal-achal jati*. *Kacha* and *pucca* food from this community is not socially acceptable to high-caste Brahman, Kayastha and Sadgop *bhadraloks*, though *siddha* is. On their part, the Lohars do not accept food from the Haris, Doms, Bayens and Bauris. There is no taboo however, on accepting *siddha* from these communities. Inter-community marriage is taboo. Putative kinship-based, or ritual-based, friendship (*sakhi*, or, locally, *sai*) is in vogue.

Lohars have access to wells and other water sources, roads, schools, crematoriums, *panchayat ghars* and houses, but they are barred entry into sanctums of temples. They have *jajmani* relations with their Brahman priests and a socio-economic inter-dependence with Napits, or Narasundars (barbers) and Dom, or Hari, midwives. The Lohars, as a community, keep a low profile in politics. However, many join processions, organized by different political parties, to Calcutta, or district towns. Lohars have not taken part in any political or ethnic movement.

A few have landlord-tenant relations as *bhag-chasis* (sharecroppers) with landowners. *Bhag-chasis* consider themselves privileged, since they share half the produce they cultivate in the landowner's field. Besides, the sharecroppers take two-thirds of the straw, while the rest is given to the landowner. The cultivator-labourer relationship is broadly of two kinds — *kisani*, or *krisani* (a seasonal contract between the labourer and landowner); and *munish*. Employees prefer to be *kisans*, or *krisans*, rather than *munish*. A *kisan*, under normal circumstances, shares a third of the yield, while two-thirds is taken by the landowner, while a *munish* is dependent on daily wages. There exists an employer-worker relationship in a rural setup when people are employed — on a daily wage basis — for casual, isolated pieces of work, such as roof-thatching or earth-moving.

The community as a whole is still backward in literacy and education, as in health and medicare. Family welfare measures have made no headway. However, the Lohars have taken to family planning. Drinking water is available all year round because of government measures taken in sinking tube wells and digging wells in different hamlets. Employment and self-employment schemes are still not within their reach.

Lohars listen to songs, plays and music on transistors — not national or international news. Roads and means of transport have given Lohars a scope to move faster and wider. Electricity is still a luxury in their mud huts, than any real need, yet people have been forced to give up using wood as fuel, since it is not available. Coal and *gul* (in areas close to towns) and cowdung cakes are used as fuel. In the interior areas, people still gather dry leaves and twigs as fuel. Lohars with land show an eagerness to utilize irrigation facilities, wherever available, since it helps produce more than one crop a year, and so, increases employment potential. Lohar landowners prefer chemical fertilizers and insecticides, as well as organic manure.

Nutrition programmes for schoolchildren are irregular. For such commodities as sugar and kerosene, Lohars depend upon rations, since these are costlier in the open market. Banking facilities have no attraction for them, yet.

R. K. BHATTACHARYA

LOHARA

The Loharas, or Lohras, are a little-known community of West Bengal. Risley says the Loharas are a sect of the Mundas in Chhotanagpur, and 'Lohra' is a synonym for 'Asura' and 'Lohar' (Risley, 1891: II: 24). But Loharas now say that the Lohars are Kamars who have been so named because *loha* (iron) is an essential item in their life-cycle rituals. The Mundas also live very close to them, but maintain a separate identity. The only surname of the Loharas is Sardar. The history narrated by the people is that they were brought from the western districts of Bengal — Bankura, or Chhotanagpur — by the English to work in indigo plantations in Nadia district, about four or five generations ago. At that time, they used to live in jungles. But now, they say that in Nadia they are mainly distributed in Mithapur, Homaeapoter, Dubli, Dismali, Chinapukuria, Mondalpukuria, Devagram Huchukdanga, Sarishdangipara, Uttar Dhaduria, Sridharpur, Moragachha, Kamalpur, Panidhali, Majdia, Narayanpur and Ujirpukuria Balarampur.

The region under study has a moderate climate and plain alluvial and fertile soil. Many rivers, including the Bhagirathi, provide natural irrigation in the region. Along with natural irrigation through rivers and rainfall, modern irrigation is provided by deep tube wells, giving the area an abundance of vegetation and crops. The Forestry Department has implemented many afforestation schemes. A wide variety of fruit plants help the people to earn money.

By the 1981 census, the total Lohara population in West Bengal was 23,799 — most of whom were settled in West Dinajpur district. The Loharas speak Bengali at home and outside, since they have forgotten their own tribal language through disuse. They sometimes speak a corrupt form of Hindi. They have no identification mark. Constitutionally, they are a scheduled tribe of West Bengal.

They are non-vegetarian and eat all kinds of fishes and animal and bird-meat, except beef. They go on annual hunts in winter, when they catch *satana*s (iguanas), *khata*s (wild cats), *khara*s (hares), *dhere*s (otters), *soret*s (animals belonging to the wild cat family), *bezi*s (mongooses), *kunka*s (birds) and *lakshmibilash* (rats). Their staple food is rice and vegetable curries, with pulses. Their cooking medium is mustard oil, *til* oil and rapeseed oil. They eat fruits occasionally, but cannot afford milk since they are very poor. They drink home-brewed *haria* and *tari* almost regularly and sing in the evenings. Even the women drink occasionally. They do not have any restrictions on any food in a particular month or season. Loharas, sometimes, smoke *bidi*s or cigarettes, and chew *pan* and *dokta* and *khaini* (tobacco products). A few of them take snuff.

The Loharas neither have any social divisions or groups, nor *gotra*s or clans. Earlier, they had such surnames as Tirki, Toppo, Har and Manja, but now, they use only Sardar. They believe they are Adivasis, or an autochthonous tribal people. Other communities also look upon them as Adivasis, Sardars, or Bunas and consider them socially low in rank.

Loharas are endogamous at the community level, and exogamous at the village level. The marriageable age for Lohar girls is nine to twelve years, and, for boys, twelve to fifteen. There is no system of paying bride price or dowry in marriage, but the groom's father gives *chadda-sika*s as *bhita-selami* (fourteen coins each worth one-fourth of a rupee) to the bride's parents. This money is given to the midwife and barber who serve the bride's family.

Marriages are negotiated, and mostly monogamous, but sometimes, Loharas marry more than one wife, if the first is barren. *Sankha*, *sindur* and *loha* are symbols of a married woman. The wife lives with the husband after marriage. *Chhara-chhari* (divorce) may be initiated by either partner and a meeting of five members is held to finalize the divorce. After divorce, the woman returns to her parents' house and is considered unmarried. If a divorcee man or woman remarries, the second marriage is called *nikah*. Widows and widowers too, may remarry.

Lohara families are mostly nuclear, though a few vertically extended one exist, too. Of late, however, the trend has been towards the former kind. Relations between members of a family are extremely cordial and close-knit. Every member respects and obeys the head of the family. Youngsters are treated with love and affection. A man, usually, has a relationship of distance with his *bhadra-bou* and a woman with her *mama-svashur*. Grandparents and grandchildren have a jocular relationship. Family elders arbitrate to settle conflicts arising over a wide variety of reasons. Sons equally inherit property. Inter-family links are in evidence at social and life-cycle crises. There has been no change in these aspects.

The responsibilities of Lohara women include housework — cooking, cleaning, child-rearing and looking after domestic animals. Some work in agriculture, and contribute whatever they earn to the family kitty. Women play a major role in the worship of household deities, but take no part in community festivals or regional politics. They do not inherit property.

After a child is born, pollution lasts twenty-one days. On the fifth, and again on the ninth day, the mother and newborn have to take a ritual bath. After the bath on the fifth day, the maternal uncle, or grandmother, selects a name for the baby. A feast, with *baria*, follows. The Loharas have no *annaprashan*. On the twenty-first day, a bath in a pond is essential, before worship at the *ghat* (bank of the pond). Red spots are drawn on cowdung with vermilion, while praying to Dharmaraj (their supreme deity).

A Lohara marriage begins with *meye-dekha* (searching for a bride); in which five members from both families take part, followed by *chhele-dekha* (approving the choice of husband) in the groom's house. *Ashirbad* or *bandhuni* (blessing, or binding) follows at the bride's house. In the first ritual, the bride's family gets gifts of *sari*s, *churi*s (bangles) and food, such as *chira* and *muri*. The groom is similarly blessed through the *bandhuni* ritual, and gifted a *ganjee* (guernsey) and a *dhoti* by the bride's family. The other rituals are: *gayehalud*, *satpak-ghora*, *malabadal*, *boubhat* and *ashtamangala*. The bride and groom may live together after the last rite held on the eighth day after the wedding.

Loharas bury their dead. After a person dies, pollution lasts ten days. On the eleventh, *sradh* rites are conducted by a priest or a *naikha* (caste-*panchayat* member). All men of the dead person's lineage — as well as the pall-bearers — have to shave their heads, pare their nails and have a bath on the tenth day. A Bengali barber serves them in this rite. The *ghate-tola* follows, in which new clothes are gifted to the members of the bereaved family by people related by marriage after they have had a bath on the tenth day. The clothes of every pall-bearer have to be cleaned by the mourning family. On the twelfth day, a *kush* (a kind of grass) idol of the dead person is made and placed on a banana leaf. The members of the bereaved family then anoint the idol with turmeric paste and mustard oil. The eldest member carries it to a water body and throws it in.

The Loharas' main economic resource is land. Some work as agricultural labourers, while others own land. Agriculture is the main source of sustenance. Some work at petty businesses — selling bullocks, vegetables and fruits — as a subsidiary occupation. A few pull rickshaw-vans. They have to depend on markets to sell their commodities. The community has no bonded labourer. A rising population has led to a spurt in the number of agricultural labourers, who are paid in cash.

The Loharas have their own traditional caste-panchayat comprising five members, headed by a *majhi*, or *karta*, or *mondal* (a hereditary post), who presides over meetings. His deputy is the *jakmajhi*, and the third in hierarchy is the *gorait*, who is like a peon to the council, delivering messages to the village folk and serving notices of meetings to villagers. His post is akin to the village *chowkidar's*, or *kotal's*. The fourth member is the *pramanik*, who serves as barber and conducts purification rites at births and deaths, and sometimes, wedding rites. The fifth is the *laikha*, who serves as priest.

The community has a regional association, which helps them to get in touch with the local administrative authorities. The functions of the caste-council are varied. It looks into social issues — granting divorce, finalizing a wedding, ruling in burglary or theft cases. The role of a modern *gram-panchayat* is to manage the distribution of various government funds among the villagers.

Their main family deity is Dharmaraj and Dharmaraj puja is held in Magh. They have other community, or village festivals, such as Dal puja or Karam, in *Shravan* or *Bhadra*, Panchabhut puja in *Kartik*, Makar in *Poush* and the annual hunting festival on *Magh*-Purnima day (full-moon day in *Magh*). Very few have visited places of religious interest. They worship all deities of the wider Hindu pantheon for the well being of the villagers. Their major fair is the snake fair at Khadaitala, though they visit other fairs, too.

The community has no tradition in the arts or crafts, but they do have certain traditions in folk music and dance. Many of them know the *Jhumurgans*, and sing them to the accompaniment of various kinds of indigenous musical instruments.

They share food with such neighbouring tribes as the Mundas, Oraons and Lodhas. Some have married into the Munda community. They have no difficulty in entering schools, crematoriums, or temples. They do have some socio-economic dependence upon certain neighbouring Hindu communities whom they serve as agricultural labourers. The Loharas have established modern inter-community links, as well, since they visit the office of the local sub-divisional officer, who is a Santal. Young Lohara boys work for local political parties. They have economic relations with the *aratdars* (middlemen who buy their goods).

The Loharas have a low level of literacy and education. Most children do not go to school. A few have studied only up to Class VIII or IX. They depend on both indigenous and modern medical treatment. They have not adopted any family planning measures. They fetch their drinking water from tube wells. They do not approach the employment exchange, nor seek assistance from any rural development agency. There is no self-employed person among them. Trains, buses, *gram-panchayat* offices and scheduled caste, scheduled tribe offices help them maintain links with the world outside.

Lohara villages mostly do not have electricity. In villages that do, the Loharas cannot afford it, since they are poor. Wood and cowdung cakes are their main fuel. They use water from shallow tube wells for irrigation. They use chemical fertilizer and insecticides. There are nutrition schemes, but, by and large, they do not avail of these. They pick up their rations from fair price shops, but have no transactions with banks.

CHANDRIMA CHOWDHURY

MAHAR

The Mahars, originally migrated from parts of Maharashtra to West Bengal in the first decade of this century, especially when workshops and colonies of the Indian Railways were being set up.

The land within the Railways settlement at Kharagpur was acquired by the railway administration some time near about 1898. Along with the establishment of railway workshops and colonies during the first decade of this century, the people belonging to the Mahar community came to Kharagpur for their livelihood and settled here permanently. Those who got employment in Railways departments also got Railway quarters for residential purposes and others started living in huts built on Railways land.

The Mahars are distributed in various municipalities of the state — especially in Kharagpur, Jhargram in Midnapore district, and also in districts like Burdwan, the 24-Parganas, Maldah and Murshidabad. They live in the plains of West Bengal, characterized by a hot summer, relatively high humidity and well distributed rainfall in the monsoon. By the 1981 Census, the total Mahar population in West Bengal was 17,706. They speak Marathi at home and with relatives, though a section — especially those in Maldah and Murshidabad districts — speak Bengali among themselves. They speak in Hindi or Bengali with outsiders. They write in Devanagari or Bengali. The men wear *pyjamas*, *punjabis* and *topis* (caps). The women wear *saris* in a typically Marathi style. Constitutionally, they are a scheduled caste.

The Mahars are non-vegetarian, but do not eat beef and pork. Both rice and *chapatis* are their staple food. They have such pulses as gram, *moong* and *masur*. *Vanaspati* and mustard oil are their cooking mediums. They eat all kinds of locally available roots, tubers and vegetables, besides seasonal fruits, such as apples, oranges and grapes. The men, occasionally, drink alcohol bought from the market. They smoke *bidis* and chew betel. They make sweets on such religious occasions as Buddha Purnima and Maghi Purnima.

No recent change in surnames or clan names has been reported. The most popular surnames of the Mahars are Hogra, Gorhe, Meshram and Shendey — also considered clan names, though everyone has forgotten the meanings of these clans. The Mahars are treated as a low caste in the local social hierarchy, though not at par with the Bhangis or Haris who are considered even lower. The Mahars consider themselves Sudras, and the others, too, hold this view.

The Mahars are clan-exogamous. Marriages are negotiated and monogamous. The marriageable age for men is between twenty and twenty-six years, and for women, between eighteen and twenty-one. *Sindur*, *mangalsutra* and *pala* are symbols of a married woman and *kangan* of a married man. Paying and receiving dowry is — in cash and kind — is socially acceptable. After marriage, the wife lives with her husband. Divorce may be sought by either partner on grounds of adultery, maladjustment or impotence. Compensation is paid to the aggrieved party. The responsibility of children of divorced parents lies with either the father or the mother. Widow and widower remarriage is permitted, though without elaborate ceremony. Of late, there has been a rise in age at marriage among the Mahars.

The Mahars live in both nuclear and joint families. Relations within the family depend upon love, respect, reciprocal duties and obligations. Wives love and care for their husbands. Parents and adult children have a relationship of mutual affection and obligation. Grandparent-grandchild relations are based on love, affection and joking. There is no relationship of distance in a nuclear family, but in a joint family, a woman has such a relationship with her husband's elder brother. A man might have jocular relations with his elder brother's wife. Mahars generally avoid conflict. Sons inherit their parents' property, and the eldest son succeeds to his father's position. Inter-family links are based on cooperation and guidance.

Women do not have a right to inherit. Their economic role overlaps with domestic activities. They have the social roles of daughter, wife, mother and grandmother. They have roles in the life-cycle rituals too. They observe fasts and cook special food at religious festivals. Their only involvement in politics is the exercise of their adult franchise. They have no specific role in family management.

The Mahars observe certain pre-delivery rituals and restrictions. Pregnant women do not venture outdoors, especially after dark. After a child is born, pollution lasts six days. A barber and a *dai* conduct the purification rites. On the sixth day, *chatti* is held, at which a feast for children, women and the old is held. There is no naming ceremony. *Annaprashan* — conducted by the family priest — is held in the sixth month for a boy, and seventh, for a girl child. A feast is hosted for relatives and friends.

Wedding rituals are elaborate, and are held at both the bride's and the groom's houses. The wedding rites are performed by a *bhikkhu*/

bhante or *upasak*, and both the families hold feasts.

Mahars cremate their dead and mourn for ten days. On the second day, men visit the crematorium; collect a few bones kept in an earthen pot, and throw them into a river. *Das-kria* is held on the tenth day. A *bhikkhu* and a Napit conduct the purification rites. A feast is held for neighbours, guests, relatives and friends. Many rituals have now been curtailed to curb expenses.

The Mahars are a landless community, and are mainly, self-employed in business. Making *thongas* (paper bags) with old newspapers and *bidi* binding is their primary occupation in West Bengal, and working as daily wage factory workers as the subsidiary occupation. They are fully dependent on the market, where the medium of exchange is money. There are neither bonded, nor child labourers, among the Mahars. Wages are paid in cash. Since the Mahars are a migrant community, almost all have lost their traditional occupation and only the primary and secondary occupations are their main sources of sustenance.

The Buddha-Vihar Society is their traditional *jati* council and the state unit of the Buddhist Society of India is the regional association in West Bengal. The Kharagpur Buddha Vihar Society is the locally registered organization, where the president is the chief. He is elected by voice vote and holds office for five years. These councils look after community welfare and give financial assistance when needed. The Mahars get in touch with these councils when their needs are not met through their own community. Ostracism or social boycott is the main form of punishment for adultery, rape, elopement or theft, but there is no from of reward. The main changes since Independence are that literate young Mahars are now more prone to becoming members of the *jati* councils, and the traditional panchayat is slowly losing its control to statutory councils which are becoming more powerful.

The Mahars are mainly Buddhists, though a section in Maldah and Murshidabad districts is Hindu. Santoshi Ma and Satyanarayan are their family deities and Hanuman Ji, Sitala, Kali and Hari the village and regional ones. All major neighbouring sacred centres are considered pilgrimages. The *bhikkhu/bhante*, or *upasak* and the Brahman priest are their religious experts. They celebrate the birth anniversaries of Buddha and of Bharat Ratna Dr. B. R. Ambedkar, besides Maghi Purnima. They attend all major local fairs and festivals too, including some with socio-religious significance.

Some of the folk songs and folklore in existence among the Mahars have been borrowed from their place of origin. The songs are sung by men and women especially at different festivals. The Mahars sometimes, use percussion instruments, at ceremonies.

A typical folk-song runs:

"Chhatramukh sani Ayodhya cha,/ Raja Nand tole majha/ Maye bapa majhe mayee bapa,/ Cabari dewacha, majhe mayee bapa,/ Cabari dewacha Nand toshe majha". (This song is sung by women when a boy is born in the family. Here, the mother praises her child, saying, "You are very beautiful; your face is so beautiful that it resembles the face of the King of Ayodhya, who was beautiful, too").

Another song runs;

"Gan raya lookar ejo/ Bhet lagreya al dejyo". (This is sung to ward off danger. "Oh, God! Please help me overcome this crisis").

Because they are scheduled castes, the Mahars are considered *jalachal* in the ritual, social and occupational fields. The Brahmans accept *siddha*, but not *pucca*, food from them. Inter-community marriages are not permitted, though there are no restrictions on ritual-based friendship. They have no problems in sharing wells and other water sources, roads, schools, crematoriums, temples, houses, or *panchayat-ghars* with their neighbours. They have had a patron-client relationship with the Brahman, *upasak*, *bhikkhu*, Napit and Dhobi for generations.

Mahars say they took part in the socio-religious movement led by Dr. B. R. Ambedkar for the uplift of backward and downtrodden communities. They have employer-worker and other forms of symbiotic relationships. Mahar businessmen have opened up modern inter-community links in their fields of work.

Literacy and education levels of the Mahars are low, though both boys and girls have some kind of formal education. Boys study up to the college level and girls up to the secondary level, since they are poor. They do not have a progressive outlook towards modern healthcare, and mostly prefer indigenous, traditional medicines. They do not have a favourable attitude towards modern family planning measures either. They get drinking water in their areas from municipal taps and tube wells. The Mahars get the facilities of various government employment programmes, though they are mostly self-employed, especially in animal husbandry.

They listen to the radio and watch television. They use all available forms of mechanized transport. Many Mahars have electricity in their homes. Firewood, cowdung cakes and coal are their fuels. They do not show any awareness of the need for environmental conservation. Since most live in urban areas, irrigation is not a matter of interest to them. Neither do they use chemical fertilizers nor insecticides, since most are landless. Nutrition programmes in their children's schools are irregular and perfunctory. They pick up their rations from fair price shops. Some avail of banking facilities, but many depend upon moneylenders and shopkeepers for loans and credit.

SUBHRENDU MAITI

MAHARASHTRIAN

The Maharashtrians, with the synonym Marathi, have been named after their state, Maharashtra, which indicates a union of *mahan* (great) *rashtras* (states). Historically, Maharashtra comprises three regions — western Maharashtra, Vidarbha and Marathwada — of which Vidarbha has an oft-narrated past, with mention in the Mahabharata. After Independence, the Government of India's experiment in bilingualism — through combining Maharashtra and Gujarat — did not work and these two separate states were formed on May 1, 1960. The Maharashtrians' history of migration to West Bengal dates back to 1890, when they settled in Calcutta and accepted jobs in the erstwhile Bengal Nagpur Railway (now South Eastern Railway)

The community has two dialects — Marathi and Konkani (northern part of the Konkan coast). The Maharashtrians are concentrated mainly in central and south Calcutta, but scattered throughout the city and other parts of West Bengal too. Calcutta is located on the coastal plains of Gangetic West Bengal, and has a moderate climate, high humidity and medium rainfall. Calcutta, the megalopolis of West Bengal, lies within 22° 33' North latitude and 88° 23' East longitude and is situated about 160 kilometres from the Bay of Bengal on the left bank of the western branch of the Ganga, called Hooghly or Bhagirathi.

The total area of Calcutta is 104.00 square kilometres, while the Calcutta Municipal Corporation covers 98.79 square kilometres. The remaining areas are under Calcutta Port Trust and military establishments. The average temperatures recorded in 1979 were 37.8° Celsius (maximum) and 14.7° Celsius (minimum). The annual rainfall in the same year was 1,321.1 mm (by the 1981 census). The Marathi speaking population in West Bengal as per 1981 census was 6771. Out of which 1,609 (896 men and 713 women) lived in Calcutta alone. Maharashtrians speak in Marathi and Konkani's speak in Konkani; both write in the Devanagari script with family, kin groups and others. Both speak in Bengali, Hindi and English and write in the Roman, Devanagari and Bengali scripts with others.

Maharashtrians — Chitpavan, Desastha, Karahade and Devdny Brahmans — are pure vegetarian, though now, some have developed a taste for non-vegetarian food. The Saraswat, Shervi Brahmans and other castes are generally non-vegetarian. Their staple food is rice or wheat. They have such pulses as gram, *tuar*, *masur*, peas and beans. Their cooking medium is groundnut oil. They eat green vegetables, roots, tubers and seasonal fruits available in the market. The coconut is an inseparable part of any *puja*. The main change in their food habits is that they are now turning to non-vegetarian diet. Those who can afford have fish, eggs and meat, since these are available in plenty in the city, as also due to the influence of the food habits of their Bengali neighbours.

Maharashtrians have pre- and post-natal restrictions on food. *Kanthal*s (jackfruit) and pineapples are taboo. After delivery, the mother is not allowed to have *cholar-dal* (gram) or spicy and oily food. Men, occasionally, have alcoholic drinks. They have such beverages as tea and coffee too, besides smoking cigarettes and chewing betel.

Maharashtrians have social divisions. Among the Hindus, there are Chitpavan Brahmans (Konkonastha, with such surnames as Marathe, Tilak, Gokhle and Sathe), Desastha Brahmans (with surnames such as Kulkarni, Despande and Ane), Karahade Brahmans (whose surnames are Karare, Dev and Karkare), Devdny Brahmans (with surnames Misra, Bagdathay and Atra), Chandra Sreni Kayastha Prabhus (with surnames of Toykar and Kirtikar), Saraswat Brahmans (with surnames such as Gavaskar, Borkar and Majumder), Shenwi Brahmans (who have such surnames as Prabhu, Walavalkar, or Pandit), Maratha Chatris (with surnames such as Bhosley, Morey, or Pawar), Maratha Vaishyas (surname — Patil), Maratha Kumbis (surnames — Wogmare, or Kupahkar), Sinpi Marathas (goldsmiths; surnames — Nagarkar and Shimpi), Lohars (surname — Tambata), scheduled castes (surnames — Ambedkar, or Mahar).

The social divisions like clans or *gotras* of the Maharashtrian Brahmans and Kayasthas are Atri, Kapi, Kashyap, Garge, Shandilya, Kandinya, Kaushik, Jamudagna, Nityananda, Babhroavya, Bhardwaj, Masty, Vasistha, Bhisnu and Ruddha. Their social divisions are based on social status and ancestry. They are aware of the *varna* order and believe — as do others — they have a high social status.

They are endogamous at the caste and community levels and exogamous at the *gotra* level. The practice of cross cousin marriage exists. They marry when adult, and marriages are negotiated, by mutual consent, or through courtship, as well as monogamous. The *mangalsutra*, green glass bangles, *bindi*s and toe rings are the symbols of a married woman. The system of *kanyadan* exists, but not bride price or dowry. After marriage, the wife lives with her husband. Either partner may divorce, with judicial approval, for maladjustment, or any other cognizable reason. Widows and widowers may remarry, as may men and women divorcees. Among certain modern, educated families, the concept of a negotiated, traditional marriage is going out of vogue. Inter-caste and inter-community marriages through courtship are gaining prominence. Maharashtrians now do not marry unless the man earns and can afford to support a family.

Maharashtrian families are mostly nuclear, though a few extended ones also exist. A woman has a relationship of distance with her father-in-law and elder brother-in-law. A jocular relationship exists between a woman and her younger brother-in-law, as well as between grandparents and grandchildren. These, however, are not very rigid among the younger generations. Property and financial disputes spark conflict. Sons and daughters inherit property equally after the enactment of the Mitakshara Act. The eldest son succeeds his father as head of the family.

Women have roles in economic activities and in social and religious rituals. They have equal status with men and decision-making powers at home. They contribute to the family income and control family expenditure jointly with men.

A woman observes four *dohare jiwan*s (predelivery eating rituals) — the first in the third month, the second in the fifth (at her father-in-law's house), the third in the seventh and the last in the ninth month of pregnancy (at her father's house). The one in the fifth month is called *panch-fale ati*, in which the mother-in-law places five kinds of fruits and rice on the *anchal* (loose end of the garment or *sari*) worn by her daughter-in-law. The one in the seventh month, *warivaran*, is when ornaments of flowers are gifted to the would-be-mother at her father's house. The woman is put on a swing and girls surround her, sing songs, in a celebration held after the full-moon night. White dresses and delicacies are gifted to the woman. The last, *charcholi*, is held in complete secrecy at the father's house and the mother-in-law presents her daughter-in-law with a green blousepiece and a coconut. A feast is held for relatives and friends.

Barasu (naming ceremony) is held on the twelfth day if the child born is a girl and, on the thirteenth, if a boy. Three names of Lord Krishna are uttered. After this, a round stone (representing the baby) is passed thrice over and under the cradle by the mother and another married woman standing on opposite sides of the cradle. The baby is passed in the same way after a sweet is placed in the baby's right hand and an ornament in the left. A priest finds out the *pashi* (planetary position) at the time of birth and decides on a suitable name. This name is whispered into the child's ears. Pollution lasts three weeks if the child born is a boy, and five, if a girl. *Zabar-catne* (tonsuring) is performed at *annaprashan* only for a boy when he is ten months old. Only Brahmans observe *janeu* (sacred-thread ceremony) between eight and twelve years of age and this is held at any place other than the maternal uncle's house.

Wedding rituals are performed according to the Vedic tradition at the bride's house, generally before twelve noon, but sometimes, they take place at dusk. Marriages are, usually, negotiated between the respective parents. Before the wedding, the groom's relatives observe *sriman-pujan* (blessing ritual) in which gifts of gold ornaments and *saris* are offered to the girl. The marriage is solemnized through *saptapadi* (holding hands and walking round the fire seven times). The priest sings Mangal-Astak songs. The *prijojon* ceremony is observed at the groom's house.

Maharashtrians cremate their dead and pollution lasts ten days. Though everyone observes death rites, the different castes have slight variations. Caste Hindus — mainly Brahmans — perform the elaborate death rites punctiliously, but some castes have cut these short. Soon after a person dies, news is sent out to relatives. The corpse is washed and covered in new clothes, bedecked with flowers and carried to the crematorium on a bier by relatives and friends, on their shoulders. Before the cremation the priest performs some rituals. The eldest son usually lights the funeral pyre. On the tenth day, relatives pare their nails, shave their heads and beards and have a bath in a river or a pond. *Tilanjali* is observed on the thirteenth, when the final purification rites are held.

Maharashtrians are mainly landless, and work in ferry services in Calcutta. They own businesses too, work in the private sector or are self-employed in general trade or transport. They have direct links with the daily market, where transactions are in cash.

Their local association is the Maharashtra Mandal, where they meet at regular intervals and hold religious, social and cultural activities. The officials are elected from among the committee members. The Mandal rewards Maharashtrians and people of other communities for good work by giving them a shawl and a coconut. The Mandal office is housed in Maharashtra Niwas in South Calcutta, where there are provisions for entertainment through staging of plays and dances which highlight their culture. The Mandal has organized the

Maharashtrians in Calcutta into a unified cultural entity through religious and secular activities. It aims at building a common platform for those away from hearth and home.

The Mandal invites Bengali personalities and academics too, on different occasions. It organizes cultural programmes to harmonize social relations with locals and extend its range of activities. It has donated money to universities and colleges in Calcutta in the memory of Gokhale and Tilak. It has also raised a special fund for charities. It runs a library where one can find Maharashtrian books, publications and journals. Anyone — irrespective of caste or community — can become a member of this if one knows Marathi. The Mandal observes Shivaji Jayanti and some other major festivals.

Their festivals have socio-religious significance. They celebrate the Ganesh Festival for ten days in Bhadrahad, from the Ganesh Chaturthi to the Chaturdashi (fourth to the fourteenth day of the lunar fortnight). A large image of Ganesh is installed and worshipped by two Maharashtrian priests at the Niwas. Every Maharashtrian in the city — whether a member of the Mandal, or not — attends the festival. A special feature is the 'Women's Day', when they exchange *haldi* and *kum-kum* (vermilion). On the tenth day, the image is taken in a procession to the Ganga and immersed. Maharashtrians celebrate the anniversaries of such Maharashtrian saints such as Ramdas, Eknath and Tukaram.

They are Hindus and have family deities. They worship Satyanarayana, Shiva, Kali and Durga. They worship Hanumanji too every Saturday. The Mandal celebrates Hanuman Jayanti once a year with pomp. Hanumanji is considered a god of health and power and holds a high place in the lives of Maharashtrians, since Ram Das (the *guru* of Shivaji) established temples and images of Hanumanji all over the country. Despite their urban lifestyle and liberal outlook, every Maharashtrian family is deeply religious. Satyanarayana and Ganesh are worshipped during morning and evening. The women get together every Thursday and read and discuss religious texts, besides singing devotional songs in the names of Vithol, Nandeva and Daneswar (a Maharashtrian saint who translated the Bhagavad Gita at the age of sixteen).

Maharashtrians are a very old and traditional community and have their own folk-tales, folklore and folk-songs, formed in combination with their mythology and regional beliefs and customs.

A typical song may run thus:

"Nakhawa balha balha japha japha,/ Machawa kinari balha balha" (Fisherman, quickly row me towards the shore — row me, row me). Both men and women sing this song.

Another song runs:

"Pret adwe yene" (If one comes across a corpse being carried down the road and it is to one's left, it is a good omen). They play percussion, wind and string instruments.

Maharashtrians have traditional inter-community relations with their neighbours from other states, but especially with the Bengalis. Except a few orthodox families, everyone shares water, *kachcha*, *pucca* and *siddha* food with the other Hindu communities. They share water sources, crematoriums and schools. Inter-community marriages take place, but putative kinship does not exist. They make no distinction in visiting shrines. They have no specific role in traditional festivals. They accept and render services in economic, social and ritual fields. There is no patron-client, landlord-tenant, cultivator-labourer, or any other form of symbiotic relationship. The community has businessmen, artists, scholars, teachers, doctors and engineers.

Maharashtrians prefer their children to study up to the post-graduate, or at least graduate, levels through the medium of English, though some prefer Hindi. They have comfortably adjusted their lifestyles to keep pace with modern advancements. They make use of all civic amenities, such as electricity, drinking water, liquefied petroleum gas and the rationing system. They listen to the radio and watch television. They get medical aid from ICDS who live in and around the centre and from private physicians or hospitals when necessary. They have saving and investment transactions with banks. Couples prefer a couple of children at the most and use modern family planning methods.

Maharashtrians have adjusted their lifestyles with that of others. Some have opted for inter-community marriage. Maharashtrian girls marrying Bengali men wear vermilion and iron and conch shell bangles. They perform Saraswati puja, which is not their custom. They have a natural liking for plays and music which they perform. The socio-political lessons they got from Shivaji, Tilak and Gokhale expanded their horizons, and till date, they have not abandoned this heritage. Many do not rigidly follow the socio-religious customs (such as wearing the sacred thread in case of Brahmans, or coloured glass bangles in case of married women), but women always wear the *mangalsutra*. They have built up good neighbourly relations with the

Bengalis in Calcutta by adopting the Bengali language and culture. They have not much interest in politics.

MADHUMALA CHATTOPADHYAY

MAHISHYA

The Mahishyas are landowners and cultivators of West Bengal. They have the caste status of clean Sudras in the *varna* order, and are, sometimes, equated with Kaivartas — a generic geographical term signifying groups living in waterlogged areas (*ke* means 'water'). The *Amarkosh* identifies Mahishyas as those born of a Kshatriya father and a Vaishya mother, or the other way round. This has been corroborated by Yajnavalkya, Parashuram, Gaurada Purana and Vyasasukta.

Mahishyas live in Greater Bengal areas bordering Bihar and Orissa states, as well as Bangladesh. They are one of the largest caste groups. In West Bengal, they have a large presence in Midnapore, Howrah and Hooghly districts. This group migrated to this region when they had to change their occupation from fishing to cultivation because of the receding seas.

Risley (1891) remarks, "... They have five princedoms in Midnapore district, and it shows their position was a commanding one". Dr. R. C. Majumdar, mentions in the 'History of Bengal' (Vol. I): "The revolt of northern Bengal, during the reign of Rama Pala and the rule of Dibya and his two successors indicated the importance of the Kaivarta caste to which they belonged". However, it is said that a vast mass of people of varied castes and communities preferred to be called Mahishyas — a generic term. It is, therefore, a confederation of many groups, including the Austro-Asiatic autochthons (Bhowmick: 1956).

Mahishyas speak Bengali with local dialectal variations, and write in Bengali too. The total population of the Mahishyas of Bengal as per 1931 census was 2,381,266.

Though there is no systematic bio-anthropological information on them, there are some university reports where we find details on the dolicho-brachycephalic head forms and variable statures and different complexions of the Mahishyas in different places, indicating a mixed heterogeneous group. They prefer all kinds of food, but in the olden times, certain items such as fish, was taboo to some groups. Their staple food is rice and special kinds of dishes are cooked at festivals and ceremonies.

Among the Mahishyas, there are several *gotras* named after the rishis — Shandilya and Parasar — and these only regulate marriages. The community had strong ethnocentric ideas in the olden days. They are aware of the *varna* order and believe they are 'clean' Sudras of a higher than normal social status, though below the Brahmans, Kayasthas and Baidyas. As a rule, they married outside the *gotra*, but now, inter-caste marriages often take place. Paying dowry is a custom, but, among the poor, the custom of paying dowry or bride price does not exist.

Traditional marriages are negotiated. The final approval of the bride is given at the *ashirwadi*, where the date and time of the marriage are fixed after consulting an almanac and a *lagna-patra* is made. Mahishyas marry when adult. Only rarely do girls marry before puberty. In these cases, *punar-bibaha* (a second wedding) takes place before the couple may share a bed. Polygyny was not uncommon, especially if a man had no child from his first marriage, but this custom is now on the decline because of financial reasons. After marriage, a woman lives with her husband, but, if her father has no son, her husband may live as a *ghar-jamai*. Divorce is permitted, and so is widower remarriage. Men have a certain edge over women in such marriages.

Mahishyas have simple and nuclear to big joint families even in these times. A woman respects her husband's elder brother like her father-in-law, and in many instances, a joint family is run with him as the head. Sons have equal right of inheritance, though daughters, of late, have a right to property. Men dominate women in running a family, but a woman is never neglected, or her position is undermined. Women perform many rituals in pregnancy. *Sadh* is held in the seventh, or eighth, month of pregnancy. The woman is gifted new clothes by relatives. After a child is born, pollution is observed. A Brahman conducts Godar-Shashti rites for the well being of mother and newborn.

A wedding has elaborate ceremonies performed with the help of a Brahman priest and a barber. The maternal uncle plays a special role in the rituals. Applying vermilion and wearing conch shell and iron bangles are common formalities.

Mahishyas cremate their dead. In South Bengal, on the fourth day after a person dies, a clay effigy is built and placed on the pyre and covered with a torn piece of cloth. A canopy is built, supported by four sticks. The articles used by the dead person are placed on it and a temple-like structure is built with banana leaves. This is allowed to drift in a river or pond with a lighted lamp placed on it. This resembles the Egyptian funeral custom. *Nam-Sankirtan* (singing devotional songs) is an essential part of the cremation rites and also held during the *sradh* later.

As mentioned, Mahishyas are both landowners and cultivators. In the historical past, they have served as soldiers, as also in many white collar jobs. There are poor Mahishyas, as well as extremely rich ones. The poor work as daily wage labourers. The village caste council looks after the formalities of the social functioning. Ostracism, fines or boycott were, earlier, forms of punishment, but traditional village caste councils have now been replaced by the present democratic *panchayat* dominated by the ruling political party.

The Mahishyas are Hindus and worship all Hindu gods and goddesses, along with regional deities, and the women observe *bar*s and *brata*s on specific days. They also make pilgrimages. Brahman priests, Acharyas or astrologers and barbers serve as their religious experts. Many Mahishyas have turned Vaishnavas and some Brahmo influence is also noticeable, especially among elites.

Brahmans never demur in accepting *siddha*, or *pucca*, food from Mahishyas. Their ritual, or ceremonial, kinship cuts across caste boundaries and reinforces social relations. They have access to all temples and shrines. They took part in some ethnic movements after a report was published on them in the 1891 census report. The All India Mahishya Samity is located in Calcutta and maintains contact with the movement leaders. Mahishyas have attained some of the highest educational levels and been employed in many white collar jobs. Their involvement in the Indian freedom struggle, as well as establishment of a parallel government in this period in Midnapore are some aspects worth mentioning.

The Mahishyas have a high rate of literacy. They make use of roads, post offices, banking facilities and the public distribution system. Some also depend on moneylenders.

P. K. BHOWMICK

MAHLI

The Mahlis are a little-known community of West Bengal. The Mahlis, Risley (1891: II: 40) points out, were a small community who lived in the Chhotanagpur region of Bihar. The caste Risley described as Mahali, or Mahili, was mentioned as Mahli in the 1931 Census. According to Risley the Mahalis were a Dravidian caste of labourers, *palanquin* bearers and workers in bamboo found in Chhotanagpur and West Bengal. Risley sub-divided the group into: 1) the Bansphor-Mahilis, who worked in bamboo; 2) the Patar-Mahilis, or basket-weavers and cultivators; 3) the Sulunkhi-Mahilis, who were cultivators and labourers; and 4) the Tanti-Mahilis, or those who were palanquin bearers; and 5) the Mahili-Mundas.

Risley found a close resemblance between the totemistic section of the Mahilis and the Santal clans, and, so, came to the conclusion that some sections of the Mahilis (Bansphors, Sulunkhis and Tantis) had originated from the Santals. The Mahili Mundas could have been part of the Munda tribe for similar reasons. The Patar Mahilis were a Hinduised sub-caste of southeast Manbhum who employed Brahmans as priests and refrained from eating beef. In the 1981 Census, the Mahlis numbered 10,827.

They are distributed mainly in Jalpaiguri, Darjeeling, Midnapore, Purulia, Nadia, Bankura, West Dinajpur, Birbhum and the 24-Parganas districts of West Bengal. They were brought to Nadia district from the West by the British to work on indigo plantations.

Their mother tongue now is Bengali, but they say they had a language of their own in the past. They live in central Bengal, where — besides deep and shallow tube wells — several rivers and canals irrigate the plain, alluvial and fertile soil that allows the growth of a variety of fruit plants, vegetables and crops. They catch frogs from the surrounding areas for export. Constitutionally, they are a scheduled tribe of West Bengal.

In Nadia district, Mahlis do not pursue the occupation of basket-weaving. However, in Purulia and Midnapore, this is their major occupation. Elsewhere too, Mahlis are better known only as a basket-weaving community.

The Mahlis are non-vegetarian but they do not kill *baraha*s (pigs) for meat. They do not eat *boal* or *guzar* fish. They have locally available vegetables and pulses with rice, which is their staple food. They eat fruits at ceremonies, but cannot afford milk. They do not have *seem* in *Chaitra*, *mulo* (radish) in *Magh*, pumpkin in *Jaishtha* and *Bhadra* and *bel* in *Jaishtha*. They chew *pan*, smoke *bidi*s and cigarettes and take snuff.

They are not aware of the *varna* order because of their tribal origin, and many are Vaishnavs who have taken Vaishnav *mantra*s. However the Brahmans, Vaishnavs and barbers are invited to their social ceremonies. The Mahlis are endogamous at the community level and exogamous at the village level. The marriageable age for women is between eighteen and twenty years, and for men, twenty-two and twenty-five. Marriages are, mostly, negotiated and monogamous. *Sankha*, *loha* and *sindur* are the symbols of a married Mahli woman. Now, paying dowry for a marriage is compulsory. Women live with their husbands after marriage. Divorce is prohibited, but if anybody wants to break the rule, he has to approach the local panchayat authorities or the court for a decision. Men may remarry after divorce or after the death of their wives, but women are not permitted to remarry. The only change in the institution of marriage is the abolition of bride price.

Most families are nuclear. Many Mahlis however live in vertically extended or joint families. Sons usually inherit property, but now daughters also get an equal share. Inter-family relations are very cordial and closeknit. A man has a relationship of distance with his *bhadra-bou*. Grandparents and grandchildren have a jocular relationship. The eldest son succeeds to his father's position.

Women are not only confined to housework, but also work as daily wage agricultural labourers in the sowing and harvesting seasons. In others, they make bamboo baskets and paper packets for grocers' shops. They contribute to the family's earnings. They have specific religious roles, besides household chores.

Pollution lasts twenty-one days after a child is born, but before that, there are certain restrictions on movement and food during pregnancy. *Setera* is observed on the sixth day after the birth. Three *kaman* rites are performed during the twenty-one days of pollution. On the twenty-first, a *puja* is offered to Shasthi Thakur.

Weddings do not take place in *Bhadra*, *Pous* or *Chaitra*. The wedding day is fixed after consulting an almanac. The services of a Brahman priest and a barber are required for a wedding. *Ashirbad* of the groom is the first rite after the date is finalized. The bride is blessed on the eve of the wedding. *Aiburobhat* is held at both the houses a day before the wedding. On the morning of the wedding day, *gayehalud* takes place. The other main rites are *nandimukh*, *sampradan*, *boubhat* and *phulsajjya*. Either the uncle on the mother's or father's side, or the bride's father, himself, performs the *sampradan*. *Phulsajjya* is the consummation rite. The last wedding rite is the return of the bride and groom to the bride's house — *dasabandhane-ghura-asha*.

The dead are cremated under normal circumstances. However the corpses of infants are buried. After a person dies, pollution lasts thirteen days. They visit a nearby *ghat*, where the rituals of shaving and giving *pinda* to the dead soul with the help of a Brahman priest are held in *ghat-sradh*. On the fourteenth day, a feast is held for relatives and friends in the *auschmukti* ritual, signifying the end of eating *hobisi* (rice and vegetables boiled in an earthen pot without oil or spices) for the sons and the termination of the pollution period. A *bostom* (a Vaishnav religious expert) also helps conduct the *sradh* rites. An annual *sradh*, called *bachharki*, has to be performed.

Earlier, Mahlis had a *jati panchayat*, but now, they are controlled by the local *gram panchayat*. In any serious dispute, they move the court. Mahlis are a Hinduised tribal community, and all their rituals closely resemble those of caste Hindus whom they consider as their reference group. Many are Vaishnavs and hold a *puja* of Gauranga Mahaprabhu on Dol Purnima day. Funds for this are collected from people in the neighbouring areas. Many have taken the Krishna *mantra*s and some worship the image of Goddess Lakshmi daily at home. They worship Manasa during the Dassehra festival and at *Bhadra* Sankranti. *Vaastu* (home and homestead land) is worshipped on Pous Sankranti day. The women observe several *Shashthi*s (the sixth day after a full-moon night).

Their major centres of pilgrimage are Puri, Mayapur, Vrindaban, Nabadwip, Hardwar, Rishikesh and Kamakshya. Their religious specialist is the Brahman or Vaishnav. The major fairs they visit are the Aranghata Jugole Kishorer mela, Santipurer rash mela, Santimar mela of Ghoshpara and the *mela*s of Mohanpur, Baupur, Habibpur and Bajitpur. Sometimes, they visit places where *nam-kirtan*s are sung. Many have embraced Vaishnavism.

The Mahlis are a landless community. All men and women earn a living by working in bamboo and basket-weaving, or as daily wage agricultural labourers. Now, agricultural activities continue throughout the year because shallow and deep tube wells have been sunk in

Nadia district. They earn a meagre income in whatever work they do. Their daily wage rate is twelve rupees. Sometimes, they till, or sow crops in, one *bigha* of land and are paid one hundred and twenty rupees, but they work on a monthly payment basis too, as *mahinder-khata* (*mali-khata* in Bengali). The place where they live is locally known as *mali-pota*. Sometimes, they allow children below fifteen years of age to work as daily wage labourers too.

The Mahlis have traditional inter-community links since they are served by Brahman priests and by barbers at religious rituals. They share *kachcha*, *pucca* and *siddha* food with all communities, except the Muslims and Doms. They do not share *kachcha* food with the Brahmans and Kayasthas. Some inter-community marriages have taken place with the Kayasthas and Paramaniks. They have no putative or kinship-based friendship. The Mahlis share wells, temples, crematoriums, roads and schools with the other communities. Mahlis have a kind of socio-economic inter-dependence on the Brahmans, Vaishnavas and Napits, though not exactly a jajmani relationship. The Mahlis have built up modern inter-community links through the panchayat offices and local political leaders, though this has not helped relieve their poverty.

The Mahlis have a low literacy level. They visit local dispensaries and hospitals for medicare. They fetch drinking water from tube wells in the area. They sometimes get jobs under the IRDP or funds from the DRDA. Their areas do not yet have electricity. Coal, wood, cowdung cakes and kerosene are their fuels. Their school going children do not get midday meals from school. They have no savings, investments or banking transactions.

CHANDRIMA CHOWDHURY

MAL

The Mals believe their name has originated from Malla Kshatriya (wrestler-soldier). They say they were employed as professional wrestlers — more appropriately as soldiers — by the *raja*s of the past (also see Risley 1891: 45). The following are their four sub-groups: 1) Raja-Mal, or Rajbansi Mal; 2) Chhatradhari-Mal, or Rajchhatradhari-Mal; 3) Sapure-Mal, or Bede; and 4) Paharia-Mal, or Dhanguria-Mal (see *ibid*: 97 and 98). Beverley (1872: 184), as quoted by Risley (p: 46), considers Mals as an offshoot of the Male (plural Males), a Dravidian-speaking tribe of the Rajmahal Hills. In course of time, the name, Male, or Maler, has become Mal. However, it should be noted that Malers and Mal-Paharias are two different communities living in these hills and the surrounding areas.

On the Mals' migration, Beverley (see *ibid*: 46 and 47) states, "These Mals appear ... to have spread over the whole of Bengal, where they have become merged in the mess of low-caste Hindus'. Respondents from the Raja-Mal sub-group say the Rajchhatradhari-Mals live in the northern part of Birbhum district; Paharia-Mals are distributed in Murshidabad and along parts on the West Bengal-Bihar border; and Raja-Mals in Rampurhat, Birbhum. The present distribution of Mals corroborates with Beverley's account more than a hundred years ago, in which he wrote they were spread over entire Bengal. Their major concentration for the past hundred years has been in Birbhum and Murshidabad districts. They are also found in Bihar and, outside India, in Bangladesh.

Birbhum is a part of the erstwhile Radh region, a laterite zone. By the 1981 Census, the total Mal population in West Bengal is 2,04,775 less than two per cent of the total scheduled caste population of the state. They speak a local Bengali dialect, both among themselves and with neighbouring communities, and write, both at home and outside, in Bengali. They have no identification mark. They are a scheduled caste of West Bengal.

The Mals are non-vegetarian, but avoid eating beef and pork. Their staple food is boiled rice, pulses (mostly *biuli*) and, depending on their means, either vegetables, or fish. Their cooking medium is mustard oil and, occasionally, *til* oil. Those who can afford give their children milk. They drink liquor brewed at home and bought from the markets. Vegetables that are taboo in certain months are radish in

Magh; *lau* in *Bhadra*; and *seem* in *Chaitra*, though, now, these restrictions are not so strict.

Though Risley writes about the four sub-castes, the Mal respondents consider each an exclusive division without marriage relations. The differentiation of these sub-groups is based on occupation. Chhatradharis serve their clients by holding umbrellas over them at weddings; Sapurias are snake charmers; Paharis earn their living by selling firewood; and Raja-Mals work mainly in agriculture. The Mals claim they have a single clan, Kashyap. Their surnames are either Mal, or Das. They consider they are a low caste, though higher than the Haris, Muchis and Doms. They consider themselves socially superior to their immediate neighbours, the Muslims. The Mals believe they are Sudras in the *varna* order. The neighbouring Hindu communities corroborate their views about their caste and community's position.

The Mals do not marry into the same *pitri-kul* (father's lineage) within at least five to seven generations. On the mother's side, one does not marry one's immediate kin and their children. The marriageable age for men is between eighteen and twenty-five years, and, for girls, between thirteen and eighteen. Marriages are, usually, negotiated and monogamous. The girl's father takes the initiative in searching for a suitable groom. Occasional love marriages rarely cut across boundaries of community. If the first wife is infertile, polygyny is permissible. The symbols of a married woman are *sindur* and conch shell and iron bangles. Dowry is paid in cash (any amount upwards of Rs. 2,000/-) and kind (clothing, ornaments and utensils). Because of this imposition, finding a suitable groom for a marriageable girl is difficult.

After marriage, the bride begins living with her husband in *Agrahayan*. If the marriage has taken place earlier, or if later, the bride has to wait until *Agrahayan* when she is sent to her husband with *tatta*. The custom of *ghar-jamai* is also followed when a man's in-laws have no sons. Both partners may seek divorce on grounds of infidelity, infertility or desertion. The traditional panchayat, or often, a few community elders conduct the divorce formalities and provide social sanction to the act. Remarriage is rare, occurring only where a widow is young and has no children, or when a widower or a divorcee wishes to marry. Village community elders lend sanction to such an occasion by attending the ceremony, though without elaborate rituals.

Two generations ago, child marriage (between six and seven years for girls and nine and twelve for boys) was in vogue. After marrying, the couple would begin living together at the husband's house only after the girl had attained puberty. Earlier, the man's family took the initiative to search for a girl and there was no dowry. Instead, the man's family used to send gifts to the girl. Instances of divorce and remarriage were frequent compared with those in the present times. On one hand, dowry has indirectly lowered the incidence of divorce since husbands have to return the amount if they seek divorce. On the other hand, the husband and wife, have to perforce carry on, even if they are genuinely unhappy, since divorce entails heavy expenses. Now divorce is often sought in a court of law.

Mal families are mostly nuclear, though a few joint or extended families do exist among the comparatively richer members of the community. In a nuclear family, the husband is head of the family. Respect, as an aspect of behaviour in maintaining inter-personal relations in a family is almost non-existent. The head of the family is feared by youngsters, though he is often a loving father. As long as children live in their father's family they are obliged to obey him, help in domestic chores, and whenever possible, take up outdoor work to help their parents. A husband-wife relationship is one of mutual obligation.

A wife is often an earning member, since women work in agriculture and as maids. Besides a woman fetches water, cooks, looks after the children and does most of the housework. The children, especially the daughters, help her in these onerous tasks. Hence a parent-child relationship is more of mutual obligation, than that of love and fear. Siblings in childhood are playmates. An elderly brother, or sister, lovingly looks after the younger ones. However, after reaching adolescence, a brother and sister maintain a distance.

In a joint family, a man has a relationship of avoidance with his younger brother's wife, and all forms of physical contact are avoided. However, a man has joking relations with his elder brother's wife. Relations between wives of brothers are sisterly, but, sometimes, become strained because of property disputes, or the strain of sharing the heavy burden of a joint family. Children in a joint family maintain the same kind of relations with their father's brothers — especially the eldest — that they have with their father. In an extended family, the eldest man is head of the family, and he runs the family on the basis of mutual obligations and understanding with his brothers. In household management, his wife plays a leading role and her sons' wives abide by her decisions. These wives maintain a distance with their father-in-law.

Property is shared equally by the sons. Mals are aware of the Hindu Code Bill, but in reality, daughters often do not stake their claim. The eldest son succeeds his father. Mal families in a village live in one or two *paras* (exclusive areas) of their own, where the major link between the families is agnate ties. Since village endogamy is not taboo, some families have affinal ties too. Besides, where there is no actual kinship — agnate or affinal — they rely on a village-based kinship that develops over time through living in the same village. This is known as *gram-samparke atmiya*. Families with agnate or affinal ties help each other in times of need. If cash or kind (paddy or seeds of crops) is borrowed, it is returned with interest. *Gaontar* (mutual exchange of labour) is another aspect of inter-family link, where the rich employ their poor brethren as agricultural labourers.

Mal women do not enjoy equality with the men. A boy in the family is preferred and attracts more parental care than a girl, who is considered a financial burden and is not encouraged to study. They are forced to dropout after the primary level. Women are never heads of the family, nor given the position of a leader — a *mondal*, or a *murubbi*. However, they can move about freely and often travel out of the village on work. They earn and do share the financial burden of the family with their husbands.

Sadhbhakshan is a pre-delivery ritual in the seventh month of pregnancy, held at the husband's house, where the woman is treated to special food. A first-born, especially a boy, is greeted with joy in the family. Apart from pollution for twenty-one days, there is no other function associated with the birth of a child. A Chamar or Dom midwife helps in the delivery. *Bhat-diani*, or *annaprashan*, is a significant life-cycle ritual, held when the child is six months old if a boy, and seven if a girl. The child is named on this occasion and the *mama*, or the paternal grandfather, feeds the child the first morsel of rice. The child is also tonsured on this day.

A wedding comprises many rites and rituals. After the marriage is negotiated, a visit to the groom's family, and subsequently to the bride's, by the two families involved is known as *na*, or *la-samandha*. Wedding rituals continue for two or three days, to the accompaniment of communal feasts and merry-making. The *barjatri* is well looked after by the bride's family after their arrival at the girl's house. A priest and a barber help conduct the marriage rites, a few of which are *gayehalud*, *nandimukh* and *satpake ghora*.

Mals bury their dead after *mukhagni* is performed by the eldest son. The *gangaputra* (or *palunt*, a derogatory term) begins the digging of the grave and relatives, friends and neighbours complete the work. Those who can afford to, cremate the dead. Pollution lasts ten days, followed by *ghat* and *kamano* on the eleventh day, ritually ending the mourning. On this day, they tonsure their heads, shave their beards and pare their nails before having a bath. The barber conducts certain rites.

Mals are, predominantly, a landless community. Some landowners among them till their own land. Some work as sharecroppers. The majority works as *munish*, *kisans*, or *mahindars* on land owned by rich neighbours of other communities, or rich Muslims. Mal women work as *kamins* in all agricultural operations, except ploughing and hoeing. Mals depend upon weekly and permanent markets in nearby towns for their daily needs. The steady rise in population has led to an increase in landlessness and the number of agricultural workers. Adolescent children — girls between fourteen and fifteen years of age and boys between ten and eleven — work as agricultural labourers too, and get wages in both cash and kind. Very few Mals work as peons, clerks or school teachers.

Mals have a *mondal* or *murubbi* as their leader — an elderly man who is considered wise and knowledgeable about their affairs and traditions. He is chosen informally by Mal villagers and the post is not hereditary. The *mondal* has very little specific function other than to arbitrate in minor disputes, or sanctioning remarriage and divorce, which he does in consultation with other village elders. He decides on the amount of fine to be imposed on a social offender. Members of other castes and communities take his help in settling issues involving Mals. The statutory council is the modern *gram-panchayat*, which controls their lives. The Mals are aware of the responsibilities of the *panchayat* and they consult its members to settle major disputes.

Earlier, a *paramanik* — with jurisdiction over a few nearby villages with a Mal population — was selected. This helped them maintain a kind of regional association. Now, the all-pervasive influence of the statutory *panchayat* has curbed the *mondal*'s power.

Mals are Hindus and worship Dharmaraj, the popular village deity of the central part of West Bengal, jointly with the other village communities. Gaya, Vrindaban and Kashi are their pilgrimages, though very few have actually had the privilege of affording these trips. Brahman priests conduct the worship of Mal household deities. Their major festival is Durga puja, when they wear new clothes. Mals, traditionally, sing folk songs at weddings.

They live in multi-ethnic villages that form part of the composite rural society. Being, mainly, landless agricultural labourers, they have been dependent — for generations — upon the neighbouring landed gentry of other communities. Traditionally, the other link they share with their neighbours is religion. *Varna* Hindus — the Brahmans, Rajputs, Kayasthas, Sadgops and Napits do not accept water from Mals and consider them *jal-achal*, though they do accept *siddha*. The Brahmans and Napits, for instance, are given *siddha* at different life-cycle rituals. Putative kinship of *ganga-jal* and *shibjal* is quite common and that with a Muslim is known as *sai*, or *sakhi*. Mals freely share crematoriums and other civic amenities with their neighbours.

Brahman priests, barbers and midwives have *jajmani* relations with their Mal clients. The Brahman priest visits them at least once a year to collect his annual dues in cash or kind. They are also paid for their services at occasions such as weddings. There has been a slow decline of *jajmani* over the years. The Mals' relations with serving castes — potters, blacksmiths, barbers and midwives — is becoming commercial too. The major, modern links are based on political affiliations, which extend far beyond their immediate neighbourhood and cut across community boundaries. All this has brought them socially closer to other communities. Mals also contribute to the general funds raised for the village Durga puja or Kali puja.

The plethora of primary, secondary and night schools and adult education centres, or colleges that have sprung up after Independence in the districts have had a marginal impact on the Mals' education level. A small section is now literate. The facilities for health and medicare are still very poor in their areas, but their attitude towards family planning is positive. Vasectomy is the commonest measure, but contraceptives are not used. Mals fetch their drinking water from tube wells and wells. Employment and self-employment opportunities are still not within easy reach and they have not risen from the position of agricultural labourers.

Communication facilities have improved of late. Metalled roads have been built over the years, though they are not maintained well. Bus services have improved too. Well-off Mals own transistor radios. Electricity is, still, mostly unaffordable. Coal, cowdung cakes and *gul* are their fuels. The schools attended by their children have irregular nutritional programmes.

R. K. BHATTACHARYA

MALAKAR

The name of the community is Malakar (meaning makers of garlands). The Malakars are referred to as 'Atashbaj', meaning makers of *atashbaji* (fireworks or crackers). However, this is not considered a synonym and neither is in regular usage. Mitra (1953: 330) says the Malakars are of three kinds: 1) Uttar-Rarhi; 2) Dakshin-Rarhi and 3) Bangaja. The community now is not aware of these *thak*s that Mitra referred to. They profess four *thak*s, but can name only three: Malakar; Dokane-Malakar, or greengrocers; and Phulmali, or dealers in flowers. According to Mitra (*ibid*), Malakars are of ancient origin.

There is a myth. A Malakar and Poddar (Sonar Bene, or Swarnakar — goldsmith) were both poor and extremely religious. God appeared, one day, in answer to their prayers. The Malakar, smoking his *hookah* (pipe) at that moment, deferentially avoided God. God blessed the Poddar, saying he would be rich, but, when the Malakar returned, God gave him an occupation with which to serve Him. Then onwards, Malakars have been making ornaments and other decorative items from *sola* (thermocol) for idols of God.

The Malakars are aware of their widespread distribution in different districts of the State. Malakars, sometimes, arrange marriages with people from faraway villages to keep the relationships within the community. They are not concentrated in any one village in large numbers. Malakars live in the eastern plains of India where the climate is warm and temperate, rainfall medium, and humidity in summer high. The major river that flows through these plains is the Ganga. The language they speak and write in, both at home and outside, is Bengali. Constitutionally, they are another backward class.

Malakars are non-vegetarian and eat meat and fish, though not beef, pork, or chicken. However, the younger generation — especially men — have it outside the home. Their staple food is rice, and cooking medium mustard oil. They have pulses of different varieties, mostly *moong*, *masur* and *kalai*. The last is their favourite. Roots, ginger, potato, yam, sweet potato, tubers and bark are eaten, and spices used are turmeric, and cinnamon. They have almost all vegetables available. They have fruits occasionally. Those who can afford milk give it to their children or the old. Tea is a common drink. Liquor is taboo. *Ole* is eaten especially in *Bhadra*. There are several restrictions on eating certain kinds of food on certain *tithis* and in certain seasons, but these are not strictly followed.

Their *thaks* (major social divisions), in hierarchical order, are the Dokane-Malakars, Malakars and Phulmalis. The basis of differentiation is occupational. Malakars of one group customarily, did not marry into another, though now, Malakars are marrying into the Dokane-Malakar group. Mitra (*ibid*) writes about three divisions differentiated on the basis of religious attributes. However, there also seem to be territorial distinctions. The Malakar group is the commonest in Birbhum and Murshidabad. The following are used in different parts of the state: Das, Chaudhury, Majumdar, Seth, Ray and Dey. A few *gotras* are: Shandilya, Kashyap and Phulrashi. The last two are totemic. The Kashyaps avoid looking at a tortoise; and the Phulrashis do not burn any *phul-gach* (flower plant).

The Malakars are a member of the *nabasakha* group of communities, and so, considered equal in status to the other eight communities of the same group. They are ranked lower than the Brahmans, Kayasthas and Baidyas. The *nabasakhas* are, however, superior to any low caste community and their position in the local social hierarchy is not controversial. However, Malakars, sometimes, claim they are just below the Brahmans — something that is not acknowledged by the upper Hindu castes. In the *Brahmavaivarta Puran*, the Malakars are listed as a Sat-Sudra (clean Sudra) *jati*. The community's role and function are explicit in its traditional caste occupation.

The community is clan-exogamous and marry neither lineage members, nor *bhayad*. The members of each *thak* try to marry within their own *thak*. The marriageable age for girls is between sixteen and seventeen, and for men, between twenty-three and twenty-four. In certain remote areas, Malakar men and women marry at even younger ages. Marriages are negotiated through relatives, and monogamous, though polygyny is allowed if the first wife is infertile. The symbols of a married Malakar woman are *sindur* and *sankha*. Paying *pan* is an accepted custom. After marriage, the wife lives at her husband's house. The *ghar-jamai* custom is followed in rare cases. Malakars do not divorce. A widower may remarry, as also a man whose first wife is childless. About three generations ago, dowry was not a custom. Instead, the groom's family sent gifts to the bride's family. There have been a couple of instances of inter-community marriages of late, though such marriages are not socially approved.

Malakar families are nuclear and relations within a family are close-knit. The husband-wife relationship is not demonstrative by social mores. The accepted social behaviour for a wife is to be respectful towards her husband and, outwardly, keep a distance from him as an expression of her womanly coyness. The closeness of their relationship is evident from their mutual dependence and co-operation. A parent-child relation is one of mutual love and affection. A father-son relationship deepens when the former assumes the role of a teacher of the craft they pursue as a living. Adolescent boys learn the skills of their traditional craft from their elder brother, father, uncle, or grandfather (both maternal and paternal). This relation of debt (in learning the craft) is fondly remembered by the boys later in life.

A grandchild-grandparent relationship is based on love, affection and joking. A man has a relationship of avoidance with his younger brother's wife, and a joking one with his elder brother's wife. Sons inherit parents' property, and daughters normally get none, though Malakars are aware of women's legal claim to parental property. The eldest son succeeds to his father's position. Inter-family links are close, yet competitive, in a healthy way. It does not go to the extent of creating factionalism among families. Indeed, they help each other by sharing tools of craft, skills and ideas.

A woman's economic role is restricted to doing domestic chores; her social role that of rearing children and looking after the family. She takes part in various life-cycle rituals. Her religious role is in observing *bratas* and *upas*. Except exercising her voting rights, a woman is not politically active. Malakar women have very little scope of earning, and so, of contributing to her family budget. However, they help their husbands with their traditional craft. Women traditionally have no rights, but many obligations.

After a child is born, *antur* (pollution) lasts a month for family and *bhayad* (those related by blood). Used kitchen earthenware is thrown away by the family and *bhayad*. *Annaprashan* is held in the sixth month if the child born is a boy, and seventh, if a girl. On this day, the child is tonsured by a barber and the family priest performs the rites. The midwife is a special invitee. The maternal uncle — and in his absence, the grandfather — feeds the child its first morsel of solid food. Relatives and friends are treated to a feast later.

A wedding comprises many elaborate rituals and merry-making. *Gayehalud*, *adhibas*, *biye* and *boubhat* are the essential rites. A barber and a Brahman priest conduct the rituals.

Malakars cremate their dead, if possible, at a riverside crematorium. Pollution lasts a month for family and *bhayad* after a person dies. Used kitchen earthenware is thrown away as a mark of mourning and these members have vegetarian food, without turmeric or oil, during the pollution period. They do not shave or pare their nails. They bathe without oil or soap and eat *habisi* thrice — in the beginning, middle and at the end of the period. Thirty days later, *ghat* and *sraddh* are held, the latter performed by a Brahman priest. The following day, a feast is held as a ritual end to mourning.

The Malakars' major economic resource is land, which individual owners control. The community comprises both landowners and the landless, though there are no agricultural labourers. The community's traditional occupation is manufacture of exquisite *sola* ornaments and decorations, encrusted in sequins, wires and spring beads; *daks* (coloured, or enamelled, thin mica or aluminium foils); and *baji* (fireworks). (For details see Mitra: *ibid*). The primary occupation of landowners is cultivation. Many of them pursue the traditional craft as a subsidiary occupation. They find their *byabsha* (business in the traditional craft) paying only during certain seasons (the wedding season, or during Durga puja).

They are totally dependent upon markets. They have neither bonded-labourers among them, nor child-labourers, though children, often help around with tools and raw material while the master craftsmen are at work. They do this out of curiosity and are encouraged to learn the craft, while the elder craftsmen get them to do various odd jobs. Since Independence, there has been a fall in the demand for and interest in, the artefacts made by them, so several have taken up other occupations (see Mitra *ibid*: 340). Educated Malakars have gone in for teaching and clerical jobs.

The traditional caste councils are mostly defunct, which is a significant change. The Malakars now have no regional association, or *sabha*. There is no traditional village panchayat either, to settle disputes among communities. The modern statutory councils' role is important and villagers have to keep contact with them to get economic assistance and to settle minor disputes. Malakars claim they had the *shateki* (literally meaning 'a hundred'), besides, a kind of community court or tribunal, held during large funeral feasts with members of the community as invitees, who were shown the utmost hospitality on these occasions. The head of the tribunal would cut a betel nut into two halves, offering one-half to the host and keeping the remaining for himself, symbolizing the opening of the session. Mitra (*ibid*: 340) writes, "Even the attempt to form a 'Malakar-Sabha' ... failed due to the extreme poverty of these caste craftsmen".

The community professes Hinduism. The Malakars' family deity is Lakshmi, worshipped on Thursdays, and the village and regional deity Dharmaraj. Vishvakarma holds an honoured place in their pantheon. All major Hindu sacred centres and shrines are pilgrimages for Malakars, especially Puri (Jagannath tirtha, where *tirtha* means 'pilgrimage'). Brahman priests are their religious experts. In Birbhum, the major fairs are the *Poush* mela at Santiniketan and Patharchapuri. In the good old days, Barabaganer mela was held at Suri in *Magh* and *Phalgun*. Vishvakarma puja is a community *puja* (see *ibid*: 330) and Durga puja is a general community festival.

In the Santiniketan mela, fireworks made by the Malakars are let off on the last day of the fair and is a spectacular sight. According to the wishes of his father, Debendranath Tagore, Rabindranath had made it compulsory for Visva-Bharati to invite local master craftsmen of fireworks for a display of his work on the last day of the Poush mela. This was a great tribute to the artisans.

The Malakars' traditional community occupation of handicrafts — now mostly a subsidiary livelihood for some — is an example of an excellent art form still prevalent in this state. Mitra (*ibid*: 337-340) gives a detailed account of their work with *sola* and *dak*, but makes no mention of their skill in making fireworks. The crafts of working with *sola*, *dak* and fireworks have not been codified by the craftsmen themselves, or by anyone else, and the techniques are transferred from one generation to another orally and through apprenticeship. So, there is little scope of reproducing any single aspect of this creative tradition, if lost.

Commensal norms are changing fast. Conventionally, the *nabasakha* castes are *jal-chal* for upper caste groups, and so Malakars can be considered *jal-chal* too. Since the days of Chaitanya Mahaprabhu they have become so. Inter-community marriages are restricted. Putative relations are gradually, going out of vogue. The community has no problems in sharing wells and other water sources, roads, schools, crematoriums, temples, houses and *panchayat* offices. Each Malakar family has a fixed Brahman priest, barber and midwife in relations maintained through generations. In certain areas midwives are from the Bauri community.

Though the Malakars show interest in discussing politics and are aware of the political situations in their respective districts, they take no direct part in political activities, other than in exercising their right to vote. They seem to have made at least one unsuccessful attempt at an ethnic movement to claim a higher social status (*ibid*: 339). A newsletter, titled '*Malakar Sammilani Patrika*' was edited from Chinsurah, West Bengal, by a Malakar advocate. This publication stopped its circulation abruptly, breaking the communication it had endeavoured to build up among the members.

A landlord-tenant relationship is not observed among the Malakars, but the landowners employ *munish* and *mahendars*, who are paid in both cash and kind. This cultivator-labourer relationship is one of mutual dependence. In their own craft, they often employ their close kin.

There is almost total literacy among modern Malakar men. Some take the advantages of higher education. Malakars have a progressive outlook on health and medicare. Malakar youths complain they do not always get loans or sanctions for projects under the government schemes meant for district improvement, or bank loans for self-employment projects.

The more educated ones are exposed to modern mass communications media, such as the radio, transistors and newspapers and are aware of regional, national and international news. Roads and transport facilities have improved, though not adequately in their villages. Theft of electricity wires from poles has posed a major hindrance in the supply of electricity to the villages.

Environmental conservation is not of much importance to them. Cowdung cakes, coal and *kola*, or *gul*, are used as fuel. Malakar landowners avail of irrigation facilities wherever available, and use fertilizer, insecticides and organic manure. Nutrition programmes at schools are irregular and perfunctory. The Malakars pick up their rations from fair price shops. However, they do not avail of banking facilities.

R. K. BHATTACHARYA

MALHAR

The Malhars are locally called Dokras, or Dhokras. They call themselves Malhars, or Marals. They have migrated from Orissa and Bastar, in Madhya Pradesh. They are found in Bankura, Burdwan and Midnapore districts of West Bengal, Gaya district of Bihar, Bastar district of Madhya Pradesh and in some parts of Orissa. The areas they live in are marked by plains with a warm and temperate climate, high humidity, a thin forest cover and medium rainfall. They speak in the Malhar dialect at home and write in Bengali both at home and outside.

The Malhars are non-vegetarian, but do not eat beef, or pork. Their staple cereals are rice and, sometimes, wheat, and favourite pulses gram, *moong* and *masur*. Their cooking medium is mustard oil. They have tea, milk and milk products. They drink alcohol, brewed at home, or bought from the market. They smoke *bidis* and chew tobacco and betel. They eat all seasonal vegetables, such as potato, *jhinga* and *kochu*. They eat vegetables in moderation, and fruits occasionally. They do not eat radish in *Magh* and *lau* in *Bhadra*. Of late, they have been having less of pulses and more of vegetables.

Rajgusti, Moralgusti, Kuliagusti, Chowdhurygusti, Chormundigusti, Tekoyargusti and Nagpuriyagusti are the seven Malhar lineage groups, which are divided into such totemic clans as Bhera (sheep), Kachhap (tortoise) and Nag (snake) that indicate descent. Lineage groups are based on respective functions in different religious and social rituals, as well as in resolving social problems. The Malhars have a low status in the local social hierarchy.

Malhars are endogamous at the community level and exogamous at the *gotra* and lineage levels. Malhars marry early, and marriages are negotiated and monogamous. Junior sororate is permissible only after the first wife dies. Vermilion, iron and conch shell bangles are symbols of a married woman. Bride price, paid in cash, is a prevalent custom. A woman lives with her husband after marriage. Divorce is permitted, on grounds of maladjustment and adultery, with the approval of the village *soloana* (caste council). Divorce compensation is paid to the wife. Both partners can seek divorce, and children of divorced parents are the liabilities of either. Remarriage of men and women divorcees, widows and widowers is socially acceptable.

Most Malhar families are nuclear, though there are some vertically extended ones. The man is head of the family, and youngsters obey him. There is a relationship of distance between a man and his younger brother's wife. The members of the family have duties and obligations towards one another. A person has a joking relationship with one's elder brother's wife, and with grandparents. Restrictions on the freedom of youngsters and poverty often strain relations in a family. All sons inherit their parents' property equally. The eldest son succeeds to his father's position. Inter-family links are reinforced at different religious and social rituals.

Malhar women gather fuel and fetch water. Besides doing the housework, the women have a significant role in the religious festivals and rituals. Malhar women tattoo people's bodies for a fee. Though the women share the economic burden of the family with their husbands, they have a low status.

Malhars observe many life-cycle rituals. *Bhujal* is observed in the seventh month for a first pregnancy. The *prasad* of the family deity is given to the pregnant woman in the fifth, seventh and ninth months. In the ninth, she has wet *chira*, with molasses and curd, on an auspicious day. *Panchute* is observed on the fifth day after a child is born and *sentera* on the seventh. They clean their house and wash their clothes on the twenty-first and thirtieth days. Certain pre-delivery restrictions are observed. Pollution lasts thirty days after the birth. *Muhechhetni* (ceremony where the child first tastes rice) is held in the sixth month if the child born is a boy, and seventh, if a girl. Cooked rice is brought from the house of a Brahman in exchange of money and the *mama* — or, in his absence, the *rajamondal* (village head) — feeds it to the child. A feast is held for relatives, and old men and women are offered a drink of alcohol.

After Malhars complete negotiations for their son's, or daughter's, marriage, the bride's father offers *charhandi-mod* (four pitchers of homemade liquor) to the bride's family. When the groom's father visits the girl to bless her, her father offers *duihandi-mod* (two pitchers of liquor). *Aiburobhat* and *gayehalud* are rituals before the main wedding ritual, which are conducted by the *rajamondal*. The bride's father, or uncle, performs *dan*. *Sindurdan* also takes place on this day. The women sing and dance throughout the day and the men play the *madal*. The bride goes to her husband's house the next day, and the groom's father holds a *bou-bhoje* (feast) on the same day, when the marriage is consummated.

Malhars cremate their dead and pollution lasts ten days. The sons of the dead pour water on a *kush* plant every day throughout the pollution period. Kaman is held on the tenth day, and the *rajamondal* conducts the funeral rites. A feast is held for relatives on this day. Expenses on rituals have been rising.

Originally, Malhars made *ghungurs* (bells), *pai* and *poa* (brass vessels to measure grain). The women worked at tattooing people and used to travel far and wide. But, after *dokra* art was introduced, many have taken up this art as a profession. Mukherjee (1978: 338) in this connection writes, "At Deriapur, near Guskara, hollow brass images, similar to those produced by Gharua folk artisans, are made in a process which should be called 'lost resin', rather than 'lost wax'. The people who have taken up this craft as a profession are leading a better life than before. They sell their finished material, such as peacock, deer and Lakshmi figurines, through the Regional Design and Technological Centre (RDTC) in Calcutta, with the help of the Deriapur Dokra Artisan Co-operative Industrial Society, which negotiates with the RDTC for such sales. The Malhars, themselves, sell their finished goods in different daily or weekly, markets.

The Malhar caste council is called *soloana*, comprising twenty-five to thirty members, including seven office bearers. The *rajamondal*, belonging to the *rajgusthi*, is head of this council. His job is to adjudicate, or arbitrate. The *mondal*, belonging to the *mondalgusthi*, is the office bearer next in hierarchy. His duty is to help the *rajamondal* and supervise community feasts. The *kuliar's* duty is to assemble people for different functions, and that of the *choudhury* to bring reluctant offenders of social codes to meetings. The *chormundi* officiates in the absence of the *choudhury*. The *tekoyar* makes cones from leaves, in which alcohol is served to members of the *soloana*. The last office bearer is the *nagpuriya*, who seats the invitees in rows.

Their social problems are resolved by their caste council, while the *gram-panchayat* — the statutory council — plans and implements welfare programmes for the area. Ostracism, physical punishment and cash fines are imposed for adultery, or disobeying the traditional council. Malhars meet at Deriapur on the last day of *Poush* and the *rajamondal* resolves the different social problems and punishes offenders, backed by the *soloana*. Donations are collected from the members of the community for a feast on this day.

Malhars are Hindus and worship Tulsi, Shiva and Raksha-Kali as village deities. Manasa is a regional deity and Shiva-tala and Raksha-Kali-tala are their local sacred centres. A Brahman priest serves them in Vishvakarma worship, while a priest from their own community conducts the rituals for Manasa puja and Saraswati puja. The *rajamondal* conducts their wedding and funeral rites. Poushparal, Vishvakarma puja and Manasa puja are significant festivals.

Malhars sing folk song during wedding rituals.

Malhars share food and drinks with other communities according to their commensal norms. The Hari or Maghaya Dom *dai* and the Napit have a patron-client relationship with them. The nomadic Malhars have wide inter-community links at the economic level, while Malhars who have settled have links with the Koras and Bagdis as neighbours. Outsiders who buy their goods come into contact with them. A few Malhars have even got prizes from the President of India for their creativity. Some hold jobs. All these activities help build up modern inter-community links with others.

Educationally, Malhars are a backward community. They prefer traditional medicines to modern ones and visit hospitals only when indigenous medicines fail. They are not very receptive to modern ideas of family planning. They fetch drinking water from wells or tube wells. Some have taken loans under the IRDP to buy brass for their craft. Malhars listen to the radio, go to the cinema and take the advice of *gram panchayat* on getting loans for business. Their localities are well connected by roads and railways and post offices are close by. Wood and coal are their fuels. They pick up their rations from fair price shops. Most cannot afford to save.

ARCHANA DATTA

MALI

The Malis are a caste engaged in providing other castes with flowers, and are also locally known as Phulmalis. A section of the community is also known as Malakars who make garlands and ornaments from flowers. Risley (1981: 60) mentions that 'Malakar' is a synonym of 'Mali'. A mythological story on their origin relates them to Lord Krishna. They are now distributed mainly in the plains of West Bengal — Midnapore, Howrah, the 24-Parnagas, Nadia and Murshidabad districts. By the 1931 Census, their population in undivided Bengal was 79,084. They speak Bengali at home and with neighbours. They hold the status of other backward class.

The Malis are non-vegetarian and eat fish, eggs and meat, but do not eat beef or pork. Their staple food is rice. They eat such pulses as gram, *tuar*, *moong*, *masur* and *urad*. They have all kinds of vegetables available in the market and use mustard oil as a cooking medium. They do not drink alcohol. They have tea, milk and milk products. They smoke *bidi*s and cigarettes and chew betel. They have fruits occasionally.

The Malis have three endogamous social subdivisions: 1) Rarhi; 2) Barendra; and 3) Athgharer-Mali. However now, the endogamous character is not as rigid as before. Malis have several exogamous *gotra*s — Alamyam, Kashyapa, Maudgalya and Sandilya; their function is to regulate marriage. They use such surnames as Mali, Malakar, Phulmali, Das and Biswas. The Malis consider themselves equal to the *nabasakha* group of Bengal. The Kamars, Baruis, Kangsabaniks and Kumbhars hold them equal in rank. They are aware of the *varna* order and consider themselves Sudras.

The Malis never marry outside their community. A man cannot marry a girl of his own *gotra*. They marry when adult; marriages are negotiated and monogamous. The symbols of married women are *sindur*, *sankha* and *loha*. Dowry is paid in both cash and kind. After marriage, the wife lives with her husband. Divorce is not socially permissible, though, nowadays, one does hear of such instances. Divorced women can marry again, without any social ceremony. Widows and widowers may remarry too.

The Malis mostly live in nuclear families, though extended ones also exist. Of late, the former kind has been gaining predominance. A man is head of the family. A husband-wife relation is one of mutual obligation. A woman has a relationship of distance with her father-in-law, and a jocular one with her husband's younger brother. Property issues spark conflict. Sons equally inherit property. The eldest son succeeds to his father's position. Inter-family links are observed at festivals, *pujas* and the life-cycle rituals.

Mali women do not inherit their parents' property. They have specific roles in agriculture, gathering fuel and fetching water. They take part in social and religious rituals. They share the economic burden of their families with their husbands, besides doing the housework. They have a lower status than men. They are not politically active; nor do they have any decision making power.

The Malis observe pre-delivery rituals, such as *sadh-deoa* and *panchamrita*. Post-natal restrictions are observed and rituals, such as Shashthi puja are performed. *Janmasouch* (pollution after a child is born) lasts a month. *Namkaran* and *bhat-deoa annaprashan* (first rice feeding ceremony) are held when the baby is six or seven months old.

Wedding rites — *gayehalud*, *adhibas*, *kanya-sampradan*, *malabadal*, *yogna*, *subhodristi* and *sindurdan* — are held at the bride's house. The bride's parents hold a feast. Consummation takes place on the third day after the wedding, at the groom's house. Pollution lasts thirteen days after the death and *sraddh* is held on the thirteenth. A feast is held for relatives.

The Malis — a cultivating caste — regard land a major economic resource, and are both landowning and landless. Traditionally, they grow flowering plants, such as *gandha* (marigold), *jaba* (china rose), *aparajita*, *dhutura*, *rajanigandha*, *bel*, *chameli* and *jui*. A few are settled cultivators. Their subsidiary occupations are working as agricultural labourers, doing government and private sector jobs and trading in flowers. They depend on the daily and weekly markets. They get their wages in cash. The number of daily wage earners and agricultural labourers has been rising because of increasing landlessness.

They have their own, traditional caste council, headed by a *mondal*. But now it is defunct. The statutory *panchayat* looks after development and welfare of the village.

Malis are Hindus and worship Satyanarayan, Lakshmi and Krishna at home, besides Saraswati, Durga, Kali, Chandi, Manasa and Sitala. The Brahman acts as their priest. Doljatra, Janmashtami and Rathayatra are major festivals. Puri, Kalighat, Mathura and Vrindaban are the main pilgrimages.

The Malis have a tradition in the art of making beautiful garlands of flowers. They have mythological folk-tales on Lord Krishna and Raja Kangsa. They have folk songs on Krishna, too.

One such song runs:

" ... *Kadambabane Radha Krishner bandhan jugale,/ Mora mala ganthi diya anu tahar charantale* ... " (We string together garlands of flowers sitting at the feet of Lord Krishna and Radha).

Malis have traditional inter-community links with all neighbouring castes in social and occupational matters. The Brahman accepts water from them, but the Malis do not share water or food with the Haris, the Muchis, the Dhobas and the Namasudras. There are no inter-community marriages, but Malis have ritual friendship, such as *sakha*, with their neighbours. They share schools, roads, crematoriums and *panchayat ghar* with others. The community has government job holders, businessmen and artists.

Malis have a low literacy rate. They use modern medicines and traditional ones, as well. They fetch water from ponds and tube wells. They get benefits under the IRDP schemes. The transistor radio is a popular medium of mass communication. They go to the cinema and watch television. Most Malis cannot afford electricity. Rain water and canal water are their main source of irrigation. They use organic and chemical manure; and cowdung cakes and coal as fuel. They avail of banking facilities, as also of the public distribution system.

AMITABHA MITRA

MALPAHARIA

The Malpaharias are a scheduled tribe community of West Bengal. They are not well aware of their origin and tradition. Risley (1891) also stated that they have no tradition worth mentioning except a vague legend that their first parents were born from a cow. The Malpaharias of Murshidabad district, however believe that they are progeny of 'Sri Ram', the Ramayana hero. Regarding the origin of the name Malpaharia, it may be stated that they call themselves 'Male' in their Malto dialect which means man. These people are not the autochthones of this state, but were the original inhabitants of Bihar. Their migration was mainly from Dumka (Santhal Parganas), Bihar and distributed in Murshidabad, Maldah, West Dinajpur, Jalpaiguri, Darjeeling, Birbhum, Nadia districts of West Bengal. According to Census 1981, their population were 17,020 in the state. They speak Malto, Bengali and Hindi in and outside home. They do not use any script, as they are mostly illiterate.

The Malpaharias are non-vegetarian and take meat, fish, egg, etc. Rice is their staple food. They eat all kinds of pulses like *urad*, *masur*, *moong*, *kesari*. They use mustard oil and rapeseed oil for cooking. They consume some varieties of roots and tubers and vegetables. Occasionally they take fruits. They drink milk and take milk products if they can afford them. They smoke indigenous *cheroot*s and *bidi*s and chew tobacco. They consume *tari*, *mad* (alcoholic drinks) regularly.

According to the statements of our informants, the Malpaharias are divided into three sections - (1) Malpaharia, (2) Kumarbag and (3) Sauria Paharia. For all practical purposes they have three endogamous groups. In West Bengal though the clan system is absent among the Malpaharias, still they have a number of *khunts* or *khoms*. These are i) Deheri; ii) Pujhar; iii) Laya; iv) Grihi; v) Singh; vi) Manjhi; vii) Ahiri; and 8) Pator (according to a published report of the Cultural Research Institute, Government of West Bengal, 1966).

They practise endogamy at the community and group levels. They generally try to follow the rule of *khunt* or *khom* exogamy, though it is not as rigidly followed as that followed by other tribals in connection with clan exogamy. That is why they try to avoid marrying members of the same *khunt* or *khom* as far as possible. They never like to choose their mates within their blood relations up to three generations — of either *bijkul* (father's side) or *dudkul* (mother's side). Such marriages — if unavoidable — are always preferred in *dudkul* side beyond three generations.

Monogamy is practised through negotiation. Age at marriage is twenty-one to twenty-three in case of boys and fifteen to eighteen in case of girls. In a few cases marriage by love or service or marriage by exchange is practised. Cousin marriage is absent in the society. Remarriage is permissible for widows, widowers and also male and female divorcees. A man can marry the widow of his elder brother, or his wife's younger sister, but cannot marry the widow of his younger brother or wife's elder sister. Bride price (*bandi*) system is present among them.

Monogamous family type is the social profile and it is patrilineal in nature. Nuclear families are dominant, a few joint families are also found. *Choddoanabhag* (14/16th part) of the parental property is inherited by the sons, and *duanabhag* (2/16th part) by the daughters. Among the sons, the elder son gets a little larger share. Succession goes to the eldest son.

They observe post-natal pollution. During these days, mothers of newborn babies do not cook for the family members. During child birth they employ a midwife from their own community. They observe *randa* (rice eating ceremony) when the baby attains three months of age. They perform the name giving ceremony in the first month and generally an uncle or the maternal uncle selects a name for the baby.

Marriage is solemnized by the *majhiya* (head of the *jati panchayat*). *Malabadal* (exchange of garlands of *tulsi* beads), *gayehalud*, *sindurdan* are the main rituals during the marriage. A day before the marriage, the girl is first married to a mango or *mahul* tree. Married women use vermilion, conch shell bangles and iron bangles as their marriage symbols. Married women also tattoo their hands or foreheads. During marriage, musicians from the Muchi or Dom community beat drums. After marriage the bride's father gives a feast to relatives and villagers. Next day the bride goes to the bridegroom's house.

They cremate their dead and observe ten days mourning. After *kaman* (purificatory ceremony), they give a feast to relatives and villagers. If any one dies due to epidemics they bury the dead, and after one year the body is exhumed and the *shradh* ceremony performed.

Though they depend on land, the Malpaharias are landless. They are mainly agricultural labourers. And a few are day labourers. Their traditional occupation was hunting and gathering, but at present this occupation is obsolete.

The Malpaharia women also work in agricultural fields, doing the weeding and transplanting work, apart from their household jobs. They have equal status with their men folk. Women do not have any decision making powers, though they contribute to family income.

They have their own traditional council known as *dashe-dashjaner*, headed by *majhiya* (head) and *gorait* (messenger).

The religion of the Malpaharias may be described as an amalgamation of tribal religion with Hinduism. They perform Dharma puja; observe *Baisakh* Sankranti, Kali puja and *Maghi* puja. They do not visit any pilgrimage centres, only youngsters attend a few fairs held at nearby villages.

They have traditional folk songs, sung by both males and females during various rituals and festivals. They also dance.

The Malpaharias accept water and food from the neighbouring communities. They also take *sidha* from others. They do not have any putative kinship. They participate in traditional festivals and festivities. Cultivator-labour relationship exists among them.

The formal educational level of the Malpaharias is low. They use both modern and traditional medicare. Their attitude towards the family planning programme is favourable. Drinking water is available within the locality. They do not use electricity. They listen to the radio. They use wood, kerosene, and cowdung cakes as fuel. They do not irrigate their fields with canal water. They use chemical fertilizers and pesticides on their agricultural fields. Midday meal scheme for school going children is irregularly availed of. They take the facilities of ration shop mainly for kerosene. They do not use banking facilities.

R. K. BHATTACHARYA, AMITABHA MITRA

MANGAR

The Mangars, "a characteristically fighting ... community ... belonging to the martial classes ... are one of the trio which toppled the Newar rule in Nepal. Recruited as combatants to the Gorkha regiments, they provide a large number of soldiers for the Indian and Nepalese armies" (Bagchi *et. al.* 1951: 56). They are also known as Magars. They have migrated from the west of Darjeeling district and are now distributed in the hills of Darjeeling. By the 1931 Census, the Mangar population in the state was 24,042, out of which 14,613 was in Darjeeling district alone. They speak Nepali at home and Nepali, Nepali-Hindi and Hindi with outsiders. They write in the Devanagari script at home and in Devanagari and Roman with outsiders. They are one of the other backward classes.

There is some bio-anthropological information available on them. Risley (1891) says the average stature is 1,587 mm. The cephalic index is 79.0 and nasal index 76.6. So their stature is below standard, the head-form mesocephalic and nose-form mesorrhine.

Mangars are non-vegetarian and have mutton, chicken, pork, eggs and fish. Their staple food is rice. They have all vegetables available in the market and such pulses as gram, *urad*, *moong*, *masur*, peas and beans. Mustard oil or lard is their cooking medium. They drink home-made *nigbur-zanr* quitc regularly. It is essential in their rituals too. They have milk and milk products and fruits occasionally. They smoke *bidi*s and cigarettes.

Mangars have no sub-groups, but those with the title of Thapa are considered higher than others and call themselves Bara Mangars. Mangars have several exogamous *thar*s — Achami, Allia, Kyagchhagi, Brahgolagi, Pongwar, Rasaili, Yangmi, Sarangi, Namazali, Ghatraj, Khapangi, Chumi, Lamjel and Pulami. Thapa, Singh and Rana are the usual surnames. Bara Mangars use only Thapa as a title and consider themselves equal to the Gurungs and the Chhetris. They are aware of the *varna* order and consider themselves Sudras.

Mangars marry within their community, though a man cannot marry a girl of his own *thar*. Mangars marry when adult; and marriages are negotiated and monogamous. *Sindur* and a green *pote-mala* are symbols of a married woman. Dowry is paid in both cash and kind. After marriage, the wife lives with her husband. Either partner may seek *chhutanam* (divorce), which though rare, is allowed with social approval on grounds of adultery or maladjustment. Divorce compensation is paid to the aggrieved party. Children of divorced parents are the liability of either parent. Men and women divorcees, as well as widows and widowers, may remarry.

Mangars prefer nuclear families, though a few live in mixed-extended ones. The man is the head of the family. A woman has a relationship of distance with her father-in-law and her husband's elder brother and a jocular one with her husband's younger brother. Sons equally inherit their parents' property. The eldest son succeeds to his father's position. Inter-family links are in evidence at festivals and rituals.

Mangar women do not inherit property. They gather firewood, fetch water and do all the housework. They do jobs outside the home too. They take an active part in religious and social rituals, but not in politics. They do not contribute to, nor control family expenditure. They have a status lower than that of the men.

Mangars observe several pre-delivery and post-natal restrictions. Pollution lasts seven days after a child is born. The naming ceremony — where the child has its first taste of cereals — is observed in the sixth or seventh month after birth.

Wedding rituals — *malabadal*, *sindurdan* and *home-jogna* — are held at the bride's house and her parents hold a feast. Consummation takes place at the bride's house after three days.

Mangars cremate their dead, though a few bury them, and pollution lasts eleven days. On the twelfth day, *sradh* is held, conducted by a Nepali Brahman priest. A feast for relatives follows this ritual purification.

Mangars are cultivators, whose main economic resource is land. They are both landowners and landholders. They grow *aman-chawal* (*aman* paddy), *odua* (ginger) and *kodo* (millet) through terrace cultivation. The majority of them are either in the Indian Army or in government service. Their secondary occupations are working as agricultural labourers and in forestry projects and tea plantations, and teaching in schools. Child labour does not exist. They depend on daily markets. They are paid wages in cash. The number of daily wage earners and plantation labourers is rising because of increasing landlessness.

Mangars have no caste-panchayat. The statutory panchayat — which looks after development and welfare of villages — are bodies for social control.

Mangars are Hindus and worship Satyanarayan, Lakshmi and Radha-Krishna at home, besides Shiva, Kali and Durga. The Mahakal Baba Temple at Chowrasta, Darjeeling, is a major sacred centre. Shivaratri, Tihar and Holi are the main festivals. The Nepali Brahman acts as a priest at pujas and life-cycle rituals.

The Mangars have a rich tradition in folk tales and folk songs. Their traditional folk songs are known as *bhailo-geet*, sung to the accompaniment of *shehnai*s (a wind category musical instrument) and *bansi* (flute). Both men and women dance.

Nepali Brahmans accept food and water from them, as do the Chhetris, Gurungs and Rais, though they do not accept water from the Damais and Sarkis. They, however, accept *siddha* food from all neighbouring communities. Inter-community marriage is not socially acceptable. They share roads, schools, crematoriums and water sources with all others, as also take part in festivals. They have a cultivator-labourer relationship with other Nepali castes. The community has doctors, engineers, government job holders, teachers and army men.

Mangar children go to schools, and their interest in modern education is more than that seen in children of some neighbouring communities. They use modern medicines, as well as traditional ones. They have adopted family planning measures and prefer up to three children. Water from mountain springs and rivulets is the only drinking water they get.

The transistor radio is a popular mass communication medium. All Mangar villages do not yet have electricity, but they avail of it wherever available. Their main fuel is firewood. They use organic manure; and spring water and rain water are their main sources of irrigation. Students in primary schools get bread. Mangars avail of rationing facilities through fair price shops. They also avail of banking facilities.

AMITABHA MITRA

MARWARI

The Marwaris are a trading community. They speak the Marwari language and have migrated to the present habitat from their original homeland, Rajasthan. The community has such sub-groups as Srimali, Rajput, Oswal, Puskarna, Parikh and Maheswari and Agarwala. The first is a Brahman, the second Kshatriya and third Vaishya by caste. The word, Puskarna, is believed to have been derived from Lake Puskar in Ajmer, Rajasthan, near which they originally lived. Srimali is derived the name of their hometown Srimal in Rajasthan. Maheswaris believe their ancestor was God Maheswar, another name of Shiva. Agarwals are thought to be descendants of King Agrasen.

According to them, King Agrasen had seventeen sons who married the seventeen daughters of Basuki, the King of *nag*s (snakes). According to a legend, the Oswals' ancestor was the Rajput king of Osanagar in Marwar. He and his followers were converted by a Jain mendicant. The Rajputs consider themselves descendants of the rulers. However, there are only a few Rajputs in West Bengal. The community is aware of its widespread distribution throughout West Bengal, as also in other states. The main concentration, however is in Calcutta, in the plains of the Gangetic West Bengal, where the climate is warm and temperate (the average temperature is 37.8° C), with high humidity.

They speak in Marwari with family and kin and write in the Devanagari script. They speak Hindi, Bengali and a smattering of English with others and write in the Devanagari and Roman scripts.

They are pure vegetarians, and do not eat even onion or garlic. Their staple food is rice and wheat. They have a variety of pulses, such as *moong*, *urad*, *tuar* and *kulthi*, besides peas and beans. Their cooking medium is mustard oil. They eat all locally available fruits and vegetables. They do not drink alcohol, but have such beverages as tea and coffee, besides milk and milk products. Smoking is not socially acceptable. Nowadays however, the younger generation has started having non-vegetarian food outside the home and even smoking. Children in some families have eggs.

The community is divided into major caste groups. They are aware of the *varna* order, in which the Brahman holds the highest status, followed by Kshatriyas and then Vaishyas. Among the Brahmans, Pushkarnas, again, are divided according to their *gotra*. For instance, the Purohit belongs to the Shandilya *gotra*, Joshi to the Parasar *gotra* and Vyas to the Bhardwaj *gotra*. The Parikhs belong to the Parasar *gotra*. Agarwals are divided into various groups, considered *gotras*, such as Singhal, Bansal, Garg, Kashyap, Konsil and Mittal. Similarly, Maheswaris are also divided into Soni, Daga, Dwark and Kopilas. Oswals are divided into Bhantia, Doshi, Nahata and Pugalia. The basis of these differentiations is mainly socio-religious and the *gotras* regulate marriage alliances, as well as descent and ancestry. Some surnames are Mohata, Bhantia, Agarwal, Jalan, Singhal, Purohit, Vyas and Kiradoo.

Marwari *gotras* are exogamous and sub-groups and community are endogamous. They marry when adult. The marriageable age has increased slightly, since girls nowadays are getting educated and acquiring jobs. Marriages are mostly monogamous and negotiated, or through mutual consent, through courtship — and so, inter-group, or inter-community marriage — are also common now. *Roli* (vermilion) and lac and iron bangles are symbols of a married woman. The modern generation does not strictly use these symbols.

Kanyadan is customary, as is dowry in cash and kind. A woman lives at her in-laws' house after marriage. Divorce — with judicial and social approval — is permissible on grounds of adultery, maladjustment and insanity, though extremely rare. Compensation is paid to the aggrieved partner and children of divorced parents are the liability of either. A widower may remarry if he has young children, or he himself is young; widow remarriage is permissible, though rare. Women divorcees marry rarely, though a man may marry after divorce. Junior sororate is permissible if the father consents to the marriage and if a dead woman leaves behind young children.

Marwari families are mostly of the mixed-extended kind, though a man who starts a new business at another place, or finds a shortage of space at his parents' house may set up a nuclear one. All the members are consanguinealy, or affinally, related to each other. A man has a relationship of avoidance with his younger brother's wife, as well as his nephew's wife, and one of joking with his wife's younger siblings, as also his elder brother's wife. A grandparent-grandchild relationship is one of joking. Sons equally inherit property, and daughters only get a share of gold ornaments at their wedding. The eldest son succeeds his father as head of family. The members of a family help each other in times of need. Property occasionally creates conflict.

Marwari women are engaged in many economic activities nowadays. They have started confectioneries and beauty parlours, or have taken up jobs as teachers and lawyers. Some also run the family business. Their social role is not restricted to rearing children and looking after the family. They go shopping when it pleases them and accompany their children to school. They have a significant traditional role in the life-cycle rituals, as also in performing religious *brata*s and *upas* for the wellbeing of the family. They worship the family deities. They have no political role, except in exercising their voting rights. Earning women contribute to family income, though family expenditure is controlled only by the men.

Pushkarna Brahmans observe *londa* before a child is born to propitiate Lord Bhairav for the baby's wellbeing. Pollution lasts forty days after the birth for those related by blood. The new mother may not enter the kitchen, or do any housework. *Chhatti* (naming ceremony) takes place on the sixth day after birth among the Maheswaris and Agarwals. Brahmans hold a *namankaran* (naming) ceremony following the position of the stars and planets at the time of the birth, determined by an astrologer. A Brahman priest, or the head of the family, names the child. *Mundan* takes place at any sacred place for both boys and girls in *Chaitra*, *Ashwin*, or *Kartik* during any odd numbered year after birth. *Annagrahan* (where the child has its first taste of cereals by the head of the family, or priest) is held between six and eight months after birth.

Janeu (sacred thread ceremony) is held when a boy is eight years old or more, or even during the wedding. The boy's head is tonsured and beard shaved before the priest makes him chant religious hymns. The boy's maternal grandparents give him new clothes, and they do not sleep that night. A feast is held on the day.

A wedding is a chain of merry making rituals. The *sagai*, or *neg* (engagement ceremony) at the would be bride's house involves the man giving a gold wedding ring to the girl and her parents giving him clothes and ornaments. After a firm date is fixed, Ganesh puja takes place. The wedding has to follow soon after, since it is believed that after worshipping Ganesh, it cannot be delayed or postponed under any circumstance. *Mayama* (establishment of a Mahamaya, or Matadi, or Durga idol) takes place on the wedding day, or a day before. *Haldat* (turmeric smearing ceremony) is performed by a host of female relatives of the bride and groom. In the *bhat* ritual, the bride's maternal uncle sends her clothes and ornaments.

The groom, upon arrival at the bride's house, is welcomed by her mother, or, if she is a widow, her *bhabi* (elder brother's wife), who puts a *tilak* (vermilion mark) on the forehead. The ritual of *phira* takes place, in which the bride and groom walk round the sacred fire seven times. Among Puskarna Brahmans, the bride leads the first three rounds, while the groom leads the rest. *Kanyadan* takes place, accompanied by chanting of *mantra*s by the priest; some money and all household items are presented to the groom. A *priti-bhoj* (feast) is held at the bride's house, and another (*sajon-ghot*) when the bride goes to her in-laws' house.

Marwaris cremate their dead and pollution lasts thirteen days. The son performs *mukhagni* at the cremation ground. The men do not shave in pollution, but shave their heads and beards only on the eleventh day; all household linen and clothes are washed. A *sradh* is conducted by a Brahman priest on the twelfth day. On the thirteenth, a feast is held for neighbouring lineage members. The bones of the dead are disposed of at the Tribeni, confluence of Ganga and Jamuna at Allahabad, in Uttar Pradesh.

Business and trade are the traditional and main occupation of the Marwaris. They came to West Bengal with the express purpose of starting business and engaged themselves in various fields, such as manufacturing mills and factories and trading firms. Some have become industrialists of repute. In fact, it would be very difficult compiling the history of modern West Bengal industry, trade and commerce without mentioning the contribution of its Marwari entrepreneurs. Some however, work in government and private jobs. They have direct links with the local daily markets. There are several industrial labourers working in various firms and industries. Child labour, or bonded labour, are virtually absent. All adult men are engaged in the family business in one way or another.

Traditional councils that exist mainly plan and implement welfare activities for the society. The names of some caste organizations are the Maheswari Sabha, the Marwari Relief Society, the Parikh Sabha and the Rajasthan Brahman Sabha. The Maheswari Sabha (established in 1914) has built a Maheswari Bhawan with thirteen branches for development: the Maheswari Pustakalaya (library), Sri Maheswari Vidyalaya (school), Maheswari Balika Vidyalaya, Maheswari Oudyogik Sikshan Kendra, Maheswari Education Board, Maheswari Club, Maheswari Byamalaya, Maheswari Sangitalaya, Maheswari Samajotthan Samiti, Maheswari Mahila Samiti, Maheswari Bhawan Samiti and

Maheswari Sabha Trust. The Marwari Relief Society (established in 1913) runs a hospital cum dispensary, employing many doctors and nurses. The caste organizations settle issues, mainly of disrespect to traditional norms.

Marwaris are basically Hindus, but some profess Jainism. The Jains are subdivided into: Digambaras and Swetambaras. Both sects propitiate the twenty-four Jain Tirthankaras, the point of difference being that the Digambaras believe a monk who owns property — or even wears clothes — cannot attain salvation, while the Swetambaras assert that complete nudity is not essential for liberation of the soul. Both Hindu and Jain Marwaris abstain from eating any kind of meat; as a rule, they have no objection in inter-marrying.

The principal family deities are Ganesh, or Ganapati, son of Mahadev and Parvati; Gauri, or Parvati, Lakshmi and Narayan. Ganesh is the 'God of Good Luck', while Gauri is symbolic of a ripe harvest, since her own body is yellow. Lakshmi is the 'Goddess of Wealth and Prosperity'. The Jains regard all Hindu sacred shrines as a pilgrimage. The main festivals are the Kumbh mela at Hardwar and Allahabad, Gangasagar mela, Holi, Gangaur, Diwali, Rathayatra, Raksha-bandhan and Mahavir Jayanti. Holi takes place in *Phalgun*. In the Gangaur festival, Gauri (Durga) is worshipped as the 'Goddess of Corn', at about the time of the vernal equinox, only by women.

During Diwali, Ganesh and Lakshmi are worshipped. Books of accounts for the new financial year are worshipped and adorned with a Ganesh idol on the front page before they are opened. Marwaris believe it is essential to gamble on Diwali day to bring good luck for the coming year. Rathayatra is of great significance,. Raksha-bandhan is observed to ward off evil spirits. Jain Marwaris organize two processions at Kartik Mahotsav — one by the Swetambaras and the other by the Digambaras, from their respective temples. Jains celebrate Mahavir Jayanti. Marwaris take part in Durga puja and Saraswati puja, as general community festivals. In Calcutta, there are a few Shiva, Hanumanji and Bhairoji temples where Marwaris pray. Swetambaras and Digambaras have their main temples in Badridas Temple Street and at Belgachia (Parasnath Temple), respectively. Their religious expert is the Brahman, whose main duty is to conduct life-cycle rituals.

Almost all Marwari women know embroidery, but this is not followed as a profession. They have their own folk tales, folklore and folk songs. There are some Bhajan Mandalis and Kirtan Mandalis, where the community gathers to sing religious songs.

Traditional commensal relations are becoming less significant now. Marwaris accept water from all other groups, except the Haris, Muchis and Doms. Brahmans, generally, accept cooked food, but not water, from the Maheswaris and Agarwals. They do not accept cooked food from Bengali Brahmans either, since they are non-vegetarians. Jains employ Marwari Brahmans to conduct the life-cycle rituals.

Marwaris have no problems in sharing water sources, crematoriums, schools and religious shrines. They supply drinking water on various occasions, such as Durga puja and Kali puja immersion processions, through their charitable trust, named Kashi Vishwanath Seva Samity. Napits and Dhopas serve them whenever necessary. The community has several entrepreneurs, businessmen, teachers and doctors. Many Bengali doctors are employed in the Marwari Relief Society Hospital (known also as the Swami Vishuddhananda Saraswsati Marwari Hospital). Marwaris are aware of the current political situation and quite a few take active part in politics.

The present generation — both boys and girls — takes full opportunity of modern education. The community has built many schools to improve their level of education. Some boys, however, opt for the family business after a minimum level of matriculation or higher secondary education. Even now, there is a trend of getting daughters married early, leading to some dropouts at the secondary or tertiary level. Marwaris are favourably disposed towards modern medical facilities and modern couples prefer family planning programmes.

Marwaris listen to the radio, watch television and go to the cinema. They avail of the facilities of roads, railways and post offices. They use electricity, coal, kerosene and liquefied petroleum gas as fuel. The community has midday meal schemes for nursery school children, funded by their caste organizations. They are extremely keen on saving and also take loans from banks — both of which they invest in business, usually for handsome returns.

SNIGDHA CHAKRABORTY

MAYARA

The Mayaras are a caste of confectioners of Bengal, with Modak, Madak and Madhunapit as synonyms. Their titles are Chowdhury and Mandal. J.N. Bhattercharya (1896: 191) writes, "The word, Mayara, is a corrupt form of the Sanskrit compound Madaka-Kara, which means a confectioner". It is a heterogeneous functional group. Informants say they are divided into four sub-groups: 1) Madhumayara; 2) Jat-Mayara; 3) Kuri-Mayara; and 4) Satyam-Mayara. Risley (1891: 89), as well as the early twentieth century census reports, referred to the Madhunapits as a separate caste formed by a splinter group of Napits who had abandoned their traditional occupation for that of confectioner. In the course of time, this group seems to have been completely integrated with the traditional caste of confectioners, the Mayaras; current informants consider Madhunapit as just a synonym for Mayara.

Mitra (1953: 56) refers to *Brhaddharma Purana*, which says the Mayaras originated from a Kshatriya father and a Sudra mother. There are two stories on the Mayaras' origins:

On the fourth day of her menstruation, Bhagawati, wife of Shiva, asked her husband to call a barber to pare her nails. She was waiting on the bank of a river while it was raining. Shiva forgot to send a barber. After waiting a long time, Bhagawati created a barber from a bubble of water, who pared her nails. Shiva, meanwhile, suddenly remembered what he had to do and created a barber from a few bones lying nearby. He sent this barber to Bhagawati, by which time the first barber had completed his task. Bhagwati asked him not to touch the feet of any other person and ordered him (Bimbhudas — since he had been created from a *bimbu*, meaning a bubble) to earn his livelihood from *madhu* (honey). So, he and his descendants were known as Madhunapit, or Madhumayara. Being created from *har* (bones), the other barber was named Harudas and ordered to work as a barber.

Another story on Madhunapits that Risley mentions goes:

A barber named Madhu shaved Lord Chaitanya's head when he became a *sanyasi*. He asked to be released from his hereditary profession. He said, having touched the head of Chaitanya, how could he ever cut the toenails of ordinary mortals? The descendants of Madhu were named Madhunapit (Risley, 1891: 26-27).

Mayaras say they have relatives in various districts of West Bengal — Bankura, Birbhum, Burdwan and Hooghly. The area where they live is characterized by flat, alluvial plains, with a warm and temperate climate, high humidity and medium rainfall. They speak and write in Bengali.

The Mayaras are non-vegetarian, but do not eat beef, pork or carrion. Their staple cereals are rice, and sometimes, wheat. Gram, *moong*, *masur* and *birikalai* are the common pulses they eat. Their cooking mediums are mustard oil and sesamum oil. They have all kinds of seasonal vegetables in moderation. Potato is a great favourite. They have all seasonal fruits, such as bananas, mangoes and litchis. They drink tea regularly, and have milk and milk products, since most of them have cows. Only a few drink alcohol. The men smoke *bidi*s or cigarettes and take snuff; both men and women chew betel.

Mayaras do not eat radish in *Magh* and *lau* in *Bhadra*. Their vegetable and fruit consumption has increased, as indeed, all other food — with people earning more.

Mayaras have four major social subdivisions, besides several non-hierarchical *gotra*s: Alimyan, Bhardwaj, Ambarishi, Madhukulya, Shandilya and Kashyap. The hierarchical order of the social divisions is also unknown. Earlier, the subgroups did not inter-marry, but, now, Madhumayaras and Jat-Mayaras do so only among themselves, since they believe the other two subgroups are culturally lower and belong mostly to Bihar. Marriages are also negotiated between people from the clan, only after converting the woman's clan name into that of her maternal grandfather's clan at the wedding. Mayaras avoid three generations from the father's side while negotiating such marriages.

There has been no change in surnames; the common ones are Das, Modak, Pal, Datta, Dey, Ash, Nandi and Rakshit. Mayaras are one of the *navasakha* groups, and believe any of the others is equal in status, while Brahmans are higher and scheduled castes and scheduled tribes are lower. The other *navasakha* groups agree with this. Mayaras believe they are Sudras in the *varna* system.

Mayaras are clan-exogamous and caste, and sub-caste, endogamous in marriage. Junior sororate is permissible. The marriageable age for men is around twenty-five years and, for girls, eighteen. Marriages are negotiated and monogamous. A second marriage is allowed only after the first wife dies. *Sindur*, *sankha* and *noa* are the symbols of a married woman. Dowry is paid in cash and kind. The wife lives in her husband's house after marriage. The Mayaras of the area under study cannot refer to a single instance of divorce; they are not aware of any divorce rules. Mayaras are aware of the present law permitting Hindu widow remarriage, but there is no such instance in their society. Widower remarriage and junior sororate are permissible only after the first wife dies. The marriageable age for both men and women has increased. Bride price, earlier customary, has given way to an ever increasing demand for dowry.

Mayara families are mostly nuclear, though mixed-extended ones do exist. Elders in a family are feared, respected and obeyed by youngsters, who are in turn, loved and cared for. There is a relationship of avoidance between a man and his *bhadra-bou* (now, however, the *bhadra-bou* shows respect to her *bhasur* only by touching his feet — strictly prohibited earlier), as between a woman and her *jamai*. *Dadu* and *thakurma* (paternal grandparents) have a joking relationship with their *nati-natni* (grandchildren), as do *boudi* and *deor* and *jamai-babu* and *shala* or *shali*.

The man maintains the establishment, educates his children and arranges their marriage. A woman looks after her children and family and does the housework. Adult sons share the family's financial burden and look after agriculture, or the family sweets business. Adult, unmarried daughters help their mother with the housework, look after the family and sew, stitch and wash clothes.

Property issues and the inability of adult sons to earn spark conflict. Sons and daughters equally inherit property. The eldest son succeeds to his father's position. Family links are brushed up at the life-cycle rituals. Relatives, as well as members of other castes, sometimes, arbitrate in property conflicts — a process through which inter-family links are maintained. Extended families are increasingly, giving way to nuclear ones.

Mayara women now have a right to inherit their parents' property equally with their brothers, but they do not usually stake their claim. Mayara women do the housework, besides looking after domestic animals. Several Mayara women also do jobs. Women have an important role in the life-cycle rituals, as well as in the worship of family deities. They are not politically active. Mayara women have a lower status than their men and are not financially independent.

Mayaras observe many life-cycle rituals: *Sadh* is held in the seventh and ninth months of pregnancy, when women neighbours and relatives are invited. The would-be mother wears a new *sari* on these days. After a child is born, *Sentera* puja is offered to Goddess Shasthi, either on the sixth, or seventh, day. This *puja* is not held on the birthday of the child's father. A Hari *dai* offers this *puja* at the Shashthitala on behalf of the family. A barber pares the nails of both newborn and mother. On the thirtieth day — at the end of *anandasouch* — mother and baby have a bath with soap and water. Those who had attended to the woman during pollution have to bathe in the Ganga for purification.

The ceremony where the child first has rice is held in the sixth month, if the child born is a boy, and seventh, or ninth, if a girl. Village deities are propitiated before the child's maternal uncle feeds him *prasad*. The barber tonsures the baby on this day, before it has a bath. A feast is held for relatives and neighbours only for a firstborn.

Mayaras have no rituals when a girl attains puberty; she only has to take a bath with soap and water on the fifth day for ritual purification.

The wedding day is fixed after negotiation, and *ashirbad* is held on an auspicious day — first in the groom's house. The bride's father blesses the groom with a gift, for instance a wristwatch or a ring. The ceremony is repeated at the bride's house on another auspicious day, with gifts of gold ornaments. On wedding day, after *nandimukh*, *gayehalud* and other rituals are performed and the *dai* offers Shasthi puja, the groom and his *barjatri* reach the bride's house in the evening. A family barber and a priest accompanies them to conduct the wedding rituals.

The main ceremony takes place outside the house. *Satpak*, *shubhodrishti*, *malabadal*, *dan* and *kusumdinga* are essential rituals. A family barber helps the bride and groom during *malabadal* and *shubhodrishti*. The groom's family barber helps the priest during *kusumdinga*, and also the groom change his dress. The bride's father, usually, performs the *dan*. A feast is held for relatives, friends and neighbours that night. The next day, the bride leaves for her *svashurbari* (in-laws' house) with her husband. *Phulsajjya* and *boubhat* take place on the third day. Another feast for relatives, friends and neighbours is held that night.

Mayaras cremate their dead. Pollution lasts either thirty, or fifteen, or twelve, days. *Ghat* rituals take place on the thirtieth, or fifteenth, or twelfth day after the death. A barber tonsures the sons, and *sradh* is conducted by a Brahman priest the next day.

The Mayaras' life-cycle rituals have changed very little. Earlier, a marriage was consummated the day after the wedding, but now it takes place on the day of *phulsajjya*. Pollution after a person dies has been cut down to fifteen, or even twelve, days. Expenses for life-cycle rituals have been rising steadily.

Traditionally, Mayaras are confectioners and experts in making sweets. This business is their primary economic pursuit, though most own agricultural land too. Many work as doctors, hold jobs, or are in such other businesses as fertilizer or clothes. No specific subsidiary occupation is recognizable. To make sweets, they buy casein from nearby urban markets; sometimes, the Goala too, supplies them milk, or casein. They have sweet shops in villages and towns, as well as in the big cities. Mayaras sell their sweets in the weekly markets. Transactions are in cash. Mayara boys begin work as assistants to their father in sweet shops. They pay their agricultural labourers in cash and kind. They believe making sweets was their original occupation. So holding jobs, or working in other businesses denotes a change of occupation.

Mayaras, now have no caste panchayat, but a regional association, Mayara Mukti, headquartered at Guskara, in Burdwan district. The main function of this organization is to arrange marriage negotiations through a monthly magazine. Their statutory council is the *gram panchayat*, which plans and implements village welfare and development. Earlier, they had a caste council, comprising *mondals* representing twenty-seven neighbouring villages. The Mayaras had to take the council's advice on marriage negotiations or *sradh* ceremonies. This custom is now defunct.

Mayaras profess to be orthodox Hindus, belonging mostly to the Vaishnav sect. Some are also Saktas. Their family deities are Narayan, Lakshmi and *Tulsi*. There is a *tulsi* plant in front of every Mayara house. Mayaras open *hal-khata* (new books of accounts) on Ganesh puja day in *Baisakh*. Their village deities are Raksha-Kali, Kalachand, Dharmaraj and Manasa. Raksha-Kali is worshipped for the welfare of the villagers, Kalachand, and Dharmaraj for protection against different diseases. Kali-tala and Shiva-tala are the local sacred centres, and Nabadwip, Puri, Gaya, Tarakeswar and Tarapith are their pilgrimages. Brahman priests conduct *pujas* for the family, as well as life-cycle rituals. Kalachand, Dharmaraj and Kali puja are the major village festivals, when fairs are organized.

Mayaras cannot mention any traditional art or craft of their own, except making sweets. They do however, have folk tales about their origin, referred to earlier.

Traditional inter-community links are maintained through rituals. The *dai*, Napit and Brahman priest are required to conduct the life-cycle rituals. They have close links with Goalas who supply them milk and casein. Since Mayaras belong to the nabasakha group, Brahmans accept water from them. They accept cooked food only from the Brahmans and water, or sweets, from members of the *nabasakha* group. Young Mayaras, however, do not follow these rules strictly. Recent inter-caste love marriages with the Telis (Kalus), Brahmans and Dhobas have established links with other communities too, although such marriages are not really acceptable in Mayara society.

Traditional *jajmani* no longer exists in Mayara society. Though there are fixed Brahman priests, Napits and *dai*s for every family, they are paid in cash and kind for their services. The community's participation in different elections has created inter-community links. Mayaras in secondary and tertiary occupations foster further links with others. Members of other low caste communities, such as the Bauris, Bagdis and Doms work as agricultural labourers on Mayara owned lands. Mayaras invite them to a feast the day the first paddy is brought home; so, a socio-economic link between communities is established.

The Mayara community has businessmen, doctors, engineers, artists, white collar job holders and teachers, though not many. Mayara political leaders operate in the village panchayats, helping establish inter-community links.

Educationally, Mayaras are a backward community. Most boys and girls study up to the secondary level since they are poor. They visit nearby health centres and are favourably disposed towards family planning. Many women get sterilized after having two or three children. Mayaras fetch drinking water from village tube wells, either installed by the government, or privately owned. Provisions for employment, or self-employment, exist in the areas where they live, but they have not got the benefits till now.

Most Mayaras own radio sets, the most common medium of mass communication. They have links with urban areas through buses and trains. Sometimes, they watch television in neighbours' houses. Mayara cultivators take the advice of agricultural extension officers and get political information through different political parties. Post offices are close by. They use electricity whenever available. Coal, firewood and cowdung cakes are used as fuel. Some draw water from canals for their fields. They use organic manure, chemical fertilizers, insecticides and pesticides for a better yield. Some children get the benefit of midday meal schemes. They pick up their rations from local fair price shops. They do not use banking facilities since they are poor. Indeed, they have to depend upon shopkeepers for credit for their business.

Even today, Mayaras do not cultivate sugarcane, or take any part in making molasses. This taboo has its origin in the myth that Bhagawati had asked them to earn their livelihood through trading in *madhu* (honey). Since the amount of *madhu* that can be procured is limited, *gur* (molasses) has become a substitute for making sweets. In spite of this, they do not grow sugarcane or make *gur*.

ARCHANA DATTA

MECH

The Meches of North Bengal are of Mongoloid origin and believed to be the western branch of the Great Kachari of Boro tribe. Such scholars as Grierson (1903: 1), Chatterjee (1951: 51) and others say the word, *mech*, has been derived from the Sanskrit word, *mlechcha*, or vice versa. It is also said that they derived their name from the fact that the Meches first lived on the banks of the river Mechi in Nepal, and came to be known as Mechi, Mechia, or Mech. The Meches of North Bengal also call themselves Bodos, or Boros, since they belong to the linguistic Bodo group.

Dr Suniti Kumar Chatterjee (1978: 667) says the Mech, Koch, Rajbanshi, Rabha, Garo, Kachari, Dimasa, Chutiya, Haijong, and Tipra (Tripuri) belong to the Bodo ethnic group. To their kinsmen in Assam, the Meches are known as 'Bardhan-ari'. On the other hand, the Mech, or the Bodo, of Assam are called 'Sanj-ari' by North Bengal Meches. About a century ago, H.H. Risley (1891: 87) reported that the Darjeeling and Jalpaiguri Mech were divided into two endogamous sub-tribes, 'Agnia-Mech' and 'Jati-Mech'. The recent field study, however, reveals no such divisions.

There are several legends and myths on their origin. Risley (1891: 87) relates one such interesting story:

The ancestors of the Meches were first dropped by gods from heaven. They fell in Benaras, in Uttar Pradesh, though this was not the place they were destined for; so, they moved northwards and reached Kachar. The youngest brother settled here and became the father of the Mech, Koch and Dhimal. Two others went further into the hills and their descendants became the Limbu and the Khambu of Nepal. This myth seems to be propounded by Brahmanical priests in order to induct the Meches into the Hindu fold.

The richness and prosperity of India were known to the world from its priceless antiques, which attracted different people, who came to the country to see and obtain these things. When India was not known by its present name and the history of India had not yet unfolded, the Meches set out from their original homeland — believed to be the headwaters of the Yang Tse-Kiang and Hoang-Ho rivers — in search of fertile land for *jhum* cultivation. And, so, the Meches reached the north-eastern and eastern corners of the present sub-continent of India and settled over a vast area, where they saw the rise, fulfilment and downfall of the Mech monarchy.

The earliest known king of the Meches was Mairong Danava, who flourished in north-eastern India long before the great battle of Kurukshetra. References to Mech kings have also been made in Indian scriptures. The story of Narak Asur, the mighty Mech king, is found in such works as the *Vishnu Purana*, *Kalika Purana* and *Yogini Tanra*. He belonged to the Mech tribe, whom the Indian *shastras* named Asura. That Narak Asur was a Mech has been indicated in a statement by Dr Suniti Kumar Chatterjee, who emphatically said the Great Mech or Bodo people are the offspring of the son of Vishnu and Mother Earth, who was no other than Narak Asur of the *Puranas*, cited above. In the epic, *Mahabharata*, the renowned king, Bhagadatta, was a great king of the Meches.

Introduction to Ferishta's History (*History of India*, Vol. VI, 1875: 553) mentions a powerful Mech named Shankal who defeated Kedar Khan of the Siwalik Hills. The political history of the Meches became comparatively clearer from the fourth Century to the twelfth Century A.D., when such authentic sources as Si Yu-Ki and Harshacharita were compiled and the Nidhanpur and Doobi copperplate grants were discovered.

Kumar Bhaskarvarman, whom the Chinese traveller, Hiuen Tsiang, visited during the seventh Century A.D., was a great Mech king of the then sub-continent of India. Mech kings reigned over almost all north-eastern and eastern India under different dynastic names. Mech king Naranarayana of Koch Behar was a worthy contemporary of Emperor Akbar, who entered into "a peaceful and defensive alliance on equal terms" with the former. King Naranarayana was the only non-Muslim monarch during Muslim rule, with whom even the Great Akbar made such an alliance. The contribution of the Meches to the history, civilization and culture of northeastern India, in particular, and entire India, in general, occupies a unique position in the history of mankind.

However, the socio-politico-religious vicissitudes through centuries culminated in the formation of different fragmentary communities, of whom the Mech, finally, came out as a little-known tribe in India.

The Meches are found in the Jalpaiguri, Darjeeling and Cooch Behar districts of North Bengal. They are found in great numbers in Assam, where they call themselves Bodos, and also in Meghalaya, Nagaland, Arunachal Pradesh and Tripura. Outside India, they are found in Bangladesh and Nepal. By the 1981 Census, the Meches numbered only

26,959 in West Bengal. Their main concentration is in the sub-mountainous regions of the Kumargramduar, Alipurduar, Kalchini and Madarihat police station areas, under Alipurduar sub-division, in Jalpaiguri district.

The Meches speak in Mech, or Bodo at home, and in Bengali and Hindi outside. The generic term, Bodo, was first used by B.H. Hodgson in 1846 to denote the Bodo group of languages. The Meches do not have a script of their own. They use the Roman, Devanagari, or Bengali scripts. They do not have any identification mark. However, the Mech women weave a special kind of dress for themselves — a typical, bright-coloured garment, called *dokhna*. Constitutionally, the Meches are a scheduled tribe of West Bengal.

Most Meches are poor, and nutritionally, the food they eat has much in common with that eaten by other low-income groups living around them. The Meches are non-vegetarians, since they think meat provides strength to the body which vegetables cannot replenish. They eat both wild pigs and those reared at home, and only a few have buffalo meat. Their staple food is rice, eaten and garnished with, and seasoned by, lentils, mustard oil, salt, chillies and turmeric and other spices. They have *dao-bidot* (chicken), *borma-bidot*, or *moi-bidot* (deer), if available, and every variety of fish. They have butter and sugar, besides such vegetables as potato, brinjal, ladies' finger, beans, cabbage, cauliflower and others. They grow, and eat, such fruits as mango, jackfruit, guava, banana, papaya and litchi, as also tubers, such as *simla-alu* and *misti-alu* (varieties of potato). Only a few well-off families drink milk, but many Meches drink home-brewed *jou*, made from rice, which is very intoxicating. They also drink alcohol bought from the market, though this is considered an extravagance. A typical Mech characteristic is chewing *goi* (areca nuts), grown abundantly in the region. Guests and visitors to one's house are welcomed and offered these nuts. The Meches have now modified their habits and manners according to the customs of the neighbourhood they live in. They have left eating meat of lizards, long-tailed sheep, snakes and field-rats. Drinking tea however, has become very popular now.

The Mech society has no social divisions, elevating, or condemning, a person to a high, or low, position. They do, however, have *aris* (septs), such as Narjinari (dry jute-leaf folk), Iswarary (god folk), Basumata (earth folk), Hazoari (hill folk) and Mochari (lion folk). Due to the great influence of Hinduism, the urge to carve out their own niche in the *jati-varna* system and social pressures from Hindu society, many Meches discarded their ancestral language and religion. Many have taken Mondal, Roy, Singha and Thakur as surnames. They have begun to speak Bengali. They were so over-zealous that those who spoke in their native language were fined. Bhutanese kings conferred such epithets as Katham, Subba and Karjee on certain leading Mech families entrusted to collect revenue for them. Some Meches have taken the title of Brahma, following the teachings of Kalicharan Mech of Assam, a follower of Sivanarayana Paramhansa. The Meches believe they are not inferior to others and that the *varna* system is a curse. Hindus, however, socially rank the Meches extremely low.

The Meches have five forms of marriage: a) *bwnanwi-lana*, or marriage by capture; b) *dwnkhatnai*, or elopement; c) *khatsonnai*, or willingly going away to a man's house; d) *gabwi-dwnnai*, or *gwrjia*, or obtaining a girl by service; and e) *swngani*, or marriage by negotiation. Mech neo-elites, nowadays, do not much care for the first form. There is no symbol for married people. Earlier, *mwdwm-thakha* (bride-price) ranged from Rs. 49 to Rs. 100, but this has now been considerably relaxed. There is no system of dowry, either. Divorce is rare, but, in such cases, the husband and wife appear before village elders and state the reasons for desiring divorce. Divorce is affected by a symbolic act of *phathwi-bichinai* (tearing of a *pan* leaf into two halves). As the two plates of *pan* leaf can never by joined together, so also the couple's separation.

Newly married couples live in a separate hut in the household of the husband's father. If the son wants to set up a *nokhor* (his own home), he does so with his parents' consent. A day before this happens, a *gubun-janai* (feast) is held. Widows or female divorcees may remarry. Mech customs allow the unmarried younger brother of a dead person to marry his *bibajwi* (elder brother's wife). Again, the elite Meches have forsaken this tradition. There have been some changes among customs followed by Mech women of late. Following Hindu custom, married women have begun to wear *sindur* and conch shell bangles. The Mech concept of family is *nokhor*, comprising man, woman, sons, daughters and brothers or sisters of the man, if any. The Meches have joint families till the man dies.

Relations in a Mech family are those of love, fear, distance, obligation and joking. A Mech man is an extremely good-natured and easy-going head of a contented, and simple, family. Loving relations exist between a husband and wife. Relations between a man and his *beoai* (younger brother's wife) are one of distance. A person has jocular relations with only the brother-in-law, *bibnang* (sister-in-law), *abou* (grandfather) and *abwi* (grandmother).

Property is passed on from father to son. However, the rules of inheritance seem vague, since after the death of a man, the eldest son manages the household affairs. If there is more than one son, they get an equal share. Married, or unmarried, daughters do not inherit anything. But, if a father wishes to give any of his daughters a share, he does so with the family's consent. The Meches have loving and affectionate inter-family links. If a person has a misfortune, either his father-in-law, or mother-in-law, or both, come to share his grief. The mother looks after her pregnant daughter in his son-in-law's house even today.

Though they do not, normally, inherit property, Mech women have an equal status and are consulted on all important matters. Women help men in transplantation of paddy and gathering fuel and fodder. They play an important role in social activities and life-cycle rituals. Mech women, however, do not take part in politics. Mech women work hard to run the family. They rear pigs, goats and birds, and weave *ari*, to be sold in the market. Every Mech woman is an expert in weaving and spinning. Teaching their daughters to cook, husking paddy, spinning and weaving are family obligations that elder Mech women have.

Mech women do not have many rigid restrictions before, or after, they give birth. A woman has to have a bath on the third day of every lunar week and sprinkle *dwi gwthar-sathnai* (holy water) round every hut in her homestead. A Mech homestead comprises four huts — one each in the north, south, east and west. The main hut is the one in the north, called *noma* (large house), believed to be the seat of the Mainao deity. She is represented by a small mud plinth erected in the north-east corner of the hut. Bathou, the chief god, is represented by a euphorbia tree, called *sijou*, planted in the northeast corner of the homestead.

After sprinkling water round every hut, the woman sprinkles the rest of the holy water on the *chithla* (courtyard) and then, from the seat of Bathou up to the seat of Mainao, Bathou's consort. The umbilical cord is cut by a *jwthwn-khlamgra* (midwife), a little while after the child is born. She ties up the cut end of the cord near the child's navel with cotton, jute, or *eri* silk thread after applying ash or clay. This is supposed to be antiseptic. Instances of the wounds turning septic, surprisingly, are extremely rare. An infant is named immediately after birth, or a week later.

When a girl has her first menstruation, she is confined in a room for three days, with her meals being served there.

A Mech wedding has several rituals. When the bride reaches the groom's house, her feet are ritually washed — in the presence of friends and relatives of both families — with water kept in a wooden keg. The marriage is considered consummated after the girl receives gifts and bows before Bathou and Mainao. Soon after, the *deosi*, or *deori*, priest invokes the blessings of Dhwrwm Thakhur, who represents the sun and the moon and Bathou and Mainao are asked to give the newlyweds offspring good health and happiness till an old age.

The Meches were earlier nomadic and used to shift their cultivation and home from one place to another. Cultivation assumed the form of *jhum*. When they became settled cultivators, they took up rice cultivation as their major economic pursuit. The main economic resource is naturally land, and they are both landowners and landless. The Meches have not been satisfactory traders or businessmen. The community does not have bonded or child labourers to any great extent. Wages are paid in cash and kind. A remarkable change after Independence is that many have sold off their land to the non-Meches and gone to neighbouring Assam. This is because of the severe pressure of an exodus of refugees from erstwhile East Pakistan (presently Bangladesh) to West Bengal.

At the time of the Bhutanese occupation of the Dooars, each Mech village had *thakhuri* (headman). Later, this post was replaced by that of a *mondal*, who was assisted by a *halmajhi*. The *mondal* decreed punishment for offences in the presence of villagers and three other *mondals*. The offender had to pay a cash fine, besides treating the village to a feast. After Panchayati Raj was introduced, the Meches took an active part. Many Meches hold important positions in the *gram panchayat*s. The traditional village council is now defunct, but modern statutory councils, such as *gram panchayat*s, have taken its place. However, minor offences are still redressed by village elders.

The Meches were, originally, followers of traditional tribal/folk religion. They have community gods and village gods. The chief community god and goddess are Bathou and Mainao. In the past, their major sacred shrine was the Kamakshya Temple. The North Bengal Meches have long forgotten their major festivals, *kherai* and *ai-hunai*. These have now been replaced by such Hindu festivals as Durga puja and Kali puja. Hinduism has had great influence on them. Christianity too, entered Mech hamlets in-mid nineteenth century, and has since then made a great impact. About fifty per cent of the Meches are now Christians. A third influence, in the early-twentieth century was that of Kalicharan Mech from Assam, who preached from the teachings of Sivanarayana Paramhansa, and drew a large number of disciples. They call this religion Bormo, or Brahma religion.

The Meches are experts in working in bamboo and make excellent *burung*s, fish traps, *chhonggrtai*s (winnowing fans) and *chhandrwi*s (sieves). They have a rich tradition in folk songs and folk tales, many of which may be lost for want of proper research. Many have already been lost after the authors died. The following folk song may be mentioned as a specimen:

"Khundung lunanwi, si dananwi sannw habab sannw/ Be swngsarkhou mabrwi bengnw, Ma baidi mohor khanw" (To spin and to weave forever, alas! All I wonder is how to hold the family together and how to weave beautiful designs)

The Meches are fond of music and the most important instruments are the *khan* (big drum), *chiphung* (bamboo flute), *serza* (guitar) and *gongna* (blues harp). Dance is important to them, the most popular form being the *bagurumba*. There are two cultural organizations in North Bengal, the Rongjali Boro Kristi Afat and Kongkoti Boro Kristi Afat. These two *afat*s try their best to preserve cultural traditions. The first is an organization of Mech Christians from Nararthali village. This cultural troupe has been highly acclaimed at cultural shows in Delhi and Calcutta, especially in the Republic Day celebrations. A dance programme of this *afat* has also been telecast by Calcutta Doordarshan Kendra. The Kongkoti Boro Krishti Afat is organized by a Mech of old Bathou faith. This group has not yet been able to make much of a mark, though they too, have toured Calcutta and the West Bengal districts.

Despite having to mingle with other communities, there remains a kind of a physical barrier between the Meches and others. In every sphere of social activity — for instance the life-cycle rituals, or socio-religious ceremonies — interaction between them and the others is almost non-existent. The Meches hold a low status in the *jati-varna* order, and, consequently, Brahmans — or even the others — do not accept water from them. The Meches, however, accept water from the Brahmans. Certain categories of Hindus accept *kachcha* and *pucca* food from the Meches. The Meches have inter-community marriages, especially with the Bengalis. Inter-tribal links within the Bodo group are reflected in marriages with the Garos and Kacharis and outside, with the migrant Oraons, Mundas and Santals. There is a strong inter-tribal solidarity and resistance against exploitation.

The Meches have no problems in sharing wells, roads or schools, or in entering *panchayat-ghars* and houses. The Meches do not have any *jajmani* relationship with the Brahmans, but they do with the Hajam and the village barber. The Meches are dependent on such other communities as the Kamars, Kumbhars and Lohars. The neo-elite Meches is politically active and attends public functions at the *taluka* and district levels. The Meches in Assam have been demanding a separate, autonomous state within the Indian Union, called Udayachal. There is a cordial relationship between share-croppers and landlords, as also cultivators and labourers.

The Meches are not in absolute majority anywhere, but live mingled with other communities. Modern education has influenced them very much. The only hindrance for them has been the medium of instruction, which is other than their native Mech or Bodo language. Poverty too, is an impediment in their children going to school. Literacy among the Meches, compared with that of other tribals, such as the Santals and Oraons, is a reasonable 26.97 per cent, considering the difficulties.

Health centres and hospitals are now within their reach. The Meches in remote villages, however, still follow their old practices of calling the *roja* (tribal medicine-man). Mech women's response to family planning programmes is promising. A few young Mech men have benefited from the Integrated Tribal Development Programme. Very few Meches are self-employed. Public Works Department roads link many Mech villages to nearby towns. Electricity is still beyond their reach, though there is a probability that, within a few years, Mech hamlets will have electricity. Their main fuel is wood. Irrigation facilities are not available. Meches use — or, indeed, prefer — chemical fertilisers. Apart from some nutrition programmes in schools, there are no such other programmes in Mech villages. The Meches pick up their rations from fair price shops. Banking facilities are now available in their areas.

The pan-Bodo movement — which originated in neighbouring Assam — has aroused some political aspirations among them. The movement of the Plains Tribal Council of Assam (PTCA) for a separate Udayachal state has pervaded the Mech society of North Bengal and they have moral support for this cause. The pan-Bodo literary movement — which also originated in Assam — the All-Bodo Sahitya Sabha, has its counterpart in North Bengal. As a result, the educated Meches of North Bengal are now demanding that their mother tongue be recognized as a medium of instruction at the primary level, to begin with.

HIRA CHARAN NARJINARI

METE

The Metes, a fishing community of West Bengal have Metia and Malla Bagdi as synonyms. The legend that explains the etymology of their name says they were made by God Shiva from *mati* or soil of his body so they were known as Metes. They claim they are a branch of the Bagdi caste and have relatives throughout the region. The Metes are the autochthons of West Bengal, living in an area, characterized by plains and plateaus, dominated by a monsoon climate. They speak and write in Bengali.

The Metes are non-vegetarian. They eat fish, mutton and chicken. Their staple cereals are rice and wheat. Their favourite pulses are *moong*, *masur* (lentil) and *biri* (black gram) and cooking medium is mustard and rapeseed oil. They eat all locally available seasonal vegetables in moderation, and such fruits as mango and jackfruit only occasionally. They have tea with or without milk in the mornings and evenings. The men like having alcohol, bought from the market, occasionally. Most men smoke *bidis* and chew betel with *dokta* (a preparation from tobacco leaves). Their consumption of pulses and vegetables has gone down.

The Metes have totemistic clans the *bogri* (a bird), or *bagh* (tiger), but there is no hierarchy among these groups. They are not aware of the *varna* system. They believe they have a low status in the local social hierarchy and this perception is corroborated by their neighbours.

They are endogamous at the community level and clan-exogamous in marriage, which is usually monogamous. They negotiate the marriage of their children at a very young age; sixteen years for boys and twelve years for girls. Vermilion and iron and conch shell bangles are the symbols of a married woman. Dowry, such as wrist watches, radios, bicycles and silver ornaments, is usually given in kind. A wife lives with her husband after marriage. Divorce is not permissible. If there is a separation between husband and wife, they and their families are ostracized. To become part of the society again, they have to perform a *yagna*, helped by a Brahman, and have to host a feast for the village community members. A woman may not remarry, but a man may, only after the death of his first wife. Recently, there has been an increase in the age at marriage and the customs of dowry and clan endogamy have become more widespread. In case of clan endogamy, the girl is transferred to the clan of her mothers brother, before marriage.

The Metes, generally, have nuclear families, but extended families are not unknown. In a Mete family, generally, the father is the controlling authority and the younger members obey him. Young boys obey him only till they are able to earn, whereupon they marry and set up home of their own. The children, normally, are afraid of their father and the eldest brother till quite an advanced age. A man and woman show affection to their children. A woman has a relationship of distance with her *shvashur*, *bhasur* and *jamai*. There is usually a jocular relationship between a man and the younger siblings of his wife, a woman and her husbands younger brothers and with ones grandparents.

Parents look after their childrens well being, while young children help their mothers by gathering such fuel as cowdung and dry leaves. They also help their mothers in catching fish. Unequal sharing of the economic burden is a flashpoint of conflict in a family. Male equigeniture is the inheritance rule. The eldest son succeeds his father as head of the family. Of late, there has been an increase in the number of nuclear families.

Mete women lead a very busy life. They go out early in the morning to catch fish, and then sell them in the market. They buy vegetables, rice, pulses and other grocery items with the money they get from selling fish. Once back home, they cook, and later feed the family. After the usual round of housework, they go out again to catch and sell fish for buying food for the night. So, Mete women play a vital role in their families. Their neighbours say they have no time to waste quarrelling, or gossiping. Sometimes, they also work as agricultural labourers in sowing paddy. They also play a role in religious rituals. But, in spite of the vital economic role they play, they have no decision making power and have a low status compared with that of men.

In the ninth month of pregnancy, they have a ritual known as *sadhana*, in which they offer *puja* to Ma Manasa and give *prasad* to the expectant mother, who wears a new *sari* and eats sweets. Neighbours and relatives are invited to a feast on this day. The ritual is observed in an elaborate manner only during the birth of the firstborn. For others, only the *prasad* of Ma Manasa is given to the pregnant woman. *Narta* is observed on the ninth day after childbirth. A barber pares the nails of the newborn and mother and a Barui *dai* offers puja to the Jalmahajan beside a pond. *Ekusha*, the purification ritual, is performed on the twenty-first day after the child is born. A barber pares the nails of mother and child, and the *dai* washes their clothes that day. The new mother may not enter the kitchen for the twenty-one days of pollution. They generally go out to catch fish when the baby is two months old, but sometimes, even as early as after twenty-one days. *Bhujno* is observed in the seventh month if the child born is a girl, and the sixth if a boy. The barber tonsures the baby on that day, when *puja* is offered to Ma Manasa and the *thakurma* feeds the child *prasad* and then rice. The maternal uncle feeds the baby rice, too.

When a boy or girl reaches marriageable age, parents launch the search for a suitable partner. Metes, generally try to marry their daughters off before they have their first menstruation. Negotiations over, the boys father visits the girls house, blesses her and gives her ten to twenty rupees. The girls father next blesses the boy. The family priest fixes the date of the wedding with the help of an almanac. *Gayehalud* take place four or six days before the wedding day. The *dai* comes in on that day to claim a new *sari* and ten to twenty rupees as tips. A barber pares the nails of the boy or the girl a day before the wedding, in ritual *adhibas*. *Nandimukh* is held on the morning of the wedding at the grooms house, and the same ceremony is performed at the brides house just before the groom arrives. The brides father, grandfather or uncle performs *dan*. In *satshighora*, another ritual, the bride sits on the *machadali* (a kind of winnowing fan) and is moved round the groom seven times. The *machadali* is carried by married men in the family. The *Dom* worships the *dhol* (drums) before *nandimukh*. He plays the *dhol* during the *sindurdan* ritual too. *Malabadal* is another ritual in which the bride exchanges her garland of betel nut for the garland of *akanda* flowers worn by the groom. The bride goes to her husbands home next morning and *boubhat* is held on that day, when the grooms father hosts a feast only for his relatives. A feast for friends and neighbours follows the next day. The consummation ceremony is held on the eighth day at the brides home.

Metes cremate their dead. Pollution lasts ten days. Relatives and members of the family of the dead place *muri* on the third day, at the spot where the person died. The ritual on the fourth day is known as *titobhat*, when cooked rice with *neem* leaves is placed on the *dopaira* in the evening. The sons pour water on the *bena* tree from the fourth to the tenth day after the death. The tenth day is *ghat*, or *kaman*, when the barber tonsures the sons and priest completes the *pinda-dan* ceremony. *Sradh* is held on the eleventh day. Relatives are invited on that day to a non-vegetarian lunch. No change is observed in the rituals of the Mete community except an increasing demand for dowry in kind.

As the Metes are a fishing community, water is their major economic resource. They are landless. They catch fish in marshlands kept fallow by others. A few of them take ponds on lease to breed fish. Fishing is the traditional occupation. Metes have great financial difficulties from *Magh* to *Jaishtha* since most of the marshland and ponds run dry during the period. The rainy season is the best period when they can catch a great deal of fish. In addition, they work as agricultural labourers and are paid in cash and kind. They depend directly on daily and weekly markets, where they sell their fish for cash. Boys and girls of the community begin helping their parents to catch fish from a very young age of eight to ten years and to catch and sell fish from the age of fifteen to sixteen years. They use *gole jal* (round nets) and *kheya jal* (casting net) in fishing. There has been an increase in the number of people engaged in fishing.

Metes elect an aged person by voice vote as *malik* (village chief), whom they consult, apart from other aged people of the community, while negotiating a marriage. If a girl marries into another caste, her parents have to call three or four *maliks* of different villages and burn her effigy, besides performing a *sradh* for her (signifying her death in the community). A feast has to be hosted for community members, as well as the *maliks*. The *malik* resolves other social problems too. If anybody is found guilty of theft, he is punished physically. The *gram panchayat* is their statutory council, which plans and implements welfare and development activities for the villagers.

The Metes are Hindus and most belong to the *Sakta* sect. The women worship Lakshmi at home. Manasa (Goddess of Snakes) is a community deity as well as a regional one. Manasa is worshipped on the last day of *Shravana*. Manasa-tala is the sacred village centre. A Mete priest, known as *deghure*, worships Manasa. Manasa puja is their biggest festival and Manasa mela is their biggest fair. Metes and the other communities sacrifice goats through the *deghure*. They also celebrate Durga puja, Kali puja and Gajan and visit such fairs as Gajaner mela and Dharmarajer mela. Since Metes have to move around in marshy land, they worship Manasa for safety. The Brahman priest, on their behalf, holds *pujas* for deities and while they enter a new home, as also observes the life-cycle rituals. The *deghure* performs only Manasa puja.

Weaving of various kinds of nets is a traditional craft of their people. Their women sing songs during *Bhadu*. They have folktales about their origin, referred to earlier.

The Brahman priest serves them in worship, and during life-cycle rituals. The Napit and the *dai* also serve them during life-cycle rituals. The Dom plays the *dhole* at Mete weddings. They also supply the *machadali* for use at weddings. Inter-community links are established through these rituals, besides such ceremonial occasions as weddings and religious festivals. Through the caste occupation of selling the fish that they catch, Metes come into contact with other neighbouring communities. The Bauris, Bedias, Muchis, Doms, Keots, Bagdis and Sutradhars are the major neighbouring communities in the area under study.

Metes do not accept any kind of food from the Bauris, Bedias, Muchis, Doms, or Bagdis. The Keots do not eat in Mete households, though Metes do accept food from them. The putative kinship of *dharma-bhai* and putative friendship of *phul* exist commonly among Metes. The regular priest, Napit and *dai* are paid off immediately for services rendered. Metes who work as agricultural labourers in the fields of other communities develop a labourer-cultivator relationship with them. The community does not have any modern inter-community links worth mentioning.

Their attitude towards education is favourable. The literacy level however, is very low. Mete boys hardly cross the primary level, and girls do not go to school at all. They depend mostly upon modern medicare methods, though traditional forms are not unknown. A woman, sometimes, goes to the hospital at the time of delivery. Many women have got sterilized after three children. The Metes draw water from tube wells and wells. They complain they get no government help.

A few Mete families own radio sets and some young boys watch television in their neighbours houses. Young boys often go to the cinema, but not women. Political parties get in touch with them only during elections. Road and railway facilities exist a short distance from their localities. Metes cannot afford electricity for their homes. They use firewood and coal as fuel. Mete children sometimes, get bread in school. Metes pick up their rations from fair price shops. Only a few can save in banks. Many have to take loans from the Baniyas or from other wealthy people during *Ashar* and *Sravan* when they breed fish. They repay this loan with interest in *Baisakh*.

ARCHANA DATTA

MIRSHIKAR

The name of the community is Mirshikar. The name of the community is also pronounced as Mirsikar. Etymologically, Mirshikar means *mir* (head) and *shikari* (hunter). Risley (1981, Vol. II, 92) observed: "Mirsikar, a chief huntsman; a low class of Mohammedans who live by snaring birds". Its synonyms are Mirsikari and Sheikh. They migrated from the Gaya, Dumka and Jamui areas to Panchakot Raj State before the 1857 Sepoy Mutiny and helped the members of the royal family during their hunting expeditions by providing them with gunpowder.

They are distributed in different villages of erstwhile Manbhum district and the Santhal Parganas and Burdwan district. They live in regions with a hard laterite soil. Earlier, kings gave them *lakhraj*, or rent-free land grant. They speak in Manbhuinya Bangla and in Bengali and Hindi within the family and with outsiders. They write in the Bengali, Urdu and Devanagari scripts. They are considered educationally backward.

They are purely non-vegetarian and their staple food is rice and pulses. They use mustard oil for cooking. They eat leafy vegetables, roots and tubers, besides all kinds of seasonal fruits. They drink tea and milk. The men seldom drink liquor. Both men and women chew tobacco. The men also smoke *bidis* and cigarettes and chew betel. They prepare special food during the Id and Ramzan festivals with *sewi*.

The major social divisions among the Mohammedans are Saids, Pathans, Mughals and Sheikhs. Mirshikars believe they belong to the Sheikh genre and consider the other three groups higher in status. There is no religious differentiation between them, but their economic and social status is identifiable. They use Sheikh as a prefix to their name. They are surrounded by Hindu upper and lower castes. These neighbouring Hindus do not consider them equal and always keep a distance.

The Mirshikars marry within the Sheikh community. The marriageable age for girls is between fifteen and eighteen years and, for boys, twenty-one and twenty-five. Marriages are usually negotiated. The *nikah*, or marriage, proposals are initiated by relatives and friends. There are no marriage symbols, except the *bindia* and glass bangles. The *denmohar* amount varies from Rs. 525 to Rs. 1,000 and is accepted by the grooms side. But now *denmohar* is only symbolic and the incidence of dowry has been increasing rapidly of late. After marriage, the wife lives with the husband.

Divorce is permitted under the condition that compensation of three months and thirteen days subsistence is paid to the wife and the *denmohar* returned. Both men and women can remarry with *nikah* rituals. Families are mostly nuclear. Inter-personal relations within the family are maintained through love, respect and fear. There are jocular and avoidance relationships between certain members of the kin. The rule of inheritance is male equigeniture and succession as head of family passes from father to eldest son. Inter-family links are maintained through reciprocity and cooperation.

Women do not have any right of inheritance, but do take part in the economic and social activities of the family. They perform every household chore, take care of children, manage family expenditure and contribute to family income. The status of women is low and determined by the *Shariat*.

A special feast, or sweets, is given in the ninth month of the first pregnancy, known as *sadh-khawa*. It takes place with the approval of the local *Maulavi*. The umbilical cord is cut by an elderly woman. On the fifth day, the bathing ceremony takes place. *Sunnat* is done when boys are between the age of three and seven.

Marriage proposals are initiated by the grooms family. The *sagan* is fixed on the third or fifth day. In *nikah*, the *kalma* (passages from the Koran) are chanted by the *Maulavi*. Wedding songs are sung and feasts are held by both families. Consummation takes place after *dwiragaman* or *ghura-phera*.

Mirshikars bury their dead. The *Maulavi* reads verses from the Koran on the fourth, tenth, nineteenth and fortieth days after the death. A feast, known as *milad*, is held for the poor.

Mirshikars are mainly landless. They work as tailors and are small businessmen. Some work as masons and in other kinds of casual labour. In the agricultural season, they work as agricultural labourers. They work as *bidi* binders and vegetable vendors too, and own chicken and mutton shops.

Moulavis, or religious priests, are much respected people and are consulted on various socio-religious matters. But the *mir* of the Mirshikars is the traditional social head. The *mir* (headman), with the help of other elderly people, and with the *maulavi*s sanction, controls the social mechanism or social norms of the community. There are other traditional officers, besides, known as *nayebs* and *chowkidars*. Social offenders are ostracized by the Mirshikars traditional *panchayat*.

As they are surrounded by the Hindu community, they condemn the killing of cattle.

Adultery, trespassing, rape and other kinds of social misbehaviour are viewed very seriously. The amount of *denmohar* is settled before community elders, in the presence of the *mir*, *nayeb* and *moulavi*. The high offices of the *moulavi* and *mir* take care of the *denmohar* during *chhara-chhari* or *talak* (divorce) and the money guaranteed has to be returned by the husband. Nowadays, the statutory *panchayat* is very effective. Mirshikars play active roles in the *gram-panchayat*, *anchal panchayat* and *zilla parishad* elections and the *panchayat* decisions are carried out by them. Conflicts over land or property, or anything that might lead to violence are decided upon by the statutory *panchayat*. A Mirshikar is one of the elected members of the *gram-panchayat*.

Mirshikars observe such Muslim festivals as Id, Sab-e-barat, Bakri Id, Muharram, Egarhi, Surifer Fatiha, Barfafa Fateha and Ramzan. They also observe *roja* (fast) on Muharram and in the month of Ramzan and chant *namaz* thrice every day. Eating pork is *haram* (blasphemy) to them. They do not eat the meat of slain animals or birds if not fresh. They sing the Jhumur songs of the region. Some are very good singers and lyricists. They are expert wrestlers, archers and gunmen. The royal hunting party of the Panchakot Raj family always keep them as bodyguards. In Muharram processions, they hold demonstrations and mock fights with swords and sticks, and utter words in the painful memory of Hassan and Hussain, who died in the Karbala war.

They sing wedding songs, and during the *Nachni* dance, the men sing Jhumur songs, mostly socio-political in nature and depicting the peoples struggle.

They enjoy the local Hindu festivals too, and make new garments to sell at festivals, such as Durga puja, Shiva-gajan and Charak. On the Tusu, Bhadu and Bandna festivals, they also make food and cakes and decorate their houses, while young children sing Tusu songs. They also sing Bhadu songs, but do not take part in any ritual. Besides, they have their own songs, such as Qawali and sing Hindi film songs.

Some Mirshikars work as members of professional bands and play the flute with Hindi songs. Sometimes, they organize *jatras* with local Hindu boys and act in these.

At least twice or thrice a year, local *maulavis* read from the Koran, as also the *haji* or *imam*. They regard all these as religious activities. During the death rituals on *chaturam* day (the fourth day), they arrange for verses to be read from the Koran and food and clothes to be given to fakirs (beggars). On the tenth day, *dasaya* is celebrated through the reading of verses from the Koran and hosting a feast for the poor. The *milad* is also held on the nineteenth day, known as *bisowa*, and on the fortieth day, known as *chaliswa*.

They maintain inter-community links with great warmth by performing the *phool* and *saiba* rituals with members from the other communities, who are invited to Mirshikar weddings or social functions and these obligations are reciprocated. They accept *kachcha* or *pucca* food from Hindus and tribals, both of whom, however, do not accept food cooked by them and accept only *kachcha* food. During Hindu festivals, they stitch new clothes.

They enjoy equal status in schools and *panchayat-ghars*. They maintain cultivator-labour relationships as *munish*, *kamins* and *bagals* in the house of local traders and big farmers. They work as *mutias* (load-bearers) in the Kashipur weekly and daily markets. They have access to drinking water sources, such as wells, ponds and tube wells. They are educationally backward. They prefer Islamic education and get *dini talim* (education) through the Koran. There is not a single matriculate among them and nobody holds a government job, except a peon in the settlements department.

They are very keen on family planning, and most are self employed. They take care about their personal health and hygiene. Practically no IRDP or NREP projects have been implemented in a Mirshikar area. They have no facilities to enjoy the benefits of the Inter-Corporate Deposit Scheme. They listen to the radio and sometimes, watch television. Those working as tailors especially in Kashipur and Adra read Bengali newspapers.

They are very keen on environmental conservation and their energy resources are wood, coal, sawdust and cowdung. They have no irrigation facilities, but do enjoy ration shop facilities. School children get one midday meal. Banks and savings and investment organizations exist in their areas.

Mirshikars are now well aware of Muslim fundamentalism. Every Mirshikar now visits a mosque and listens to the speeches of *maulavis*. In the name of Islam, they are now organizing themselves and they identify themselves as Sheikhs. They are very vigorously asserting themselves and use a special kind of typically Muslim *kurta*, *topi* and *pyjamas*. They prefer the Urdu and Arabic languages to he local languages as their medium of instruction.

P. P. MAHATO

MUCHI

The Muchis are a well known caste of West Bengal with such synonyms as Ruidas, Das, Chamar, Charmakar, Rishi and Rabidas. Arisona, Darshana or Ruidas, Barohajare and Choumu or Chamar are their four subgroups. Various legends about their origin are in vogue in this area. One is that Muchiram, the ancestor of the caste was created from the sweat of Narayan. The name of Muchiram as their ancestor is also referred to by Risley (1891: 95).

They are predominantly concentrated in Bankura, Birbhum, Hooghly and Burdwan districts. The areas under study are characterized by plains with a warm and temperate climate, high humidity and medium rainfall. The total Muchi population in West Bengal in 1981 was 7,11,024. They speak and write in Bengali. They belong to the scheduled castes category by the Constitution.

The somatometric data of Bengal and serological information of the states of Uttar Pradesh and Madhya Pradesh are available. According to Risley (1981), Chakladar (1936), Majumdar and Rao (1960) and Roy Chaudhury (1952), all cited by Gupta and Dutta (1966), their average stature varies from 1,613.94mm to 1,641 mm.; the cephalic index varies from 77.03 to 79.22; and nasal index varies from 68.98 to 75.2. Serological information was collected by Majumdar and Kishen (1947) and Kumar (1966) on Chamars. The p gene ranges from 13% to 14%, q gene from 26% to 32% and r gene from 54% to 61%.

The Muchis are non-vegetarian, but do not eat beef, pork or carrion. They eat rice and, sometimes, wheat as staple cereals. Masur (lentil) and black gram are their favourite pulses. Mustard and rapeseed oils are their cooking mediums. They eat all locally available seasonal vegetables and fruits in moderation. They drink tea, and the men, occasionally, have alcohol, either brewed at home, or bought from the market. Those who can afford it have milk and milk products. They smoke *bidi*s and chew tobacco and, sometimes, betel. They do not have bottle-gourd or radish in *Bhadra* and *Magh*, respectively. Of late, there has been an increase in the use of pulses and decrease in the consumption of fruits.

Sub-castes, or subgroups, lineage and social divisions regulate marriage alliances. The Arisonas are at the top of the social ladder, followed by the Darshanas, Barohajares and Choumus, respectively. Some claim that the Darshanas are at the top of he hierarchy, followed by the Arisonas. Sai Bangsha, Gantro Bangsha, Porshuni Bangsha, Moral Bangsha and Paramanik Bangsha indicate lineage names of the Darshana subgroup. Lineage also indicates ancestry. They have a low social status locally and believe they are Sudras in the Varna order.

They are endogamous at the community and sub-caste levels. The Darshana subgroup follows lineage exogamy too. Marriages are usually negotiated and monogamous. Vermilion and iron and shell bangles are symbols of a married Muchi woman. Dowry is paid in cash and kind. A woman lives with her husband after marriage. Divorce is sought on grounds of adultery and maladjustment and takes place with social approval. If the husband is at fault, he has to return all the things he received from his wifes father during the wedding. Children of divorced parents are the liability of either father or mother.

Widows, widowers, men and women divorcees, may remarry. Remarriage of a woman is known as *sanga*. Junior sororate or levirate is permissible only after the death of the first spouse. Recently, there has been an increase in the age at marriage, dowry has gradually replaced bride price, and the incidence of divorce has recorded a decline.

Muchi families are mostly nuclear, though vertically extended ones exist too. The father is the head of the family, and younger members obey him. The fathers responsibility is to earn for the family and the mothers to look after the familys health and need for food, besides being hospitable towards kin. Sometimes, she shares the economic burden with her husband. Adult sons share their fathers economic responsibilities, while adult daughters help their mother in household chores.

In a family, there is a relationship of distance between the *jamai* and *shvashuri*, and between a woman and her *shvasur* and *bhasur*. A jocular relationship exists between a woman and her *deor*, or between a man and the younger siblings of his wife, and between grandparents and grandchildren. Unequal sharing of the economic burden and workload and, sometimes, property issues cause conflict within a family. Equigeniture is an inheritance rule and the eldest son succeeds to his fathers position. The number of nuclear families has been on the rise with the breakup of extended ones and both men and women can now claim the rightful share of their fathers property, instead of only sons.

Women take part in agricultural operations, rearing of domesticated animals and housework. They also take part in religious rituals, attend political meetings and shoulder a large part of the familys economic burden, besides controlling family expenditure. However they still have a low status in the community.

Muchis have various life-cycle rituals. They observe *bhaja sadh* in the fifth, or seventh, month of pregnancy and *sadh* in the ninth. Panchute and Shasthi puja are post-delivery rituals. A Hari or Muchi Dai helps in the delivery. Pollution lasts thirty days, after which the new mother may enter the kitchen. *Annaprashan* is observed in the sixth month if he child born is a boy and in the seventh if a girl. They bring *prasad* from the house of a Brahman in exchange of *sidha* food and the mama feeds it and cooked rice to the child.

When boys and girls attain a marriageable age, their parents hold negotiations for a suitable match. After these are finalized, the girls father, *mama*, *mesho* (husband of the mothers sister) and other elderly persons attend a blessing ceremony at the boys house. The boys family blesses the girl on wedding day. *Nandimukhu* (or *nandimukh*), *Gayehalud*, *malabadal* (with garlands made of basil leaves and durba grass), *shubhodrishti* and *sindurdan* are essential marriage rites. The brides father hosts a feast on the wedding day, while the grooms father holds one on the third day after the marriage. The marriage is consummated at the grooms house.

Muchis cremate their dead and observe a mourning period of fifteen days. *Ghat* rites are observed on the fifteenth day and *sradh* on the sixteenth, followed by *tel-machh* on the seventeenth. They hold a feast for relatives on this day. The bones of the dead are disposed of in the Ganga. Now, however, pollution lasts fifteen days after a person dies, instead of thirty. An increase in expenses of rituals has been reported.

Traditionally, Muchis are tanners, makers of shoes and drums, and sometimes, musicians. Now, many work as agricultural labourers, cultivators, share-croppers and in petty businesses too. The Barohajares and Choumus weave baskets. Muchis have direct links with the daily or weekly markets where transactions are in cash. There has been a rise in the number of agricultural labourers, who are paid in cash and kind.

Muchis have no caste-*panchayat*. The statutory *gram panchayat* plans and implements welfare and development activities for their area. Earlier, they had *mondals* and *paramaniks* as members of the caste council, who used to address different social problems, or help in marriage negotiations. Now, such posts have been abolished.

The majority of the Muchis are Vaishnavas, who worship Lakshmi, Narayan and Tulsi as their family deities and Kali, Durga and Gopinath as village deities. Didima, or Shitala-ma, is a regional deity. The Brahman priest serves them in worship and life-cycle rituals. Gajan, Kali puja and worship of Didima are festivals with socio-religious significance.

They have some folk-tales about their origin, one of which has been referred to earlier.

Traditionally, other communities do not share cooked food with the Muchis, except Doms, but do share *sidha* food. Their participation in such traditional festivals as Gajan, Kali puja and Didimar puja also helps to establish inter-community links. They have a patron-client relationship with the Brahman and a landlord-tenant and cultivator-labourer relationship with Muslims and other higher caste Hindus. They have established links with others in the religious and economic spheres of life. They have a few doctors, job-holders or political leaders among them, and inter-community links have been established through their efforts.

Except a few, Muchis are educationally backward. They do use modern medicare and react favourably towards family planning programmes. They fetch drinking water from tube wells. Many have taken loans under the IRDP for agricultural purposes, to buy bullocks for ploughing, or to run petty businesses in husking rice.

They listen to the radio, go to the cinema, take advice from agricultural extension agencies for farm operations, and get various kinds of information through political parties. Their localities are connected by roads, railways and post offices. They cannot afford electricity at home. Firewood is their main source of fuel. They use canal water to irrigate land and organic manure, chemical fertilizer and pesticides for a better yield. Their children get free midday meals. They collect their rations from fair price shops. They cannot avail of banking facilities since they do not earn enough. On the contrary, they sometimes buy groceries on credit.

ARCHANA DATTA

MUNDA

The Mundas are a well-known tribe of West Bengal. They are also known as Mankis in some parts of West Dinajpur district of West Bengal. They have several subgroups, such as Kharia-Munda, Munda-Majhi, Kol-Munda, Bhumij-Munda, Mahali-Munda, Nagbanshi-Munda, Savar-Munda and Manki-Munda. The ethnographic account and history of the Mundas are very rich. They have migrated from Bihar and are now distributed in Midnapore, Purulia, West Dinajpur, Maldah, Jalpaiguri and Darjeeling districts of West Bengal.

Their total population figure is 2,30,016 in the state, by the 1981 Census. They speak the Munda and Sadri dialects at home and in Bengali, Hindi and Sadri with outsiders. They write in the Devanagari and Bengali scripts at home and in Devanagari, Bengali and Roman scripts to others. They hold the constitutional status of a scheduled tribe in West Bengal.

They are non-vegetarians and eat meat, fish, eggs, chicken and pork, but never consume beef. Rice, wheat and maize are their staple food. They eat all kinds of vegetables, fruit only occasionally and pulses, such as *urad*, *tuar*, *moong*, *masur* and *kesar* are also taken. Mustard oil is their cooking medium. They regularly drink *pachai* or *tari* brewed at home or bought from the local market. They have milk and milk products and smoke *bidi*s, cigarettes and indigenous cheroots. They chew betel leaf.

The Munda subgroups are Kharia-Munda, Munda-Majhi, Kol-Munda, Mahali-Munda, Bhumij-Munda, Manki-Munda, Nagbanshi-Munda and Savar-Munda. They have several exogamous clans, such as Bojra, Bhengra, Sal, Beng, Bar, Ashar, Bag, Bagela, Ghagher, Machhli, Hemram, Karketa, Hansa, Kiri and Nag. They have a high perception of themselves. They regard the Santals and the Hos as social equals and the neighbouring castes believe the Mundas are socially higher than the Haris, Dom, Kandras and Muchis.

They are endogamous at the community level and exogamous at the clan level. They prefer adult marriages. Marriage by negotiation, service, mutual consent and elopement are the common forms of acquiring mates. Marriages are, usually, monogamous, though non-sororate polygyny, junior levirate and junior sororate are also permissible. Married women use *sindur* and glass bangles as symbols of marriage. Bride-price is paid in cash and kind. After marriage, the bride lives with her husband.

Divorce is permissible, with social approval, on grounds of adultery, maladjustment, cruelty, or insanity. Either husband or wife can seek divorce and compensation is paid to the aggrieved party. Children of divorced parents are the liability of the father. Widows and divorcees may marry again.

Mundas prefer to live in nuclear families, though a few live in mixed-extended families. A woman, normally, has a relationship of distance with her father-in-law and her husband's elder brother. There is a jocular relationship between a woman and her husband's younger brother, as between grandparents and grandchildren. Conflict arises out of property matters. Parental property is inherited equally by the sons and the eldest son succeeds to his father's position. Inter-family links are evident during festivities, rituals and religious functions.

Women play various roles in their day-to-day life. They gather fuel, fetch water and help their husbands in agriculture. They have other roles in social and religious rituals. They take part in other economic activities too, and contribute their earnings to the family kitty, though they do not control family expenditure. They have a low status and no power in social control or in the political sphere.

Mundas observe various life-cycle rituals. During pregnancy Munda women do not eat fish, which has been caught on a hook or tortoise speared with a harpoon. In the seventh or ninth month, *sadh* is held, at which the woman eats food according to her liking. A Hari or Bhangi midwife cuts the umbilical cord and cleans the mother and newborn. *Ekusia* (pollution), normally, lasts twenty-one days. Now, a few observe pollution for nine days, called *narta*. On the tenth day, the naming ceremony is held. The rice-eating ceremony takes place in the sixth month if the child born is a boy, and, in the seventh, if a girl.

Marriages are generally negotiated. The father of the groom sends a *dutam* (intermediary) to the father of the bride. A Brahman suggests a date for the wedding after consulting an almanac. Rituals, such as *tasang-ojo* or *telkharhi*, are an essential part of the wedding and most rituals are observed at the bride's house. The bride, seated on a *mandoa* (a flat seat made of bamboo) and facing eastward, is carried round the groom four times. Their hands and garments are then knotted together by a priest in a ritual called *hath ganthi*, or *anchal ganthi*. After this they exchange garlands. The groom puts vermilion in the parting of the bride's hair with a piece of copper and then puts a (*kharu*) iron bracelet on her wrist which the bride believes to be the sign of a happy married life. Next, a ceremonial feast or *bhojmarhi* is held.

Several rituals mark a funeral ceremony. Mundas have their own cremation ground, but bodies of children are buried. Pollution lasts ten days. Fowl, rice and vegetables are offered to the dead soul and the sacred fire ceremony marks the end of the pollution period.

The Mundas are into agriculture. Their natural resource is land. Almost all Mundas cultivate land owned mostly by caste Hindus. The mode of contract is locally known as *barga chas* (share-cropping), in which the cultivator bears all the agricultural expenses, while the land-owner pays the revenue and gets half the total production. Mundas are employed as seasonal, or full-time, agricultural labourers working on a daily wage basis. Very few own land. Their traditional occupations were hunting and gathering food, fuel and fodder, but nowadays they are mainly cultivators. Besides, they work in government offices and in the private sector. They are also engaged as skilled labourers. They have direct links with the daily and weekly markets, where transactions are in cash.

Mundas have a traditional panchayat headed by a *mondal*, or *majhi*, a hereditary post. Generally, the man who first sets up a village is selected as the *mondal* by the others. The other members are selected by voice vote. The function of the tribal panchayat is to exert social control. There is a statutory *panchayat*, which looks after the welfare and development programme for the villagers.

The Mundas believe in their indigenous religion. A few profess Christianity. They have many religious festivals, such as Dhuria puja, which they perform in May or June in the belief that it will bring rain; *Ashari*, which they observe in July to make their agricultural operations trouble free, and to have a bumper crop; *Karam* in August or September; *Garam* in January; Sitala in February; Bandhna Parab, a cattle caressing festival, in October or November; and Sharur in March or April. They have their own priest who performs the rituals and pujas.

The Mundas have a very rich tradition in folk songs, folk tales and folklore. Both men and women take part in dances during rituals and festivities.

The Mundas accept water and food from all neighbouring tribals and castes. But Brahmans do not accept water from them. Mundas do not marry outside their community. They share drinking water sources, schools, roads, crematoriums and *panchayat ghars* with the other communities. They take part in such festivals as Dassehra and Holi, along with local Hindus. They have a patron-client or landlord-tenant relationship with their neighbours. The community has businessmen and job-holders in the government.

They are now aware of the need for education and send their boys and girls to schools and colleges regularly. They prefer modern medicine and make use of family planning methods and programmes. They fetch their drinking water from such sources as tube wells and ponds. A few have got loans under the IRDP. They own transistor radio sets, watch television, go to the cinema, and make use of railways and roads for communication. They use firewood, coal and cowdung cakes as fuel and rainwater and canal water for irrigation. They use organic manure and chemical fertilisers too. Their children get bread at school. They also make use of rationing facilities and are dependent on money-lenders and shopkeepers.

AMITABHA MITRA

MUSAHAR

The Musahars believe they have four *khunts* — Maghaiya, Dosadh, Musahar and Dhangar. They have little knowledge of their origin or history of migration. They are aware of their distribution in three adjacent districts — Burdwan, Birbhum and Murshidabad — and across the state boundary, in the Santhal Parganas of Bihar. Their major concentration is in northern Bengal. The other three Musahar *khunts* are found in areas where the Musahars live. The Musahars live in hamlets, away from the main village area where the upper castes live. They sometimes live in the same area with other low castes.

Musahars live in the plains of West Bengal, which have a temperate, warm and humid climate. The major river in the area is the Ganga, and Musahars — other than those in Purulia and Bankura — have settled in areas not very far from the river. The areas have seen severe forest denudation, and so, there is medium rainfall. The total Musahar population in West Bengal was 17,628 by the 1981 Census. They speak a corrupt Hindi dialect at home and with relatives. They speak to their Bengali neighbours in Bengali and to members of the other three *khunts* in their Hindi dialect. They write — if at all, since almost every Musahar is illiterate — in Bengali. Constitutionally, they belong to the scheduled castes.

Musahars are non-vegetarians — in fact, they eat all edible items ("*sab kichhu khai*"), but do not consume beef or snakes. They eat pork, snails, *gugli* and *jhinuk*. Their staple food is rice and *kalai*, or *kala-kalai*, pulses. Their cooking medium is mustard oil. They eat all available edible roots, tubers and vegetables, except bark. Most vegetables and potatoes are eaten with their skins or jackets on. They have milk and tea occasionally. They are extremely fond of alcohol and drink both homemade and the commercial variety of alcohol. Adult men and women have large quantities of rice beer, an essential item in any festivity or social gathering. There is no restriction on any food in any season or on any occasion, other than mourning.

Members of the Musahar *khunt* consider themselves hierarchically superior to the other three. The Maghaiyas come next, followed by Dosadhs and Dhangars. The basis of differentiation is not clear, though there are minor occupational differences. The Musahars are mainly daily wage agricultural labourers; the Maghaiya do an assortment of daily wage labourer's jobs — such as digging wells, breaking stones and laying roofs; the Dosadhs, besides laying roofs, work as daily wage labourers at road construction sites; and the Dhangars as daily wage agricultural labourers, and also sell firewood. They brew *toddy* from palm juice and sell it in the market.

The Musahars use Ray, Ray-Musahar, or simply, Musahar as a surname. They make no claims regarding their position in the local social hierarchy. All four *khunt*s are social equals and observe no commensal restrictions, though they do not marry into another *khunt*. The Musahars attempt to explain their hierarchical status by saying they are considered a low *jat* by both the neighbouring Hindus and Muslims. Neighbouring upper castes consider them a scheduled caste — that, traditionally, has come to be associated with low social status — which, in fact, they are.

Musahars do not marry their *bhayad*, nor close kin, such as one's maternal uncle's daughter or the daughter of one's mother's sister. Girls get married by age twelve. Boys, usually, marry by age sixteen to eighteen. Marriages are negotiated and monogamous. The negotiations are done through relatives. *Sindur*, *sankha* and *loha* are symbols of a married woman. *Sankhas* are not always worn, since they break easily, which is considered to bring bad luck. The dowry system does not exist. After marriage, the wife lives with her husband. On rare occasions, the husband lives with his wife's family in the *ghar-jamai* system — neither the preferred choice, nor socially honourable.

Divorce is permitted on grounds of incompatibility and infidelity, but not infertility, since they believe it is *maliker-khela* (an act of God). Both husband and wife have equal right to seek divorce and initiate proceedings. A person may not remarry if the spouse is alive. Divorcees, widows and widowers may remarry.

Musahars, mostly have nuclear families, though there are a few joint and extended families among them. A few families are a combination of joint and extended families. Relations within a family — especially between parent and child — are free of such constraints as fear or deference and affected modesty between husband and wife. Children are loved and cared for, and are obedient. Husband and wife, as also parents and grownup children, have relations of mutual obligations. Confrontation is not a regular feature of inter-personal relations. Grandparents and grandchildren have jocular relations, and so do a man and his elder brother's wife, while a woman has a relationship of distance with her husband's elder brother.

Customary rules of inheritance stipulate that a quarter of a dead man's property be distributed equally among his daughters, and the rest equally between the sons. After a woman dies, her property is shared equally only by her daughters. The eldest son succeeds to his father's position. Close inter-family links and interactions are in evidence at festivities, life-cycle rituals and community *pujas*. The other aspects of inter-family links, such as mutual exchange of *bagar* labour, are not practised, though they do employ fellow Musahars as daily wage labourers. On rare occasions, small amounts of money are lent to a family, which later repays the loan without any interest.

Women have multiple roles, the prime one being housework. The main social role is bringing up children. They also have an active role in the life-cycle rituals. Women are almost at par with men as earning members of the family. They work as *reja*s (daily wage labourers), though not at the same rate of payment — they get a rupee less than what a man gets. Women contribute to the family income.

After a child is born, pollution lasts seven days for family and *bhayad*. On the fifth day, a barber pares the nails of everyone and clips off a little hair from the child's head. The mother has her first bath after the delivery. On the seventh day, the barber again pares the nails of everyone and the pollution ends ritually. After a couple of months, the parents name the child, though there is no ceremony. When the child is one to one and a half years old, he gets his first taste of solid food, fed first by the parents and then by relatives in the *bhat-khawani* ceremony.

A wedding comprises several rites: three days before *biya*, *gayehalud* is held thrice a day for three days. There are songs and dances galore to the accompaniment of drums played by Muchis hired for the purpose. On the wedding day, the groom is accompanied to the bride's house by the *barjatri* (relatives and friends). The bride's family arranges for a priest and a barber to be present. The next day, the groom's family organizes *basi-biya*, and, a day later, a feast. The *mondal* of the Musahar village plays an indispensable role at a wedding.

Musahars cremate their dead. Either the eldest, or the youngest, son performs the last rites. The Musahar *mondal* officiates, and, with the help of his messengers, informs Musahars in nearby hamlets of the death. Many villagers are present at the cremation and are served alcohol by the bereaved family. After a person dies, pollution lasts ten days for family and *bhayad*. There are restrictions on certain kinds of food in this period. The *bhayad* eat vegetarian food cooked without oil or turmeric. Those that are close to the dead, for instance the sons, eat *atap* (rice dried in the sun), and molasses, without salt, and milk. On the eleventh day, a barber pares the nails of the mourners and tonsures the sons of the deceased. On the twelfth, a feast is held to end pollution ritually. A significant change in the Musahars' death rites is the presence of a Brahman priest and barber. They have also curtailed the mourning period, though in certain places, the old custom of a month of pollution is in vogue.

Though the Musahars are mainly landless, they consider land as a major economic resource. An insignificant few are individual proprietors of land. For others, the traditional, and primary, occupation is working as labourers on the agricultural land of their rich Hindu and Muslim neighbours. Their subsidiary occupations are working as daily wage non-agricultural labourers, brewing and selling illicit liquor and poaching for snake-skins and rearing pigs. Musahars are totally dependent upon markets. There are no bonded labourers among them. There has been a gradual rise in the number of Musahar labourers working on agricultural land and plantations.

Children below the age of fifteen years are often sent out to work as daily wage *reja*s (apprentice agricultural labourers) and wages are paid in both cash and kind. As non-agricultural daily wage labourers, payment is usually, only in cash. A few who are *kisan*s (seasonal agricultural labourers), are paid in terms of a share of the produce. Women and children who work as *reja*s are given a rupee or two less than men. There have been no major changes since Independence, except that a few work as menial staff in offices. Their scheduled caste status has greatly helped them get such employment.

Each Musahar hamlet has a *mondal* as chief, and the post is hereditary, passed on from father to the eldest son. One or more messengers, called *chharidars*, in each hamlet help the *mondal* convene a *majlis*, or meeting, of villagers over which he presides. These messengers have the responsibility of informing the villagers of such meetings. A *majlis* is convened when an issue concerns the wrong-doing of any Musahar. The offender is fined and the money is spent on liquor served to the assembled villagers. Musahar do not allow any member to go to court. Instead of allowing a member of the community to spend money on legal aid, the Musahars make him spend the money on themselves.

There is no traditional *gram panchayat* for settling disputes among communities. The Musahars have a lukewarm attitude towards modern statutory councils. Since Independence, the community has, somehow, maintained its old mechanism of social control and has, so far, not given in to the forces of modern, politically controlled statutory councils.

The Musahars are Hindus. Kali is a regional deity. The Musahars do talk about local shrines and pilgrimages, though the concept of pilgrimage (or *tirth*, *tirth-jatra*, or *tirth-darshan*) is not common. Some visit the *Babar-than* (shrine of the *Baba*, or Shiva) at Jamalpur, Katwa and Burdwan. Brahman priests are their religious experts. The Musahars' major fairs and festivals are all local. In *Baisakh*, the Musahars living in the neighbourhood visit a *mela* at Bishnupur Kalibari, in Behrampur. The Musahars say their major *puja* is *Surjay* puja (worship of the Sun God) in *Phalgun*, and a major festival, held at intervals of five to seven years, since it is very expensive. A Brahman priest conducts the *puja*. All the items needed for the *puja* — clothes, sacrificial goats, and, even drums — must be white and are covered with white cloth. Members of a *bhayad* jointly organize the *puja*. A major change is that Brahman priests are now their religious experts.

The Musahars have a tradition in music. *Gan-bandha* (composing songs) in traditional tunes — at weddings and other festive occasions — is quite common. Their main musical instrument is the *madal*.

The Musahars are a *jal-achal* community and social acceptance of food, in any form, by upper castes from them is beyond question. Inter-community marriages are not reported, except a few instances where the Musahars have married into their own *khunt*s, namely the Maghaiyas. The Musahars are, traditionally, barred entry into temples and houses of the upper castes, though there are no restrictions on their access to roads, schools, crematoriums, *panchayat ghar*s and wells and other water sources — the Musahars share tube wells with other low caste communities, though they do not have a chance to share these with the upper castes since the latter live away from low caste residential areas. Schools and *panchayat ghar*s are modern, secular institutions that guide the lives of the Musahars.

Traditional socio-economic inter-dependence exists between the Musahars and their Hari midwives and Muchi drummers. The Musahars' involvement in politics is minimal; they only exercise their voting rights. The Musahars main inter-community links are based on the relationship with their landowning neighbours.

The Musahars show no great interest either in literacy and education, or in health and medicare, though family planning has made some progress among them. They have no drinking water problem, since most Musahar hamlets have tube wells. They know nothing about rural employment programmes and self-employment through bank loans is a difficult feat. They are not, particularly, exposed to mass communication media. They cannot dream of installing electricity at home. They have made no conscious effort towards environmental conservation. They have no use for irrigation or fertilisers since they are landless. The Musahars pick up their rations from the public distribution system. They do not avail of banking facilities.

R. K. BHATTACHARYA

NAGAR

The Nagars are a little known community of West Bengal. They are also popularly known as Nagar-mondal or simply as Mondal in the region. They identify five subgroups among themselves, namely – (1) Nagar-mondal; (2) Chain; (3) Dhanuk; (4) Polos-nagar; and (5) Tior. Risley has described them as a "small cultivating caste of Bhagalpur and Santhal Parganas". "The affinities of the Nagars are obscure. They have lost their original sections", wrote Risley, "and the whole caste now professes to belong to the Kashyapa *gotra*, a section name borrowed from the Brahmanical System and inoperative for the purpose of controlling intermarriage. They are divided into five sub-castes – Jethaut, Pulauns, Nagbansi, Kathantia, Bhatnagar," (Risley, 1891; 120). However, today they claim themselves to be the original inhabitants of the region where they live. They are identified mainly at the local level. The ethnographic account about the community has been found to be more or less true. The Nagars perceive of their present distribution in Milkilalpur, English Bazar, Maldah proper, Dhulian, Nimtita, Bisnupur, Basudevpur, Sandaspur, Mehrapur etc. in the district of Maldah of West Bengal. According to 1931 Census their population in Bengal was 16,164. They speak the local dialect of Bengali among themselves and Bengali with others. Bengali is the only script used by them. They belong to the other backward class category of communities.

Rice and wheat are their staple food. They are non-vegetarians, but do not take beef and pork. Various types of roots and tubers are consumed generally as vegetables. Tea and milk are their common beverages. Some of the men take alcoholic drinks occasionally from the market. Many of them are habituated to smoking *bidi*s, cigarettes and chewing betel.

The subgroups mentioned above are the only social division recognised by them. Though marriage within the same group was prohibited in the past, it is not the case at present. Hierarchical differentiation among these groups is recognised at social level to regulate marriage. All of them are affiliated to Kashyap *gotra*, which has no special function. All along they have been using 'Mondal' as their only surname. They consider the Hari, Kurol, Muchi and Dom to be of lower social status than their own. They recognised the Brahman to be the only community of higher social status than themselves. All the rest of the communities of the region are treated as equals. Thus, they claim themselves to be of middle status in the regional social hierarchy. Others think of them to be neither lowly placed nor untouchables, but to be of middle social status at the regional level.

Marriage within their own community is the common practice. As has been already mentioned marriage both within and outside one's own subgroup prevails among them. Both hypergamy and hypogamy is allowed. Marriage with father's sister's daughter is not altogether absent among them, though it is not always favoured. Marriages are generally settled through negotiation after the boys and girls become adult. Excepting a few, most of the persons marry only once in their lifetime. *Sankha* (conch shell bangles) and *sindur* or vermilion are the recognised symbols of married women. *Kanyapan* or bride-price mainly in kind and a token of Rs 5/- in cash was the normal practice in the past, but of late *barpan* or dowry both in cash and kind has become the common practice among them. After marriage the bride may come to live with her in-laws along with her husband or the couple may set up their independent household separately. *Charpatra* or divorce is looked down upon in their society, and even then if any such case occurs it is never accepted cordially. Both widows and the widowers are free to remarry. A widower may marry as per his choice, whereas a widow is generally allowed to remarry a widower only. Both junior levirate or remarriage with the younger brother-in-law of the widow and junior sororate or remarriage with the younger sister-in-law of the widower prevail as preferred types of remarriage. The recent changes in the institution of marriage among the Nagars are that marriage outside one's own subgroup, comparative increase in the age at marriage for boys and girls and the practice of bride-price giving way to dowry.

Both nuclear families or the families comprising husband, wife and their unmarried children and extended families comprising either parents and their married sons or married brothers exist side by side, but the former type of family predominates. Relationship of strict avoidance is observed between a woman and her husband's maternal uncle. Relationship with elder brother's wife, younger brother and sister-in-laws and also with the parent-in-laws of sons and daughters is that of joking and friendliness. Paternal property is equally inherited by all the sons and daughters, both married and unmarried. Succession to family headship descends through male line from father to the eldest son. Comparative rise in the number of nuclear families, and equal right of inheritance even for the married daughters due to the provision made in the law are the changes noticed in the institution of family.

Apart from performing a major part of the daily household chores, women have a direct or indirect role in agriculture, animal husbandry, collection of fuel and bringing potable water. Traditionally the young women among them generally remain confined within their house and do not go out to work in the field or as wage labourers. However of late, some young women have started going out to earn for their family due to their poor economic condition. Besides these, women play important roles in the performance of most of the socio-religious rituals. They however, do not have any direct role in the political sphere and in the mechanism of social control. Women in the community enjoy equality with the men and participate in the decision making process in the family; contribute to the family income and at the same time exercise control over the expenditure of the family.

Sadhbhakshan is the only ritual associated with pregnant women, wherein they are fed with their choicest food and presented with new clothes, in the seventh month of pregnancy. Only in case of the first child the ritual is performed at her parental house. Child birth generally takes place at home, with the help of a *dai* or midwife from the Hari or Muchi community. Birth pollution is observed for twelve days. *Shashthi* or naming of the child on the sixth day, *kheuri* or purification on the twelfth day, *mundan* or tonsure of the child and *annaprashan* or first rice feeding, are the important rituals performed by the Nagars, following the birth of a child. Rituals connected with marriage are performed at the bride's residence under the *mandap* or *pandal* with the help of a Goswami Brahman priest. Marriage feast is hosted by both the parties concerned at their respective places. *Chukti* or token payment of Rs 5/- as fee for the marriage contract, *kanyadan* or ritual offering of the bride, by her father to the bridegroom in marriage, *sindurdan* or application of vermilion to the bride, *boubhat* or reception of the bride at the bridegroom's place and *ashtamangala* or return of the bride along with the bridegroom to her parental house for about a week, are the important rituals performed in connection with marriage. Under normal conditions the newly married couple consummate their marriage on the night of *boubhat* at the bridegroom's house.

The dead are cremated. However, children who die even before having the first set of teeth are buried. The ritual of *mukhagni* or offering fire to the funeral pyre is performed by the eldest son at the death of his father and by the youngest son at the death of his mother. *Asouch* or death pollution is observed for thirteen days. The person who offers fire at the funeral observes *habisi* or *dudhmukhi*, all through the pollution period, or they take self-cooked vegetarian food without oil, only once a day. The ritual of *khaurkarma* or purificatory shaving and tonsure of the primary members of the family is performed on the twelfth day. This is followed by the ritual of *agradani* or ancestral worship and offering *dan* or presentation through the Agradani Brahman or degraded category of Brahman. The Agradani Brahman is not allowed to perform any ritual inside the house. The ritual of *sradh* is performed on the thirteenth day through the Goswami Brahman priest. The things that were presented to the Agradani Brahman as *dan* namely umbrella, shoes, etc. are not used by the sons of the deceased person for a period of one year.

Land is the main natural resource of the Nagars. They are basically a landowning community, though landlessness is not altogether absent among them. Land is held under individual proprietorship. Agriculture has been their traditional primary occupation. Wage labour, petty business and service in different private and government organisations are the common secondary occupations for them. Elderly women of the community earn by selling rice, pulses, parched and puffed rice in the local market. They have direct link with the market and the mode of exchange is cash. Bonded labour does not exist among them, but their children also work to augment the family income. Payment of wages is generally in cash. Inadequate size of landholding and landlessness are the reasons for many of them to become primarily dependent on wage labour, service and petty business. The informal council of elders, headed by the *moral* or headman is the only body to deal with the problems at the community level. The members of the council are elected by voice vote. They are aware of the existence of modern statutory ., that implements welfare and development programmes of the government, for the people of the region in general. Problems of land disputes, theft, fighting, etc., within the community are dealt with by the informal council of elders by imposing cash fines or social boycott.

The Nagar profess Hinduism. Kumorparmeshi and Gramdevi are the deities recognised among them at the family and village levels respectively. Most of the deities of the wider Hindu pantheon are also recognised by them. Service of a Brahman priest is hired for the performance of rituals connected with birth, marriage and death. Kalimandir or the temple of Kali, temple of Gramdevi, temple of Manasa and other Hindu temples of the neighbourhood are sacred centres commonly visited by them. Baidyanath Dham, Gaya and Deoghar are regarded as the centres for pilgrimage. Durga puja, Kali puja or Diwali, Manasa puja, Holi and Sitala puja are their major festivals of socio-religious significance.

Decorating the floors and walls of houses with floral designs on different socio-religious occasions is the art form commonly practised by their women. There is no craft known specifically to them. Only the women sing folk songs on different socio-religious functions in the family. They do not play any musical instrument themselves but hire the Muchis to play music on the occasions of birth and marriage in the family.

Traditionally they do not accept food and water from the Teli, Hari, Muchi, Kurol and the Dom. Though all the neighbouring communities, including the Brahman accept food from them, some however, may also refuse to accept food from them, on purely personal grounds, not necessarily connected with their community affiliation. Inter-community marriages, however, are of late taking place among them but only occasionally. Putative kinship can be established with any person from the neighbouring communities through exchange of new clothes. Linkages with other neighbouring communities are reflected through amicable sharing of the water sources, religious shrines, crematorium and other public places with them. Though they do not have any specific role in the festivals, linkages with the neighbouring communities are traditionally maintained through participation in the traditional Hindu festivals. In terms of the cultivator-labourer relationship and landlord-sharecropper-tenant relationship, linkages are established with various other communities of the region. Traditional linkages with the Brahman, Napit, Hari, Muchi and other village menials are established and perpetuated through rendering and receiving of services. Of late, modern linkages with various other communities are also established through the petty businessmen, service holders, teachers and the *panchayat* level leaders of the community at their respective levels.

They have a favourable attitude towards education. Many of their boys have studied up to college level and girls up to higher secondary level. Poor economic conditions, lack of interest on the part of either parents or pupils are the common reasons behind discontinuing study. Some of the girls also are forced to dropout for the envisaged problem of getting suitable bridegroom for them. Though most of them make full use of modern medicare facilities, they have not completely discarded their indigenous medicare system. Many of them favour family planning through adoption of modern methods, including sterilization of men. Some of them still do not realise the usefulness of family planning nor favour it. Drinking water is made available to them within the locality by the statutory *panchayat* through tube wells. Though no provision of employment is made available to them under any scheme, many of them have benefited through IRDP loans in getting self-employment in agriculture, animal husbandry, confectionery and general business. They are exposed to most of the modern means of mass media and communication namely — radio, newspaper, roads, railway, post office, etc., available in the region. Electricity is not used by them due to its non-availability. Firewood, cowdung cakes, kerosene, dry leaves, and tree branches constitute their main sources of fuel. Natural rainwater still continues to be the main source of irrigation for most of them, as they can not afford to make use of the available facilities of irrigation. Both organic manure and chemical fertilisers are used by them. No provision for nutrition, either for the mother, or her children, is made available to them under any scheme. Most of them feel highly benefited by the provision of fair price shops by the government. They favour the banking system for saving and borrowing loans, but some of them still depend on the local shopkeepers and money lenders temporarily.

BADAL KUMAR BASU

NAGESIA

The Nagesias or Nagasias are "a small Dravidian tribe" of West Bengal The etymology of the name Nagasia shows that it has come from 'nag' i.e., snakes. They are locally called Nagasia-Kisan as they think both the communities have come from the same stock. Risley mentions that the Nagasia have been divided into two sub-tribes i) Telia Nagasia and ii) Sinduria Nagasia (1891:122). The present day Nagesias are aware of the above mentioned two groups but they say that at present they do not maintain any differentiation with each other. It is also mentioned that "the names Sinduria and Telia have reference to this practice. Their sections bear totemistic names which occur among the Mundas and among many other Dravidian tribes" (*ibid*). History says that the Nagesias were original inhabitants of Chhotanagpur and migrated to the different parts of West Bengal especially to the tea plantation areas of Darjeeling and Jalpaiguri in the distant past. They were brought to these regions by the British during the colonial period as tea plantation labourers and were given land for their permanent settlement. At that time they began to settle permanently in different parts of north-eastern India, stretching from the banks of the river Mechi to all the villages of Assam. The Nagesias claim that their original homeland was in the Sarguja district of Madhya Pradesh. The Nagesias know about their distribution in different parts of the districts as well as state. They are concentrated in small numbers in the different parts of Terai and Duars regions of West Bengal. At the time of marriage negotiations they at times require to go beyond the limit of their individual regions. They live in the foothills of the Himalayas, and the climate varies from moderate to cold during various seasons. There are however, dense and thin forests in some parts of their inhabited areas. Snowfall is not found in the inhabited regions of the Nagesias. According to 1981 Census their total population in West Bengal is 7745. The Nagesias speak Sadri language while they communicate with members of their own community as well as with other local tribal communities. They speak Hindi and Bengali with outsiders and use two scripts, viz., Bengali and Devanagari. Male members wear a cloth like *Kupni* or *lengti*, the length of which is about 72" and breadth about 36". Besides, they wear a turban also. Their traditional male dress is called *bhagoa*. Female members generally wear a petticoat and a blouse without any covering cloth or *sari*. But when they go outdoors they wear *saris* and ornaments made of silver, glass, etc. The community belongs to the scheduled tribe category.

The Nagesias prefer non-vegetarian dishes. But poor economic condition does not permit them to take non-vegetarian items regularly. They eat meat, pork, fowl, rat, pigeon, *ban murgi* (wild fowl), etc. They do not take beef. The Nagesias take rice as staple food. Locally available pulses, cereals, roots, tubers, vegetables, etc., are taken as food items. Locally available leafy vegetables (which grow in the wild), are their common items on the menu. These are called *jangli sak*. They take fruits on rare occasion specially apple, orange, grape, etc. Seasonal fruits like mango, jackfruit, palm, etc., which are available in the locality are taken occasionally. They can not afford milk for their children. Generally it is taken as a medically prescribed diet. Some of them take tea without milk. Both males and females take alcoholic drinks. They generally prepare *haria* (rice beer prepared with rice, water, etc.) at home, and take it very frequently. Besides, they purchase *haria* and *cholai* (country liquor) from the local markets on several occasions. Some of them prepare *cholai* in their homes. The Nagesias prepare special food on several religious occasions. At the time of *Karma* or *Karam* puja females prepare *pithe* (cake) with rice and molasses. At the time of *dausi*, i.e., at the time of Kali puja, they arrange *Banda parab* where they worship cattle and offer pigeon or cock and *haria* which are eaten afterwards by the family members. Significant change in food habits is that the Nagesias frequently take *roti* (handmade bread) of wheat or maize as staple food instead of rice. At present many of them use rapeseed oil as cooking medium in lieu of mustard oil.

The Nagesias are of two types viz., i) Sindria Nagesia, those who use *sindur* (vermilion) in their marriage ceremony and ii) Telia Nagesia; those who substitute oil instead of vermilion in the marriage ritual. Among these groups, the Telia Nagesias are considered to be a higher ritualistic group than the Sindria Nagesias. The basis of differentiation between these groups is religious. Previously these groups were not intermarrying groups, i.e., marriage alliances were restricted among them. At present they do not maintain any function of social sub-divisions. They use 'Nagasia' as their surname, which is considered as the *gotra* name also. They think that this has come from the word *nag*, i.e., snake. Some of the Nagesias mention their surname as Nagesia-Kisan as they consider that both belonged to the same stock and are considered equal. The Nagesias have no perception of the *varna* order. They say that all tribes are equal and in their tribal religion *varna* order is not recognised.

Endogamy at the community and *gotra* level is practised by them. The Nagesias do not marry their nearest blood related kin. Junior sororate and levirate are permitted among them. Marriageable age varies between eighteen and twenty-five years in case of a male and between fifteen and twenty years in case of a female. Negotiated marriage is generally preferred but marriage by mutual consent is not a taboo. Sometimes young men woo their sweethearts with offerings of flowers for their hair and present ornaments as tokens of love. Polygynous marriage is not a taboo but due to their poor economic condition almost all of them remain content with one wife. A married woman is recognised by her *sindur* on the forehead and in the parting of the hair. The Nagesias practise the custom of paying bride-price. Residence after marriage is patrilocal i.e., the wife comes to live in her husband's house. *Chutachuti* (divorce) is permitted on grounds like maladjustment between husband and wife or impotency. Young widowers or widows can remarry, but no elaborate ceremony is performed, as in the case of usual marriage. Significant changes that have been observed are that i) age of marriage has been increasing; ii) symbol of marriage is not followed just after few months of marriage and a married woman cannot be recognised by outsiders without interrogation; iii) dowry has been introduced instead of bride price.

Most Nagesia families are nuclear. Inter-personal relations within the family are based on respect and love between husband and wife and between parents and adult children; children get scolded when they do not obey the order of elders. Avoidance relation is found between husband's elder brother and younger brother's wife. Obligation is noticed between husband and wife and between adult sons and parents. Joking is permitted between husband's younger brother and elder brother's wife and between grandparents and grandchildren. Conflict and confrontation are not generally observed among them. On rare occasions conflict is noticed between husband and wife specially when husband becomes intoxicated and shows laziness in work. Male equigeniture is the common rule of inheritance and eldest son succeeds as head of the family. Inter-family linkages are based on economic assistance, mutual help and cooperation, exchange of goods, services, and participation in several festivities.

The right of inheritance has been provided to women, but they feel that they should not stake their claim after the demise of father.

Women engage themselves in the collection of fuel, fetching water and other domestic duties. They look after the children and take care of the welfare of the family members. They have innumerable roles in rituals associated with birth, marriage and death. Women perform *upas* (fasting) on different religious occasions for the welfare of self as well as of her family members. They are little interested in political activities and even a number of them do not cast their votes in elections. The Nagesia women play an important role in family management by making contributions to the family income. They are employed in tea gardens to collect tea leaves on contract, thus they earn money which is spent for the family. Besides, some of them earn money by selling *baria* in the markets and on roadsides in tea garden areas. In fact, Nagesia women are hard working and they discharge various duties and obligations in day-to-day family life.

The Nagesias observe a few pre-delivery rituals. Pregnant women do not move freely specially in the night in order to avoid evil spirits or ghosts. After conception, the members of the family pray to ancestors for a male child and easy delivery. Sometimes they sacrifice a fowl or goat for this purpose. After birth of a child, they observe three days as pollution period. The umbilical cord is cut by an old and experienced lady of their own community, either by a snail shell or a sharp piece of bamboo. The Nagesias sometimes invite a barber for birth purification. There is a special ceremony for name giving. Within six months of birth of a child they fix an auspicious day for name giving. Old members of the family as well as neighbouring lineage members are invited.to attend the ceremony. They keep water in a *thala* (plate), and then place a little *atapchal* (unboiled rice) in the water while uttering the names of forefathers. The *atapchal* is kept on the water very slowly so that the grains may float on the water. Female members from the mother's side, and male members from the father's side of the newborn baby, sit on either side of the plate. One from each side places a rice grain on the water in the plate while suggesting a name for the child. If the grain sinks the suggested name is rejected. When a grain floats on the water and touches the previous floating grains, the forefather's name which was uttered is given to the child. Besides, they may also give a name to the child based on the day of birth. For example, Somra (for male) or Somri (for female) if the child is born on a *sombar* (Monday), Mangla (for male) or Mangli (for female) if the child is born on a *mangalbar* (Tuesday), Budhua (for male) and Budhni (for female) if the child is born on a *budhbar*

(Wednesday), and so on. A major part of the marriage rituals are performed at the house of the bride. An old and experienced male member performs the marriage ceremony as priest. They perform *gayebalud* function. Bridegroom puts a drop of mustard oil or *sindur* on the forehead of the bride and then the priest touches the forehead of the bride and groom and by blessing them ensure a happy married life. *Haria* (rice beer) and meat are served as special items to all relatives, members of the groom's party and other invited guests. They sacrifice a goat at the time of the marriage ceremony. There is no *mantra* or sacred text for conducting the ritual part of marriage. The marriage ceremony is performed at night and next morning the bridegroom and bride go to the groom's house, where his parents arrange a bridal feast that night. Liquor is a compulsory item on the menu. There is no formal day for consummation of marriage.

The dead are usually cremated. Some of them bury their dead also depending on the availability of firewood and the weather. The mourning is observed for thirteen days. After death they lay the body on a common cot or cover it with a new cloth and carry it to the funeral place, escorted by those neighbours who are able to attend. Sometimes the funeral procession proceeds with music. After cremation members of the deceased collect the charred bones which are brought in an earthen vessel and kept behind the house for a few months. On an auspicious day the eldest son of the deceased throws the urn in a sacred river for peace of the deceased soul. Sometimes they invite a Napit for purificatory ceremony. He pares nails of the neighbouring lineage members and shaves the heads of the sons of the deceased. Sons keep a *tiki* (on the back of the head the Napit spares a few tufts of hair and shaves rest of the head) if either of the parents dies. On the thirteenth day of death they arrange a feast with drinks and meat and all neighbouring members and guests are invited to participate in the function. On this occasion food and drink are offered to the dead in the same way as food is given to a living being. The cremation ground is always near a river, stream or a forest. The significant change observed in funerals is that at present the Nagesias curtail many of the rituals as they think rituals are expensive. Besides, a few Nagesias observe one day's mourning period instead of thirteen days due to their poor economic condition.

Land, their main economic resource, is controlled by individual proprietors. The community is a combination of both landowning and landless people. Agriculture is the traditional occupation of the community which is considered their primary source of income. Share-cropping, day labour, tea plantation labour etc., are their subsidiary occupations. Link with markets exists directly and the medium of exchange is cash. There is no bonded labour among the Nagesias. The extent of landlessness and the number of labourers working in agriculture, plantation, etc., are comparatively high among the Nagesias. Due to poor economic condition the Nagesias are compelled to engage their children in the agricultural fields and its allied pursuits. Payment of wages is generally made in cash. Since Independence there has been a little flow of immigrant labour in the tea plantation areas. Many people from the adjoining areas have come and settled permanently, and most of them maintain their livelihood through settled cultivation. But these immigrants also engage themselves in the tea estates, where the supply of labour force is thus ensured from the surrounding region. As a result it has been seen that most of the Nagesias are poor and are not in a position to come at par with the other communities.

The Nagesias have no traditional *jati* council and regional association. In their inhabited area they select a head man who generally settles primary disputes regarding parental property, matrimonial settlement and other petty matters related to their *samaj*. There is no traditional village *panchayat* for settling disputes among various communities. Forms of punishment depend on the extent of wrongdoing. The role of modern councils is important. They keep contact with these councils for economic assistance, settling serious disputes, etc. The significant change observed is the establishment of 'Adivasi Mahasabha'. As tribal people they become members of the Mahasabha and the general secretary of the 'Adivasi Mahasabha' tries to help in their development through the Office of the Scheduled Castes and Tribes Welfare Development. At present the power of the headman has been reduced to some extent due to class consciousness and political consciousness among the people in general.

The Nagesias mainly profess Hinduism and believe in ancestor worship. The faith in spirits is most common among them. They think that man's power is restricted and that he has access to limited areas, but through ancestor worship they can acquire power of a far-reaching and compulsive kind. The spirits of ancestors are called very often and worshipped annually by them. They recognise Darha, the village god of the Munda and observe the Sarhul festival like them, (Risley: 1891: 122). Maharaja, Mahadev, Kali, etc., are considered as village and regional deities. As they profess Hinduism, all major Hindu sacred centres are regarded by them as centres for pilgrimage. No formal priest is required for their ceremonies. Charak mela, Poush mela, Rash Utsab mela, etc. are the major fairs in their inhabited areas. Besides, they organise Karam festival, Bandna Parab, etc. which are performed in different seasons in the year. Due to their Hindu religious faith the Nagesias consider Durga puja, Kali puja, Rath utsab, etc., as general community festivals. Change of religion and extent of adaptation observed are that the Nagesias believe in all Hindu gods and goddesses though they have their own belief in tribal religion and ancestor worship.

Their handicraft is limited to making and repairing a kind of *chatai* (mat) from grass. They have inherited a number of folk song, folklore etc., which are considered as oral tradition of the tribal communities. These are sung by both male and female members of the community during several festivals including lifecycle rituals. They perform music and dance at the time of singing on different religious occasions.

As a tribe, the Nagesias are considered as *jal-achal* to the Hindu castes, who do not accept *kachcha* or *pucca* food from them. The community approves inter-community marriages with the Kisans. They do not face any bar regarding access to and sharing of wells and other water sources, facilities of roads, school, crematorium, entry to temple, houses, *panchayat ghar* etc. In reality, Nagesias do not maintain any patron-client relationship. However, at present they invite Napits in their ritual ceremonies. Modern inter-community linkages are not noticed among them. Their participation in political activities was intense only during the period of the 'Naxalite Movement' which was considered as an agrarian armed revolution in West Bengal. A good number of them cultivate land on sharecropping basis and the relationship between landlord and tenant is maintained through love and mutual co-operation. Besides, a good number of them work as agricultural labourer, tea garden labourer, etc., and the relationship between the two groups is maintained by way of love, help and cooperation.

Literacy and education among the Nagesias is almost nonexistent. Poor economic condition and lack of incentives do not permit them to send their children to schools. Health and medical care is poor. Family planning has had no impact among them. Dug well water is used for drinking. Employment and self employment schemes have made little impact on the Nagesia community. Various tribal development schemes of the government have brought in improvement of a few members of the community. A negligible section of them have radio sets. Communication has improved and the villagers take advantage of the communication system. Electricity is not found in their locality. They use wood, dried leaves and twigs as fuel. Irrigation mainly depends on rainwater. They do not use chemical fertilisers and insecticides. The Nagesias complain that those who send their children to Hindi medium schools do not get any facility of nutrition programme. They avail themselves of the public distribution system. Banking facilities in terms of savings and investment have made no impact among the members of community.

SUBHRENDU MAITI

(*Top left*) A Kayastha female. (*Top right*) A Khaira Female. (*Bottom left*) A Kharwar couple. (*Bottom left*) A Khatik belle.

(*Top*) A Lalbegi couple. (*Bottom left*) A Limbu family.
(*Bottom right*) Mother and daughter: Mahar

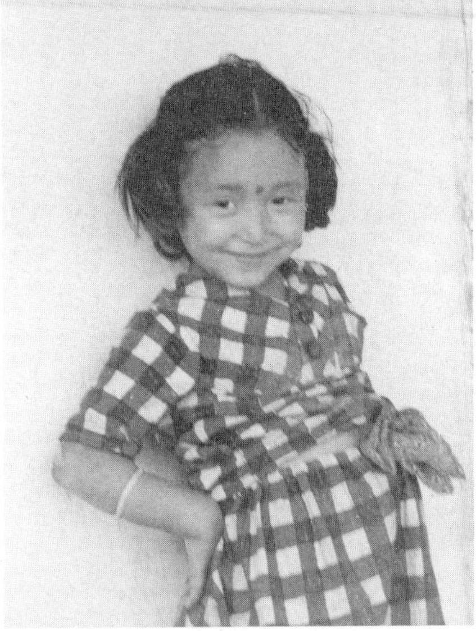

(*Top left*) A Mahishya male. (*Top right*) A Mangar girl. (*Bottom*) Craftsmen at work: Malhar.

(*Top*) Mech: traditional dance. (*Bottom*) A female weaver: Mech.

(*Top left*) A Mech family. (*Top right*) Playing on a musical instrument: Mech. (*Bottom left*) Washing clothes: a Munda mother. (*Bottom right*) A Namasudra male.

(*Top left*) A Pod male. (*Top right*) An old woman: Rabha.
(*Bottom*) Agricultural operation: Rabha

(*Top left*) A Rabha musician. (*Top right*) Busy in domestic work: Rabha women. (*Bottom*) A Santal wedding

(*Top left*) A Rajbanshi family. (*Top right*) A Subarnabanik family: . (*Bottom*) A couple: Tiyor

NAMASUDRA

The Namasudras are a well known community which previously had various synonyms like Chandal, Chanral, Nama etc. They derived their name from Namas or Lomosa Muni. They mention the names of their subgroups as Seuli, Kora, Kishoi, Nolo, Mecho, Nuni and Chasi. According to their own version of the history of their origin, they were born of a marriage between a brother and a sister (who were the son and daughter of Namasa Muni), whom Namasa Muni imprecated to become Chandal caste due to violation of rule. Children born of this marriage are the ancestors of the Namasudra caste. There is another history of the Namasudras that they were a non-Aryan caste of eastern Bengal, engaged for the most part in beating drums and cultivation. The derivation of the name Chandal is uncertain and it is possible conjecture that it may have been like Sudra, the tribal name of one of the aboriginal races whom the Aryans found in possession of the soil. Unlike the Sudras, the Chandals were debarred from entering even the outer circles of the Aryan house, and from the earliest times they are depicted by Sanskrit writers as an outcaste and helot people, performing menial duties for the Brahmans, and living on the outskirts of cities, apart from the dwellings of the dominant race. They are distributed today in the whole of West Bengal. Their main concentration may be found in the district of 24-Parganas. Many of them have migrated from the east and all are living in the plains having a moderate rainfall and high humidity. Their population figure, according to 1981 Census, is 1,692,233 in West Bengal. Their language and script in all respects is Bengali. Their constitutional status is that of a scheduled caste. The Namasudras in Bengal are of low height (short stature) medium head form (mesocephalic) and medium nose form (mesorrhine) according to D. N. Majumder and C. R. Rao (1960).

Vegetable consumption of the Namasudras is moderate. They are a regular non-vegetarian, but do not consume beef, pork or buffalo. Their staple food is rice along with vegetables and pulses of various types. They cook food in mustard oil and rapeseed oil. They take tea, milk and milk products. They consume seasonal fruits occasionally. Many of their men consume alcoholic drinks regularly purchased from the market. They chew *pan*, smoke *bidis* and cigarettes, and use snuff.

The Namasudras are divided into seven distinct social divisions such as Sonuli, Kora, Kishore, Nolo, Mecho, Nuni and Chasi. All these divisions are occupational, but they are not sure about the hierarchy of these subdivisions. These groups are not endogamous today. According to the Namasudras themselves they have two clans; Kashyap and Shiva. Their surnames are Mondal, Biswas, Sarkar, Sardar, Kirotonia etc. The community perceives their low Sudra rank and places themselves in the Sudra group. The others also place them in the same rank.

The Namasudras practise endogamy at the community level. Their clan is both exogamous and endogamous. When the clan is endogamous they avoid five ascending generations of the father in marriage. They practise adult marriage. Negotiation is their primary mode for acquiring mate. Monogamy and junior sororate are the rules of marriage. Dowry is paid both in cash and kind. Patrilocal residence is the rule of residence after marriage. Divorce is permitted and both the partners can seek divorce with judicial approval. Divorce compensation is given to the aggrieved party. Children are the responsibility of either father or mother or both. Remarriage is permissible in all cases. Increase of age at marriage, strict observance of marriage symbols and bride price giving way to dowry are changes in their marriage customs.

The Namasudra families are mostly of the nuclear type. Some vertically extended families also exist. Avoidance relation is maintained between *bhasur* (husband's elder brother) and *bhadrabau* (younger brother's wife), between *mamasasur* (mother-in-law's brother) and *bhagnebau* (sisters son's wife). Respectful relation is maintained between parents-in-law and their sons-in-law and daughters-in-law. Joking relation is maintained between brother-in-law and his wife's brothers and sisters, between elder brothers wife and husband's younger brother and between grandparents and grandchildren, Conflict arises in the family due to unjustified division of parents property, restriction on the freedom of youngsters, challenge to the authority of elders. The rule of male equigeniture is followed in dividing parental property. The eldest son succeeds his father as the head of the family. Inter-family linkages are also maintained on every ceremonial occasion like birth, marriage and death and religious rituals like Satyanarayan puja, Lakshmi puja etc. Rise in the number of nuclear families and decline in that of vertically extended families are the changes in family structure.

The Namasudra women do not get their father's property. Their women have a role in agriculture, bringing potable water, animal husbandry and in other external activities like service, mid-wife's job, maid servant's jobs etc. Some weave mats at home. They have roles in ritual and social ceremonies. Their status is equal to that of men. They contribute their income to the family budget, and have power to control family expenditure.

The Namasudra observe pre-delivery restriction on food, and movement of pregnant women, and observe rituals like *sadhbhakshan* (special food items cooked for the pregnant woman in an auspicious month of pregnancy and on an auspicious day). They observe a pollution period of twenty-one days for a male child and thirty days for a female child, after birth and call it *phulasouch*. Mother and newborn baby become purified after three *kaman* rites (i.e., cutting nails and taking bath and holy water or *santi jal* from a temple). The last *kaman* is done on the last day of the pollution period, when *puja* is also offered to Shashthi. One *kaman* is done on the day after birth, and another on the ninth day called '*natta*'. They perform another rite on the sixth day after birth called '*chhayrate*'. A pregnant woman can not cross a river on the day of full moon or on the day of new moon. If she has to go anywhere she must keep some '*bel*' leaves (marmelos leaves) or *tulsi* (basil) with her. They have *annaprashan* (first feeding of rice) or *mukhebhat* ceremony. There was a custom of *ditiyobiya* (second marriage) when child marriage was prevalent. *Ditiyobiya* was performed after marriage, after the first menses. Their marriage follow the rites like *ashirbad* (blessing of bride and bridegroom by elderly person in both the houses), *gayehalud* (smearing turmeric paste on the bride and bridegroom), *abhuti* (oblation to the ancestors), *sampradan* (giving the daughter in marriage), *boubhat* (first serving of rice by the newly married bride, to relatives and friends in her father-in-law's house) and *phulsajjya* (bride and bridegroom spending the night on a floral bed). The marriage rituals are performed in both the bride and bridegroom's houses. A *Chhatnatala* (*pandal* or marriage booth) is also erected in the bride's house. Feasts are arranged in both the houses. The nuptial ceremony is performed in bride's mother's residence. They do not have the custom of confining the bride and bridegroom in '*basar*' (a room for keeping bride and bridegroom awake for the first night of marriage), because of the *Manusamangal* story of Behula and Lakshminder in which Lakshminder was bit by a snake while in the '*basar*'. During their marriages, the paternal grandfather's father whom they call *pothakurdada*, *matul* (maternal uncle) and *barajamai* (eldest son-in-law) have some special functions. *Pothakurdada* and *matul* must only be present and the *barajamai* is supposed to go through the *baran* ceremony (formal reception) first, before the new bridegroom. They have a system of making ceremonial friendship in marriage. After returning of the bride to her father's house (after three or five or seven days after *phulsajjya*) with the bridegroom, they both visit any one's house together without wearing any footwear. This function is known as *dhulapaye lagan deoa*.

The Namasudras cremate their dead in a burning *ghat*. They observe a pollution period of eleven days after death. They perform *dasa* (tenth day's rite) on the tenth day after death, which is also known as *'ghatkaman'* performed on the bank of a river or pond. In this rite they shave their hair and pare their nails, and give *pinda* to the deceased. On the eleventh day they perform *sradh* ceremony. The twelfth day is known as *jiren* (i.e., stoppage of all work). On the thirteenth day they perform *terodosa*. On this day they cook fish or other non-vegetarian food for the first time after death in the family and on third day they invite their relatives (*jnati*). They have also annual *sradh* ceremony known as *bachhar kri*. During the pollution period after death, they take only *'habisi'* (*arua* sun-dried rice boiled with vegetables in an earthen pot). The sons of the deceased wear *kachha* (a white and new cloth) during pollution period. Ancestors are worshipped in *sradh* ceremony. Bones are thrown in water. These rituals are being curtailed nowadays days, as they are becoming expensive.

The Namasudras are mainly a landowning community. They also have among them a large number of day labourers, who have come from the east and settled in many districts of West Bengal. In lower Bengal some are also engaged in *jalkar* (fish cultivation in stagnant water in paddy fields) as owners. Besides agriculture, they serve as day labourers in agricultural fields and brick fields. Some are service holders and businessmen; some are in the occupation of *bidi* binding and mat weaving. Some also know the art of image making, masonry, carpentry etc. They are directly linked with the daily or weekly market. Their wages are paid in cash.

The *jati panchayat* of the Namasudras does not exist any more. They are now living under the control of modern *gram panchayat*, which implements the government's plans and programmes for the general welfare of villagers; and also tries to settle disputes over land, property and theft etc.

Hinduism is the religion of the Namasudras. Many of them have embraced Vaishnavism and are followers of the Matua sect. Their family rituals are Bhagabati puja in the month of *Baisakh* (April-May), Manasa, Sitala, Bipadtarini, Itu or Ghot and Lakshmi puja on every Thursday. On the day of Poush-Sankranti i.e., the last day of the Bengali month of *Poush* (December-January) they observe *pitha parab* ceremony. Bastu puja is also a very important festival of the Namasudras. Their village deities are Manasa, Basanti, Shiva, Kali, Saraswati, Durga etc. They also observe Dak-Sankranti or 'Dhane Sadh' on the last day of the month of *Ashwin* (September-October). On this occasion they offer the paddy plant various kinds of food items, like *'sadh'* ceremony of a pregnant woman, for better yield. Durga, Kali, Saraswati, Bipadtarini etc., are their deities of the wider Hindu pantheon. Places like Puri, Nabadwip, Tarakeswar, Mayapur, Deoghar etc., are their sacred centres for pilgrimages. Their sacred specialist is a Brahman priest. Their major fairs take place on the occasion of Charak, Baruni mela and Rathayatra. The Matua sect, organised in the late nineteenth century by Sri Harichand Thakur and his son Sri Guruchand Thakur, has been a remarkable socio-religious movement among the Namasudras. Following the *sahajiya* tradition, the Matua philosophy discarded casteism and preached equality of all human beings. Consequently it became popular among the people of lower order in Bengal. Recently, since 1986, there has been an attempt to revitalise the sect and give it an organisational form in the shape or Matua Mahasangha, with it's headquarter at Thakurnagar in the district of North 24 Parganas. Mat weaving is their only traditional craft.

The community has traditional inter-community linkages, as they are served by the Brahman priest, and barber. They establish putative kinship during marriage. Inter-community marriages are very few among them. They do not face away trouble in sharing wells, water sources, roads, schools, temples and crematorium etc. They exchange water, and *kachcha*, *pucca* and *siddha* food with other communities like the Brahman, Kayastha, Baiti etc. They exchange these with the Baiti, Pod etc., but they do not give *sidha* food to the Muchi, Dom etc. There is no *jajmani* system at present. They sometimes maintain sharecropper-landowner relationship by giving half of the produce. Cultivator-labour relationship is maintained by payment of wages in cash and it varies from season to season and place to place, from Rs. 12/- to Rs. 15/- per day. The modern inter-community linkages are also very prominent, as their children are going to schools and collages, some are office goers and they have contact with middlemen, owners of brick fields, paddy fields and *jalkars* etc. They have scholars, teachers, doctors, administrator, engineers and political leaders among them.

Educationally the Namasudras are sometimes very advanced and sometimes totally illiterate. They are availing themselves of the educational grants for the scheduled castes. Both traditional and modern medicare facilities are used by them. They prefer up to three children. They use tube well water for drinking. They take loans for self-employment through IRDP or DRDA programme. They communicate by bus, train, cinema, television, newspaper etc. They use electricity. As fuel they use wood, cowdung cake, coal, kerosene etc. They irrigate their fields with rainwater and from shallow tube wells. They use chemical fertilizers and insecticides for better crops. They get their rations from fair-price shops and avail of banking facilities.

CHANDRIMA CHOWDHURY

NAPIT

The Napit is a *nabasakha* group of West Bengal. Risley mentions several titles like Barik, Bhandari, Baidya, Khyaurakar, Nara-sundar, Paramanik, etc. which "are borne only by Napits who practice medicine" (1891 : 112) some of the titles referred to by Risley are used as surname and these are not to be considered as title at present. According to Risley (1891: 124) the Napits of West Bengal were of fourteen subgroups: Anarpuria, Bamanbene, Barendra, Uttar-rarhi, Dakshin-rarhi, Paschim-rarhi, Mahmudabaz, Samtagram, Khotta, Haldar-Paramanik, Kolia-Paramanik, Hansedaha-Paramanik and Mujganji-Paramanik. The present day Napits of West Bengal are not aware of all there groups. They maintain that they have seven groups which are Barendra, Uttar-rarhi, Dakshin-rarhi, Paschim-rarhi, Satgharia, Haldar-Paramanik and Hansedaha-Paramanik. The last two groups are found in 24-Parganas and the remaining five are found in other parts of West Bengal. Risley says *(ibid)*. "Napit, the barber caste of Bengal, descended, according to one opinion from a Kshatriya father and Sudra mother, and according to Parasara from Kuveri father and Pattikar mother. Some, again, ascribe the origin of the caste to an act of special creation on the part of Shiva, undertaken to provide for the cutting of his wife's nails". All are myths regarding the origin of the Napit community. Risley also mentions that "the caste is clearly a functional group, formed in all probability from the members of respectable castes who in different parts of the country adopted the profession of barbers" *(ibid)*. The Napits are aware of their present day distribution in different districts of the state. At the time of marriage negotiation they at times enquire about their groups and sometimes go beyond the limit of the individual districts. Areas inhabited by the community are warm and temperate and are the plains of eastern India. Humidity is high during summer and rainfall is medium to high. As per the 1931 Census the total population of the Napits in West Bengal was 451,068, their maximum concentration being in the district of Midnapore (36, 047). The written and spoken language of the members of this community both at home and outside is Bengali. The male members while moving round for their profession carry several instruments like razors, scissors, *narul* (nail cutter), in a small bag which sometimes identifies them as members of the Napit community. The community is an other backward class.

The Napits are non-vegetarian i.e., they eat fish, egg, meat of goat, ram and fowl. They do not eat pork, boal fish, *chang* fish and *sal* fish. Their staple food is rice, and cooking medium mustard oil. Pulses like *masur, kolai, mug, khesari*, etc., are eaten by them. Roots, tubers and bark used as food items are ginger, garlic, turmeric, potato, yam, *kochu*, *thore* (inner stem of the banana trunk), etc. Besides, throughout the year they eat a variety of leafy vegetables. Seasonal fruits are taken occasionally and as medically prescribed diet. Tea is their common drink. Milk is considered as a nourishing drink and it is taken especially by the children and old people. Light home made alcoholic drink known as *tari* (made of date palm or palm juices) is taken by a good number of adult male members. Alcoholic drinks available in the local markets and *bhatikhanas*, are also consumed frequently by the male members.

Women observe *brato*, *upas* and prepare several food items on certain *tithis* and in certain seasons. There are also a number of restrictions as regards items of food which are not eaten on several *tithis* and in several seasons. They do not eat *kalmi sak* (a kind of leafy vegetable) in the month of *Bhadra* (Bengali month). At the time of *Janmastami* (birth day of Lord Srikrishna) they prepare *naru* (made of coconut and sugar/ *gur*) and several items like *chal bhaja*, fried gram, pea, ground nut, etc. which are offered in the name of Lord Krishna, and afterwards distributed to all family members. Females also observe *brato* on that day. Males are not very particular in observing restrictions on food items.

It is already mentioned that the Napits of West Bengal have been divided into fourteen subgroups, though they maintain only seven groups at present. All the subgroups are primarily based upon territorial distinctions and refer to the early settlements of certain *amin* divisions of the caste. Among these divisions the Uttar-rarhi Napits claim to be of a higher rank than the Dakshin- and Paschim-rarhi, and support their claim by the tale that "one of their ancestors was so skilful an operator that he used to shave the Raja of Nadia without waking him" (Risley: 1891: 125). The three Rarhi sub-castes are not strictly hypergamous and these three groups intermarry. Risley *(ibid)* writes about the Anarpuria Napits who are differentiated on the basis of occupational practices. Anarpuria Napits do not practice the profession of the caste but make their living by trade, medicine and clerical works. The Napits of West Bengal generally use the following surnames in different parts of the state: Manna, Pramanik, Barik, Khawash, Rana,

Halder, etc. Pramanik and Barik are the most common surnames among the Napits of Medinipur. A few *gotras* like Moudgolla, Karkota, Kashyap, etc., are found among the Napits of Medinipur. All the *gotras* are totemic. Some of the Napits claim that their main mantra is Krishna *mantra*.

The social standing of the Napit caste is high. They are included in the standard couplet of 'Parasara' defining the *nabasakha* group, and Brahmans take water from their hands. As per local social hierarchy they are subordinate to the Brahman, the Vaidya, the Karan, the Mahishya and the Kayastha. They are superior to the scheduled castes and scheduled tribes. The Napits have no clear concept of their position in Hindu *varna* order. However some of them claim that they belong to the Sudra order due to their occupational practices; the claim is generally acknowledged by the local Hindu castes. The community's role and function in various ritual ceremonies are many in terms of their traditional caste occupation.

The Napits practice clan exogamy. They marry neither their lineage members nor blood-kin. Age at marriage for males varies from twenty-one to twenty-five years, and for females, sixteen to twenty-one years. In some of the interior rural areas age of marriage comparatively goes down for both the sexes. The socially sanctioned mode of acquiring mates is through negotiation. Monogamy is the general from of marriage; however polygyny is practiced when first wife is barren. A married woman is recognised by the *sindur* (on the forehead and in hair parting) and *sankha* (conch-shell bangle). Sometimes *palar churi* (lac bangle) is also considered a marriage symbol. The Napits practice dowry both in cash and kind. Their residence after marriage is patrilocal. Divorce is permitted among them, due to reasons like adultery, maladjustment, cruelty and insanity. In such cases compensation is given to the wife's parents. A male can remarry as a young widower, or in case his first wife is barren. But in such cases no elaborate ceremony is observed.

The Napits live in nuclear and mixed extended families. Interpersonal relations within the family are close-knit. Relation between husband and wife rests on love, respect and mutual co-operation. Besides, the wife does not publicly demonstrate her close relationship with the husband. Sometimes, she maintains a distance from the other family members and expresses womanly coyness to her husband. Relationship between parents and children is of love and affection. Avoidance relationship is found between husband's elder brother and younger brother's wife, and joking relationship is found between husband's younger brother and elder brother's wife, and between grandchildren and grandparents. Conflicts and confrontations arise due to unequal distribution of property, and restricting the freedom of youngsters. Sons inherit their parental property. Succession is patrilineal. Inter-family linkages are of mutual cooperation and dependence. Besides, exchange of daily essential commodities between and among the family members of the Napit society is a common occurrence. Sometimes, exchange of curry and rice is observed if relatives arrive suddenly at lunch or dinner time. Rising tendency towards formation of nuclear families is the significant change among the Napit community.

Women do not inherit parental property under normal circumstances though the Napits are aware of a daughter's legal claim over her parental property. Women play their respective role in domestic chores. In her social role she is also responsible for rearing children and looking after the general welfare of the family. She actively participates in a number of rituals associated with birth, marriage and death. Her religious role is specific and is performed through the observance of *brata* and *upos* on certain occasions for the welfare of her near and dear ones. Women do not actively participate in political activities except casting their vote at elections. In general, women do not have any scope to earn through employment or to contribute such earnings to their family budget. In fact women enjoy only a few rights, though their duties and obligations as per social norms are explicit and many.

The Napits observe twenty-one days as birth pollution period. The mother and her newborn baby observe one month as pollution period which is called *antur*. On that day one of the members of the Napit community comes and pares nails of the mother and her child. The umbilical cord is cut by the *daima* who belongs to the Hari community. The Napits invite an Acharya Pandit or a *jyotish* to prepare a horoscope of the newborn baby. They arrange a special ceremony for name giving. The Acharya Pandit gives a specific name to the child in consultation with the elder members of the family. Name giving ceremony is done within the six months of age of a newly born child. *Annaprashan* ceremony is observed when the male child is six months old, and seven months old for a female child. The first morsel of food is customarily given into the mouth of the child by his *mama* (maternal uncle). The family priest is called to perform the ritual associated with the ceremony. On that day they invite a male member from their own community who shaves the head of the child. The midwife is an invitee guest on that day. On that day the father of the child arranges a feast where neighbours, friends and relatives are invited.

Two days before the marriage the prospective bridegroom and bride, through her guardians, perform *nandimukhi sradh* for the propitiation of their ancestors. This is followed on the next day by *adhibas*, and on the wedding day, the bridegroom is smeared seven times with turmeric and mustard oil, and after bathing he is dressed in a red silk wrapper. The bride is also smeared with turmeric paste and mustard oil. This ceremony is performed by married women whose husbands are alive. A Brahman priest solemnizes the marriage ceremony by uttering *mantras* or sacred texts. After marriage the bride and the bridegroom are taken to the *basarghar*, where they spend the night in the company of a number of young women, friends of the family, who enjoy the privilege of teasing the bridegroom. Next day morning the bride is taken to the bridegroom's house where she stays for a week, and consummation usually takes place on the third day of marriage. On that day the bridegroom's father arranges a feast which is known as *boubhat*.

The dead body is cremated, and after the death of a person his family and the neighbouring lineage members observe a month's pollution. In the deceased's family cooking is prohibited for three days after the death. On the fourth day they ceremonially start cooking and observe a ritual ceremony known as *chaturtha*. Only lineage members are invited to take food that evening. If any unmarried person dies, the cremation ground is kept on watch for three consecutive nights with a view to stop any evil activity by the *tantriks*. Thirty days after the death, *ghat* (taking ritual dip after shaving and paring nails by all the lineage male members of the deceased) ceremony is performed and on the 31st day they observe *pindadan* and *sradh* ceremony in an orthodox fashion. This ceremony is presided over by a Brahman priest. The day after *sradh*, a feast known as *aspanna* is arranged to mark the day from which onwards the mourners are allowed to eat normal food. The Napits sometimes curtail various rituals, due to their poor economic conditions, and increasing prices.

The Napits consider land as their major economic resource. Control over land lies in the hands of individual proprietors. The community has a combination of landowning and landless people. The traditional occupation of the community is that of barber i.e., nail paring, hair cutting, ear-cleaning, shampooing and body massaging.

The primary occupation is cultivation, especially for those who own land. The traditional occupation as well as day labour, rickshaw pulling, etc., have now become subsidiary occupations among a number of members of the Napit community. Their traditional occupation is maintained through *jajmani* system, i.e., in the house of the neighbouring communities the barber ship is often considered as a hereditary post as is that of the Brahman priest, *dhopa* and *dai*. Besides, their traditional occupation is dependent on markets (for shaving, hair cutting and the like), as they also set up shops, hair dressing saloons, etc., in the markets and other urban areas, and remunerations are paid in cash. Their traditional occupation is sometimes considered as a business especially when their services are required at different ritual ceremonies connected with birth, marriage and death. The Napits have no bonded or child labour among them. A good number of them are landless and as a result they are found to be engaged as agricultural labourers, day labourers, etc., by the neighbouring landowning families. Payment of wages is both in cash, and kind. The Napits pare the nails of Hindu females as well as males and their presence is required on various family occasions. After birth of a child he pares the nails of the mother as well as her baby and ceremonially makes them free from the birth pollution. At the houses of Muslims he is also present on a specific day of the pollution period. In several ritual ceremonies the Napits get money, new clothes and other necessities like rice, pulses, oil, salt, and turmeric, etc. At marriages, as has been mentioned above, their presence is essential and "for some castes he performs the function of a priest" (Risley: 1891: 128). At present the educated Napits have gone in for various services like teaching, clerical jobs, factory work, etc.

The traditional *jati* council is nonexistent among the Napits. The modern statutory council is important among them. They keep contact with the members of the modern statutory council's members for economic assistance, settling disputes (mainly property and other serious family matters), etc. Small feuds, matrimonial disputes, etc., are primarily settled by their own community members. Some times they take help from old people and other educated persons of neighbouring communities. Social boycott and cash fines are the primary forms of punishment. Adultery, rape, theft, etc., are considered as serious offences. All these offences are mainly settled by the *panchayat* members of the locality. Giving social prestige is considered a reward by the members of the Napit community.

The community professes Hinduism. Risley writes "most Napits are Vaishnavas, and comparatively few Saktas or Saivas are found among the caste" (*ibid*, p. 127). Family deities of the Napits seem to be Damodar (Narayan) *sila*, Shasthi and Lakshmi who are propitiated on certain days and on certain *tithis*. Sitala, Basudhara, Shiva, Mahamaya, Hari, etc., are considered as village and regional deities. All major Hindu sacred centres and shrines are regarded as potential centres for pilgrimage by the members of the Napits. They employ Brahman as priests, who are received on equal terms by other members of the sacred caste. In Medinipur the major fairs are Baisakhi mela, Rather mela, Rashmela, Poush mela, Shiva Chaturdasi mela and Charak mela. Some of the Napits are at present found to be observing Vishvakarma puja due to their occupational practice i.e., barber ship. Besides, they observe Durga puja, Kali puja, etc., as general community festivals. At present Santoshi *mata* puja has become popular among the married women of the Napit community. This is held on Fridays. Except for a brief period in the early part of this century, the Napits have not attempted to organise any socio-religious movement in terms of claiming any higher status in the social hierarchy.

In different saloons and hair dressing centres the Napits make various styles of hair cutting and dressing among the younger generations which are borrowed by the today's youth from the film stars. Before dressing hair they ask the customers about their choice of hair style and do so as per their instructions. These designs may be considered as art of the Napit community. Besides, ladies at present prefer several hair styles, like V cut, U cut, Bob cut, etc., in beauty parlours where a good number of Napits work, or run the business. In ritual ceremonies especially in death, the male Napits make *fulghat* (made of banana bark and sticks) which is offered to the deceased by married daughters at the time of *sradh*. This offering is done with the help of Brahman priest by chanting sacred texts. The Napit have specific oral traditions which are observed at the time of marriage ceremonies. They utter several folk tales, rhymes, etc., at the time of marriage and tease both bride and bridegroom with practical jokes.

The Napits of West Bengal are considered an important functional community and accordingly they have a greater linkage with almost all Hindu communities in respect of life cycle rituals. Besides, they are considered as a member of the *nabasakha* group and as a result they maintain a good network of relationships with the neighbouring communities through various social and occupational purposes. They are considered as *jal-chal* group. Ritual-based kinship like *dharambhai*, *kaka*, etc., is found among a good number of the Napits. The community faces no problems regarding access to and sharing of wells and other water sources, facilities of road, school, and entry to temples, houses, *panchayat ghar*, etc. The community has separate crematorium. A good number of Napit families have specific relation with several communities and this relation is maintained through generations on the basis of *jajmani* system. In general the Napits do not show special interest in direct political participation except exercising their right of voting at elections. However they show interest in political discussions, and are aware of the present political situation. Except some perfunctory attempts in the early part of this country, the Napits have attempted to organise any ethnic movement claiming higher status and higher social position in the caste hierarchy of West Bengal. A good number of Napits work as sharecroppers, and as a result maintain good relations with landowning families of neighbouring communities. Relationship between cultivator and labour is based upon mutual respect and cooperation. Those who are engaged in labour earn their wages both in cash and kind. In times of crisis especially in the months of *Bhadra*, and *Ashwin* (Bengali months), sharecroppers and labourers face economic problems, and as a result take paddy, rice, money, etc. as *dadan* (short term loan) from landholding families. This is repaid after harvesting season, sometimes also through manual labour.

Though a few of the male Napits are literate, yet they are educationally backward. This is perhaps due to their poor economic condition and lack of incentives. Health and medical care is poor. Only a few of them take interest in family welfare programme. Tube wells in the adjacent areas have solved the problem of drinking water. Employment in government schemes has made little impact upon them. Food for work scheme has also made a small impact. Self-employment schemes have not created any headway among them as most of them complain that they are hardly considered by the authorities in terms of sanctioning their schemes and providing with loans. Transistors are used by a small number of families. They take advantage of the mechanised transport system. Electricity is not found in the Napit inhabited areas. Straw *lara* (lower portion of the straw), dried bamboo leaves and barks, broken twigs of trees, *patkati* (jute sticks), cowdung cake, *tus* (bran), *cigra* (husk of paddy), etc., are used as fuel. Irrigation depends only on rain water. Those who own land, show a positive attitude towards use of chemical fertilisers and insecticides. But most of the time they use organic manures like cowdung, ash, etc. Nutrition programmes are not run systematically for school children. The villagers collect rice, wheat, rapeseed oil, kerosene, etc. from the ration shops. The Napits do not have much inclination towards saving and investment in the locally available banks.

SUBHRENDU MAITI

NAT

The Nats are "a dancing and musician caste" of West Bengal having synonym 'Natta'. The word Nat has probably come from *'nattak'* or *'natak'*, i.e., performance or performer of drama, dance, music, etc. The Nats have migrated from different parts of Bangladesh to various areas of West Bengal in the early part of the twentieth century. Risley says "Nar, Nat, Nartak or Natak is a dancing and musician caste of Eastern Bengal" (1891: 129). History reveals that "the Nats were brought to Bengal from Bihar during indigo plantations and they gradually turned to agricultural labourers" (Das: 1966). This contention is not supported by the present day Nats of West Bengal. The Nats are predominantly distributed in the districts of West Dinajpur, Darjeeling (Siliguri region), Jalpaiguri, Koch Behar, Nadia and its adjoining areas. They live in the plains of West Bengal where the climate is warm and temperate. Rainfall is medium and the humidity rises high during summer. As per 1981 Census, the total population of the Nats in West Bengal is 3376. Principal language is Bengali which is spoken at home as well as with outsiders. They use the Bengali script. The constitutional status of the community is scheduled caste.

The Nats are non-vegetarian. They prefer tortoise meat, but they do not eat pork or beef. Rice is their staple food. Locally available food grains, roots, tubers, vegetables etc., are generally eaten by them. Fruit and milk are taken as a nourishing and medically prescribed diet. The Nats use mustard oil for cooking. A majority of them drink tea. Alcoholic drinks are normally avoided, though it is not a taboo. Female members prepare several food items on certain occasions and in certain seasons. They also observe several beliefs regarding taking of and restriction on food items related to several *tithis* and days. For example on the day of Lakshmi *purnima* and on Sundays, female members prepare *naru*, a sweet made of coconut/*til* and sugar. The devotees of Sri Sri Anukul Thakur take vegetarian food.

The Nats have been divided into four groups viz. i) the Manchrang Nat or those who perform *natak* (drama etc.) in the *rangamanch* (theatre or stage); ii) the Gawar Nat or those who perform dance, music and organise *band party* in several rituals and festive occasions; iii) the Bratya Kshatriya or those who maintain their livelihood through other occupations different from those two professions; and iv) the Karwal Nat or who were once proclaimed as a criminal group. Among these four groups the Manchrang Nats seem to be higher in status than the other three groups due to their rich professional activities. Hierarchically the Gawar Nats are in the second position as they assist the actors by performing music. The Bratya Kshatriya Nats are in the third position as they live by occupations which are not regarded as the traditional among them. The Karwal Nats once maintained their livelihood by criminal activities and accordingly they are considered as a distinctive caste, believed to posses the stigma of pollution by Javeh as conceived by the above three groups. The basis of differentiation among the Nats is occupational. Natta is their popular surname though a good number of them use several surnames like Nandy, Sarkar, Barman, Ray, etc. Clans like Kashyap, Aliman, Bharadwaj, etc., are found among the Nats of West Bengal. The community members claim their position to be Sudra which is acknowledged by the other communities too. The role or function of the community in the social hierarchy is not explicit.

The Nats practise both clan endogamy and exogamy. The age at marriage ranges between twenty-one and twenty-six years for boys, and for girls it varies between sixteen and twenty-one years. Marriage by negotiation is their mode of acquiring mates. Monogamy is their general form of marriage, and a married woman is recognised by her *sindur* and *sankha*. Previously payment of bride-price was the practise but at present that has given way to dowry. After marriage the wife comes to live in her husband's house, and she becomes a member of her husband's family. Divorce and remarriage are permitted by them, but not unless it is absolutely essential. Adultery and impotency are the primary reasons for divorce. A young widow, widower, male or female divorcee can remarry, but no elaborate ceremony is observed in such cases. Previously the Nats preferred child marriage but at present adult marriage is their common custom. Besides, inter-community marriages are permitted among members of the Nat community nowadays.

The Nats live in nuclear and mixed extended families. Inter-personal relations are close-knit. Relationship between husband and wife is maintained through love, respect and mutual co-operation. Avoidance relationship is found between husband's elder brother and younger brother's wife and between father-in-law and son's wife. Relationship between parents and sons depends on love, respect and moral obligation. Joking is permitted between elder brother's wife and husband's younger brothers and sisters. Conflicts and confrontations arise due to unequal distribution of parental property, and challenge to the authority of elders. Sons inherit the parental property and succession follows the male line. Inter-family linkages are based on mutual co-operation and exchange of goods and services.

Under normal circumstances women do not get any share of parental property. Through collection of fuel, fetching of drinking water, etc., they play their economic role. In social life women take a keen interest in rearing children and look after the welfare of their family members. They play a specific role in a number of rituals connected with birth, marriage and death. Their religious role is performed through *brata*, *upos*, etc., and through preparation of several food items on certain occasions. Women do not take an active part in political activities, except exercising adult franchise. A few women earn money through employment, but in general they do not take any part in controlling family expenditure. It can be said that women enjoy few rights, though their duties and obligations as per social norms are many and explicit.

The Nats observe a few pre-delivery rituals. Pregnant women are not allowed to move freely outside, or do any heavy household work. *Sadh* is given on an auspicious day in the fifth, seventh, or ninth month of pregnancy. It is given by the parents of the pregnant woman. After the birth of a child the Nats observe one month as pollution period. The umbilical cord is cut by a *dhatri* (midwife) who generally belongs to their own community. On the sixth day of birth they arrange *chhay Shashthi* for the welfare of the newly born child. All family members take vegetarian dishes for one month. Used earthenware from the kitchen is thrown away in a selected place after the birth of a child. Services of a Napit and a *Dhopa* are required for the birth purificatory ceremony. *Annaprashan* is observed after six months of birth in case of a male child, and in the seventh month in case of a female child. The head of the child is shaved by a barber, and the family priest is invited to perform the ritual part of the ceremony. The grandfather puts the first morsel of food into the mouth of the child and then the maternal uncle gives *payesh* (a sweet dish of *atàp chal* or sun-dried rice, milk and sugar) into the mouth of the child. He presents new clothes, ornaments, utensils and sweets to the child. On the day of *annaprashan* the family members organise Narayan puja or Mahaprabhu puja for the welfare of the newborn. Marriage is an elaborate and long ceremony of rituals consisting of *gayehalud*, *nandimukh*, *sradh*, *adhibas*, *biyia*, *basibiye* and *boubhat*. A Brahman priest solemnises marriage before a *hom* or sacred fire. *Sindurdan* is an important ceremony in the marriage ritual. It is done on the day of *basibiye* (second day morning) by the husband who puts *sindur* (vermilion) in the hair parting of the bride three times, with help of a gold ring or an iron instrument while uttering sacred *mantras*. Then elder female relatives put *sindur* on the bride's forehead, and in her hair parting, blessing her and wishing her a happy married life. Services of a Napit are also required to conduct a part of the marriage rituals. The second night of marriage is observed as *bishrati*, and on the third night of marriage the new couple are ceremonially allowed to cohabit in a bed and consummation of marriage is formally done on that day. The dead are cremated; and a period mourning of thirteen days is observed. As a symbol of mourning the members of the family as well as the community neighbours take vegetarian diet devoid of turmeric and oil. From the second to the tenth day after death, the eldest or youngest son offers rice, bananas, fruits, etc., on a banana leaf to the spirit of the deceased in the courtyard. On the tenth day *ghat* and *dosa shradha* are performed with the help of a Napit and a Brahman priest. On that day members of the funeral party take curd and *chire* (flattened rice) in the house of the mourner. *Sradh* is performed in an orthodox fashion on the eleventh day of death. On the thirteenth day members of the deceased's family arrange a feast (rice with fish) where neighbours, relatives, members of the funeral party etc., are invited, and from this day the mourners are free to eat normal food.

Performing drama, dance, music and organising band parties on several festive and cultural occasions are the traditional occupations of the Nats of West Bengal. These are considered as their major economic activities. The Nats are mainly a landless community. Their subsidiary sources of income are service, running grocery shops, repairing watches, torches, radios, etc., rickshaw pulling, hair cutting in saloons etc. They are mainly dependant on markets. Bonded labour is not found among them. A few children found to be employed in hotels, restaurants and in other families as servants, are considered as child labour among them. Those who work as day labourers or earn through any other means, are paid in cash.

In their hamlet they select an aged and knowledgeable person as a *moral* (headman), who settles primary disputes and other disputes related to marriage, among the members of their community. Selection is done in a meeting on the basis of unanimous decision. They live in the municipality areas and accordingly they take advice for settling various disputes and economic assistance from the members of the municipality. Forms of punishment depend on the extent of wrong done. A significant change that has been observed is that they sometimes consult political leaders for economic assistance, and other welfare activities among members of their society.

The community professes Hinduism. A number of them are followers of Vaishnavism. Radhakrishna, Lakshmi, Shasthi, etc. are worshipped as their family deities. A number of them are devotees of Sri Sri Anukul Thakur, especially those who have migrated from the Pabna district of Bangladesh to which Sri Sri Anukul Thakur originally belonged. Shiva, Kali, Sitala, etc., are considered village and regional gods and goddess for whom the community members organise *puja* from time to time. Temples of Shiva, Burikali, etc., are their major sacred centres. They employ Brahman priests as sacred specialists. The community members attend various fairs and festivals associated with the *pujas* of Shiva, Durga, Basanti, Kali and the like. The Nats sometimes visit the shrines of *pirs* and offer *sinni* (concentrated milk mixed with *ata* wheat flour and sugar) for fulfilment of their desires.

The oral traditions which are observed among them are generally borrowed from the local regions, and sometimes these are taken directly from modern and western songs. They are professional musicians and as such they are experts in music played with the help of different musical instruments like clarinet and saxophone, cornets, and trumpets, trombone, pocket cornet, *junguni*, big drum, side drum, circular pitch etc. They have a special dress which is worn at the time of organising a musical party. The Nats claim that the famous opera named "Natta Company" is their traditional community opera. Besides, they say that the famous actors like Shri Dulal Natta, Sri Makhan Natta, etc., are members of their community.

The Nats are considered as a *jal-achal* community. The Brahman and the upper castes do not accept *pucca* food from their hands. In several ritual ceremonies the Brahman accept *kachcha* food and *sidha* from them. They make marital relationship with the Kayastha, Kumbhakar, Laha (the communities whose surnames are Laha) and the like. Ritual based kinship like *dharam bhai*, *dharam ma*, etc., are observed among them. The Nats do not face any problem as regards access to the sharing of wells, facilities of roads, schools, crematorium, etc. They maintain *jajmani* relation with the Brahman, Napit, *Dhopa* (washer man) etc. for socio-economic inter dependence. Except exercising adult franchise they do not get involved actively in any political activities. They establish linkages with different communities due to their traditional and other different occupations. The Nats had made an unsuccessful attempt to organise a political/ethnic movement for claiming better position in the socio-economic hierarchy of Hindu society. Those who have agricultural land maintain a good relationship with the sharecroppers and other agricultural labourers.

The percentage of literacy and education is not high among the Nats. This is perhaps due to their poor economic condition and lack of incentive. The Nats complain that they do not get facilities for their health and medical care from the health centres as per their requirements. They are cautious about family planning. They collect drinking water from tube wells and sometimes from the tap which is situated outside the locality. The Nats complain that they do not get any loan for maintaining traditional occupation under the employment guarantee schemes. However a few of them got loans for purchasing rickshaws under the self-employment scheme. They use radios and visit cinemas. The Nats avail of the mechanised transport system. Electricity has reached their vicinity. Even though they live within the urban centres, they try to plant fruit bearing trees. This is not only a measure towards environmental conservation, but enables them to get fruits in different seasons. Wood, coal, *gul*, cowdung cake, etc., are their fuel sources. Use of irrigation facilities, fertilisers, etc., is not in vogue, as majority of them are landless and live in urban areas. Nutrition programmes are perfunctory. The Nats purchase essential commodities from the nearest ration shop. Some of them avail themselves of the opportunity of banking systems for savings and investment.

SUBHRENDU MAITY

NEWAR

The Newars are a business community. They are also known as the Pradhan. Due to their long association with rulership, they have assumed the name "Pradhan". At present they have no subgroups, though subgroups existed in the past. The Newars are said to have a complicated the complex organisation of their own with an elaborate caste hierarchy, comparable to that of the Hindus, consisting of the Brahmans, the Kshatriyas, the Vaishyas, and the Sudras" (Bagchi *et. al.* 1961: 53. 54). They migrated from the west and are now well distributed throughout the hill areas of Darjeeling district. The area is covered with thin forests; the climate is cool with medium rainfall and light snowfall. According to the census of 1931, the Newar population is 12,640 of which 10,235 live in the district of Darjeeling alone. They speak Nepali and use the Devanagari script at home. With outsiders they speak Nepali, Nepali-Hindi and Hindi and use the Devanagari and Roman scripts. They hold the constitutional status of other backward classes.

The Newars are non-vegetarians. They eat fish, egg, meat, fowl, and beef, (buffalo) but never take pork. Rice and wheat are their staple food. They take pulses like *mug, kalodal, masur, urad* etc. They consume roots and tubers, and vegetables which are available in the local market. They use mustard oil as cooking medium. They take fruits occasionally. They take milk and milk products. They drink tea, and take alcoholic drinks *nighar janr* (home made brewed alcohol). They also purchase it from local market. *Nighar janr* is an essential item in rituals and festivals. The men smoke *bidis* or cigarettes regularly.

The Newars have several exogamous *thars* namely, Shresthi, Malankar, Kashi, Sakule, Kiritipura, Koushila, etc., the function of the *thars* is to regulate marriages. The Shresthi regard themselves higher than the others. The Newars use Pradhan and Shresthi as their surnames. They regard themselves lower than the Brahman and the Chhetri and equal to the Gurung, the Rai the Mangar, etc., but higher than the Bhujel, the Kami, and the Damai etc. They recognise *varna* order and place themselves as Vaishya. Their self-perception of rank at regional level situates them at the middle, and other castes also reciprocate.

The Newars practise endogamy at community level and exogamy at the *thar* level. The age of marriage is fifteen to eighteen for girls and twenty to twenty-six for boys. Marriage by negotiation is the only accepted mode of acquiring mates. They practise monogamy. The symbols of married women are *sindur* (vermilion) and *potemala* (bead necklace) of green colour. Dowry in cash and kind is present among them. After marriage the bride lives with her husband. *Chhutnam* (divorce) is rare; social approval is necessary for those who want divorce. Divorce due to adultery and maladjustment is permitted, but the cases are very few. Either party can seek for *chhutnam.* Children are the liability of either mother or father. Compensation is given to the aggrieved party. Widow remarriage and remarriage of divorced women are permitted. Widowers and divorced men can also remarry. Changes have been reported regarding increase in age at marriage nowadays.

The Newars prefer to live in nuclear families, though a few have extended families. Avoidance relationships are present between daughter-in-law and father-in-law; and between husbands elder brother and younger brothers wife. Joking relationships are found between elder brothers wife and husbands younger brother and between grandparents and grandchildren. Fathers property is equally shared by the sons. Succession goes to the eldest son. Conflict arises within the family regarding the share of property. Inter-family linkages and cooperation are observed during rituals and religious functions. Changes in family type have occurred in recent days. Extended families are declining and the number of nuclear families is rising.

The Newar girls or women do not inherit their parental property. Women have roles in the collection of fuel wood or firewood, bringing potable water from nearest *dhara* (springs) or from small rivulets, and collection of fodder for domestic animals. They work as tea leaf pluckers in tea gardens and also work in tea gardens as day labourers. They take part in religious functions and in rituals. Women also take part in family management and contribute to family earnings. They have a low status without decision making powers within the family and have no place in mechanisms of social control, and in political spheres.

The Newars observe some rituals on the occasion of birth, marriage and death. They observe pre-birth rituals like *brata* for the health of the child. Pregnant women observe restrictions on some kinds of food, and avoid hard work before childbirth. They observe twenty-two days *chhutak* (pollution) period after childbirth and during this period the mother of the newborn cannot enter the kitchen. Name giving ceremony of the newborn is held on the fifth day for girls and on the seventh day for boys. The family priest gives a name to the baby. The Brahman priest calculates the sign of the zodiac, and a member (among relatives) who has the same sign of zodiac as the baby, feeds first rice to the baby. Parents of the baby arrange a feast for the villagers and relatives

Both brides and bridegrooms parents select an auspicious day for the marriage. Marriage is performed at the brides residence. The Brahman serves them as priest and recites *mantras*. A few major rites during the marriage ceremony are *gayehalud, kanthamala badal* (exchange of garlands), the bridegroom applies vermilion on the brides forehead (*sindur dan*), and makes her wear *potemala*, and *napak*, etc. A feast is given by the brides parents. Consummation of marriage takes place on the third day at the bridegrooms house.

The Newars cremate their dead. They observe thirteen days pollution period after death, and during this period they never take non-vegetarian food, they take only boiled rice, with boiled potato, *ghee* etc. On the thirteenth day, *sradh* is performed with the offering of rice, potato, *ghee*, curd, parched rice and sweetmeats. The Brahman officiates in the *sradh* ceremony. Relatives and neighbours are invited to participate in the ceremony, and a feast with *nigher jnar* and meat is arranged for them.

The Newars are a business community. Many of them are landowners. Their traditional and present occupation is agriculture (terrace cultivation) and business. Those who live in the city or town areas are dependent on the only traditional occupation of business. The other occupations that they pursue at present are labourer in tea gardens, agricultural labourer, government and private service, defence service, etc. They are linked with daily and weekly markets where mode of wage payment is cash. Some of them are landless and work as daily wage, or agricultural labourers. Tea plantation labourers are increasing in number these days. There is no child labour or bonded labour in the Newar community.

The Newars have no traditional caste *panchayat* today. They regard old people highly, and if any dispute arises they take the matter to the aged persons of the village, and obey the decision given by them. The statutory formal *panchayat* is present after independence, and looks after the various welfare and development programmes for the villagers.

The Newars profess Hinduism. They regard *kuldevata* as their home deity. They also worship Sansari deo Kali, Vairab, Shiva and Mahakal.

Mahakal baba temple at Chowrasta, Darjeeling is their main sacred centre. Other sacred centres are the Shiva temple at Dhudia, Kali temple at Naxalbari, etc. The Nepali Brahman performs the role of a sacred specialist in rituals and religious functions, among the Newars. They attend Shivaratri mela at Mahakal temple, Shiva temple at Dhudia, and *Rathayatra mela* at Rath Khola, Naxalbari regularly.

At present, the Newars have no knowledge of any handicraft, though in the past before migration it is reported that "their artistic qualities were attested by the excellent painters and sculptors found among the Newar. Work in metals and woodcarving also bear the stamp of their artistic creativity" (Bagchi, *et. al*. 1961: 54) They have no oral tradition like folk songs but have rich folk tales myths and folklore.

The Newars are a *jal-chal* community. The Brahman, the Chhetri, the Gurung, the Rai, etc., accept and exchange water with them. They also exchange *kachcha* and *pucca* food with them. They do not exchange food or water with the Kami, the Sarki, etc. However, they accept and exchange *sidha* food with all communities. The Newars never encourage inter-community marriage. Putative kinship is found among the Newars with the Chhetris, the Gurungs, the Limbus and the Rais etc. They share drinking water sources like rivulets, springs, etc., roads, crematoriums, schools, etc., and visit religious places with other castes. They have among them businessmen, scholars, teachers, government, servants, political leaders, defence personnel, etc. They have patron-client relationship with the Brahman, landlord-tenant and cultivator labour relationship with the Brahman, the Gurung, the Bhujel, the Limbu, the Sarki, etc.

The progress of education has been poor among the Newars. But, nowadays, a few boys and girls study up to college and secondary levels respectively. They make use of modern medicare facilities and also use some traditional medicines. They prefer family planning. Small rivulets and *dhara* (springs) are their main drinking water sources. Few of them get IRDP loans for small businesses. The transistor radio is very popular among them. They also visit cinemas and watch television programmes. They use electricity where available. They use wood for fuel. Irrigation is through rainwater and spring water. They use organic manures and chemical fertilizers, and insecticides etc. They enjoy the facilities of post offices and banks. Saving is favoured and they do not depend on moneylenders. They use ration shops as per their needs.

AMITABHA MITRA

NIKARI

The Nikaris are a Muslim community. The word Nikari is derived from the Persian word *nek* means good. Thus, *nek* and *kari*, i.e., Nikari stands for 'doer of good work'. They prefer to introduce themselves as Dalasayad or Dafadar. People of the other communities call them as Nikari or Nikiri. Dafadar, Sarkar, etc., are their titles. They have a belief that they are born of Soleman Paigamber the Badsah of Jins and a daughter of a fisherman. Risley (1891: 133) and Siddiqui (1974: 50) have noted them as fishmongers. They are mostly concentrated in the districts of Burdwan, Hoogly, Howrah, Murshidabad, 24-Parganas, and in Calcutta. These areas have monsoon climate. The Nikari people speak and write in Bengali.

They eat beef, buffalo meat, etc. Rice and wheat are their staple cereals. Besides lentil (their favourite pulse), they consume gram and *moong* also. Mustard and rapeseed oil are their cooking media. Potato is their main vegetable. Tea is used as a hot drink. They consume fruits occasionally and vegetables moderately. The increase in the use of pulses and vegetables and decreases in the use of fruits are the only changes in their food habits.

The Nikaris enjoy a low status in the social hierarchy.

The community is an endogamous group. Consanguineous marriage is permissible. They negotiate marriage of their sons and daughters when they become adults. Monogamy is the common form of marriage, but non-sororal polygyny is permissible. *Den-mohar* (bride price) is promised for future payment. Rule of residence is patrilocal. Divorce due to adultery, maladjustment, etc., are permissible with social approval. Only husband can divorce, and compensation is to be given to the wife. Children are the liability of father in such cases. Remarriage of male and female divorcee, widow and widower is permissible. Junior sororate is allowed after death of the first wife, whereas junior levirate is permissible but not practised. Increase in age at marriage, and practice of dowry by some, are the changes in marital affairs. A few marriages with the Sheikhs are also reported.

Both nuclear and extended families are found among them. The boys and girls love and respect their parents. Their parents, in their turn also love them. In a family, avoidance relationships exist between *shvashuri* (wife's mother) and *jamai* (son-in-law). *Shvashur* and *bhasur* (husband's father and husband's elder brother) are also avoided. Joking relationships are found with wife's younger brother and sister, and elder brother's wife and grandparents. Property, restrictions on the freedom of youngsters and unequal sharing of work load among the women cause conflict in a family. They follow the Muslim rule of inheritance, i.e., daughters get a lesser share of father's property than sons. The eldest son generally succeeds to his father's responsibility. Rise in the formation of nuclear families is the only change in family structure.

The Nikari women take care of their domestic fowls and sometimes sell eggs and the birds secretly to buy some items of their own choice. They also take part in ritual observances. They enjoy a low status.

The Nikaris observe *sadh* as pre-delivery ritual, only for the first child. They observe *kaman* on the fifth day after childbirth. The *dai* (mid wife) cleans the house and washes their clothes on that day. The barber comes to pare the nails of the family members, the baby and its mother. Another *kaman* is performed on the twenty-first day. The *dai* comes to wash the clothes of the baby and its mother. The mother is allowed to enter the kitchen after five days. But some families allow the same only after twenty-one days. The new mother can perform *namaz* (prayer) after forty days. They shave the hair of the baby on the first day of its birth. They observe first rice eating ceremony on the sixth month of the male child and seventh month of the female child. For this they offer *kshir* and *sinni* (sweet preparation) along with prayers at their mosque. Then any of the parents or grandparents feeds a small portion of this *kshir* and *sinni* into the mouth of the newborn. *Sunnat* (circumcision) is done for the male child. When boys or girls reach the marriageable age they arrange marriage. They avoid the month of *Ramzan* and the fortnight of Muharram for fixation of the date for marriage. *Gayehalud* (smearing of turmeric on the body) is performed as a marriage ritual at both the houses, of bride and bridegroom. The main marriage ceremony is observed at the bride's residence. The bride's father arranges a feast on this occasion. Marriage is consummated at the groom's residence on the marriage day itself. *Olima* is observed on the second day of marriage. The groom's father arranges a feast on this occasion.

The Nikaris bury their dead. They invite their relatives and members of the *jamat*, one from each family, (who perform *namaz* in the same mosque) for a feast on the fortieth day.

The Nikaris sell fish. They also depend on fruit gardening (especially mango gardens). They take ponds (to cultivate fish), and gardens on lease from others. Most of them are landless. Only a few possess land of their own. Some are service holders or agricultural labourers. They take fish or mangoes to the daily or weekly markets and sell them for cash. They pay the fishermen in cash and kind. It is reported that the number of leasers among them has increased.

They have no separate council of their own, but the *soloana*, i.e., members of the *jamat* try to solve the problems of the community, if it fails, they go to the panchayat, the statutory council of the village. Physical punishment, cash fine or rebukes are imposed on the guilty person.

The Nikaris are followers of Islam. Mosque is their local sacred centre, whereas Furfura Sharif and Mecca are their pilgrimage centres. Id-ul-Fitre, Id-uz-Zoha, etc., are the important religious festivals. The *Maulavi* — who may be from another Muslim community — serves them as religious teacher and officiates during birth, marriage and death rites.

The Nikaris have a folk tale about their origin which is: "Soleman Paigambar was the emperor of the *jins* (fairies). One of the Jins was his personal servant. Soleman used to go for nature's call keeping his ring in the custody of that servant. One day the servant wore Soleman's ring and got the appearance of Soleman. Then Soleman went to his hundred wives and asked them not to allow the servant into the Begam Mahal, and went away. On his way he saw a fisherman trying to catch fish in vain. He stopped there and consequently the fisherman could catch a lot of fish. The fisherman asked his identity. He replied that he was a common man. The fisherman took him to his house, and thus he prospered in his fish business. The fisherman was then converted to Islam, and he gave his daughter in marriage to Soleman. The issues of that pair became Nikaris or Dalasayad."

The Nikaris do not take water from the Dhawas (another Muslim community) but exchange cooked food with the Sheikhs. They accept *sidha* food from other communities when they work as agricultural labourers in their fields. The Hajam performs circumcisions, and he is paid in cash and kind for his services, thus a patron-client relationship is established among them. Their business transactions with other communities establish inter-community linkages at the economic level. They have a few teachers and service holders and modern inter-community linkages are also established through them.

The Nikari boys generally study up to the secondary level; whereas girls study up to the primary level only at *madrasas*. They prefer modern medicare, but they also have faith in *jalpara* (use of sacred water: a traditional method) from the *maulavi* or *hafej*, for curing some diseases. Their response to family planning is quite disappointing. They collect potable water from tube wells. They have taken loans from co-operatives or IRDP or banks for agriculture and fisheries. The Nikari people listen to radios and visit cinemas. The cultivators make contact with the agricultural extension officers for the betterment of their crops. Political parties meet them prior to the elections. Their localities are connected by roads and railways. They cannot use electricity as it has not reached their area. Wood and coal are used as fuel. They get irrigation facility from canals and tanks. They use organic manures, chemical fertilizers and insecticides for better yields. Their children get midday meals from *anganwadi*. They draw rations from fair price or ration shops. Some of them deposit their money with the local banks. They also take advances from *aratdars* (whole sellers) for fruit gardening and fishing.

ARCHANA DATTA

NUNIYA

The Nuniyas are a scheduled caste of West Bengal. They are also commonly known as Chauhan in the neighbourhood. Salt making was their traditional occupation and the name has been derived from the word *nun* or salt. They speak of four subgroups among them, namely — (1) Bachgotra Chauhan (2) Audhia (3) Kharbat and (4) Beldar. Risley (1891: 135) has mentioned seven subcastes among them, which are (1) Awadhia or Ayodhiabasi (2) Bhojpuria (3) Kharaont (4) Maghaya (5) Orh (6) Pachainya or Chauhan and (7) Semarwar. They claim to be the original settlers of the region. Regarding their origin and migration Risley has mentioned that the Nunia or Noniyan had been "a Dravidian Caste of Bihar and Upper India engaged in cultivation, saltpetre making, and various kinds of earth work. The caste seems to have no traditions except for a silly story that the Awadhia are descended from an ascetic named Bidur Bhakat, who broke his fast on salt earth, and being thereby disqualified for the higher life of meditation was condemned by Ram Chandra to betake himself to the manufacture of saltpetre. This throws some light on the origin of the Nunia. It seems, however, to be generally believed that they are closely connected with the Bind and the Beldar, and venture the conjecture that the Bind may be the modern representatives of an aboriginal tribe from which the Nunia have branched off as saltpetre makers and the Beldar as earth workers. All three groups are now endogamous. The hunting and fishing proclivities of the Bind seem to suggest that they are the oldest of the three, while the totemistic sections of the Nuniya stamp them as Dravidian. The Beldar are probably a more recent offshoot, but the fact the name Beldar (mattock-bearer) assumed by members of any caste when employed on earth work renders it difficult to determine their precise affinities" (Risley, 1891: 135). The Nuniyas think that their community is mainly distributed in the districts of Maldah, West Dinajpur and Burdwan of West Bengal and in Darbhanga of Bihar. As many as 41, 531 of them were found in West Bengal during the census enumeration of 1981. They speak Khotta or a mixed dialect of Bengali and Hindi and use the Bengali script.

Rice is the staple food of the Nuniyas. They are non-vegetarian, but do not consume beef or pork. Roots and tubers are generally consumed as vegetables. Fruit is an occasional delicacy for them. Tea and milk are their common beverages. Men are habituated to consuming alcoholic drinks procured from the markets. They smoke *bidis* and cigarettes and chew betel and *khaini* or tobacco mixed with lime.

Though the Nuniyas often talk of as many as seven *khoms* sub-divisions, they can recognise only four of them, namely 1. Audhia. 2. Bachgotra Chauhan, 3. Kharbat, and 4. Beldar. Hierarchical differentiation among the different *khoms* is recognised at the social level to regulate marriage. Rai is the surname used by them all along. They themselves perceive that they enjoy a middle status in the regional social hierarchy. Other neighbouring communities however consider them to be of a low status, as that of the Beldar, but not as untouchables. They generally marry within their own community but outside their own *khom* or subcaste. Marriage with brother's children, sister's children and cross cousins does not prevail among them. Though child marriage was prevalent in the past, adult marriage has become the common practice among them at present. Marriages are generally settled through negotiation, but sometimes the poor settle it through *douga* or marriage by purchase, to get relief from the expenses involved in marriage. Monogamy is the common form of marriage. *Sindur* or vermilion and *lahichudi* or lac bangles are the recognised symbols of married women. Dowry in both cash and kind prevails among them. After marriage the couple may stay with the parents of the bridegroom or they may set up their own household separately. Both husband and wife can divorce with mutual consent or agreement. Adultery, barrenness, lack of a male child, impotency, maladjustment etc., are the common reasons for divorce. Divorce compensation is given to the parents of the wife or to the husband, as the case may be. Liability of the children in divorce cases generally lies with the mother. Widows, widowers and divorcees are free to remarry as per their choice. Remarriage with husband's younger brother and wife's younger sister prevails and is often preferred. A man can also remarry the widow or divorced wife of his brother-in-law. The nuclear type of family, comprising of husband wife and their unmarried children, predominate over the extended type, where parents and their married sons or married brothers live together. A relationship of avoidance is maintained between the *bhasur* or husband's elder brother and his *bhai-bou* or younger brother's wife, and also between the *mamasasur* or husband's maternal uncle and his *bhagina-bou* or wife of nephew. The relationship with elder brother's wife, brothers-in-law, sisters-in-law and parents-in-law of children is that of joking and friendliness. Paternal property is equally inherited by all the children, irrespective of whether married or unmarried. The widower mother also has claim to an equal share, provided she has not remarried. Succession descends through male line from father to the eldest son. A rise in the number of nuclear families, and decline in the number of extended families, is the change noticed by them in the institution of family.

Apart from performing major part of the routine household chores, women have a role in animal husbandry, collection of fuel and fetching of potable water. Women play an important role in the performance of socio-religious rituals. They also contribute to the family income through working as wage labourers. They have direct and indirect role in political spheres as well as in the mechanism of social control. They enjoy equal status with the men in the community. Women along with men exercise their right in the decision making process and exert control over family expenditure.

The ritual of *khir-khouki* is observed in the seventh month of pregnancy, wherein the woman is fed her choicest food along with *khir* or sweet dish prepared by boiling rice, milk and sugar. The ritual is generally performed at the parental house of the pregnant woman; Childbirth generally takes place at home with the help of a midwife from among the Hadi or Muchi community. Birth pollution is observed for nine days and first purificatory bath is taken on the first day with five pitchers full of water of *indara* or ring well. The ritual of *mundan* or tonsure is performed at an auspicious time, decided by a Brahman according to the *panji* (almanac). Rituals of marriage are performed at the houses of both the bride and the bridegroom; and a feast is also given by each party. *Panchui*, marriage rituals performed by Chatri Brahman at the bride's house, *boubhat* or reception of the bride at her in-laws' house and *chautha* or return of the bride along with her husband to her parental house for nine days, are the important rituals performed in marriage among the Nuniyas. The dead are generally cremated, but the dead bodies of children of five years and below are buried. The son or grandson offers the sacred fire at the funeral. The person who offers the fire at the funeral is called *aginkarta*. *Chutia* or death pollution is observed for thirteen days. All though the period of *chutia*, the *aginkarta* abstains from taking oil, turmeric and non-vegetarian dishes. Other members of the family abstain from taking non-vegetarian items. *Kheur* or shaving and tonsure and *ghatkria* or *sradh* conducted by the Chetri Brahman, are the important rituals performed among the Nuniyas following a death in the family.

They do not depend on any natural resource for their livelihood, but mainly survive on their individual labour, *Khoa-surki bhanga* or making stone chips by breaking boulders and stones, is reported to be their primary occupation at present. They are basically a landless community. Only a very few of them have small portions of land. Different types of wage labour have been the major source of their secondary income. They are primarily a labourer community and often shift to any type of earning that they can get hold of. They have direct link with markets, and the medium of exchange is cash. Though bonded labour system does not exist among them, their children above ten years do work to earn for the family. Landlessness has been the basic reason for their becoming a labourer community. In course of time there has been a change in their occupation in terms of the shift from their traditional occupation of stone chip making to any type of wage labour.

Problems of adultery, theft, feuds etc., at the community level are dealt with by the informal council of elders of the community through imposition of cash fines or social boycotts. The members of the council are elected by votes. No formal council exists at the village level to deal with the problems involving more than one community. The inter-community problems are handled by the informal council of village elders as and when situations arise. They do not have chieftainship among them. They are aware of the existence of modern statutory *panchayat* for the welfare and development of the area and public in general.

They profess Hinduism. Taru, Bir and Bhagwati are the deities recognised at the family level and that at the level of the village as a whole is Goraiya. Deities of the wider Hindu pantheon, namely Shiva, Durga, and Kali etc. are also recognised by them. The temples of Shiva and Durga are the local sacred centres commonly visited by them. Kashi is reported to be regarded as the centre for pilgrimage among them. Chhat, Holi and Durga puja are the major festivals celebrated by them. The services of Chetri Brahman are hired for performance of the rituals connected with birth, marriage and death.

Painting the floors and walls of houses on various socio-religious occasions is an art commonly performed by the women. Both men and women sing folksongs on socio-religious occasions in the family.

Only the women participate in traditional dance. They hire musicians from among the Hadi and Muchi communities as and when desired.

Traditionally they do not accept food and water from the Hadi, Muchi, Dusadh, and Chamar etc. All the communities in the neighbourhood are claimed to accept food and water from them. Marriage with other communities does take place but only occasionally. Putative kinship of *yar* (friend) can be established with all the neighbouring communities through exchange of new clothes and food. Besides these, linkages with other communities of the region are maintained through amicable sharing of water sources, religious shrines and crematorium. Patron-client and cultivator-labour relationship also helps in establishing linkages with other communities like the Chetri Brahman, Hadi, Muchi, Naia or barber etc.

They have an unfavourable attitude towards education. Most of their boys dropout before completing the primary level of education; whereas majority of the girls do not study at all. Poor economic condition, the need to earn for the family, an overall apathetic attitude on the part of the children and their parents towards education, are the reasons for this. They favour and make full use of modern medicare but they have not altogether discarded their indigenous medicare. They favour family planning and try to restrict the number of children to two to three, by adopting modern methods, except sterilization of women. Drinking water is made available to them within the locality by the statutory panchayat through tube wells. Few of them who possess some land have benefited through IRDP scheme of giving loans. They are exposed to mass media and communication facilities, such as radio, cinema, road, railway, newspaper, post office etc. Though electricity is available, they cannot afford it. Dry leaves, cowdung cakes and wood constitute their main fuel resources. The few land holders among them can not afford to use fertilizers or irrigation facilities, and hence generally depend on rainwater. No nutritional scheme has been made available to them as yet. They get the benefit of fair price shops. Most of them are not able to use banking facility or obtain loan due to their poor economic condition. They depend mainly on the local moneylenders and shop keepers for their requirements, and are thus indebted to them.

BADAL KUMAR BASU

ORAON

The Oraons are widely dispersed over the State but are mainly distributed in north Bengal especially in the district of Jalpaiguri, and the western fringes of the State which cover the districts like Midnapore, Purulia and Bankura and in the Sunderbans and its adjoining zones of 24-Parganas district. The Oraons have generally migrated to the state from the Chhotanagpur area of Bihar as seasonal or permanent migrant labourers in tea gardens, or as those engaged in the reclamation of the Sunderbans, and various construction works. They belong to the proto-Australoid ethnic stock. According to the 1981 Census, their population in West Bengal is 4,37,574. The Oraons call their language Kurukh. They also speak Sadri. Oraon children know little about Kurukh. Nowadays the adults speak among themselves in Kurukh but use Bengali and Hindi while communicating with the outsiders. They use both Bengali and Devanagari scripts. Some highly educated, and Christian Oraons use the Roman script. They are included in the list of scheduled tribes. The women tattoo their bodies and wear a necklace made of a thick twisted cord on which coins are threaded.

The Oraons are non-vegetarian. However, Bhagat Oraons are strictly vegetarian. A few Christian Oraons consume pork, but by and large they do not eat beef or pork. Mutton, goat-meat, fowl, fish and eggs are eaten with relish. Rice is their staple food. They also consume some locally available pulses and vegetables along with rice. They consume non-vegetarian food occasionally. Consumption of vegetables and seasonal fruits is very poor. Tea has gained popularity as a beverage. Milk is generally not taken unless the person is weak or sick. They however, prefer to take alcoholic drinks like *baria* (rice beer), *daru*, *mahua* or *illi* (*mahua* spirit) and *cholai* (country liquor). They smoke *bidis*, cigarettes, and indigenous cheroots, and chew tobacco with lime and betel leaves.

The social organisation of the Oraons is characterised by the existence of totemic clan divisions, e.g. Lakra (tiger), Tikri (young mice), Kujur (a kind of fruit), etc. A man of the Kujur clan cannot eat the *kujur* fruit; he even cannot sit under the shadow of a *kujur* tree. A Kujur woman, even though no blood relations can genealogically be traced with her, stands in the position of a sister to him, and he cannot marry her. Although marriage amongst the Oraon are primarily governed by the rule of clan exogamy, genealogical or blood relationship up to three generations are now generally considered a bar to marriage even with a member of a different clan.

One interesting feature of the traditional Oraon village organisation — now totally absent — was the existence of '*dhumkuria*' or bachelor's dormitory, where all the bachelors of the village, from the age of about nine and above, would sleep at night. There they learned their tribal lore, were initiated into sex-rites, and under direction of their elected office-bearers participated in different tribal activities, including marriage and other ceremonies of the village, annual hunts of the *parha* and *jatra* and dances associated with agricultural and other production cycles. Similar to the dormitories of the bachelors, there were dormitories of the maidens also. They would gather at nightfall in the village dancing ground or *akhar* or *akhra* and through dance, music and love-making, time would roll at frenzied speed up to late hours in the night.

Dancing and music of the Oraon, however, are not only for individual pleasure, but these have definite social ends. They are believed to stimulate helpful forces of the nature so that the earth may be fruitful, the Oraon may be blessed with an abundance of animal and vegetable food, and the fertility of man and of the rest of creation may increase.

The Oraons are endogamous. Marriages between first cousins, members of the same clan, boy and girl who are related to each other by milk relation, i.e., who have suckled milk from the same mother are forbidden. They prefer adult marriage. The girl and boy get married, when they are between fifteen and twenty-five years, and between fifteen and twenty-six years respectively. Late marriages are common among the Christian Oraons. Many married women use *sindur* (vermilion) as a symbol of marriage. Bride-price is to be given as a traditional norm but nowadays dowry is often accepted in cash, or kind, or both. Divorce is granted with the approval of the panchayat due to barrenness, bad nature and laziness of the wife. If the husband is found to be guilty, he loses his bride-price. They follow the rule of patrilocal residence after marriage. Widows, widowers and divorcees may remarry. Widow or widower remarriage is known as *sagai* and is performed without elaborate rituals.

They live mostly in nuclear families. However, various forms of joint or extended families are not uncommon. The Oraon family has a patrilocal structure. The father or any other eldest male member is the central figure in the family. All authority is vested in him and lineage or descent is traced through him. All property belongs to him and is inherited equally by his sons.

The women take charge of infants and children not only for rearing but also for initial socialisation. They perform all the household work. They work as labourers and take part in light agricultural operations. They contribute their income to the family. They also purchase essential commodities from the market. They however, do not have any right of inheritance or succession excepting inheritance of movable property like ornaments, utensils etc., from their mothers or mothers-in-law. They actively take part in communal singing, dancing, socio-religious rites and rituals. They do not have any role in political activities, except exercising their franchise. Very recently, a few Oraon women have been elected as members of the three tier statutory panchayats.

During pregnancy, the Oraon woman takes care of herself. She covers her body fully to protect herself against the evil eyes. She neither goes to burial or cremation grounds nor attends any death rites. Thunder is also considered harmful. When a woman gives birth to her first child, her father offers a sacrifice of pig or fowl to the spirits in a ritual known as *jodakamna.* Delivery takes place in the house. Only women are allowed near the birth-bed. The two mid-wives who generally come from their own community are known as *kushrain*. According to their traditional customs, the newborn is bathed with *kanji pani* (rice water that has been kept in an airtight pot for many days). Within three days from birth, the father of the child offers a grey coloured fowl to the *pahan* (priest) for sacrifice. The delivery of the child makes the whole house ritually unclean. After a week or so the mother purifies herself by anointing herself with oil mixed with pounded turmeric and takes a bath. She also puts a vermilion mark on the stone or wood that is kept near the water bodies. This is done in order to appease *dari* (spring) spirit. On the seventh or eighth day after birth *danda katta* or *palkhansa* i.e., cutting the evil teeth is done. Rice-beer and eggs are offered to Dharmesh (God) and to the ancestral spirits by the *pahan*. The rest of the eggs are distributed to the children. Guests are treated with rice-beer and a delicious meal. Various other birth rites include the name giving ceremony and hair shaving as well as birth feast.

The marriage is initially negotiated with *agua*, i.e., matchmaker. When both the families have agreed to the proposal, the girl's father invites the relatives of the boy to his house, in a ceremony known as *lotapani*. The girl receives some presents from the boy's father, which is known as *lotapani sari*. Afterwards, the boy's family invites the girl's party and entertains them with rice-beer and a meal. The ceremony is known as *chuna tamku* or *sanipahi*. In *koha-pahi* ceremony, the bride's party again pays a visit to the bridegroom's house and fixes the wedding day, and amount of bride price, which generally varies from five to nine rupees. The bridegroom's party also send some presents to the bride's house. The various pre-marriage ceremonies include *karsa bhanda* (burning of paddy stock within a decorated pot), *benja-pitri* (cutting of a mat prepared from reed into seven equal parts) etc. The marriage is performed under the *mandwa*. The boy and girl stand on the stone, facing east, the girl in front, the boy's hand resting on her shoulders and his toes touching her heels. Then both the boy and girl promise to live in a lifelong company and share sorrow, joy and burdens with each other. Then onwards they are treated as husband and wife. A piece of linen, coloured with turmeric is then put for a few moments around the newlywed couple as a screen, until a woman sprinkles water with the mango twigs. The newly married couple jumps off the stone and enters into a room. The women then start the *benja lasna* (marriage) dance. After the dance, both bride and groom are again brought to the *mandwa* for *sabha-sinduri*. Both of them sit on a mat. The senior invitees throw *arwa* rice (raw rice) and wish them health and prosperity. The persons assembled there offer gifts like money, utensils, household articles etc. The invitees are entertained with a feast and offerings of *haria* (rice-beer). Marriage is consummated at the bridegroom's house.

The dead are generally buried and sometimes cremated. The remnants of the bones are picked up by the female members of the family. The bones are washed and wiped with a new piece of cloth. The bones are then put into a pot. The place where the deceased is cremated is cleaned with diluted cowdung and half-boiled rice is put there in three *sal* leaf plates. The ceremony is known as *harbori*. In *ekh mankhna* ceremony, they take back the shade of the deceased in the house where the deceased person breathed his/her last. The bones of the deceased are carried in a procession to the *kunddi*, i.e., family grave. On arrival at the *kunddi*, a man takes and dashes the pot with the bones against the *pulki* stone (memorial stone). The women then clean the *pulki* stone and anoint it with vermilion dissolved in oil. The *pahan* (village priest) sprinkles turmeric water over the *pulki* i.e., memorial stone. The men and women then leave the place, take a purificatory bath and go home.

Land is their main economic resource and is controlled by lineage, clan or individuals. However, most of the Oraons work as plantation labourers, agricultural serfs and workers engaged in various unorganised sectors mainly as labourers. To most of the Oraons, the economic importance of forests has been considerably reduced due to large scale deforestation. Traditional occupation of the Oraons is cultivation, hunting and food gathering. Though agriculture remains the main occupation, a good number of the Oraons are employed as tea plantation labourers in Jalpaiguri and Darjeeling district. Among the ex-tea garden labourers of Jalpaiguri district there are a few rich *jotedars*. A few of them have received higher education and have entered government services. An overwhelming majority of the Oraons all over the state, however, are either share croppers or agricultural labourers. In West Dinajpur district, some are reported to have entered business successfully. Community hunting is a rare occurrence among the Oraons nowadays.

They have the traditional panchayat (community council) at the village level. *Mahato* or *morol* is the headman of the council. *Charidar* is the assistant to the headman and *paramanik* is the messenger. They decide cases of social and religious importance. They have the *parha* or regional council composed of a number of villages. Each *parha* is known by the number of villages it encompasses. The *mahato* of the *raja* (king) village is known as *parha raja*. The others are *dewan*, *kotwar*, *panery*, *panbharwa* and *mukatwa* villages. The *parha* organisation with the superior position of the original settler family has practically died out. The new leadership that is emerging draws its sanction from its capacity to tackle government officials rather than supernatural deities. The three tier statutory *panchayat* mainly deals with developmental and welfare activities. The *parha* council now exists in almost vestigial form.

The Oraon profess faith in tribal religion and Hinduism. Their supreme deity is Dharma. They also believe in a host of spirits like Chala Pacho, Kalmai or Chandi, Sarnaburia or spirit of sacred bush, Mahadania bunga, Devi mai, Gaon-deoti, Bir-belas, Cando-belas, Bura-Buri, Panch-balai and so on. They also worship Hindu gods and goddesses. They celebrate the traditional festivals of Sarhul, Karma, Phagu, Sohurai, Dussehra, Asri, Nawakhani and so on. They participate in Hindu festivals; viz., Durga puja, Kati puja, Kartik puja, Manasa puja and Sitala puja, Lakshmi puja, Satyanarayan puja etc., and these are celebrated in their houses. They also offer *Hari lot* (offer in the name of Lord Hari). The *pahan* is their sacred specialist.

Tribal dances are performed but these seem to have lost their significance. No longer are these dances associated with tribal belief and action with production cycle and the Oraon themselves look upon these as only interesting and not curious relics of the past. In fact, tribal opposition to such dances have been reported from certain areas. The Oraons have commensal relationship with the neighbouring Santals, Mundas, Nepalis, Rajbanshis and others. They accept food and water from them. They have ceremonial friendship with other communities. They have landlord-sharecropper, cultivator-labourer mortgagee-mortgager relationship with them.

Owing to poverty, and distant location of schools, the Oraons have poor literacy. They use indigenous medicine. They also avail themselves of modern medicine facilities. Their attitude towards family planning is favourable. They fetch drinking water from tube wells and dug wells. They are covered under government employment programmes. There is no electricity in most of the villages. They use firewood. Irrigation facilities are absent. They avail of ICDS. In hours of crisis, when they need money, they go to the moneylender.

A large number of Oraons have been converted to Christianity. The totemic clan division with their food and marital taboos also remains among them. But while non-Christian Oraons observe tribal endogamy, Christian Oraons can also marry Christian Mundas. Unmarried Oraon youths are not required to observe any food restriction with respect to their Hindu and other tribal neighbours, but after marriage, all traditional restrictions are rigorously enforced. Being a community who allow premarital sex relationship, marriage among the Oraons in the plantation areas has thus lost much of its significance as an institution to confer sex-rite. On the other hand from what has been described above, marriage appears to have an extra significance as an agency for regulating inter community social-political relationship in the area.

PABITRA KUMAR GUPTA

ORIYA

The name of the community is Oriya. Its synonyms are Odra and Uriya. Risley (1981: II: 150) said "Orha, Ourha [are] synonyms for Uriya, a native of Orissa". The term Oriya had been derived from the ancient *janapada* 'Odra' which later on shaped into the term 'Orissa'. As they are a worrier community and fight with *Khanda* (sword) and shield, they are also termed as Khandayat or Kshatriya. According to mythical story when goddess Durga was fighting with demon Mahishasur, she created a large army through her sword. These soldiers were later on called Kshatriya and founded the ancient civilization and culture of Orissa. According to key informants the Odra people came from outside India by sea. Later on they became soldiers for the king of Orissa. So the title 'Mangaraj' was given to them. They migrated to neighbouring Singhbhum district of Bihar and Purulia district of West Bengal in the fifteenth century, when Gajapati King of Orissa selected them as bodyguards of Sri Chaitanya Dev during his travel to Mathura from Puri. Later on after getting 'Lakhraj' land grants from the Dhalbhumgarh and Barabhum Rajas, they settled in these jungle parts of the country as border guards and regular soldiers of the local chiefs. They have subgroups defined in terms of territorial divisions, like Jajpuria, Singbhumia, and Barabhumia etc. But they intermarry with each other. They use surnames such as Rout, Samal, Senapati, Mangaraj, Jena, Barik, Paul, Biswal, Jethi, Maiti, Dandapat, Digar etc. The social divisions are clans or *gotra*, like Nilkantha, Nageswar, Kashyap, Sandilya, Bharadwaj, Basistha, Maharshi, Nag-Rishi, Jata-Rishi etc. They are found in Barabazar and some other parts of Purulia, Bankura and Jhargram, Rohini Nayagram, Gopiballavpur, Belpahari of Midnapur etc. In West Bengal both inside and outside the family they speak in Oriya, Manbhuiya Bengali, and Bhanjabhumiya dialects and use Bengali, Devanagari, Oriya and Roman scripts.

Rice is their staple food. They use pulses regularly. They take all kinds of leafy vegetables, tubers and roots. They are purely non-vegetarian but do not eat beef or pork. They take all kinds of fishes from rivers and ponds. They drink milk and tea. Male folk only in exceptional cases drink liquor bought from the markets. They chew tobacco and both males and females use betel with or without tobacco. Male folk smoke *bidis* and cigarettes. They live in the plateau region where ponds and rivers are very near to their habitat.

As mentioned earlier they are divided into a number of clans and they practise clan exogamy. The community recognises the *varna* system in Hindu hierarchical order and places the Brahman at the top and claims to be Kshatriyas. They consider Nene, Sunri, Moira, and Napit etc., as clean castes and place the Santal, Kudmi, Bhumij, Kora Mudi, Muchi, Dom, and Kharia etc. as polluted or *ajalchal*.

The Oriyas are endogamous and practise clan exogamy. In some rare cases marriage in the same clan or *gotra* is fixed. They practise *kanyadan* rituals. Monogamy is the rule. The process of acquiring mates is initiated from the bride's side. Marriage by negotiation is common; love marriage is also allowed within the community. Inter-caste marriages are looked down upon. Divorce is not allowed if initiated from the side of females. Desertion of the wife by the husband is however allowed. There is no *sangha* or widow marriage. Junior levirate is allowed. But junior sororate is allowed only if the first wife is issueless. Previously bride price was found among them, but now dowry has replaced bride price. Dowry claimed by the bridegroom's side is heavy. *Kanyadan* is practised by them. Previously the girls were married before attaining puberty. But now the age of marriage is between eighteen to twenty years for girls and twenty to thirty years for boys. Their marriage symbols are vermilion and iron bangles.

The family type is mostly nuclear but vertically extended families and joint families are also found. They have got avoidance and joking relationship with their fixed kin members. Property and challenge to the authority of elders are the major points of conflict and confrontation. The rule of inheritance is male equigeniture. Females do not inherit, and succession to the official authorities goes to the eldest son.

Women enjoy a very low status within their community. They only work inside the house. No outside work is done by the women; even in serious decision making issues women are not consulted. In the seventh month of pregnancy, the pregnant woman is served with her favourite food in a ritual known as *sadbhaksan*. The umbilical cord is cut by a Hari woman. On the ninth day the *narta* or purification ceremony is done with the help of the Napit, Dhopa, and Brahman. They observe puberty pollution ritual for three days. Searching for a suitable bride is done by the nearest kin or *ghatak*. *Kanyadan* ritual is performed through the Brahman. Marriage is performed on a *bedi* and to avoid any mishaps, the bridegroom first marries the *Sawra* tree. They observe *basarghar* and *phulsajjya* rituals. Both the parties arrange feasts for the kin and relatives. They have the *diragaman* ritual too. During the time of marriage the sacred thread wearing ceremony is performed.

Dead bodies are generally cremated, and in exceptional cases only, corpses of infant females are cremated. The death pollution is observed for ten days. On the second day the *kai-pani* and on third day the *tita-bhat* rituals are done in the name of the deceased ancestors. *Sradh* ceremony is done on the eleventh day and a feast is given on the eleventh and twelfth day. The rituals are performed by a Brahman, Vaishnav and kin members. They use open air for toilets for defecation.

They are very fond of cleanliness and use soaps, detergents etc. They use *sal*, *datan* for cleaning their teeth. Both males and females use *gudaku* for washing their mouths.

The Oriyas are agriculturists; mostly marginal farmers and agricultural labours. They also own small business or work in different occupations like those of mason, carpenter, vegetable seller and small grocery shop owner etc. Only a few persons are engaged as primary teachers and also in Government and other jobs. Some are working as industrial labour. They engage agricultural labour or annually contracted labour from different communities, and pay wages in cash or kind.

Social control is exerted through the *jati panchayat* or caste council. Some time the village *soloana* also does the same. The *jati panchayat* office bearers are *pradhan, nayek, kakhari, ghatwal, digar, sardar* etc.

They worship Baram, Rankini, Shiva, Durga, Kali, Kothari, Radha-Krishna, Garamthan, Kalnagini, Manasa etc. They sing Tusu, Bhadu, Karam, Jhumur songs and participate in Bandna, Jitua, Sarul festivals. They decorate the walls during the Bandna festival and decorate floors with *jhunti* or *alpana*. The women folk do not dance, only the males participate in *kirtan* songs and also dance during Shiva-Gajan festival. They believe in *dahin* and to control them, they call *ojhas*. They sing and dance with *Karam* songs. The women folk also sing regional Tusu songs.

Besides all those, Bandna rituals and festivals are shared by them. They prepare chains of paddy and hang it in house and decorate the floors with *alpana*. They also decorate the walls during the Durga puja. They observe the regional Jitua or Jita festival with great care and pomp. They are experts in village *Jatras* and perform different

Jatras directed by themselves and produced by the village *soloana*. The males do not perform Chou or Paika dance but they patronize the whole Shiva Gajan festival and take the leadership in different social and cultural gatherings. They maintain inter-community linkages with the Brahman and Vaishnav whom they treat as *jajman* and they have *goun-ghar* or *bartani* relation with the Kamar, Kumbhar, Napit, Dhoba, etc. They also invite the Doms and Sahis to special performances. They maintain putative relationship with the Kudmi, Gour, Bhumij, Bagal, etc., in the name of *phool* and *saiha*. They give *uvla* clothes to their respective ceremonial friends. They accept *pucca* and *kachcha* food from the Brahmans only.

Their literacy rate is very poor. However, female education is now increasing. Their womenfolk welcome family planning measures. They visit nearby health centres occasionally. But they have strong faith in traditional medicines. Drinking water facilities have been made available to them; they prefer energy conservation. Some are enjoying electricity facilities. They enjoy the benefits of the rationing system, post office and bank facilities. They use chemical fertilizers for cultivation and prefer to irrigate their lands through traditional methods and through pump sets.

PASHUPATI PRASAD MAHATO

PAHARIYA

The Pahariyas are a hill community of West Bengal. Local people call them Pahira or Pahida. The word Pahira or Pahida was derived probably from Kudmali dialect. The Pahariya means inhabitants of the hills. They mostly live on the hilly western parts of Purulia covered by forest. At present, the forest of this region is not so dense. The area is marked by excessive heat in summer followed by a cold winter. Rainfall is medium. They speak and write in Bengali and claim themselves to be the offshoot of the Bhumij. According to Basu (1969: 399 - 416) they are also found in Singhbhum and Ranchi districts. He refers to them as Pahira, having a population of more than 330 individuals in the Ayodhya hills of Purulia district during 1963-64.

So far as bio-anthropological information is concerned only one study has been done among the Pahariyas of West Bengal by Basu (1969: 399-416). He has referred to the Pahariyas of the Ayodhya hills as northern Pahira. In anthropometric data twelve measurements are found among the northern Pahira. Mean values of stature and body weight are 1530.26 mm and 90.02 lb for male and 1421.36 mm. and 77.15 lb for females respectively. In serological data, only ABO system has been studied among them. Their gene frequencies are as follows: p-o. 0.3726, q-o. 0.2309, r-o. 0.3962. Besides ABO blood group phenylthiocarbomide taste (PTC) has also been done among the Pahariyas of this area. It is found that 58. 45% are taster. Basu also has referred to their sex ratio as 43.59, net productive index 2.89 and child-woman ratio 74.24.

The Pahariyas are a non-vegetarian community. They take all kinds of fish and meat except beef. Rice with starch is their staple food. They also consume maize and millets which are also as preferred as rice. Consumption of pulses is casual while lentil is consumed more than the other pulses. The medium of cooking is mustard oil. The Pahariyas consume large amounts of green leaves and vegetables like *kurol saq*, *arsa saq*, fig, curry of *jihur* flower, soup of tamarind, wild potato, etc., collected from the forest. Sometimes, if rice with starch is not available in sufficient quantity, they take a bowlful of soup of *kurol saq*. They consume *bhela*, *aola*, blackberry, mango, kend, etc., in plenty from the jungle. Most of them have milch cows so they can afford milk for their children. Some of them take tea. They distil indigenous liquor from *mahua* and prepare beer from rice. All the members of the family take alcohol at least once a week and it is generally on the day of *hat* (weekly market). Besides, they also take alcohol on different religious or social occasions. Decrease in consumption of pulses due to increase in prices, and decrease in consumption of vegetables and fruits due to clearance of jungles, are the major changes in food habits of the Pahariyas.

Clan or *gotra* are their only social division. Luthimachi (a kind of fly), Berhal, (a kind of insect), Titachhali (mushroom) etc., are their clan names. No hierarchical order is maintained among these clans. The only function of these clan divisions is to regulate marriage alliances. Pahariya is their common surname. Some of them use Sing Pahariya as surname. The Mahato, Tambuli, Napit, Mayara etc. and the other neighbouring clean caste Hindu communities are thought to be higher then the Pahariyas in social hierarchy. The Ghasi and the Hari, the neighbouring scheduled caste communities are thought to be lower than them, where as the Santal, the Bhumij, etc., the scheduled tribe communities are thought to be equal to them in local social hierarchy.

Endogamy at the community level and exogamy at the clan level are the common marriage rules of Pahariyas. Junior sororate or levirate is permissible only after death of the first wife or husband respectively. The Pahariyas generally marry off their daughters around thirteen, and boys around twenty-three years of age. Marriage by negotiation is the common mode of acquiring mates. Monogamy is the general form of marriage in the Pahariyas society. One can marry again due to barrenness or death of the first wife. Vermilion and iron bangles are the symbols of married women. However, vermilion is used generally during different religious and social occasions. Twelve rupees is their obligatory bride-price given in cash at the time of marriage. The bride goes to live in her father-in-laws' house after marriage. Divorce may occur due to adultery or maladjustment. *Majhi* (leader) and *laya* (priest) try to settle the matter amicably at the initial stage. Even then if the bride leaves the house of her husband, he is excommunicated. The husband has to offer a feast with rice and meat to get re-admitted into the community. The children are the liabilities of either parent. Remarriage of both males and females is permissible. The only exception is that, the ritual of *malabadal* (exchange of garlands), is not performed in *sanga* (remarriage) of a women.

A boy forms a separate establishment after marriage, so, the nuclear family is the common pattern of the Pahariya society. But vertically extended families are not unknown. As the father is the head of the family the youngsters obey him and show respect. Young children are loved and cared for by the parents. Avoidance relation is found between *shvashuri* (mother-in-law) and *jamai* (son-in-law), daughter-in-law (son's wife) and husband's father, between younger brother's wife and husband's elder brother. It is the duty of the parents to provide maintenance to their children. As soon as the boys and girls can go to the forest independently they start collecting forest products, and become assets to their parents. Joking relations exists with wife's younger brothers and sisters, with grandparents etc. Conflicts mainly arise between husband and wife due to the husband's addiction to alcohol. Male equigeniture is the rule of inheritance. Generally eldest son of the *majhi* or the *laya* succeeds to the post of his father. Interfamily linkages are maintained through different religious and social functions.

Women do not inherit their father's property. They share the economic burden with their male counterparts equally. They work as agricultural labourers, take care of domestic animals, fetch potable water, collect *jhang* and *shal* leaves, and fruits and vegetables from the jungle and sell those in the market. They also have a role in the life cycle rituals. Generally, the Pahariya women control family expenditure. Despite all this their status is low.

The Pahariyas observe *sadh* ceremony in the ninth month of pregnancy. Generally, it is the duty of the girl's mother to perform this ritual. No pre-delivery restriction is observed by them. They observe *narta* ritual on the fifth, seventh or ninth day after childbirth. The barber comes to pare nails of all family members as well as of the child and the mother. The *laya* (priest) takes the new mother to a tank for a bath and offers some mustard oil, vermilion and wine to a particular place to perform worship. He also gives a name to the baby on the same day. Their relatives come to see the new child with some gifts known as *mukh dekhni*. They observe a pollution period for twenty-one days. On the twenty first day the *dhai* touches the tip of a hot *hansua* (sickle) around the umbilicus of the baby to cauterize the spot. This is known as *chirikara*. The barber shaves the baby's head and both mother and child take purificatory baths. The mother can enter the kitchen from that day. The mother cannot take fish and meat till the baby begins to consume them. They observe *mujhutan* or *bhujano* ceremony (first feeding of cereals) in the fifth month for a male child and in the seventh month for a female child. Generally, the maternal or paternal grandmother gives the first rice into the mouth of the child.

When boys and girls attain the marriageable age their fathers begin to search for a suitable partner. The boy's father generally, comes to see the girl. If he is satisfied, members of the community decide whether this marriage will take place or not. They generally arrange marriage in the month of *Agrahayan* (November-December), *Phalgun* (February-March), and *Baisakh* (April-May). First the boy's father comes to bless the girl with new clothes, and subsequently the girl's father also blesses the boy with new clothes. *Gayehalud* ceremony (smearing of turmeric) is observed five or seven days before the main marriage ceremony. The *laya* comes in the morning of the main marriage day. He offers mustard oil, vermilion and *kajal* (collyrium) to the river. *Adhibas* (the last eating of rice in unmarried condition), ceremony is also performed on the day of marriage. *Satpak ghora* and *malabadal* are other marriage rituals. So is *sindurdan* (smearing of vermilion in the hair parting of the girl). A feast is given by the girl's father on that day. The girl goes with her husband to her father-in-law's house the next day. A grand feast is arranged on the third day of marriage in which the members of the girl's family are also invited. It is known as *baharater bhoj*.

The dead are cremated. The eldest or youngest touches the mouth of the corpse with fire before cremation. After which they bury the bones. On the third day after death the family members smear their bodies with oil and take a bath, which is known as *telkhole*. They take *muri*, *khoi* etc., on the third afternoon and vegetarian food with rice in the evening. They offer food to the dead soul on that day, it is known as *titabhat*. They observe a pollution period of ten days. The tenth day is the day of *ghat*. The barber comes to pare the nails of family members and to shave the males. The Dhoba also comes to wash their clothes on that day. On the eleventh day the *basi sradh* ceremony is performed and they invite their relatives to a non-vegetarian lunch on that day. No change is observed in lifecycle rituals except rising expenditure due to increasing prices.

Forests are the main economic resource of the Pahariyas. Forest resources are controlled by the government. Pahariyas are mainly a landless community. They are dependent on forest products. They collect timbers, *shal* and *ghong* leaves and different vegetables like *karla*, wild potato, *kundri*, mango, etc., from the forest and sell them in markets in the plains. They make brooms from bamboos and also sell them to the plain dwellers. As they cannot go to the forest in the month of *Ashar* (June-July), *Sravan* (July-August) and *Bhadra* (August-September), they have to work as agricultural labourers in the plains, during that period. Some of them also work as casual labourers in the forest department. The Pahariyas have a direct link with the markets. They carry the forest products themselves to the local weekly and bi-weekly markets. They generally, sell their products for cash, but sometimes they purchase rice in exchange from the villagers of the plains. Some people have milch cows. They supply milk to the plain dwellers regularly. With clearance of forests, the number of daily wage, casual labourers and agricultural labourers has increased. Eight or nine year old boys and girls also work as agricultural labourers. Agricultural labourers are generally paid in kind, i.e., the female and child labourers are paid four *pailas* (2 kg) of paddy and rice or *muri* (puffed rice) to eat once in a day, whereas the male labourers get five *pailas* of paddy and *muri* in the morning and rice at noon. A great change is observed in the economic life of the Pahariyas after the acquisition of forests by the government. Previously, they used to produce lac from trees of *kusum*, *palash*, plum, etc., and by selling it in the market they could earn a lot of money. They also used to burn forest wood, excluding lac producing trees, and sell charcoal to the plains dwellers. But today these sources of income have been totally lost to them.

The *majhi* (leader) and the *laya* (priest) control the social life of the community. They try to mitigate the conflicts between husband and wife. They excommunicate a person whose wife leaves him; and he has to arrange a feast to the community members, for his re-entry into society. They punish the persons guilty of theft either physically or by imposing cash fines. They also take the final decision regarding the settlement of marriage, of a boy or a girl of their community. *Layas* control the religious and ritual aspects of the community. The statutory panchayat looks after their welfare through different development activities, e.g. it has started a school for the primary education of Pahariya children, the block employees sometimes come to advise them regarding their health. Previously the *majhi* and the *laya* were the only responsible persons to solve problems and look after the prospects of the community. With the formation of the statutory councils after Independence, their (*majhi's* or *laya's*) responsibility has somewhat decreased, as members of these statutory councils look after such problems.

The community profess tribal religion. Gram *thakran* is their village deity, whereas Karmaburu, Baghut, etc., are their regional deities. They perform Rohin puja in the month of *Baisakh* (April-May), Ashari puja or Murgi puja in the month of *Ashar* (June-July). This latter puja is performed for wealth, just as goddess Lakshmi is worshipped by the Hindus. Manasa puja is performed in the month of *Sravan* or (July-August) or *Bhadra* (August-September) for the safety of the family members from snake bite. Garaya puja is performed in the month of *Kartik* (October-November) for the welfare of the domestic animals. They also worship Baghut on that day. Dharam puja is generally done in the month of *Aghrayan* (November-December) for the welfare of the family. They offer a *puja* to Karmaburu on that day. Yatra puja is done in the month of *Poush* (December-January). Tusu puja is done by the tender girls in the same month whereas Maghi puja is performed in the month of *Magh* (February-March) for the welfare of the village. Baghut puja is also done in that month for safety of their lives from fierce animals in the forest. Karma buru, the place of Gram *thakran* etc., are their major sacred centres. *Laya* is their sacred specialist. He performs different religious and social rituals. *Bandna parab* related to Garaya puja and *Karam parab* are their major festivals. Durga mela at Urma during Durga puja festival and Gajaner mela during Gajan, etc., seem to be their only fairs. Now, some of them are initiated by the Hindu Vaishnava Gosain, which is an indication of slow Hinduisation.

The Pahariyas have no traditional art and craft but they have some traditional songs. One of those is sung at the time of bidding farewell to husband's sister by the *boudi*, "*Ek mutha kshudi chale, Pushlo more sangika, Kone desher kara bagale, Niya gelo more sangika*" (My companion is brought up with a handful of broken rice. Now an unknown herdsman has taken her away.) *Danshala* is their traditional dance which is performed by boys and girls during Bandna and Karam festivals.

The Pahariyas maintain linkages with other communities in different ways. The Ghasi and the Hari women work as *dhai* (midwife) during delivery, the Dhoba and the Napit are called for purification. The Pahariyas also work as agricultural labourers of the Mahatos and other clean caste people having agricultural land. They also sell forest products to the neighbouring communities living in the plains. The

Malhar come to the Pahariya village for tattooing them. The Pahariyas also go to them in the neighbouring market places for getting tattooed and to buy *ser* or *paila* (measuring vessel) from them. The Hindu Vaishnav Gosain indoctrinates them. They accept cooked food from the neighbouring houses of the Mahato, the Gosain, the Tambuli, the Mayara, etc., the clean caste Hindus but not from the the Santal, the Hari, the Ghasi, the Dhoba, the Tanti, the Kamar, etc. Modern community linkages are present only in the form of cultivator-labourer relationship and selling of forest products to the neighbouring plain dwellers. They exercise their electoral rights and political leaders meet them during elections.

Educationally the Pahariyas are a very backward community. Some of their boys read up to the primary level, whereas the girls do not go to school at all. Lack of initiative of their guardians as well as teachers is the main cause for this backwardness. The Pahariyas believe in *bhuts* (ghosts or evil spirits), so they are also dependent on *ojhas*. The *dhai* attends to the woman during child birth. Nowadays they also go to the doctor for curing diseases. The Pahariyas are not aware of family planning; they have five to six children on an average. They collect potable water from springs, wells or tube wells. Some have received IRDP loans for animal husbandry. Only a few Pahariya families possess radios. The men visit cinemas frequently, whereas females do so occasionally. Members of different political parties come to them during election. Roads, railways, and post offices are far away from the Pahariya village. Electricity has not yet reached them. They use wood as cooking fuel, as it is easily available in the forest. A few have meagre amounts of agricultural land. They are totally dependent on rainwater for their irrigation, and use organic manure more than chemical fertilisers and insecticides. The Pahariyas have to draw their rations from distant places. They can not save any money as their income is very low. They have to depend on loans from the shopkeepers as well as from the neighbouring well-to-do people of other communities.

It may be said that since the Pahariyas live in inaccessible areas, the fruits of modern development have not reached them, and their seclusion is responsible for their backwardness.

Archana Datta

PAKHIMARA

The Pakhimaras are one of the least known gypsy communities. In West Bengal they are commonly known as Pakhmara. In course of their wandering bird catching expeditions, the Pakhimaras often cross the boundaries of different districts and states. In Chanchal block of district Maldah, the locus of the present study, they are popularly known as the *Lolua*. The Pakhimaras themselves report that they are also known as the *Kurmi*. The group of Pakhimaras under study are reported to have set out on a bird catching expedition from Dumka and Pakur of Santhal Parganas district of Bihar bordering West Bengal. For a major part of the year, especially during the winter and summer months, they are reported to be on the move, constantly from one place to another, on bird catching expeditions. They generally move in groups of 15-25 persons from place to place in search of birds. During the rainy season, movement from place to place and bird catching become extremely difficult for them. In view of these, most of the Pakhimaras are reported to stay generally either in the school premises, or in abandoned settlements at Dumka and Pakur, their so-called home. The Pakhimaras themselves could not tell anything about their origins. The Pakhimaras, in fact, do not seem to have a permanent settlement of their own at any place. In course of their yearly rotational settlement encampments at different places of the districts of Murshidabad, Maldah, West Dinajpur etc., of north Bengal the Pakhimara normally do not stay at one place for more than a fortnight at any stretch. They speak a mixed dialect of Hindi and Bengali among themselves and with others. In view of the fact of being totally illiterate the Pakhimaras do not have the scope of using any script.

Except in the event of death, the meals of the Pakhimaras normally do not consist of vegetables on most days. Chicken and beef never constitute a part of their food. Meat of different types of birds and pork are reported to be consumed regularly by them. Rice is their staple food. *Mung, musoor* and *arhar* are the pulses generally taken by the Pakhimaras. Mustard oil is their common cooking medium. Tea is generally taken from the market. Alcoholic drinks are occasionally consumed from the market. Among the Pakhimaras consumption of fruits is reported to be almost nil.

Pakhmara and Kurmi are reported to be the only two surnames used by the Pakhimaras all along. The Pakhimaras claim themselves to be higher than the Musalman (Muslim), Hadi, Muchi and Dom. Though they place themselves just below the communities of the Kahar, Dhanuk and Mushahar, the Pakhimaras consider these communities as their fellow brethren in terms of social status. The Pakhimaras are commonly identified as the *Lolua*, or as *jajabar* (wandering/gypsy) lowly placed people who visit the area once in a year for about a fortnight to catch birds, sell their indigenous medicines and also for begging.

The Pakhimaras generally marry within their community. Though hypogamous marriages are not prohibited, it is in fact a rare event among the Pakhimaras. Adult marriage is the general practice. Marriages are mostly settled through negotiation between the parties concerned. Though monogamy is the general form of marriage, polygamy is not completely unknown. *Sindur* (vermilion) is the only symbol of married women which is not observed very strictly. After marriage the bride joins her husband within the wandering group comprising mostly his agnates. On issues like adultery, maladjustment, impotency or barrenness etc., either party may resort to divorce simply by mutual consent. No compensation is reported to be paid to any party for a divorce. Liability of the children particularly that of the younger ones, usually lies with the mother.

With regard to remarriage a great deal of flexibility seems to exist among the Pakhimaras. A widow can even remarry an unmarried boy. A widower is free to remarry even an unmarried girl if and when available. Both the male and female divorcees are free to remarry as per their choices. Remarriages may also take place in the form of junior levirate and junior sororate, subject to availability of partners.

Most of the wandering groups of the Pakhimaras consist mainly of nuclear families. Avoidance relationships are almost absent among them. Joking is generally not restricted within specific categories of relatives. There hardly any scope of accumulation of property by wandering gypsy communities, and in fact nothing in the form of property is found among the wandering groups of the Pakhimaras. The question of rules of inheritance and succession in regard to property is therefore irrelevant for them. The linkages between the constituent families of the Pakhimara encampment are reported to be as good as that between the members of a family. In matters relating to occupation, socio-religious rituals, the Pakhimara families often remain in close contact with each other through regular mutual cooperation.

As it has already been mentioned, there is no scope of any right to inherit property by the women, or for that matter by the men as well, among the Pakhimaras. Apart from collecting fuel for cooking, fetching potable water, the women play a major role in the different socio-religious ritual performances of the family and the group. The women do not have any role in the political sphere. Through door to door begging in and around the encampment, the women are reported to make a considerable contribution to the family income and they also participate in its management.

There is no ritual performance before childbirth among the Pakhimaras. They rarely go to hospital for delivery. Deliveries in the encampment of Pakhimaras are generally attended to by Chamar women, and they are paid in cash in lieu of their services as midwives. Birth pollution is observed for nine days. With the completion of pollution period a barber is called to pare the nails of child and mother, and then both of them are given a purificatory bath. After about six months the ritual of *mukhbhat* (first rice feeding) is observed, and group mates are invited to a feast arranged on this occasion. Marriage rituals are generally performed at the bride's parental camp. Marriage feast is given by both the parties at their respective camps. No sacred specialist from any other community is reported to be required for performing the marriage rituals among the Pakhimaras. In the case of child marriage, which takes place rarely, the ritual of *gaona* is observed after the bride attains her puberty. Consummation of marriage takes place in the camp of the bridegroom and no ritual is reported to be performed for the same.

Dead bodies are always cremated by the Pakhimaras. The ritual of offering the sacred fire to the funeral pyre is reported to be performed by the eldest son. Death pollution is observed for thirteen days among them. Except the prohibition on consumption of meat and fish, no other restriction on food during the pollution period is reported to exist among the Pakhimaras. The ritual of *mundan* (tonsure) is performed on the ninth day followed by *sradh* on the tenth day of pollution. All death rituals are performed by elderly persons of the wandering group. The family members of the deceased person get purified by hosting a feast for all the members of the encampment on the thirteenth day. The married daughters who have gone to other wandering groups are reported to observe the pollution period for one month.

Forests, ponds, lakes and marshy land adjacent to the encampment area are the natural resources on which the Pakhimaras mainly depend. They do not have any control over the resources. The Pakhimaras are a totally landless community. Catching birds with the help of *log* (elongated and detachable bamboo shafts), *khoncha* (sharp pointed iron harpoon head) and *natha* (indigenous adhesive), and selling medicinal oil are the traditional and primary occupations of the Pakhimaras. Begging in areas around the encampment happens to be the traditional and primary economic pursuit of the women. Apart from the medicinal oil, sometimes they also sell birds in nearby markets. The *natha* or indigenous adhesive is prepared by boiling the latex of *dumur* (fig), and *bargach* (banyan) trees. It is reported to be very effective for catching birds by using a stick smeared with the same. Pakhimaras generally catch birds like *ghugu*, *harial*, *pankauri*, *paira* (pigeon), *bank*, *tia* (parrot) and *badur* (bats), etc. They prepare their own bird catching implements and appliances such as the *log, khoncha, natha* etc. Their link with the weekly or daily markets depends on their distance from their encampment. However, the Pakhimaras always keep in touch with the market, and the transaction is only in cash. Children below the age of fifteen years generally accompany the women for begging.

The Pakhimaras do not have any formal or traditional caste council or regional association. An informal body of elders, constituted from among the persons of the group, is reported to be the only platform for settling disputes among them. The Pakhimara wandering groups generally remain outside the purview of any modern statutory *gram panchayat* due to their frequent change of location. For the offences of adultery, rape or theft *jarimana taka* or cash fine is reported to be the usual form of punishment awarded by the body of elders among them.

They profess Hinduism. There are no specific deities at the family, *gotra*, village or regional level among the Pakhimaras. However, Durga, Kali, and Bhagabati are the deities worshipped by them. Durga puja is their main festival. Shivmandir (temple of Shiva) is their common sacred centre. The sacred abode of Paharsingh at Katihar is the centre of pilgrimage for them. The deity of Paharsingh is reported to be propitiated by offering *patha* (he goat), or *suor* (pig) as *bali* (sacrifice) by the Pakhimaras. *Bhagaban ke darkhasta* or praying to god for a better catch of birds and the wellbeing of family members are the main reasons for which they worship or propitiate the abovementioned deities. As has already been mentioned, the Pakhimaras do not employ any sacred specialists from other communities. Elderly and experienced persons from the community generally act as sacred specialists for the performance of different socio-religious rituals.

Tattooing on the bodies of both men and women seems to be the only art known to them. On the occasions of marriage, birth etc., in the family most of the men and women of the Pakhimaras group sing folk songs and participate in group dancing.

It may be mentioned here that though the members of a wandering group of the Pakhimaras interact with the communities of the Muchi, Hadi, Chamar, Napit (Barber) etc., on the occasions of birth, marriage and death, the relationship is generally more a matter of occasional interaction rather than permanent linkages as such. In fact there is no scope of establishing linkages with other communities through regular interactions over a considerable period at a particular place or locality. Commensal norms in regard to non-acceptance of food and water is reported to being observed by the Pakhimaras with the communities of Muslim, Hari, Muchi, Dom. Except the Kahar, Dhanuk, Mushar etc., who are considered to be nearest to the status of the Pakhimaras no other community generally accepts water and food from them. Putative relationship or *dosti* is generally reported to be established with the persons of other wandering groups of their own community without any ritual. The Pakhimaras do not face any hindrance in regard to sharing of water-resources, crematorium, temple or shrine etc., with other communities. They generally do not come within the purview of any type of a patron-client relationship with any other community.

By and large most of them are illiterate. Because of their wandering way of life the scope of sending their children to schools appears to be almost absent. Pakhimaras are reported to be mostly dependent on indigenous medicare. In regard to the different development programmes of the government no impact is reported to be there on the Pakhimaras simply for being remaining outside the purview of the schemes.

BADAL KUMAR BASU

PALIYA

The Paliyas are a large community and has the synonym of Poliya. "The name Paliya is said to refer to the *palayan* (flight) of the supposed Kshatriya ancestors..." (Risley: 1981: 4923). There is historical foundation of their origin from the Kochh or Kshatriya (*ibid*, 1981: 491-500). They are mainly distributed in the plains of West Dinajpur and Koch Behar districts of West Bengal, and the area is known to be a moderate climate zone with medium to high rainfall. The total population figure for the Paliyas in the state is 1,16,819 (census - 1981). They speak Bengali among themselves and also with outsiders. They use the Bengali script both at home and with neighbours. The Paliyas hold the constitutional status of scheduled caste in the state.

The Paliyas are non-vegetarian. They eat fish, meat and eggs. They do not take beef or pork. Rice is their staple food. They take all kinds of pulses, like *mug*, *masur*, *urad*, gram, etc. They take varieties of vegetables, roots and tubers which are available in the local market. They use mustard oil as their cooking medium. They take fruits occasionally. Tea is a common drink for them. Only men take brewed alcohol, locally known as *deshi madh,* purchased from country liquor shops. They use milk for nourishment of children and aged persons. They take milk products. They smoke *bidis* and cigarettes, and *hookkah* regularly. Both men and women chew *pan* (betel leaves) and *supari* or *gua* (betel nuts).

The Paliyas have three subgroups placed in hierarchical order: the Paliya Kshatriya, the Paliya and the Paliya Rajbanshi. They have several *gotras*. The *gotras* are, Kashyap, Sandilya, Modgaula, Gautam, Bharadwaja, Batsya, etc. The *gotras* are exogamous in nature. They use surnames like Sarkar, Deb, Das, etc. They consider Brahmans as higher than themselves. They regard themselves equal to the Kayasthas, and rank themselves higher than Kumbhars, Dhobas, Kansaris, etc. Brahmans, Kayasthas, Baidyas consider the Paliyas as equal to the Rajbanshis. They recognize the *varna* order and place themselves as Kshatriyas.

The Paliyas practise community endogamy, and subgroup endogamy. However, nowadays a few do not practise subgroup endogamy. They rigidly follow the rule of *gotra* exogamy. They prefer adult marriage and marriage by negotiation is the common practice. They prefer and practise monogamy. The symbols of marriage for married women are *sindur* (vermilion), *sankha* (conch shell bangles), and *loha* (iron bangles). Dowry exists and is given in cash and kind. After marriage, the bride lives with her husband. Divorce due to adultery and maladjustment is permissible with social or judicial approval. Either party can divorce. Children are the liability of either parent. Divorce compensation is given to the aggrieved party. Divorced men and women can remarry. Widow and widower remarriage is also permissible. The only change reported is that they have discarded child marriage and at present prefer only adult marriage.

The Paliyas prefer to live in nuclear families. However, a few of them have mixed extended families. They maintain avoidance relationship between daughter-in-law and father-in-law, between a man and his younger brother's wife. Joking relationship is found between elder brother's wife and the husband's younger brother, between grandparents and grandchildren. Conflict is observed on the property issue. Parental property is inherited equally by sons. Succession is by the eldest son. Women traditionally do not enjoy the right of inheritance. A recent change observed is the rise in number of nuclear families.

Women have various roles in society and in day to day life, like collection of fuel, fetching potable water, etc. They have roles in social rituals and in religious spheres of life and they do household activities. Women do not have any decision making power within the family. They have lower status than the men.

After child birth, the mother of the child is considered unclean for seven days. *Namkaran* (name giving) ceremony is done at the time of the *bhatdeoa* (first rice giving) ceremony, performed when the child is six or seven months old. A Brahman is called on that day for the purpose. During this ceremony the relatives and friends are invited and fed. The marriage is generally settled by the parents. On the day of marriage the bridegroom goes to the bride's house. The ceremony is performed by a Brahman. Marriage rituals are performed at the bride's house. The rituals are *adibas*, *kanyadan*, *homyogna* (fire worship), *sindurdan* (applying vermilion on bride's forehead), *malabadal* (exchange of garlands), making her wear *sankha* (conch shell bangles) and *loha* (iron bangles), etc. The priest recites hymns. A feast is arranged for the invitees.

The Paliyas cremate their dead bodies. They observe a pollution period for eleven days. On the twelfth day they perform the purificatory ceremony. An Agradani Brahman (a Brahman of lower order than the priest) is engaged and he conducts the sradh ceremony, in which offerings of sun-dried rice, sweets, etc., are made to the departed soul and to ancestors up to three generations on the father's and mother's side. This offering is known as *swapindakaran*. Relatives and friends are given a feast on the same evening.

The major economic resource of the Paliya is land. They have among them both landowners and landless people. Their traditional and present occupation is agriculture. Paddy is their main crop, though they also cultivate *pat* (jute), *pan* (betel), etc., as cash crops. The other occupations that they pursue are business, Government service, day labour etc. They have direct links with the local daily market, where transactions are in cash. As many of them are landless, the number of agricultural labourers has now gone up.

The Paliyas have a traditional *jati panchayat* or caste panchayat. The caste panchayat consists of three members, headed by the *morol*, a post that is not hereditary. They have a state level regional association. A statutory *panchayat* also exists for welfare activities of the villagers.

The Paliyas profess Hinduism. They worship Narayan, Laxmi, Chaitanya Mahaprabhu, etc., as their home deities. They also worship Lord Krishna, Shiva, Durga, Kali, Saraswati, etc. The Brahmans do the job of sacred specialists. They visit the temple of Bhabani (at Balurghat), and other popular pilgrimage centres like Puri, Varanasi, Mathura, Haridwar, etc. They have major festivals, like Gambhira, Charak, etc.

The Paliyas have a rich oral tradition of myth oriented folktales, folk songs and folklore. The instruments played while they sing folk songs are *khol*, *jhun jhuni*, etc. One example of their folk songs is given below. This song is sung by the bride's side.

"...... *Chiko chiko mai ge tor kapale Te ache Kalo masena tor bade ache*......"

(It means - oh poor girl, a dark groom is there for you.) They have folk dances which are performed in the *gambhira* festival, and *gambhira* dance is regarded as the main performance in this region of the state.

The Paliyas have the traditional inter-community linkages with the Brahman, the Kamar, the Chhutor, etc., and these linkages are maintained by way of rituals, and occupational activities. They accept food and water from the Brahman, the Kayastha, the Rajbanshi, etc. The Brahman, the Kayastha, etc., also accept water and food from them. They have putative kinship with their neighbours. They share wells, roads, schools, crematorium with others. They have businessmen, scholars, doctors, political leaders who have greater interaction with the larger society.

A few families take good care to educate their children. They use modern medicare and traditional medicines. They take the family welfare measures. Drinking water is mostly fetched from wells and tube wells. Radios and transistors are very common among them. Some of them get IRDP loans. Electricity has not yet reached most Paliya villages. They use chemical and organic manures. Irrigation mainly depends on tube wells, canal water and rainwater. They use coal, wood, and cowdung cakes as fuel. They make use of banking facilities, and the rationing system.

AMITABHA MITRA

PAN

The Pan are an immigrant community. They are also known as Pan Tanti. According to Risley, the Pan are a low weaving, basket making and servile caste scattered under various names throughout the north of Orissa and the southern and western part of Chhotonagpur (Risley : 1981 : 155). They are spread over a large area of the country and appear under several different names, the origin of which it is now difficult to trace (*ibid* : 157). They have migrated from Balasore district of Orissa. At present they live in the districts of Midnapur, and the 24 Parganas of West Bengal. Their population figure is 9,328 in West Bengal (1981 census). The climate of the area inhabited by the Pan in West Bengal is warm and temperate, associated with medium rainfall and high humidity. Soil is lateritic in nature. They speak Bengali and Oriya at home and with others. They use Bengali and Oriya script both at home and with neighbours. They hold constitutional status of scheduled caste in West Bengal.

The Pan are non-vegetarian. They take fish, egg and meat. They do not eat beef. Rice is the staple food. They take pulses like *mug, masur, kalai*, etc. They take various kinds of vegetables, roots and tubers which are available in the local market. Tea is compulsory drink for adults. They take alcoholic dinks occasionally and purchase it from the market. They can afford milk only for children. They take milk products. They cannot afford fruits regularly except on certain festive occasions. They smoke *bidi* and cigarette. They chew betel regularly. They also use *khaini* (chewing tobacco).

The Pan have four social sub-groups. The sub-groups are Pan, Raj Pan, Buna Pan and Pan Vaishnab. The basis of differentiation is based on hierarchy, occupation and on social status. In the hierarchical order, the Pan sub-group claim a higher social status than the other sub-groups. They have taken cultivation as a new and major occupation instead of pursuing their traditional occupation of weaving. Buna Pan includes those who weave cloth only. Raj Pan are the cane worker and basket weaver. These three sub-groups are intermarrying groups. The Pan Vaisnab do the job of priests for the community. The Pan Vaisnab are an endogamous group. The Pan use various surnames like Das, Pan, Patra, etc. The exogamous *gotra* names are Kashyapa, Vyasa, Sandilya, etc. They regard the Brahman, the Kayastha, the Karan, the Raju, etc. as ranked higher than the Pan, and they rank themselves equal to the Kamar, the Mall, etc. They regard themselves higher than the Bhuinmali, the Hari, the Kandra, etc. in local social hierarchy. They recognise the *varna* order and place themselves as Sudra. The Pan practise community endogamy. They also practise sub-groups exogamy and endogamy which was stated earlier, i.e. the Pan, the Buna Pan, and the Raj Pan may intermarry. The Pan Vaisnab practise endogamy within their sub-group. They prefer adult marriage and the age at marriage varies from sixteen to twenty years in case of girls and twenty to twenty four years in case of boys. They prefer marriage by negotiation, and practise monogamy. Junior sororate marriage is permissible. Married women use *sindur* (vermilion) and *sankha* (conch shell bangles) as their symbols of marriage. Bride-price is very rare. At present they practise dowry. The dowry is given in cash and in kind. After the marriage, bride goes to live with her husband. Divorce due to adultery, maladjustment, insanity is permitted with social approval. Either party can take the initiative to seek divorce. Divorce compensation is given to the aggrieved party. Children are the liability of either mother or father. Widow or widower can marry again. Divorced men as well as women are allowed to marry again. The widow can marry her deceased husband's younger brother, however, she is in no case, allowed to marry the elder brother of her deceased husband.

The Pan have mostly nuclear families. A few extended families are observed. Within the family, the eldest male member is regarded as the head of the family. Love and respect are always present between husband and wife. Children are treated with love and affection. Avoidance relationship is found between daughter-in-law and father-in-law. Joking relationship is found between elder brother's wife and husband's younger brother. Conflict arises on the property issue. Father's property is shared equally by the sons. Succession goes to the eldest son. Inter-family linkages in and outside the community are present. Neighbours are called as and when necessary to conduct various activities during the social, ritual and religious functions. The Pan who weave cloth, need constant supply of cotton thread. If supply is short, they frequently get cotton thread as loan from their neighbours. This mutual loan system is common to them to make full use of the looms as idle looms affect their economy adversely.

Women do not inherit parental property. They have economic role in the family, such as, collection of fuel, fetching potable water, etc. They also have roles in social, rituals, religious functions. They have no roles to play in matters of social control and are not given decision making power, and they do not control family expenditure. However, they participate in economic activities and contribute their earnings to the family. They also do the household job. They have low status than the men.

The Pan observe pollution period for six days after child birth. They perform a ceremony known as *sashti* on the sixth day. They observe and perform *namkaran* (name giving ceremony), *bhat khaoa* (first feeding of cereal) ceremonies in the sixth month in case of boys and in the seventh month in case of girls. Parents select an auspicious day for marriage of their son/daughter. Bridegroom goes to the bride's house to marry. Services of a Pan Vaisnab as a priest is necessary to solemnize the marriage. Marriage rituals are performed at bride's house and the rituals are *malabadal* (exchange of garlands), *sindurdan* (smearing vermilion in the parting of bride's hair) etc. A feast is arranged by the bride's parent. The Pan cremate their dead. They observe twelve days as a period of mourning. They observe *shradh* ceremony on the thirteenth day and offer rice, parched rice, curd, mustard seed, etc. to the deceased soul. The Pan Vaisnab and the Agradani Brahman do the job of priests. A feast is arranged for the *shradh* ceremony.

The Pan are traditionally a weaving caste. At present they weave cloth and also depend on land. They are both landowning and landless people. Other than settled cultivation and cloth weaving, they do the job in government. and private sectors, business, working in industry, labour in agricultural field, etc. A few do the cane work and make basket and weave mats. They have link with the market directly or through middle men. Payment of wages are in cash. As regards change, it may be mentioned that their original or rather traditional occupation was weaving, but now many of them have taken to cultivation.

The Pan have their *jati panchayat*. The post of chief is usually filled through an election or sometimes by voice votes. Statutory *panchayat* exists and it looks after the welfare and developmental programme of the village where they live.

The Pan profess Hinduism. They worship Lord Krishna, Satyanarayan as their home deity. They also worship Manasa, Sitala, Shiva, Durga, etc. The Pan Vaisnab (a sub-group of the Pan) do the job of a priests, however, nowadays the Brahman come to give services in the rituals and in religious functions. Shiva *mandir* (temple) Radha krishna *mandir*, etc. are their sacred centres. They go to Puri,

Varanasi, Kalighat for pilgrimage. Holi, Rathayatra, etc. are their main festivals. Weaving of cloth, basket making, mat weaving, cane work, etc. are the major crafts prevalent among them. They have rich oral tradition of folksongs, folklores, and folk tales. A sample of the folk song is given below :

"...*mora pantanti barohati kapor bune tante baccha pali, pet pali basi panta bhate*... ". (It means - We the Pan Tanti weave a *saree* twelve hands long, and so we maintain our livelihood.)

The Pan are a *jal-chal* community. They accept water and food from the Brahman, the Karan, the Kayastha, etc. The Brahman, the Kayastha, etc. also accept water and food from them. They do not accept water and cooked food from the Hari, the Behera, the Dom, etc. They do not prefer to marry outside their community. They share wells, tubewells, roads, schools, crematorium with others. They have patron-client, landlord-tenant relationship with the Brahman, the Raju, the Mahishya, etc. The community has teachers, government. service holders, businessmen etc.

The Pan are aware of the need for education. They prefer to send their children to schools. They use modern as well as indigenous medicine. They prefer family planning and use modern methods like tubectomy. Drinking water is available through tubewells, ponds, wells, etc. A few of them get I. R. D. P. loan to get handlooms, cotton threads, etc. They use transistor radio, visit cinema, use roads, post offices, etc. They use firewood, cow-dung cakes, kerosene oil, etc. as their fuel. Irrigation is only through rain water. They use organic manure and chemical fertilizer in agricultural land for better yield. Children get mid-day meal at school. They make use of ration facilities. They depend on moneylenders and on *mahajan* for subsistence.

AMITABHA MITRA

PARJA/PORJA

The Parjas are one of the least known communities in West Bengal. They are also known as Porja. Regarding the origin and migration of the Parjas it is said that they are originally an offshoot of the Gonds who reside in the centre and east of Bastar State and adjoining Jaipur Zamindari of Madras. The Parjas themselves have a story somewhat resembling that mentioned in the Madras Census Report of 1871 regarding their origin. It has been mentioned that "their ancestor was the elder brother of the first Raja of Bastar when he lived in Madras, to the south of Warangal. From there he had to flee on account of an invasion of the Muhammedans and was accompanied by the Goddess Danteswari, the tutelary deity of the Rajas of Bastar. In accordance with the command of the Goddess the younger brother was considered as the Raja and rode on a horse, while elder went before him carrying their baggage. At Bhadrachallam they met the Bhatras, and further on the Halbas. The Goddess followed them, guiding their steps, but she strictly enjoined on the Raja not to look behind him so as to see her. But when they came to the sands of the rivers Sankani and Dankani, the tinkle of the anklets of the Goddess could not be heard for the sand. The Raja therefore looked behind him to see if she was following, on which she said that she could go no more with him, but he was to march as far as he could and then settle down. The two brothers settled in Bastar, when the descendants of the younger became the ruling clan, and those of the elder were their servants, the Parjas. The story indicates, perhaps, that the Parjas were the original Gond inhabitants and rulers of the country. Their sept names are Gondi words, and their language is a form of Gondi, called after them Parji. Parji has hitherto been considered a form of Bhatri, but Sir G. Grierson has now classified the latter as a dialect of the Oriya language, while Parji remains a local and very corrupt variation of Gondi, considerably mixed with Hindi form" (Russel and Hiralal, 1916). The Parjas of Soongachi Tea Estate of Jalpaiguri themselves reported to have migrated from Surjankota village in Vishakhapattanam *thana* of district Jaipur and settled in the tea gardens sometimes around 1949. Madras is generally referred to as the homeland by the Parja. Apart from Soongachi tea estate the Parjas are reported to be distributed in various tea gardens of Jalpaiguri district e.g. Killote, Lankapara, Gergenda, Keron, Lakhipara and Ambari tea estates. Jalpaiguri district has a moderate climate with low hilly terrain, plain and marshy land, moderately humid, thin to medium forest and a medium range of rainfall. The Parjas speak an Oriya dialect among themselves and Hindi with others. Some of them can also speak and understand Bengali. Though Oriya is reported to be the script traditionally used by the Parjas, they have also started learning and using Devanagari and Bengali script after their migration to the present habitat. The concept of vegetarianism as such cannot even be perceived by the Parjas. Most of them take tea as non-alcoholic beverage. Both men and women almost regularly drink home made *baria* (rice beer). They do not eat beef.

As reported, (i) Khonda Parja; (ii) Jodia Parja; (iii) Peng Parja; (iv) Parenga Parja; and (v) Godwa Parja are the subgroups among the Parjas in their hierarchical positions respectively. Though the subgroups were traditionally endogamous, after their migration they are no longer so. Social hierarchy was the only basis of differentiation among the subgroups. Following are the names of *gotra* reported among the Parja (i) Kora (sun); (ii) Ontal (*nag* snake); (iii) Phangi (eagle); (iv) Balu/ Bhalu (bear); (v) Kilo (tiger); (vi) Kachim (tortoise); and (vii) Mach (fish). The exogamous totemistic *gotras* used to have clusters among themselves, in the sense that the Kora, Ontal, Bhalu and Kilo *gotras* settle marriages with one another but not with the *gotras* of Kachim, Phangi or Mach. Similarly the latter *gotras* also had separate cluster for the purpose of arranging marriage with one another. After their migration because of practical inconvenience, the rule has slowly been limited to the extent of *gotra* exogamy at present. Irrespective of their group or *gotra* affiliations all the Parja families of the settlement live in solidarity through mutual help cooperation and fellow feelings. Parja also happened to be the only surname used by them all along. In social status the Dom, Chamar and Ghasi are considered lower, whereas the Dora, Chetri, Brahman Karan, Teli, Mali, Kumar, Goala etc., are considered to be higher than the Parjas. Generally the Parjas are known as *Madrasi* (from Madras) or *Oriya* (from Orissa) by other communities inhabiting the tea garden settlements.

In most of the cases marriages are generally arranged within their own community but always outside ones own *gotra*. Though betrothal is completed at an early age, the actual marriage generally takes place after they become adult. *Mangabara* or marriage by negotiation is the usual mode of acquiring mates among the Parjas. Apart from this, sometimes marriages also take place through *rajikhusi* or love and courtship. Monogamy is the normal form of marriage. Both the forms of junior levirate and junior sororate are prevalent among the Parjas. Prevalence of cross cousin marriage and marriage between maternal uncle and niece among the Parjas indicate their similarity with the communities of south India. Traditionally a sum of Rs. 25/- to 50/- was given as bride-price in a *mangabari* (negotiated) marriage. This amount used to be generally paid as *mai sariluga* meaning the cost of upbringing the bride by her mother in her womb and there after. But at present there is no rule of either any bride-price or dowry as such among the Parjas. Generally a newly married couple sets up a new apartment within the household of the bridegrooms parents. In the tea garden if the man is a permanent employee he can be provided with a separate house after marriage. *Charachadi* or *kuhaboli* (divorce) can be obtained through approval of the informal panchayat for maladjustment, want of male child, impotency etc. In case a woman seeks divorce, which is a rare event, she is required to pay the amount spent in the marriage. Generally the father has the responsibility to maintain the children in case of a divorce. Only a nursing child stays wit its mother. Remarriage of widows, widowers, and male or female divorcees is prevalent among the Parjas. A widow generally prefers to remarry a widower, or her deceased husbands younger brother. A widower, male or female divorcee, is free to remarry any one as per their choice. Introduction of the liberty to settle marriages with any of the five subgroups, and abolition of the custom of paying either *maisariluga* (bride-price) or dowry are changes reported in the institution of marriage since their migration.

Many families are comprised of father, mother, their married sons, unmarried sons and daughters. The presence of nuclear families of married couples with unmarried children is also quite high among the Parjas. The younger members show respect to and obey their elders while they in turn love and take care of them. Women in a family have respect and status on their own right as tea garden employees. Husband and wife attach importance to each other in family matters apart from their bio-social role of obligations and expectations. The relationship between *sasura* (husbands elder brother) and *guari* (younger brothers wife) is that of avoidance. The relationship with wifes younger siblings, husbands younger siblings, *amibha* (fathers father), *dada* (mothers father) and *samadhi* (offsprings parent-in-laws) is that of mutual joking and friendliness. Parental property is inherited equally by all the sons generally. But sometimes the daughters are also given some share of it depending on their personal relationship with their brothers. A widow can enjoy or maintain herself on her deceased husbands property only so long she remains a widow and does not remarry. Comparative increase in the number of nuclear families and increase in the degree of self respect and status of the women since their settlement in the tea gardens are the main changes in their family life, as perceived by the Parjas.

Apart from doing the main household chores, the women play an important role in most of the socio-religious performances at the family level. In most families women play a very important economic role by substantially contributing to the family income, as many of them are employees of tea gardens. This has enhanced the status of women among the Parjas in terms of independence and respect. Though as employees the women do take part in the programmes of the tea garden labour unions, they in fact do not play any political role as such. They follow instructions of their male family heads in exercise of their franchise during the elections.

No pre-delivery ritual has been reported among the Parjas. Experienced elderly women from their own community act as midwives. Birth pollution is observed among the Parjas for eleven days. On completion of the sixth day, the ritual of *chatiari* or *navigirana* is performed by *mama* or maternal uncle of the child. The ritual *chutnitana* or purification is performed on completion of the eleventh day.

The rituals of marriage are performed at the residence of the bridegroom. The proposal of marriage is discussed with the *guru* or *disari* (their own sacred specialist) in the presence of the parents of the bride, her maternal uncle and the *agua* (go-between). Prior to the day of marriage the rituals of *grahasankat bidhi* is performed at the brides place. On the following morning, i.e., on the day of marriage the bride is taken to the bridegrooms house by her party. The ritual of *grahasankat bidhi* (or the ritual to ward off the effect of bad omen if any) is performed in the house of the bridegroom. These marriage rituals are performed by the *guru* or *disari* in the *madua* (*pandal*) outside the living room. Generally *maisari* is given in kind, i.e., clothes to brides mother and maternal uncle, or in cash called *jolataku*, followed by *samdhijodajodi* or *samdhibat* or exchange of clothes between the parents of the bride and bridegroom. A feast is arranged to entertain the guests and invitees after the ritual of *chuman* or blessing of the couple. On the following day *bidai* (send off of the brides party) is arranged through the ritual of *khasichatka* or killing of a he-goat for feeding the brides party. After nine days the ritual called *anibadauni* is performed whereby the newly married couple visits the brides house for the first time. They are offered fish and *kekra* (crab). After three days the ritual of *sotdekhna* is performed to send off the bride with her husband. Since adult marriage is the general practise, consummation is expected to take place at the bridegrooms residence following completion of the rituals of marriage with the send off ceremony for the brides party.

The dead are cremated, except in the case of children, who are buried. The grandson is preferred to offer the sacred fire to the funeral pyre. One who performs the ritual is called *joideva*. Death pollution is observed for three days. During all these days the *joideva* takes bath in *mahi* (hot water with turmeric) and abstains from fish, meat, *haldi* (turmeric) *piyaj* (onion), *lasun* (garlic) and oil and offers food in the name of *dumadokra*. On completion of the third day of pollution, the ritual of *sradh* is performed by going to the *bejorna* (a place near the spot of cremation) and offering *pindabhat* to *dumadokra* with *kalamurgichana* (black chicken) and taking a bath on the way back to home. Then *chutkachuta* or purification of family members and the house is done by sprinkling hot water mixed with turmeric. Later on, depending on ones economic ability, *suddhikriya* or *gami* or *bud* may be performed on the tenth day, or after a year. It is believed those for whom *gami* is not performed, will be unable to take rebirth.

Land was the major economic resource on which the Parjas depended, prior to their migration to the tea gardens. They were mostly share croppers or *goti* of different land owners or landlords. The Parjas were mainly a landholding community but not landowners. But after their migration to the tea estates of the district of Jalpaiguri, the Parjas began to earn their livelihood mainly as tea garden labourers and this became their primary occupation. The unemployed male and female Parjas work as casual wage labourers in tea gardens, and outside the tea estates, or work as casual labourers during the peak (rainy) season in the tea gardens. Working in the cultivable land allotted by the tea garden management is the only secondary occupation of the majority of the permanent employees of the tea estates. Apart from the well developed daily market, the Parjas depend on the weekly market of the garden itself that takes place every Friday; the weekly payday of the labourers. The medium of exchange in the market is always cash. There is no bonded labour among the Parjas. It has already been mentioned that for the majority of tea garden labourers in India, landlessness was the major factor behind migration and settling down in the tea gardens of Jalpaiguri district as labourers. There are no child labourers among the Parjas. Apart from wages in cash, various subsidies e.g., food grains at subsidised rates, free accommodation, drinking water, free fuel, medical care, educational facilities for children etc., are provided to all permanent employees of tea estates. For supplementing the family income and providing maintenance for the unemployed members, the permanent employees of the tea estates are also provided with some amount of cultivable land by the garden authority. Though the employees cultivate and consume the crops grown on the land, the tea estates owners remain owners of the land. These lands are liable to be taken back by the authority after retirement of the permanent employees. Landlessness leading to migration from original homeland, and subsequently settling down in the Dooars and Terai regions as tea plantation labourers has been the revolutionary change in the economic life of the Parjas in course of the last thirty-five to forty years.

Generally an informal panchayat body consisting of elderly and knowledgeable persons of their community settle minor disputes among them. Generally in cases of adultery, rape or elopement, the guilty are either socially boycotted, or fined in cash by the panchayat. The tea estates generally remain outside the purview of the modern statutory panchayat of the area. For matters of serious concern the Parjas also approach the labour union of the tea garden of even the judicial court at Jalpaiguri or local *thana* to seek redressal of problems and disputes.

The Parjas profess Hinduism. *Nishani Deota* is the common deity for all the Parjas. Worship of their deceased parents, is common among all Parja families. *Nishani Munda* or the sacred abode of the village deity is an important sacred centre of the Parjas. Babadham in Deoghar and Majhkund patal in Rajasthan are considered to be the important centres of pilgrimage. Their *guru* or *disari* performs the role of sacred specialist. They do not engage any specialist from outside their community. Worship, propitiation, performance of rituals of birth, marriage, death and protection from evil spirits are the main roles played by the *Gurudisari*. *Chaitparab* connected with community hunting expeditions of *tingribet* and *barabet*, and *Kaorapuja* connected with *kilosgau* and *betal rao* (folk songs) for harvesting and protection from small pox are the major festivals of the Parjas. A few cases of change of religion into Christianity and other animistic tribal religions have been reported among them. Though they are excommunicated, they can be taken back into the community again with ritual performance and payment of fine imposed on them. The converts generally discontinue their traditional religious practices.

The art of tattooing on parts of the body of both men and women was prevalent among the Parjas. At present they do not like it, Basketry is almost a community craft for the Parjas and they make articles like *kolki*, *dala, tipni, kula, tali, chatodi* (cap), *tarla* etc. Both men and women take part in singing folksongs. On various socio-religious occasions among the Parja music is played mostly by the Dom, using instruments like *kirdi, tamok, dhapu* and *mohri (sahanai)*.

In course of working together in the tea plantation and living in the same area of settlement the Parjas and various other communities often interact with each other and certain linkages are established among them. On different socio-religious occasions they mutually cooperate and extend help to each other. The Parjas do not accept food and water from the Tanti, Dom and Ghasi (horse dealers). On the other land, it is reported that the Brahman, Chetri, Dora Koran, Teli, Goala etc., do not accept food and water from them. As already mentioned, though some inter-community marriages have been taken place among them, they have never been accepted as legitimate marital exchanges establishing linkages with other communities. Inter-community marriages, in fact are looked down upon in Parja society till date. *Maitorgot* or putative relationship can be established with persons from any other community through the ritual of tying of *aampata tulsi-tama* (mango and *tulsi* leaf along with a piece of copper) on the wrists and mutual exchange of clothes and food among the concerned parities. The Parjas freely share all public amenities, i.e., water resources, roads, schools, crematoriums, temples, hospitals etc., with other communities. Except contributing subscriptions to the labour union fund of the tea garden and at times participating in some meetings and processions of tea garden labourers, they have no political activity.

The Parjas have expressed their favourable attitude to education. In their present settlement in tea gardens, they have the facility, for the first time, to send their children to the school run by the tea garden authority. Girls do not generally study beyond the lower primary level; because by the time they come to that level, they become potential wage earners in plantations and prefer to support their family, rather than go for studies. Some of the boys of course, go to nearby higher secondary schools. Most of the boys who had opted to go out of the garden school for further studies generally continue their study up to higher secondary level and then look for a job in the tea garden. The Parjas still have considerable faith in their indigenous medicare system. *Guru guruniani* is their indigenous medical man who is still consulted by most of the Parjas. By being in regular touch with the hospital run by the garden authority, they are gradually gaining faith in modern medicines. In an ailment or disease they first try indigenous medicines, and will approach the tea garden doctor only if uncured. They favour family planning schemes, but do not want to undergo an operation. They have their own method of birth control. A maximum of three children is considered ideal for a couple. They are provided with tap water facility by the garden authority in the settlement itself. The unemployed members of the Parja families either go out to work as wage labourers or are casually employed as labourers in the garden itself during the rainy season. They are well exposed to most of the means of mass media and communication, e.g., transistor, newspaper, video, cinema, roads, buses, railways and post offices etc. Though they do not have electricity in their settlements at presently, they have been assured by the garden authority that it will be made available very soon. As has already been mentioned earlier, the Parjas do not have any problem of fuel because it is provided by the garden authority free of cost every year to every permanent employee. Natural rainwater is the only source of irrigation used for the land provided to them by the management. Though nutritional schemes were introduced for school going children by the authorities, they became irregular after sometime. They are provided with food grains by the garden authority at subsidised rates. Most of the Parjas cannot afford to save any amount in the bank. Provident fund and gratuity are the only accounts in which they save for their future lives.

BADAL KUMAR BASU

PARSI

The Parsis are an ethno-religious minority community in India. The name of the community is also pronounced as Parsees. The historical root of the Parsi Zoroastrian community can be traced to the pre-Islamic history of Persia. The Zoroastrian dynasty came to an end when the army of the last king Yezdozard was defeated by the Arabs in the battle of Nahavand in the year AD 641. A long process of conversion by the Muslim invaders followed and thousands of Zoroastrian were converted into Islam by force. Later, a few hundred Zoroastrians left Iran and came to India by the sea route and landed on the island of Diu in AD 697. In the year AD 716, they came to settle at Sanjan on the west coast of Gujarat. From the west coast they started settling in various other parts of the country and considered India as their motherland. The recorded history of the Parsis of Calcutta begins with Dadabhoy Behramji. Banaji came here in AD 1767 from Surat. Till their migration to India, there were no sects or subsects among his followers of the religion of Zarathushtra. In Iran they had divided themselves into four classes on purely occupational basis. The major concentration of Parsis in West Bengal is in Calcutta. In Calcutta the Parsi population is spread throughout the city. But their main concentration is in central Calcutta. Geographically, Calcutta is situated on the Ganga delta with flat land surface. The city experiences a warm and temperate climate; with an average maximum temperature of 37.8° Celsius in summer and minimum temperature of 14.7° Celsius in winter. The average annual rainfall is 1320 mm, and high relative humidity is recorded during the monsoon season. The total population was 1220 in 1985, and the number of Parsi families in Calcutta was 448. The Parsis have adopted the Gujarati language as their tongue after migrating to India. But the Parsis mainly speak in English among themselves. While speaking with others they use both English and Hindi and in some cases Bengali. But they use Roman script for writing among themselves and others.

The Parsis are non-vegetarian. They take both beef and pork. Some special dishes are e.g., *dhansak, prawn patia, patra machi, vermicelli* etc. They eat both rice and wheat, all kind of pulses roots and tubers. They generally use ground nut oil, safflower, and sunflower oil for cooking. In the Parsi community both men and women drink and smoke occasionally.

Originally Parsis had four classes based on occupation namely: (a) the *Alhornon*, the priestly class; (b) the *Rathaeshtaran*, the military class; (c) the *Vastryosor*, the agricultural class; (d) the *Hutokhonan*, the artisans, tradesman and manufacturers. After their migration to India Parsis were very few in number. So, it was not possible to keep all these classes. Only priestly class has kept its identity and all others were grouped as '*Behedin*'. Now, the Parsis in India are divided into three groups, i.e., *Shahenshai*, *Kadmis* and *Fassalis*. The division is based on the mode of following the Parsi calendar. The *Yezdozardi* (Y. Z.) year of the Parsi is counted from 16th June 632 A.D., on which date Yezdozard III, the last Sassanian Emperor of Iran ascended the throne. In those days to make up the equivalent of the extra day added every leap year in the western calendar, and extra month called the 'Kabiseh' was added after every 120 years. The Parsis after migrating to India have observed the Kabiseh only once, but the followers of Zarathushtra who remained in Iran somehow failed to add the extra month on a single occasion after the invasion of the Muslims. About 200 years ago, it was noticed that Parsi Zoroastrians in India were one month ahead of Irani Zoroastrians. So, few Parsis in India, particularly in Surat and Bharuch started following the calendar observed by Irani Zoroastrians. As this sect based their now practice on what they considered to be ancient tradition, they came to known as 'Kadimi' presumably meaning "ancient" later corrupted to 'Kadmi'. The rest of the Parsis in India were labelled as 'Shahenshai', meaning 'of the city' but the word is popularly interpreted as 'Royalist'. A certain section of the Parsis felt that the proper day on which to commence the New Year was the Jamshedi Navroz day which always falls on the 21st March. This section formed themselves into a new sect called 'Fasslis' means 'season' in about the year 1906. It may, however, be noted that the Shahenshai, the Kadmis as well as the Fassalis start their New year with the month of Farvardin as the first month of the year, though each of them starts the year at a different time. Thus among all these three sects, there are two classes known as the Alhornan (priest) and Behedin (non-priest). They have changed their surnames when they came to India. They had taken surnames according to their profession or the place where they have settled, e. g. Contractor, Engineer, Ankelsaria, Bharucha, Bulsara, etc. It is interesting to note that they have some surnames which were originally the titles of the local Gujrati community, i.e., Desai, Mehta, Munshi, Modi, Patel etc.

The Parsis are very strict regarding their marriage rules. The Parsis follow endogamy within the community. There is no restriction on marriage within the same surname level. The Parsis follow the Parsi Marriage and Divorce Act No. XV of 1865. According to this Act, a Parsi can not marry some relatives, e.g., grandfather, step mother, sister, first cousin etc. So, they generally do not marry near relatives and persons within the same family tree. Adult marriage is the rule in their community. They strictly follow monogamy. Their symbol of marriage is wedding ring. They practice dowry system in both cash and kind. Their original rule of residence was patrilocal but now neolocal is also common. Marriage can be dissolved when either party is continuously absent for seven years or is of unsound mind, is involved in adultery bigamy, rape or infected with some infectious disease and if the person ceases to be Parsi. Compensation is given to the wife if her income is insufficient to support herself. Minor children are kept in the custody of either mother or father. In Parsi society the remarriage of both widowed and divorced male and female is common.

They have both nuclear and mixed extended types of family. Inheritance among the Parsis is controlled by the Parsi Succession Act No. XXI of 1865, according to which a son receives twice as much as the widow, and a daughter half as much as the widow's share of the property of a man. Eldest son succeeds father as head of the family. The Parsi women in Calcutta have an important role in economic activity and social functions. The Parsi women have 'The Calcutta Stree Mandal' with the principal object of extending help to the needy Zoroastrians residing in and around Calcutta and to assist them in improving their conditions. Women have more or less equal status in a modern Parsi family. They participate in economic activity, contribute to family income and in some cases control family expenditure also.

During pregnancy, the modern Parsis have no religious ceremonies or rites. On the completion of the fifth month of pregnancy, one day is celebrated and known as 'panch masiu'. Similarly, a day is observed on the completion of the seventh month, and is known as 'aghari'. These days are observed as auspicious day only in the case of first pregnancy. These are observed not in accordance with any religious ceremonies or rites. On the day or 'aghrani' the expecting mother is presented with clothes by her parents, relatives and friends and especially by the family of her husband. The husband is in turn presented with clothes by his wife's family. Sweets are sent out as presents by the husband's family to the bride's house and to near relations and friends. Among these sweets one prepared in the form of coconut, has a prominent place. A coconut typifies a man's head and so it is a symbol of fecundity. Some of the customs, observed on these occasions are more Indian in their origin and significance than originally Persian or Zoroastrian. After delivery, the mother in enjoined to remain apart from others. She may not touch fire, water and furniture of the house. This period, as described in the Pahlavi and Persian books lasts for forty days in all cases of delivery. The birthday of a modern Parsi child and especially the first birthday is an important day. No religious rites or ceremonies are necessary. This ceremony consists of the recital of prayers is honour of the thirty-three different *yazatas* (angels). After prolonged contact with the Hindus in India, the present day followers of Zarathushtra have adopted several Hindu customs and ceremonies. But the religious parts of the ceremony, where the priests take part, is originally Persian and is conducted in the Pazard language. The nuptial ceremonies of the marriage day are preceded by several other ceremonies. When the match is arranged, an auspicious day is fixed for the betrothal. On the betrothal day first ladies of the bridegroom's family go to the house of the bride with some special utensils, e.g., *thali* (plate), rosewater container, lamp container, water container, container to carry vermilion, raw rice, coconut, sugar and flowers and present her a silver coin. Then the ladies of the bride's family go to the house of the bridegroom with the bride. Rings are exchanged on this day in the presence of friends and relatives. The modern Parsi term of this ceremony is '*adravvun*'. According to the Parsi custom, a girl's name is always connected with her husband's, in religious ceremonies after the betrothal. The next ceremonial occasion is that of '*divo*' (light). On this day an oil lamp is lit in the house of each party. The next important occasion is that of '*adarna*'. On this occasion, the dowry (if any) given by the bride's father, is presented to the bridegroom's family. The marriage festivities generally last for four days. The first of these is called '*mandavsaro*' when a twig of a mango tree is planted near the door. The second and the third days '*varadh-patra*' (religious ceremonies in honour of the dead) are performed. Zoroastrian marriages are performed in the evening. It must be celebrated in the presence of an *anjuman* (assembly), who can bear witness to the event. The Parsi marriage is a contract between two persons. This marriage ceremony is performed in a temple and the feast is given by both sides.

Zoroastrians do not bury their dead because they believe that the evil associated with death would pollute the good earth. For the same reason the corpse cannot be disposed of at sea or cremated. Zoroastrians believe the vulture and other similar creatures were created to devour the corpse. In India today the dead body is placed in a *dakhma* (Tower of Silence). But in India and abroad, where no Towers are available, dead bodies are buried in *aramgah* (burial grounds reserved for the Parsis). The ceremonies for the dead, which are enjoined by the scriptures are, *chaharum* (on fourth day), *dehum* (on tenth day), *siruz* (thirtieth day), *salruz* (three hundred and sixty-sixth day). These ceremonies are prescribed as obligatory only during the first year.

There have been many illustrious entrepreneurs in the Parsi community. They were in the jute, shipping, textile and liquor business. Parsi entrepreneurship lost its importance after Independence. Today Parsi men and women are mostly engaged in government and private services and have scaled heights in their careers. Many are at the top of the city's most prestigious companies, and many more have made their mark in professions. They have direct link with the market. The medium of exchange is cash. There is no child labour among them.

There are various associations related to the religious, social and economic activities of the Parsi community in Calcutta. They are: Fire Temple, Calcutta Zoroastrian Community's Religious and Charity Funds, The Honourable Sir Dinshaw Manekjee Petit Zoroastrian Library, Calcutta Parsee Amateur Dramatic Club, Calcutta Parsee Club, The Parsee Zoroastrian Association, etc. The Parsee Zoroastrian Association is also referred to by the state government in various civic matters including recommendation of names of the delegates to the chief Parsee Matrimonial Court.

The Parsi community being an ethno-religious group has a common religion, i.e., Zoroastrian. They do not have any deity. They pray to *Ahura Mazda* (god almighty) and utilize the service of *Atash Behram* and *Atash Adaran* (sacred fire) as a transmitter to carry their prayer. In the Parsi community, any male member of the priestly family can become priest. According to the ancient customs, the rights can be revived by a descendent of a priest up to third generation. It then dies and can no longer be exercised. The role of the *dastur* (sacred specialists) is to worship, perform birth, marriage and death rites. There are many holy days in the Zoroastrian year and all are taken as festival days. The holiest day is Zarathushtra day. It is celebrated on the eleventh day of the tenth month. Other festival days are Pateti

(New year day), Khordad Sal (the birthday of Zarathushtra), *Farvardian-nu-Jashan* (ceremony of the dead), Jamshedi Navroz (nature's birthday), historical events etc.

The Parsi community have oral traditions of folk tales and folk songs. Their oral tradition and folk tales depict the life of Zarathushtra, and also the various stages of the development of this religion. Parsis have folk songs which are common Gujarati songs. The modern Parsi community is fond of western music, light music and classical music. They also participate in dance, both modern and traditional.

They accept water from other communities and exchange water with everybody. Inter-community marriage between Parsi and non-Parsi community is not common. In fact a Parsi Zoroastrian woman is excommunicated, when she marries a non-Parsi. A non-Parsi Zoroastrian woman can not become Parsi Zoroastrian by marrying a man of that community. The Parsis participate in traditional festivals like Holi, Diwali etc. The community has entrepreneurs, businessmen, executives, administrators, engineers, doctors.

Parsi boys and girls both take higher education. Many of them study up to post-graduate and even higher levels. After completing their studies, boys start earning to support the family; girls either get married or start earning. They make use of only modern medicare. Their attitude is favourable towards family planning. Couples prefer one or two children. Drinking water from tap is available within the locality. They listen to radio, watch television, visit cinema. They use electricity for domestic purpose. LPG is used as fuel. They avail themselves of ration distribution through fair price shops and have favourable attitude towards savings.

The main distinctive feature of the Parsi community is that they are very strict regarding their religion. According to Parsi Zoroastrian rule a non-Zoroastrian can be converted to the Zoroastrian religion, but he or she cannot be termed as a Parsi Zoroastrian. He will not enjoy any facility provided by the Parsi Zoroastrian funds. Parsis cannot adopt any child according to their custom and religion.

SMITA SENGUPTA

PASI

The Pasis are one of the well known communities of Bihar and Uttar Pradesh. A number of them are residing in Barrackpur subdivision of North 24 Parganas of West Bengal. They are also called Paswan. Their surnames are Chowdhury, Paswan, Pasi, Saraj, Prasad and Ratna. Pasis have four subgroups. The sub-divisions are Byadha, Tirsulia, Kaykhoash and Gaidudhya. According to some there is another subgroup. Traditional occupation of the Byadha and Tirsulia, was that of cutting palm trees and preparing and selling toddy. Other two groups were agriculturists. They have a story about their origin. They were born out of the sweat of Parasuram at the time of his *nikshatrikaran* (eliminating Kshatriya *varna*). Though Risley (1891 : II : 166) said that their traditional occupation was selling country liquor, nearly half of the Pasis of Naihati and Bijpore region are working in different factories. According to the Pasis, they are distributed in all the districts of Bihar state, but in West Bengal they are mainly distributed in places like Jagaddal, Naihati, Bijpur, Bhatpara, Kanchrapara, Halisahar, Ranaghat in Barrackpur subdivision of North 24-Parganas. The habitat of the community is the Gangetic plains of lower Bengal. Their total population according to the 1981 Census is 21,367.

The language of the Pasis in West Bengal is Hindi. Their dialect is Hindi. Their script is Devanagari and they use it at home and with kin groups. They can speak and understand Bengali. The Pasis have no identification marks in respect of dress and ornaments. Their constitutional status is that of scheduled caste.

They are a non-vegetarian group of people. They do not eat beef, tortoise and pork. They usually take varieties of fishes and meat. Their staple food for lunch is rice along with *dal* (pulses), vegetable curry and fish. They usually take *roti* (hand made bread) with vegetable curry and *dal* (pulses) for breakfast and dinner. They drink alcoholic drinks almost every day. Their attitude is that since they have to work hard alcoholic drinks are essential. They purchase it from the market as well as they consume the homemade *tari*. They sometimes take milk according to economic condition of the family. Those whose first issue is a son, never eat *chalkumra* (a kind of gourd) in the month of *Jaistha* (May-June). They have changed some of their food habits, because in West Bengal they do not get *makai* (maize) or *marua* (a kind of grain) which had been their staple food in Bihar.

Social hierarchy was present in the past among their four divisions. The two groups who used to cut palm trees and sell liquor were ranked low. Each group was an endogamous unit some ten years back, but now-a-days there is no marriage restriction among these four subgroups. Occupation was the only basis for group differentiation. Their only clan or *gotra* is 'Parasuram'. The self-perception of the community itself, as well as the opinion of other communities of the locality is that they rank very low because they belong to the scheduled caste category.

Endogamy is the marriage rule of the Pasis. The age of marriage for girls is fifteen or sixteen years, and eighteen or nineteen years for boys. Negotiation is their primary mode for acquiring a mate. Monogamy is the form of marriage, *sindur* (vermilion), and glass bangles are the marriage symbols for their women. Dowry in both cash and kind is given at the time of *tilak* (first marriage rite). Residence is patrilocal after marriage.

Divorce is permitted. Men and women, who want divorce, seek permission from the *samaj panchayat*. The *panchayat* holds a meeting and decides who is guilty between the spouses; the guilty man or woman is forced to pay a cash penalty to the *samaj panchayat*. Permission and decision of the *samaj panchayat* are absolutely necessary for a divorce or for securing post-divorce maintenance. Remarriage is permissible for both men and women after finalization of divorce by the *panchayat*. Remarriage is allowed after the death of one spouse. In Risley's book (1891: II: 166) this form of marriage has been mentioned as the *sagai* form. The widow is not expected to marry her husband's younger brother. The only change in marriage institution is that marriage is nowadays allowed among four subdivisions, which was not possible even some ten years back.

The Pasis prefer to live in both vertically and laterally extended families. Number of nuclear families is very few among them. They narrate that in their homeland in Bihar their families consist of ten to forty members. But in West Bengal their family size is four to ten members. The inter-personal relations are marked love, fear, avoidance, obligation, joking, conflict and confrontation. An avoidance relationship is maintained with husband's elder brother and joking relation is found between elder brother's wife and husband younger brother, between a man and his wife's brothers and sister's and between grandparents and grandchildren. Rules of inheritance and succession are also through male line. The eldest son succeeds his father. Inter-family linkages are very much strong in their society because in every marriage ritual and also in other festivals they meet and sing religious songs. No significant change is observable in respect of family except the deteriorating economic condition of the Pasi community, as they are not getting proper employment. In West Bengal they are also not getting any facility offered to the schedule castes.

The amount of property owned by the Pasi community of West Bengal is really insignificant. After the death of her husband, a woman has the right to inherit his property. If a woman is the only child of her parents she has a claim on her parents' property. Pasi women are mostly illiterate and that is why their participation in white collar job is nil. Sometimes widows are found selling by the street side as they have lost their husbands and have no other alternative to manage their households. Family or household management is the sole responsibility of the women folk.

The Pasis observe a birth pollution of *soamahina* (five weeks), irrespective of the sex of the child. On the sixth day after birth, the mother of a newborn baby takes a bath after the cutting nails etc. For the first four to five days she has to take turmeric as well as molasses and ginger as indigenous medicines for a quick recovery. Another bath and cutting of nails etc. are arranged on the twelfth day and it is called *barohi* and this is a semi-purificatory rite. After *barohi* the woman is allowed to enter the kitchen or put vermilion on her forehead. After the completion of pollution period of *soamahina*, some women from the neighbourhood or from among the relatives come and sing religious songs. Sweets are distributed among them from the house of the new born baby and this ceremony is called *kothakara*. Some rich families among them observe *annaprashan* like the Bengalis. In case of a female child after her first menstruation they say that *"a totka lena porega"* and this *totka* (a rite) is called *bandhankata*. In this rite they hang a rope with some knots at equal distances. The newly menstruating girl cuts the rope taking two knot spaceful of rope and half of the rope between the second and the third knots. After this the girl has to take a bath with two and a half *poa* (altogether *arhaipoa* water a *poa* is one fourth of a *seer*) of water. This rite is also called '*arhaibandhankatano*'. During this ritual they pray to god for an early marriage of the girl.

Marriage of the Pasis starts with the binding rite called *chhenka*, when the bride's family visits the groom's house and gives some money to the groom's family. It is a symbol of consent for the marriage, i.e., they express willingness to have affinal tie with the groom's family members as well as their opinion that the residence of the groom has come up to their expectation. When the groom's party gives their consent to the marriage, i.e., when bride is chosen by the groom's party, the bride's family once again visits the groom's family and gives three to four thousand rupees as binding money. After the final settlement of the marriage another rite known as *tilak* is done, in which the bride's family is informed of the expected amount of dowry. If the bride's family is unable to pay the dowry as per demand they plainly explain their inability and under no circumstances is the marriage retracted. Their marriages generally take place within the months of May and June. *Lagan* is settled by the Brahman priest and who is called *pandit*. Just one day before the marriage ceremony they have another rite known as *ghatoan* in which parents of the bride and groom in their respective houses remain on fast for the whole day and listen to *Satyanarayana katha* (recitation from the book on Satyanarayan Puja) sitting by the side of the *Maro* (marriage booth). *Maro* is prepared two days before the marriage. For preparing a *maro* they bring five new bamboos with some branches at the top and these are erected on the ground enclosing some space in the middle. The tops of the five bamboos are bound by red coloured papers or ribbons. A bunch of *kush* (a kind of grass) is put on the top the *maro* as it is considered a good omen. After the preparation of the *maro*, some Pasi women come from the locality and sing some religious songs. Then the family distributes some mustard oil and *Veligur* (a kind of molasses) to the visitors. This festival is known as *matimangra*. After the *Satyanarayana katha* a small pitcher is worshipped and all the gods and goddess are invoked for blessing the marriage. Then the mouth of the pitcher is closed with some mud because it is feared that evil spirit may enter the pot. They prepare a *sugga* (a wooden slab on which eight to ten birds are engraved) and they keep it hidden in the *maro*. It is a good omen and they keep it in both the houses of the groom and the bride. In the bride's house the bridegroom's party search until they find it, and in bridegroom's house the bride's party have to do so. The relatives and friends who come to see the bridegroom and the visitors put some coins or rupees on a plate according to their wish and means. This is called *duar*. Nowadays a few Pasi families arrange a feast during marriage like other communities. On the day after the marriage the bridegroom returns with the bride to his home. On this day they celebrate *sohagrat*; it is their consummation of marriage. They also perform *boubhat* on the next day of *sohagrat*. Previously they had a system of second marriage called *gaona*. When child marriage was prevalent the bride used to reside in her father's house till her first menstruation. After menstruation, *gaona* was performed (almost like marriage ceremony excluding dowry etc.) and it was held in any odd year i.e.; third, fifth or seventh year after marriage. At present *gaona* is performed just one year after the marriage or simultaneously with the marriage because nowadays child marriage is not practised. A Brahman priest and a barber are essential for a Pasi marriage. The barber carries the water (with which the groom had taken a bath) to the bride's house, as the bride has to take her bath in that water. The barbers of the both parties must be present at the time of marriage as they carry out the orders of the priests. There is a system of payment to the priest and the barber at the time of marriage. If the bride's party pays Rs. 2/- to the barber or the priest, the groom's party must pay Rs. 4/-. Nowadays total payment made to the priest is Rs 70/- to Rs 80/- and a *dhoti*.

They cremate their dead at the burning *ghat*. The pollution period lasts for ten days. They hang a pitcher from a *pipal* tree or a banyan tree and the person who does *mukhagni* (lights fire to the mouth of the dead) and the other family members have to fill that pitcher with water after taking his bath for ten days. They believe that the soul resides with them for ten days and after *sradh* it goes to the other world. The chief mourner takes only one meal a day and he cooks it himself. Married daughters have no function after the death of their parents unless there is none in her father's lineage. On the tenth day they go to the river side and the sons get their hair and all family members get their nails cut by the barber. On the twelfth day they perform *sradh* ceremony, which is sometimes called *barohi*. A vegetarian feast is held on the twelfth day and it is known as *kachcha*. On the thirteenth day (they call it *terohi*) they invite friends and relatives to a non-vegetarian feast.

According to the Pasis, three fourths of them living in Barrackpur sub-division, work in different factories; and one-fourth still practise their traditional profession like *gachhkata* (extracting palm juice), and making and selling *tari* (country liquor). They now extract palm juice throughout the year. They cut *khajur* (date palm) trees from the month of *Bhadra* (August-September) to *Magh* (January-February) and *tal* (palm) tree from the month of *Phalgun* (February-March) to *Sravan* (July-August). The man who extracts the palm juice sells it to another at wholesale price. The second man sells it to his customers at the price of fifty paisa per glass. Palm trees are taken by the Pasis on lease. Pasis in West Bengal are a landless community.

The Pasis have a traditional *jati panchayat*. The head of the institution is called *chowdhury*. There are one secretary and ten to eleven members. At the time of necessity, *chowdhury* calls all members to come meet and settle disputes or cases of divorce etc. There is also a sub-committee formed by the members of the *panchayat*, whose duty is to collect a subscription of Re. 1/- from each Pasi family of the village for running the *panchayat*. Sometime between 1950 and 1952 the Pasis had a Mahashabha (meeting) at Belur in Howrah district.

Hinduism is the religion of the Pasis. Their family deities are Lakshmi and Narayana. They occasionally arrange Lakshmi and Narayana *Katha* (readings from the books of stories on Lakshmi and Narayana) and listen to these stories. They observe *narat* in the month of *Chaitra* (March-April) and *Kner* in *Ashwin* (September-October). This nine day festival ends on the day of *Mahalaya*. In *narat* festival they worship deities like Kali, Sitala, Tara etc. They also observe *Tijparab* in the month of *Sravan* (July-August) in which unmarried girls worship *Kijri* for getting good husbands. After *Mahalaya* they make offerings to the deceased and this period is called *pitripaksha*. They observe Holi, *Ekadasi*, Ramnavami, Chhatparab, etc. They worship Hanuman and Brindhachal. Residing in Bengal they have give subscriptions for Durga puja, Kali puja, Lakshmi and Saraswati pujas performed by the Bengalis. They wear new clothes during Bengali festivals. Their major sacred centre is Gangasagar mela. Before going to any place of pilgrimage they first visit Gangasagar. They visit many places like Gaya, Kashi, Ayodhya, Mathura, Brindaban, Rishikesh, Badrikasram, Gangotri, and Tarakeswar for pilgrimage. In all socio-religious ceremonies they engage a Brahman priest of Bihar whom they call him *pandit* and who is their sacred specialist. They visit various fairs like Charak mela, Ratha Yatra mela etc.

The Pasi has traditional inter community linkage with the Brahman priest and barber. It is mentioned by Risley (1891) that the rank of the Pasis was socially below the Tatwas and much the same as Binds and Chains. But in West Bengal, the Pasis say that their place is higher than Kamar and Dusadh. They further say that still in their place of origin (Bihar) many castes do not take water from their hand, but in the urban setting there is no such restriction. They now accept water, *kachcha*, *pucca* and *sidha* food from the communities like the

Brahman, Kayastha etc. They exchange such food with those who are socially equal to them. They do not accept these from the Hela and Dom. In West Bengal there is no restriction on the Pasis in sharing wells, water source, road, crematorium, temple etc. They maintain some symbiotic relationship with those from whom they take palm trees on lease for collecting palm juice.

They maintain modern inter-community linkages in various ways, i.e., their children are going to schools and colleges; some are service-holders in factories and offices. Among the modern inter-community linkages it may be mentioned that a number of persons from the Pasi community were put up as candidates in Municipality election.

The level of education among the Pasis is still very poor. Percentage of male students studying in schools is much higher than that of girl students. Girls read mostly up to class IV. There are only ten to twelve matriculates. B.A. or M.A. degree holders are rare in the studied area having a population of two or three thousand.

For their medical necessity they go to the E. S. I. Hospital or consult doctors at their own cost. The Pasi community does not like the family planning programme as only one or two educated persons have got themselves sterilized. The remaining Pasis have the idea that a baby is born only with the grace of god and so they have no right to check its birth. They listen to radio, watch television programmes and visit cinema. They receive information through extension agencies and political parties. The roads, railways and post offices exist nearby. For drinking the Pasis use tap water. The Pasi community, though residing in urban centre, is unable to use electricity due to poverty. Pasis live in rationing areas and take advantage of the public distribution system. Their children sometimes get bread from their schools. Cowdung, coal, kerosene are used as fuel. It can be stated that no Pasi is getting any kind of facility offered to the scheduled castes. It is very difficult for them to get scheduled caste certificate from any government office.

CHANDRIMA CHOWDHURY

PATHAN

The Pathan community has neither a synonym nor a title. The etymology of the name Pathan is traced from the word *fatehan* meaning to win victory. The Pathans think that their ancestors won victory in wars and thus came to be known as Pathan. The Pathans maintain that like any *jat*, they are divided into four *thaks*. However, while naming the *thak*, they mention five names, viz., 1) Niaji Pathan, 2) Sur Pathan; 3) Jilam Pathan or Zalem Pathan; 4) Guria or Garia Pathan; and 5) Beteli Pathan. The Pathans, as Moslems trace their history from Arabia. They maintain that the first ever Moslems were from Arabia whence this faith originated and was propagated. They consider Afghanistan as the original abode of the Pathans and trace their ancestry from there. They deliberately remain oblivious of the fact of Islamic proselytism. They rather, speculate a historic past when their Middle Eastern Moslem ancestors came in the company of Moslem invaders and later settled in the country and married local women. They consider themselves to be the descendants of those unions. The Pathans are aware of their global distribution. They are observed to be specific about their local distribution. According to them, a good number of them are found across the state's border in the district of Santhal Parganas, Bihar. They further state that they are found in the districts of Malda, Murshidabad and in the north-western part of Birbhum district. They are found in almost all districts of West Bengal. The environment of their natural habitat in this state the plains of eastern India, is a warm and temperate climate with high humidity and medium rainfall. The language/dialect spoken at home in certain areas is Hindi. Those who are literate among them, write in Bengali, even while writing letters to their kin. With outsiders both spoken and written language is Bengali.

The Pathans are non-vegetarian. The concept of non-vegetarianism is expressed in terms of inclusion of meat, fish, etc., as food items. As non-vegetarians, they include both beef and meat of buffalo in their food. Like all other Moslems, they consider pork a taboo. Their staple food is rice. They prefer *masur dal*; but they consider it not easily digestible. Instead they find *kala kalai* as a suitable variety of pulses for them, as it is easily digestible and it keeps them physically cool while working in the field for long hours in the sun or while doing hard physical labour. There are certain local notions, depending on which they classify some items of food as having cooling effect on one's health, while the others as hot, i.e., producing heat in the body. Edible oil is extracted from mustard seeds. (Mustard is a popular crop in most of the districts in the state). A variety of roots, tubers, bark, etc., constitute food items. Turmeric, ginger, potato, sweet potato, yam, etc., are commonly eaten. The most common vegetables are brinjal, greens, gourd, bean, etc. Fruits are eaten occasionally and seasonally, and on festive occasions, e.g., during the month of Ramzan. Children of rich Pathan families are provided milk by their parents, while poor Pathan children have to do without it. Tea is a common drink. As per Quranic instructions alcohol is a taboo for Moslems. However, the Pathans admit that a few among them do indulge in drinking toddy as well as liquor. For liquor they depend on the market and toddy is, at times, extracted from palm trees owned by individual families. They have a preference for the meat of animals and fruits supposedly eaten in Arabia, e.g., meat of camel or fruits like dates. They do not eat birds and animals that are taboo according to the writings of the Koran. They conventionally avoid eating mushroom, crab, tortoise, snail, etc.

The Pathans have a stereotyped notion of social divisions among them. These divisions are, in a way, territorial and, to some extent, based on the assumed temperamental disposition of each of these groups. The Niazi or Niaji Pathans are found in Birbhum and are considered temperamentally peace-loving. Another group known as Sur Pathan found in Malda are also peace-loving. The Jelam or the Jelem Pathans are found in Murshidabad. The Guria or Garia Pathan are a nomadic group (hardly seen these days) and are supposedly soldier-like in their attitude. There is another division of the Pathan known as Beteli who are stubborn, hot-headed and can break into a fit of temper in no time. However, their anger subsides easily. They use Khan (meaning Pathan) as their surname. They place themselves in the third position in the locally perceived hierarchy of the Moslem communities. They place the Sayads at the top of the hierarchy and reckon the Sheiks' position as second in the hierarchy. The Sheiks who dominate in number over all other Moslem communities in the state have a similar notion about the hierarchy. Though the Moslems have a local social hierarchy almost parallel to that of the Hindu social hierarchy, they do not have any *varna* to support it. The neighbouring Hindus hardly show any interest as regards this hierarchy. They regard the Pathan as a socio-ritually lowly Moslem community and the upper caste Hindus expect the poor Pathan to work for them as labourers like members of any low caste/community. The rich Pathans in practice, however, compete with the upper caste Hindus almost as equals in the socio-economic and political spheres. They too employ the members of the Hindu low caste communities as well as poor Moslems of various communities as labourers either in their cultivation or for doing odd jobs like earth-moving, thatching etc.

The Pathans go by the marriage rules prescribed in the Koran. According to rules, they are usually not permitted to marry across their respective generations and within the same generations they are prohibited to marry their brothers and sisters, including half-brothers and half-sisters. Fosterage or milk relationship counts like blood relationship as per the rules. Due to this they are not allowed to marry their foster brothers or foster sisters. The rules in the Koran stipulate that in establishing the marriage tie with a woman, her faith (obviously Islam) is to be taken into consideration, but not her social position. The local Moslems do not conform to this rule, rather they try to strictly limit their marriages within their respective communities (or *kam*, as the local Pathans define it). Age at marriage for males is between twenty and twenty-five years, while females are married between the age of eighteen and twenty years. The prevalent mode of acquiring mates is by negotiation. For negotiation the Pathans use their kin network and do not usually employ a matchmaker. Monogamy is commonly practised and favoured. As per Islamic traditions the Moslems, however, are allowed polygyny. Bride-price (*den mehr*) and dowry, both are in practice. *Den mehr* is as per the Islamic traditions (*Shariat*) and it is an integral part of a marriage contract. There are Koranic injunctions regarding this in *sure*: 4, *Ayet*: 4 and 25 and also *sure*: 2, *Ayet*: 236. *Den mehr* constitutes the money and valuables promised to be given to the bride by the groom. A part of this promised amount is actually given at the time of the marriage. *Pan* or dowry is a recent innovation among the Moslems and Pathans mention Hindu influence as the cause of its origin. It is given both in cash and kind. Residence after marriage is patrilocal and exceptions are made only in the case of a *gharjamai*, when the husband comes to live with his in-laws. Divorce as well as the necessity of precautions to guard against it has been dealt with in detail in the Koran. Divorce is looked upon and talked about as a male prerogative. The Pathans state that a husband can seek divorce on the basis of any one of the following faults of the wife: (i) adultery; (ii) suspicion that she may kill him; (iii) change of religion; and (iv) barrenness. There is a Koranic injunction as regards post-divorce maintenance for the period of *iddat* (or waiting), but no such maintenance is normally provided for. Except for the observance of *iddat* for about three months by both the divorcees there is no specific rule regarding remarriage. The principal ceremony of marriage and remarriage is the same.

Nuclear families dominate the other types of families in Pathan villages. As regards interpersonal relations within the family the Pathans talk about the different ideal aspects that should be practised with a view to maintaining relations between husband and wife. The first and foremost demand on the part of the husbands on their wives is the unconditional devotion of their wives to them. The other thing that they talk about is purdah. Husbands should take adequate measures to keep their wives in purdah and wives on their part, should try to observe it. These, however, constitute a kind of thinking aloud of the rich Pathan or, in general, of the rich Moslem and is a result of the formal *woaz* (talks) given by *mullahs* on different religio-festive occasion like *milad*. In their daily life there is not much scope of practising such high ideals, e.g., purdah, especially by poor women. The wives in general, are loyal to their husbands, but there is nothing like unconditional obligation on their part towards their husbands. The relations between them are of mutual dependence and obligation. They jointly take the responsibility of the family. Parent-child relation is of love and affection. The relation of affection and joking (*akud neksa*) is between grandparent and grandchild. The Pathans follow Moslem rules of inheritance as outlined in the Koran. One important feature of these rules is that generally, but not always, the male takes a share double that of the female in his own category. The rules are complicated because there are shares for the ascendant, the spouse, the descendant, and the collateral, e.g., there are shares for the deceased's parent, his or her spouse, and children and in certain cases uterine sibling. Succession is patrilineal. Interfamily linkages are multifarious-linkages based on their membership of the same community; sharing of the same hamlet; practice of one and the same religion; adherence to the similar sect, namely, Sunni, and the same school of thought, Hanafi, inter-linkages of kin both affined and agnate; and village-based kinship, friendship and interest group of social, economic and political nature.

Women's right of inheritance is religio-socially and legally acknowledged. They have a right to inherit part of the properties as mothers, wives and sisters. Their right to inheritance is, not always, properly honoured, especially when parental properties are concerned and brothers are there to inherit them. However, brothers are often found obliged towards their sisters when they forgo their part or whole of their claim. The obligation is frequently shown is terms of taking social, economic or educational responsibilities of sisters' children or in terms of maintaining a good and helpful relation with their sisters. Women's major economic role is household management and their important social role is that of mothers i.e., rearing and initial training in the socialization of children. Women have no active role in political activities. Women contribute to family income whatever little they can earn by way of selling eggs of domesticated birds to itinerant traders or any other trade.

Birth of a male child is announced by *azan*. On the fifth day (locally known as *panchute*) the child's head is shaved by a barber. This custom, according to the Pathans, is a typically Moslem custom. They observe a period of pollution after the birth of a child and the period is called *antur*. They, unlike the local Hindu communities do not throw away earthenware used in the kitchen after birth. They employ midwives belonging to the Hadi community for deliveries. They have a prescribed name giving ceremony called *agika*. Most people skip this ceremony as they find it expensive. During *agika* either goats or cows are slaughtered. The parents of the child do not eat the sacrificial meat of the animal. Unlike *agika*, circumcision or *khatna* is a must for every male child. It is done by a Moslem *Hajjam* or barber. Every parent tries to arrange it at an early age for the child. Celibacy is not religio-socially accepted by any Moslem community. The principal ceremony of marriage is contractual. Marriages are not held on the following dates of the Moslem lunar months as these are considered inauspicious: first, eleventh, twenty-first, third, thirteenth, twenty-third, fifth, fifteenth, twenty-fifth, seventh, seventeenth, twenty-seventh. The month after Muharram (the first month of Hijrat year) is known as *teji* (i.e., strong) month and no marriage is held during this month. The first formality in marriage is a visit on the part of the groom's side to the bride's home. On the day of this formal visit the date of marriage is settled. There is normally an interval of five, seven, or nine days between the day of the visit and the date of marriage. This period is called *lagan*. During *lagan, gayehalud* and merry-making begin. *Gayehalud* is smearing of a paste of turmeric in mustered oil with *sondha* (a sweet smelling plant) on the bodies of both groom and bride. The bride's party visits the groom's house after the abovementioned formal visit by the groom's party is over. When the bride's party comes to the groom's home *mehendi* (i.e. *henna* or *mehendi*) is applied. There is no ritual attached to consummation of marriage.

After the death of a person, a forty day period of mourning is observed. This is called *chalisha*. The deceased is washed; dressed and buried. Seven small pieces of new cloth are required while washing a dead man and for washing a dead woman nine pieces are needed. Four more pieces of new cloth are used while burying the dead. All these pieces are known as *kaphan*. The Moslems do not use any coffin for the corpse. Before interring the dead all the assembled Moslems at the graveyard say the *janaja* or last prayer facing the west. If the *wakt* (time) of any of the normal daily five time *namaz* coincides with that of the *janaja*, then the *janaja* is read only after the time of daily *namaz* is over. *Akad bandha* is considered an important occasion. This is child marriage under certain exigent situations. For example, a dying parent may wish to see his or her child's marriage, or under certain circumstances for the sake of keeping a promise parents or guardians of both the bride and groom may arrange a marriage of this kind. The bride goes to her in-laws only when she comes of age.

The major economic resource is land for the Pathan inhabitants of the pre-eminently agricultural districts of the state. The community is a combination of both landowning and landless categories. The rich Pathans, who form a small section of the community, have land on which they can subsist. The poor Pathans constitute another section, not very small in size like the former, are either completely landless or have very little landholding. The rest of community hold lands which is on the one hand not enough for them to subsist on and on the other hand not as small as holding as that of the poor Pathan. These middle class cultivators have taken up a number of non agricultural occupations. Those who possess land exercise control over it. Ownership of individual proprietors is practised as regards land holding. For generations the Pathans are known to be cultivators. They claim that in the distant past they were soldiers. At present the Pathans living in rural areas of the state are primarily a community of agriculturists. As subsidiary means of livelihood they have gone in for a number of occupations such as *paikari* (trade in cattle), pisciculture and business in fish, and petty businesses, namely, grocery, tailoring, etc. The community is dependent on markets. There are no bonded labourers among them. Among the Pathans not many are completely landless. According to the Pathans there is a marginal rise in the number of labourers working in agriculture. Child labour is observed among the poor Pathans who send their young boys to be work as *bagal* (cowherd) or domestic agricultural servants (i.e. *mahendar*) in the homes of the rich. Payment of wages for a cowherd or a domestic servant is in both cash and kind. For *bhagchasi* (share-croppers) and seasonally or annually employed agricultural labour (*i.e. kisan*), payment is made in kind. Since Independence the major change perceived is the proliferation of opportunities of earning, such as pisciculture, trade in fish, petty business etc.

The traditional caste or rather community council of the Pathans is made up of elderly, respectable Pathan villagers. The council or the panchayat deals with a number of assorted issues of social, religious and economic importance. Its jurisdiction does not generally extend beyond the residential zone of the Pathans within a village; it settles cases of divorce, property inheritance or discusses problems of development of the village mosque or *idgah*. It is slowly losing its importance and social support because villagers apply to more powerful bodies like statutory panchayat or law courts, for redressed of grievances or for reparation for wrong. The Pathans do not have any regional association. There exists no traditional village panchayat for settling disputes among various communities. The major change since Independence is the introduction of modern statutory councils whose role has become important in the work-a-day life of the villagers especially in terms of the involvement of these councils in introducing various governmental schemes of development and employment in rural areas.

The community professes Islam and its members belong to the Sunni sect and follow the *Hanafi* school of thought. The Pathans have faith in *pir* (saint). The regional *pir* is Satya Pir who is propitiated by offering *sunni* and this is done in order to get over personal and familial crises. The various local *dargahs* or *pirs* are regarded as sacred shrines and devout Pathans visit these *dargahs*. One of the fundamental Islamic religious obligations for the rich Moslem (*maldar*) is the *haj* or the pilgrimage to Mecca. According to the prescribed rule of *Shariat* this is done during the twelfth month of Zul-Haj. The Pathan, who has accomplished his pilgrimage to Mecca, is known as Haji. A Haji is highly esteemed by the members of the community. Qualified *mullahs* act as sacred specialists among the Pathans. These *mullahs* are non-Pathans, mostly Sheiks. During *urs* at different *dargahs*, fairs are held. These local fairs attract a large number of Pathans. The following major Moslem festivals are celebrated by the Pathans: Muharram in the month of Muharram; Idu'l Fitr on the first of Shawal and Idu'z Zuha on the tenth of Zul-Haj. These fairs and festivals have religious significance. Besides, these provide the villagers with opportunities to break away from their daily routine of work. Through the observance of the festivals the Pathans experience the communal solidarity and unity of their community.

The Pathan women are good embroiderers. They make beautiful *kantha* from old used clothes to be used as bedclothes. They also make palm-leaf mats with beautiful coloured designs on them. These arts are unfortunately giving way to modern popular fashion like knitting woollen garments and caps. There are traditional Moslem songs which are sung with *dhol* (a drum-like musical instrument) during marriage and circumcision ceremonies. Women take an active part in these festivities.

The Pathans as a community of Moslems are a *jal-achal* community for the Hindus. *Jal-achal* has almost become an archaic concept. Commensal restrictions are confined to women. Connubial norms of marrying within one's own community are observed. However, the Pathans do not categorically decry a union between a member of their community and any one from the other local Moslem communities. Putative kinship and friendship are almost non-existent among the Pathans. The Pathans are free to share with others facilities like road, school, *panchayat ghar*, etc. The Pathans live in their separate hamlets or residential zones in a village inhabited by many communities, and they are observed to have their own wells, tube wells and other water sources. Upper caste Hindus, in general, live apart from both the Moslem and the low caste Hindu and under normal circumstances they are not required to share wells, tube-wells and other water sources with neighbouring communities of the Moslems and the low castes. However, there is no strict social taboo as regards access to and sharing of such resources. Patron-client relationship is observed between the Pathans and their servicing castes like the Hadis (from whom they engage midwives), the Napits (barber) and their Moslem Hajjams for circumcision (the barbers themselves prefer to be called Khalifa). The rich Pathans are observed to take keen interest in politics and a few among them are successful in becoming members of different statutory councils. Share cropping is becoming obsolete, as it is not a paying proposition for landlords especially under the present government order. As per the present governmental injunctions, the landlord gets a share of 25% of the produce, while the share-cropper takes the bulk of 75% and the landlord is required to bear the cost of inputs plus irrigation tax. In the case of *kisani* (contractual seasonal/ annual employment of labour), a *kisan* is given one third of the produce of the land that he tills. (Besides, he is given an amount of straw so that he can thatch the roof of his hut) The production cost of the yield such as cost of inputs (e.g., seed, manure, even taxes to be paid to the government for irrigation i.e., canal water) is borne by the owner of the land or the master (*munib*); while the *kisan* puts in his labour to raise the crop.

Literacy is fairly high among the Pathans belonging to the richer sections of their community. There are however, very few cases where the Pathans have succeeded in achieving higher education. The poorer section in general lags behind in literacy and education. Health and medical care including family welfare is in a poor state among the members of this section. In contrast the rich section shows interest in health and medical care. Besides, the members of this section have taken to family planning. Oral contraceptives are in use among them. There is no observable scarcity as regards drinking water. Employment under various rural employment programmes has not opened up any opportunity for the members of the community. However, for a handful of Pathans, self-employment through bank loans has opened up new vistas. Communication facilities it terms of road transport have improved. Educated Pathans take interest in reading newspapers and listening to news bulletins over radios, transistors and televisions. Regular stealing of wire from electrical poles has hindered supply of electricity in many rural areas. Villagers as such have not been involved in any environmental conservation programme or scheme. As regards energy resources, the Pathans are observed using coal, cowdung cakes and dried mustard plants as fuels. The Pathans are found eager to accept irrigation and innovations for cultivation. Nutrition programmes in schools are of irregular nature. Rationing system is popular. Instead of going in for savings and investment in banks, the rich Pathans are in the habit of taking advantage of post office for the purpose.

R. K. BHATTACHARYA

PATIKAR

The Patikars are a community of small craftsmen. Patial and Paital are their synonyms. The word 'Patikar' was derived from *pati* (a kind of mat). The caste profession of the community is making a kind of fine mat (*shital pati*). Before Partition (1947), the major concentrations of the community were found in Dacca, Cumilla, etc. Now, they are found in Assam (Dibrugarh, Cachhar), 24-Parganas, Calcutta, Hooghly and Coochbehar districts of West Bengal. They live in the plain areas with medium rainfall and high humidity. They speak and write in Bengali.

The Patikars are a non-vegetarian Hindu community. Rice and wheat are their staple cereals. Lentil and *moong* are the favourite pulses. Mustard oil and rapeseed oil are their cooking media. They consume all types of seasonal vegetables and fruits available in the market. Tea is a common drink for most members of the community, while milk is also consumed by those who can afford it. Alcoholic drinks are not preferred by them. They smoke *bidis*, sometimes cigarettes, chew betel or tobacco. They do not eat radish in the month of *Poush* (December-January) and *Magh* (January-February), *lau* (bottle gourd) is not taken by the mother whose first child is male, in the month of *Jaistha* (May-June) and *Bhadra* (August-September).

The Patikars have different *gotras* like Moudgalya, Goutam, Alimyan, etc., whose only function is to regulate marriage alliances. Since it is a lesser known community, some of them identify themselves as Kayasthas. The Patikars perceive themselves, equal to other *nabashakha* groups. People of other communities also do not think them lower than the *nabashakhas* The Patikars think of themselves as Sudras in the *varna* order.

The Patikars practise caste endogamy and *gotra* exogamy. Junior sororate is permissible only after the death of first wife. The marriageable age for boys is around twenty-eight and for girls around twenty. Negotiation is their mode of acquiring mates. Monogamy is their common form of marriage. Vermilion, lac, iron as well as conch-shell bangles are used by their women as marriage symbols. The Patikars give dowry in cash and kind. The girl lives with her husband, at her father-in-law's house after marriage. No case of divorce is reported. Remarriage of a woman is not permissible. Marriageable ages of both boys and girls have increased, and dowry, instead of bride-price, has recently been introduced in their society.

Nuclear type of family is the common family pattern of the Patikars. But extended family is not unknown to them. In a family, youngsters obey their elders. The elders in turn love the young. Avoidance relationship is maintained between *shashuri* (mother-in-law) and *jamai* (son-in-law), *betarbou* (daughter-in-law) and *shvashur* (father-in-law), younger brother's wife and *bhasur* (husband's elder brother). Reciprocal duties and obligations tie the family members with each other. Joking relationship exists with wife's younger sister and brother, husband's younger brother and sister and with grandparents. Restrictions on the freedom of youngsters and poor pecuniary condition sometimes create conflict among the family members. Both sons and daughters get equal share of father's property, but the daughters normally do not claim their share. The eldest son succeeds to his father's responsibility. Inter-family linkages are maintained through different ritual performances and ceremonial occasions. Breaking up of the extended family structure, relaxation in avoidance relationship and acceptance of women's equal right to father's property are changes in their family life.

The role of women in the economic affairs of the Patikars is substantial. Women prepare *pati* (mat). They also train their children in this art. They play a significant role in ritual and socio-religious performances. Financial control lies mainly in the hands of male members as women possess low status.

The Patikars observe *saptamrita* in the seventh month and *sadh* in the ninth month of pregnancy as pre-delivery rituals. Many restrictions are imposed on the pregnant lady. She may not look at a snake, nor go out at night etc. At present restrictions on the pregnant lady has been relaxed to some extent. Sasthipuja is observed as post delivery ritual on the sixth day after childbirth. The new mother and the baby take a clean bath on that day. The barber comes to pare the nails of the mother and the baby on the twenty-first day. Soda water is collected from the Dhoba (washerman) to wash the clothes, and other things (this is a part of ritual). They observe post-delivery pollution period of thirty days. The new mother enters the kitchen after taking a purificatory bath and prepares *payesh* (a sweet preparation of milk and rice) on that day. They also invite some relatives on that day. The mother does not go out at night or at mid-day up to the sixth month of the baby. *Annaprashan* (first feeding of cereals) is observed in the sixth month for the male child and seventh month for the female child.

The *mama* (mother's brother) feeds the *prasad* of any deity into the mouth of the child followed by rice. After first menstruation, a Patikar girl does not go out of the house for four days and takes the purificatory bath on the fifth day before sunrise. The Brahman priest comes and feeds her a mixture of *sabri kala* (a kind of banana), cow's milk, cowdung and urine of an ox, *ghee* and dew's water as well as honey after chanting some *mantras* (incantations). The marriage ceremony takes place in the bride's house. The months of *Chaitra* (March-April), *Bhadra* (August-September), *Ashwin* (September-October), *Kartik* (October-November), and *Poush* (December-January), are avoided in fixing the marriage date. The ceremony of *pakadekha* (finalisation of marriage) is performed in the boy's home. The father and other elderly persons of the girl's side come to the boy's home for the finalisation of marriage on that day. *Gayehalud* (smearing of turmeric), *satpakghora* (moving around the bridegroom seven times), *shubhadrishti* (exchange of glances), *malabadal* (exchange of garland), *sindurdan* (smearing of vermilion on the hair parting of the girl), etc., are the marriage rituals. *Dan* (handing over) is performed generally by uncle of the girl or her elder brother. Both the boy and the girl destroy garlands of *shola* (cork) of each other then they exchange their garlands. *Sindurdan* ceremony is performed on the next day of the marriage, *boubhat* (giving rice to the bride) and *phulsajjya* (consummation) ceremonies are performed in the house of the bridegroom.

After death, cremation is the mode of disposal. *Dasha* ceremony is performed on the tenth day of death. Participants of the funeral procession are invited to a feast on that day. *Ghat* is performed on the twenty-ninth day. The soda water from the Dhoba is essential to use for washing their clothes and other things. Thirty days are observed as mourning period and *sraddha* ceremony is performed on the thirtieth day. The thirty-first day is known as *machh chhowni*. They invite guests, kin and relatives on that day to a non-vegetarian feast. Increase in expenses for ritual performances is reported.

The Patikars are landless. *Mutra*, a wild plant is the only raw material from which mat is prepared. Male folk are generally engaged in hawking the merchandise in the urban and rural areas of Gangetic Bengal as well as in north Bengal. Sometimes middlemen also collect the material from the craftsmen. They sell their merchandise in different daily and weekly markets in exchange of cash. Now, some of them are engaged in different services or in self-employment.

Although the community had its caste council in the past, it does not exist now. As they live mostly in urban areas, municipality are their statutory councils. Some of the Patikars get bank loans to carry on their business with the recommendations of the municipalities. Any conflict with the neighbouring Patikars or other people is solved by the political parties or elderly persons of their locality.

The Patikars belong to the Vaishnav sect of Hinduism. They worship Radha and Krishna and often go to the temple of Radhagobinda, while Tulasi and Lakshmi are their family deities. The Patikars being craftsmen worship Vishvakarma. The Patikars visit sacred centres, shrines and pilgrimage centres like other caste Hindus. The Brahman is their sacred specialist who serves them during different life cycle ceremonies as well as in other religious performances. They participate in fairs and festivals of the locality along with other communities. Ashtaprahar Nam Sankirtan, Durga puja, Kali puja, etc., are their religious festivals whereas Satimar mela on the day of Doljatra is the major fair of the locality.

Women make *alpana* (floor painting) in different religious performances. Making of *pati* (mat) is the specialised handicraft of this caste.

The Patikars accept and exchange food and water from and with other communities who are eligible to provide water to the Brahman. Patron-client relationship exists with the Brahmans, the Napit, etc. As they are a very small community they have to establish social linkages with other neighbouring communities. Modern linkages are established through their business, service, etc.

Now, most of their sons and daughters study up to secondary level and some up to college level also. They avail themselves of the modern medical facilities whenever it is necessary, but traditional medicare is not unknown to them. Some of their women get sterilised after three children. Drinking water is fetched from municipal taps. Some of them take loans from banks for mat making. They listen to radio, visit cinema and watch television. The Patikars get information through different political parties. Their localities are well connected by roads and railways. Post offices also exist near by. They use electricity for domestic consumption. Cowdung cakes, coal and kerosene are used as cooking fuel. They avail of ration from fair-price shops. A few of them save money and deposit it with the banks. Sometimes they purchase grocery items on credit.

ARCHANA DATTA

PATNI

The Patni community is also known by their synonyms Maheswar and Ghatwal (as are always known at the *ghats*). Their other synonyms are Paturi, Patanni, Dom Patni (Risley, 1891: 170). The Patnis think they are so named because they are meant to carry a person to the other bank of a river in a thin boat and as their service is always at a *ghat*, so they are called Ghatwals also. The Patnis may have also derived their name from the term *patta nayaka* (captain of army as reported in the 1951 Census). The Patnis have several sub-groups, like: Jat Patni, Ghat Patni, Balami or Ghatwal, Dom Patni, Machhwa or Nagarchi (*ibid*). There is also a history about their origin (*ibid*), which relates them to Madhava who has ferried Rama across a river on his way from Ayodhya to Mithila. Regarding their migration the Patnis inform that many of them have migrated from East Bengal (presently Bangladesh) after partition in 1947. According to the Patnis they are distributed in areas like Najarnagore, Halisahar, Kankinara, Naihati, Puro, Taki, Dholtitha, Amtala, Goalpota, Sangrampur and Baduria and in the surrounding localities of the district of 24-Parganas. They also name distant places like Hooghly, Nadia, Medinipur, Murshidabad, Malda and Siliguri in Darjeeling district as their other places of settlement.

Sufficient rainfall and the fertile soil conditions of the region permit the growth of various kinds of vegetables, crops and fruit plants (mango, coconut, litchi, guava etc). The jungles of Sunderbans have an abundance of wild animals like deer, snakes and Royal Bengal Tigers. A number of rivers supply the area with plenty of fishes. According to the 1981 Census the total population of the Patnis in West Bengal was 22,466. The language and script of the Patnis is Bengali at home and with outsiders. The constitutional status of the Patnis is that of scheduled caste.

Patnis are a non-vegetarian group of people but do not eat beef, pork, or buffalo meat. Their staple food is rice with vegetables, fishes and pulses. They consume locally available varieties of vegetables and fishes. They also consume locally available fruits, but very rarely due to poverty. Some of them drink alcoholic drinks purchased from the market. Due to poverty, Patnis can not consume milk, but they sometimes take tea in the morning. They avoid radish in the month of *Magh* (January-February), pumpkin in the month of *Bhadra* (August-September) and *sajina* in the month of *Chaitra* (March-April). There is no significant change in their food habit, but they are not getting their proper food due to poverty. In the past it was customary for the villagers who used to avail ferry service to offer vegetables and other kinds of food to the Patnis instead of money as ferry charges. But this practice is no longer in vogue.

According to some, they have only one *gotra* or clan that is Aliman, but some have the opinion that they have another *gotra* and that is Kashyapa. But their *gotra*s has no function as for a long time, marriage is allowed within the some *gotra*. Their surnames are Halder, Biswas, Das and Sarker. They do not know the meaning of their surnames. The Patnis are a low caste people according to their own self-perception as well as in the opinion of the other people in the locality. But they consider the Muchis and Methors as lower than themselves in the social hierarchy. They say that they do not accept water from the Muslims, but in actual fact they have to take water from their hand and vice-versa. Sometimes the Brahmans also have to come to their houses on the occasion of certain ceremonial feasts.

The Patnis marry within their community and that means the community is endogamous. Marriages generally do not take place within the same village. Marriage is allowed within same *gotra* or clan. Negotiation is the primary mode of acquiring mates. Age at marriage is sixteen to seventeen years for girls and twenty-two years for boys. Monogamy is their form of marriage. *Sankha* (conch-shell bangle), *sindur* (vermilion), and *loha* (iron bangle) are the marriage symbols for a Patni woman. Dowry is paid both in cash and kind in their marriages. The amount of dowry varies from Rs. 2000/- to Rs. 20,000/-, according to economic condition of a family. After marriage the Patnis follow the rule of patrilocal residence. The Patnis have no case of divorce. Separation only takes place if one of the partners is mentally unbalanced or if there is mutual dislike. In earlier days those who separated after divorce were ostracized by the society. Remarriage is very rare in case of females, but the male members can marry again after death of one's wife. A woman can remarry only if she is widowed at a young age.

Most of the Patni families are of the nuclear type. A very few vertically extended families also exist. The husband is the head of a family. Husband and wife are bound by love, respect and cooperation. Children are treated with love, affection and care. Elder members are all respected by younger members. Avoidance relationship is observed between *bhasur* (husband's elder brother) and *bhadra bau* (younger brother's wife), between maternal uncle and his sister's daughter-in-law i.e. between *mamasasur* and *bhagnabau*. Some kind of avoidance relationship is also maintained between mother-in-law and son-in-law. Grandparents and grandchildren relationship is of joking. Joking relation is also found between the *jamai babu* (elder sister's husband) and the younger *sali* or *sala* (wife's younger brother and sister). The Patnis own very little property, which is inherited by the sons. Daughters do not get any share of their father's property. The eldest son succeeds his father as the head of the family. The Patnis maintain inter-family linkages through their life cycle rituals. The only significant change in the relationship pattern is that avoidance relationships are no longer so rigid.

Women do not inherit their father's property as after marriage they do not usually come to claim their shares. Patni women have no economic role outside their house. They only look after family management, household ritual performance, and children's upbringing.

After birth the Patnis observe a pollution period of twenty-one days for a male child and thirty days for a female child. They become purified on the day of Sasthipuja on the thirtieth or twenty-first days, after three successive *kaman* (paring of nails and taking of bath and *santijal* or holywater) rites. One *kaman* is done just after birth, another on the ninth day and it is known as *natta*. The third *kaman* is performed on the day of Sasthi puja. The Patnis have the rite of *sadhbhakshan* (taking of desired food) in the seventh or ninth month of pregnancy of woman. A pregnant woman is never allowed to cross any river or canal and eat *pitha* (an indigenous cake prepared with rice powder). The Patnis have *annaprashan* (ceremonial first rice feeding of a child) and it is done in the sixth or ninth month for a male child and in fifth or seventh month for a female child.

The Patni marriage starts with the rite of *pakadekha* or *chhele asirbad* in which first the bridegroom and then the bride are blessed by the elders of the opposite parties in their respective homes. A few days before the actual day of marriage, they have a ceremony of *aiburobhat* in both the houses. In this ceremony bride and bridegroom take their last meal or rice in their unmarried state of life. On the marriage day some married women fetch water from the river known as *jolsoa* by which *nandimukh* (ancestor worship) or *briddhi* is done. *Sampradan* in which the bride is ceremonially handed over to the groom is done by the father or uncle or elder brother of the girl. *Gayehalud* ceremony is also performed in both houses on the morning of the marriage day. After smearing of the bridegroom the remaining portion of the turmeric paste is sent through a barber to the bride's home, along with other *gayehalud tatta* or gifts, such as fish, clothes for the bride, curd etc. After *sampradan* the bride and bridegroom reside in the *basarghar*. Next day morning they perform *basibiya*. The Patnis have *pakasparsa* or *boubhat* (ceremonial rice serving by the bride) and *phulsajjya*. *Phulsajjya* is their marriage consummation rite. They also have *astamangala* or *joreasha* rite. Nowadays the Patnis observe a pollution period of thirteen days instead of thirty days. On the thirteenth day they go for *ghatkaman* (cutting of nails of all the family members and shaving of head of the sons). On the fourteenth day they perform *Sradh* and on the sixteenth day they perform *terodasa.* In *terodasa* rite, the Patnis offer a non-vegetarian feast to the *antiyo* and *kutum* (affinal and consanguineal relatives) and in this ceremony *ansh* food or food with fish or meat is first prepared in the house where death has occurred. They have also annual *sradh* or *bacharkria*. The only significant change in their life cycle rituals is that they have shortened their pollution period after death.

The Patnis are a landless community. In the region where the present study has been conducted, they are mainly engaged in the occupation of ferry service. Many of them have also lost their service due to construction of bridges on the river. Some have joined other occupations or have started a business. But many found themselves in a difficult situation as they neither had sufficient funds to start a business nor skills for other types of occupation. As for other occupations some have become boat mechanics, some are engaged in cleaning the sand layer of the river bed, some are in the occupation of rickshaw van puller and some are working in the shops as helping hands. The Patnis have kitchen gardens as subsidiary occupations. They do not encourage their children to take employment as their children are going to schools. In general the Patnis are for a long time suffering from extreme poverty. Their occupation shift from primary to secondary and tertiary sectors is not very significant.

The Patnis have never had a *jati panchayat* in the past as they have always been busy with their work did not have the time to meet together or listen to each other. However, they have had one meeting at Naihati in Barrackpur sub-division of North 24-Parganas. At present, they are under the control of the modern statutory councils such as *gram panchayat*, from which they get various kinds of loans or special facilities for being a schedule caste. There is no traditional village *panchayat* for settling disputes etc. But in some cases such disputes are settled by the modern *gram panchayat* members. The only significant change that has occurred is that instead of *gram sava*, the *gram panchayat* is now the statutory council of their village.

Hinduism is the religion of the Patnis. They worship various family deities like Manasa or Lakshmi and perform Bastu puja, Goal puja, Barathakur puja, Satyanarayan puja with offering of *sinni* as *prasad*, Sitala puja etc. Patni women observe *bratas* like Ghat puja, Arandhan, Kuli mangalbar, Shivaratri, Neel etc. Kalimandir is the abode of the village deity of the Patnis. Their regional deities are Durga, Kali, Basanti, Lakshmi and Saraswati and Shiva. All the *pujas* and *bratas* are performed with a view to ensure the wellbeing of their community. The Patnis visit places like Nabadwip, Mayapur, Puri, Kashi, Haridwar etc. as their places of pilgrimage. Brahman priest is their sacred specialist, who attends to every religious ritual. Their major fairs are Ratha Yatra Mela, Charaker Mela, and Baruni Mela. Their major festivals are Durga puja, Charak and Basanti puja.

The Patnis maintain some traditional inter-community linkages as they are served by the Brahman priest and barber. The Patnis do not take water or cooked food only from the hands of Muchi, Methor and Muslims. They accept *kachcha*, *pucca* and *sidha* from the Malo, Tiyor, Kapali, and the castes of higher rank and exchange these with the Malo, Jele etc. They accept *sidha* from the Hari, Muchi etc. Some inter-caste marriages have also taken place between the Patnis and other castes like the Kapali, Pal, Kamar, Teli and Jugi. They have *gurubhai* relationship with others as in both the villages many Patnis are the disciples of the some *gurus* of Nabadwip. The Patnis do not face any difficulty in sharing water sources, temple, crematorium, schools, etc. They have no *jajmani* system but they have some sort of economic inter-dependence on some other communities like the Jele (fishermen) etc. as they serve as boat mechanics or take lease of ferry service. They also have modern inter-community linkages, as their children are going to schools, as they have to go to *gram panchayat* office for seeking facilities as members of a schedule caste, and as many of them are in the ferry service. There was once a movement to designate themselves as Mahishya, as is evident from the census report of 1951. There is a type of auction or *dak* in the ferry *ghats* for giving lease of ferry ghat, but many Patnis have no money to avail themselves of this economic opportunity. Employer-worker relationship is maintained by addressing each other as *dada* and *bhai*.

All the children of the Patnis are going to schools, but in general the level of education among Patnis is still very low. Some of their children are also getting scheduled caste grants from their respective schools. Women are found to be studying up to class VIII standard. A very few of the Patnis are matriculates. For health and medical care they consult the village dispensary as well as hospital and use both traditional and modern medicines. Some Patni women have undergone sterilisation after two or four children. They use tube-well water for drinking. Some of the Patnis are taking loans from DRDA (District Rural Development Agency) for purchasing boats etc. Some of them have become self-employed by taking the above mentioned loans. The habitat of the Patnis is connected with the outside world by ferry or bus service. Electricity is still out of their reach. The energy resources of the Patnis are wood and cowdung cake. Under the nutrition programme the children of the Patnis sometimes get a piece of bread from their schools. They avail themselves of the rationing facilities. As they have very meagre funds they do not use banking facilities either for savings or for investment. Houses of the Patnis are mud built with tile roof.

CHANDRIMA CHOWDHURY

POD

There is a great controversy about the origin of the Paundra Kshatriya caste of West Bengal. In describing Chandal or Namasudra caste Risley stated that Pods are one of the sub-castes of the Namasudras. In the 1951 Census of West Bengal (Mitra, 1953), there is a description of the Pods: "Pods of West Bengal are depressed and SC caste. According to Brahmavaivarta Purana Paundras are descended from a Vaishya father and a Saundika (Sunri) mother...Pundra was the name of prince of the Lunar dynasty. Son of Bali and brother of Angu, Vangu, Sukwa and Kalinga. Pundra is also the name of a tribe and the name of a country, Paundras are inhabitants of Pandra and may not be identical with Pundras. Puandrakas are distinguished from Pundras in Mahabharata Sabha 52.16. A Pundra tribe is mentioned in Vishnu Purana 2.3.15 along with Kalingas and South Indians. One Vasudev was their King (Hari 160, Matsya 46-27, Mahabharata Sabha 30-20)...So in Classics, Pundras and Paundras are not always distinguished. It may be that Pundras and Paundras were the same or it may also be that they were different. How far the present Pods or Pundras represent the ancient Pundras or Paundras, well known Khotriya tribe, will always remain a matter of opinion".

Risley in his *The Tribes and Castes of Bengal* (1891: II: 176) stated about the four subdivisions or sub-castes of the Pod community like Bagunda, Bangla, Khotta, or Mauna and Uraiya. Among these sub-groups the first two were found in 24 Parganas and Jessore districts of Bangladesh, the third in Mursidabad and the fourth in Midnapore, and Balasore district of Orissa. In the District Gazetteer of 24 Parganas, (1911) by O'Malley, there is some information about the Pod community of the 24 Parganas, i.e., they were divided into four groups like (1) Chasi Pod, (2) Mecho Pod, (3) Tanti Pod, and (4) Bhasa Pod. Each sub-caste had its own caste *panchayat* to punish their members for offences against caste or social laws. The Chasi Pods had a superior status to others and claimed to be of Kshatriya origin. Cultivation was their occupation. They also called themselves Bratya Kshatriya or Padma Raj. They were allowed to marry Mecho Pod (accept girls, but never give their daughters in marriage to Mecho Pod boys). *Bhasa* means floating and the Bhasa Pods were found in considerable number in Sagar Island. Bhasa Pods practised widow marriage and for this they were looked down upon by other sections. The Pod headman was called *sardar*. In the region under study a different set of sub-groups among the Pod community were found like (1) Dhulepure; (2) Bajitpure; (3) Baruni; (4) Medinipur; and (5) Sadpure. The present day members of the caste state that the Pods or Paundras are those who were dispersed or stood back with fear or were in mothers' womb at the time of *nikshatriaization* (elimination of Kshatriya caste) by Parasuram. According to them, previously this caste was a warrior caste or Kshatriya caste as mentioned in the Mahabharata. Sometimes they also mention that they have originated from the Pandavas of Mahabharata. Their synonyms are Pod, Pundarika, Padmaraja, Punro, Paundra and Pundari, according to 1951 Census. Their titles are Mondal, Adhikari, Roy, Das, Nayek, Patra, Haṇli, Baulia, Gayen, Mistri, Bir, Sunder, Halder, Bachhar, Chaukidar. Pramanik, Naskar, Biswas, Burman etc. There was a caste journal which used to come out during British period. The name of the periodical was "*Paundra Kshatriya Patrika*". One of the ministers, Sri Rajendra Nath Sarker from the Paundra Kshatriya caste tried to revive that journal, but it is no longer published. After partition many Pods have migrated from East Bengal (now Bangladesh), but they have cultural similarity with Pods of eastern part of the 24 Parganas (Basirhat sub-division) district, as is evident from the field study. They are distributed in many villages of 24 Parganas like Kaugachi, Gobindapur, Karundia, Dakshin Bhabia, Abad Kharampur, Kharampur, Ramanandapur, Silkuni, Bhurkhunda, Chimta, Kharidanga, Sandeshkhali, Hingulgange, (Kanakhagore), Gosaba etc. They cannot state their sub-caste wise distribution. The natural environment of the area is like that of lower Bengal which permits the growth of a variety of vegetable crops and fruit plants, with the Sunderbans infested with wild animals. According to the 1981 Census their total population in West Bengal was, 1,536,197. Their major concentration is in 24 Parganas. A large number of the Pods are also found in Medinipur, Howrah, Hooghly and Murshidabad. The language and script used by them is Bengali in all respects. The community has no identification marker. Their constitutional status is that of scheduled caste. The staple food of the Pods is rice and *roti*. They generally consume three major meals per day during the agricultural season i.e., rice for two meals and *roti* for one. In lean seasons, only a few can afford this type of food. They say that more then half of their population are living in very poor economic conditions and for several months they have to live on wheat with vegetables and pulses. There is an abundant supply of fish in their surrounding fisheries but these are beyond their reach. They use mustard oil for cooking. The Pods are a non-vegetarian group of people but do not consume beef, pork or buffalo. They occasionally consume fruits when these are available locally in different seasons and as per the advice of doctors. Many of them drink alcoholic drinks. Sometimes they purchase it from the market; they also brew it with the juice from their own palm trees. They do not take radish in the month of *Magh* (January-February). As the economic condition of the community is deteriorating, there has been an inevitable change in their food habits, i.e., majority of them are now consuming more wheat than rice, which is very costly.

It has already been mentioned that their caste was divided into four groups. But at present there is no stratification and the groups are not also endogamous. The members of the caste cannot state the basis of this group differentiation. They have *gotras* like Kashyapa, Sandilya, Jugavansi, Lakshmir Barputra and so on. But these clans or *gotras* have no function, because marriage within the same *gotra* is allowed. As their social status is very low it is noticed in different places, that they are changing their surname from Purkait to Purokayastha. As they are a scheduled caste, their social status is low, but they claim to be a Kshatriya caste. To other people however, the Paundra Kshatriyas still appear to be a community of lower order. Paundras are aware of the *Varna* order. Before 1977, they had a caste panchayat and the *moral* (headman) was the chief of that panchayat.

Endogamy is the marriage rule of the Pods. Age of marriage for girls is from eighteen to twenty-five years, and for boys from twenty-one to thirty-five years. Negotiation is the primary mode of acquiring mates. Monogamy is the form of marriage. *Sankha* (conch shell bangle), *sindur* (vermilion) and *loha* (an iron bangle) are the marriage symbols for women. Dowry is paid both in cash and kind and the amount varies from Rs. 1000 to Rs. 10,000, according to the economic condition of the family and character of the bridegroom. Sometimes they have to sell their land for daughter's marriage. Divorce is allowed and sometimes it occurs in an informal way with the decision of the *panchayat* members. Remarriage is also allowed for both males and females. But older widows do not like to remarry. The significant changes in their marriage pattern are an increase in marriageable age for girls, and increase in the amount of dowry.

Majority of the Pod families are of nuclear type, but a few vertically extended families also exist. Families are bound by a set of interpersonal relations of love, fear, avoidance, obligation etc. Inheritance is still patrilineal. Succession is also through the male line. Inter family linkages are there in different social ceremonies. Women of the Pod community do not enjoy the right of inheritance, and in poorer families they have economic roles such as working in agricultural fields and catching small (*chara*) prawns from the river for about three months in a year. They also have a role in family management and contribute to the family income.

After the birth of a male child their pollution period lasts for twenty-one days, but for a female child it lasts for thirty days. They become purified after three *kamans* and *Sasthipuja*. *Kaman* is a rite of cutting nails and taking bath for purification. One *kaman* is done after birth, the second *kaman* is done on the ninth day after birth and it is called *natta*. After *natta* the mother and new born baby are semi-purified. Some observe *annaprashan*. For *annaprashan* they bring some *prasad* from a temple and feed it to the new born at the age of six or eight months for a boy and five or seven months for a female child. They perform all their social ceremonies after consulting a Brahman priest and an almanac. Marriage starts with *ashirbad* and ends with *phulsajjya*, including other rites like *gayehalud*, *aiburobhat*, *gayehalud tatta* (which is carried by barber), *jalsoa*, *nandimukh* or *abhhuti*, *sampradan*, *sindurdan*, *basibiye*, *santaliphela* (the bride has a rite to repay her debts to her parents with a plateful of rice grains) and *subho-chandipuja*. The bride has to keep a *kajal lata* (stibinum vessel) and *kalar moch* (portion of banana plant) and the groom has to keep a *jati* (nut cracker) and *kalar moch* for all the time during their marriage. *Phulsajjya* is the marriage consummation rite.

They have shortened their pollution period after death. They cremate their dead due to poverty.

Land and water (to some extent) are the major economic resources of the Pods. The community is a combination of both landowning and landless people. Half of the total population have land, but not all have sufficient land. Only a few families can fully maintain themselves with the earnings from their land. Many of these landowning families can only grow provisions for five to six months in a year. For the rest of the year, these landowners have to work as day labourers along with other landless people. They own their land as individual proprietors. The day labourer's wage is Rs. 10/- for nine hours' duty from 6 am to 12 o'clock and from 3 pm to 6 pm. Due to lack of education there is no occupational shift from primary to secondary or tertiary sectors. Their only choice is day labourer's job. However, it was found in the village Pitambara of Diamond Harbour sub-division that many take to making palm molasses for four months during the lean season. In north Bengal, especially in Malda, the Pods also grow silk worms.

Before 1977, the Pods had a caste panchayat and the headman was *moral*. But after the formation of *gram panchayat*s in 1977 all village disputes are settled by the *gram panchayat* members. In some villages the previous *moral* is also called for settling many disputes. Many Pods are now members and *pradhans* of the *gram panchayat*s.

Hinduism is the religion of the Pods. The month of *Baisakh* (April-May) is their '*Dharam Mas*' and in this month they worship God Shiva and give *jhara* (a small pitcher full of water is hung over a basil plant) to the *tulsi* plant. In this month they also perform *Goalpuja* on the first day of the month. They worship goddess Shani every Saturday and it is called '*Barathakurerbar*'. Besides these, they perform Bipadtarini, Jaimangalbar, Jamai Shashthi, Rannapuja, Manasapuja, Janmashtami, Durga Shashthi and Astami, Bastupuja, Banabibir puja, Asok Shashthi and Astami, Basanti Shashthi, Charak, Neel and Sital Shashthi. Their village deities are Manasa, and Banbibi. Their regional deities are Durga, Saraswati, Kali, Basanti, etc. Their major sacred centres are Haridwar, Kankhal, Brindaban, Deoghar, Kashi, Gaya, Prayag, Mathura, Rajgir, Puri, Badrinath etc. Their sacred specialists are Brahman priests and barbers who provide them with specialised service. Their major fair and festival is Charak. There is no significant change in religious behaviour, but goddess Santoshi ma is being worshipped by many of their women on Fridays.

They have traditional inter-community linkage, as they are served by the Brahman priest and the barber. In the area where the field survey was undertaken, it was found that the same Brahman priest's family had been serving them for generations, though this priest does not serve their caste alone. At present, they have no commensal restrictions for *kachcha*, *pucca* and *sidha* food, as there is a group for singing religious songs (*Hari Sankirtan*) in which men from various caste groups like the Muchi, Bagdi, Kahar, Karmakar, Brahman and Kayasthas are involved. There are a few incidences of inter-caste marriages with the Kumor and Kayastha. But inter-caste marriages are not cordially accepted either by their family members or by members of their community. Nowadays families across community lines are mixing in different social ceremonies. They do not face any trouble in sharing temple, water source, village path etc. They establish modern inter-community linkages, when their children go to schools. They visit block or sub-division offices, become *pradhans* of *gram panchayats* or become disciples of Anukul Thakur, Balak Brahmachari, Swamijis of Belurmath and Swamijis of Chaitanyamath and Gauriomath of Nadia etc. They do not like to give their land permanently on lease for share cropping, as many sharecroppers become landlords after cheating their masters. The landlord himself cultivates and they sometimes employ day labourers on wage basis from any community like the Kahar, Muslim etc.

The standard of education is still not high. Only one-third of their male members are matriculates, and only about 5 per cent of the literate boys are graduates. Women of the present generation are going to school, but their percentage of literacy and level of education is not high. For health and medical care they visit local dispensaries like Bhabanipore and Bhabia and Basirhat or Taki hospitals. More than three-fourth of the married women are sterilised as part of a family planning measure. After operation, Rs. 130/- is paid to the woman who undergoes sterilization after three or four children. Many of the Pods therefore complain that for getting money some of their women go for sterilisation but due to lack of post-operative care and diet, many of them die subsequently. Their drinking water is procured from tube wells. For employment they have to register their names at the Employment Exchange. The Pods are found to be taking various governmental developmental loans available from DRDA (District Rural Development Agency) the amount of which varies from Rs. 1200/- to Rs. 6000/- for household industry. An agricultural loan is also available. With these loans many of them have started parched rice making business. Half of this loan is to be paid back to the government and half is given as subsidy. With the aid of this loan many men and women have become self-employed. There is another government scheme for the rural poor i.e., NREP Scheme. In this scheme all the village poor are employed in construction work such as cutting of soil, construction of village road and school building etc. Their means of communication are bus or ferry, newspaper and radio set. Electricity has not entered their houses. They sometimes irrigate their fields from shallow tube-wells. Their fuels are jute sticks, cowdung cakes and wood. They use chemical fertilizers like urea, phosphate, potash, sulphate etc. They use various insecticides available in the market. There is no midday meal programme. They use rationing facility. Their money transactions (getting government loan etc.) are done through banks.

CHANDRIMA CHOWDHURY

PORTUGUESE

The Portuguese in West Bengal are a community having a synonym "Firingi". They are also identified as "Christian", due to non-existence of such community in the neighbouring areas. The word has come from 'Portugal' – the place from where they originally migrated. The Portuguese are at present found only in the Midnapore district of West Bengal. The story of their migration to the village Mirpur is quite interesting. It is said that in the year 1770 when this region was being threatened by Maratha raiders and sea-pirates from Arakan, Chittagong etc., who were known as *mag*, the queen Janaki Devi of Mahisadal Raj brought twelve Portuguese gunners from the erstwhile Portuguese colony of Bandel (in Hoogly district of West Bengal) to protect her estates from these plunderers and this particular village Mirpur was given to them for their settlement. In lieu of their service they were given (*niskar*) rent free land. These Portuguese settlers were habituated to alcoholic drinks and "used to molest the local Hindu women. Consequently the Metropolitan Bishop tried to bring these Christians into the fold of his administration. A Bengali preacher was sent to baptise the women living with those Portuguese gunners. This Bengali Christian took much initiative and made arrangements for their marriage according to Christian rites" (Bhowmick: 1976: 121).

Mirpur village is situated just near the bank of the river Rupnarayan and the confluence of river Hoogly under the Mahisadal police station of the Midnapore district of West Bengal. Actually this village stands on the river frontier, on the eastern side of the tract and it is about one mile south of Geokhali which is a market and ferry station. The soil of this region is alluvial and the climate is warm and temperate. Humidity is high during the summer and rainfall is medium. According to a survey made in 1982, the total population of the Portuguese in Mirpur village was 450. The spoken language of the members of this community both at home and outside is Bengali. The script used by them is also Bengali.

The Portuguese are non-vegetarians. They do not have any restrictions on taking of any meat like that of pig, cow, goat, etc. Rice is their staple food. Pulses like *mug, musur, kalai,* etc., are generally used and seasonal roots tubers and bark, *thor* (i.e. inner portion of the banana trunk), etc., are their general food items. They use mustard oil for cooking. Vegetables which are grown by them and also those available in the market are normally eaten. Besides, they purchase oranges, apples, etc., on several religious occasions. Milk is generally taken by the children and old people. Taking tea and other non-alcoholic drinks like coffee, water of green coconut, etc., is a common occurrence. They take alcoholic drinks of and on. These are generally purchased from markets. The Portuguese arrange special food at the time of Christmas. On that day they prepare special cakes and sweets and buy oranges, lozenges etc. from the market which are distributed among members of their own community, as well as outsiders and invited guests of other communities. They arrange prayers in churches and thereafter the abovementioned food items are distributed.

The Portuguese community of Mirpur has no social division as such. Basically they are divided into two religious groups i.e. Roman Catholic and Protestant. They do not maintain any hierarchy between the two groups. No connubial restrictions have been found between Roman Catholic and Protestant religious groups because marriage alliances between the groups usually take place. Two churches are situated in the two different parts of the village. One Bengali Christian who baptised the women, married to the Portuguese gunners was successful in constructing a church. It is ascertained that in the beginning all the Portuguese gunners i.e., the first settlers, belong to the Protestant faith. Due to a misunderstanding with the others, one person having the surname Rota, came to Calcutta and changed his faith and accepted the Roman Catholic creed. After that a few churches had been set up here at the initiative of the Catholics. Therefore, two churches with their respective organizations are functioning in this village. They use traditional Portuguese surnames such as Iraq, Pereira, Teaser, Tessera, Rozario, D'cruz, Nunis, Lobu, Rota, etc. Besides, other surnames are also met with due to immigration and local conversion. These surnames are Mitra, Mukherjee, Mallick, Biswas, Gorai and the like. Like surnames both Portuguese and Bengali names are in use. Due to this we come across such queer combination of names and surnames like Bijay Tessera, Benjamin Biswas, etc. Here 'Bijoy' is the name borrowed from the Bengalis and surname 'Tessera' is their traditional one. This is due to their prolonged intermixing with the Bengali communities. The traditional names are Luis, Arthur, Lucas, Benjamin, etc., and the Bengali names are Bijoy, Basanta, Ajit, Prabhat and the like.

The Portuguese of Mirpur village are Christians and they have been living in this region since 1770. Previously they used to drink heavily and led an unrestricted social life which kept them away from the neighbouring villagers on all social occasions. Due to the reasons stated above they were treated as "mlechha" (untouchable) or foreigner by the orthodox Hindu society, at that time.

The Portuguese practise community endogamy. As they do not have any clan, they restrict their marriages within the Christian religious group. They marry neither their lineage members nor their blood kin. Marriageable age varies from eighteen to twenty-five years in case of females and from twenty to thirty years in case of males. The mode of acquiring mates is through negotiation. They are strictly monogamous. Marriage is permitted between persons having the same surname. As Christians they do not have any special marriage symbol. Putting of *sindur* on the forehead and the use of *sankha* have now become the symbols of marriage and this may be due to their close proximity with the neighbouring Hindu communities. System of dowry is prevalent and it is paid both in cash and kind. The amount of dowry depends on the economic conditions of the bride's parents. They are patrilocal. On rare occasions the system of *gharjamai* is practised. Divorce is permitted on grounds like physical inability of either of the spouse, adultery, maladjustment in the family, etc. At the time of settling divorce they take assistance from the *'katikist'* (priest of the church) and other elder persons of their community. Post-divorce maintenance depends on the decision taken by the *'katikist'* and other members who generally sit together for settling divorce. Remarriage is permitted but it is allowed after divorce or death of the spouse. Following changes are noticed in the institution of marriage; i) age at marriage has been increasing; ii) love marriage has been noticed; iii) *sankha* and *sindur* are being used as marriage symbols, etc.

Two types of families viz. nuclear and joint are found among the Portuguese. Inter-personal relations are maintained through mutual love, respect and assistance. Relationship between husband and wife depends on love, respect and obligation. Children are treated with love and affection. The girls are trained in domestic duties by their mothers and boys follow their father, paternal uncles, grandfathers, and other senior members of the family. Adolescent children are found to obey their father and other elder male members of their family and their obedience is perhaps due to fear of punishment. Avoidance relationship is found between husband's elder brother and younger brother's wife. Joking relationship exists between elder brother's wife and husband's younger brother and between grandparents and grandchildren. Conflict and confrontation between the members of the family arise in different situations like inability to share family expenditure, litigation on property etc. Though the Portuguese are aware of the legal position held by women as regards inheritance of parental property yet sons inherit parental property under normal conditions and daughters are deprived of their rights. Succession is patrilineal. Inter-family linkages are based upon cooperation and mutual exchange of goods and services among the members of the community. At present younger generations are found to live separately just few months after their marriage.

It is already mentioned that right of inheritance among the women is often transgressed. Their economic role is confined to duties and their social role is to look after the wellbeing of their husband, children and other members of the family. They participate in a number of rituals associated with the various life-cycle rituals. They have a religious role. They enjoy freedom to go to churches and other religious and social gatherings. Women do not actively participate in political activities. There is usually no scope for women to earn through employment and as such women have no scope to escape from domestic duties in the family. In fact, there is hardly any traditionally prescribed right for women, but their obligations in the different spheres of life are many.

The Portuguese of Mirpur do not have any special ceremony in connection with birth. They do not observe any pollution period as such. Umbilical cord is cut by an experienced woman of their own community, and the placenta is buried near the house. On this occasion they do not require the services of the barber, washer man or priest. After one and a half month of birth of a child, parents bring the newborn child to their respective church for 'Baptism' (Christening ceremony). The deacon or a clergyman comes and performs the ceremony. Sometimes the local '*katikist*' does the duties of a deacon. A Sunday is fixed for such a ceremony. On this occasion a ceremonial name is given to the baby by the clergyman at the church. *Annaprashan* or rice eating ceremony is a prevalent custom among the Portuguese of Mirpur. In case of a male child, *annaprashan* is held when the baby completes six months of age. In case of a female it is held in the seventh month. Unlike Hindus they do not consult the almanac for fixing *annaprashan* day. It is fixed considering the availability of the kin during the function. On this occasion maternal uncle feeds the first morsel of food into the mouth of the child, or in his absence by the grandfather. Usually on this occasion a *ghusi* (red thread) is tied on the waist of the baby. There is a slight difference in the *annaprashan* performance of the Roman Catholics and Protestants. Protestants prepare *payesh* (a sweet dish made of rice, milk and sugar) which is fed to the baby with the help of a silver coin, but the Roman Catholics only feed sweets. The child is reared in the home up to the age of five. Thereafter he/she is admitted to the village primary school.

Marriage generally takes in the bride's parent's house and negotiation is done with the relatives with the help of a *ghatak* (go between). When everything regarding the marriage is settled they arrange a formal ceremony which is known as *pantola*. The prospective bridegroom and his relatives bring a packet of *batasa* (a kind of sweet made of sugar) and distribute these among the members present from the prospective bride's house. After this the date of the marriage is intimated to the deacons of respective churches of each party. Prior to the formal marriage ceremony the deacons declare the names of the bride and the bridegroom for proper intimation of the villagers on three consecutive Sundays. If nobody objects to this marriage then the date is finally fixed. This is known as *bandaka*. Before betrothal, female members from the bridegroom's house visit the house of the bride, and after finalising matters related to the marriage, elderly married women apply vermilion on the forehead of the bride. Ceremonial application of turmeric paste on the bride and bridegroom is made for three consecutive days prior to the day of marriage. A new piece of cloth dyed yellow, is given to them and application of turmeric paste is followed by a ceremonial bath, on each occasion.

On the wedding day the bridegroom comes to the house of bride with his party and afterwards both bride and bridegroom are brought to the church where all the villagers assemble to record their witness on the occasion. The 'Bishop' of the church solemnizes the marriage and then starts the wedding prayer. The 'Bishop' offers two rings to the respective bride and bridegroom which are give to the 'Bishop' by the respective party. Bridegroom puts vermilion on the forehead and hair parting of the bride with the help of the ring. Then the bridegroom presents his ring to the bride and simultaneously the bride presents her ring to the bridegroom which is treated as marriage bond. After that the bride and the groom are taken to the bride's parent's house where bride's mother receives and offers milk and cream to the couple. On the same day a wedding feast is given to the villagers.

Then the new couple goes to the bridegroom's house. They remain there for three days. After three days bridegroom's parents arrange a bridal feast which all villagers and relatives attend. The newlywed couple stays there for three days and then goes to the bride's house. They remain there for a day or two and then finally return to the home of the bridegroom, taking with them the presents given to them on different occasions related to the ritual. Consummation is possible immediately after the marriage.

The dead are buried according to Christian customs. Both Protestants and Roman Catholics use the same burial ground. No burial takes place during the night. After death, the dead body is brought to the respective church and it is cleaned with water. Perfume is applied on the body of the dead before it is brought to the burial ground and then it is buried and a prayer is offered. They do not observe any mourning period. Seven days after of the death they assemble at the church and arrange a mourning prayer under the leadership of the '*katikist*'. On 2nd November every year they assemble at the burial ground and arrange a mourning prayer for the peace and happiness of the souls of all deceased persons.

The Portuguese maintain a register where the date, place, time of birth and date of *baptism* are recorded. Besides, they maintain a record of marriages and deaths also.

Land is considered as major economic resource of the community. Control over land lies in the hands of individual proprietors. The Portuguese are mainly a landowning community. Previously they were brought to this region as gunners, but at present agriculture is their primary occupation. Service in government and non-governmental organisations are considered as subsidiary sources of income. A few of them are engaged in porter's jobs for carrying goods and luggage in Geokhali, by which they earn money. For essential commodities they depend on markets. They have no bonded labour among them. The extent of landlessness and the number of labourers working in agriculture is significantly low among the Portuguese. Child labour is not observed among them. For agricultural purposes, they generally employ labourers from the Muslim community. Payment of wages for agricultural labourer as well as for other forms of labour is both in cash and kind. After Independence a few of them have given up the agricultural profession and taken up jobs in the Navy, factories and dockyards. Besides, due to their Christian religious faith a few of them have got an opportunity to get jobs in missionary organisations.

The Portuguese have their own religious council which is known as "Christio Samaj". They have no regional association. The above mentioned 'Samaj' has a communal headman who is selected by the villagers on the basis of his qualities and attributes. He generally settles simple disputes related to socio-political affairs. While settling disputes he discusses with the elderly members of the village and acts on the joint decision. Petty thefts, drunkenness, etc., are taken as serious offences. Form of punishment is determined by the nature of the misdeed. Both cash fine and social boycott are imposed as punishment. The role of modern statutory councils is important. They have considerable participation in the present *panchayat* system and accordingly they try to contact the members of the councils for settling serious disputes related to land and property.

The Portuguese profess Christianity. It is already mentioned that there are two churches situated in the village Mirpur. The priest or *katikist* of the respective church is regarded as sacred specialist. Except Jesus Christ they do not worship any god or goddess. Churches of different places are regarded as major sacred centres. The role of priests is very important. From birth to death of a person they play roles in various life cycle ceremonies. The priests (*katikists*) keep regular contact with the heads of their respective churches and intimate their service and religious activities to the respective Bishops in Calcutta. In addition to this they hold services every Sunday and on Good Friday/Easter Saturday and Christmas day which are related to their Christian religion. From time to time they convene religious gatherings in the churches for enlightenment of the children in general. Besides, female members of the Portuguese community arrange special prayer to Jesus Christ at their individual houses for recovery and welfare of family members. On many ceremonial occasions they go out from their houses in a procession to the churches or any other festive place in batches and enjoy the occasion. They attend local fairs though those are not of any special significance in their life. Normally they do not observe any regional festival nor do they contribute to or participate in any such festival.

The Portuguese have no specific art and craft. Oral traditions which are observed among them in different ceremonials are mainly borrowed form the sacred texts of the Bible. On different occasions they arrange prayer, music and church choir also.

Inter-community linkages are cordial but restricted to some extent. For example, they do not take an active part in any festival of the

Hindus or Moslems who live around their village. Conventionally they are considered as *mlechha* (unclean) by the neighbouring Hindus. Inter-religious marital exchanges are prohibited if there is such a case then the person concerned is required to change his religion. They do not have any restriction on making putative friendship. They do not face any problem as regard access to and sharing of tube-wells facilities of roads, schools and regarding entry to temples, houses, *panchayat ghar*, club, etc. They maintain a kind of patron-client relationship with the priest/*katikist* or Bishop of the churches. They also maintain modern inter-community linkages. They take active part along with neighbouring Hindus and Moslems in exercising their voting rights at election times. They maintain a good relation with the neighbouring communities in respect of various economic activities related to agriculture which is based on mutual dependence and cooperation.

Most Portuguese males of the present generation are literate. There are two primary schools in the studied village of which one is run by the Government of West Bengal and the other is run by the Roman Catholic Christian Mission. Children from the Portuguese community not only get facilities from these institutions but they also avail themselves of the opportunities from the missionary schools of Calcutta with which they maintain contact through the Bishops. The Portuguese have a progressive outlook as regards health and medical care. Both male and female members go and consult doctors about planning their families. At present they do not face any problem of drinking water. They are aware of the various rural employment programmes and sometimes they take advantage of self employment through different government agencies. Radio, newspaper, television and local newspapers are found in many families. The Portuguese village is situated near to Geokhali (which is the largest centre of the locality) and as a result their village is well connected by bus and ferry service. Electrification has reached the village and most households use electricity. Environmental conservation and energy resources are not anything that primarily concerns the members of this community. Wood, coal, cowdung cake, straw, etc. are used as energy resources. Irrigation facilities are not availed of. Cultivation depends on rainwater only. Chemical fertilisers and insecticides are used by them. Midday meal, feeding programme at schools are availed of by them though these are irregular. The Portuguese collect essential commodities from the M. R. shop. They take loans and other facilities from the Mallabhum Gramin Bank, situated at Geokhali.

When Portuguese gunners came and settled in Mirpur village a good number of women from the low caste neighbouring communities were abducted and compelled to live with them. Ultimately those women lost their relations with parental families as well as social status and began to live with them. This type of social life compelled neighbouring Hindu communities to avoid the Portuguese gunners as well as women who used to live with them.

Owing to such isolation, the missionary organisations came forward and took a keen interest in their betterment by giving all sorts of help and assistance. As a result a good number of them are found to be employed in many factories, dockyard and missionary organisations. Besides, the present generation is trying their best to wipe out illiteracy and other social vices through their contacts with outsiders. They marry only members of Christian communities. They sometimes try to find Portuguese boys or girls from Calcutta for prospective marriage alliances. For instance, Sri Rajit Tessers of Mirpur married a Portuguese woman who lived in Calcutta but is originally from Goa (which was once ruled by the Portuguese). He contacted that lady through the Bishop of a missionary organisation of Calcutta.

SUBHRENDU MAITI

PUNJABI

The Punjabis are a linguistic minority group in West Bengal. The Punjabis took their name from their habitat Punjab. The Punjab is made up of two Persian words *Panj* (five) and *aab* (water, the 5 rivers namely Jhelum, Chenab, Ravi, Beas, and Sutlej). In the Vedic ages it was called "Sapta Sindhu" i.e., land of seven rivers. The word Punjabi generally conveys the impression of a particular community, having a beard and wearing a big turban on the head, commonly known as Sikh. It is easy to define Sikh as a religious community. The Sikhs though form the bulk of the Punjabi population. However, there are also Hindu and Muslim Punjabis. The Sikhs are the disciples or *shishya* who accepted the institution *Khalsa* founded in 1699 by Guru Govind Singh, their tenth and last Guru. Today the Sikhs and other non Sikh Punjabis are to be found in almost every part of west Bengal. Their major concentration is in the city of Calcutta, mainly in Bhawanipur, Burrabazar, Kidderpur, Metiabruj, Dunlop, and B. T. Road areas, and also scattered all over the state and Calcutta, where the study has been made. Calcutta is located on coastal plain land with moderate climate, high humidity and medium rainfall. Calcutta, the chief metropolis of West Bengal, lies within 22°33' north latitude and 88°23' east longitude. It is situated about 160 kilometres from the sea on the left bank of the western branch of the Ganges, called Hooghly or Bhagirathi river. The area of Calcutta district is 104.00 square kilometres. The remaining areas are under the Port and Military establishments. The average temperatures recorded in 1979 were 37.08° Celsius maximum and 14.7° Celsius minimum. The annual rainfall recorded in Calcutta in the same year was 1321.1mm (according to 1981 Census). The Punjabi population in Calcutta was 23,995 according to 1981 Census, comprising 13,729 males and 10,266 females. They speak in Punjabi and use Gurmukhi script within the family, kin-group and with other Punjabis. They speak in Hindi, Bengali, English and use Devanagari and Roman scripts with others. The Sikh Punjabi males can be identified by their turbans and beards. However the Punjabis as a minority group are defined by language, food habits, common traditions, and folk culture.

They are usually non-vegetarian. The Sikh Punjabis who take *amrit* (sacred water) are strictly vegetarian. They take wheat, rice as their staple food. Pulses like gram, *urad*, *moong*, *masur*, *moth*, peas and beans are used by them. Groundnut oil and pure *ghee* are used as cooking medium. They take green vegetables, roots, tubers, and seasonal fruits as available in the market. Men take alcoholic drinks occasionally. They take milk and milk products like *ghee*, sweets etc. They do not as a traditional custom, smoke *bidis*, cigarettes etc. although a few chew betel. Nowadays some Punjabis especially non-Sikh Punjabis smoke and use tobacco products. Here many of them take rice every day while rice is served only occasionally or at regular intervals at their native place.

The Punjabis are divided into Sikh and non-Sikh Punjabis. The Sikhs have social divisions. Brahman Sikhs (who propagates the fundamental principles of Guru Govind Singh's teaching, clan — Mujhal), Jat Sikh (agriculturist, clans — Gil, Sidhu, Dhafiwals, Dhilons, Sindhu, Mann etc), Khatris (principal occupation is commerce, clans — Bunjahi, Bahri, Sarin, Kohkram), Aroras (trader, trade and clans — Bahri, Bunjahi), Mahtams and Mahtons (partly vagrants and hunters and partly agriculturists, clans — Dupaich, Puri, Khatti, Babat, Jhalwal), Sairis (mainly found in military service and have liking for gardening, clans — Boli, Pawan, Goddi, Manger), Tarkhans or Ramgarhias (carpenter, clans — Dhoman, Khatti Matharu, Gade, Tharu), Nais (barber, clans — Gola, Bahgu, Bhatti, Kokhar), Chhimbas (calico printer clans — Sippal, Khakhar, Bhatti) etc. The Hindu and Muslim Punjabis are also divided into several castes and sub-castes and segments. The social divisions of the Muslim Punjabis are based on caste hierarchy and social status which regulate marriage alliances, indicate social status and ancestry. They are aware of Vedic *varna* system — Brahman, Kshatriya, Vaishya and Sudra. However Muslim Punjabis do not recognise the *varna* system. They enjoy a high social status, according to their self perception. In their neighbours' perception also, they occupy high position within the social hierarchy.

They practise endogamy at community level and exogamy at *gotra* (clan) level. They do not practise consanguinity in marriage. They practise adult marriage and acquire mates by negotiation, mutual consent and courtship. They practise monogamy. Married women have no marriage symbol. Dowry in kind prevails. Rules of residence after marriage are patrilocal. Either party can seek divorce with judicial approval for maladjustment or any other legal reasons. Widow remarriage, widower remarriage, male and female divorcee remarriage, levirate and sororate are permissible. Among some educated and modernised families some changes are noticed, as they do not favour negotiation and traditional marriage systems. Some prefer intercommunity marriage and marriage through courtship. In general, marriage at early ages are not preferred, at least not until the boy becomes independent and can earn his own livelihood.

Although there are nuclear type families, majority of them live in extended families. They have avoidance relationship between daughter-in-law and father-in-law, younger sister-in-law and elder brother-in-law. They have joking relationship between elder sister-in-law and younger brother-in-law, grandparents and grandchildren, and with wife's siblings. With advancement of learning and adoption of modern culture, avoidance and joking relationships are not observed among present generation very strictly. Conflicts and confrontations occur mainly on property and financial disputes. All the sons inherit property equally. The eldest son succeeds his father as the head of the family, according to their rules of succession.

The women participate in economic activities, social functions and rituals. They have lower status than men and do not have decision making power. Most of them do household jobs. Some women contribute to the family income as they are engaged in service or teaching. They also control family expenditure jointly with men.

The Punjabi Sikhs observe post-delivery pollution for twelve days when the mother is confined to the room with strict seclusion for first five days. On the thirteenth day the whole of the house is cleaned and washed and the *purohit* (priest) performs *yagna* (offering in the sacred fire). On the thirteenth day after birth or any odd day a name is given to the child. The *granthi* or any elder member of the family opens the Granth Sahib (holy book of the Sikhs) at random. The first letter of the first line on the left hand page, at which the book opens, must be the initial letter of the name to be given to the infant. However in case of the Punjabi Hindus naming ceremony is observed on the eleventh day. Male children are tonsured in the first, third or fifth year of birth. *Janeu* (sacred thread wearing) ceremony is observed by the male Hindu Punjabi Brahman during their adolescence. The Punjabi Muslims observe birth rites as per Islamic norms. When a Punjabi Sikh boy is around five or six years of age, he wears a turban for the first time ceremonially. The ceremony is called *dastarbandi*.

Among the Punjabi Sikhs marriage rituals are performed according to Sikh tradition at the bride's residence. The bride's parents give a feast for the marriage. They arrange a reception ceremony at the bridegroom's house. Marriages are generally arranged through direct communication between the parents of the boy and girl and also by sending messages through friends, priests and kin. They also observe betrothal ceremony, popularly known as *sak, sargai* or *kurmai*. The following procedure is usually adopted in a Sikh marriage. Before departure of the bride-groom for the bride's house, for marriage, the bride-groom is dressed in yellow, wreathed by a *sera* (a garland of flowers) and crowned with a *mukut* (head dress), made of mica and tinsel paper, with hanging golden threads covering the face. A Brahman ties the *kangua* (seven knotted bracelet) on the boy's wrist. Then the *barat* (marriage procession) starts with the bridegroom mounting on a mare, followed by males also mounted, as many as possible. Before reaching the bride's house her father and relatives receive the party which is known as *milni*. In the past Sikh marriages were celebrated according to Hindu rites, but with hymns of the fourth Guru, sung by female members, instead of Hindu songs. Presently most of them have completely given up the Hindu rituals. They circumambulate the Granth Sahib and Sikh priests read hymns of their holy book. After that the couple goes round the sacrificial fire four times. The first *laon* (round) is interpreted to represent *pragrithi marga* (path of fourth-going) the second to mark the approach of the disciple to the true Guru (purification and realisation of self), the third round to mean *niurith marg* (turning home words) and the fourth and the final round as union of self with the supreme. This ceremony is termed as *anand*. After *anand* the *khat* ceremony is held. On this occasion father and relatives of the bridegroom and his followers are presented with gifts. Nuptial rites are, as a rule celebrated on the night of marriage. On the next day the ceremony of *got kumala* is observed in the bridegroom's house. Where marriage follows betrothal, it should take place in the first, third or fifth year, as even years are considered unlucky. Certain subsidiary customs are also observed before and after marriage. Those are *maiyan* (confinement of both bridegroom and bride for seven or eight days before marriage), *vari* (presentation of ornaments etc., to the bride by the bridegroom's father), *Khat* (reciprocal gifts by the bride's father) and three other rapidly declining customs as: *chhand* (bridegroom's intelligence test taken by bride's relatives), *lassi mundi* (picking up of an article from a milk tray) and *muthi kholna* (physical test of the couple).

The Punjabi Hindus perform certain marriage rituals at the groom's residence, while the main marriage rituals are performed at the bride's place. Marriage is consummated at the groom's residence. The Punjabi

Muslims observe marriage rituals as per norms prescribed in Islamic tradition.

The dead bodies of both Punjabi Sikhs and Hindus are cremated while those of Muslims are buried. Dead bodies of children under five years of age even in case of Punjabi Sikhs and Hindus are usually buried. The Punjabi Sikhs observe pollution for ten days. Death rituals are prevalent among the Sikhs. Dead bodies of Sikhs are carried to the cremation ground while reciting "*shabods*". The body is put on the funeral pyre and set on fire. After cremation the ritual of reading the *Granth Sahib* commences and is terminated on the tenth day after death. The Punjabi Hindus observe pollution for eleven or thirteen days and observe *sradh* ceremony. In case of Punjabi Muslims they read *janaja namaj* before the corpse is buried. On the fortieth day some Muslims arrange religious discourses and give alms to *fakirs.*

Another ritual some Sikhs observe is *amrit pan* (drinking sacred water). An auspicious date is fixed for this ceremony, which is observed generally by spiritual minded Sikhs. On the determined date they fast and attend the *gurdwara* (house of Guru) with a devoted mind. The *Granthi* or priest gives each a few *Batasas* (sugarcakes) which they are advised to put into a pot of water and shake well. This water is known as *amrit* (sacred water), which they drink. At the time of drinking *amrit* the *granthi* makes them read some oaths and also some hymns from the *Granth Sahib*. The principal oaths that they take are for leading an honest and spiritual life and for abstaining from non-vegetarian meals. The persons drinking *amrit* together are called *dharam bhai*.

The Punjabis in West Bengal are mainly landless. They are engaged in business and Government service. They also work in industries, textile (weaving and dyeing) mills, and wood, priests, skilled and unskilled labourers. They have direct link with the daily market where the mode of exchange is cash. They are also self employed in general as well as are in transport, business etc.

They have a local association. Panjabi Biradree, where they meet at regular intervals for mutual cooperation and welfare. Officials are elected by secret ballot. As regards changes in mechanism of social control they do not depend on traditional systems of caste councils. Any fine or punishment by such councils can neither be imposed nor implemented.

Most of the Punjabis are Sikh by religion however some Punjabis follow Hinduism or Islam. The sacred specialists of the Punjabi Sikhs are from the same community. They perform birth, marriage and death rites. Their festivals are of socio-religious significance. They observe the festivals of Guru Nanak's birthday, Baisakhi, Guru Gobind Sing's birthday and Diwali. Guru Nanak's birthday is celebrated on Kartik *purnamashi* (full moon day in November). Preceding that day, forty-eight hours' *akhand path* (continuous reading) of the holy *Adi Granth* by a series of readers reading it in turns is observed in every *Gurudwara*. A day before the birthday of Guru Nanak, a grand procession is taken out. It is led by five holy men followed by *Adi Granth* on a carrier. Behind it several parties of singers follow reciting hymns from the *Granth*. The other members of the procession participate in reciting the hymns in chorus. In Calcutta a procession is led from the *Gurudwara* at Bhawanipur to that at Burrabazar. In the morning devotees gather at the Gurudwara make voluntary offerings and salute the *Granth* by half way prostrating before it and then sit down and listen to the praise of God. With regard to Guru Nanak's birthday there are some controversies. Some believe that Nanak was born in *Baisakh* (April-May) but the celebration was transferred to the month of *Kartik*, due to some reason or other. Guru Gobind Singh's birthday falls in December-January. It is a three day celebration as in the case of Guru Nanak, consisting of *akhand path*, processions and congregation with great pomp and perfection. *Baisakhi*, another important festival of the Punjabi Sikhs falls in the first half of April. It is celebrated as birthday of *khalsa*. This is also a three day celebration at big centres and one day celebration at other places. *Kirtan, kathas*, lectures and *langars* form essential parts of the day's function. Hindus also join the Sikhs in this celebration. *Diwali*, mainly a Hindu festival has been adopted by the Sikhs as one of their main festivals. Their sixth Guru, Hargovind, arrived at Amritsar on the Diwali day after twelve years' imprisonment at Gwalior. Moreover the major *gurmatos* of Sikhs were held on this day in the eighteenth century. The day is observed with *kirtans, kathas*, lectures, *langars*, illuminations, fireworks etc., and lastly with distribution of sweets. The Punjabi Hindus accept the deities of the wider Hindu pantheon and observe major Hindu festivals like Holi, Diwali etc. Many Punjabis are the followers of the Arya Samaj and Nirankari Sect. The Punjabi Muslims profess Islam and observe Muharram, Idul Fitr, Iduz Zuha and so on.

Punjabis being a very old and traditional community, they have their own folk tales, folklore, folk songs in combination with their mythology and zonal beliefs and customs. They use the *dhole*, and wind, string, and valve instruments for music. Both men and women participate in singing.

The Punjabis have traditional intercommunity relationship with residents of neighbouring areas. They accept and exchange water, *kachcha* food, pucca food, and *sidha* food with other communities. They share water sources, crematorium, schools etc., with others. Putative kinship (*dharam bhai*) exists. Those who drink *amrit* together in Gurdwara are called *dharam bhai* (religious brother hood). In visiting shrines they make no distinction. In economic, social and ritual aspects they receive and render service. The community has businessmen, scholars, white collar job holders, teachers, administrators, engineers, doctors and members of defence services.

They prefer higher education for boys, but general education for all. Boys study up to postgraduate level and girls up to graduate level. They have comfortably adjusted themselves to the modern lifestyle. All civic amenities like electricity, piped water, and food rationing are utilized by them. They like entertainment through radio, and television. They avail themselves of modern medical aids from I.C.D.S. centre and also from private physicians or from hospitals according to their needs. Their attitude to family planning is favourable. Couples prefer two or three children and use modern methods of family planning. Transaction through banks, savings and investments are popular among them. Some take loans for the purpose of transport business or to construct their houses, from the nationalised banks.

MADHUMALA CHATTOPADHYAY

RABHA

The Rabhas of North Bengal live mainly in the districts of Jalpaiguri and Cooch Behar. In Jalpaiguri district, they live in the thanas of Kalchini, Kumargram and Alipurduar — all under Alipurduar Sub-division. The Rabhas of Cooch Behar are found only in the thana of Tufanganj Sub-division.

The names of the Rabha inhabited villages are given below:-

Jalpaiguri District:	Cooch Behar District:
1. Poro Basti	1. Bansraja
2. Kodal Basti	2. Bharea
3. Puarpar	3. Haripur
4. Damanpur	4. Bhandijilash
5. Chikliguri	5. Mughabhog
6. Kamakhyaguri	6. Chhatrampur
7. Madhya Kamakhyaguri	7. Purba Chikliguri
8. Proba Salbari	8. Chengtimari forest
9. Raidak forest	9. Atiamechar forest
10. Chhipra forest	10. Takuamari forest
11. Tashikbil	
12. Bara Salbari.	

The Rabhas are matrilineal. They are divided into a number of *husuks* or gotras. Children get mother's *husuk*. Marriage within the same *gotra* is prohibited. Sexual relation between boys and girls of the same *husuk* is not permitted as the Rabhas believe that the members of the same *husuk* originated from the same stock. Some of these *husuks* are totemistic in nature. Totemic objects are prohibited for eating, using, killing or planting.

Some important *Husuks* are given below :-

Husuk	*Totemic Objects*
Banda	Curd/Milk
Bantao	Brinjal
Chinchet	Ginger
Darboth	Banian tree
Durunga	Peacock and peahen
Kantram	Dank and Kora
Dalangsa	Boal fish
Kama	Rat
Logobak	Boal fish

Moijipran	Boal fish
Moijidong	Boal fish
Mositak	Deer
Pomrei	Tortoisc
Unichandal	Peacock
Unichidangbaria	Bhati

Two stories have been collected; one about the origin of Pomrei *husuk* and other about the source of Masitak *husuk*.

1. Long ago, one day the members of a household were taking their meal. At that time a tortoise came to take some rice. It was instantly killed with a sharp *gaien*. The meat of the tortoise was cooked and served. But as soon as one took its meat, he began to sink down into the earth. All the members who took the meat of the tortoise faced the same consequence. When the head male member came home from the farm, though he was astonished to see the fate of the members of his family, he realised what the matter was. The remaining meat of the tortoise was immediately thrown out. As soon as it was done, all members came out of the earth. From that day, the members of Pomrei *husuk* identified their origin with the tortoise. Eating of tortoise-meat has been prohibited.

2. One day seven sisters were husking paddy. At that time a fawn came there. The fawn was attacked with the *gaien* and it died. Before its death the fawn cursed them. Since then Rabhas belonging to Mositak *husuk* have believed that they originated from he-deer. Hunting of deer and eating of its meat are prohibited for the members of the Masitak *husuk*.

Runtuk is the house-deity. In every Rabha house she is placed in the north-western corner of the house upon a bamboo platform. In all the festivities of the house, *Runtuk* is worshipped first. Fowls and pigs are sacrificed. *Chakot* or liquor is the main material of *Runtuk puja*. *Bashek* is regarded as the sister companion of *Runtuk*. She is similarly worshiped by the Rabhas. There is no image of *Runtuk* or *Bashek*. An earthen pitcher full of rice is placed upon the bamboo platform. An egg (*Tauchi*) is placed upon the rice. The mantras uttered by the *Deosi* at the time of worship of *Runtuk* and *Bashek* are given below:-

Hal Jal ji neu Hal jal ji nai Sona nagau na bau Sona gktang na ou. Hattirai tasai Ghara bau tasai Hal jal ji neu Hal jal ji nai.

Free translation :

Oh. *Runtuk* and *Bashek*, you are two sisters. Oh *Runtuk*, the golden house is yours. Oh *Bashek*, you are offered a silver house. Be pleased with us. Do not be angry. Do not go away on elephant's back. Oh *Runtuk*, Oh *Bashek*, be pleased with us.

Nuor Bai is regarded as the goddess of welfare. She is worshipped for the well being of newborn child and mother. *Buluarai* is regarded as an evil god or *apadevata*. The *Huji* (priest and medicine man) controls him by means of some magical performances. Along with *Bulua* his two sisters *Pania* and *Ganch* are also worshipped. Evil Spirits of the dead are called *Joura* by the Rabhas. *Joura* is also done away with magical performances of the *Huji*. Ganga Raja is worshipped by the Rabha agriculturists for good harvest. *Rishi* is their chief deity. *Jaga* is his wife. *Rishi* and *Jaga* are reminiscent our Shiva and Kali. They have no images. Once in the month of *Baisakh* each year *Rishi* and *Jaga* are worshipped. They are also worshipped before marriage ceremonies. Every Rabha who has the means should once a year sacrifice a hog or fowl to *Rishi*. Now most of the Rabhas have become Hinduized. The Hinduized Rabhas worship Kali, Shiva, Narayan, Vishvakarma, Vishabari and other Hindu deities of the locality.

Like the Meches, the Rabha women were experts in weaving and spinning. Every Rabha house was a centre of *Endi* industry. Today only among some forest Rabhas, this indigenous industry survives. The training-cum-production centre established at Narthali (Jalpaiguri) is helping the Rabha women in this matter.

Kaal and *darshi* are the two principal musical instruments of the Rabhas. *Kaal* is made of reed. It is a long pipe of 5 to 6 feet. There are holes through the reed. The sound of the *Kaal* is just the PU-U-U. *Dangshi* is like a *dhak*, (a sort of drum) small in breadth. A folk tale has been collected relating to the origin of *Kaal*. It runs thus:-

Once upon a time there was an epidemic. In a village, all the members of a family died of Cholera. The house remained vacant. A traveller became fatigued, in the evening he saw a solitary house. He took shelter on the *macha* of that house. Darkness began to increase. At dead of night, a host of phantoms appeared. They got the scent of a living man in the house. They said — "Where is gog rice, it flavours like that. If we could get, we would eat". (*Diyci Bhogmai Menaauta, Kaun Masna Maun Sana Maun*). Thus saying they began to dance. Their leader sat on a *shham* and began to play with it — "Ting Biding Chak karbar Ra-Ba..." Hearing the sound of instrumental music, the ghosts danced again and again. All of them said in one voice, "we do not fear anybody, we not fear any weapon. We shall only fear the sound PU-U-U. . ."

(Hindangba michang, banduk ba khingchang PU-U-U Tane se khirang).

Hearing this, the man became more frightened. He began to think over the sound of PU-U-U.... For survival even in midst of darkness he began to find out a pipe of reed to make the sound PU-U-U.... He found one such pipe in the *macha* and started to play on it. When the sound PU-U-U-was heard, all the ghosts ran away. The man drove away hosts of ghosts as and when they came, with the help of that instrument. In the morning, the man came down from the *macha* and went away. This is how the *kaal* was made and used. *Kaal* and *Dangshi* are used in all the festivals of the Rabhas.

Some Rabha folk songs are given below:-

1. *Chika Jareing pan jejeng Ghughu Mangsa Hepcha Okai Malam Malam Banaiv Okai Aoan Hepa.*

Free translation:-

In the far off branch of a dead tree, a dove is weeping. It has lost its mate. Why are you weeping alone?

2. *Tausa Magnsa chiao chiao Bai chongor Tanga Tin pradhan Babu Aa Nudur Peng Bang Panga.*

Free translation:-

Like the chickens we humbly request the babu. We hold his feet and inform him of our pains, but in vain. (This refers to their economic plight).

3. *Shyal Kairenga Hoa Hoa Bantang Damii chai Okai Aango Nana Dekan Chani Ripak Dai.*

Free translation:-

By the side of the brinjal farm, jackals bark — Hukka hua-hua —. When my friend is with me, whom shall I fear?

4. *Sairga lau lau Puiman Neyia Ukan Bakan Tia Nu Aang Na Na Na Pa Taka Rang Tam Pia.*

Free translation:-

A green parrot flies in the blue sky. Oh girl, I shall purchase you with money (This refers to the dowry system).

5. *Ji Sing Phaleng oingai Tou Kanta Seka Okoi Akana Hepa Gancha Ganch Baneing Otho gai Dhaleng Keka.*

Free translation:-

Like a white hen, the sky is clear. Now it is dawn. At that time, you came with *pan* and *guya*, you have come to me with tears. (This reflects the sentiments of the lovers).

6. *Neng Duku Le U Ang Palau Nunga*
Sari Hasai Naiman Nakcheng Retihiya.

Free Translation:-

I have taken Jakui. Please come and take Kalui. Let us catch fish in the Bura river. (The Rabhas both males and females are expert in fishing. Fishing has been referred to here).

7. *Juta Karap Karap Kharam Karap Karap Nini Kabak Naita Hathi Chakiriang Mushi Chakiriang Dubal Bisin Dabal Nini Kabak Nita*

Free translation:-

He is annoyed with me. Sounding the shoes he is going away. Please turn him back. He is going to be *mahut* or *maishal*. He is going away. Please turn him back. (The daily quarrels of husband-wife resulting from and in love are reflected here).

8. *Bauchaur Pidan Sakphaijau Shung Doban Pui Jau Nai Logau Laogau Nang Bausun Din Skfaijau. .... ne*

Free translation:-

The Happy New Year is coming. Our minds are happy. Let us go enjoy this joyous day.

(The agriculturist Rabhas enjoy during the harvest)

9. *Parang Butul Parjau Shung Rasang Sakjau Nini Ini Kaurau Doan Namparai Puijau ...... Ne*

Free translation:-

Flowers are blooming. Our mind is also developing. Words of love are in the air. (A full blossomed flower is the symbol of love).

10. *Au Anao Gagraiju Kaum lau Kapcha Kauntang Kapchuju*
Au Anao Maslalanju Chang Hauma Navnaau Chang Lana Naungau

Free translation:-

On my dear sister, you are not a good weaver. You do not know how to live. Nobody will marry you.

(The Rabha girls who are not skilled in weaving are not chosen by the youths for marriage)

11. *Ka Kabak Ha Kabak Kundu Lug Sau Ne Palao Ham Kapcha Dukhu Ham Kapcha Chang Hauna Naungau Chang Lana Naungau Ha Kabak Damag Tai Nang.*

Free translation:-

Oh my brother-in-law, you do not know to make a bamboo, you do not know to make a good basket. Who will marry you?

(The Rabha girls do not accept a boy as husband unless he is expert in manufacturing fishing apparatus and the like).

The Rabhas are mainly cultivators. They also earn by running poultry farms and piggeries. The Rabhas who live in reserved forests work as Government labourers. They produce rice, wheat, pulses, vegetables, etc. Their daily economic life centres round weekly markets. The medium of exchange is cash. Among the Rabhas there is no bonded or child labour. Traditional village council exists. It is called *Mara Sen* (*Mara* — Men, *Sen* — Elders). *Pare* is the traditional headman. The Rabhas have adopted the statutory *panchayat* System (three tier). Inter-community and inter-*bustee* (slum) disputes are settled by the *Mara Sen*.

The Rabhas maintain inter-community relationship with the Meches, Oraons, Rajbanshis, Jalia Kaibartas, Naths and Sahas. They take food and water from them. They have ceremonial relationship with the Rajbanshis. *Mitar* and *Panichita Maobap* are very popular. The Rabhas have cultivator-labour or -share-cropper and mortgagee-mortgager relationship with other communities.

The Rabhas are mostly illiterate. They have their own medicine men and medicines. Now they get modern medical facilities. Family planning programmes do not attract them. They use tube-wells and wells for drinking water. New employment programmes of the government have covered the Rabhas. Road transport and Post Offices have now reached the Rabha villages. There is no electricity. Irrigation facilities are not available. Modern manures are used. They get benefits from the ICDS projects. They are not accustomed to banking. They mortgage land to money-lenders when they are in need of money.

DR. PABITRA KUMAR GUPTA

RAI

The Rais also claim to be known as Kirat Rais. The *thars* or clans are the only subgroups among them. They are identified both at the local and regional levels. They claim to be the original settlers of the region. They perceive their distribution in Algarh, Songche and Laba in the district of Darjeeling and in the adjoining district of Jalpaiguri of West Bengal. They inhabit the hilly terrain region with cold climate, medium rainfall, and occasional snowfall during winter. They speak Nepali and Hindi and use Devanagari and Roman scripts.

The Rai are occasional non-vegetarians and also eat pork. Rice and wheat are their staple food. Roots and tubers are consumed generally as vegetables. Tea and milk are common beverages for them. Alcoholic drinks are taken occasionally from the market by both men and women. Fruit is taken only occasionally. They are habituated to smoking *bidis* and cigarettes and chewing betel.

They have among them seven *thars* or clans, namely (i) Thulung; (2) Kulung; (3) Khaling; (4) Chamling; (5) Bantawa; (6) Baing; and (7) Yakha or Deon. Marriage within the same *thar* is traditionally prohibited. Hierarchical differentiation among the different *thars* is recognised at social level to regulate marriage. They have been using 'Rai' as their surname all along. They claim to be of middle status in the regional social hierarchy. Other neighbouring communities of the region also recognise them as of middle social status.

Marriages are generally settled within their own community but outside one's own *thar* or clan. Hypogamy or marriage with women of higher social status prevails among them. Marriage with brother's and sister's children, father's sister's daughter and mother's brother's daughter does not prevail among them. Most of the marriages are settled through *mangni* or negotiation but marriage through *bhagarlanu* or by courtship and elopement is also not unknown among them. Adult marriage is their common practice. Most of them marry only once during their lifetime. *Sindur* or vermilion and *pote* or coloured bead-necklace are regarded as sacred symbols of married women. Presentation of *suar* or pig as bride price is the custom prevailing among them. After marriage the couple either stays with the parents of the bridegroom or they setup their own household independently. Both husband and wife can divorce with mutual consent and social approval of the informal council of elders of the community. No compensation is however, paid to anybody in divorce cases. Adultery, maladjustment and cruelty are the common reasons for divorce. Liability of the children lie with both father and mother, but if the children are minor they generally are the liability of the mother. Widows, widowers and divorcees are free to remarry as per their own choice. Both the practices of junior levirate or remarriage with husband's younger brother and junior sororate or remarriage with wife's younger sister prevail.

Nuclear families, comprising husband, wife and unmarried children, and extended families, with parents and married sons or married brothers, both exist, but the former type predominates. Relationship of avoidance is observed between the father-in-law and daughter-in-law, and also between husband's elder brother and his *buari* or younger brother's wife. Relationship with younger brother and sister-in-law, elder brother's wife and between the parents-in-law of sons and daughters is that of joking and friendliness. Paternal property is equally inherited by the sons only. Succession to family headship proceeds though the male line from father to eldest son. The growing popularity of the nuclear type of family is the only change perceived by them in the institution of family.

Besides performing a major part of the household chores, women of the community have a role in agriculture, animal husbandry, and fetching potable water. They also have direct and indirect roles in economic the sphere through contribution to the family income mainly as agricultural labourers and petty vegetable sellers. They play important roles in most of the socio-religious functions. Women also have direct and indirect roles in political spheres and in the mechanism of social control. They have equal status as that of the men in the community. Women have equal say in the decision making process and exercise control over family expenditure.

Childbirth generally takes place at home with the help of *dhai-mai* or midwife either from the Kami, Damai or from their own community. Birth pollution is observed either for eleven or thirteen days. The first purificatory bath is taken on the day of birth. *Naoran*, *china*, *cheor*, tonsure of the male child in the third year and *bhatkhilai* or first feeding of rice to a male child in the sixth month and in the fifth month to a female child are the rituals performed following childbirth. Marriage rituals are performed at the bride's residence through a *Baon* or Brahman priest. Marriage feast is given by both the parties. Sending the gift of *rakshi* or country liquor to the bride's house, and *sindur-pote* and *khada* or exchange of garlands of cotton between the bride and the bridegroom are the important rituals performed in a marriage.

Dead bodies of adults are cremated but those of children up to five years are buried. Death-pollution is observed for five days. The eldest son of the deceased offers fire at the funeral, called *debate*. They abstain from taking salt, oil, rice and non-vegetarian food during the days of pollution. *Kria*, *nanglo* or offering food to the deceased and the ancestors and *bijna* or general feast to the villagers are the rituals observed following a death.

Land has been the traditional natural resource on which they depend. They are basically a land owing community having individual proprietorship. Agriculture on terraced and plain land is their traditional and primary occupation. Working as *coolies* or porters and labourers, selling of agricultural products, carpentry and service in various government and private organisations are their main sources of secondary income. They have direct links with both daily and weekly markets and the medium of exchange is cash. Bonded labour does not exist among them but children above twelve years work to contribute to the family income. Inadequate size of land holding and landlessness in some cases are the reasons for many of them to become *coolies* and tea plantation labourers. Wages are always paid in cash.

The informal council of elders of the community deals with the problems of adultery, disputes over land and water, theft, fights etc., at the community level. Problems involving more than one community of the village are dealt with by the village elders as and when the situation arises. The members of the council of elders of the community are selected by voice votes. The elders of the community solve problems at the community level by imposing cash fines or social boycotts. They are aware of the existence of modern statutory *panchayat* for the implementation of general welfare schemes of the government, construction of roads and providing water facilities for the general public in the region.

They profess Hinduism. Deities are recognised at the family, *thar*, and village levels. *Kul* is the deity at the *thar* level and that at the village level is *devithan*. Married women are prohibited entry at the *devithan*. Deities of the wider Hindu pantheon are also recognised among them. The service of a *Baon* or Brahman priest is hired by them for the performance of rituals associated with birth, marriage and death. Temples of Lord Shiva and Goddess Kali are the sacred centres commonly visited by them. The temple of *Mata* in Kathmandu in Nepal, Benaras and Kashi are recognised by them as their centres of pilgrimage. Dassehra, Saoni Sankrat and Nayapuja are their major festivals, of socio-religious and economic importance. Change of religion is not altogether unknown among them, but pre-change practices are retained to some extent by converts.

Tattooing on different parts of the body is the only art form prevailing among them. Carpentry, basketry, knitting and stitching by women for household consumption are some common crafts practiced by them. Folksongs are often sung by women on different socio-religious occasions. They do not play any musical instrument themselves but hire musicians from other communities when required. They, however, do not participate in any traditional dance.

Traditionally they do not accept food and water from the Darji, Kami, Sarki, and Christian. Except the *Baon* Brahman and Chetri, all the other neighbouring communities accept food and water from them. Inter-community marriages are not completely unknown among them. Linkages with most of the communities of the region are maintained through amicable sharing of the water sources, religious shrines, crematorium and other public places with them. The putative kinship of *mit* (friend) with most of the neighbouring communities also helps in maintaining linkages with them. Putative kinship is established through exchange of rings and clothes. The wife of one *mit* avoids the *mit* of her husband. Patron-client, landlord-tenant and cultivator-labour relationship with various other communities also help in maintaining traditional linkages with them. Small entrepreneurs, different types of service holders, teachers and defence service holders of the community by way of their inter-action with various other communities create new types of modern linkages at their respective levels. Leadership, however, has not emerged from among them at any level as yet.

They have a favourable attitude towards education of both boys and girls. Many of their boys have studied up to the college level, and girls up to the secondary level. The need to earn for their family, and the social problem of getting suitable partners for highly educated girls, are the common reasons for discontinuation of studies for boys and girls respectively. Though they generally make use of modern medicare, they have not altogether discarded their indigenous medicare system. They show a favourable attitude towards family planning, and prefer to restrict the number of children to three, by adoption of various family planning methods including sterilization. Drinking water is available to them from the *jhora* or natural stream flowing near their settlements and also from taps installed by the statutory *panchayat* within the settlement. Some of them have benefited through the old man's pension scheme of the government. Apart from agriculture, many of them are self-employed and have taken up poultry farming, animal husbandry, and transport business etc. Most of them are exposed to mass media and communication facilities, such as radio, television, cinema, road, post office etc, available within their neighbourhoods. Railways are, however, far away from the settlement. They have benefited from the availability of electricity. *Dalla* or cowdung cakes, firewood, coal, and kerosene constitute their main fuel resources. No irrigation facility is available to them and they mainly depend on natural rainwater and water of the *jhora* or stream for irrigation. They use both natural compost and chemical fertilizer in agriculture. They make full use of fair price shops. They favour the system of saving though banks, and are not permanently indebted to shopkeepers and moneylenders.

BADAL KUMAR BASU

RAJBANSHI

The Rajbanshis are a cultivating and landowning community of north Bengal. They are also known as Desi or Bahey. "The history of the origin of the Rajbanshi is a mystery. It is said that they belong to the great Bodo family that entered India in the 10th century B.C., from the east and settled on the banks of the Brahmaputra and gradually spread over Assam and the whole of North Bengal" (Sanyal 1965 : 10). Hunter notes that "in ... Jalpaiguri and Koch Behar, the name Rajbanshi, which literally means 'Royal Race' is adopted by the cultivators and respectable men, that of Koch being restricted to labourers and specially to the palanquin bearers." (Hunter, 1877:x:347-348). Risley describes that Koch, Koch-Mandi, Rajbansi, Palliya, and Desi belong to a large Dravidian tribe of north eastern and eastern Bengal amongst whom there are grounds for suspecting some admixture of Mongolian blood. The transformation of Koch into Rajbansi, the name by which they are now known in Jalpaiguri, Koch Behar, is a singular illustration of the influence exercised by fiction in the making of caste. Now the great majority of Koch inhabitants of northern Bengal invariably describe themselves as Rajbansis or Bhanga Kshatriyas. They are thoroughly Koch under the name Rajbansi. There is no historical foundation for the claim of Rajbansis to be a provincial variety of Kshatriyas. (Risley, 1891 : 1 : 491).

The area, where the Rajbanshis live is traversed by innumerable streams. The main rivers are the Tista, Mahananda, Jaldhaka, Torsa, etc. The average soil is sandy loam. Heavy rainfall (varies from 150 to 220 inches annually) causes soil erosion, and the land being situated in the sub-montane area of the Himalayas with forest on the north is generally damp. They have two sub-groups, i.e., *barabhag* and *chhotobhag*. At present they are distributed mainly in the northern parts of West Bengal and their number, as per 1981 census, has been 2,258, 760. They speak Bengali and use Bengali script with kin and outsiders. They hold the status of scheduled caste in West Bengal.

The Rajbanshis are non-vegetarian. They eat fish, egg and meat, but refrain from taking pork or beef. Rice is the staple food. They also take vegetables, roots, tubers and varieties of pulses available in the market. Some of them take alcoholic drinks occasionally, and they purchase it from market. Women do not take alcoholic drinks. They smoke *bidi* and cigarette, chew betel frequently, and take milk and milk products. They take fruits occasionally.

Bio-anthropological information on somatometry is available on them. According to Risley, the Rajbanshi have below mean stature (1607mm), dolichocephalic head (75.3) and mesorrhine noise (76.9) (Risley, 1891). They have also below mean stature (1603 ± 3.60mm), dolichocephalic head (75.78 ± 0.20mm), mesorrhine nose (72.36 ± 0.48) (Roy, 1946).

The Rajbanshis have two social sub-groups, known as *chhotobhag* and *barabhag*, of which later is hierarchically high in status than the former. They have among them several exogamous *gotras*, such as Kashyapa, Sandilya, Bharadwaja, Goutama, Savarna, Kapila, Batsya, Maudgala, Parasara, etc. In the local social hierarchy since the early nineteenth century, they have been claiming a status equal to that of the Kshatriyas a claim substantiated by their association with the Cooch Behar Raj They are aware of the *varna* order and some place them as Sudra. According to Chatterjee, "they are proud to call themselves as Rajbanshis and claim to be called Kshatriyas" (Chatterjee, 1951 : 60-66). According to Porter, "all Rajbanshis claimed to be recorded as Kshatriyas at the beginning of the 19th century" (Porter: 1932 : 474).

The Rajbanshis marry within their community and practise *gotra* exogamy. They practise and prefer adult marriage by negotiation. Monogamy is the usual form of marriage. The Rajbanshi women use *sindur* (vermilion), *sankha* (conch shell bangles) and *noa* (iron bangles) as their marriage symbol. They practise dowry in cash and kind. There is no fixed cash amount for *pan* (dowry). Bride goes to live with her husband after her marriage. Either party can seek for divorce due to adultery, maladjustment, etc. and divorce is permissible with social or judicial approval. Divorce compensation is given to the aggrieved party. In case of divorce, children become the liability of either of the parents. Divorced men and women can marry again. Widow and widower remarriage is also permissible. The various marriage forms described in Sanyal's study indicate a tribal culture of the Rajbanshis. But gradually they discarded those libertarian practices and adopted the more accepted wedding rituals of the Hindus. The other discernible change is their abandonment of child marriage in favour of adult marriage in recent times.

The Rajbanshis prefer nuclear families. A few of them have mixed extended families. They maintain avoidance relationship between daughter-in-law and father-in-law, between a man and his younger brother's wife. Joking relationship is found among the elder brother's wife and husband's younger brother, between grandparents and grandchildren. Conflict is observed on the property issue. Parental property is inherited by sons, and it is distributed equally among them. Succession is by eldest son. Women do not have right of inheritance. Rise in the number of nuclear families is the recent change observed.

Women have various roles in day to day life. Collection of fuel, fetching potable water, etc., is the woman's role. Women participate in economic activities also. They never till the land with plough, although they help the men to weed the jute, paddy land to prepare and sow paddy seeds for nursery of winter paddy (*amon dhan*), to transplant seedling in the fields and help cutting the paddy plants when the paddy is ripe. Women also look after the kitchen garden. Whatever they earn, they contribute it for family expenditure. They do household job and enjoy low status than the men. They have roles in social and religious functions. But they do not appear to have any role in political activities or in social control. They do not even enjoy decision making power within the family.

A pregnant woman is not considered unclean and is allowed to go about her regular work and do all cooking and household work without restriction. But she is not allowed to attend any funeral. After child birth, the mother of the child is considered unclean for seven days. She is not allowed to enter the kitchen. After seven days, her nails are pared off and her clothes are washed in water. *Namkaran* (name giving ceremony) for the child is arranged also at the time of the first rice giving ceremony. *Bhat choa* (first feeding) is done both for the boy and the girl child. This is done when the child is five or six months old. An *Adhikari Brahman* (priest) is called on that day for the purpose. The maternal uncle (*mama*) has the first claim to officiate in the first feeding. During this *bhat choa* ceremony the relatives and friends are invited and fed. Music with *dhol* (drum), *kashi* (symbol or gong), *bashi* (flute), etc., is played by the *Baidyakar* at this time. The marriage is generally settled by the parents or by the elders of the family. On the day of marriage the bridegroom's party goes to the house of the bride. An *Adhikari Brahman* is called to perform the ceremony. Marriage rituals are performed at bride's house. The rituals are *odibas*, *kanyadan*, *hom*, (fire worship), *sindurdan*, *malabadal*, etc. While doing these, the priest recites hymns. A feast is given to the invitees and songs are sung by the women with music of *dhol*, *kansi*, and flute. On the next day of the marriage, the bride and bridegroom start for the boy's house. An *andhon* ceremony is performed on the day after the arrival of the girl when she distributes food to the relatives of the boy. The Rajbanshis cremate their dead. The eldest son of the dead person performs the rite of *mukhagni*. They observe pollution period for eleven days. On the twelfth day, sons of the deceased person shave their head and do the purification ceremony. An Agradani Brahman (a Brahman of lower order than the priest) is called. He conducts a *shraddha* with sun-dried rice, ripe plantains and sweets. The offering is made to the departed soul and to ancestors up to three ascending generations on the father's and mother's side if they are dead. This ceremony is known as *swapindakaran*. In the same evening the relatives and the persons attending the funeral are given a feast with rice, vegetables, curd, etc.

The major economic resource of the Rajbanshis is land. The Rajbanshis have among them both landowning and landless people. They are traditionally agriculturist and agriculture is their primary occupation. Two kinds of paddy, '*aus*' and '*aman*' are cultivated by the Rajbanshis. They also cultivate *pan* (betel) and *pat* (jute) as cash crops. A few are dependent on fishing which is also a part of economic life and it is also a side business for a few who earn some extra money by selling the catch. The other secondary and subsidiary occupations are government services, working as agricultural labourers, etc. They have direct link with the daily and weekly markets and the mode of wage payment is in cash. Due to landlessness, the number of daily wagers, agricultural labourers are increasing day by day.

The Rajbanshis have traditional caste or *jati panchayat* and a regional association in the state. Caste *panchayat* is consisted of three officials. The *moral* is the head and the post is not a hereditary one. There are also posts of a deputy and a messenger in the *jati panchayat*. The regional association (Rajbanshi *samaj*) has several branch offices in each district of the state. Statutory panchayat is present for the welfare of the villagers.

The Rajbanshis profess Hinduism. They worship Narayan, Lakshmi, etc. as home deity. They also worship Shiva, Bisahari (snake goddess), Durga, Kali, etc. Brahmans do the job of priests. In all ceremonies related to marriage, child birth, *shraddha*, the Brahman priest is called to officiate the rituals. They visit local shrines like Baikunthapur temple (Shiva temple) of Jalpaiguri, temple of Mahakal, Jalpeswar (Jalpaiguri), temple of Bhabani, Chak Bhabani (Balurghat, West Dinajpur), etc. They also visit pilgrimage centres like Puri, Kashi, Brindaban, etc.

They have rich folk songs, myth oriented folk tales, etc. They sing folk songs like, *bhedei, kheligan, meceni khela gan, bas khela gan, chorok pujar gan, budma gan* etc. One common example of the *budmu gan* (rain inducing song) is given below. This song is sung exclusively by the women folk at the onset of monsoon.

"*deoa tui borsek re*
goa dhuia mui
bari nagi jao
baria kanote
jemon deoa dur durae
oi moton chengri gila
pherketai......"

(It means – Oh sky, do please send some rain. I shall wash my body and go home. As clouds roar and rumble in the north-western sky, so my mind of the young girls run and roam about.)

They have folk dance like *mechni khela nach, dham* dance, etc. They play *mokha bansi* during the song sing in Bisahara puja.

The traditional inter-community linkages are maintained. The Brahmans take water and food from them. They accept water and food from the Paliya, the Kayastha, the Kamar, etc. They do not accept food from the Hari, the Dom, etc. They accept *sidha* from all the neighbouring communities. They do not marry outside their community. They share wells, tube wells, roads, schools, etc. with other communities. They participate and enjoy all the *pujas* and festivals in their locality. They have traditional *jajmani* system of relations with the Brahman, the Dhoba, and the Kamar. They observe other linkages and relationship with the Paliya, the Munda, the Sadgop, etc. in their day to day life. There are teachers, doctors, government service holders, political leaders, etc. within the community.

Nowadays, they are aware of the need of education, and boys and girls study up to college level. They use modern medicine and also use traditional medicine. They prefer family planning programme. Tube wells, ponds, rivers, etc., are their sources of drinking water. A few of them have received IRDP loans. Transistor radio is one of the common mass media. They avail the facilities of roadways, post offices, banks, etc. Electricity, fuel wood, kerosene, cowdung cake are their main fuel resources. Irrigation is through the canal and river water. They use chemical fertilizer as well as organic manure. They avail the facility of public distribution system.

AMITABHA MITRA

RAJPUT

The community called Rajput is also known by its other synonyms, Rajput Khatriya, Chhatri or Chhetri. On inquiry about the etymology of their caste have, they inform that any one calling himself a 'Surjabangsiya' is really a Rajput Kshatriya. The community has no sub-group in the region of West Bengal where they have been studied. But they have some sub-groups as Suryabansi, Chandrabansi, Sombansi, Agnikul, Bhojpuria, Jadubansi etc. in Bihar (Risley; 1891 : II ; Appendix, 117-118), Malwe, Mar Rajput in Chotanagpur, and Balgori, Baradai and Mulki in West Bengal (Burdwan). Existing literature on the history of the Rajput Kshatriya reveals that they were a fighting and landholding caste of northern India, who claimed to be the modern representatives of the Kshatriyas of classical tradition with markedly Aryan caste feature. Besides these Aryan Rajputs, the large group designated indifferently by the name Rajput or Chhatri includes many families of doubtful, or non-Aryan descent whose pretensions to membership of the twice born warrior caste rest solely upon the circumstances that they have or are supposed to have some sort of proprietary domination over land. "The tradition of the tribe", says Risley, "goes back to the dateless antiquity in which so many royal pedigrees seek refuge. According to the usually accepted version there are two branches of Rajputs, the Surajbansi or solar race and Chandrabansi or Lunar race. To these must be added the four Agnikulas or Fire tribes. Surajbansi Rajputs claim descent from Ikshwaku, the son of the Manu Vaivaswat, who was the son of Vivaswat, the Sun, Ikshwaku, it is said, was born from the nostril of the Manu as he happened to sneeze. The elder branch of the solar race sprang from Ikshwaku's eldest son Vikukshi, and reigned in Ayodhya at the beginning of the second or Treta Yuga. Another son named Nini founded the dynasty of Mithila. The lunar race affects to be descended from the moon, to which they trace through Ayus, Pururavas, and Budha or Mercury, the son of Soma by Rohini or by Tara, wife of Brihaspati. The Agnikulas or Five Tribes are supposed to have been brought into existence by a special act of creation of comparatively recent mythological date". (Risley : *op. cit*, 185). Migration of the community might have taken place almost seven generations ago, when they settled in different districts of Bengal, in various services, and holding sufficient land also. After the partition in 1947 many come from the eastern part and settled in different districts of West Bengal.

As the community perceives, they are distributed at present in the surrounding areas like Basirhat town, Asokenagore, Khatra, Sulkuni, Barasat, Bangaon, Gobardanga etc. in the North 24-Parganas districts. They mention that they are also distributed in Purulia, Burdwan, Howrah, Hooghly, Mursidabad and Bankura.

As the area (under study) falls under the continuation of Sunderban (Biosphere Reserves) it is not far from the Bay of Bengal which allows a warm and temperate climatic condition characteristic of coastal region of West Bengal. Again such climatic condition along with sufficient rainfall, and natural fertility of alluvial soil condition permit the growth of a variety of crops (jute, rice, oil seeds, sugarcane), vegetables (almost all the vegetables of West Bengal), fruits (mango, coconut, jackfruit, *lichi*, *sapeta*, date palm etc) and timber plants. The jungles of Sunderban have an abundance of wild animals like tiger, deer, snakes, birds etc. A number of rivers in the area supply plenty of fish to the region and elsewhere. Their language and script at home and in relation to others is Bengali. For some, a generation ago their language was Bhojpuri. A sufficient number of them have reading, writing and speaking knowledge of Hindi and English. The census figure available for their total population in 1931 census was 1,56,978.

The Rajput Kshatriyas are non-vegetarian. Their concept of vegetarianism and non-vegetarianism is like that of the Bengalis, but they do not eat beef, pork and the meat of buffaloes. Egg is also eaten by them. They consume fish very frequently. Their staple food is rice for lunch and dinner. They also take *roti* (hand made wheat bread) during breakfast. They consume pulses like *mung* or *moong*, *masur* (lentil), *beuli or muskalai* (black gram), *chholardal* (gram), *matardal* (peas) etc. They consume varieties of locally available seasonal vegetables. Their vegetable consumption is plenty as they cultivate various kinds of vegetables. Their fruits consumption is also plenty as they have sufficient number of fruit bearing plants. The Rajput Kshatriyas take tea in the morning and evening. Since many of them rear cattle, they take milk also almost regularly. A very few of them have the habit of taking alcoholic drinks purchasing from the shops. They never take pumpkin in the month of *Bhadra* (August-September) and radish in the month of *Magh* (January-February). Their food habit has totally changed and now it is very similar to that of neighbouring Bengali people.

It has already been mentioned that the Rajput Kshatriyas have sub-groups, but the informants covered in the present field study appear to be unaware of these. The basis of differentiation is mostly Indian classical myths. Their clans are Bharadwaj, Sandilya, Kashyapa, Batsa and Goutam. They have other *gotras* which are very similar to Brahmanical *gotras* (Risley : 1891 :II: App. 122). Marriage is not permitted within the same *gotra*, but due to necessity they are not following strict exogamy rule at *gotra* level in their marriage. There is a very significant change in their surname. Their original surnames was Singh, but now they adopt the surname Sinha Roy, because there is no Singh like surname in the Bengali communities, while Sinha Roy is one of the Bengal surnames. Most probably they have taken this surname in order to appear as Bengalis before the neighbouring communities. But to the outsiders they state that they are Suryabangsiya. Their other surnames are Babu, Barik, Barman, Khan, Maulik, Mondal, Raut, Sipahi, Thakur, Samant etc. They as well as others perceive them as Chhetri or Kshatriya in *varna* order.

They are following endogamy rule in marriage at caste level. Exogamy at clan level and village level is practised in their marriages. The marriageable age for girls is fifteen to twenty years at present and for boys it is twenty-five years. Negotiation is the primary mode for acquiring mate. Monogamy is the form of their marriage. *Sankha* (conch shell bangle), *sindur* (vermilion) and *loha* (iron bangle) are the marriage symbols of a Rajput Kshatriya woman. According to them, dowry is paid in their marriage both in cash and kind and the amount paid varies from a minimum of Rs. 10,000/- to a maximum of Rs. 50,000/- They follow patrilocal residence after marriage. Incidence of divorce is almost nil among them. For settling any divorce case they have to move to a court. Remarriage is allowed for males. For females however it is prohibited. The most significant changes are increase of marriageable age for girls and increase in the amount of dowry.

The percentage of nuclear and vertically extended joint families among them is almost equal. Each of these families is headed by a male member and everybody respects him and obeys his command. Inter-personal relations are very cordial. Husband and wife are related to each other by love, respect and mutual cooperation. Children are treated with love, affection and care. The children learn to respect their elders from very childhood. Some avoidance relationship is maintained between *bhasur* (husband's elder brother) and *bhadrabau* (younger brother's wife). Joking relationship is found between *deor* (husband's younger brother) and *baudi* (elder brother's wife), between *thakurdada* or *dadmosai* or *thakurma* or *didima* (grandparents) and their *nati* or *natni* (grandchildren) and between younger *sali-sala* (wife's younger brothers and sisters) and *jumaibabu* (elder sister's husband). Inheritance still follows the line from father to sons but in a very few cases daughters are also getting the same on the basis of the present law. Succession rule also allows the eldest son to succeed his father as the head of the family. Inter-family linkages are also a very prominent in their society on all social or ceremonial occasions like birth, marriage, death, *sradh* etc. The major changes that have taken place in their society in respect to their family structure is that they are now following all the behavioural patterns of kinship like their Bengali neighbours.

Their women have now the right to inherit their fathers' property as per the present Hindu Code Bill, but they do not always exert their right. Like other Bengali women they devote themselves to household work. They cook food, serve it to the family members, nurse the young and old, look after their livestock, wash garments etc. They have role also in household ritual performance as well as they participate in others' ritual activities particularly in feminine role like *striachar* etc. With the increase of female education, some of them are now taking white collar jobs.

Like the neighbouring Bengalis they observe a pollution period of twenty-one days after the birth of a male child and thirty days after a female child. There are also three *kaman* (cutting of nails and taking of bath and *santijal* i.e. holy water from a temple etc.) rites. One *kaman* is done just after birth, the second *kaman* is done on the ninth day and it is known as *natta* and the third *Kaman* is done on the day of Sasti puja, i.e. on the twenty-first day or thirtieth day. On the sixth day they observe another rite known as *chhay sasthi*. Name giving rite is performed on the day of *chhay sasthi* or on the day of *annaprasan* (first rice eating ceremony). In the name giving rite they write five selected names on the *bat* (banyan tree) leaves and five candles with fire are put on those leaves. The name against the candle which gives the biggest flame is selected for the baby. They have *annaprasan* ceremony. In childhood their boys have to undergo *upanayan* (sacred thread ceremony) which is an initiation rite and they say their ritual performances are similar to those of the Brahmans.

At present their marriage rite is very similar to that of the Bengali people. It starts with *asirbad* (blessing) in which both the partners are blessed with some gifts by each others elderly family members. Other associated rituals performed in the marriage are almost similar to these of the other Bengali people. These are *gayehalud*, *nandimukh*, *jalsoa*, *abbhutic*, *basibiya*, *boubhat* and *phulsajjya*. They stated that a slight difference can be observed in the function under the marriage booth. The bride wears *sankha* (conch-shell bangle) and *sindur* (vermilion) in *chatnatala* (marriage booth) and the function of *basibiya* is also completed in the same night. They say that it takes two hours to complete a Bengali Brahman marriage, while their marriages take four hours. A Kanuajia Brahman is essential for uttering the marriage *mantras* (reading of sacred hymns for marriage). They regard Brahmans with the surname of Misra as Kanaujia Brahmans. They say that other higher caste Brahman can serve in their other pujas. Their marriage rite comes to an end with *phiruni* (coming back of the newly married couple to the bride's house) which is also termed *joreasha* by other people of the locality. *Phulsajjya* is their marriage consummation rite.

After the death of a person they cremate the dead body at a burning *ghat*. Some of them carry the body to any one of the well known burning *ghats*, located by the side of the river Ganga i.e. Keoratala or Nimtala in Calcutta. They observe a pollution period for twelve days after death. On the twelfth day they go far a *ghatkaman* (cutting of nails and hair and shaving) at a river side. On the thirteenth day, they perform *sradh*. On the fourteenth day they observe *terodasa*, i.e., *gnatibhojan* or *anttiyakutum bhojan*. It is the first day for cooking non-vegetarian food after death in the family and only relatives are invited to this feast. On the day of *sradh* they have another feast for the Brahmans only. They have annual *sradh* ceremony, which they call *bachhar kria*. The most significant change that has taken place in their life cycle ritual is that they are following their rituals almost in the same way as the neighbouring Bengali people, except a few marriage rituals.

The Rajput Kshatriyas are primarily a landholding community of West Bengal. They say that at present one third of them are office-goers and some are engaged in business. They own their land as individual proprietors. Landlessness is almost nil among them. Traditionally the Rajput Kshatriyas are a warrior caste, but seven or eight generations of their in Bengal they have become a landholding community. Service and business are their subsidiary occupations. They sell their excess produce in the market directly in exchange of cash and sometimes middlemen also purchase their produce. There is none in their community who serves as day labourer. So there is no question of child labour.

The Rajput Kshatriyas never had a *jati panchayat*. All their social disputes are primarily settled by the elderly persons. For more serious matters they have to go to court. The present *gram panchayat* has very little utility for them. They say that the developmental programmes are mainly implemented for the scheduled caste people. They have applied for such loans, but it is not yet sanctioned. If they have to take agricultural loan they have to keep their land in mortgage.

Hinduism is the religion of the Rajput Kshatriyas. They worship goddess Lakshmi and Narayan regularly as their family deities. They have the other deities and the religious observances in their family in different months of the year are *barathakurer bar*, i.e. worshipping the deity of Soni on Saturday, Bipadtarini, Itu, Kali, Mangal Chandi, Sibratri etc. They worship Sitala, and perform Bastu puja, Manasa puja, Kali puja, Durga puja etc. Their regional deities are Durga, Kali, Basanti, Siva, Saraswati, Sitala, Manasa etc. They visit places like Gangasagar, Nabadwip, Brindaban, Tarakeswar, Kasi, etc. for pilgrimage. Their sacred specialist is a Brahman priest. They prefer Brahmans with Misra as surname whom they regard as Kanauj Brahmans. Their major fair is Hazratala *mela* which is held on the occasion of *charak* and it is a night long *mela*. They also visit other fairs in some distant villages on the occasions of Baruni and Ratha yatra. Their major festivals are *charak*, (Shiva puja), Durga puja and Basanti puja On the occasion of *charak* many of them remain as *sannyasi*. Some remain in saffron colour dress and observe some restriction for a month in the month of *Chaitra* (March-April). They also become *sannyasi* in the month of *Sravan* (July-August). Their religious pattern has totally changed due to their contact with the people of Bengal through generations.

They have traditional inter-community linkages with the priest's family whom they call Misra Brahman or Kanauj Brahman. On inquiry about their norms of water acceptance they reply that '*Jaler arek nam jiban*' i.e., the other name of water is life or in other words, they do not observe any restriction about water acceptances. Now according to them even the higher caste Brahmans are also taking water from the Muslims' house. When water is acceptable, there cannot be any restriction about taking cooked food if the food is served in a clean way, though they still avoid the Dom, Muchi, etc. They have no putative friendship, but they may have *gurubhai* (disciples of the preceptor or *guru*) relations, as many of them have taken *guru diksha* (*mantra* or some words from a *guru*) from the Brahman. They do not face any difficulty in sharing of pond or well or a temple. It is already stated that they have linkages with some Brahman families having the title of Misra for their priestly job, but it is not clear how far it is a *jajmani* relationship, because those Brahman families are not totally dependent on their client. They have some modern inter-community linkages as their children are going to schools and colleges. Some of them are service holders, some of them visit *panchayat* office or *block* office for agricultural loan etc., and they invite other caste people on ceremonial occasions.

In production relation they have ties with their neighbouring Muslim day labourers. In some cases they give their lands for sharecropping. Half of the total production is given to the landlord and all the cost of the cultivation is borne by the cultivators. Cultivator-labourer relationship is maintained by payment of cash wages and the wage rate varies from Rs. 7/- or Rs. 8/- to Rs. 10/- or 12/- in different types of agricultural or non-agricultural seasons.

Many of them are graduate and post-graduate degree holders. Many of them are doctors and engineers. They say that roughly ten percent of their women are graduates and the rest have studied up to VII or VIII standard. All their children are going schools and colleges. For their medical necessity they go to a dispensary first and for further necessity they go to hospitals.

They use water from tube wells for drinking. They register their name in employment exchange office for employment. They find difficulties in getting DRDA loans and as a result none of them are self employed. They get newspapers, and watch television and video in even remote villages. Many of them use their own cars, hired tempos for transportation. Electricity has not yet reached some of their houses. They are using cowdung cake, coal and kerosene oil as their fuel. For irrigation they have their own shallow tube-well or they hire it from others. They use various kinds of chemical fertilizers like phosphate, urea, sulphate etc. They use gamaxine powder, folidol etc as pesticides. Under the nutrition programme their children get a piece of bread from their school up to class IV. They get ration from their village ration shops. They have money transaction with Sagar Gramin bank as well as many banks at the town. They have some savings. Sometimes they have to take loans from these banks also.

As other observations it can be mentioned that the Rajput Kshatriyas mostly live in concrete houses and they have linkages with some low castes whom they invite as religious singers. They belong to such castes like the Muchi, Bagdi, Kahar etc. who are honourably served food also.

CHANDRIMA CHOWDHURY

RAJPUT SOLANKI

The Rajput Solankis form an endogamous immigrant community of erstwhile Rajputana and Saurashtra who are at present settled in the western and southern parts of West Bengal. Having a migratory legend of martial tradition of historic time, they are now a settled community of landowners and landed aristocrats, who have taken seriously to settled agriculture in the completely different eco-cultural setup of fertile West Bengal. The Rajputs constitute an important social group in Hindu society representing the Kshatriya *varna*, the second of the four-tier classificatory system of ordering of Hindu *varna* ladder, who are mythically considered to have been originated from the arms of Brahma, and enjoy a status next to Brahmans. The old name of Kshatriya is still commonly used but the designation Rajput, or son of a king, has now superseded it as the standard name of the community. The term Solanki (Chalukya or Baghel) has been referred to as one of the thirty six Rajput clans by British ethnographers. The Solankis claim themselves to be Agnivanshi (or Agnikula) referring to a myth that when the Kshatriya were slain by Parashurama, gods and men, particularly the Brahman, felt the loss of their protectors keeping in view the danger of invasion by the demons. The sage Vishwamitra, once a Kshatriya, who had raised himself to the status a *Brahma Rishi* through penance, determined to revive the race that had been exterminated, and moved the gods to assemble for this purpose on Mount Abu in Rajputana. Four images of *durba* grass were thrown into the fire and called into life by appropriate incantation. From these sprung the four fire groups, Parmar, Solanki, Parihar and Chavhan. The *Mahavavishya Puran* also refers to the above mentioned myth. Russell and Hiralal (1975:II:465) mention that "their original name is said to have been Chaluka, because they were formed in the *Chalu* (palm) of the hand". "The Baghel Rajput are a branch of the Chalukya or Solanki, one of the four Agnikula or those born from the fire-pit on Mount Abu. In the tenth century A. D., the Solanki Rajput established an independent kingdom at Anhilwara in Saurashtra which included parts of southern Rajputana. Hoernle (1905:1-14) mentions that "they apparently migrated from Rajputana to Gujarat, which had formerly been known as Lata, obtained its present name. The principal king of this line was Sidh Raj Solanki". Mularaja was the founder of the Solanki dynasty. The ancient capital of the Solanki has been identified with the modern town of Patan, situated in Baroda. Mularaja reigned for fifty-five years and was succeeded by his son, Chandraj. During the reign of Bhim I, Sultan Mahmud of Ghazni led an expedition against the celebrated temple of Somnath in A. D. 1024. King Jaisingha Sidrao, however, re-established Gujarat. Kumarpala was considered to be the greatest king of the dynasty. At the end of the 13th century A. D. the Baghel Solanki assumed the power in Gujarat. In the year A. D. 1297, Alauddin Khilji invaded Gujarat, defeated its king Karna II, and took possession of the province which was ultimately burnt to ashes by the Tarter representatives. During this period, many Solankis left their home on the pretext of seeing the Jagannath Dev of Puri. Travelling through many holy places, such as Dwaraka, Haridwar, Brindavan, Benaras, Gaya, etc., the Solanki Rajputs entered the well known *pargana* of Kedarkunda of the district of Midnapore in the then Orissa kingdom. As they came in three batches numbering 1400, 552 and 80 respectively, the present society of the Solanki Rajputs is still divided into three sections. The legend is referred to in Rajputana Kulachi and Sarada Kahiru. The Solankis came to the *pargana* of Kedarkunda by the famous embankment with the name of Nanadakapasia, the remains of which are still visible. They took refuge in a deserted shrine known as Chapaleswar Shiva or Kedareswar Shiva. During that period, two saints named Paramananda and Ramananda visited the shrine, and were shocked by the deplorable condition of the *pargana*. They requested Debnath, the chief of the Solanki Rajput group, to take charge of ruling the place. Through the negotiation of Parmananda and Ramananda, Debnath was appointed as the sub-king of the *pargana* under the king of Orissa, Bhanudeva II. He defeated and expelled the plunderers. He also defeated two oppressive kings named Dali Bhunya and Kalat Sinha. Later on, Debnath renovated the temple of Chapaleswar Shiva. He was later renamed Birsinha. Being a sub-king, he rose to power and prestige and ruled for several years. He built a fort at Birsinhapur the remains of which are still visible seven kms south of Balichak railway station in the district of Midnapur (West Bengal).

Shamsuddin Eliyas Shah, the Sultan of Bengal (1342-57) declared war against Orissa and raided the frontier province during the reign of Bhanudeva III. In this war the Rajput Solanki king Birsinha fought with the Muslim general of Eliyas Shah and was defeated in the battle. In consequence of this, the Solanki Rajputs left the battle field and discarded their sacred threads in a forest after burning fire. The place is still known as *'sootchharah'* (place of discarding sacred thread) village. After that they hid themselves and took refuge in many Bengali houses of the district and neighbouring areas.

In common parlance the Rajput Solankis of Bengal are also referred to as 'Sukli' in rural areas. Etymologically the term 'sukli' has come from Solanki as an abbreviated form. The Sanskrit lines mentioned by Kashyap Sarveswar Santanam depict them as:

Solanki Sukulo Nama Bhedah Kshatriyasambhava Sthito Rajputanakhye Deshe Bharatbhumishu

(The above lines mean that there is no difference between Solanki and Sukul in terms of connection and that the Solanki Kshatriya lived in the Rajputana region of India.)

O'Malley mentioned that the Sukulis were a small cultivating caste peculiar to the district of Midnapore. They claimed to be the descendants of a Solanki Rajput named Bir Singh who came to Midnapore about six hundred years ago.

Risley (1981: 274) attests to the information of O'Malley and adds that they built 'a fort at Birsinghpur in pargana Kedarkunda. The remains of the fort are still visible. It is flanked by two large mounds, called Mundamarui and Gardamarui, the former of which is said to cover the heads, and the latter the bodies, of seven hundred Bagdis who were slain by Bir Singh because they could not pronounce the word *hesh*, meaning a mat made of date-leaves. The legend goes on to say that after a time Bir Singh himself was defeated, and that his followers then discarded the sacred thread, changed the name Sulanki to Sukli, and settled down as cultivators.

In West Bengal the Rajput Solankis are distributed in the districts of Midnapur, Howrah, Hooghly, 24 Parganas (South), 24 Parganas (North), Burdwan, Bankura and in the city of Calcutta. Their eastward migration has led them to settle in the plains where the climate is moderate with coastal impact. The region experiences both high and medium rainfall. They speak amongst themselves in both Bengali and Hindi and use the script of Devanagari and Bengali, which comes under the Indo-Aryan group of languages. With others, they speak in Bengali, Hindi and in English and use the scripts of Bengali, Devanagari and Roman. Both men and women put on ceremonial dresses during ritualistic performances.

As regards their present day food habit, they are occasional non-vegetarian and consume egg, meat, fish and chicken. The staple food consists of both rice and wheat. Pulses include gram, *tur*, *urad*, *moong, masur*, etc. The cooking media include groundnut oil, mustard oil and *ghee*. They are non-alcoholic in their drinking habit. The drinks include milk, tea and coffee. They smoke tobacco and chew betel leaf. The major changes noticed in the food habit include a shift from vegetarianism to non-vegetarianism, decrease in the use of pulses and vegetables, and preference for rice over *roti*.

This endogamous community comprises set of exogamous *gotra* (clan) which are based on the names of sages and saints, viz:- Atri, Bhardwaj, Gautam, Vyas, Kashyap, Vishwamitra and Vasistha. Though earlier ethnographers have used the term 'Solanki' as one of the clan names of the Rajput, nevertheless, it emerged as the caste name. Although clans and castes seem to be very different kinds of social units, Levi Strauss (1966) believes that the latter may in some cases, at least, have developed from the former. This process of transformation of clan units in to castes seems to project a complex economic specialization and division of labour. However, 'Solanki' remains an endogamous entity. They place themselves in the Kshatriya order of *varna* system of Hindu social stratification. After their settlement in West Bengal, a change of surnames has taken place, as they have adopted many surnames of the local neighbouring castes. This adoption of surnames is the result of a process of acculturation taking place in a plural society.

Among the Rajput Solankis, consanguineous marriages are forbidden. Monogamy is the form of marriage, being practise at an adult age where negotiation is the mode of acquiring mates. The symbols of marriages for a married woman include vermilion mark on the forehead and in the hair parting, conch-shell bangles, iron bangle, red coral bangles and toe ring. Dowry is paid both in cash and kind. Rule of residence after marriage is patrilocal. Divorce is permissible in their society, and it is settled through judicial procedure. The main reason behind a divorce is maladjustment between the mates. Either party can initiate the divorce suit. Compensation is paid to the divorce wife as per the decision of the court of law. Children become the liability of either of parents. Remarriage is allowed for both male divorcee and widower. Sororate and levirate are permissible. The major changes noticed in the institution of marriage include a rise in the age at marriage and liberalisation of rules for remarriage.

They prefer to live in mixed extended type of families, though nuclear families have also been reported. Avoidance relationship is maintained between father-in-law and daughter -in-law and between a married woman and her husband's elder brother. The flow of time has relaxed thc avoidance relationship to a great extent. Joking relationship is permissible with husband's younger brother and wife's younger sister, husband's younger sister and between grandparents and grandchildren. Though, at the present day, property is inherited through equigeniture, it remains nevertheless an issue of conflict and confrontation amongst the shareholders. The eldest son succeeds his father as the head of the family. The structural change noticed in the unit of family incorporates the disintegration of extended families and functional change includes only the approval of equigeniture in inheritance rules.

The women in their society are given important responsibilities in the social, religious and ritualistic spheres of life, and are considered at per with their male counterparts. The family management depends on their skills and labour.

The life cycle rituals are observed ceremoniously, keeping in view the traditional norms of the society. Pre-delivery rituals and restrictions are observed by the expectant mothers. On the seventh month of pregnancy a rituals named *sadh-bacchant* is observed when the expectant woman is offered food items of her choice. During this ritual she is attended to by married women only. On this day she puts on either a red or a green sari and red or green bangles which signify fertility. In olden days, during parturition, she was attended to by a midwife. But now they prefer hospitals, except in a few remote rural areas. After parturition, she and the baby are kept in seclusion for five days. On the sixth day, *chatti* or *shasthi* is performed when manicuring is performed by a Nai woman. Purificatory bath is taken by them. In earlier days, a second phase of pollution period was observed till the child attended thirty nine days of age but now this custom is on the wane. For naming the child an astrologer is consulted. He also prepares the zodiac chart of the new born baby after the Hindu almanac. The zodiac chart provides with the *rashnam* (starname) of the baby. When a female baby attains six months of age and a male baby attains seven months of age, *annaprashan* (first feeding of cereals) ceremony is performed. They also undergo *mundan* (tonsure) ceremony on this day. Ceremonial tonsure and first feeding of cereals are done by the maternal uncle of the baby. Traditionally the Rajput Solankis practised the custom of ear-piercing for the boys, and it is in practise till recent days. When a boy attains five years of age his earlobes are pierced with a sharp needle and rings are put on and he is ceremonially handed over a sword which signifies chivalrous nature of marital tradition. The males undergo the *janeu* (sacred thread) ceremony which is now being abandoned. It is now practised ceremonially to mark the occasion only.

Marriage among the Rajput Solanki is a religious bond. Neither negotiation nor the marriage is performed between *shayan ekadasi* (eleventh day of lunar orbit in *Sravan* i.e. July-August) and *utthan ekadasi* (eleventh day of lunar orbit in *Agrahayan* i.e. November-December). Parental negotiation is the mode of selection of mates. After the fixation of marriage, a ritual named *tilak* is performed at the boy's place when elderly relatives of the bride visit the house to bless the groom. The betrothed is offered a *tilak* mark on the forehead with the help of *rorhi* (red ochre) and turmeric paste. He is also given a tray containing five types of dry fruits like almond, date-palm, cashewnut, etc. The ceremony is marked with vegetarian feast offered by the groom's parents. On the day of marriage the bride and the groom have to smear their bodies with turmeric and oil paste, at their respective houses. Marriage is held at the bride's house. The marriage procession is led by the groom who is received at the entrance of the house of the bride by the bride's mother and other elderly women. No male members are allowed to perform these reception rituals. The groom and his relatives are taken to *janbasa* (reception room). The rituals connected with marriage are performed at the *marwa* (marriage booth) which is constructed by the bride's mother's brother or the bride's father's sister's husband or the bride's elder sister's husband, inside the courtyard. Marriage rituals are performed according to Vedic rites which are conducted by a Kanaujia Brahman priest. Along with the chanting of sacred hymn, circumambulation is done for seven times around the sacred fire. A sword is held tight above the sacred fire by both the bride and the bridegroom and an oath of lifetime union is taken, being repeated for three times. A knot is tied as the insignia of marital knot in their clothing. The bride and the groom return to the groom's house in the following morning where they are received by the groom's sisters. The groom's elder sister puts on a *tilak* mark on the forehead of the groom with the help of *rorhi* (red ochre) and turmeric paste. She remains the same lady who had put on similar sort of *tilak* on the forehead of her brother (the groom) when he had set on for marriage. These *tilaks* are known as *vijay tilak* (victory symbol). The consummation of marriage takes place on the third day of marriage at the groom's house. Both the parties offer marriage feasts at their respective houses on respective days, viz. marriage day and consummation day.

Disposal of dead is by cremation. It is customary on the part of the eldest son offer fire to the pyre. Being the chief mourner he performs the rituals connected with death. The death pollution terminates after the performance of *sradh* on the fourteenth day. A funeral feast is offered on this day. The charred bones of the deceased are disposed off in the flowing water at a pilgrimage centre.

They profess Hinduism. They worship the deities of a wide Sanskritic pantheon. Apart from these, they also propitiate regional deities. A Kanaujia Brahman priest officiates in their rituals, both religious and social. The main festivals participated by them are Holi, Rakhi and Bhai duj. During Rakhi or Raksha Bandhan and Bhai Duj, rorhi (red ochre) is used by the sisters to put on a *tilak* mark on the forehead of the brothers. Shiva in the name of Kedareshwar Shiva or Chapaleshwar Shiva is worshipped and is given the prime importance.

The Rajput Solankis maintain a set of oral tradition which includes folk songs, folk lore and folk tales. Women are proficient in folk songs which are sung during the birth of a child and during marriage of an individual. As a result of constant pressure of acculturation, some of the tales seem have incorporated various elements drawn from the dominant cultural tradition of the region.

Though the Rajput Solankis inhabit multiethnic locales, they have nevertheless their traditional allegiance towards their community council. Being regional in nature, the community council elects and nominates members by voice vote. However, adult franchise is also practised on special occasion. This homogeneous body at the present day mostly takes into cognizance the matrimonial affairs pertaining to the community. However, planning and implementation of welfare and developmental activities are also looked into.

At the level of traditional intercommunity linkage, they accept and exchange food and water from the communities who are either equal to them or are higher to them. Connubial relations across communities are strictly prohibited, whereas commensal norms have been relaxed at the modern day, particularly in the urban areas. In rural areas, they share the water resources, crematorium, religious shrines, etc. with other communities. They participate in traditional festivals which include Raksha Bandhan, Holi, Dussera, Deepawali, etc. Relationship relating to patron-client, landlord-tenant and cultivator-labour exist. In earlier days, they used to receive and render services to the feudal lords. At the modern level of inter-community linkage, they have representatives in the fields of trade and business, scholarly profession, art, administration, medicine, defence services, politics, etc. This has strengthened the intra-group solidarity upholding the sense of ethnicity and regionalisation among them.

Economically the Rajput Solankis are well off. Their tradition, was to render services to the feudal lords as soldiers. Apart from this they also practised agriculture which they still continue. At the present day, they are a class of land aristocrats. However, share-cropping is also done by a few individuals. Modern day economic pursuits have enabled them to adopt white collar jobs and professions. This occupational mobility is the result of modernization and migration from rural to urban sectors.

Modern day development programmes have created a dent in their life and culture. Education has proved to be favourable for them, the facility of which is availed of irrespective of sex. They have positive attitude towards both indigenous and modern medicines. They prefer family planning. Drinking water is available within their locality. They listen to radio, watch television, cinema and avail themselves of the modern civic amenities provided by the Government authorities and voluntary agencies. They use electricity and also avail themselves of the facilities of roads, railways and post offices. In rural areas they use walk and rain water for irrigation. They use chemical fertilizers and insecticides. Immunization facilities are also availed of. Facility of getting of food items though fair price shops is available to them.

GAUTAM KUMAR BERA

RAJU

The Rajus are a cultivating caste of West Bengal. The Rajus "claim descent from a Raja Chaurang Deb" of Orissa (Mitra, : 1951 : 80). In the distant past, they migrated from Orissa to the southern part of the Midnapore district of West Bengal. At present they are mainly concentrated in the Contai sub-division of the Midnapore district. Their population in the undivided Bengal as shown in 1931 census was 56,778 and in Medinipur alone it was 54,764. They speak Bengali and Oriya with outsiders and only Bengali at home. They use Bengali and Oriya scripts at home and use Bengali, Oriya and Roman scripts with outsiders. They hold the status of other backward class.

The Rajus are non-vegetarian. They eat fish, meat, egg, etc. Rice is their staple food. They take all kinds of vegetables which are available in the market. They take pulses like, gram, *moong*, *masur*, etc. They use mustard oil as cooking media. They do not indulge in alcoholic drinks. They drink tea and milk and take milk products. They smoke *bidis* and cigarettes. They chew betel nuts and leaf.

The Rajus have several exogamous *gotras* like, Kashyapa, Alammyan, Maudgalya, Sandilya, etc. The function of the *gotra* is to regulate marriage. They use various surnames, as Ghosh, Pal, Dutta, Jana, Mahanti, etc. The Rajus rank themselves equal to the *nabasakha* group of Bengal. They are aware of the *varna* order and place themselves as Sudra. They rank themselves below the Brahman, the Karan, the Kayastha, etc., and higher than the Dhoba, the Muchi, the Behera, etc.

They marry within their community. But a man can not marry a girl who belongs to the same *gotra*. They prefer adult marriage. Marriage by negotiation is the only mode of acquiring mates. They prefer monogamy. Married women wear bangles and use vermilion as symbols of marriage. They practise the dowry system and dowry or *pan* is given either in cash or in kind. The bride goes to live with her husband after marriage. Divorce is not permitted in the society. However, nowadays divorce is reported, though the cases are rare. Divorced women can marry again if they are young and issueless. Junior sororate is permissible. Widows and widowers can remarry. A recent phenomenon is the liberalisation of rules for remarriage.

The Rajus prefer to live in a nuclear family, though a few mixed extended families are also there. The relation between the husband

and wife is of love and respect. They maintain avoidance relationships between daughter-in-law and father-in-law, between husband's elder brother and younger brother's wife. Joking relationships are found between husband's younger brother and elder brother's wife, and between grandparents and grandchildren. Conflicts arise on property issues. Parental property is equally shared by the sons. Succession to family rights goes to the eldest son. Emergence of nuclear families through breaking up of big joint families is a recent phenomenon.

The Raju women do not have rights of inheritance. Women have roles in the agricultural field, particularly in sowing seeds, collecting fuels, bringing or fetching drinking water from the ponds or tube wells. They have roles in social ritual and religious, functions as well. They participate in outdoor jobs and also do household duties. They contribute their earnings to the family management though they do not control the family expenditure. They have low status than the men. They do not participate in economic activities. Inter-family linkages are observed during the life cycle rituals like birth rites, marriage ceremonies, death rites, as well as during festivals and *pujas*.

The Rajus observe pre-delivery rituals like, *astamaita sadh*, *panchamrita, astneur*, etc. They observe *sasthi brata* after child birth and observe 10 days' pollution period. The name-giving ceremony and first feeding of cereals are performed when the baby is six months old. They perform marriage rituals at bride's house and the rituals are *gayehalud*, *ashirbad*, *malabadal*, *sindurdan*, etc. An Utkal Brahman does the job of a priest. A feast is given by the bride's parents to the invitees. The nuptial ceremony is performed on the third day at groom's residence. They cremate their dead and observe eleven day's pollution period. On the eleventh day, they arrange the purificatory ceremony and *shraddh* ceremony is performed on the thirteenth day. A feast is given to the relatives on such occasion.

The major economic resource of the Rajus is land. They have among them both landowning and landless people. They are traditionally agriculturists and agriculture is their primary occupation. The secondary and subsidiary occupations are government service and running of groceries, small business etc. They are also engaged as agricultural labourers. They depend on daily and weekly markets. Their link with the market is both direct and through middle man. Wages are paid in cash. Due to landlessness, recently agricultural labourers are increasing in number.

The Rajus have traditional caste panchayats and the panchayat consists of three members. Members are selected through voice votes, and a senior member acts as the head or *morol*. Statutory *panchayat*s exist to look after the developmental and welfare programmes of the villagers. The Raju profess Hinduism. They worship Narayan, Jagannath, etc., as their home deity. They also worship Lord Shiva, Krishna and goddesses like Durga, Manasa, Sitala, and Saraswati. The Brahman priests, normally the Utkal Brahmans, officiate in their religious ceremonies. Rathayatra, Dolyatra, Shivaratri, etc., are their main festivals. They visit Puri, Chandaneswar, Varanasi, Haridwar, etc., as their major pilgrimage centres. The Raju have myth oriented folklores and folktales.

The traditional inter-community linkages are observed with the Brahman, the Kamar, the Dhoba, etc., in their day to day life. The Brahman, the Kayastha, the Karan, etc., take food and water from them and in this sense they are a *jal-chal* community. They do not take water from the Muchi, the Hari, the Kandra, etc. They do not marry outside their community. They share roads, drinking water sources, schools, etc. with others. They have landlord-tenant, cultivator-labour relationships with their neighbours. The community have teachers, local political leaders, government and private service holders, etc.

The Rajus are aware of the need of education, and they send their children to the schools. They use modern medicare and family welfare methods. They prefer three children. They also use traditional medicines. Wells, tube wells, and ponds are their sources of drinking water. They have not benefited much from the IRDP. The transistor radio is one of the common mass media used by them. They visit the cinema, enjoy television etc. They use electricity. Coal, cow-dung cake, fuel wood, etc. are their main fuel. Irrigation is through canal water (like Satmile Canal). They use chemical and organic manure. Their children get midday meal at schools. They use banking facilities and public distribution systems.

AMITABHA MITRA

RAJWAR

The Rajwars inhabit the Chotanagpur plateau and are distributed over the tract adjoining the three statcs of West Bengal, Bihar and Orissa. In Bihar, they are found in Singbhum and Ranchi districts. In Orissa, they are found in Banai, Gangpur, Jashpur, Sarguja, Udaipur, etc. In West Bengal, their major concentration is in the district of Purulia. However, some families also live in Bankura, Birbhum and Medinipur. In Purulia Thana, their origin is shrouded in mystery, W. W. Hunter (1877) termed as "semi-hinduized aborigin". The neo-literate claim that they are descendants of a militant race on whom the local *rajas* used to rely for defence. Drawing similarly with the origin of the name of Marwari from Marwar some theorise that they came from a land called Rajwar. Local myth traces the origin of the community from the marriage of Mahabharata's Arjun with snake princes Ulapi. They speak the same form of Bengali as is spoken in Purulia, i.e. the so-called western from of Bengali. According to the estimate of one voluntary organization of the community, the number of Rajwar in Purulia in 1984 was 1,46, 531 (72,319 male, 74,212 female).

In Purulia the Rajwars are considered to be a scheduled caste. In the villages of Purulia the Kudmi Mahato and other dominant castes do not take water or cooked foods from them. But this form of social discrimination is uniformly practised everywhere. Majority of the Rajwars are poor landless agricultural labourers, eking out a precarious existence. When asked what is their traditional occupation most of them gave preparing flattened rice as the traditional occupation.

They are non-vegetarian. Taking beef or pork is prohibited. During festive occasion indulging in rice-beer is not a taboo but an accepted from of social practice.

Not many Rajwars seem to be aware of the divisions that are there in their own community. Of the few who know there is no unanimity of opinion. One group hold that there are fourfold divisions of the community, each division having a number of clans:-

Division Clans

1. Bhumihar: Nagbangsi, Dumra, Sangatkoira, Bagbanwar, Mahula, Singan, Laya, and Singtoar
2. Angar: Madhurekha, Mera, Bura
3. Jhuintihar: Sabdarekha, Sagarchita, Supad
4. Khorriar: Sandilya, Gobasanti, Manja

The second classification given, substitutes the last two divisions with Kathie and Albans. All the four divisions are territorial divisions. Intermarriage between the groups is not prohibited but discouraged on the ground of differences in ritual observances. Of the clans the distribution of Albans appear to be widespread. Clan exogamy is rigidly followed.

When a girl attains eight-ten years or twelve-fifteen years of age she is deemed fit for marriage. Now the latter age-bracket is preferred. Two forms of marriage are recognised — marriage by negotiation and *sanga* marriage. For marriage by negotiation the services of a matchmaker who is a knowledgeable male of the locality is requisitioned. There is no fixed official for this purpose. Traditionally, paying bride-price (Rs. 2/-) was the rule, but now it has been replaced by dowry. Residence after marriage is patrilocal. Among the landless agricultural labourers, the new bride and bridegroom after their marriage resides with the parents for sometime. When economic conditions permit, the new bride and bride-groom construct a new hut within the parental compound and live separately. Divorce is resorted to for three reasons, a) incompatibility; b) adultery; and c) for killing cow. Remarriage or *sanga* marriage is practised after desertion, divorce or death of a spouse. For this no ritual or elaborate ceremony is resorted to. Only the girl is given a new *sari* and *sindur* (vermilion) is applied on her forehead by the groom. Desertion or divorce is nowadays not very frequent. In the past divorce was frequent. This change has come about because of change from bride-price to dowry. A movement was started among the community against acceptance of dowry. On January 30, 1983 the *Rajwar Samaj Sudhar Samiti* was floated by some young men of the community. The Samiti asked the two parties entering into marital relation to fill in a form and declare formally that they have not accepted or given dowry. The young men of the community claim that the incidence of taking dowry has come down but the people in general assert that behind the formality of disclaimer, taking of dowry is going as usual and the officers of the Samiti are lining their pockets.

Because the majority of the families are landless and indigent, the predominant form of family is nuclear. Among the landed peasantry the extended family is frequently found. The inter-personal relationship within the nuclear family and extended family, or to more specific, between the landless and landed families, is different. Among the landless, the boys in particular, become independent when they reach adolescent stage. The girls as reported earlier, go out of their family and village through arranged marriage. During childhood children live a happy and free life with parents remaining busy in procuring food for their family members. Child beating or scolding are not rare in these families but occurs when the children pester their parents or become too recalcitrant. In the evening when all members get together over a crackling fire during winter or gather round a cot (*khatia*) in the open during summer mutual grooming, gossiping and other emotive family scenes are in evidence. In the extended family the role of father as a *karta* (head of the family) similar to Hindu joint or extended family is more in evidence. The father or *karta* is respected and held in some form of awe. The dependent relationship first between husband and wife and then between parents and children gradually build up around the nexus of land and agricultural activities. The sons depend on their father for education and sustenance. Among the landless families the sons earn as they reach adolescent stage and support their parents to some extent till they get married and set up their own independent family. In the landed family sons have to depend on their father even after they get married. They become independent only when their parents get old and are unable to look after the family. The property, if there is any, is shared by sons equally but the eldest son is given a little extra in recognition of his ordinal position.

The status of women in the community has undergone a sea-change since Independence. It has already been pointed out that the practice of bride-price has been replaced by dowry. Consequently girls are deemed to be a burden on the family. In the landless agricultural labourer family the women perform a useful role as a co-earner. Their movements are much freer. In the traditional occupation of preparing flattened rice their role is of sole importance. The men folk performed the role of procuring the raw material only. The women prepared the flattened rice and frequently sold it in the market place or hawked it in the village. But even then the subordinate role of the women was evident through the pattern of interaction. This subordinate role is found in more intensified form in the landed families. There the free movement of the women is lost. They are mostly confined within the four walls of the family dwellings.

The Rajwar villagers live exclusively in their own hamlets when they are in sufficient number. In the Para *thana* area of Purulia district there are some villages where the Rajwars are either the sole or the dominant occupants. The members of a *para* (hamlet) are agnatically related. Economic and social cooperation such as formation of work-group in agriculture, in helping in hut-construction in exchanging information about marriageable bride and bridegroom, in marriage ceremony, is frequently found. Reciprocity and cooperation are frequent among the members of the minimal lineage. The intensity of interaction and cooperation tapers off as the circle of agnatic kin widens. The majority of Rajwars are landless. In villages where landed families are present, working in the houses of close relatives as labourer or annual agricultural labourer is not discounted but said to be not an ideal working situation.

The Rajwars are often referred to as a community of extremely low order. Water and cooked food is not accepted by the Kurmi Mahato and other dominant communities. Yet, the forms of this past stigma of pollutant level are different compared to those in the Hindu caste villages. The stigma of pollutant level stops at some negative form of interaction. In public places they are not discriminated against. In tea shops a Kurmi Mahato can be found to enjoy a cup of tea along with a Rajwar. Even a *bidi* is accepted from a Rajwar. Rajwars can participate in village *bandhna parab* or *gajan* festivals.

An aged woman belonging to Hari community operates as a midwife. She cuts the umbilical cord with a mollusc shell and deposits it in a hole dug in the middle of the floor of the room where birth has taken place. She then lights a fire and tends the baby and mother. On the fifth day of the birth ashes of the fire is collected in a *Panshbara* (winnowing fan). This along with an old broom is taken to a *dopotha* (village road crossing) and left there. Before that all the women members of the house is subjected to a spell of *mantras* so that evil spirits do not attack them. The mother is given special diet for five days. For the first two days she is given only milk. On the third day she is given *kuthii* and flattened rice. On the fourth and fifth she is given garlic, turmeric and *jhalbhat* (hot rice). On the sixth day a special ceremony called *naran* is held to mark the end of the pollution period. The lineage members and mother along with the new born baby are given oil and turmeric pastes. A *Maghaia napit* (naturalised barber from Bihar) is called who ritually pares the nails of the members of the family. On the twenty-first day the father of the new mother sends four new clothes and rice. The first rice ceremony is help on the ninth month when the parents of the new mother bring one goat, rice, etc. to the grandchild's house and entertain them. On the next day the grandchild's own parents and relatives entertain them.

The marriage ceremony of the Rajwars has many similarities with those of the other communities living in Manbhum. No priest is required for performing marriage rituals. Only the barber woman and the Hari woman who worked as midwife are involved from other communities. The Hari woman's service during the birth of the bride/bridegroom is given social recognition by giving her a *sari*, some sweets and one rupee. The ritual part of the marriage is not negligible but more important is the interarticulation of matri-and patrilineal relations. The role of the match maker is taken up voluntarily by an adult male member of the community. After the negotiation is settled it is solemnized by two ceremonies held in bride and bridegroom's houses. This is done by giving a *dhoti* to the bridegroom and a *sari* to the bride. Previously rupees two used to be paid to the bride as bride-price along with a *sari*. The marriage ceremony is held spanning over three days. The first day is spent in bride's place. On the appointed day, which is determined nowadays by consulting an almanac, a square area of roughly 5' x 5' is marked out on the open courtyard. This place is cleaned and smeared with cowdung. Four poles are erected and a temporary roof is made by covering it with *Sal* and mango leaves. On the floor of this place a *sidha*, *bahara* and mango fruits are placed together for consecrating. In case of the bride, instead of mango, *mahua* fruit is placed for consecration. This consecrated place is called *chamratal* where marriage ritual is solemnized. In this place a winnowing fan containing seventeen different articles are placed. The articles are one cloth, four and half kg of rice, half kg of brinjal, mirror, comb, *sindur*, powder, ribbon, droppings of goat, leaves and fruits of *bherri* tree, husk of paddy, perched rice, grounded fried rice, garlic and flattened rice. Another important ceremony is called *amlakhawa* or eating mother's sister's, father's sister's and mother's saliva with molasses in a mango leaf. Under the roof of the *chamra* vermilion is applied on the forehead of the bride four times. The fifth one is applied on the floor of the *chamra*. After coming to bridegroom's place an iron bangle is put on the left wrist of the bride. On the third day bride is required to distribute salt to all the women during the ceremonial feast and save some for herself. In this feast previously it was compulsory to entertain the *manjhi* (chief of the village).

If death occurs in the family a pollution period of ten days is observed. When death is confirmed the dead body is brought out of the hut and kept by the side of the *tulsi tala* (Ocimum plant). The dead body is anointed with mustard oil and turmeric paste. On the bier a winnowing fan containing soil of the middle portion of sleeping-room, *durba* grass, paddy, and iron bangle, are placed. After the dead body is placed on the burring pyre, fire is touched on the mouth of the dead body by means of a torch dipped in *ghee*. This is done usually by the eldest son who stands by the side of the pyre with his back to the pyre. After the dead body is burnt some bones are collected in an earthen pot. On five leaves of *palash*, a small portion of ash, a portion of a flesh of the cock sacrificed at the pyre, parched rice backed on the dying fire, grass collected from the ground underneath the eaves of the hut of the dead man, are placed on the ash and water is poured on it. While coming back to the village a ritual called *kantaduari* is observed. This is a simple ceremony performed at a junction of two roads designed to discourage the spirit of the dead man to travel back to the village. This is done by placing some throne on the road junction. A big stone is placed on the throne and people who accomplished the dead body jump over the stone one by one. The pall bearers take bath in the pond and come back after placing a portion of the banyan tree's outer layer and a pinch of earth in their mouth. The consecration procedure is completed by making them touching fire made from paddy husk. All the earthen pots of the house are discarded. For three days food is cooked without salt or turmeric power. On the fourth day close relatives are given a feast called *titabhat* (bitter rice). On the seventh, ninth and tenth day water and *nim* stick are offered to the spirit of the dead person at the village pond by a Bihari (*Ojha*) Brahman. On the tenth day a barber shaves the heads of male family members. On that day the Brahman is offered sweets and fruits of which some portion is left for the consumption of the family members. This completes the mortuary ritual.

The majority of the Rajwars are poor landless labourers. The traditional occupation of preparing and selling flattened rice is no longer a paying occupation. Agriculture and working as agricultural labourer are the principal sources of occupation. Some people have taken to making different objects from bamboo and selling them in market or village. Both the male and female members of a household work as agricultural labourers. They visit local weekly *hats* regularly. Where urban markets have come up, such as in Purulia, Jaipur, Para, they visit there regularly to sell flattened rice or bamboo objects. The Rajwars have *jajmani* relationship with Hari, Napit and Bihari Brahman castes.

Previously the Rajwars used to be ruled by a well-organized territorial organization. The head of the village used to be a *manjhi* whose post was hereditary. A cluster of nine villages used to constitute a *pagan* headed by a *paranoid*. The *paranoid* used to preside over the cases of religious ostracism. At present this territorial organization is defunct. In its place the modern statutory *panchayat* system has been able to integrate them with the other communities in a network of relationship where the young members are playing useful roles.

A recent development among the Rajwar has been the formation of pressure group called *Rajwar Sudhar Samiti* formed by young educated male members of the community. The *Samiti* publish a journal with the aim of informing the community about the state of the affairs. The *Samiti* particularly points out similarly of the Rajwars with other tribal and semi-tribal communities of Chotanagpur. The *Samiti* launched a strident campaign against the evil practice of dowry.

The community profess to practise Hinduism but a close look at their religion and rituals seems to point to a semi-Hinduised status very similar to that of the Bhumij or Kurmi Mahato of the district. They do not have separate village deity of their own. They follow the festivals common to Purulia district such as Bandhna, Bhadu, Tushu, Gajan, Jita, Rohin etc. The last named festivals observed during the month of *Jaistha* (May-June) have special significance. During this festival it was customary among the Rajwars in the past to pay homage to their village chief. Another festival, reported by some villagers, is called Barhula Puja. It is observed on the last day of the month *Magh* (January-February). The Rajwars also have a tradition of ancestor-worship on the occasion of Rohin puja. This puja is performed by *laya* or village chiefs. Visiting sacred places has not been reported although traditional Hindu sacred places are known to them.

The Rajwars do not have any tradition of song or dance of their own. Nowadays in many villages the Rajwars have set up their own Cho dance group. Like other community they participate in Bhadu, Tushu songs. They too have a tradition of marriage songs common in Purulia.

In Cho dance group and in political activities the young people find an outlet to participate in intercommunity activities. In political activities of various hues people are forging linkages with other communities. A section of landed Rajwars now prefer to join the political movement launched by the Jharkhand Mukti Morcha. The movement does not seem to have mush support among the landless. We have already pointed out common ground of intercommunity interactions.

According to one estimate provided by *Sudhar Samiti*, there were 17,103 literate people in 1984. Two hundred and fifty-seven boys and girls passed School Final. Thirty-two boys have gone for higher education. Facilities for modern health care are very poor in Purulia. The traditional practise of *gunin* and witchcraft is still prevalent. So is the case of supply of potable water. In many villages there is only one well. Facilities of communication in villages are poor. Young educated boys of well-to-do families are going for business due to lack of employment facilities. The district of Purulia is one of the most backward districts in the country. The developmental process started in the early sixties has hardly affected the people's lives.

DIKSHIT SINHA

RANGREZ

The Rangrez are little known community of West Bengal. The group, identified mainly in the city of Calcutta, belongs to the Muslim Sunni sect and came from Rajasthan and for this they are also called Marwari Rangrez. They have synonyms like Rangrez, Rangarej, Rangraj, Ramgri, Ram gredh, Bhawas, Ramjari etc. They are also called Lilgar. The name of the community has been derived form *rang* of colour, and *rez* or *rekhtam* or pouring. The community have several surnames like Lodhi, Chohan, Solarki, Gori, etc. The community states that they are called Rangrez due to their engagement in the occupation of using *rang* or colour. They have migrated from Rajasthan about 50 to 60 years ago. The community perceives its distribution in many places of Calcutta like Burrabazar, Baubazer, Jorasanko, Park Street, Collin Street, Sagar Datta Lane etc. as well as in Rajasthan and Bihar. The community has been studied within the environment of Calcutta. Their exact population figure is not available. But according to a rough estimate about eight thousand of them are living in Calcutta. The language or dialect they use at home and with the Kin group is Rajasthani. The script used by them is Urdu. They also use Hindi, Bengali, and English language when they speak to others. The community has an identification mark. The ladies use red skirt after marriage. While others from Rajasthan use skirts of various colours, the Rangrez ladies use only red skirts or *laltilak* or *tilaklugri*. The constitutional status of the Rangrez community is Muslim other backward class.

The Rangrez is a non-vegetarian community. They take beef, meat of goat and fowl. Their staple food is rice and *roti* (hand made wheat bread) with various vegetables, pulses and salad. Some of them take alcoholic drinks. They take milk and milk products. They chew *pan*, smoke cigarette and *bidi*. Sometime they like snuff. They use mustard oil, or rapeseed oil for cooking. Taking of crab is prohibited for them. After taking crab one cannot take part in *roja* (a religious observance). They take fruits and other special food (*verne*) on ceremonial occasions. They break their fasting after *ajan* by taking *khejur* (date palm fruit) or salt.

The Rangrez community has no segmentation or groupings in respect of occupation or clan that could be placed in a hierarchical order. Only they have two economic groups i.e. rich and poor. They can take any job, low or high, but that does not affect their social status. According to their customs, marriage can take place across such economic barriers. But they prefer to marry within their community, in which the ladies wear red skirt with yellow *dopatta* (a light veil like cloth with which upper portion of the skirt is covered). About half of their marriages take place within the city of Calcutta and in the remaining cases, marriages alliances are sought their homeland. Marriageable age for girls is from fifteen to twenty years and for boys it is from twenty-one to twenty-five years, Negotiation is the primary mode of acquiring mates. Now monogamy is the form of marriage. As it has already been maintained their marriage symbol for their ladies is wearing of a red skirt along with a yellow *dopatta* after marriage. After marriage women is not allowed to stay in front of her mother -in law, father-in-law, and husband without wearing her red skirt. They give gold etc. in marriage but not in the form of dowry or bride price. They follow the rule of patrilocal residence after marriage. They say that in 99% of marriages there is no problem. Only in 1%, *talak* or divorce takes place. In case the wife is being divorced, the husband pays the stipulated amount of *mehar* (promised bride-price) if unpaid, and children became the responsibility of the father. Remarriage is also allowed both for male and female divorces. In case of women, however, they have to wait for three months after divorce, which is called the period of *iddat*, if she wants to marry again. Two changes have occurred in respect of their marriage. One is the increase of marriageable age and the other is preference for monogamous marriage.

The Rangrez families are of both vertically extended type and nuclear type. Inter-personal relations are cordial and well knit. Younger members respect their elders and the elders are very affectionate to the junior members. Property is inherited equally by all the sons. The succession rule gives the eldest son the right to succeed his father as the head of the family.

Inter-family linkages also become evident on the occasions of death, birth, marriage and other religious ceremonies.

Women have no right to get father's property. Usually they have no economic role outside their house. They have roles in house-keeping, child rearing etc. They have important role also, i.e., they have to read *namaj* (religious prayer).

The Rangrez observe forty days pollution period after birth. They call the period as *napak*. During this period the mother of the new born baby does not do any work, can not even reads *namaj*. After forty days the mother and the baby are required to take a bath, and the baby has to cut his or her head hair. After the completion of the *Napak* rite, the pollution period comes to an end. Name is given to the baby by any person, and they go to the mosque to give name to the baby. Boys undergo ten *khatua* or *sunnat* or *musalmani* (circumcision) ceremony within five years of age. *Aquiqa* is celebrated for both boys and girls during their childhood.

Marriage ceremony takes place in the house of the bride. It takes seven or eight days to complete the marriage rites. On the first day they put *mehandi* (hena for colouring or decorating hands). Then for five days, close women relatives of both the partners put *pithi* (a mixture of turmeric paste, mustard oil and *joa* or a kind of cereal) on the bodies of the bride and bridegroom after singing at their respective houses. After that the partners give *salam* (respect) to their elders and then the partners take their bath and sweets are distributed among the women. Then the bridegroom is transferred to his grandparent's house for two days. From, there, along with the *punch* (*panchayat* members), the bridegroom with his marriage dress goes to the bride's house. Here the *maulabi* (their religious priest) asks both partners to express loudly of their approval of marriage for three times in front of the witnesses. Then both of them utter the same and come in marriage contracts with the help of *maulabi*. Then the marriage is solemnized with a feast. In the feast seven types of sweets which they call *varni* are offered as these are considered to be a good women indicating a successful marriage. After that the bride goes to the house of the bridegroom where she holds *sohagthali* for getting blessings of the elders. Then *sohagrat* (the first night the husband and wife spend together) is observed. If the bride is matured she can stay at husband's house and if she is a minor she has to remain in her parent's house till *ruksati* (maturity). In case of a death, the Rangrez community has the custom to inform their relations and friends in the neighbourhood. Then they give a bath to the dead body, spray perfume on it and dress it in new clothing. Before proceeding to graveyard, they can go to local mosque at the burial ground for reading *namaj* (their religious uttering). Before putting the dead body in the grave they take off the old garments and dress the dead body with a bag-like white garment made of four metres of cloth. They observe no pollution after death, only they console the family members of departed. They think that the soul of the departed comes back on the fortieth day. So they arrange a ceremonial function on the fortieth day.

On this day they read Koran, perform *namaj*, distribute food among the poor.

As the community is named *rang* (colour) *raj*, the community maintain its livelihood on occupations which have something to do with colour. They have shops of varieties of chemical colours and other chemical ingredients necessary for colouring. They bring colours and chemicals from Delhi and Madras. They dye varieties of clothing, from Nylon to woollen, from old to new, in front of their shops. They also dye threads on a large scale to supply them to the weaving centres. They supply colour to the *sari* printing shops and factories. Many of them are engaged in *sari* printing. The medium of exchange in their business is cash. Many of them inherit shops from fathers or forefathers. They employ their relatives or friends, mostly from their own community, in big dying centres or factories. They do not usually employ labourers below fifteen years of age.

The Rangrez have no permanent council but when there is a dispute to solve it they call five or six elderly and knowledgeable persons to form a court of their own and the case is placed before them for arbitration. Generally the council deals with the cases of misdeeds, inter-community marriage and divorce. They generally do not go to the law courts.

The Rangrez community, is Muslim by religion and belongs to the Sunni sect. Their only religious place is the *masjid* (mosque). Sometimes they visit *majar* (the place where a Muslim saint is buried). They visit the *majars* of Gajapur, Jaynagore, Majilpur, Phurphura. They also go to Ajmer Sarif. Some fairs are also held at these *Majars*. The other religious festivals which they observe are Sabe barat, Ramjan, Id, Bakri Id, Muharram etc. Their sacred specialist is maulabi.

Normally they do not accept from or exchange *kachha*, *pucca* or *sidha* food with other communities, though sometimes they exchange food with other Muslim castes and communities. They do not face any discrimination regarding the use of road, school, water sources etc., though they have their own schools, crematorium etc. With many communities (Hindu or Muslim) the Rangrez have relationship of inter-dependence through selling and purchasing of colours. The Rangrez have also some educated persons among them, who keep contact with many leaders and political parties.

Though literacy rate is not very low among them, the standard of education is not at all high. One or two holders of C. A or L. L. B. degrees may be found among them. But women rarely study beyond the primary standard. Till now they do not favour birth control measures. For health and medical care they go to dispensary or hospital. Majority of them are self employed. They use electricity. They use all modern communication facilities, such as newspaper, television, radio, road, bus and tram. They receive weekly rations and also have banking transaction.

CHANDRIMA CHOWDHURY

RAUTIA

The Rautias are a small cultivating community. Ganjhu is their title, which means leader. They are divided into two endogamous sub-groups, viz., Chhotagahari and Baragahari. Although the community can not define the etymology of the word Rautia, but Risley (1891, 199-209) said that the name Rautia suggests some connection with Rajputs, and Mr. Beames (cited by Risley) has noticed that the cognate term Raut is used in some districts to denote an inferior Rajput. The Rautias state that they are *khunt katti* who have cleared the virgin forest land for the purpose of cultivation. According to the informants their ancestors came to Bengal from Bihar about six generations ago and acquired a piece of land to get it cleared and cultivated. Risley (1891, 199-209) said "They formally dwelled in Singhaldwip (Ceylon), and migrated to Barhar in Mirzapur. In the time of the Emperor Jahangir some Rautias were serving as sentinels in the fort at Gwalior when Maharaja Durjan Sah of Chutia Nagpur was imprisoned there for failure to pay his tribute to Delhi. During his confinement the Rautias treated the Raja kindly and he repaid their good offices on his release by giving them lands in Pargana Panari of Lohardaga". In West Bengal they are found at Kagha village of Purulia district and may be found in the district of Midnapore also. Their kin and relatives are in Bihar. According to the informants the Rautia are also found in Orissa. The Rautias live in the plateau area which is dominated by warm and temperate climate with medium rainfall and low humidity. The area is surrounded by forests. The Rautias speak within the family and kin groups in Panchargania dialect and with others in Hindi or Bengali. They use Devanagari as well as Bengali scripts.

The Rautias are non vegetarians. They take all kinds of meat, fish and eggs, excepting beef, pork, fowl, eggs of hen, etc. Rice is their major staple food. *Chapatis* of wheat, millet are also taken by them. Some times they prepare millets as rice. *Urad* (black gram) is the major pulse used by the community because they produce it on their land. Other pulses consumed by the community are *boot* (gram), *moong*, lentil, *hurthi*, *ghangra*, etc, which are also occasionally produced in their agricultural fields. They use mustard oil as cooking medium. *Surguja* is also used occasionally. They consume potato, brinjal, cauliflower, tomato, arum, etc., produced in their fields or bought from the market. Besides they collect green leaves of *matmati, chokra* etc., and wild bitter gourd, wild *kundri*, fig, etc., from the forest and consume them. They prepare a kind of soup of *sonla* leaves with starch and consume it. They take all kinds of fruits either purchased from market or collected from the forest. *Kend, piyal, bhela, dhelapaka* etc., are the consumable wild fruits. They drink milk and tea. Socially they do not take any kind of alcoholic drinks, but some of them consume alcohol purchased from market. The males smoke *bidi*, *chuti* (indigenous *bidi*) and *ganja* whereas both males and females chew tobacco leaf (*khaini*) with lime. They do not consume *ole* (arum) in the month of *Kartik* (October-November) and *mulo* (radish) in the month of *Magh* (January-February) and *shim* (Kidney-bean) in the month of *Chaitra* (March-April), etc. Consumption of pulses, vegetables and fruits has decreased.

It is already mentioned that the Rautias are divided into the Chhotagahari and Baragahari. The Baragahari ranks higher than the Chhotagahari. Children of the concubine of a Rautia and their descendants are known as Chhotagahari. People of Baragahari do not arrange marriage of their sons or daughters with the Chhotagaharis. They also do not accept water from them for fear of losing caste. But the Rautias of this area do not know the rule of re-entrance into the society as there is no Chhotagahari in this area. They are also divided into a number of totemistic clans viz. Kachhap (tortoise), Katoyar, Lathur, Kumhar, Karkoyar, etc. Clans regulate marriage alliances. The Bhumij, the Chik-Baraik, the Ghasi, the Mahto, the Brahman, the Napit, the Vaishnava etc., are their neighbouring communities. They place the Brahman, the Vaishnav and the Napit in higher status, the Ghasi and the Chik-Baraik in lower status and others in equal status.

Endogamy at community level and exogamy at clan level are the marriage rules of the Rautias. Junior sororate or levirate is permissible after death of wife or husband respectively. The Rautias marry off their boys at the age of twenty to twenty-five years, and girls between the age of ten and fifteen years. Negotiation is the mode of acquiring mates and monogamy is the form of marriage. Iron bangle is the principal symbol which is strictly worn by the married woman. The married women also wear vermilion and *sankha* (conch-shell bangles) if their economic means as well as time permit. The payment of bride price in cash is obligatory, the value of which is nine rupees. The girl lives with her husband in his father's home after marriage. Divorce is permissible with social approval and it occurs due to maladjustment. Compensations are given to the aggrieved party. Both parties can divorce, and children become the liability of either mother or father. Remarriage of both male and female are permissible. Remarriage of a female is known as *sanga*.

Vertically extended family is the common family pattern of the Rautias. Nuclear families are also found. Father is the head of the family. Youngsters obey and respect him and other elderly persons. The elders, on their part, show affection to the younger. Avoidance relation exists between wife's mother and daughter's husband, son's wife and husband's father, husband's elder brother and younger brother's wife. Joking relation is found with husband's younger brother, with wife's younger brother and sister and as well as with grand parents. Property and restriction on the freedom of youngsters are major points of conflict in a family. Inheritance and succession pass through the male line. All the sons get equal shares of father's property. The eldest son succeeds to his father's responsibility. Inter-family linkage is maintained through ritual observances and religious occasions.

The Rautia women work as agricultural labourers, as well as work in their own agricultural fields. They take care of their domestic birds and animals. They collect fuel from the jungle, and fetch potable water as well as water for cooking from wells. They also participate in the worship of Shiva and festivals of Karam, Tusu, etc. The Rautia women share the economic burden of their family with the male members. They also control the family expenditure. But they enjoy lower status when compared to their men.

The Rautia women observe *sadhoury* (a pre-delivery ritual) on the seventh or ninth month of pregnancy. Pregnant women are not allowed to cross a river, or to consume fish, mutton, jackfruit etc., after five months. *Chhathi* or *narata* is observed on the sixth day or ninth day after child birth. Clothes for all young family members, rice, garlic, *kurthi* (a kind of pulse), mustard oil, turmeric, *chira* (parched rice) etc., are sent on that day by the girl's family, only on the birth of the first child. The barber comes to shave the head of the child and pare the nails of all the family members as well as of the new mother and baby. *Dhai* (midwife) comes to attend the baby and its mother up to nine days and washes their clothes. The Dhoba comes to wash the clothes of other family members. On the twenty-first day of child birth they observe *ekusha*. The barber comes on that day also to pare nails of the baby, its mother and all the family members. *Dhai* comes to give the purificatory bath to the new mother in the river. *Nayan* (the priest-*naya*'s wife) offers *puja* to Lakjumra (village deity) and makes a spot around the umbilicus of the baby with the help of heated *bansua* (sickle) as a preventive measure against infection. They perform *mujbutan* (first feeding of cereals) in the sixth month for a female child and in the seventh month for a male child. The paternal or maternal grandfather of the baby gives *khsir* (sweet preparation of milk and rice) into its mouth.

When boys and girls reach marriageable age their parents negotiate their marriage. The boy's father first goes to see the girl. Then girl's father goes to see the boy. When the negotiation is completed *bartu* (blessing) ceremony is observed in the girl's house first. *Gayebalud* ceremony is performed three, five or seven days before the marriage ceremony. *Kuanr bhat* is another performance on the marriage day. In this ritual the unmarried boy or girl takes food in the houses of neighbours, who may belong to other caste groups. The Rautias do not take food in houses of other castes, either of the same status or off a lower status, than themselves, after marriage. The Gosain comes to the bridegroom a day before marriage and utters *mantras* in the ear of the bridegroom, if it has not been done before hand and gives him the sacred thread to wear. *Ghee Dhali* (pouring of *ghee* in the fire) is performed by the Brahman priest before going to the bride's home. This ritual is observed in the bride's home after arrival of the bridegroom. Sprinkling of water by the bride and bridegroom on each other, exchanging of garlands of *akanda* flowers, *hastabandhan* (binding of hands of the bride and bridegroom), *dan* (handing over) and *sindra dan* (smearing of vermilion known as *matali sindur*) are the major rituals of Rautia marriages. During *dan* the hands of the bride and the bridegroom are tied together with thread and the thread is held by the bride's mother into the room and bride's father sits near the bride and bridegroom under the *maroa* and both of them utter the *mantras* of *dan*. The bride goes with her husband to his father's home on the same day. On the day after the marriage ceremony the bride and bridegroom as well as *lookdin* (an old lady of the bride's family) go with the *nayan* to some place outside the village boundary and offer a *puja* and sacrifice three or five hens. Then all of them take baths there. This worship is done to drive out evil spirits. The members of the bride's home are invited for a feast on that day in the bridegroom's house.

Burial after touching fire in the mouth of the corpse by the eldest or the youngest son is the mode of disposal of the dead. Firstly, one of their community members digs three strokes to start the grave, and then others complete the digging. They observe a pollution period of ten days. On the tenth day the Brahman comes to perform *dashakarma* (a death rite) near the river. The *Napit* (barber) comes to shave the heads of the sons of the deceased. On the eleventh day the Brahman performs *tilapat sradh* (a death rite). Relatives, kin and neighbours are invited to a vegetarian feast on that day. No change is found in the ritual performances, except increasing expenses due to increasing market price and introduction of vegetarian meal in place of non-vegetarian meal on the day of *tilapat sradh*.

Land is the main economic resource of the Rautias. They cultivate their own land as well as other's lands on share cropping basis. Agriculture is their traditional occupation. Some of them also work as agricultural labourers. A few of them are engaged as labourers in railway departments. Some of them also work as masons. They themselves market their agricultural produce in the weekly markets of Purulia as well as at adjacent markets of Bihar. Produce is sold for cash. Previously, none of them worked as agricultural labourers, but at present many of them have to depend on this. The agricultural labourers are paid in both cash and kind. *Gram panchayat* is their statutory *panchayat*. They plan and implement welfare and development activities of the village as a whole.

The Rautias follow both folk religion and Hinduism. Generally all the members of this community take *mantras* from the Vaishnav *guru* during their childhood. *Tulsipir* (basil plant), Ma Manasa, etc., are their family deities. Women light lamps and *dhup* (incense sticks) in the evening and give a coating of cowdung around the *bedi* every morning. *Gramthan*, *Lakjumra*, etc., are their village deities. The Brahman priest comes to perform marriage and death rites where as the *naya* (priest) from a tribal community performs other rituals and religious worship. They observe *Rohin* in the month the *Jaistha* and sow seeds on that day. They worship *Gramthan*, their village deity, in the month of *Ashar* (June-July) for the welfare of the village. Manasa puja is performed in the month of *Sravan* (July-August) to save the lives of family members from snake bites. *Karam* festival is observed in the month of *Bhadra* (August-September). Durga puja and *Godhan* puja are performed in the month of *Ashwin* (September-October) and *Kartik* (October-November) respectively. Worship related to harvesting known as *Thakurmai ana* (bringing of *Thakurmai* meaning paddy) is performed in the month of *Agrahayan* (November-December) Tusu is observed in the month of *Poush* (December-January). First ploughing is done on the first day of *Magha* (January-February) known as *Akan yatra*. Shiva *chaturdashi* is observed in the month of *Phalgun* (February-March), whereas the first sowing of paddy is done by some persons on the day of *Akshaya tritiya*, and Shiva puja is performed in the month of *Chaitra* (March-April). Durga puja, *Godhan* puja, Tusu, etc. are important festivals of the Rautias. Durga puja and Tusu have socio-religious significance whereas *Godhan* puja has socio-economic significance which is observed for the welfare of the domestic cows. *Bendhabejha* and worship of *Gramthan* are the two traditional festivals in which they participate along with other communities. Harihara mela and Satighat mela are important fairs of the Rautias. Previously, the Rautias, used to perform Durga puja as joint efforts, but very recently they perform the same individually.

They sing songs during marriage, Karam, Tusu, etc.

The Bhumij, the Chik Baraik, the Napit, the Brahman, The Ghasi, the Mahato, the Vaishnav, etc., are the neighbouring communities of the Rautia. They do not eat in the houses of all those communities except the Vaishnavas and the Brahman. They accept *sidha* food from the Mahato and the Napit. *Phul, Sai,* are the friendship terms of the Rautia. Their participation in *Bendhabejha* festival and worship of *Gramthan* also establish inter-community linkages with other communities.

The Rautias work as share croppers or as agricultural labourers. So, an economic relationship has been established with the cultivators. Patron-client relationship has been established with the Brahman, the Bhumij (as priest), the Ghasi (as mid-wife) etc. A few members of their community are holding white collar jobs, they have members in *gram panchayats* and the members of this community attend different political meetings. So, inter-community linkages have been established in economic and political levels.

Educationally, the Rautias are a backward community. A few boys have acquired secondary education. Girls rarely go to school. The Rautias depend mostly on traditional medicare. If this treatment fails then they go to the hospital. Some of the Rautia women get sterilized after four children. They collect their potable water from nearby wells and tube wells. The Rautias do not get any help from the government. A few families possess, and listen to radios. They visit cinemas, but women rarely visit cinema shows. Members of different political parties come to them during elections. Roads are accessible, but railways are far off from their locality. A post office is situated nearby. They do not use electricity. Wood, cowdung cakes, coal dust, etc. are their cooking fuels. The Rautias have to depend on rain water for their cultivation. They use organic manure, chemical fertilisers as well as insecticides for their agricultural crops. Their children do not get any facility of midday meal schemes. The Rautias avail themselves of the rationing facility through fair price shops. They sometimes have to take their daily necessities from the grocery shop on credit. The Rautias are mostly dependent on agriculture which is not well developed for want of proper irrigation facilities. It is quite difficult for them to save money in the bank or post office.

ARCHANA DATTA

SABAR/SAVARA

The Sabar are a community of snake charmers in West Bengal. In Sanskrit, the word 'Savara'/'Sabar'/'Savar' simply means a 'corpse'. Roy mentions that "from Herodotus, however, we learn the Scythian word for an 'axe' was 'sagaris' and as 'g' and 'v' are inter-changeable letters. Savara is the same word as 'Sagar'. It seems therefore not unreasonable to infer that the tribes who were so called took their name from their habit of carrying axes. Now it is one of the striking peculiarities of the Savaras that they are rarely seen without an axe in their hand. But at present the Savara are found to carry a spade (*khanta*). Perhaps the spade has replaced the traditional axe" (1986:20). The Savara are divided into four groups placed in a hierarchy, these are 'Basu', Angada', 'Kalketu' and 'Jara' Savara. Some of the informants say that they are divided into five groups viz. Basu Sabar, Muslim Sabar, Lodha Sabar, Mahato Sabar and Akoti Sabar. In the Ramayana and the Mahabharata "they had been described as *kirats* or *vyadhas*, meaning hunters. Their traditional home was forest and their occupations were collection of forest produce and hunting and shooting games and birds and snaring and piercing them. According to them they are descendants of Jara Savar, who killed Lord Srikrishna by a poisonous telescopic spear in the Dwapara Era (age of the Mahabharata). Some of them say that the Jara Savar was Angada, son of Bali the king, who was the king of Vanaras (monkeys) in the Era of Treta (age of the Ramayana) " (Bhowmick: 1976). The Aitareya Brahmana has described the Savara as the elder sons of Viswamitra. The Puranas described them as "Dakshina Parthavasinah and Vindhyamaulike (Matsys Purana) i.e. the aborigines of the Vindhya Mountains". Roy mentions that "the Savara are the neighbours of the Kol group of people. The relation that subsisted once between the Kols and the Savaras could be ascertained on the basis of some facts relating to the language and social conditions of those who retain in one form or another the old name 'Sabara'" (Roy: 1986: 11). There are many references of snake charmer available in the Bengali literature, 'Manasa Mangal'. It is mentioned that the goddess Manasa or Goddess of serpents was worshipped from pre-Aryan time and after-wards she was gradually assimilated into the Aryan culture. It is also said that "once the Bengali *sapurias* (snake charmers) maintained their economic life by wandering throughout India" (Roy: 1986: 17). According to Roy "by instinct and habit the

Savaras are considered to be a semi-nomadic snake-charming community of West Bengal, who are often found in lower Bengal, an area infested by a great variety of poisonous snakes. Although these Savaras maintain their permanent settlement, they often prefer to live a wandering life" (1986:33). The Sabar are distributed mainly in the districts of Medinipur, Purulia, Bankura and its adjacent areas of West Bengal. These areas constitute the easternmost part of the country. Climate is warm and temperate and the humidity is high during summer. Rainfall is heaviest in July and lowest in November and April. The trees of economic value that grow in this region are *sal*, *mahua*, banyan, palm, mango, *nim*, bamboo, etc. Many of the animals that abound in the region, such as rabbit, different varieties of fowl, and ducks, are hunted by the Savara. According to 1981 census total population of the Sabar of West Bengal is 37,247. The written and spoken language both at home and outside is Bengali. Women generally tattoo their bodies and use various kinds of ornaments like ear rings, *churis*, silver bangles, etc. The community is a scheduled tribe.

The Sabar are non-vegetarian. They do not take beef and pork. Rice is their staple food. Locally available vegetables, roots tubers and bark (*thore* i.e. inner portion of banana trunk) are eaten by them. Mustard oil is the medium of cooking. Seasonal locally available fruits like mango, date-palm, palm, *jam*, etc. are taken off and on. But fruits like apple, orange, grape, etc. are taken as prescribed diet. Male members sometimes take tea. Due to their poor economic condition they cannot afford milk for their children and other members of the family. Both male and female members take country liquor which is generally purchased from markets. At the time of several festive occasions they arrange for alcoholic drinks as one of the drinking items. They arrange special food (fruits, vegetables, etc.) which is to be eaten on certain occasions and in certain seasons. For instance, on the day of *ambubachi* (seventh day of Ashar month in Bengali year) they arrange milk and mango which are distributed to all family members with a belief that nobody will be bitten by poisonous snakes for a year. Besides, they maintain a number of restrictions as regards items of food which are not to be eaten on certain *tithi* (auspicious day) and in certain seasons. These days male members are not very particular in observing these restrictions. At present most of them are habituated to taking *roti* (hand made bread) at night instead of rice. Pulses are taken very occasionally by a good number of families due to high price and it is seen that most of the families take rice with leafy green vegetables such as *susni, gime, chikni, thankuni*, etc. These are grown in abundance in different fields.

The major social divisions among the Sabar have already been mentioned above. Among them the Basu Sabar claim to occupy a better hierarchic position than the other groups. They claim that their social position is not inferior to that of the Brahman. According to them one 'Basu Sabar' is engaged as priest in the temple of lord Jagannath of Orissa. The Basu Sabar never touch water from others, except from the hands of a Brahman. The Angada Sabar catch birds but never kill or eat them. This group comes under the second hierarchic order. The Kalketu group occupies the third position and is mainly dependent on snake charming. In the last rank of the hierarchy the Jara Sabar are placed as they sell different types of medicinal plants and poison extracted from the snakes. The social divisions of the Sabar are primarily based upon their occupational practices. The Lodha Sabar and the Mahato are now regarded as separate communities in West Bengal. The Sabar have forgotten the traditional occupation of the Akhoti Sabar. At present they cannot identify themselves according to their traditional activities. The Basu Sabar, who claim the highest social position than the other groups due to their priesthood in the temple of lord Jagannath in Orissa, are engaged as snake charmers in West Bengal. Other groups also depend on snake catching and snake charming and they do not maintain any differentiation between one group and another. The Sabar say that they have *gotra* like Sandilya, Kashyap, Vyasa, Maudgalya etc. The totemic object of the Sandilya is 'sal' fish. The Kashyap *gotra* has originated from the name of the sage 'Kashyap'. The totemic object of this *gotra* is 'tortoise'. The 'Vyasa' has originated from the name of sage Vyasa. The Sabar say that the 'Maudgalya' has originated from the noted sage 'Maudgalya' mentioned in the Puranas. The members of each *gotra* do not observe any taboo or prohibition with regard to their totem. The Sabar claim their position is not lower than that of the other Hindu castes. "For maintaining higher status they always try to make relationship by marital bond with the other castes" (Roy: 1986:168). They are considered as a low community by the local Hindus. At present they do not place themselves in any *varna* order or in any other hierarchy. In 'Matsya' and 'Vayu' Puranas they were treated as 'Kshatriya'. According to Manu they are treated as 'Sudra' as they gave up all sorts of relationship with the Brahmans and Brahmanical culture.

The community is an endogamous group and practises both clan endogamy and exogamy. They do not make any marriage relation with the descendants of father's brother and mother's brothers. Marriageable age for males varies between eighteen and twenty-five years and that for the females between fifteen and twenty years. Now they prefer negotiated marriage though marriage by purchase of offering bride-price is a common custom. Though polygyny is permitted, especially in case of barrenness of the first wife, monogamy is the general form. They permit junior sororate as well as junior levirate. *Sankha* and *sindur* are symbols of marriage. They follow the custom of paying bride-price. The Sabar after marriage follow patrilocal post marital rules of residence. Divorce is permitted if either of the two does not wish to continue as married couple on grounds like adultery, maladjustments, impotency, etc. The Sabar allow widowers/widows to remarry. Such type of marriage is called *sanga* marriage. They do not observe any elaborate ceremony at the time of remarriage. Increasing age at marriage, remarriage by elopement/love/service, introducing dowry (both in cash and kind) are the significant changes noticed in the above aspects of the institution of marriage:

Majority of the Sabar families are nuclear. Inter-personal relations within the family are well-knit and this well-knit unit of their social fabric constitutes the nucleus of their traditional society. Relationship between husband and wife depends on love, respect and reciprocal duties. As the head of the family the husband is mainly responsible for its proper maintenance. Wife assists the husband in the family pursuits and in the successful performance of social and religious ceremonies of their family. They are not only sex partners, but partners in economic life too. A relation between a man and the wife of his younger brother is marked by many restrictions and taboos, all of which are intended to prevent slightest physical contact or indeed, any kind of familiarity between the two. A joking relationship exists between the women and the younger brothers of her husband. Conflict and confrontation exist to a lesser extent in a family. The sons inherit the property of their father in equal shares; the eldest son sometimes receives a slightly larger share. In absence of son or daughter, the property goes to the brother's son and in his absence, to the closest male kin. A man having no son may keep his son-in-laws as *gharjamai* and by custom he inherits the property of his father-in-law. Succession is patrilineal. Inter-family linkages are close knit and cordial. Economic assistance and making group solidarity among the different families are the modes of forging inter-family linkages. Broken family, joint or extended family and polygynous family are found in a few cases among the Sabar community.

Under normal circumstances, women in the Sabar family are deprived of the right of inheritance. Their role is confined to the domestic chores i.e. collection of fuel and fodder, fetching water and other household activities. They are also given much importance in the social, ritual and religious life and are permitted to play their respective roles except during periods of delivery and menstruation. It is their duty to clean and plaster the sacred place and to procure and supply all the requirements of their proper propitiation. A woman carries the sacred pot containing food and other articles for offering to the sprits of the deceased ancestors during the memorial services. Women do not participate actively in any political activity except exercising their right of voting at the time of different elections. Women do not have any scope to earn money through employment and as such they have little to contribute as to their family budget. Occasionally they contribute to family income by making mat with the help of date-palm leaves. Though there is no such prescribed right for women yet their obligation in social, ritual and religious life are many and explicit.

The Sabar observe a few rites and rituals during pregnancy. Besides the restrictions, the guardians take vow to offer fruits, rice or to sacrifice a goat to the local deity for the welfare of the expectant mother and the child. After parturition they observe birth pollution for a period of one month. They take services of a *dai* and barber for birth purification. After delivery, the body of the baby is cleaned with lukewarm water and then anointed with oil and turmeric paste by the midwife. The new born child and the mother take bath in the pond on the day of final purification. They take help from the Brahman/Gosai at the time of name giving. *Annaprasan* is observed in the sixth month after birth of a male child and in case of a female one it is held in the seventh month. Any full moon day is selected for the ceremony. The Sabar do not observe any ceremony or perform any puberty rite for either sex. Generally a menstruating woman is considered ritually impure and she is not allowed to do any household work or take part in any socio-religious function in the family for a period of seven days. Marriage is an elaborate ceremony and at the time of marriage an elderly person of the community is asked to conduct the ceremony. Marriage is generally avoided in the months of birth of both the bride and the groom. Certain rites and rituals are performed on the day of marriage in the houses of the groom and the bride. Both bride and bridegroom are anointed with oil and turmeric paste by a group of female members in their respective houses. Malik or headman is invited as special guest who presents three betel-nuts and five betel leaves as a symbolic gift. The actual marriage ritual starts immediately after the arrival of the bridegroom and his party at the residence of the bride. The priest formally ties the hands of the bride and bridegroom together by uttering *mantras*. Then the groom puts vermilion on the forehead of the bride, as well as on her hair-parting by the tip of a nut-cracker. After this ritual the bride and the bridegroom bow down in front of an earthen pot which has been worshipped on the day and then they encircle the marriage booth thrice and then go inside the room. A feast is arranged in the night by the bride's parents where all neighbours, relatives and friends are invited. Next day morning the new couple reach the groom's house where groom's mother receives them and presents an ornament or a silver coin to her daughter-in-law. On that day groom's father arranges a feast. Consummation of marriage takes place immediately after the marriage. Generally, the Sabar cremate their dead body and a period of ten days is observed as mourning. After death, the dead body is laid upon a mat and the mouth of the dead is tied with a piece of cloth. A sickle or scythe is placed near the head of the dead to protect the body from being possessed by spirit. In case of father, the eldest son touches fire at the mouth of the deceased and in case of mother, the youngest son does the same. At the end of burning, especially when the head bursts out, a few pieces of the charred bones are collected in a new earthen pot which is thrown into the nearest river later on for peace and happiness of the soul. Members of the bereaved family take vegetarian diet devoid of oil and turmeric. The chief mourner offers fruits, rice, etc. to the deceased soul in front of the courtyard. On the last day of mourning i.e., on the tenth day, they perform *ghat* where a priest and a barber are invited to conduct the important part of the ritual. The *sraddh* is performed on the eleventh day of death. A feast is given to the villagers and to those who participate in the funeral ceremony. On the twelfth day the family members of the deceased put oil and turmeric ritually on the foot of the priest and from this day onwards all restrictions are waived and the family members lead a normal life. The Sabar have curtailed many of the ritual items due to their poor economic condition. Some of them bury their dead body as they think cremation is more expensive than burial.

Major economic activities of the community are snake charming, hunting game and birds, fishing and its connected activities. Control over the resources lies in the hands of individual family members. The Sabar are mainly a landless community. Their traditional occupation is snake-charming, hunting and fishing. Agriculture, share-cropping, day labour, etc. are the subsidiary occupations of the community members. A few of them earn money by engaging in professions like those of gunin, ojha etc. in their locality. The community's dependence on market is total. Barter system is not found amongst the community members. They do not have any bonded labour and child labour. Children are often found to assist their parents in their traditional economic pursuits. Those who work as day labourer earn their wages both in cash and kind. The Sabar were originally food gatherers and hunters, who maintained their livelihood by collecting edible roots, tubers, fruits, herbs from the forests and hunting and killing animals. After deforestation in and around their habitation, they shifted from the forest areas or forest fringe to other localities for their livelihood. As they lived in the forest, they did not know the methods of food production, especially agriculture. So they continued the occupations like snake catching and snake charming, and "took monkey dancing, angling of rods, mat-making, etc. which are as alternatives to them and feed the regional economy without creating any maladjustment into the system" (Roy: 1986: 44).

The Sabar have their own caste council known as 'Sabar Samaj' or *desh*. The above mentioned council is generally formed by the adult male members of the community. The office of the headman (*malik* or *mukhia*) is held on hereditary basis and traditionally passed from father to the eldest son. In the absence of a son, a suitable near kin of the village is elected to hold the office. The *malik* generally solves all disputes which primarily concern the different family members of the community. The *malik* holds the highest position and is unquestionably obeyed by others. In all ceremonial functions the decision of the *malik/mukhia* is considered as final. The mode of punishment depends on the nature of guilt. They do not have any prevalent form of giving reward. Modern statutory councils play very important role for settling serious disputes and for providing economic assistance, etc. Following changes have taken place since Independence (i) sometimes headman is not selected on hereditary basis, (ii) at present the power of the headman has been lessened to some extent due to class consciousness, spread of education and political consciousness of the people in general.

Most of the Sabar profess Hinduism. Roy mentions that "a process of 'Brahmanisation' is prevalent among them, but their magico-religious practices are considered as non-Aryan traits. Gradually they have become hinduised by Aryan culture" (1986: 146). Hindu gods and goddesses are worshipped by them. Kali, Sitala, Hari, Shiva, etc. are worshipped as village and regional deities. They visit all temples and shrines as sacred centres for pilgrimage. They employ Brahman priest as sacred specialist. The community members visit all fairs in the locality which are held on certain *tithi* (auspicious days) and in certain seasons. The Sabar observe a number of festivals which are mostly of regional origin and have been adopted by them due to contact with the neighbouring Hindu caste people. These are celebrated either on family basis or on village or community basis.

The Sabar prepare mat, bag, etc. with the help of date palm leaves and *babui* grass which may be considered as their handicraft. The oral traditions which are observed among them, mainly borrowed from the sacred texts of 'Manasa Mangal' where they always try to focus the story of Behula and Lakhindar, who died in the *basarghar*, as a result of bite by a poisonous snake named Kalnagini. These songs are mainly sung at the time of snake charming. Besides, they have a number of oral traditions which are observed at the time of propitiating spirits and other magical practices and at the time of catching snakes. Two examples are given below:

1. *"Sita khullen Tiburi Lakshman Katilen pap Sei analey pure galo amukar hat pa Fatashni, Pujishni, Kalamerey ja Kar Anga, Sita, Ramchandrer Anga."*

(Sita would lend the word; Lakshman extracts its poison of the sores of your burnt hands and feet. So the wounds can not suppurate. By the grace of Sita and Ramchandra, these will dry up).

O, Sita dilan kundali Lakshman dilan pa Jhothr sap southi tha Ram Dilan kundali Sita dilan pa -Jhottier sap southi tha Gurur Anjai tha athu -Jodi Noru charu Iswar Rang jang thaley bish bhuru".

(It is generally uttered at the time of snake catching and narrates an episode from the Ramayana.)

The Sabar are considered as *jal-achal* community. Inter-community marital exchanges are not permitted though they try to make relationship by marital bond with the other communities. They try to establish rituals based relationship with the neighbouring communities as *dharam baba*, *dharam ma*, *dharam bhai*, etc. They do not face any problem sharing of wells, facilities of roads, schools, etc. They maintain patron-client relationship with the Brahman, *dal* and Napit. Except exercising adult franchise they do not actively participate in political activities. The Sabar maintain their livelihood primarily by snake catching, snake charming and selling snakes. Naturally they establish a good relationship with the different communities for maintaining their socio-economic inter-dependence. Those who work as day labourer, agricultural labourer, share-cropper, etc. maintain a good linkage with the landowners and the persons who employ them. Female folk go to the market for selling mats and as a result they come into contact with groups of people for establishing a socio-economic relationship.

Level of literacy among the Sabar is poor. They have no progressive outlook towards health, medical care and family planning. Drinking water is available within their vicinity. They avail themselves of the opportunity of employment and self-employment schemes. A few of them keep radio sets. They make use of the advanced communication system. Electricity has not reached their areas. The Sabar are not aware of environmental conservation. Wood, dried leaves, cowdung cake, etc. are used as fuel. Irrigation mainly depends on rain water. Use of chemical fertilisers and insecticides is not vogue among the community members. Mid-day meal, feeding programme at school, etc. are irregular. They collect rice, wheat, kerosene oil, etc. from the nearest ration shop. The community members do not avail themselves of the banking facilities for savings and investments.

It is noticed that a section of the Muslim community is also known as Savara. They are distributed mainly in the Police stations of Bhagwanpur, Nandigram and Khejuri in Medinipur district. These Muslim Savara are mainly dependent on agriculture, day labour, etc. Besides, they also catch non-poisonous snakes like water vapour (Natrix piscator), *dhamna* (Ptyas mucosus) and *go-sap* (Varanus flaviscene). Skins of these snakes are stripped and are sold to the agents who come to them of and on and buy these snake skins in cash. Not only they catch snakes but they also catch snakes but they also catch birds by harpoon, locally called *nala*. Varieties of birds like heron, dove, skylark, etc. are caught and used as food. Sometimes they sell these to the neighbouring poor communities.

Female members of this community make mats from date-leaves which are collected from the neighbouring date-palm tree owners. They supply one mat to the owner in exchange for the leaves of five date-palm trees. Sometimes it depends on the quantity of leaves of the tree. A few old women sell some stationary goods like soap, bangle, red thread, comb, vermilion, lac dye, etc. to the womenfolk of neighbouring villages and thereby earn a little money, rice, vegetables, etc.

This community is also identified as Savara in the locality for their professional link with snake catching and hunting birds. The socio-religious life of this community is, however, similar to that of the Muslim community. They establish marriage relationship only within the Muslim community and practise cross-cousin and parallel cousin marriages. This community professes Muslim religious faith and go to the mosque and other Muslim shrines for prayer like other Muslim communities.

SUBHRENDU MAITI

SADGOP

The Sadgops with synonyms of Chasa, Chasi, etc., are known as a cultivating caste of Bengal. Sarkar, Roy, Mandal, etc., are their titles. Sadgop means good cowherd. They have a belief that they are descendants of Gopal of the Pal dynasty. They are divided into two subgroups, viz. (1) Kulin or Kongar Sadgops and (2) Moulik Sadgops. Paterson (1910: 21) referred that original settlement of the Sadgop dynasty was at Gopbhum. Risley (1891: 212) said that they were supposed to have separated themselves from the Goalas by abandoning pastoral pursuits and taking exclusively to agriculture. For this reason they also introduce themselves as Chasa or Chasi. Risley (1891: 212) said that they had two divisions (1) Paschim Kuliya, who lived to the West of Bhagirathi and the (2) Purba Kuliya whose settlements were on the east of that river. The separation between the two is said to have taken place in the time of Ballal Sen. They are mostly found in the districts of Bardhaman, Hooghly, Birbhum, Bankura, Midnapore, 24-Parganas and Murshidabad. The areas are characterised by plain terrains, warm and temperate climate, high humidity and medium rainfall. Their population during 1931 (census, 1931: 240) was 5,50,813. They speak and write in Bengali. The community bears no identification mark or special constitutional status.

Somatometric information is available on the Sadgops. According to Majumdar and Rao (1960), as cited by Gupta and Datta (1966: 309) their average stature is 1646.67mm., cephalic index-76.85 (mesocephalic), nasal index- 74.99 (mesorrhine).

The Sadgops are a non vegetarian community. However they do not eat beef (cow and buffalo) and pork. Rice is their staple cereal. Pulses like *biri kalai* (black gram), *masur* (lentil), *moong* (green gram) and some times *teora* (chickling vetch) and gram are common to them. They use mustard oil as cooking medium. Among the roots, potato, sweet potato, arum, radish, etc., are preferred by them. They take all seasonal vegetables like brinjal, cabbage, etc., and all seasonal fruits like guava, mango, banana etc., which are available in the village. Generally, most of the families can afford milk for their family members as they have cows. Tea is also used by them as a regular drink. Some members of the Sadgop community drink alcohol during different festive occasions purchased from the market, thought it is not the universal feature of the community. The Sadgops take *masur dal* with green mango and take bath with mango juice on the day of *ambaruni* (a ritual performed to increase the production of mangoes) in the month of *Chaitra* (the twelfth month of the Bengali calendar). They do not take radish on the day of Ganesh puja in the month of *Magh* (the tenth month of the Bengali calendar). At present some of the members of the Sadgop community prefer *roti* (homemade wheat bread) to rice at night. Use of pulses has decreased due to the increase of price. Consumption of vegetables has increased with its increasing production, whereas fruit consumption has decreased with its decreasing production.

The Sadgops have two sub-groups as referred to earlier, Kulin and Moulik. Previously, the Kulin Sadgop was a hypergamous group. But, at present, such restriction is not followed. The Sadgops are divided into a number of *gotras* viz. Sandilya, Madhukulya, Kashyap, etc. There is no hierarchy among these groups. Generally, *gotras* are considered for marriage alliances. They think that the Brahman and Kshatriya are higher than them whereas all the *nabasakha* castes are placed in a lower status. They recognise their place in the *varna* system as Vaishya and as a member of *nabasakha* group.

Clan exogamy and caste endogamy are the marriage rules of the Sadgop community. The Sadgops marry off their daughters generally around the age of twenty years and their sons around the age of twenty-five years. Marriage by negotiation is the common mode of acquiring mates. Monogamous marriage is the common rule of their society, at present. One can marry again (it may be junior sororate) in case of death of the first wife. *Sindur* (vermilion) *shankha* (conch-shell bangles) and *noa* (iron bangle) are the marriage symbols of their women. Dowry in cash and kind are also prevalent among them. Patrilocal residence after marriage is the rule of the Sadgops. Divorce is sought if the wife suffers from any incurable disease, if there is maladjustment between the spouses or if the husband is guilty of adultery. Members of the Sadgop community generally go to court for judicial separation. Remarriage of widows or female divorcees is still not acceptable in Sadgop society. A few cases of such remarriages are reported mostly with other castes. No ceremony is observed in these cases. Remarriage of widowers or male divorcees do take place, but with a very simple ceremony. Previously, the father of a girl of Maulik Sadgop had to pay Rs. 101/- as *man* (honour) to the father of a boy of Kulin Sadgop during the marriage ceremony. The practice has been abandoned now. Negotiation of marriage within the same *gotra* was strictly avoided by them; but at present, some marriages are negotiated within the same *gotra*. In such cases the girl is ceremonially transferred to the *gotra* of her maternal uncle during the marriage ceremony. The age of marriage for both boys and girls has been increased. Bride-price was the prevalent rule of the Sadgop society; but nowadays they have changed over to dowry. Earlier, divorce was not recognised, but at present it is accepted.

Extended families are a common feature of the family structure of the Sadgop community. An extended family generally breaks after the death of the parents. The eldest person (generally father) is the head of the family. The younger members love and show respect to their parents. Generally, all younger members of a family are afraid of the head of the family. Avoidance relation is observed between *bhasur* (husband's elder brother) and *bhadra bou* (wife of younger brother) and between *shvasur* (husband's father) and *betar bou* (son's wife). Joking relation is found between *thakurda* (father's father)/*thakurma* (father's mother) and *nati/natni* (grandchildren), between *boudi* (wife of elder brother) and *deor* (husband's younger brother). Joking relation is also found between *shala* (wife's younger brother) or *shali* (wife's younger sister) and *jamaibabu* (elder sister's husband). The duty of the head of the family is to maintain the establishment. Another responsibility of his is to teach the younger boys the technique of cultivation. Married women look after the comfort of children and other members of the family and take care of the maintenance of crops after harvesting. Adult female members help the head of the family in agriculture, whereas adult unmarried women help their mother or *boudi* in household work. Conflicts and contradictions are mostly related to property, unequal sharing of economic burden, and disobeying attitude of young boys. Equigeniture is their rule of inheritance. The eldest son succeeds father's responsibility. Inter-family linkage within the community is maintained mostly through the ceremonial occasions and ritual performances. Break in the extended family structure after the death of the parents is a significant change in the Sadgop family. Decreasing reverence to the elders, relaxation of avoidance relation between *bhasur-bhadrabou* and *shvasur-betarbou* and disobeying attitude of youngsters are the changes in the inter-personal relations. Male equigeniture to equigeniture is the change in the rules of inheritance of the Sadgop community.

At present the Sadgop girls have a right to claim equal share of their father's property along with their brothers. They are not economically independent. Most of them are engaged in household work. Though they do not participate directly in agricultural work, they do the work of maintaining crops after harvesting, besides their household work. They also take care of domestic animals. The girls at quite a young age take part in different sports, cultural programmes, recitations, etc.; whereas the young matured girls go to enjoy *jatra*, cinema, etc. performed in the village or in the neighbouring village. The married women have an active role in ritual and religious performances. Women worship Lakshmi daily. Some of the Sadgop women are engaged as nurses, teachers or in service and they contribute to the family income. Generally, with a few exceptions they do not control family expenditure. Their women have no decision making power and enjoy a low status.

The Sadgops observe a number of rituals on the occasion of birth, childhood, marriage, and death. During pregnancy the Sadgops observe *bhijie khaoa* in the fifth month. The pregnant woman does not take rice on that day. She takes wet *chira* (parched rice) with yoghurt, fruits, sweets, etc. They observe *bhaja sadh* in the seventh month and *sadh* on the ninth month. They invite their relatives and kin, specially the married ladies from the bride's father's side on the occasion of *bhaja sadh* and *sadh*. They offer *puja* to their *duordhara thakur* (family deity), Narayan, Maheshwara, etc. on the occasions of fifth, seventh, and ninth month and the pregnant lady wears the sacred flowers on her arm. After childbirth they observe *atkoure* on the eighth day. The *dai* (midwife from the Hari community) offers Shashthi puja in the Shashthitala on behalf of the family on the ninth, eleventh, twelfth, fifteenth or seventeenth day. The *dai* also attends to the new mother or the baby during the pollution period. A barber comes to pare the nails of the baby and its mother on the day of Shashthi puja and on the thirtieth day (when pollution period comes to the end). A Brahman comes to perform Jalkumari puja on the day of Shashthi puja. Total period of pollution is known as *anandashouch*. The new mother and the baby take a clean bath with soap on the thirtieth day. It is obligatory for them to take bath in the river Ganga after the thirtieth day for purification. The name giving ceremony is not observed by them. The Sadgops perform *annaprashan* (first rice eating ceremony) in the sixth or eighth month for a male child and in the seventh month for a female child. On the day of the rice eating ceremony they offer *puja* to the village deities as well as to their *duordhara thakur* (family deity, most of the time it is situated in a place distant from their residence) if any, and the *prasad* is fed by the maternal uncle into the mouth of child. The barber comes on that day and shaves the head of the baby completely before bathing. They invite their relatives and neighbours on that day for a luncheon feast. At present the Sadgops do not observe any restriction or ritual during puberty of a girl.

After negotiation, the Brahman fixes a date for the marriage on an auspicious day with the help of an almanac. *Ashirbad* (blessing) ceremony is also observed on an auspicious day in the bridegroom's house. The bride's father and other elderly persons of the bride's family visit the bridegroom's house to bless the bridegroom and give him some gifts on behalf of the bride's family. The same ceremony is also observed in the bride's house on another auspicious day. On the fixed date of marriage, after *nandimukh* and *gayehalud* and other rituals performed by women the *barjatri* (marriage party) reaches the bride's house with the bridegroom. A family barber and a priest also accompany them to complete the marriage rituals. The marriage is performed at *chhadna-tala* (the place ear marked for the main marriage ceremony). The binding portions of this part of the ceremony are *satpak*, *subho-dristi*, *malabadal*, *dan*, *kusumdinga*, etc. The bride's family barber assists the bride and the bridegroom during *malabadal*, (exchange of garlands) whereas the barber of the bridegroom's family helps the priest during *kusumdinga* as well as help the bridegroom to wear the new clothes. *Dan* generally is performed by father, mother, uncle or aunt. A grand feast is given by the bride's father on that night. The relatives, neighbours and friends are invited for the feast. In the morning of the second day, the bride goes with her husband to his house. The relatives and kin are invited to attend the *boubhat* ceremony on that day. *Phulsajjya* (consummation ceremony) is observed on the third day night in the house of the bridegroom. The kin, relatives, neighbours and friends are invited to a great feast at night arranged by the bridegroom's father.

Cremation is the mode of disposal of a dead body. Either thirty or fifteen days are observed as mourning period. They dispose of bones in the Ganga. The *sradh* ceremony is performed on the thirty first day. The day after *sradh* is known as *bas sradh*. The Brahmans, relatives, kin and neighbours are invited to a vegetarian luncheon feast on the day of *bas sradh*. On the day after *bas sradh* they arrange a non-vegetarian feast and invite only their kin and relatives. This ritual part is known as *anshpanna* or *anshture*.

The ritual parts of the life cycle of the Sadgop community show some changes. The rituals after the birth of a child have been shortened. Previously they used to observe *panchute* on the fifth day, *sentera* on the sixth day for a male child and on the seventh day for female child. As child birth does not take place at home, so, those rituals have become almost obsolete now. Earlier a Sadgop girl would not see the sun for four days at the onset of first menstruation. On the fifth day the married women would sing and dance in the mud which was prepared by them. After that the family barber would pare the nails of that girl and she would wear new clothes after taking a bath. But with the introduction of adult marriage such rituals are not observed now. Previously, *gayehalud*, *nandimukh*, etc., were performed on the preceding day of marriage. It is observed on the day of marriage at present. Earlier the Sadgops had to observe a mourning period for thirty days. But at present some of them observe this mourning period for fifteen days only.

Land is the principal economic resource of the Sadgop community. They themselves individually exercise control over the land. They are mostly a landowning community, albeit, some of them are also landless. Agriculture is the traditional primary occupation of the community. At present some of their members, after taking education, are being engaged in business and service. Some are also engaged in the business of vegetables, paddy or as share croppers, etc. These are subsidiary sources of income of the community as a whole. Some also work as agricultural labourers. The small cultivators carry their produce, especially vegetables, to the nearby daily, weekly or bi-weekly markets, and some of them dispose of their produce through middlemen. Barter or any other form of exchange system is absent. At present, landlessness of the Sadgop community has increased and as a result there is an increase in the number of landless agricultural labourers. The Sadgop boys start work in the agricultural fields after eighteen years age. The labourers work in other's agricultural lands in lieu of payment in cash and kind. It is noticed that increasing economic crises inspired the members of the Sadgop community to change their agricultural economy from subsistence to commercial level. They are trying to produce crops of high yielding varieties to get higher returns from land so that they can market the surplus. Engagement of some of their members in service also shows that the community is slowly shifting from primary sector to the tertiary sector of occupation. Increasing landlessness is another change of the Sadgop community.

At present the Sadgops have no caste *panchayat*. *Gram panchayat* is their statutory council. They have a village committee also which is formed by members of different castes. This committee generally controls the religious festivals, settles the disputes of land or settles the case of theft of vegetables, etc. If the village communities fail, the members of the Sadgop community go to the *panchayat* for adjudication. There is no form of punishment or reward in Sadgop society. The members of the village communities only rebuke the person for his fault.

Previously, they had a caste council and the members of that council would control the problems and prospects of their society. But it does not exist now.

The Sadgops are a Hindu community and they worship all the gods and goddesses which are common to other Bengali clean caste Hindu people. Some of them are Shaktas and most of them are Vaishnavs. Hari, Lakshmi, Narayan, etc., are their family deities; Shiva, Narayan, Dharmaraj, Manasa, Shashthi, Kali, etc. are their village deities. Shiva temple, temple of Narayan and Dharmaraj, Kali tala, etc. are their local sacred centres, whereas Gaya, Triveni, Prayag, Kashi, Vrindaban, etc., are centres for pilgrimage. The Brahmans who serve them as priests are received on equal terms by other members of the sacred order. The priest attends a Sadgop family on different occasions related to their life cycle rituals and worships. Durga puja, Kali puja, Dharmaraja Gajan, etc., are major festivals of their village whereas they attend the fairs related to Dharmarajer Gajan, Pirer mela, etc.

Previously, the *moral* of the caste council of a village took responsibility to conduct those festivals and fairs but now the young members of the village irrespective of caste take initiative for the same though they take advice from older persons for their success. The Sadgop women draw *alpana* (floor paintings) during *pujas*.

Traditional inter-community linkages are established through different ritual and religious performances and socio-economic activities. A Brahman priest serves a Sadgop family on the day of Sasthi puja, marriage, *sradh* and worship of Lakshmi, Narayan, etc. A *dai* (midwife) from the Hari community serves them during ritual observances after the birth of a child, *annaprashan*, marriage as well as during death rituals. Traditional socio-economic linkage is observed with the Kumor who supply them with earthen pots, whereas the Kamar supplies and repairs agricultural implements. The Dom supply them basket, *kulo* (winnowing fan) etc. Previously, all of these communities were linked up in the form of *jajmani* system but today they are paid in cash and sometimes in both cash and kind against their services. Being a cultivator community they get service also from the Santal, the Bauri and the Namasudra whom they recruit as agricultural labourers. They are also paid now in cash and kind and a traditional inter-community linkage is maintained through their services. The community agrees with the statement of Paterson that the Sadgops actually stand at the head of the Bengal agricultural castes (Paterson, 1910: 63). The older Brahmans only accept uncooked food from them sitting in a separate row, but the younger generations do not follow this norm. Traditionally, they themselves did not take food in the houses of scheduled castes. This system is also gradually disappearing. They establish ceremonial kinship with a Brahman family during their thread wearing ceremony as *bhiksha ma* or *dinkara ma*. Previously, due to child marriage a girl after coming back to her father's home would go back to her husband's house after one year. With the introduction of adult marriage this system is not in vogue but to maintain that social custom they go to any neighbour's house of her father's village belonging to a separate caste and stay there for sometime and come back with the husband. In this system the girl establishes a relation with the woman of that house as *dinkara ma*. They participate in Durga puja, Kali puja, etc., the traditional festivals. Modern inter-community linkages are found through their participation in different elections and in political activities. The members of this community attend political meetings. They have also sent their members to *Gram panchayat* as well as to Legislative Assembly and a socio-political linkage has been developed through these activities. The businessmen, engineers, doctors etc., from the Sadgop community establish a modern inter-community linkage through their services. On the other hand a Sadgop cultivator goes outside his village to market his produce or *fariah*s (middlemen) from other communities come to him to collect the produce and a kind of economic linkage is thus developed with other communities.

The Sadgops have shared the benefit of development programmes with other communities. In general their boys are getting education up to class X and their girls up to class VIII. But a few girls have studied up to graduate level and a few boys have crossed the post graduate level also. The boys drop out from studies because they have to look after agriculture. On the other hand, girls drop out from studies due to social reasons. At present the community is aware of the modern medicare system. But primitive medication has not altogether disappeared from their society. The *ojhas* are called upon in cases of snake bite, hysteria and such other diseases. They have faith in *maduli* (when they suffer from a chronic disease). The members of the Sadgop community are also much apprised of family planning. Generally, Sadgop women get sterilised after two to three children. Potable and cooking water is drawn from tube wells, whereas water from tank is used for cooking purposes.

A number of the Sadgop villagers have taken loans through the IRDP for the business of amplifiers, paper bags or to purchase a sewing machine, etc. They have also taken *krishi* (agricultural) loans from block development offices. Many of them have taken loans from banks to purchase pump sets. Radios are found in most of the Sadgop houses. With the increasing road transport facilities they often go to visit cinemas and to purchase clothes at nearby urban and semi-urban markets. They also have railway facility. Post office facility exists in all the villages where the Sadgops are living. Although electricity is available in some of the areas, domestic consumption is still limited to the affluent families only. Coal, wood and cowdung cakes are the major fuel resources of the Sadgop community. Canal water, shallow tube well, and river lift irrigation are their major irrigation systems. Many of them also have pump sets for lifting water from the tanks to irrigate their agricultural fields. Use of chemical fertilisers, insecticides and pesticides are very common among them to get better crop yields. They also have midday meal scheme, ration shop facilities and banking facilities. Some of them also have small savings in banks and post offices.

ARCHANA DATTA

SAHIS

The Sahis have their origin according to the local people, in some Maratha stock who visited this region of Bengal to look after the horses of the then kings. In course of time, these small groups of people nestled into clusters around the villages and slowly assimilated with the regional social system. It is observed that they are in alignment with some so called people of lower order, like the sweepers or the Hadis. Their distribution is limited. Some of them refer to their existence in a few places near about Sarenga, in Bankura district. A few of them have been accommodated in the Medinipur Municipality where they are working as sweepers in the District Hospital. Naturally, their traditional habitat is in some terrain, having forest or in a lateritic topography. They speak in distorted Bengali, with a peculiar accent of their own. They are now a part of the greater social system without any historical background. Their constitutional status is not identified as scheduled caste, but attempts are afoot to identify them as sweepers.

Though they are non-vegetarian to some extent, they never touch beef or pork. Fish from the nearby river supplements their food supply along with the available vegetables, either from the market or from the locality. Rice is their staple food and all of them are in the habit of taking rice beer or toddy which they purchase from the locality. They domesticate cattle and consume milk.

They have three exogamous totemic clans or *gotras* namely, Sal, Sankha and Paira. Very recently, they have started a slow process of alignment with some similar groups of people, having surname of Kadma, Mukhi, Sahis and Sikira with unidentifiable groupings. These *gotras* are matched only to provide mates, as their marriage takes place outside the *gotra*. The all India *varna* conception is not known to them, except their despised position in society, in which they are placed almost at the lowest rung of the ladder.

Marriage takes place when they attain adulthood. Marriage is arranged by negotiation by the elderly members of the community when a sum of Rs. 12/- is paid ceremonially by the father of the groom to the bride's father. Vermillion mark is placed on the forehead of the bride in presence of the kinsmen and neighbours. Nowadays this system is in a process of decay, as per the local condition. Instead a bridegroom demands something as dowry from the bride's father. There is no formal divorce system, either for the man or his wife. Either of them, however, can refuse to stay together, Simple nuclear family is in vogue and love, affection and emotional ties are there to keep the family going. They possess no immovable property, except the house and this is handed down from generation to generation.

Women work equally with the men and as such, they have equal status, though cooking job is confined to them alone. Pregnancy has no special advantages for them, except that other members take a little special care of them. A pregnant woman has no restrictions on food intake or movement. After the birth of the child, the umbilical cord is cut by a midwife of their own caste inside the house or near the edge of the veranda. After delivery a mother is not allowed to take rice except a small quantity of flattened or parched rice, and she is given glasses of boiled water to drink for three days. On the fourth day rice with curry made of green banana and papaw and boiled pulses are served to be eaten on a *sal* leaf. After this for about fifteen days, she takes only this type of food, and parched rice only at night up to the twentieth day. A ceremony takes place on the twenty-first day. This is known as *ekusia*. On this occasion cash is given to a local degraded Brahman who blesses the baby. On the sixth day of birth, worship of goddess Shashthi is done in a confinement room which is arranged by the midwife. During the worship, nine cowrie shells are placed on a raw cowdung ball. Then a Brahman comes and propitiates an earthen pot, filled with water and mango-twigs and receptacle for collyrium. This is immersed on the twenty-first day when *ekusia* is done. On the ninth day, ceremonial paring of nails is done by a barber in lieu of little cash. Nowadays the marriage ceremony is performed by a priest. This system has been started recently. Previously the headman i.e., the *mukhia* would solemnise marriages when the bridegroom used to come in a procession to the bride's place. Turmeric paste is now applied on the body of the bride and the groom early in the morning of the wedding days. Songs are sung by the female members when the eldest son-in-law has to take the leading part. The pandal or the marriage booth is demarcated with four *sal* poles and four small banana plants. Four earthen pots dyed in yellow colour are placed in the four corners while an earthen plate is placed in the middle and the palms of the bride and the groom are tied by means of a red thread, with nine coils. After applying vermilion mark on the forehead and hair parting of the bride, the marriage is taken as consummated. The following day, the newlywed couple proceed to the house of the groom.

As a rule the dead body is cremated. The head of the departed person is placed to the north and the eldest or the youngest son of the deceased applies fire to the mouth of the dead body. A new piece of cloth is given as shroud on the body. Death pollution would last for one month and no priest was necessary before. Nowadays this mourning period lasts for nine days. On the tenth day, purification ceremony takes place with the help of a degraded Brahman.

They possess no land or any other property and therefore they are mainly landless. They are now trying to get employment as sweepers in hospitals, health centres and other places. They have a traditional caste council known as *desh*. The *mukhia* is the headman, who looks after the interfamilial disputes. Earlier also, if they used to face any difficulty they used to rush to the king, who employed them as horse-keepers originally. Politically, they now cast votes in favour of the *panchayat* members. Only Brahman priests attend to their marriage and death rituals. Cattle caressing festival or *Bandna* or *Tusu* are the regional festivals, in which they take part. They have no formal worship of their own. They participate in Shiva Gajan, Durga puja etc.

They are considered as a group of despised people and, as such, they have no relationship with other groups around them. They are not much aware of the advantages provided to them by the government through the *panchayat*. But nowadays they face difficulties about their status. They maintain commensal relationships with other Hindu low castes, viz., the Muchi, the Hari etc.

The Sahis are practically illiterate. They do not get the facilities of IRDP. Children do not get midday meals in school. They avail themselves of road, rail and facilities of post office and ration system.

P. K. BHOWMICK

SANKHAKARA

The Sankhakaras are an artisan caste dealing in conch shells found in West Bengal. They are also known as Sankhapanika/Sankhari. Etymologically *sankha* means conchshell and *kar* means artisan or craftsmen. The study was conducted in Bishnupur Municipality, in the district of Bankura, West Bengal.

A good number of folk stories are present regarding their origin. Some says they are disciples of sage Agastya Muni who had initiated them to the craft. So the saint or *muni* is regarded as *guru* and progenitor of their community; while others claim that they are descendants of Lord Shiva and his consort Parvati. The Sankhakaras or Sankhabaniks are in the fold of artisan castes which were stratified in different periods of history. They belong to the *nabasakha* group. According to the *Brahmavaivarta Purana*, the Sankhakaras along with nine other castes were born of an illicit intercourse between Viswakarma, the celestial architect and a Sudra maiden Ghreetachi or Ghrtachi, a celestial nymph who was born as a Gopa girl by Indra's curse. But in *Brhaddharma Purana*, the Sankhakaras, as one of the twenty *uttama sankara upabarna bivaga*, are described as the offspring of a Brahman father and a Vaisya mother. However, Risley (1891) stated that tradition ascribes the origin of the caste, as of the goldsmiths, jewellers and Kansaris, to one Dhanapati Sadagar of Karnata from whose third son Srikanta, the Sankharis believe they have descended and his *guru* or spiritual guide was Agastya and the Sankhari have the Brahmanical *gotras* and observe the same table of prohibited degrees as the higher castes. Agastya Muni, according to them, rid the world of a formidable demon known as Sankha Asura by cutting him with the semicircular saw used by the shell cutters. Whatever their origin may be the Sankharis claim themselves to be Vaishyas; but they are clean Sudra according to H. H. Risley's scheme.

In earlier times this community was distributed mainly in West Bengal and East Bengal (presently Bangladesh). After Partition of Bengal (after 1947) population migrated to India and settled in West Bengal. The major centres of their concentration are in the Districts of Bankura, Hooghly, Calcutta, Burdwan, Nadia, Birbhum and the 24-Parganas (both North and South). The study was carried out in Bishnupur, situated in Bankura district and its distance from Calcutta city is 205 km. The area has tropical climate, medium rainfall and low humidity.

Bengali is their main spoken language and mother tongue, but some know English and Hindi as well. They use Bengali script.

They are non-vegetarians but do not eat beef. They take fish, eggs and meat (both goat and chicken). Rice is their staple diet for both lunch and dinner; though sometimes *roti* (handmade bread) may be taken at night. They also consume various pulses (mainly *masur* and *moong*) and vegetables. They use mustard oil and rapeseed oil for cooking. The consumption of fruits, milk, milk products and other non-alcoholic or alcoholic drinks depends upon the pecuniary condition of the family. They, however, do not brew any alcoholic drinks in their houses. They smoke *bidi*s mainly and take betel leaves also.

In earlier days they consumed only fish but nowadays they also consume meat, chicken etc., and have become more and more habituated to using pulses and vegetables. They prefer *roti* mostly at night. The young generation prefers smoking cigarettes to *bidi*s.

The Sankhakaras practise endogamy, though they are divided into a number of clans or *gotras* such as Madhgolla, Sandillya, Parasara, Maurishi, Bhimrhishi, Gautama etc. There is no differentiation of hierarchy. Clan and lineage regulate marriage alliances and indicate the ancestry and descent of these craftsmen. Yet marriage within the same clan and outside the clan or *gotra* is practised. There are several surnames or titles such are Bhadra, Bardhan, Nandi, Datta, Nayak, Hazari, Karuri etc.

They know the Hindu *varna* system and the position of their caste in the *varna* system. They are clean Sudras; the community's own perception (also of other communities) about their social status at the regional level is that they enjoy a middle position.

Endogamy (community, clan/*gotra* level) is the rule of marriage. Both clan exogamy and endogamy are followed by the Sankhakara society. They also practise monogamous marriage. A widower is only allowed to marry a second time, but the widow is not permitted to do so; junior sororate is permitted in their community.

In earlier days, the age for marriage was eighteen/nineteen to twenty-eight/thirty years for boys and twelve/thirteen years for girls. There is a proverb which is related to the age difference between the husband and wife of the community: "*Ram jokhan gargarabaae, Sita thakhan jal garabae*" (When the wife Sita is able to work (mature/ adult) her husband (Ram) goes to his death bed old and unable to work). The average age for marriage has now increased to twenty-five to thirty-five years for boys, and eighteen to twenty-eight years for girls.

The main reason for this change as put forward by them is their changing economic condition. Hypogamy and hypergamy marriages are socially accepted at present. Though marriage by negotiation is more common, marriage by courtship is also observed at present. The matchmaking in marriage in most cases is done by the relatives of the family of either bride or of groom or both.

The symbols of marriage are the wearing of conch shell bangles on both hands, iron bangles on left hand and vermilion marks on the forehead and parting of hair by married women. All these indicate the married status of Bengali Hindu women.

Conch shell bangles have symbolic and sentimental social and cultural value in Bengali Hindu society. The widows and unmarried women and girls are forbidden to wear these bangles.

Bride-price was the social norm till the early twentieth century but has since changed to dowry. There is however no fixed amount of dowry, usually it is received in the form of articles like ornaments, furniture etc. *Kanyadan* is the main aspect of the marriage ceremony. They follow the rule of patrilocal residence after marriage.

Divorce was not permitted in the earlier period. However, mutual separation was found, but in negligible number. With the enactment of Hindu Marriage Act during post Independence period, the society has no other option but to accede to legal divorce and hence some cases are found. Regarding remarriage in the society, only a widower/divorcee is allowed to marry a second time. But in case of a widow/divorced/separated woman remarriage is still socially proscribed. Some of the changes in the institution of marriage are the higher age at marriage, system of bride price giving way to dowry etc. Joint or mixed extended family is the most common form of family, though nuclear family is also found.

The inter-personal relationships between different members in the family vary according to the nature of relations with one another. The relationship between husband and wife, father/mother and children, brother and sister are of love, affection, fear etc. The joking relationship appears between husband's younger brother and elder brother's wife, wife's younger sister and elder sister's husband and between grandparents and grandchildren. Conflict and confrontation arise in the family primarily due to property, and secondarily due to the craving for freedom by the youngsters.

Presently the Sankhakaras follow inheritance rules as per the Hindu law wherein both male and female offspring have equal right over parental properties. In earlier days, however, only the males used to inherit. The succession to family headship is through male line only and the eldest son has an edge over others.

Presently, some of the major changes that have been observed in the family structure are the formation of nuclear families, and subsequent declining of extended (joint) family system and the observance of the rules of inheritance and succession as per Hindu law.

The status and role of women vary in different spheres of life. She collects fuel wood, brings potable water and performs social, economic and religious activities. A woman, though debarred from marrying after becoming a widow, is considered nonetheless to be an economic and social partner of her husband and due consideration is given to her views. Women often contribute to family income and control family expenditure.

Being a clean Sudra caste, they take the help of a barber, washer man, or priest during social ceremonies. They also interact with *mahajans*, moneylenders, employers, and employees etc.

After marriage the daughter goes to live in her father-in-law's family. During pregnancy the would-be mother is allowed neither to do hard work, nor go to the cremation ground/burning *ghat*. After the seventh month of pregnancy, women go to the temple and offer a *puja* to the family god for a bright future. Pre-delivery rituals and restrictions are observed in the community. Post-delivery pollution period for a new mother is twenty-one days and some post-natal restrictions on mother are also observed.

They follow a number of rituals after the birth of a child, namely, worshipping of Shashthi, Sitala and Narayan on the sixth day by a priest and *ekusha* on twenty-first day, name giving ceremony in the third month and the *annaprashan* (first rice feeding ceremony) in the ninth month in case of a male child and seventh month in case of a female child.

In case of marriage they observe betrothal ceremony and several other ceremonies related to marriage. The marriage rituals are performed at both bridegroom's and bride's residences. Post-marriage and pre-marriage ceremonies are observed by both the bride and the bridegroom's parties. The number of invitees on the occasion of marriage depends upon the economic condition of the concerned families. The invitation is not restricted within the caste members only, but also covers other communities who live in Bishnupur or other areas. The ceremony is usually arranged by the father or the guardian of the family. Their invitees present something either in cash or in kind or both according to their ability, to the newlywed couple. The marriage ceremony is observed in the bride's residence and post-marriage ceremonies and rituals are observed in the groom's residence. The marriage arrangements pass through several stages viz. (1) search of a spouse; (2) seeing the bride and groom; (3) betrothal – preparations for marriage and *ashirbad* ceremony; (4) actual marriage ceremony; and (5) post-wedding ceremony. Feasts are given by both the families in a marriage.

Cremation is the norm of disposing dead bodies, and only a son or any other male relative is allowed to apply fire to the funeral pyre. The pollution period in earlier days was observed for thirty days, but it has now been reduced to fifteen days only. After cremation, they collect some unburned bones and put them in an earthen vessel or pot and immerse it in the nearest river or in the Ganga, as early as possible. During the pollution period, ancestor worship is observed. They observe elaborate rituals in the *sradh* ceremony.

No change in the form of rituals can be observed, except only the fact that rituals are becoming more and more expensive than in the earlier years.

The Sankhakaras are a landless community. Their major economic pursuit is preparing conch shell products. Besides, they are also engaged in service, business, etc. There are a good number of persons who still practise the traditional craft as a subsidiary occupation, even though they are primarily engaged in service, business, or are students or self-employed.

Conch shell is the main raw material obtained by them from various sources. Further, the price of conch shells vary to a great extent, mainly because its collection from the seabed is a laborious job and the quantity of collection depends on seasonal condition. Since the artisans are not economically well off, barring a few, they have to depend solely on conch shell dealers, traders and *mahajans*. Thus they are at the mercy of the above three agencies. The government agency sometimes sells raw material to the artisans, but the quantity is too meagre to meet their requirements. Three modes are prevalent for the procurement of raw materials and marketing of finished products. In the first mode, the craftsmen purchase raw material from the *mahajan* or trader and sell back the finished products entirely to the particular trader or the *mahajan*. In the second mode, we find contractual labour of craftsmen (*bani* labour) wherein they are supplied with raw materials by traders or *mahajans* and are asked to supply the finished products as per the requirements of the said traders, in exchange of labour charges only. In the last mode, raw material is purchased by the artisan and finished products are sold to agencies or to the actual user.

The conch shell products are mainly conch shell bangles and shell horn (musical instrument). Bangles are of various types, sizes and designs. The name of the designs are *lot*, full *lot*, *kankan*, *udayer pathe, matar, lichnchot, dhansheesh, lata, pal kata, makar mukh, sankha, sankhaful, sankha padma, panchgachi, satgachi, naygachi, rang khilan* (coloured bangles with vavle), *kar sankha* (broken parts of conch shell fixed with the help of *puttine* (paste) and made into bangles. The other conch shell products are finger rings, vermilion pots, incense stands, ear-rings, hairclips, hair pins, buttons for shirts and *punjabis*, necklaces and beads of the necklaces and powdered conch shell.

For purchasing tools and implements, they visit local shops owned by different castes. However, the saw is purchased from Burdwan either by themselves or through agents. The transaction for purchasing raw materials and selling finished products is done for cash only. The *sankharis* (craftsmen) are dependent on the moneylenders. The rate of wage varies according to the type of work, and is paid in cash. The labour charge in this particular craft is similar in case of male, female and children also. They collect subsidiary raw materials from the local market against cash payment generally. Sometimes they collect it from Calcutta or from any fair, against cash payment. Some of the Sankhakaras earn their subsistence from service (government/private), teaching in educational and musical institutions, business, rickshaw pulling, hawking etc.

During the pre-independence period, the raw materials were available more easily and the demand was quite reasonable. But now the picture is quite different.

Thus we see that this craft economy with the old traditional method cannot sustain the community at the minimum level of subsistence due to new demands in social and economic life of the changing society. To meet this demand they have to work from morning till night. A few of them, being frustrated in this pursuit, have adopted other occupations (trade, labourer, service etc.) with a view to making some extra income as their craft industry has become less profitable. Of course this has helped them to have new types of interaction with other communities.

Marketing and capital investment are their vital problems. So this community with its traditional craft should be encouraged by ensuring easy availability of raw materials and fair markets for their finished products as well.

A caste council exists among them and it is locally known as *soloana*. The body consists of selected craftsmen of their community whose functions during earlier days were organising ceremonies and rituals, thereby bringing each member of Sankhakara or Sankhari community closer to one another, looking after the interest of the craftsmen by procuring raw materials, marketing and controlling the price of finished products, and lastly even in the social sphere controlling social norms etc. The punishments inflicted by the council are physical embarrassment, cash fine and social boycott and the main crimes which it deals with are adultery, rape and theft. The role of the *soloana* has changed considerably of late. It gives loans and advances to poor artisans and performs religious ceremonies from the *soloana's* own bank account. Yet in the field of craft it has now only negligible control.

The religious beliefs and practices are reflected in the rituals and festivals of the community. They are Hindus and the Sankhakaras are Vaishnavs by faith. They observe several religious ceremonies in order to appease deities like Radha-Krishna, Durga, Kali, Manasa, Saraswati, Lakshmi etc. Their community deity is Agastya Muni. The family deities are of different forms. Their sacred centres are Nabadwip, Brindaban, Kashi, Gaya etc. Their sacred specialist is a Brahman priest who performs all the rituals and rites of the community. *Muni puja* (sage Agastya – a mythological *rishi* or saint) and Viswakarma puja (the celestial architect) are observed by them for betterment of their craft and for the well-being of the community as whole. The *Muni puja* takes place on the twenty-eighth of *Bhadra* and Viswakarma puja on the thirtieth of *Bhadra*, i.e., the day of *sankranti* (the last day of the month). Economic urge, social conditions, environment, and superstition all play an important role in urging them to practise religious performance. They follow the Bengali calendar beginning with the month of *Baisakh* and ending in *Chaitra*. The Sankhakaras are full of life and have a good sense of humour. They paint their walls and floors at the time of worshipping different deities (god and goddesses). The special craft of the community is to make conch shell articles like bangles, wind blown instruments, hair pins, finger rings etc. They have their own oral traditions, folk songs, folk tales, folklore etc. During marriage ceremonies and religious festivals they sing those songs. The Tusu Song (a folk song) is very popular among them. They themselves sing the songs of Tusu and perform those rituals connected with the function. They also sing the songs of Lord Krishna and Radha and organise the *puja* of Madan Mohan which goes on continuously for seventy-two hours i.e. *chabbis prahar*. They use mostly wind and string instruments. Musicians of Bishnupur Gharana are famous in our country. Some of the Sankhakaras of Bishnupur are employed as classical music teachers in some localities and in many other places in India.

The workers and craftsmen spend their leisure time in gardening, repairing houses and tools used for their particular craft, listening to radios, reading papers, watching cinemas and performing *pujas* in the house and in the locality. The children and youth of the Sankhakaras also involve in Bratachari (a kind of physical training introduced by Gurusaday Dutta).

They come in contact with other communities during their day-to-day life, since they are living side by side with many other communities in multi-ethnic setting. In every sphere of life the Sankhakaras come in contact with other communities and interact and even join in their social and religious ceremonies. They purchase their daily necessities from dealers belonging to other communities. They make friends belonging to other communities and attend their marriages. Inter-community marriage also takes place. They share common wells, ponds and other water sources, and cremation grounds and religious shrines with other communities. They celebrate Kali puja along with the Subarnabaniks of the area with whom they have close interaction. They supply conch shell bangles to the goddesses on the occasion of festivals.

In the economic sphere too, they come in contact with the people of several other castes and religious groups and interact with them unhesitatingly. For procurement of raw materials they previously had close contact with several Muslim traders who deal in conch shells. They have a long association with the blacksmiths i.e. Karmakars for the supply of saws and other tools and implements. Subsidiary raw materials are purchased from dealers belonging to other castes. Some of the workers (*bani* labourer i.e. contract labourer) belong to other castes of the locality. Because of modern transport and communication facilities, even people of Tamil Nadu, Maharashtra, etc. visit them. The traders of other cities, both far and near places, also establish contact for either supplying raw materials or for purchasing finished products. Some of the members of their community are engaged in business, teaching etc. There are also creative artists (engraving, music etc.), engineers, scholars and government /non-government service holders among them and they establish contact with various other communities at their respective spheres. Previously the Sankhakaras had an aversion towards imparting education to their children, but after the introduction of the programme of free education they have started sending their children (both boys and girls) to school. With the establishment of health clinics, hospitals and medical units run by welfare organisations, they have started taking advantages of the above agencies. They use both modern and traditional medicines but prefer modern medicines and modern method of family planning. Drinking water is taken from tube wells sunk by the government and wells sunk individually. Regarding benefit from employment and self employment programme, several females are employed under the government relief association schemes, for which they receive Rs. 600/- per month as labour charge. The males have received bank loans for purchasing rickshaws under the self-employment programme. Some individual craftsmen have also benefited after receiving loans from government agencies. Improvement of communication facilities had several impacts over the community. Their finished products have gone not only to distant parts of India but also outside India and a few of them have achieved distinction as master craftsmen. They have also established contact with several persons in distant areas. In the social sphere too, it has left its impact, like increasing number of marriages at distant places. The communication of the area with other places is maintained by means of postal services. The other means of communication are the bus services, and train services from Bankura. The means of cultural communication are post office, newspapers, magazines, radios, television and cinema. They receive various types of information through extension agencies, political and voluntary agencies. Electricity has also radically changed their methods of production. Innovative machines have been introduced which are run by electricity and thereby the rate of production has increased manifold. Their main fuel resources are cowdung cakes, coal, wood and kerosene. Regarding the nutrition programme, the people have also been benefited through midday meal at the primary school level and there are ration shops (fair price shops) for purchasing food grains and other things. For savings purpose they use several banks and post offices but in day-to-day life they depend heavily on money lenders and shop-keepers.

RITA GANGOPADHAYAY

SANTAL

Etymologically, the name Santal is a corruption of Saontar and was adopted by the tribe after their sojourn in the country about Saont, for several generations. Saont is an obscure village in Medinipur (*Skrefsurd*). Before their stay in Saont they are said to have been called Kharwar. However, Santal has come to stay; they refer to themselves as *hor* which literally means man. There are no sub-groups. According to known history, there home is in the Chotanagpur plateau and the surrounding plains. They settled in Palamau, Hazaribagh and part of Birbhum district at a remote period. The book that contains the story of their origin and history is called *Mare Hapram Reak' Katha* (the story of ancestors).

Their present day distribution is over Bihar, West Bengal, Orissa, Assam, Meghalaya, Tripura in India and in parts of Bangladesh and Nepal. Their highest concentration is in the Rajmahal Hills and the neighbouring areas. They are a migratory community. Their major concentration in West Bengal is in Medinipur. They love to live clinging to the skirts of hills and forests. They are found in the different lateritic zones of West Bengal.

In physical appearance the Santal of West Bengal are characterised by such features as short or below medium height, long head shape, broad facial profile and a short or moderately broad nose. Serogenetic studies among the Santal of Medinipur show about 52-58 per cent of gene O and an excess of gene B (26-27 per cent) over gene A (17-21 per cent). They show lower incidence of R_2 (10 per cent) than R_1 (75 per cent) gene complex and a very high incidence of Hp^2 allele (86-99 per cent) for haptoglobin marker and G-6PD deficient individuals in a relatively higher proportion (14 per cent). They are found to be affected with Beta thallasemia (4 per cent), sporadic incidence of HbAS (below 2 per cent) and Haemoglobin E (1 per cent) has also been reported (Choudhury *et al*, 1966).

The language they speak is Santali, a non-Aryan Austro-Asiatic family of language related to the Mundari group of languages. It has no script of its own but recently there has been some work done to introduce a script called *ol-chiki*. However, most of their written literature was sponsored by Christian Missionaries using the Roman script. Roman script has been associated with Santali for the past hundred years, before which not much effort had been made to codify their history or origins. The Santals when talking to non-Santals use either Hindi or Bengali. Among themselves they speak Santali. Their language is highly idiomatic and metaphoric.

Santals can be easily identified by their physical appearance and clothes. Santal women usually wear two pieces of cloth, one for their upper portion from the waist across left shoulder and one for their lower portion from the waist to just below the knees. Sometimes they wear a *sari* wound round their waist to form a long free flowing skirt and the other end going across their left shoulder and being highly tucked into the waist band. Santal men wear a loin cloth when working and a longer *dhoti* when going visiting. Both men and women are fond of using a piece of cloth as a shawl. Santal woman decorate their hair with flowers and silver hair pins joined symmetrically to a central round piece of silver in the centre. They are fond of silver jewellery. They bear marks of tattoo on their arms, neck and chest.

The Santals are constitutionally a scheduled tribe. They constitute the largest homogenous tribe of the Indian subcontinent.

They are non-vegetarians eating practically all kinds of meat and fish. Generally they do not eat beef or buffalo. They eat pork and meat of all fowls. They also eat rats. Their staple food is rice and seasonal vegetables. They soak the cooked rice overnight in water and then they have it with roasted chillies. They are fond of both puffed and flattened rice. They rarely drink milk; even children are not giving cow's milk as they traditionally believe that only the calf has the right over the cow's milk. They use mustard oil for cooking their food though they often smoke their fish and meat instead of frying it in oil. They are very fond of home made brewage made from rice and they call it *handi*. This rice beer is their daily drink, the men drink more regularly at home and in shops, while women drink occasionally only at home or at homes of relatives. On the whole there are no social taboos about drinking. Young unmarried women rarely drink. *Handi* is part of all Santal festivals. It is intimately related to their way of life. They sometimes drink alcohol which they do not prepare at home.

The Santals are divided into twelve patrilocal exogamous clans: Hansdak, Murmu, Kisku, Hembrom, Soren, Marandi, Tudu, Baske, Besra, Pauria, Core, Bedea. Of these the Bedea clan no longer exists. According to myth Santal clans originated as a means to avoid incest. In the beginning it is said that each clan was occupational–the Kiskus were chiefs or *rajas*, the Hembroms courtiers or princes, the Murmus priests, the Sorens fighters or soldiers, the Tudus blacksmith, drummers and merchants and the Baskes traders. The remaining four–Besra, Core, Pauria, and the Hansdak clans were hunters and cultivators. Class distinction, however, rapidly disappeared for there are no Santal legends that show them operating. "On the contrary...clan bears no relation to occupation" (Archer 1974: 24). The Santals are well-known for their democratic equality (*ibid*: 24).

The clan is used as a surname. The clan as such has no function in maintaining hierarchy; all clans are treated at par. According to the Santals, the world is divided into *hor* and *diku* meaning non-Santals irrespective of what the other communities are. However, this does not mean that they are unaware of the *diku* world, but the most important thing is that they are not Santals, thereby traditionally not comparable. They are aware of their own minority status. The Hindu and the Muslim referred to the Santals as *majhi*, the areas they occupy is called *majhi para*, and generally ascribe a low position to the Santal.

Marriage rules are simple. Clan endogamy is strictly forbidden. Each clan has a number of sub-clans or *khunts*. It is only in exceptional cases that the sub-clans have any practical significance. The boy cannot marry into his mother's *khunt* (Archer 1974:25). Santals practise negotiated marriage, in which the first step is the appointment of a matchmaker who is trusted as a friend by either family, and he is given the responsibility to find a suitable girl in another village. There are ways in which marriages are arranged by the boy and girl involved in a love affair. The other forms of marriage are i) by elopement — this is attempted when neither of the two families is in favour of the match. The boy and the girl run away together to another place. In this type of marriage the couple come back after sometime and their marriage may be celebrated officially; ii) by discovery — if a boy and girl decide to get married, then they start publicising their union as a result of which the boy's and girl's parents agree to their wedding or treat their union as a marriage; iii) marriage by capture — sometimes the lovers decide to force a union by resorting to 'capture'. In this case the boy captures his girl and forces her on his parents and their union is recognized as a marriage. Capture is resorted to by the girl too in which she takes the boy to her house and forces the boy's parents to accept her as his wife. Any arrangement by which a boy and girl live together openly as man and wife and are not subjected to tribal boycott is a valid union. However, none of these marriages are regarded by the Santals as 'good' marriages as in these cases every one suffers loss of dignity.

Marriage among the Santals is regarded as an important aspect of life. It is a time when their social capability is tested, and either they come out of it with dignity, or they emerge with a loss of dignity. Since their sons and daughters are involved in this maintenance of social dignity, they are expected to behave in ways upholding their parent's position. Marriage is symbolised by vermilion in the parting of the hair and tattoo marks on the right side of the body; before marriage she is tattooed only on the left side. Age at marriage for girls is between fifteen to eighteen years and boys it is sixteen to twenty-two years.

The system of bride price is followed, and is paid only when the marriage is finally settled. The bride price used to consist of one cow and rupees twelve. However, dowry has made inroads in Santal life. Bride price was simply a custom, whereas now the girl's parents have to procure sufficient dowry to be able to get a good catch. This is one of the recent changes that can be noticed in this community.

After marriage the bride lives in her husband's home. Divorce is sanctioned in the Santal community. Divorce is sought on many grounds – frigidity, barrenness, mental incompatibility and illness. Divorce may be sought by both men and women; and divorce is finalized in a particular way. The village council is called which after hearing both sides gives the verdict for or against and usually a ceremony is held in which the parties involved tear mango leaves into two from the middle. At the time of divorce, the husband pays an amount decided by the council as divorce money. From both the male and the female perspective, divorce is unsettling and dislocating. The girl loses her status as a married woman; she has to return to her father's home and has to share in the housework. The dislocation and the frustration are so much that a second marriage becomes inevitable. It is difficult for a divorced woman to find a suitable husband. There are no particular rules regarding remarriage.

Santals usually live in nuclear families. The family or household is an important aspect of their life. Each family or house is represented by its head in the village council. The person who is at the head of the family is respected and obeyed. He is accorded respect by those who do not belong to his family; in fact heads of families show mutual respect for each other. The Santal possesses great refinement of speech and a breach of this is fined. However, between some relatives like wife's brothers and husband's sister, grandparents and grandchildren and their spouses and that between son/daughter with father's sister's husband, there exists a joking relation. Rules of avoidance are the most important rules for maintaining tribal integrity. Rules of avoidance have to do with the concept of incest. The first rule is that a Santal may not have relations with non-Santals and clan endogamy is strictly forbidden.

Rules of inheritance and succession follow line of patrilineal descent. Inter-family linkages are on a formal level. "A kind of 'anarchy' (a Weberian concept) exists which according to Weber is the coexistence and cooperation within the community" (Hrach n. d. 229). It may not be so true today, however, in their inter-family interactions a social distance is maintained that is not based on commensal norms or hierarchy or any other social institution, yet each family is conscious of their own as well as other' privacy. Houses do not crowd into each other; nobody just drops in, except during festivals when visits are conducted in a formal way. Their interaction is on a retrained key. Yet the village is the essence of these people – the *hor ato* or Santal village presents a picture of unity. Most of Santal communal activities centre around the road or *kulhi* on which village council meets, on which dances are performed during festivals as well as signifying a sacred institution as far as behaviour is concerned.

Women do not enjoy the right of inheritance, but otherwise, women are not discriminated against socially. They have an important role in economic activities. They collect fuel, fodder, look after household work and go out for work in the fields and construction sites etc. Socially undue pressure is not put upon them. Breach of conduct is punishable in both men and women. Women can obtain separation for ills done to them; like abandonment, pregnancy out of wedlock, unwanted attention of males etc. Girls are not discriminated against as compared to boys; boys and girls are treated alike. Girls are patiently taught the ritual songs and dances and the ways of greeting guests. Girls are free to mix with boys but when there is breach of conduct both the boy and the girl are punished. Women do not generally change their surname after marriage.

At birth the arrival of the baby is announced using euphemisms like–there's a new guest. When asking about the sex, it is asked if the new guest carries things on the head (for girls), or on the shoulder (for boys). Birth is a simple process aided by the midwife who attends on the mother during birth and for some days after it, receiving payment in cash and kind. After birth the news is sent to the priest. Birth pollutes everyone including the Santal spirits of the village, as well as the house spirits, and especially the people of the house where birth has taken place. A ceremony for cleansing is an important ceremony by which pollution is removed which enables the members to participate in all communal activities. This ceremony is performed on the third, fifth or any subsequent odd day. On this day *neem* leaves are mixed with rice water. This ceremony is called *neem dak' mandi*. However, in cases of impending social events this purification ceremony is performed much earlier so that the village as a whole can participate in the festivities. On this day the child is named. The announcement of the child's name formally admits him to its clan and comes under the protection of the clan *bongas*.

Rites for adolescence were once in practice but are not in evidence these days. However, apart from a formal ritual, boys and girls who have reached adolescence are treated differently than when they are younger. Responsibilities are imposed upon them in the sense that they are allowed to participate in adult activities in household management and economic activities. They are also allowed to care for the *bongas*. However, the change is so gradual that there is an imperceptible shift from one stage to another. Adolescent boys are seen whiling away their time in play, maybe of less boisterous kind.

Chaco Chatiar ceremony, a ceremony of confirmation for boys was held during this stage of transition. But, now it is held when the boy gets married. This is certainly a local innovation and the ceremony itself has taken on certain Hindu dimensions. The day before the marriage ceremony the priest ties sacred thread around the boy rather like that of a Brahman, and propitiates the clan *bongas* with annual sacrifice, usually fowl. *Chaco Chatiar* ceremony is used for the recalling of the early history of the Santal. The significance of this ceremony has markedly decreased over the years.

Marriage is an important life cycle ritual among the Santal and one marvels at the various types of unions which they can conceive of as marriage. Their attitude is practical and realistic. A respectable marriage is one which is arranged by negotiation and follows certain rituals. Then the boy and the girl are presented with clothes and gifts; and as most marriages are held in the summer months, this is treated like a betrothal. The bride price is customarily paid before the actual ceremony, though in richer families dowry is found to be in practise. For the wedding a wedding booth is erected which is square in structure canopied with *sal* and mango branches. This day onwards the boy and the girl are smeared with oil and turmeric. The priest is entrusted to make a sacrifice to the *bongas* of the village. The *jogmajhi* supervises the anointing of the boy and the girl. The marriage party of the groom arrives at the girl's village and it is not unusual to see these days a band party accompanying the groom. The groom is dressed in marriage garments, usually a *dhoti*, and a shawl like cloth, and on his head a conical cap made of *shola*. There is much dancing and singing around the wedding booth and much drinking of rice beer. There is no well appointed time for the actual ceremony. During the wedding the family ancestors are worshipped. The girl's party then goes to receive the groom's party where the groom is welcomed by the girl's mother, after which the bridegroom is taken round the village. In each house of the village a little sugar and water is put in the bridegroom's mouth. After this the headmen of the two villages meet. The groom is then presented a *dhoti* from the girl's side and the girl likewise puts on the *sari* brought by the groom's party. The bride is then put in a basket with her head and face covered with a cloth. The groom is seated on the shoulders of some men to be at the same height as the bride, during which time he dabs her forehead with vermilion. After this their clothes are tied together, they circle the wedding booth thrice. The feast is then held. The next day the bride and groom leave the village amidst much singing and dancing. However, there are no hard and fast rules regarding rituals and many more may be instituted or the ceremonies may be dispensed with especially the details. All marriages are marked with singing, dancing and drinking; the feasting is almost redundant as they drink so heavily. The bride is adopted by the *bongas* of her husband's clan after this.

Death is another important aspect in their lives. When a Santal dies, the family and village all cooperate in disposing his body. Usually the dead are cremated, before which the body is smeared with oil and turmeric. Sometimes a sacrifice is also made. The period of pollution usually lasts for five days after which cleaning and washing is performed at the dead man's house. Only after this the dead man formally joins his ancestors. The bones of the dead are thrown into a river after the period of pollution. A sacrifice is also performed. A feast with rice beer is arranged by the dead man's family. There are special funeral songs which are sung during this time. Only after the household has been purified, is it allowed to propitiate *bongas*, or take part in ceremonies and arrange weddings. A year after death a special ceremony for appeasement of the spirit of the dead is arranged.

The traditional council of a Santal village comprises of the headman or the *majhi baram*, assistant headman or the *jog majhi*, priest or the *naeke*, and messenger or the *godet*. It also includes one adult male member from each household, who is usually the head of the family. Thus every household is represented in the council. The designated posts play a leading role in decision making, but it is never without consensus. However, each of the members are men of importance in their own right in the village, each is an elder of the village. Yet, the headman who holds a prestigious post cannot be regarded as more than first among equals (Sommers 1977:95, 58). Apart from the village, sometimes we find a council that caters to a few villages together. The *pargana* council is made up of groups of elders, each group with its headman, representatives from each of the villages in the parganas. The *pargana* elects one person from among themselves to serve as the *parganic* for a life term (*ibid*: 103). However, this council is becoming more and more obsolete and its importance has declined considerably. During the course of field work the Santal respondents mentioned the existence of such councils in the past. The council that has most significance today is the village council. This council can impose fines on those found guilty, can provide a platform for those who have some grievances, give a hearing to anybody's complaint, can help in bringing about rapprochement between two warring parties. Punishment is in terms of fine in cash which is spent in entertaining the assembled council. There are no rewards. However government having spread its arms into every nook and corner have somehow overshadowed local indigenous councils. Thus the changes that are noticed are the greater involvement of statutory bodies in the lives of people which provides for some regional representation.

The tribals practise tribal religion. The gods they worship are represented in nature, like mountain, trees, and stones. *Thakur jiu* or the creator, created them as well as the things on earth. The lesser god or *Maran buru* which means big mountain, acting as the behest of the *Thakur jiu* guided the Santals on their journey in order to find the true land of the Santal. Whenever taking food or *handi* Santals always offer a little in the name of their ancestors and *Maran buru*. Santal religion cannot be understood without a probe into their *bongas* or spirits who rule and influence their every movement, thought and feeling. The village groves, forests, as such, are the homes of the *bongas* who maintain a bitter sweet relation with the Santal.

Ancestors who die join the *bongas* and it becomes the sacred duty of every Santal to keep the *bongas* happy. The *bongas* are periodically worshipped by sacrifice of fowl and other rituals. The major *bongas* indicated by *sal* trees are *Maran Buru*, *Moreiko Turuiko* (the five-six), and *Jaher Era* (the lady of the grove). A *mahua* tree set apart from these three represents *Gosai Era*. Apart from these there is present in every Santal village, a sacred place made of a raised mud platform under the shade of a tree near the headman's house called *maintain*. The villagers gather at this spot to honour the founder's sprit. Each homestead has a separate dwelling place for ancestors in the interior of the main hut. The Santals are highly superstitious and have strong belief with witchcraft. (For details, see Archer 1974: 26-31).

The Santals have the following major festivals: *Erok'* (during the summer before sowing), *Janthar* (late September, a festival to prevent illness after harvesting and for increasing produce), and *Sonrae*. This last is the longest and most important festival after harvest. The first day of the festival is called *um* or beginning; second day is called *jel daka* on which day meat and rice are eaten; Third day is called *khuntoi* a day for veneration of cattle sport; forth day is called *jale yale* which is a day for visiting; fifth day is called *haku katkom* (the word literally means fish and crab, on this day the Santal usually go for fishing). The sixth or last day is called *sakrat* when traditionally the headman makes a gesture of relinquishing his position when he is formally asked to continue, as well as the day for hunting and for games. The dancing and the singing start from the third day and drinking continues throughout. It is a festival of merry-making, special songs are sung for each day. It is indeed a rejuvenating festival of joy. Poor or rich, *handi* is brewed and at least for these five/six days there is unbounded fervour in these people.

There are some evidences of religious conversions — most of the conversions are into Christianity. The noticeable change among the Christian Santal is noticed in their drinking habits which have acquired the connotation of sin and in their aspirations for education jobs, and other amenities of life.

The Kharwar movement in 1871 is a landmark in Santal history as a socio-religious movement. It was a form of revival of Santal traditions and signified the rise of the clean or *safa hor*. However this has become part of history and many Santal respondents could not say much about it.

At the very simple level, Santals paint the walls of their houses, tracing animal/bird motifs. Otherwise they do not have special artistic abilities. Their literary culture is very rich, probably the richest in the tribal world. Their songs – specific for different occasions, show the extent these people have made use of euphemisms and imagery. No better tribute could be paid to their literary richness than the one that has been paid by W. G. Archer (*"Hill of Flutes – Love and Poetry in Tribal India: A Portrait of the Santals"*, 1974). Far back in 1861 they drew the attention of E. G. Man who too was impressed by their songs and took the trouble of getting some of them translated. Being largely an oral tradition, at least for a long time, it is indeed remarkable to observe the richness of their literary traditions. Their dances are graceful and signify the spirit of unison. It becomes even more evident that these people are really cooperative and perceive themselves as one.

Traditionally the *hor* is not supposed to have any truck with a *diku* or non-Santal, ritually or socially. Occupationally too, there are few traditional links. Commensal norms with other communities being non-existent, there is no question of acceptance/exchange. It is difficult to come across putative friendship. When Santal live as part of a larger village, their area is often marked out clearly as separate. In their locality they have their own facilities of water. However, nowadays, restrictions on sharing water, road, school, panchayat etc., have been removed statutorily.

The modern day picture shows economic dependence of the Santals on the non-Santals for employment, for livelihood. Enjoining a scheduled tribe status has brought them into the forefront in the sense that they can now pitch in their bit with the greater group of other tribes and other backward groups. Rarely are they found in isolation, they have to live in a poly-ethnic situation and thus participation in a plural society is thrust upon them. However even in all this they maintain a low profile. They keep to their own group as well as to themselves.

The political movement which they are associated with is the Jharkhand movement since Independence in which their demand is for a state of their own. However, the Santals are not alone in this demand; other tribes have joined them, as well as some political interest has become vested in this movement.

Literacy, education and health and family welfare have made sufficient inroads into their lives due to the planned developmental programme of our government. As a scheduled tribe they enjoy special status in terms of reservations in schools, collages and jobs. They are provided with special schools and crèches for their convenience. It is difficult to make a true estimate of the use made of these facilities. They come under the purview of the Tribal Welfare Office which runs many schemes for employing them or making them trained for the secondary or tertiary sectors of economy so that they do not have to fully depend upon agriculture. However, the tribal belts certainly appear to be benefiting from these programmes. All India Radio runs a Santali programme daily in the evening to which those who have a transistor set are avid listeners. Communication means are available to the Santals which they use increasingly as they travel quite widely in search of employment. Electricity even though provided in some villages has not entered into Santal homes due to their poverty. Santals are conscious of natural conservation, *i.e.,* they are found to exploit the natural resources especially forest to the extent of their need. They depend on dead dry leaves for fuel. One of the main functions of women is to collect dry leaves for fuel. Irrigation of their fields is provided by government canals. In agriculture it is found that Santals have taken to innovation slowly, but in areas where there are plural societies, the Santals have adopted many of the innovation.

The common nutrition programmes existent is found in the midday meal provided in crèches to the children where they spend a major part of the day (10 am-5 pm). Other feeding programmes are organized lackadaisically.

The picture of the Santal remains incomplete if we do not record our first impressions on entering a Santal village. There is an atmosphere of serene calmness and feeling of pervading peace. This characteristic has been heightened by all the writers in the past as well as present. The village appears harmonious, the children enjoy their childhood, nobody hustles them or uses strict disciplinary measures on them, and rather they are given a status suited to their role. The relation of the village to children is like that of an extended family in terms of belonging and caring. The dignity of these people strikes the most untrained eye. Their contentment comes through, they ask for very little of life – a full stomach, head fuzzy with drink and the Santal yearns for little else (Man 1867: 18).

KUMKUM BHATTACHARYA

SARAK

The Saraks, a small community of Chotonagpur have Mandal, Mahashaya, etc. as their titles. It is thought that the term 'Sarak' has come from '*sravaka*', in Sanskrit, i.e., a listener. The listeners of the valuable sermons of Thirthankar were known as 'Sravaka'. The Saraks of Purulia (the studied area) are divided into Atharasika and Mahat. This division was also referred to by Bhattacharyya (1986 : 230), but he also mentions five other subdivisions, viz. (1) Panchakotdhiya (2) Nadipariya (3) Birbhumiya (4) Tamariya (5) Tanti Sarak. These latter five subdivisions cannot be located now in the area where the field work has been undertaken. Coupland (1916 : 84) mentioned that their original homeland was somewhere near Gazipur of Uttar Pradesh, although they themselves cannot recall their history of migration. Mitra (1953 : 58) has given the various accounts of their origin from *Brahmavaivarta Purana, Brhaddharma Purana* as well as from *Jatimala* : *Brahmavaivarta Purana* referred to their origin from Jola father and Kuvinda mother. *Brhaddharma Purana* referred to their origin from Malakara father and Sudra mother, whereas *Jatimala* referred to the origin of Saraks from Napit father and Kuverin mother. The Saraks of the studied area identify their relatives in Purulia, Bankura, Bardhaman and Medinipur districts of West Bengal as well as in Dhanbad district of Bihar, whereas Tarundev Bhattacharyya (1986) says that they are also found in Birbhum, Ranchi and Santhal Parganas. The Saraks live in the plains and plateaus characterised by warm and temperate climate, low humidity and medium rainfall. They speak and write in Bengali.

The Saraks are pure vegetarian and they retain all the prejudices of the Jainas with regard to eating the flesh of any kind of animal. Onion, garlic and lentil are not generally taken and these are strictly avoided in ceremonial feasts. Rice is their staple cereal. But some persons take *roti* (wheat bread) at dinner. Black gram is their common pulse dish. Mustard oil and rapeseed oil are their cooking media. They moderately consume all seasonal vegetables, produced in their agricultural fields as well as available in the market. Seasonal fruits are consumed by them occasionally. Most of the Sarak households domesticate cows and buffalos, so they can afford milk for their family members. Tea is a very common drink but none of them take alcohol. Their male members smoke *bidi*s or cigarettes, chew tobacco, and some of them use snuff. Many of their male and female members chew betel. The Saraks do not consume radish in the month of *Magha* (January-February) and any type of vegetable of bitter taste as well as roasted brinjal on Sunday. Earlier, they preferred to takc milk instead of tea. They used to cultivate sugarcane and prefer to consume molasses but decrease in production of sugarcane has compelled them to reduce consumption of molasses. Increase of pulse consumption and decrease of vegetable consumption and introduction of onion and garlic in their food by some of them are the other changes in food habit of the Sarak people.

Among the two sub-divisions, the Atharasika follow hypergamy and the Mahat. Dharmadev, Adidev, etc. are their *gotras*. Atharasika is higher than the Mahat in local social hierarchy. Those social divisions regulate marriage alliances whereas *gotras* indicate descent also. At present titles are also used in surnames. Some of their members with titles like Behara, Acharya, and Gayen have taken Maji as surname. As cultivators, they think themselves as Vaishya in *varna* order. They think themselves lower than the Brahman and the Kayastha and equal to the Tili, Kalu, etc., whereas Tanti and other neighbouring scheduled castes are thought to be lower than themselves in social hierarchy. The Vaishya community however thinks the Saraks are lower than them in social hierarchical order.

The Saraks practise endogamy at community level and exogamy at *gotra* level. Junior sororate is permissible only after death of the first wife. The Saraks marry their daughters around the age of eighteen years and their sons around twenty-five years. Marriage by negotiation is the common mode of acquiring mates. Monogamy is the general form of marriage in the Sarak society. A man can marry again due to barrenness or death of the first wife. Vermilion, conch-shell bangles and iron bangles are the symbols of married women. Nowadays, the Saraks have to pay a high amount of dowry in cash and kind. So, they try their best to negotiate marriage of their girls among the families from where they can also bring girls in exchange. Their bride goes to the father-in-laws house after marriage. Divorce is not recognised by them. They forbid widows to remarry. Increasing age of marriage and introduction of dowry instead of bride-price are only changes in the Sarak society.

The extended family is the common family pattern of the Saraks but nuclear families are not unknown to them. In a Sarak family, all the members obey the eldest person of the family and it is obviously the father. Avoidance relationship exists between *bhasur* (husband's elder brother) and *boasin* (younger brother's wife), daughter-in-law and father in law. Joking relationship is found between *nanad* (husband's younger sister) or *deor* (husband's younger brother), *boudi* (elder brother's wife) and with *shala* and *shali* (wife's younger sister and brother) as well as with grandparents. The Sarak boys help their family through the participation in different activities viz. they take their cows in the field for grazing, carry food for their elders to the field, collect grass for their domestic cows, etc. They begin to do those works from about twelve years of age. Property, restriction on the freedom of youngsters and unequal sharing of work load are major points of conflicts and confrontation among the family members of the Saraks. Male equigeniture is the rule of inheritance. Generally, the eldest son of the *malik* (leader) succeeds to the post of his father. Different ritual and religious occasions are major platforms of inter-family linkage. Ethnocentrism of the Saraks is very strong. The Saraks help each other in every ritual performances related to life cycle. No change is observed in the family life of the Saraks except an increase in the number of nuclear families. The Sarak women do not inherit their father's property. They participate in agricultural operation like sowing and transplanting with their male members. They also take care of their domestic animals. They bring potable water from tube wells. Some of them boil and husk other's paddy in lieu of cash. They observe *shat shashthi*, Lakshmi puja, etc. Some of the Sarak women are attached to Mahila Samity and a few of them are involved in political activities too. The mother's decision is honoured during marriage of a boy or a girl but they do not control family expenditure, and male authority is dominant in family affairs.

The Saraks observe *namasi* (a pre-delivery ritual) in the ninth month of pregnancy of a girl. The pregnant girl does not cross a river or does not go out alone after evening. They observe *pansh bara* or *panchute* ritual on the fifth day or *narato* on the ninth day after child birth. All the family members take purificatory bath on that day, but the mother and the baby take purificatory bath on the twenty first day known as *ekushar snan*. Pollution period for other members of the family is over after *narato* whereas the pollution period for the mother and the baby is over after *ekusha* (twenty one days). They observe *annaprashan* ceremony (first feeding of cereal) in the sixth month of a male child and in the seventh month of a female child. On the first day, one of the grandparents or any elderly person of the family gives *prasad* of any village deity into the mouth of the child, whereas on the third day maternal uncle puts rice into the mouth of the child. When the girls and the boys reach marriageable age, their father begins the search for suitable partners for them. When a negotiation is completed, the boy's father goes to bless the girl. They take advice of a Brahman priest to finalise the date of marriage. *Adhibas nandimukh, sattee, subhadristhi* (exchange of glances), *malabadal* (exchange of garlands of *akanda* flower), *dan* (handing over), etc. are the marriage rituals of the first day. In *sattee*, at first seven persons from the bride groom's party move around the bridegroom for seven times then the bride moves around him for seven times. On the second day, *kusumdika* ceremony is performed. After that the bridegroom gives vermilion on the hair parting of the bride. *Bandapan* or *bandanir bhoj* is another ritual of the second day of the marriage. The girl goes to her husband's home on the third day. The father of the boy gives a feast for their relatives on the fourth day of the marriage. Their rule of invitation to their community members is somewhat different from other general Hindu castes. After finalisation of the date of marriage they only communicate the date to their relatives, kin and other members of the community. There are two types of invitation (1) *eksupurir nemantanna* (invitation with one betel nut); and (2) *duisupurir nemantanna* (invitation with two betel nuts). The head of the family invites the guests of two betel nuts personally and they are generally close relatives of the person concerned. They prepare a list for guests of one betel nut, and then make a lottery. The community members of the village participate in this lottery and take the charge of invitation of a village according to the decision of the lottery. Generally, two community members of a village are sent to a place with a list. They only go to the village and give the list and betel nuts to the *malik* (leader) of that village. Invitees of two betel nuts come to attend the marriage ceremony in the girl's house on the first day, whereas the invitees of one betel nut come on the day of *bandapan*. Earlier, the guests from the bridegroom's side would not take food until the *sindur-dan* (smearing of vermilion on the hair parting of the bride) ceremony was completed. But now this system is not strictly adhered to. Another change noticed is that rituals are becoming expensive. Burning is the mode of disposal of the dead body. Their pollution period is over after thirty days and the day is known as *ghat*. *Sradh* ceremony is performed on the thirty first day after death.

Agriculture is the major source of economic subsistence of the Saraks. Most of the families of this community possess agricultural land. Agriculture is their traditional as well as primary occupation also. At present, many of them are engaged in service and various types of business. Animal husbandry is their subsidiary occupation. They depend on daily as well as weekly markets. Generally, they sell their agricultural produces through middleman in exchange of cash. But, while production is abundant they themselves carry their produces to the wholesale centres. They pay to their agricultural labourers in cash and kind both. A gradual shifting from agriculture to the secondary or tertiary sectors is the only change in economic activities of the Saraks.

The *malik* or the caste leader controls the Sarak society and the post is hereditary. The *malik* takes part in the completion of marriage or death ritual or to solve any social problem, such as maladjustment between husband and wife or conflict between two brothers related to property etc. The *malik* tries to solve any social problem with the help of other responsible persons of their society. The *gram panchayat,* the statutory council, plans and implements welfare and developmental activities. They have a regional association known as 'Sarak Unnayan Samaj'. Dapunia Shiva temple is their gathering place. If a big social problem arises, the Sarak people assemble there and discuss means to overcome the problem.

The Saraks of West Bengal say that their ancestors were Jainas but now they have completely adopted Hinduism except the vegetarian food habit and some *gotras* like Dharmadeb, Adideb, etc. They claim that majority of them are followers of Vaishnavism. A *Tulsi mancha* (a small basil platform) is found in front of each and every Sarak house. Each of the Sarak family worship Lakshmi and Narayan as family deities. Shiva temple, Durga temple etc. are their village sacred centres. Dapunia Shiva temple is their regional sacred centre. They have a Shiva Mandir Unnayan committee. One person is elected by voice vote to take the responsibility of the temple. This Shiva temple indicates their devotion to Shiva also. All the Sarak families have to donate some amount of money after marriage or after a death ritual to the account of the temple. They go to all sacred centres of the Hindus for pilgrimage. The festivals related to Shiva puja, Gajan, Harikirtan, Dole Purnima, Durgapuja, Tusu, Bhadu, etc. are their major festivals. Fairs, related to Poush Sankranti in different areas, are attended by the Saraks.

The Sarak women make frescos on the walls of their houses during major festivals. They also sew artistic *kanthas*. Folk songs are sung by women on different occasions. The traditional inter-community linkages of the Saraks are same as the other agriculturist communities. They take the service of the Brahman priest during different life cycle rituals as well as during Lakshmi puja, Satyanarayan puja, etc. The Napit and the Kamar are two other communities with whom the Saraks have *jajmani* relation. They get a portion of paddy harvest for regular shaving and hair cutting, whereas the Kamar gets the same for repairing agricultural implements. The Tanti supplies thread of the waist for the new born baby, the Bauri serve them as *dai* (mid wife). All of them receive payment in cash as well as kind for their services. The Bairagi sings *namkirtans* (devotional songs) in the morning throughout the month of *Kartik* (October-November) and gets three bundles of paddy stalks directly from the field during harvesting. It is stated that earlier the Saraks thought of themselves to be equal to the *nabashakhas*. They give *sidha* to the Brahmans, the Bairagis, the Napit, the Kamar etc. Generally, no occasion arises for taking *sidha* from the other communities. Previously they did not take cooked food from any other community except the Brahman but at present they take cooked food from any *jal-chal* community. The Brahman and the Kayasthas used to take cooked food in their houses if it was cooked by a Brahman. Marriages with other communities is not reported, and if at all it happens the involved persons are not accepted by the community. *Phul* and *gangajal* are the two terms of friendship with boys or girls of other communities. For a boy, *viksha ma* (the kinship term) from the Brahman community is not uncommon. The Saraks participate in activities of different political parties. They have representatives in different levels of *panchayat*.

The Saraks seldom work as agricultural labours of other communities. But they take the similar service from other communities. They sell their agricultural produce through the *fariah* (middleman) who come to their houses. They also take their produces to the big *mahajans* of other communities in the markets. A few medical practitioners, engineers, teachers, etc. are found among them. Modern inter-community linkages are established through them.

In general, the boys of this community receive education up to Secondary standard, whereas the girls receive education up to class VIII standard. The Saraks go to the doctors for medical aid but traditional medicare is not absent in their society particularly for snake bite, measles, chicken pox, etc. A few Saraks have undergone family planning measures such as ligation and vasectomy. Potable water is fetched from wells, tube wells and rivers. The Saraks also avail themselves of loans from IRDP to purchase cows, bullock-carts, pumps, sewing machine, starting shops etc. Most of the Sarak families have radio sets, and a few have television also. They visit cinemas frequently. They also go to the extension agencies for the betterment of their agricultural pursuits. People from different political parties also visit them. They have also road and rail connections with their villages. They consume electricity when it is available. Coal, cowdung cakes and fire wood are their common fuel. A few have *gobar* (cowdung) gas plants also. They do not have any irrigation facility excepting pump irrigation from the tanks. Mostly they have to depend on rain water. They prefer organic manures to chemical fertilisers and pesticides. The Saraks get modified ration from the fair-price ration shop. Some of them can save money with bank or post office. Saraks generally take loans from their relatives or employees during their need. Many of them purchase grocery item on credit throughout the month and pay the amount at the beginning of the following month.

It is observed that the Saraks are a very conservative, quiet and law-abiding community. They live peacefully with other communities. Generally, they construct their cowshed at the entrance of their house, so that, the lower caste people who work as their cowherds need not enter the house to tend the domesticated animals. They serve sweet dishes at the beginning of any feast, the practice being different from those of the other communities. The speciality of the community is to maintain a ***Lakshmir-handi*** (an earthen pot symbolising good luck). They keep valuable things in that pot and open it only on Poush Sankranti if it falls on Thursday. The Saraks have reported that if dacoits come to any Sarak house they first search for that pot.

ARCHANA DATTA

SARKI

The Sarkis are a small community, known also as Mistri or Karighar as they work on leather. They have migrated from the west of Darjeeling district and at present live in Siliguri, Kalimpong, Kureseong and Sadar sub-divisions of the Darjeeling district and Alipurduar sub-division of Jalpaiguri district. They live in the hills as well as in the foot hills, where climate is cold, with low humidity, associated with medium rainfall and light snowfall in high attitude areas. According to the census of 1981, their population was 11,292 in West Bengal. The Sarkis speak Nepali and use Devanagari script at home. They speak Nepali and Bengali, and use Devanagari and Bengali script with others. The Sarkis hold the constitutional status of a scheduled caste.

The Sarkis are non-vegetarian and eat fish, meat and egg. Their staple food is rice. They take all kinds of pulses like gram, *urad*, *moong*, peas and beans, *masur*, etc. They take vegetables, roots and tubers which are locally available. They use mustard oil as cooking medium. Fruit consumption is moderate. They drink brewed alcohol regularly. In some rituals taking of alcoholic drinks (home made *nighar jhanr*) is essential. They also purchase alcoholic drinks from the market. They take milk, milk products, and smoke *bidi* and cigarette.

The Sarkis have no social sub-divisions or subgroups. They have several exogamous *thars*, like Boshel, Rangtel, Mongrati, Vishnugi, Purkuti, Rokha, Boilkuti, Upurkuti, Langhel, Tolangi, Baramsakha, Koiralo, Kawolakuti, Achhami, etc. The function of the *thar* is to regulate their marriage and these *thars* have no hierarchical stratification. The Sarkis use *thar* name as their surname. They recognise *varna* order and place themselves lower than the Chhetri, the Gurung, the Rai, the Mangar, etc. They place themselves in the same rank as that of the Damai, the Kami etc. In their own self perception, they stand to hold a low social status.

The Sarkis practise endogamy at community level, and exogamy at *thar* level. The age of marriage is seventeen to twenty in case of girls and seventeen to twenty-five in case of boys. Marriage by negotiation is the only mode of acquiring mates. They practise monogamy. The symbols of marriage for married women are vermilion and *potemala* (bead necklace) of green colour. Bride-price is present among them. The bride lives with her husband after marriage. *Chhutnam* or *chharachhari* (divorce) due to maladjustment is permitted with social approval but the cases are very few. Both parties can seek for *chhutnam*, and children are liability of either mother or father according to the decision of the *mondol* of the caste *panchayat*. Widow remarriage and remarriage of divorced women is permitted. Widower and divorced men also can marry again.

The Sarkis prefer to live in nuclear families, though there are a few extended families. Avoidance relationship is present between daughter-in-law and father-in-law, joking relationship is found between elder brother's wife and husband's younger brother and between grandparents and grandchildren. Father's property is inherited equally by all sons. Succession in matters of family headship and rights goes through the male line. Inter-family linkages are observed during ritual and religious functions. A rise in the number of nuclear families and decline of extended family system, are the changes reported in recent times.

Women do not get any share of the parent's property. Women take part actively in outside work like collection of fuel wood, fetching drinking water from rivulets and *jhoras* (springs). They work as tea leaf pluckers in tea gardens. Women also take part in the family management by way of contributing money, as they work as tea leaf pluckers in tea gardens. They have no role in political spheres except that of casting vote in *panchayat*, or assembly election. Women have a low status with no decision making power within the family and no place in the mechanisms of social control.

The Sarkis observe certain life-cycle rituals. They impose pre-delivery restriction on mothers and observe a few rituals before child birth. They observe twenty-two days' pollution period after childbirth. In this period the mother of the newborn cannot enter the kitchen. Name giving ceremony of the newborn baby is held sometime between the fifth and the eleventh day. A Brahman officiates in the ceremony. The first rice eating ceremony is held when the baby is six months old. The Brahman priest calculates the sign of zodiac and a member of the family, who has the same sign of zodiac with the baby, feeds the first rice to the baby. Parents of the baby arrange a feast for the villagers and relatives. Both bride's and bridegroom's parents select an auspicious day for the marriage. A token amount of bride-price (Rs. 21/-) is paid as an essential custom. Nowadays the normal practice is giving bride-price in kind. The bridegroom goes to the bride's house with musicians from the Damai community. The Brahman conducts the marriage ceremony. A few major rites during the marriage ceremony are *gayehalud*, *malabadal*, i.e., exchange of garland, *sat-pak* and *sindur-dan* in which bridegroom smears vermilion on the bride's forehead. The bride's family gives a feast to the bridegroom's party and to the villagers. After the ceremony, bride goes to her husband's house on the next day.

The Sarkis both cremate and bury their dead. They observe thirteen days pollution period. On the first day, sons of the deceased person cut the nails and shave their heads. During pollution period, they do not eat fish, meat or egg. On the thirteenth day, *shraddh* is performed with offering of rice, meat, *ghee,* potato, etc. along with sweetmeats. The Brahman officiates in the ceremony. Relatives and neighbours are invited to participate in the ceremony, and a feast is given to them with *nighar jhanr* or *roksi* (brewed alcohol).

The Sarkis are mainly a landless community. Their traditional and present occupation is leather work or making of shoes, and cover of *khukri* (knife). The other occupations that they pursue at present are agricultural labour, business, government and private services, and labour in tea gardens. They are linked with daily and weekly markets and they get their wages in cash. Due to their landlessness, the number of daily wager, agricultural labourer and tea plantation labourers has increased in recent times. Child labour exists in the Sarki community. A Sarki son inherits the skill of making shoes from his father.

The Sarkis have their own caste council, consisting of the *mondol* (head) and a *parmanik* (assistant). The posts are not hereditary. They also have an All India Nepali Scheduled Caste Association at Darjeeling. Statutory formal *panchayat* has been functioning after Independence. The statutory *panchayat* looks after the various welfare and development programmes among the villagers.

The Sarkis profess Hinduism. They regard *kuldevata* as their home deity. They also worship Shiva or Mahakal, Lakshmi, Durga, Satyanarayan etc. Mahakal temple at Chowrastha, Darjeeling, and Shiva temple at Dhudia are their main sacred centres. The Nepali Brahmans act as sacred specialists of the Sarki families in rituals and in religious functions. The Sarkis attend Shivaratri mela at Mahakal temple, Darjeeling and Shiva temple at Dhudia. They also attend *rathayatra* fair at Rothkhola, Naxalbari.

The Sarkis have the knowledge of a particular craft. They are specialised in leather work. They have very rich folk songs, folk tales and folklores. They play the flute while singing a folk song in festivals and women participate in dance and sing songs during rituals.

The Sarkis are *jal-achal*. The Brahmans do not accept water from the Sarkis. But the Damai, the Kami accept water from them. The Chhetri, the Rai, the Gurung, the Newar, the Limboo accept *kaccha* and *pucca* food from the Sarkis. The Brahman and other castes take *sidha* food and exchange *sidha* food with the Sarkis. They do not prefer inter-community marriage. Putative kinship is found between the Sarkis, and the Damais, the Limbus, the Rais, etc. They share drinking water sources like *jhora* (springs) and rivulets, schools, roads, crematorium, etc. with others. They participate in traditional festivities like Mahakal puja. Rathayatra, Dassehra etc. They have cultivator and labour relationship and other forms of relationship with the other castes in the village, like the Brahman, the Gurung, the Kami, the Limbu, etc. The community has businessmen and some of the community members hold white collar jobs in government organizations and in the private sector.

The Sarki boys normally study up to higher secondary level and the girls up to primary level. They use traditional and as well as modern medicare. Attitude towards family planning is favourable. Rivulets and springs in the hills are the drinking water sources. The Sarki do not get DRDP or IRDP loans. Electricity is not available to them. They use transistor radio as mass media. They visit cinema. They take facilities of post offices as these are often situated nearby. They use fuel wood or firewood as fuel. Children get bread as mid-day meal in schools. They use the facilities of the rationing system. They do not take the advantage of banking facilities. They depend on money lenders and shopkeepers.

AMITABHA MITRA

SAYYAD

The name of the community is Sayyad. Sayyad is often used as a title by the members of the community with a view to point out their exalted social position. Sayyad is spelt in English in a number of ways. The story of origin of the Sayyads is based on written history. They came from the direct descendents of the prophet Mohammed through Ali and Fatima (the prophet's daughter). But the history of migration of the community to remote rural areas of Bengal and other parts of India is an unrecorded matter. Though the Sayyads claim their world-wide distribution they are not very specific about the areas of their global distribution. They, however, name Arabia, Persia, Pakistan, Bangladesh and India as a few of the areas of their distribution that they know of. The rural Sayyads are observed to know very little about their distribution within this State. It is, to some extent, due to this reason that for marital ties they do not need to go to distant places, they marry close kin. They name the following districts where members of their community are found: 24-Parganas, Hooghly, Bardhaman, Birbhum and Murshidabad. The Sayyads belonging to the Shia sect are found in Murshidabad. The natural environment that the Sayyads share with other communities in the state is climate-wise warm and temperate having high humidity. The terrain they inhabit is the plains of West Bengal denuded of forests. The Sayyads in this state are Bengali speaking both at home and outside. The script used is Bengali both while writing to kin and outsiders; however, there are small sections among them who feel proud to disclose that at home they speak Urdu. The Sayyads belonging to the Shia sect are Urdu speaking. The Urdu speaking Sayyads find it appropriate and honourable for them to write to their relatives in Urdu. The community is a part of the Moslem minority.

The Sayyads are non-vegetarian. The general local concept of non-vegetarianism is inclusion of fish and meat as food items. There are codified instructions for all Moslems regarding food, lawful and unlawful (see the Koran chapter II, V, VI and XVI). Accordingly, the Sayyads eat beef and meat of buffalo, but strictly avoid pork. There are certain local innovations, e.g., fish without scale is considered a taboo. The staple food is rice. They take a variety of pulses. They prefer *masur* and *kalai*. Oil from seeds of mustard is used as edible oil. All kinds of edible roots (radish, sweet potato, and ginger), tubers (yam, potato); bark (cinnamon), vegetables (brinjal, tomato, cabbage, cauliflower, and gourd) and fruits (mango, banana, date, orange, apple, guava, and jack) are eaten. Some among the Sayyads consider mushroom a taboo, while others among them eat it, Milk tea, sherbat are common drinks. Alcohol is a taboo, known as *haram* or sinful. There are not strictures on any item like special food among the Sayyads.

The Sayyads are divided into two religious sects of Sunni and Shia. The Sayyads of Shia sect in Murshidabad use Meerza (not Mirza) as their surname. The Sayyads of Sunni sect use, in fact no surname, rather they use Sayyads as a title and prefix it to their names. The community knows of its high or rather the highest social status among the Moslem. They unguardedly compare their social position among the Moslem with that of the Brahman among the Hindu. They try to consciously shun this kind of comparison as they and other Moslem communities repudiate the existence of any social hierarchy among the Moslem. However, in practice they strive after maintaining a dignified social position e.g., unlike all other local Moslem communities, the Sayyads avoid ploughing their field with their own hands and this inhibition about ploughing distinguishes the upper caste-communities among the local Hindus. The community is accepted by the Hindu upper caste-communities as members of the secular category of *bhadralok* (respectable people). The local Moslem communities place the Sayyads at the top of their social hierarchy as they are linked to their prophet through his daughter as they traditionally avoid ploughing which, in the local context, characterizes their superiority to others, Besides, the Sayyads are often found to be descendants of celebrated families of *pir* (saint) or *nawab*. The Sayyads are, in general rich people. The neighbouring Hindus find them in secular and socio-economic terms as their equal.

The Sayyads follow Islamic marriage rules. According to the rules they are prohibited to marry their i) daughter (including step-daughter); ii) sister (uterine and foster); iii) father's sister; iv) mother's sister; v) mother (including foster-mother); vi) brother's daughter; and vii) sisters daughter. Besides they cannot marry their wife's mother and son's wife. Age at marriage for men is between twenty and twenty-five years, while for women, age at marriage is between seventeen and eighteen years. Brides need not be younger to grooms. Negotiated marriages are practised. Negotiation is done through relatives. Women kin frequently take more active role in the negotiation of marriages.

The match-maker is referred to as *mosata* or *ghatak*. Monogamy is practised. There is, however, provision in the Islamic rules, to have more than one wife. There is no marriage-symbol. A form of bride-price known as *den mehr* is a must for every Moslem marriage. Gifts to the bride are given either in cash and kind or in kind alone. Two items of ornaments namely, *nath* (nose-ring) and *tika*, worn on the forehead just near the parting of women's hair are always included among the items given as *den-mehr*. Dowry or *pan* is an innovation and is in practice now. The Sayyad are patrilocal after marriage. *Gharjamai* system is practised but it is not preferred. Divorce rules are according to the Islamic or Moslem laws (see Koran chapter II). According to the rules women and men have similar rights regarding each other. The divorce is called *talak*. However, when women seek divorce, they are often deprived of the portion of *den mehr* that remains due to them from their husbands. This sort of divorce is known as *khula*. In practice no post-divorce maintenance is given. Rules of remarriage conform to the prescribed Islamic rules. In the case of women, a remarriage is possible only after a period of *iddat* (or waiting). For a divorcee the *iddat* is for about three months, while for widow four months ten days.

Nuclear families predominate among the Sayyads. The Koran deals with, in great detail, the ideal relation that the husband and wife should maintain between themselves. Though there is no evidence that a Moslem community goes by the word of the Koran, yet there is a possibility that the Koranic ideal norms influence the actual behaviour. The husband expects respect, love and submissive attitude from his wife. She should look after his well-being. In return the husband loves his wife and looks after her welfare. Children are taught to show deference and respect to their father. The relation of avoidance between husband's elder brother and younger brother's wife is maintained. Grandparent-grandchildren relation is that of joking. Relations of conflict and confrontation between and among brothers' wives are proverbial. Close-kin marriages such as parallel cousin marriages often assuage strained relationships that exist between brothers' wives. Generally, the husband's younger brother maintains terms of joviality with elder brother's wife. Islamic rules of inheritance are practised by the Sayyads. However, these are not practised to the letter. After the death of a husband, the wife is given one-eighth and the rest is divided into two shares of six *annas* and ten *annas* (an *anna* in this context denoting one-sixteenth of the whole). The deceased's daughters share equally the portion containing six *annas* of property; while the sons divide equally among themselves the rest of ten *annas*. The descendants of Murshidabad royal family complain that these rules were violated by their predecessors, by their practice of primogeniture. Succession is patrilineal. Inter family linkages are close and manifold. The families living in a village feel a kind of solidarity because i) they consider themselves as social equals and they are often otherwise tied up by nuptial bond; ii) they profess the same religion Islam which, as it is prescribes daily and periodic congregation of its followers; iii) they feel secure, as a minority, to maintain their unity. In the past the community had a predominance of joint families.

As regards right of inheritance the female, generally, but not always, takes a share which is half of that of the male in her own category. Equity and fair dealing are, however not always observed in matters of inheritance by women. Women's activities pertain to their role in household management. Their main social activities are rearing of their children and looking after the well-being of their husbands and children. According to the Islamic tenet women have prescribed religious activities to preserve their faith, namely offering *namaz* five times a day. Women are not found to indulge in political activities except exercising their power of adult franchise during elections. As insignificant number of women have taken up jobs in the tertiary sector. The major handicap that the Sayyad women face in taking up jobs or any outdoor activity are their observance of *purdah*. Girls are allowed to go to schools, but as they grow up their movements are restricted and often they are not permitted to pursue their studies. Pressure of habits and social and family opinion act in a subtle way and in many a case women accept voluntarily the observance of *purdah*.

After the birth of a child (among some only for a male child) *azan* (summon to prayer) is called aloud by a male, preferably by the grandparent not for prayer but for proclaiming the birth of the child. The first child is usually born at the home of the mother's parents. The child's head is shaved by a barber within a few days after the birth, because the hair, with which the child is born, is considered defiling. The name giving ceremony or *agiqa* is customarily held within twenty-first days after the birth. *Aqiqa* consists of sacrifice to Allah in the name of the child, of two goats for a boy and one for a girl. The parents of the child do not take of this sacrificial meat. In the district of Birbhum the Sayyads do not observe the custom and parents eat the sacrificial meat. According to the custom a quarter of the sacrificial meat is distributed among the poor; another quarter to the kin and the rest is kept for consumption in the family. In case the parents cannot afford it, the ceremony of *aquiqa* can be skipped. During childhood the most important rite for a male child is the circumcision or *khatna*. This is done by Moslem barbers. For a few days before circumcision women of the family accompanied by their female friends and relatives from within the community beat *dhol* (drums) and sing songs in the evening. The principal ceremony of Nika (marriage) among the Sayyads is contractual. For accomplishing this part of a mullah acts as a *kazi* (or judge). An agent is employed and he, on behalf of the bridegroom proposes the marriage to the bride. Two *gawa* (witnesses) are also appointed to listen to bride's answer accepting the proposal. The *nika* is solemnly conducted. The groom's party gives a fee to the *kazi* for his services. A day before the *nika* is solemnly conducted. The groom's party gives a fee to the *kazi* for his services. A day before the *nika*, the bride is made to dress up and put on her ornaments and she is made to sit up till the small hours of the morning. An assembly for women gather around her and beat drums and sing songs, know as *sehera*. After *nika* two feasts are held–one is known as *nikar dawat* (*dawat* means invitation) and the other one is *dawate walima*. Like local Hindu and other Moslem communities the Sayyads too practise the custom of *gaya halud* (smearing of a paste of turmeric, mustard oil etc, on the body of the bridegroom and the bride). After the death, the family observes a period of mourning for forty days locally known as *chalisha*. Disposal of the body is done according to the set Moslem pattern: the body is washed and dressed up anointed with *atar* (scented oil) and is carried to the graveyard on a bier. The pall bearers bath before touching the bier. A deep grave is dug taking special care to keep the walls inside smooth. Before interring the dead all the assembled relatives and friends read *janaja* for the dead person. After *janaja* earth is thrown upon the grave. After the burial the assembled kin and friends are fed by the bereaved family.

The Sayyads' major economic resource is land. They exercise control over the land that they possess. The community is mainly landowning. Ownership of land among the Sayyads is on the basis of individual proprietorship. The Sayyads claim no hereditary or traditional occupation. In rural West Bengal they live mainly on agriculture. An educated section among them have gone in for various white-collar jobs and professions like teaching or jobs in bank. As subsidiary occupation they have taken up business and trade. None among them works as a labourer. The community is wholly dependent on market. There are no bonded labourers in the community. There is no child labour either. However, children from other neighbouring communities are employed by the rich Sayyads. Payment of wages made by the Sayyads is both in cash and kind. However, the *kisan* or agricultural labour on annual contract is paid in kind (a share of the produce) along. Since Independence a number of educated Sayyads (including women) have gone in for jobs in tertiary sector.

The Sayyads are generally not found to be exclusively living in a hamlet or village of their own. They live in company with other Moslem communities. The most common Moslem neighbours are the Sheiks, the numerically dominant Moslem community in the State. The traditional community council is usually comprised of all Moslem communities inhabiting a village. In the traditional community council the Sayyads are observed to hold positions of importance by virtue of their high social status. Generally, the village mosque is the seat of the council. The council sits when a villager or villagers call on it to settle an issue or a dispute. The council tries to amicably resolve it. The council can dress down a wrong-doer or a party at fault and this act amounts to public disapproval of the offence. The council is not empowered to reward a person for his good deed. The council also sits for discussing issues concerning general welfare such as repairing the mosque, appointing a *khatib* (i.e. *mullah*). The role of modern statutory councils is mainly developmental and these bodies are not supposed to look after any particular community. Since Independence the major change that is reported, is diminishing role of traditional panchayat as the members of the community often seek redressal of their grievances through court of law.

The Sayyads profess Islam. Majority of them are Sunni by sect in this State, but there are a few Sayyads of Shia sect living in the district of Murshidabad. Satya Pir is the regional deity. The major centre for pilgrimage is Mecca. The *mullahs* play the role of trained sacred specialists and they belong to no particular community. Their services are professional and they coming from various Moslem communities get themselves, professionally trained from Islamic educational institutes viz. *madrasahs*. A major local fair is held in the month of *Chaitra* (March-April) at Pather Chapuri near Suri in Birbhum. There is a shrine of a *pir* (Moslem Saint). According to the Sayyads, Idul Fitr and Iduz Zuha are two major Moslem festivals.

The Sayyad women have a tradition of sewing designed bedspread locally known as *kantha*. They sew a few other varieties of bedclothes known as *byathun* (thick coverlet) and *sujni* (bed cover) tastefully decorated with sewed multicoloured design. These are made of old clothes, especially old *saris*. They ornament artistically pillowcases with needle work. Some of them have good ability for tapestry. The women folk are slowly losing interest in these works, as these are time-consuming works for art. Instead, these days they are trying their hand is knitting woollen garments. Some Sayyad women have taken to *kantha*-sewing as a means of earning in Birbhum.

As far as norms are concerned regarding commensality the Hindus following their dictum consider the Sayyads *jal-achal*. However, Hindus of the lower social order employed in the homes of these landowing Sayyads do not go by the edict of the Hindus of upper social status and they freely accept water and *kachcha* food from the community. The Sayyads maintain no commensal relation with certain Moslem communities of lower social order such as the Patua, the Momin, and the Abdal. As regards connubial norms, the Sayyads repudiate ideally any restriction of intercommunity marital exchange among various Moslem communities. But, in practice they marry they daughters within their own community. However, Sayyad men are found to marry non-Sayyad women of so-called upper Moslem *jat* (community). The Sayyads do not have to share wells and other water sources with the upper caste-communities as they live residentially apart from the Hindus of upper social order and in some Sayyad households there is provision of either tube well or well. The Sayyads maintain socio-economic interdependent relation with their midwives coming either from the Dom community or from the Hadi. The members of the community have active participation in political activities and they have elected representatives from their community in various statutory councils. As landlords they have tenants from different neighbouring communities. They try to employ their own poor Moslem brethren as tenants and as agricultural labourers.

The literacy among the Sayyads is high compared to that among any other Moslem community of the State. A small section of them have gone in for college and higher education. There is a positive attitude among the members of the community as regards modern health and medical care. The family planning programme has, to a certain extent, achieved its goal. Drinking water is available within the locality. There are, however, complaints that tube wells seen is different localities do not last long as those are not of good quality. As regards self-employment, a few among them have gone in for contractorship and fishing. The Sayyads are found to take advantage of modern innovations and often they can afford such facilities. The following are the innovations that they either have accepted or are ready to accept if opportunities come: i) electricity; ii) environmental conservation; iii) irrigation (both deep tube-well and canal facilities); iv) fertilizers (chemical; organic manure is not a new concept, they are using it from time immemorial); v) pesticides; and vi) banking facilities. The community, though they avail themselves of the facilities of ration and nutrition programme (wherever and whenever possible) are critical about both quality and quantity of the materials that are given.

The Moslem communities in general and Moslem communities of upper social order in particular have a tradition of cooking tasty dishes both vegetarian and non-vegetarian. They have many exciting recipes, which are never known by their next door neighbours living for generations by their side. The Moslem communities of higher social status are found to have cultivated a taste for serving food elegantly to their guests. Besides, they are particular in learning and maintaining *adap* (etiquette). Some moneyed Sheiks have taken up Sayyad as their title. They are known as pseudo-Sayyad or locally *paisar* Sayyad meaning Sayyad by possession of money or wealth.

R. K. BHATTACHARYA

SHAH OR SHAH FAQIR

There is no available etymological account of the name Shah, except that the Shahs themselves mention two kinds of Shahs viz., Badshahs (emperors) and Faqir Shahs or Fakir Shahs (or Darvesh) meaning Moslem religious men vowed to poverty and austerity. The Shahs consider themselves as *aulia* (i.e. one who sings the praises of Allah). They are unable to provide any history of their origin. They consider themselves local to the areas where they live in. One would expect that the Shah as mendicants would have a better perception as regards their spatial distribution; but actually they can give information regarding their distribution only at the local level, not even at the district level. The Shah Fakir are found in different districts of West Bengal, e.g., Birbhum, Murshidabad, Nadia, Malda, etc., and across the state boundary too. Areas inhabited by the community are warm and temperate and are plains of eastern India. There is one main river, the Ganga and a few minor rivers and rivulets flowing through the plains. There are thin forests in some districts of West Bengal. The Shah, however, live in villages having their own *pada* (or hamlets) and these villages are located away from forests, in the midst of cultivable expanse and are marked with fruit trees; tall, and large, shady trees and trees considered having medicinal value like *nim*. Among themselves they speak at home local forms of Bengali sprinkled with Hindi, Urdu and Arabic words. The script used at home as well as outside home is Bengali. While speaking to non-Moslem in Bengal villages, they do not use non-Bengali words. Though there is no identifying mark as such to distinguish the community from others, there are noticeable items in his attire and gait when a Shah Fakir goes out as an almsman. He looks like a moving collage due to his garments which are stitched with a number of multi-coloured patches. He wears a cap and carries a pair of long iron pincers in his hand which he uses to beat time with while singing. Besides, he carries a shoulder bag and sometimes some of them are found to carry one or two tame birds of prey either on their shoulders or in their hands. This spectacular sight of a Shah Fakir on a village road or in the entrance of a mud hut is however, slowly becoming few and far between. Their Moslem identity at times can be assessed by such signs like beard, cap on the head, absence of *sankha* and *loha* in the case of married women. They form part of the Moslem minority of our country.

The Shahs are non-vegetarian and by non-vegetarian they mean those who eat meat, fish, egg etc. They eat beef but strictly avoid pork, tortoise, crab, and snail (*guguli*). The staple food is rice. They prefer to eat *kalai* and during winter months they eat *masur*. These are the two varieties of pulses that are most popular among them. Often they boil these pulses tied in a cloth, along with rice and then mash them mixing in onion, chilli, salt and mustard oil and this they eat with rice as an item on the menu. As oil seeds, mustard seed is used. The common roots that are used as food items are turnip, ginger, turmeric, sweet potato etc. The most common farinaceous tubers used for food are potatoes. Edible starchy tuber of yam is also eaten. Bark does not constitute any food item except cinnamon which is used as a spice for only special foods. As vegetables they eat a variety of *shak* (greens) and are very fond of *pater shak* (a particular variety of greens) as a substitute of *dal* (pulses) during summer months. Besides, *jhinge*, *brinjal*, *gourd*, etc., as vegetables are eaten. Seasonal fruits like mango, jackfruit, and palm are eaten. Besides, papaya, guava, banana can be included as edible fruits of the Shah. Those who can afford it, provide their children with milk. They drink tea often, though without milk, though they prefer it with milk and sugar. Alcohol is tabooed. According to the Quranic rule it is *haram* (sinful). Clandestinely, some among them drink, The Shah consider date, meat of *dumba* (broad tailed sheep, not a local variety), or meat of camel as special food as according to them these are the items of food particular to the Moslems of Arabia, the land from where their faith of Islam was propagated. On the day of Idu'z Zuha after their Id prayer in the morning, their breakfast should consist of roasted meat, preferably of cow, slaughtered in accordance with their traditions.

There are no major social divisions or groupings among the Shahs. They think that there are four *tarika* (ways) of leading life as believer and these are: i) Shariat; ii) Tarikat; iii) Marefat; and iv) Hakikat. Shariat is for those who venerate Allah in the course of leading a normal family life. Tarikat is for those who try to lead a life devoted to Allah by keeping themselves aloof from family life. Marefat is for those who venerate Allah by delegating their responsibilities to others, while in Hakikat, the person completely removes himself from his family. The Shah Fakirs consider themselves to belong to the order of Marefat. The rich among them are not in favour of their status of mendicancy and they look down upon this way of life, and at times they surreptitiously disown their connections with their poor brethren, especially those who still follow their traditional way of life. It appears that after a generation, they may give up their surname 'Shah' to renounce their connections with the community. The Shahs claim that hierarchically their position is just below the Sayyad, whom all local Moslems consider to be at the top of their hierarchy, because they are thought to be direct descendent group of the prophet Muhammad through Ali and Fatima (the prophet's daughter). Further, the superior position of the Sayyad is defined by the single fact that they avoid ploughing the field with their own hands. (This abstinence from ploughing distinguishing a community as hierarchically high is a Hindu concept). The Shahs also claim that they do not plough with their own hands and that they lead a distinctive dedicated life of mendicants, and thus in terms of equality, no community (except the Sayyad) is equal to them, rather all other Moslem communities are subordinate to them. The neighbouring Moslem communities like the Sheikh, Pathan regard the Shahs' claim of superiority as a tall claim of a community of beggars. The local Hindus never consider them as anything higher than that of a class of Moslem beggars. The Hindu and Moslem neighbours of the Shahs consider them as a class of relatively poor people and employ them as agricultural labourers. With certain nearby Moslem villages inhabited by non-Shah communities, the Shahs have a kind of jajmani relation for performing the duties of *tahal* (patrolling) in the early pre-dawn hours in the Moslem month of Ramzan to awaken the Moslem for his pre-dawn breakfast (*shiori*). During epidemics too they are called to patrol the villages.

The Shahs as community of Moslem have special rules for marriage which are common to all Moslem and they are specified in the Quran (see verse 23 of chapter 4). The rules in general, prohibit marriage between kin belonging to different generations. Within the same generation, only marriage between brother and sister is not allowed. Besides, there are certain local innovations, *e. g.,* the Shahs considering their superiority do not like to marry their daughters to Sheikh or Pathan or the other Moslem communities who they reckon to be socially inferior to them. They, however, think that there should not be any social taboo for them to marry girls from inferior communities. The logic of the argument here is that a woman coming of an inferior status will, as a wife, take a subservient role of a married woman towards her husband, but a girl coming from a superior status would not accept an obsequious role. Age at marriage for males is from twenty to twenty-two years and for females it is between sixteen and seventeen years. The most prevalent mode of acquiring mates is through negotiations. As regards forms of marriage monogamy is of general occurrence. Polygyny is very rarely practised. It has Quranic sanction (see verse, i.e., *ayat* 3 of chapter, i.e., *sura* 4) Bride-price known as *den meher* is an important and essential custom. There are Quranic injunctions regarding this. *Den meher* is publicly decided in terms of cash and kind proposed by the bridegroom to his bride while seeking matrimony. Dowry or *pan* among the Shahs is still at a nascent stage. The demand of *pan* is not in force. Concerning rules of residence after marriage they are found to be patrilocal. The Shahs have codified rules regarding divorce. Divorce is almost a male prerogative. Women at the time of divorce can fight for their dues such as promised amount of *den meher* from their husbands, post-divorce maintenance; when they have male support from their parent's homes like brothers. Divorce or *talak* is formally made either by elderly members of the community residing in the village or by legal proceedings through a court. There are no specific rules regarding remarriage except that after annulment of a marriage the wife has to observe a period of *iddat* (waiting) before forming any new union. The period of *iddat* is roughly three months. The following are the changes noticed: marrying across the various Moslem communities of Sheikh, Pathan etc.

Pattern, rather types and forms of families are mainly nuclear. Joint and extended families are not altogether absent. Inter-personal relations within families are guided in the light of the kind of knowledge that they acquire by way of their experiences as trainees in leading the life of mendicants. In their childhood, in an endeavour to learn songs, playing musical instruments, and other details of the art of the mendicant friars, and to listen to stories, they become fairly close to their grandparents, parents and uncles whom they often consider as *gurus* or preceptors. There is a general feeling that unless pupils have genuine regard for their teachers and parents and unless the elders bless them they can never be thoroughly proficient in their art nor would find access into the domain of wisdom. This philosophy works deep into the mind of the Shah. In their workaday life fathers and sons may differ in opinion from one another on various issues, the relation may not show an overtone of respect or regard, but sons, as they maintain, feel reverence for their fathers, and it is customary to pay obeisance to their fathers and teachers on the eve of a traditional performance like playing a musical instrument or singing a song. The relation between grandparents and grandchildren is that of love, affection and joking. Normally there is no public demonstration of affection between husbands and wives. There is love and care on the part of wives towards their husbands. Parents and adult children often maintain a relation of mutual affection and obligation. There is not much scope to have a relation of conflict and confrontation in a nuclear family because of strained relations between the following members: i) mother-in-law and daughter-in-law, which often leads to a situation where the relation between father and son becomes non-cordial in families; ii) sisters-in-law, which can at times, bring brothers to loggerheads. The relation of avoidance is not observed in a nuclear family. In an extended family, the husband's elder brother is avoided by his younger brother's wife. There is hardly any relation that can be described as a relation of fear. However, adolescent children are found to obey their father and in an extended family their uncles too. This obedience may be out of fear of punishment. The Shahs follow the Moslem rules of inheritance. Some important features of the rules are i) both the male and the female have their shares. Generally the male takes a share double that of the female in his own category; ii) shares are there for the following categories — Husband/wife, descendant, ascendant and collateral. Succession pattern is patrilocal. Internally linkages are very close. The residential pattern is close-knit. Houses are often piled onto each other. As they sometimes marry their first cousins both brothers and sisters are found living side by side with their families. In fact, all families of a hamlet have direct or distant kin relations among themselves. Besides residential pattern and kinship, one other important reason of their closeness is their religion. Members from different families (though not many) come to the mosque in the village to offer *namaz* (prayer) five times a day. Twice in a year all male members of the community in the village congregate to offer their *id* (festive) *namaz*. Most of them observe the same in their respective villages. Economic assistance and help is the other aspect that forges interfamily linkages.

Right of inheritance as stated above is stipulated for women, but women's share is not equal to that of the male. As per the Quranic rule a sister's share on parental property is half of that her brother. A widow gets either a fourth (when the husband leaves no child) or an eighth (if the husband leaves children) of her deceased husband's property. However, in actual practice there are observable variations. Equity and fair dealing is not observed in all matters related to women's shares. Due to observance of *purdah*, Shah women try to avoid outdoor activities such as collection of fuel and fodder for cattle, if any, goats and sheep. Women have innumerable roles as wife, mother and sister. In life-cycle rituals they have their roles. Their religious role is prescribed by the Quran and Hadith. But only a few among them keep to the prescriptions of these sacred texts. The women's role in family management consists in organizing household chores, accomplishing them and/or getting them done. Occasionally they contribute to family income by selling eggs of hens and ducks reared at homes. The poor among them employ themselves in the homes of the rich for doing certain household chores like preparing puffed rice, parboiling paddy and the cash or kind earned thus is contributed towards the family income.

Birth of a male child is proclaimed by *azan*. This is a Moslem custom. After parturition the mother observes pollution for twenty-one days and during this period she does not offer prayers nor does she consider herself *paksaf* (ritually clean). The period of pollution is not very strictly observed. For name giving they have a special ceremony known as *aqika*. However, those who cannot celebrate it skip this ceremony. *Aqika* consists of a sacrifice to Allah in the name of the child, two goats for a boy and one for a girl. The sacrificial meat is divided into three equal parts — one for consumption in the family and the other two parts to be distributed among kin and the poor and the orphans respectively. During childhood the most important ceremony observed is circumcision which is done by special Moslem barbers who is paid in cash for his service. On the day of circumcision the maternal uncle of the child is specially invited to attend. For a few days before the occasion women of the family especially young and fun-loving ones beat *dhol* (drums) and sing songs till late in the evening. Though this kind of merry-making is considered anti-*shariat*, it is being traditionally practised. When a barber visits the village on invitation he is requested by the poor parents to perform the rite for which he is paid only nominally. During adolescence there is no particular rite or ritual. Marriage is rather an elaborate ceremony. The principal ceremony of the marriage is contractual. On the day of the marriage after the arrival of the groom and his party two *sakshi* or *sakkhi* (witnesses) and an *ukil* or *vakil* (agent) go to the bride and formally puts to her the proposal of marriage. The bride receives the proposal from behind the veil. After she agrees the groom is informed and his agreement to the marriage is formally sought. When he too, agrees, the marriage is solemnized as per Islamic *shariat* (traditions). Sometimes only the principal ceremony of marriage is held while all social and cultural paraphernalia are postponed. This is known as *akad bandha*. After this the bride waits till a proper social ceremony is held and only after that she goes to live with her husband. Except in the latter form of marriage as described above, consummation of marriage is possible immediately after the marriage. The Shahs bury their dead. A lot of care is taken after a person dies. The body of the dead person is washed (*gosol*). They dress it in new clothes and put *atar* (scented oil) on it. The corpse is carried on a bier to the graveyard where all the assembled Moslems offer *janaja namaz* for the dead person before he is buried. Earlier the groom, if he could afford, would come riding a horse to the marriage *shamiana*, but at present the custom is becoming obsolete as it is difficult to procure a horse.

The major economic resources are land as well as water. Quite a few among the Shahs own land and thus are privileged to exercise control over land. Some of them also own ponds, but often jointly with others. The Shahs are a combination of both landowning and landless categories. Those who possess land, have individual proprietorship. Traditional occupation of the community is begging, or in refined terms religious mendicancy. At present the primary occupation for this community is cultivation either as owners or as labourers, and as subsidiary they have a number of callings, viz., *paikari* (dealers in cattle), pisciculture and trade in fish, business like grocery, singing and playing musical instruments as bandsmen of the locally organized body of musicians within the community, odd jobs of repairing umbrellas or of locksmith etc. The younger generations of the Shahs look down upon their traditional calling of mendicants and they consider their elders who are in this profession as a class of beggars or *pakhmara* (those who depend on the meat of birds that they hunt; this euphemism is meat for those who carry birds of prey). The younger people think that odd jobs are better than begging and in reality, this attitude has driven them to opt for any profession or work that has come handy to them. The community's dependence on market is total. A form of barter is practised when paddy is exchanged for items of daily necessity at grocer's shops or from itinerant traders of vegetables and fruits, like brinjal, cauliflower, tomato, *sharbati alu*. There are no bonded labourers among the Shahs. The extent of landlessness and rise in number of labourers working in agriculture is significantly low among the Shahs. Boys from the age of twelve years begin working as *mahendar*, *i. e*, cowherd-cum-agricultural helper and this can be considered as presence of child labour among the Shahs. Payment of wages for agricultural labourers as well as for other forms of labour is both in cash and kind. Following changes have come about after Independence or more correctly, since people have accepted the government induced planned transformation in agriculture in the seventies and have since successfully achieved a qualitative development of agriculture and consequently agriculture-based economy: i) the Shahs have given up the profession of begging in the present generation; ii) they have instead become proficient in cultivation, trade, business and the other vocations.

Elderly males as well as some literate and enterprising young men constitute a traditional 'caste' (or *jati*) council of the Shahs. It is a kind of an acephalous and amorphous body. But it certainly takes decisions on matters that are brought to its notice. The issues on which it passes judgements range from petty quarrels to inheritance of property. The poor among the Shahs come for assistance to this council on issues like divorce, inheritance of property. The council normally sits at a public place like the village mosque. The above-mentioned *jati* council of the Shahs can punish a miscreant by imposing a fine or just by admonishing him. The role of modern statutory councils such as *gram panchayat*, *panchayat samiti*, is specific, as without consulting these councils no development work can be undertaken by government agencies like the block office. Following changes have taken place since Independence as regards mechanism of social control among the Shahs : i) literate enterprising young man of the community are becoming members of the *jati* council in greater numbers; ii) traditional *panchayat* is slowly losing its control over the community, while statutory councils like *panchayati raj* institution are becoming more and more powerful.

The Shahs profess Islam. They belong to the Sunni sect and they follow Hanafi School. There are *pirersthan* (abode of a saint) in certain villages these are most often built of mud resembling graves upon which terracotta horses and elephants are placed as offerings to *pir* by the devotees. Beside the existence of these village *pirs*, *Satya Pir* can be regarded as the regional *pir* of the Moslem. These *pir* are propitiated by offering *sinni* (sweets) to bring good luck to villagers and to drive out evil things such as disease, epidemics from villages. The major sacred centre or shrine within easy reach is Data Pirer Sthan and Patharchapuri near Suri. Further away are Ajmer Sharif, Ajmer,

Rajasthan and Dargah of Khwaja Moinuddin Chisti Saheb, Delhi. However, as per the scripture, Mecca in Arabia is the only centre pilgrimage. The role of sacred specialists, viz., *mullahs* (*i.e.*, learned Moslems in Islamic theology and sacred law) is varied. As officiating priests in village mosques, they conduct the prayers, read *khodba* (the scripture), they give sermons (*waz*) and run *maktab* (Islamic educational centre). As *kazi* or Moslem Jurist, they solemnize marriages. The major fairs are *urs* or congregations at regional shrines of Pirs on their anniversaries such as Data Pirer Mela at Patharchapuri. The major festivals are the two Ids, e. g., Idu'l Fitr and Idu'z Zuha. The significance associated with these festive occasions are: Idu'l Fitr forms the completion of the month long fast of Ramazan, i.e., Roza and Idu'z Zuha is the commemoration of the prophet's Ibrahim's willingness to offer his only son Ishmael as a sacrifice in obedience to Allah's command. The change reported recently in the pattern of religious behaviour and organization is as stated below:- due to communication facilities people take initiative to visit different shrines and sacred centres.

Their handicraft is limited to making and repairing of musical instruments that they play. They do not dance but music is part of their life. They inherit a number of their traditional songs of the Fakir. They are proud of their celebrity late Lalan Shah Fakir of erstwhile East Bengal, now Bangladesh. They live in a milieu where love for music develops on its own. In spite of their diversification of professions in this day and age, they still form small musicians groups composed of three or more persons. Some among them compose and set the tune to their songs.

As Moslem, the Shahs are *jal-achal* to the Hindu. No *kachcha* or *pucca* food is accepted by the Hindu from them. However, there is no taboo regarding acceptance of *sida* or *sidha*. As for other Moslem communities there are no doctrinal restrictions in maintaining commensal and connubial relations with the Shahs; but the general norms among the socially high Moslems are to avoid the Shah with respect to commensality and marriage. The norms are not always strictly followed. Putative friendship based on kinship and ritual across the community are not many. As Moslems, the Shahs are not allowed to enter temples and Hindu houses. However, this kind of discrimination is never questioned, as the Shahs on their own have no intention to violate such norms. Besides, there is no bar regarding access to and sharing of wells and other water resources, facilities of road, school, entry to *panchayat ghar*, etc. The Shahs maintain a kind of patron-client relationship with the neighbouring Moslem communities with a view to earn by singing special songs during the month of Ramzan or during calamities like epidemic. Their participation in political activities is not of any importance, in the sense that they do not have any elected representative from among them holding positions at *zila parishad*, *anchal samity* etc. The Shahs who practise mendicancy, do not hold plough in their hands. Those who own land among these mendicants, give it to share-croppers belonging to their own community. A few comparatively rich Shahs employ members of their community as *munish* or *mahendar* (agricultural day-labourer). However, a good number of poor Shahs are employed by the rich neighbours belonging to both Hindu and Moslem communities.

Literacy and education among the Shahs is poor. Poverty seems to be one of the main reasons for the poor literacy and education. Those who have become well-off, endeavour to get their children educated. Children are taught elementary Arabic in *maktab*. But this leaves no impact on them, as they hardly keep themselves in touch with the language when they grow up. Health and medical care is poor. Family welfare as such as in terms of planning has made no inroads among the members of the community. Tube wells in Shah hamlets have solved the problem of drinking water. Employment in government schemes and self-employment through government loans have made no headway among them. Communication has improved and the Shahs along with the neighbouring communities take full advantage of this improved communication system. Transistors are in use, but mainly to listen to songs. They do not feel any need for electricity. Dried leaves and broken twigs of trees, cow dung, coal, *gul*, etc. are used as fuel. Those who own land, show a positive attitude towards irrigation, use of chemical fertilisers and insecticides as well as organic manure. Nutrition programmes are irregular for school going children. Public distribution system is popular. Kerosene and sugar are the two most sought after items from ration shops. The Shahs have not yet shown any interest towards banking facilities.

The profession of mendicancy is becoming obsolete and along with it a way of life. There has been no deep study on these people. Some of the musical instruments such as *sarangi*, a stringed instrument, are not locally available these days. Specimens of the instruments should be collected and preserved. Changes noticed in the songs and their presentation should be recorded. It is not uncommon to find the Shah Fakirs singing songs in praise of Radha and Krishna and they love and sing songs of the Baul, a Hindu sect of the Sahajiya who also lead a life of mendicancy. According to the Shahs the Moslem people are fond of the songs and they are often requested to sing these songs. Thus they include such songs in their repertoire and even compose songs of these kinds. Unlike the Kirtaniya or the Baul, they do not dance while singing.

R. K. BHATTACHARYA

SHEIK

The Sheik is used as both title and surname. Etymologically, the respondents claim descent from the Arabs but when pressurized to give exact details, they admit their origins as converts from Hindu low castes.

According to the Sheik respondents their distribution is not only pan-Indian but pan-world, i.e. they are distributed all over the world. However, it must be noted that whenever they talk about their global spread or brotherhood, it is with reference to Islam, the tradition to which they belong and not with particular reference to themselves as Sheiks. Sheiks in West Bengal are to be found in Hooghly, Birbhum, and Murshidabad in large numbers.

They speak Bengali and use the same script. Their speech is usually interspersed with Urdu/Arabic words. Generally, their dress does not bear any distinctive indications to mark them out from the members of other communities who live as their neighbours. However, during festive occasions men can be seen sporting ***kurtas*** from Lucknow. Another distinguishing mark is often a well-kept *noor* (pointed beard) that some men keep. Little boys are distinguishable because of circumcision. They enjoy the status of a minority community.

In their food habits they are non-vegetarian, eating both beef and buffalo meat. They do not eat pork in any form. Their staple food is rice, *dal*, (*maskalai*), boiled potatoes, seasonal vegetables if they can afford it, and all kinds of fish. They do not eat crab and snail. They take locally grown fruits like mango, jackfruit, papaya, and *tal* (fruit of the palm-tree) which they usually cook in the form of a *pakora*. About consumption of alcohol, their attitude, in general, is that as it is banned by the laws of the Koran, it is bad to drink. Nevertheless they indulge in it though they do not brew their own drink at home. Milk is a drink rarely available to their children, as a result of which children persist in sucking breasts even at advanced ages of four or five years. The milk produced by the buffaloes and cows is sold, and very rarely kept for the children.

There are no taboos about prohibition of food. There is marked preference for some desert fruits such as date palms and raisins, especially when there are guests.

As such there are no social divisions among the Sheiks. Believing in the egalitarian principles of Islam, they reiterate the absence of any sort of hierarchy or social divisions. However, economy plays an important role in the formation of class structure which is twofold in nature, rich and poor. This stratification is fluid in nature, i.e., mobility from one stratum to another is possible and there are evidences of such mobility, both upward and downward within two or three generations. As there are only the rich and poor, the division is between those owning land and the other existing as landless labourers serving those who own land, respectively. This kind of social stratification has social overtones of maintaining distance between classes and creation of different social worlds, though in ideal terms they profess egalitarianism.

The Sheiks are part of a plural society in which their participation and competition is with the dominant communities around them. In such a setting they perceive themselves as belonging to a status higher than the Hindu low-castes such as the Dom, Muchi, Hari, and Bagdi. Within the Muslim community they perceive their hierarchic position as being just below the Sayyad who are at the top. The position they designate to the Santal, a tribal community, dwelling side by side with them, is one below that of the Hindu low-castes.

In the local social hierarchy the Hindu castes generally look down upon the Sheiks; the upper Hindu castes do so actively, while the lower castes do so passively.

The special rules for marriage among all Muslims are same. On the whole they follow the Koran, the holy book of Islam. According to these rules a man is prohibited to marry his: i) mothers (including his grandmothers through the father or mother); ii) daughters (including granddaughter or great granddaughter through son or daughter); iii) sister (including full sister or half-sister); iv) father's sister (including grandfather's sister); v) mother's sister (including grandmother's sister); vi) brother's daughters; vii) sister's daughters; viii) foster mothers (including those with whom he has milk-relationship); ix) foster-sisters; x) wife's mothers; xi) step-daughters; and xii) son's wives. The rule in general prohibits marriage between kin belonging to different generations. Within the same generation marriage between siblings only is prohibited. These codified rules are not known in its details by all – in fact during negotiations for marriage, learned people of the community, i.e. the *kazi* or the *maulavi*, are called for consultation and interpretation of the rules.

Age at marriage for girls is sixteen to twenty years and for boys it is twenty to twenty-six years. Since marriages take place within kin, e.g., parallel and cross cousins, most marriages are arranged by parents. Very few love matches occur, which are not socially looked down upon if it is within the same community. Polygyny is provided for in the Koran. Polyandry is prohibited – a woman can take a new husband only after the death of her former husband or when there is divorce. There are no apparent symbols of marriage, except glass bangles. However, Hindu influences of *sindur*, *loha*, *shankha*, *pala* (vermillion, iron bangle, conch-shell and red shellac bangles) can sometimes be seen, especially on women who are employed outside the village.

There is the custom of *den-mohar*, a kind of bride-price which is fixed at the time of marriage with the help of the *kazi* and the *ukil* (agent). Part of the bride-price is given in kind, and part is promised in cash. Dowry is a recent phenomenon borrowed from the neighbouring Hindus. Among the rich Muslims, the practice of giving and taking dowry is quite prevalent. After marriage, the bride resides in her husband's home, though there are cases of *ghar jamai*.

Divorce as well as the necessity of precautions to guard against its abuse has been dealt with in detail in the Koran (*sura*: 2, *ayat*: 228-232, 236, 237 and 241; *sura*: 65, *ayat*: 1 to 7 and *sura*: 33, *ayat*: 49). After the annulment of a Muslim marriage the wife has to observe a period of *iddat* (waiting) for three months before forming any union. During *iddat* the husband is supposed to maintain his wife. Usually divorce is initiated by the husband and the woman has to play a subservient role. *Den mohar* is rarely paid by the husband after divorce as "justifiable" reasons are shown when initiating divorce. Remarriage is allowed according to Koranic laws — in cases of both men and women. The changes that are noticed are largely in the dowry system and in some marriage customs which have been borrowed from the neighbouring Hindu communities.

Due to the very nature of their marriage systems, families in appearance look like joint and extended families. There is however, constant division of property, even of the homestead due to quarrels and poverty due to which many nuclear families live under the same roof, each having some place of their own and a separate oven for their cooking. Inter-personal relationships are seen to follow lines of kinship and rules of marriage. In a family, the husband dominates the wife, the husband being the bread winner, while the wife's role is to look after the domestic side. The sons and daughters help their parents with light work. Among the poor, a son from a young age helps his parents by working as *mahendar* (servant) in another family. A son is expected to look after his parents in their old age. A son's wife is expected to be respectful and courteous and obedient to her husband's parents. The relation between a son's wife and his father is one of respectful distance. Sisters try to maintain close relations with their brother because of property and as well as the fact that there is always the possibility of affinal ties between their children. The Muslim are on joking terms with their elder brother's wife, with their wife's younger sisters and brothers, and with grandchildren and grandchildren's spouses. Instances of conflict and confrontation are quite common between father and son, between brothers, between sisters-in-law, and between co-wives. These conflicts and confrontations result in division of homes, homesteads, land and other property.

The Muslim rules of inheritance follow Koranic rules. Generally the male takes a share double that of the female in his own generation. A Muslim can make a will/testament for only one-third of his property. Succession pattern follows from father to son. However, in spite of the detailed and well-spelt out stipulations in the Koran, especially regarding the shares of daughters or women in general, it is not unusual to find cases where the daughters received no share of their deceased father's property, justified on the basis that a considerable sum of money had been spent on their marriage. Women often forego their share in the property in favour of their brothers for the sake of alliances that may be formed between their children. The complexity of rules stem from too many close kin of both sexes; parents, children and multiple spouses. These rules bound the kin into a corporate body and for this reason its members are likely to be mutually adjustive.

Inter-family linkages are quite strong and based on reciprocity. Many families are related to each other as kin, resulting in more home-to-home visiting, being aware of each other's state–financial, social, familial. Because of the two-fold stratification of the society into rich and poor, it is not unusual to find that master and servant are related to each other.

Changes that have occurred are to be found in the increasing number of nuclear families thus making a dent in inter-personal relations with extended kin. Rules of inheritance are often not followed to the letter in the case of women.

Women have right of inheritance and their share is stipulated in the Koran. However, as has already been mentioned, their share is sometimes not given to them. Women have an important role in managing the home economy. Collection of fuel and fodder is part of their duty for which they manage to get their children involved. Socially they have roles to play during marriage, death, birth and other rituals. During the life-cycle rituals, women sing long into the evening. This practice goes against the tenets of Islam but has become a local tradition. At the time of death, it is the women who prepare the body for burial when the deceased is a woman. The Muslim women practise their religion in the privacy of their homes. The practice of *purdah* can be felt, differing from village to village, though it is more or less approved by the Muslims being part of the codes of Islam. However, as women have to do a fair amount of work outside, it becomes difficult to maintain *purdah* inside the village though outside the village they try to maintain *purdah*. They are barred from entering the general mosque; they sometimes have their own mosques though it is not common. Some Muslim women take an active interest in contributing toward the family income by starting small business like poultry supply, looking after grocer shops, or lending money on regular basis. Nowadays, there are cases of educated Muslim girls who are employed in state government or central government organizations. Muslim girls from a young age are given basic training in their traditions and this is highly approved behaviours. It is not unusual to come across women highly well-versed in the Koran though otherwise illiterate.

Rules and rites associated with life cycle rituals are thoroughly codified in the Koran. The birth of a first child takes place usually in the wife's natal home, and this practice may not be followed for subsequent births. After the birth of a male child, a customary call is given, not for prayer but for proclaiming the birth. Some devout Muslims well-versed in Islamic rules read a brief summary of Islamic doctrine in the left ear of the new born. After child birth the mother observes pollution for seven days after which, on the seventh day the barber shaves the child's head and pares the nails of both mother and child. After shaving, the child is bathed, the mother also bathes and her period of pollution is over. This ceremony is called *aqiqa*. On this day the child is named by parents, grandparents and other close kin. Two goats for a boy and one for a girl are sacrificed but this depends on the financial status of the family.

Circumcision is the next important ritual in the life of a Muslim boy who has to be circumcised within the seventh year. It is performed by a barber. Usually at a time many boys are circumcised together as it is difficult to obtain the special barber.

The principal ceremony of marriage is contractual. However, their long residence in a dominantly Hindu environment, a host of Hindu influences are observable and a host of non-Islamic rites have evolved. Marriage rites start with the sending of *lagan*, a complete set of new clothes in a new suitcase. Then there is the ceremony of applying turmeric on the body of the groom and the bride. On the day of the marriage the groom is accompanied to the bride's house by villagers and relatives, known as *barat*. The following morning the bride and the groom are sent away with all their belongings. After the marriage the bride and the groom return to the bride's natal home for a few days where the couple are invited to visit her kin, called *astamangala*. These are some of the non-Islamic traits that have crept into their customs. The marriage ceremony called *nikah* is simple. A contract is drawn with the amount of *den-mohar* written and with the consent of both parties about terms and conditions. The *kazi* goes to take the consent of the bride thrice. The bride sits behind a curtain and answers from within her consent. Of all their life cycle rituals, Muslims specially extol their funeral rites as very distinctive and sophisticated. They wash the body of the dead person with perfumed soap taking special care to wash the mouth, clean the teeth, nostrils and lower parts of the body, dress it in new clothes, smear scented oil and dig a grave for it to put it in. Special care is taken to keep the walls inside smooth. The grave has to be deep inside to be able to sit comfortably inside. The corpse is carried on a bier by pall bearers who have to bathe before touching the dead body. The last *namaz* (prayer) called *janaja namaz* is read. The body is placed with its head to the north and feet to the south and face turned to the west. All the assembled people then throw earth on the grave. The people who come to see the dead are fed after the burial. The richer the dead person, bigger the gathering and more elaborate the feast. On the fortieth day after the death of a person, his family if it can afford it, arrange *nailed* (religious discourse) and give alms to *fakirs*.

The major sector of economic activity of the Sheik is agriculture, but not all own land. For irrigation of fields they depend on canals built by the irrigation department. As already mentioned the community is comprised of both landowning and landless people. The landowning people are involved in agriculture and the landless people form the agrarian dependents or landless labourers. Those owning land consider themselves as peasants and involved in the primary sector. Some landowing people have also taken to fishing as secondary source of income. Some others are engaged in small business like grocer's shops, tea-stalls, etc. Young boys of poor families work as *mahendar* (servant) from a young age and their terms of payment is in both cash and kind. Girls are not sent to work in others' homes but have to be engaged in all sorts of domestic work. Certainly, land-man ratio has changed drastically wherein cultivation of smaller pieces of land has become uneconomical. The members of this community are innovative and are looking out for the sources of income. Some educated youth have taken to private tuition as a means of augmenting their income.

Being an egalitarian society there is absence of a special caste council like body which assembles to settle disputes and other matters pertaining to the community like divorce or disputed property division. The representatives are elderly respected people. They have power to chastise and admonish but not to levy fines. These days because of spread of the power of the *gram panchayat*, people show more interest in trying to enter this statutory body which promises access to the larger power structure as well as opportunity structure. To be a member of the *gram panchayat* involves a lot of prestige.

The religion of the Sheiks is Islam. Their only god is Allah and the major sacred shrine is the mosque which is part of every Muslim dominated village. The mosque is an identifiable landmark when locating a Muslim village. The mosque is primarily a meeting place where they are prescribed by their religion to congregate for prayer five times a day. The time for prayer is announced from the towers of the mosque and this call is referred to as *azan*. A portion of the premises of the mosque is used as a school or *maktab*, for educating young girls and boys in the holy scripture. It also serves as a shelter for travellers or *musafirs*. The mosque is maintained by the concentrated efforts of the Muslim living in the village, employing and maintaining a *khaki* or a Maulavi who looks after the mosque. He leads the prayers, gives *azan* and runs the *maktab*.

Like the mosque, the other prominent landmark one often comes across in the village is the *idgah* which is also a place of prayer. On the occasion of the two major festivals of Id, the Muslims congregate within the open arena of *idgah* for prayer. Regarding places of pilgrimage Muslims have a very global attitude – Mecca is the ultimate dream for them but which is practically inaccessible because of the huge expense involved. Near home is the place of *Data pir* which is near Suri, the district head-quarters of Birbhum, West Bengal. Ajmer Sharif is also a favourite place of pilgrimage.

The sacred specialists have an important role to play in the community of the Muslims as a whole. They are the teachers and interpreter of the holy texts. They impart and maintain Islamic traditions. They also act as revivers of Islam, to revitalize the sprit of Islam. They have been specially trained to take on the role of sacred specialists. The network of Islamic tradition maintains an overall uniformity in its different socio-religious practices and performances carried out in the same way by Muslims spread all over the Islamic world. The network also maintains the "induced solidarity" of the Muslim as a community. The source of all these are the sacred Islamic texts. The Muslim festivals are held according to lunar months. Muslims celebrate the birth anniversary of the Prophet Mohammed. Muslim festivals are Muharram, to commemorate the martyrdom of Hossain, grandson of Mohammed; Sabe Barat, which means that god on this day registers all actions men are to perform in the ensuing years; Roza, the month of the Ramazan feast in which the holy Koran was revealed; Idu'l Fitr is the festival of completion of month long fast of Ramazan; Idu'l Zuha in commemoration of the prophet Ibrahim's willingness to offer his only son Ishmael as a sacrifice obedience to god's command. This festival is popularly known as Baqrid or Bada Id. The local fair of some significance to the Muslims is the fair held at the shrine of *Data pir* which is held usually in the month of *Chaitra* (March- April).

Recent visits to Muslim villages indicate the fact that the youth are actively involved in the socio-religious activities of the village, especially in their involvement in the activities of the mosque and the *Idgah* are marked. It is not that they are always upholding the ideal tenets of Islam but they apply their energies in the paraphernalia of their faith.

Muslim girls and women are fond of embroidery and weaving mats. Their designs are religious in nature. They do these during the rainy season when they are confined indoors because of rains, and a young girl is expected to know how to embroider bedcovers, table linen etc. Mats are woven in the season after harvesting. Men are sometimes seen knitting fishing nets. The Muslims take pride in their handicrafts and these items are carefully stored to be used only on special occasions, and during weddings it is given as part of the trousseau.

Traditional inter-community linkages are occupational in nature rather than ritualistic and social. During childbirth, the midwife is from the Hindu caste of Hari as they do not have a Muslim mid-wife. With the midwife, the relationship is of transaction in cash and kind. However, the family of midwives serve for generations. Other sectors of inter-community linkages are in the economic sector of agriculture. Muslims work as day-labourers in the fields of Hindu landlords; this relation is in a way reciprocated as Hindu agricultural labourers work in the fields of Muslim landlords. Muslim house builders are called to build and repair Hindu houses. They are also called to catch fish from Hindu village tanks during Hindu festivals and rituals. Nowadays yet another inter-community linkage may be seen between educated Muslim youth and Hindu students through private tuition. Other types of linkages evidenced in the economic sphere lies in the business dealings with non-Muslims in the market places or at the local level.

However, commensal norms, i.e., acceptance or exchange of water and food, are traditionally absent between Muslims and Hindus, connubial norms of inter-community marital exchange are practically absent. Evidences of putative friendships are rare.

Politics has worked as a great equalizer between communities and it has emerged as the bandwagon everyone desires to jump on. Muslim participation in politics is active.

Attitudes on the whole towards literacy, education, health, medical care are positive, though it is not often possible for them to take advantage of these facilities due to their financial difficulties. However, larger school attendance and increase in visits to primary health centres nearby or hospitals at the district levels are indicators of the extent developmental programmes have made inroads. Muslim girls usually do not go beyond the primary school level but well-to-do families try to send them on for further education. Muslim boys are encouraged to continue their education. Ambivalence of attitude can also be observed, as the parents expect their school going children to help them during harvesting (in the case of boys) and domestic work (in the case of girls), thereby disturbing them during study.

Attitude toward family planning is quite ambivalent; in some cases it is quite negative. Use of contraceptives is supposedly against the tenets of Islam, though increasing number of children impairs the mother's health. There are many cases of women who have gone in for ligation or other permanent modes of contraception, there are also many who do not believe in it justifying it in various socio-religious ways.

Mass media and communication have helped in opening out the world to these users of Islamic network. This network is not only aided, it is made faster and time saving. Innovative as they are, the extent of available information helps in the participation in the larger plural society. Use of agricultural innovations and technology has been able to spread its message of advantage in this community because of easy channels of communication with an egalitarian background.

No description of this community can be complete without an appreciation of their participation in the plural society in which they are usually found. Muslim villages are contiguous to villages occupied by other communities. Rarely do we find villages composed of various sections of Muslims like the Sayyad, Sheik, and Pathan etc. The inter-community hierarchy is not of much consequence, rather their position in the plural society in terms of economy, opportunity structure and the power vested in them, that is of more importance and this determines their interactions and inter-linkages with other communities. Another important point that can be made is when borrowing cultural items from other communities, it is seen that they prefer borrowing from the communities occupying a higher status or one that is dominant compared to them.

KUM KUM BHATTACHARYA

SHERPA

The Sherpas are a well known community of the State. The word Sherpa is derived from the Tibetan word "Shar-va" meaning the people of the east. They have migrated from the north-west and west to the Darjeeling district. There is a long history of Sherpa migration. However, in a nutshell, this community existed in places like Solu, Khumbu, Parak, etc., which were in Tibet up to A. D. 1792. Since A. D. 1768, Prithvinarayan Shah and his successors followed the policy of expansion of the Gurkha empire. This led to the Tibeto-Gurkha war in A. D. 1792. The Gurkha army under the command of Damodar Pandey penetrated into Tibet and occupied Kerrong, Kuti, and the surrounding areas of the Himalayas. Unfortunately the Tibetan army could protect neither their community nor their home land. They had to face a great defeat due to the hindrances of snow and difficulty of crossing the ranges of the great Himalayas. Naturally after the war this community along with their home land came under the authority of Nepal and all the Himalayan people of Tibetan origin were collectively identified as 'Bhotay' (in Nepali term). In course of time, a group of Sherpas migrated to the north-eastern regions of pre Independent India such as Darjeeling, Kalimpong, etc. (Bell : 1922). The Sherpas mainly live in Darjeeling hills at the altitudes of 4000 ft. to 9000 ft. Their population figure was 14,195, according to the census of 1981. Their mother tongue, Sherpa, belongs to the Bhotia group of the Tibeto-Burman family of languages. The Sherpas speak Tibetan and Nepali language at home and speak Hindi, Nepali and English language with outsiders. They use Devanagari and Tibetan scripts at home and use Devanagari and Roman, with outsiders. After Independence they came under the scheduled tribe act of 1956, and are now considered as a scheduled tribe.

They are non-vegetarian and eat meat, egg, beef (cow and buffalo), yak, etc. Wheat is their staple food, though a few consume rice also. '*Thukpa*' (made from wheat) is their principal diet. Normally they do not take pulses; however, nowadays some of them take pulses like *moong*, peas and beans, etc. They are very fond of alcoholic drinks like *roksi* (made from *marua*), *chhang*, *goto*, etc. They do not smoke. They take milk and milk products.

The Sherpas have territorial clans like Solu, Khumbu, Parak, Mende, etc. These clans have several *ru*, the main purpose of which is to regulate marriage. The Sherpa *ru* are Chiwa, Garza, Gola, Goarma, Khambaza, Lama, Pinasa, Salakha, Tkhaktu, Khapa, Shang-gu, Lukpa, Mormin-Cho, Chu-Sherwa, Lak-Shinda, etc. They use Sherpa as their surname or use their *ru* name. They regard all the communities like the Bhotia, Lepcha, Tamang, Rai, etc., as of the same status as themselves.

The Sherpas practise endogamy at the community level, i.e., they marry within the society. But they maintain exogamy at the level of *ru*. A man can not marry a girl of his own *ru*. They prefer and practise adult marriage, and the mode of acquiring mate is by negotiation. They practise monogamy. Married women wear *bokhu* and *pandhe* (a female dress) as symbols of marriage. They pay dowry in cash and in kind. Bride-price system now gives way to dowry system. A few family living in the interior hills still practise bride-price system, in which a token amount of Rs. 121/- is to be given. After marriage, bride lives with her husband. Divorce is not permitted. Junior sororate is permissible. Widower remarriage is permissible, but widow cannot remarry.

The Sherpas, nowadays, prefer to live in nuclear families. However, a few still live in mixed extended families. The father is the head of the family. The relation between husband and wife is of love and cordiality. The relation between mother-in-law and son-in-law is of avoidance. Conflict within the family can be observed and the conflict arises on such issues as restrictions on freedom of the youngsters or challenge to the authority of the elders. Father's property is inherited by sons equally; daughters do not get any share. The eldest son succeeds his father as the head of the family with all social and ritual rights. During festivals and rituals, inter-family linkages can be observed. A recent change is the rise in the nuclear families.

Women have various roles in their day to day life, like collection of fuel woods, fetching drinking water from the springs, participation in social and ritual functions etc. They also participate in economic activities, and can be found selling woollen garments during leisure time. They contribute their earnings to the family management, but do not control family expenditure. They have low status than the male members of the society.

The Sherpas observe pre- and post-delivery restrictions. Post-delivery pollution for seven days is observed by them in the case of a male child and for three days if it is a female child. Marriage rituals are performed at bride's house. A *Lama* presides over the ceremony.

Sindurdan at the time of marriage is done, but they do not regard it as a symbol of marriage. A feast is arranged by the bride's parent. The nuptial ceremony is held on the third day after marriage at the groom's residence. They bury their dead. They observe thirty-nine days' pollution period. After seven days the *lama* propitiates the deceased soul. On the thirty-ninth day the purification ceremony is held.

The Sherpas are mainly a landless community, though they depend on land. They are horticulturists. Their traditional and present occupation is to produce potato in the hill terrain. The other present occupation is to work as porters in hill towns like Darjeeling, Kalimpong etc. The corps of special porters used in all the Mount Everest expeditions and other rock climbing expeditions is recruited almost entirely from the Sherpa community and they have proved their worth on every important Himalayan expedition. The subsidiary occupations are business, service in government and private sectors, etc. Child labour is reported. The mode of exchange is through cash. The recent change observed is that, due to landlessness, they are largely being engaged as day labourers and as plantation labour in tea gardens.

The Sherpas have traditional councils for settling disputes among themselves. The council consists of two members and the head is selected by voice vote. The statutory *panchayat* looks after developmental programme and welfare of the villagers.

The Sherpas profess Buddhism. They worship Buddha Bhagawan, Snage, Guru Rimbuchhe, Jherambochhi, etc. The *lama*s are their traditional sacred specialists. The *lama* is often from same community or from the other neighbouring groups, such as the Lepcha, or the Tamang. *Gompha* is their traditional sacred centre. They visit the *gompha* at Ghoom during Buddha Purnima.

The Sherpas have no traditional art, except only a few women knitting woollen garments and selling them in the local market and in the Darjeeling city market. They have rich folk tales and songs. An example is given below :-

"*Keene Am-i-Ke shum,*
Sani Ab-i-So shum
Soh-ihala..." (Mother gave birth and father made me a man).

The *lama*s take water and food from the Sherpas. They have ritual *miter sahin* (*dharam bhai*) with other communities. They share drinking water sources, schools, roads, etc., with others. They have cultivator-labour relationships with the Nepalese communities. The community have government service holders, teachers, political leaders, etc.

The Sherpas are little educated. They use modern medicine and folk medicine, and take the facilities of the family welfare programmes. Springs and rivulets are their main water sources. Very few of them get IRDP loans. The transistor radio is the only mode of mass media. Sherpa villages are mainly devoid of electricity. Fuel wood is their only fuel. They do not use fertilizer in their potato fields. Children get bread at their schools. They avail themselves of the facilities of ration system. Attitude towards savings is not favourable and they depend on money lenders and shop keepers.

AMITABHA MITRA

SIKH

The Sikhs are also known as 'Sardarji'. The Sikhs are a religious community. The word Sikh is derived from the Sanskrit word *sisya* which means disciple. Guru Nanak Dev was the founder of Sikhism. The Sikhs are defined as the followers of Guru Nanak Dev and of nine other Sikh *gurus*. The Sikhs are of two types, *viz.* Sahajdharis, i.e. apprentices or beginners who do not keep long hair but believe in the Guru and follow some Sikh tenets, and Amritdharis or those who have been formally baptized. Both these subgroups recite *Gurbani*. The Amritdharis, in addition, put on the symbols decreed by the tenth master Guru Govind Singh as members of the Khalsa.

The history of the Sikhs of West Bengal and especially of Calcutta is as old as the history of Sikhism. Guru Nanak Dev first visited Calcutta during one of his 'Udasis' on his way to the Lord Jagannath temple in Puri. The Sikh Sangat Gurdwara at Burra Bazaar is associated with the visit of Guru Nanak Dev to Calcutta.

The history of the Sikhs of West Bengal is indeed the history of the Sikhs of Calcutta. The Sikhs after migrating to Calcutta dispersed in search of job opportunities to the adjoining sub-urban areas and different districts of West Bengal in course of time.

They are divided into various ethnic subgroups like Khatri, Jat, Mazhabi, Arora and so on. The titles Singh and Kaur are used by men and women respectively. The Sikhs are widely distributed throughout the state. They are, however, concentrated in the towns and cities like Calcutta, Kharagpur, Asansol and so on. The contact of the Sikhs with the state government goes back to the British period when they came to this state as bodyguards, transport owners, *darwans*, defence personnel etc. During the First World War the Sikhs were part of the military contingents that were sent to different countries by ship from Calcutta. After the war, the Sikhs were employed in government offices, jute mills and private organisations as *darwans* (security guards). The Sikhs were also recruited as drivers in 'Indian Taxi', a company established by the Britishers. Later on they also started their own transport businesses. During the Second World War many businessmen sold their business houses to the Sikhs at very low prices. Sikhs diversified their business mainly in the field of *dhabas* (restaurants), transport, textiles and so on. Their population as per 1981 census was 49,054 individuals. They speak Punjabi among themselves and Hindi and Bengali with the members of other communities. Similarly, they use Gurmukhi script among themselves and Devanagari and Bengali with others. They can be easily identified by their turban, flowing beards and moustaches. The men wear *kurta* (a kind of small jacket) and *pyjama*, or trouser and shirt and a turban while the women wear *salwar*, *kamiz* (loose fitting shirt), and *dupatta*. Some of the ladies have also started wearing saris recently.

They are both vegetarian and non-vegetarian. Non-vegetarian food includes chicken and mutton. Their staple food is *roti* (bread), and *dal*, i.e. pulses. They consume locally available roots, tubers, leafy green vegetables and fruits. Tea, milk and milk products like *lassi* (yoghurt) are their favourite drinks. The various other favourite dishes include *sarson-da-sag* (leaves of the mustard plant), *makki-di-roti* (bread made of maize flour). Mustard oil, groundnut oil and *desi ghee* (made from clarified butter) are their medium of cooking. Nowadays they have also started taking fish and rice. Men take alcoholic drinks on special occasions. The use of tobacco and tobacco products is totally prohibited. The increase in the consumption of fish and rice are the recent changes in their food habits.

They are endogamous. Various groups of Sikhs, viz. Khatri Sikh, Ramgharia Sikh, Jat Sikh, Mazhabi Sikh and so on marry among their own groups and observe *got* exogamy. There is still geographical endogamy. Malwa, Doaband, Manjha persons still prefer to select the mates from their own respective eco-cultural zones. However due to the impact of migration, marriages within inter-cultural zone, and inter-state marriages are also observed. Their social position in regional social hierarchy is fairly high. They prefer adult marriages which are arranged with the help of *vichola* (mediator). They mostly seek marriage alliance from Punjab or in few cases they also select mates locally. The local selection of mates is a recent development. They practise monogamy. There is no marriage symbol. A few married women however, use vermilion. Payment of dowry is not obligatory but dowry may be given in the form of cash or kind or both depending upon the financial condition of the bride's family. The post-marital residence is patrilocal. Divorce is very rare but is allowed due to maladjustment. Remarriage of widow, widower, divorced male or female is permissible. Recently the age of marriage has been increased.

They live in both joint and nuclear families. Any avoidance relationship is not observed strictly. It is replaced by respect towards elders. Rule of inheritance is patrilineal. The eldest son gets the succession.

Women do household jobs. A few are also employed. The Sikh women are treated as equals with their men folk. They contribute their earnings to the family and share the economic burden with their husbands in the family.

The Sikhs observe a number of rituals on the occasions of birth, marriage and death. Pre-delivery rituals and post-natal restrictions on the mother do exist. The post-natal pollution period extends for thirteen days. At the birth of a child, a drop of honey placed on the tip of *kirpan* over which the *mul mantra* has been read, is put into the mouth of the newborn. After that a prayer is offered. A passage is read from Guru Granth Sahib and the first letter of *Shabad* is regarded as a key letter and the congregation is asked to suggest a suitable name beginning with that letter. The name is approved and announced with *jaikars* (*Bolay so Nihal sat Sri Akal*). The ceremony is known as *namkaran*.

During the childhood, the *amrit-chakhna* ceremony is observed either in the house or in a Gurudwara. The Holy Book is opened. The *panj piyara* (five Khalsas) who possess all the five symbols sit in front of the Holy Book. The recipients after taking a bath and putting on new clothes stand up with folded hands. Then one of the five Khalsas tells them about the principles of Khalsa and asks them to signify their acceptance. After the recipients have given their consent, one of the five Khalsas offers a prayer for the preparation of *amrit*. They sit in a circle for the preparation of *amrit*. They place an iron vessel in the centre with some water and *batasa* (sugar pellets) on it. One by one they come in front of the vessel and recite Japji, Jap, Saheb, ten *swayyas*, *chaupai* and Anand Sahib while stirring the water with a sword. Then the five Khalsas stand up and offer a prayer. The *amrit* is then ready for distribution. Each candidate is called to receive the *amrit*. He makes a cup of his hands and drinks five handfuls uttering "*waheguru ji ka Khalsa, waheguru ji ke fateh*". Then *amrit* is poured five times in his eyes and five times in his hair. Each time the candidate utters the above *mantra*. Whatever is left in the vessel is drunk by the candidates one after another. Then each candidate recites *mul mantra* five times. One of the five Khalsas then tells the candidates to the vows of the disciples and the commands of Guru Govind Singh. Hereafter they are known as Khalsa. They consider Guru Govind Singh and Mata Saheb Kaur as their father and mother respectively. They are to offer *nit-nam* (daily prayer), to contribute or use *daswand* (one tenth of their income) regularly for religious and charitable purposes and to wear five *kaka's*. They are to keep away from four *kurkahats* (misdeeds) namely the cutting of hair, eating *halal* meat, adultery and use of tobacco. If they do any of these misdeeds, they must be re-baptised. They are also to refrain from doing certain misdeeds called *tankhas*. After the ceremony one of the five Khalsas offers prayer and reads from the Granth Sahib. If a candidate is one who formerly professed another religion he is given a Sikh name. At the end, all the baptised Sikhs eat *karah prasad* out of the same vessel.

Marriage takes place either at the residence of the bride or in a Gurudwara according to the Sikh tradition of *anand kharaj*. The relations of the boy pay a visit to the house of the girl where they are entertained. Some sweets are given to them for the boy. This meeting is held in the presence of *Guru Granth Sahib*. The bridegroom along with his friends goes to the bride's residence or to the Gurudwara where the bride is also present. The parties sing hymns, offer prayers and welcome each other. Early morning of the next day, the two parties assemble in the presence of *Guru Granth Sahib* and after *asa-di-var*; the bride and the bridegroom are seated in front of the Holy Book. Then the *granthi* (priest) or any person asks the couple and their parents to stand up and invoke god's blessing. Then he tells them about the new phase of life they are about to enter and their respective duties. After that the scarf of the bridegroom is placed in the hands of the bride and the couple stands up. Then the *lavan* (four hymns) are read out from the 'Holy Book'. After the recitation of each *lavan* the couple go round the *Guru Granth Sahib*, with the bridegroom in front followed by the bride. The musicians or *sangat* repeat the same *lavan*. At the end of each *lavan* the couple bow down and take their seats. Thereafter *Anand* is read out. After *Ardas*, *karah prasad* is distributed.

They cremate their dead and observe mourning for ten days. The friends and relatives read *Japji* or *Sukhamani* or perform *sadharan akhand path* (recitation). Generally the bereaved family keeps a *path* on the *Guru Granth Sahib* in the house or in the Gurudwara. On the tenth day friends and relatives attend the *bhog* ceremony and then a prayer is offered for the solace of the departed person. The ceremony ends with the distribution of *karah prasad*.

Their main resource in urban areas is business while both land and business is their resource base in rural areas. They are also engaged in industry, government and public service. They own workshops, repair shops, motor parts shops, petrol pumps etc. A few Sikhs are also cloth merchants, tailors and *dhaba* (restaurant) owners. A good number of Sikhs are policemen, defence personnel, security men, government officers, teachers, administrators and scientists.

They have their own association which is known as Gurudwara Prabandhak Committee. The role of the association is to plan and implement measures for the welfare of the community and to preach their religion. *Akal Takht* is their supreme religious authority and is empowered to punish any Sikh for the violation of religious norms.

They follow Sikh religion and worship in the Gurudwaras. The *granthi* is their sacred specialist. He comes from the Sikh community and performs rituals associated with the life cycle events and gives religious teachings also. They celebrate Diwali, Dussehra, Baisakhi, Sahidi Diwas, Lohri and the local *puja* with the Bengali. They also observe the birthdays of Guru Nanak Dev and Guru Govind Singh when processions are taken out and congregational prayers and recitation from the *Guru Granth Sahib* are held.

The folk song is generally accompanied by the playing upon *dholak* (drum). *Gohri* is a marriage song. Among the Sikhs *boli* and *tappa* are quite popular. *Bhangra* is their most popular folk dance. Both men and women participate in folk song and folk dance.

Inter-community linkage is maintained by the collective performance of different rituals and festivals. They accept and exchange water and foods with other communities. They have employee-employer, cultivator-labourer and landlord-tenant relationship with other communities.

They are highly advanced community. Boys and girls are given higher education. They have positive attitude towards modern medicare and family planning methods.

The contribution of the Sikh towards development of education and culture of the state is worth mentioning. They established Khalsa High School in Bhawanipur in 1933. Desh Darpan, a daily Punjabi newspaper was published since 1930. They also published Navi Prabhat. Khalsa Gazette was published from 1950 to 1980. Sajjari Pairh was established in 1968 by the Punjabi Sahit Sabha, Calcutta as a quarterly magazine. However, since 1978, it is published as a monthly magazine.

SWARAN SINGH

SIYALGIR

The Siyalgirs are a very small community of the state. They have migrated from the Saurasthra region of the Gujarat state at a distant past, according to Mitra, "six or seven generations ago" (Mitra : 1953:81). The distribution of the Siyalgirs is confined only to the plains of Mohanpur police station of the Medinipur district. They use Bengali script at home and with outsiders.

The Siyalgirs are non-vegetarian. They eat fish, egg, meat, etc. Rice is the staple food. They take all kinds of vegetables which are available in the market. They consume pulses like *urad, mug, masur,* etc. They use mustard oil for cooking. They occasionally consume alcoholic drinks. They drink tea and milk products. Fruit consumption is limited and occasional. They smoke *bidi*s and cigarettes.

They have no social divisions. All of them belong to a single *gotra* and Kashyapa is the *gotra* name. They use their surnames as Baraik/ Barik, Das, Jana, Patra, etc. They regard themselves higher than the Muchi, the Dom, the Bhangi, etc., and they rank themselves below the Kamar, the Kumbhar, the Napit, the Karan, etc.

They practise community endogamy. Due to a single *gotra*, they marry within the *gotra*. However, they avoid marital relationship with three ascending generations in father's line. They practise adult marriage and prefer marriage by negotiation. They prefer monogamy. Married women use *sindur* as a symbol of marriage. Bride price in cash and kind is present among them. After marriage wife lives with her husband. Divorce is permissible with social approval and the reasons for divorce are adultery, maladjustment and barrenness. However, cases of divorces are very rare among them. Either party can seek for divorce. Children are liability to either mother or father. Divorce compensation is given to the aggrieved party. Divorced men and women can marry again. Widow and widower remarriage is also permissible. Nowadays, incidence of divorce shows a rising tendency.

The Siyalgirs prefer to live in nuclear families though there are a few extended families. Father is regarded as the head of the family. Avoidance relationship is found between daughter-in-law and father-in-law, joking relation is observed between husband's younger and elder brother's wife. Conflict arises in the family on property share. Father's property is inherited equally by the sons. Succession of father's social and ritual rights goes to the eldest son. The recent change is a rise in the number of nuclear family.

Women do not inherit their father's property. The women have various roles in their day to day life. They have roles in the collection of fuel wood, bringing and fetching drinking water, fishing in canals, etc. They have roles in social, religious and economic activities of life. They have no roles in political activities. They contribute their earnings from selling fish to the family management; however, they do not control family expenditure. They have low status than the male members of the society.

They observe some pre-delivery restrictions. They also observe post-natal pollution and restrictions. Normally, they observe seven days pollution after childbirth. Name giving ceremony and the ceremony of first feeding of cereals are observed on the sixth or seventh month of the baby. Marriage ceremony is performed at bride's house in the presence of a priest from their own community. *Malabadal*, *sindurdan*, etc., are the main rituals in the marriage ceremony. Marriage feast is given by bride's parents. Nuptial ceremony is performed on the third day after marriage. They cremate their dead bodies. They observe thirteen days pollution period after death. They perform the purification and *sraddha* ceremony on the thirteenth day. On that day they arrange a feast for the relatives and for the villagers.

The major economic activity of the Siyalgirs is selling vegetables and fish in the local market. They are a landless community. As regards their traditional occupation, Mitra observed that "some sell fish some sell groceries, some cultivate, some make and sell bamboo mats and a few are cultivators" (Mitra :1953:81). They have direct link with daily and weekly market and the form of exchange is through cash. Due to landlessness, the number of day labourers is increasing among them.

The Siyalgirs have a traditional caste panchayat, which consists of three official members selected through voice votes, of which the senior most member acts as a chief. The statutory *panchayat* exists to look after the welfare activities of the villagers.

They profess Hinduism. They worship all the gods and goddesses of Hindu religion, like Saraswati, Lakshmi, Manasa, Durga, Kali, Shiva, etc. Brahmans normally do not attend any of their religious functions. However, nowadays a few Utkal Brahmans attend as a priest to their rituals, worships, etc. They observe Janmasthami as a great festival. They visit Puri, Jaleshwar, Haridwar, etc., the pilgrimage centres.

The Siyalgirs do not take water or any kind of food from the Muchi, the Dom, the Hari, the Bhangi, etc. The Brahman, the Kayastha, the Karan, the Kamar, the Mahishya do not accept water from them and in this sense they are a *jal-achal* community. However, the Kayastha, the Karan, the Brahman, etc. accept *sidha* from them. They share drinking water sources, roads, crematorium, schools, *panchayat ghar*, etc., with others. They have cultivator-labour relationship, and other symbolic relationships with others.

They are not aware of the benefit of education and only a few boys attend schools. They use folk medicine and also use modern medicines from government health clinics. Wells are their main water source. A few among them get IRDP loans to construct permanent stalls in the market. They use transistor radio as a means of mass media. They do not use electricity. Coal and cowdung cakes are the fuel which they use for cooking. They are beneficiaries of the public distribution system, but do not use banking facilities. They depend on moneylenders and shop keepers.

AMITABHA MITRA

SOUTH-INDIAN

The South-Indians are an immigrant community from the four southern states, i.e. Andhra Pradesh, Karnataka, Kerala and Tamil Nadu. The community has titles like Rao, Menon, and Nair etc. They are mainly concentrated in Calcutta. In Calcutta they are spread throughout the urban complex. But their main concentration is around Lake Market, Deshapriya Park, Lake Gardens, and Monohar Pukur Road in South Calcutta. They have sub-groups like Kannadigas, Malayalis, Tamils and Telegus. They can be identified at national level. The community has both ethnographic and historical account. The South-Indians are found mainly in four South-Indian states and metropolitan cities. Geographically, Calcutta is situated on Ganga delta with flat land surface. The city experiences warm and temperate climate with an average maximum temperature of 37.8° Celsius in summer and minimum temperature of 14.7° Celsius in winter. The average rainfall is 1320 mm and high relative humidity is recorded during the monsoon season. They speak in Kannada, Malayalam, Tamil and Telugu languages within family and kin groups and use Kannada, Malayalam, Tamil, Telugu and Roman script for writing. They speak in English, Bengali and occasionally in Hindi and write in Roman script to communicate with others. The South Indian women are identified by their dress, ornaments like nose stud, *thali* etc. and by the flower worn in their hair.

The South-Indian have mixed food habits, while the Hindu Brahmans are pure vegetarian, the other castes and Christians are non-vegetarian. Their staple food is rice. They use *tur, urad* and *moong* as pulses. Their common dishes are *rasam* (curry), *sambar* (pulses with mixed vegetables), and *dahi bhat* (curd rice). Their common snacks are *dosa, idli, upma, utthapam, vada etc.* As cooking medium they previously used linseed and coconut oil, but now they prefer groundnut oil and rapeseed oil. They consume roots and tubers. They consume very little fruit. The South-Indians in general prefer coffee over tea. They take milk and milk products. They smoke cigarettes and chew betel. There are changes in food habits among them. Nowadays many of them take different items of non-vegetarian food, prefer *roti* to ricc as staple food and their consumption of fruit has also increased.

They have social divisions based on lineage and sub-caste. This differentiation is based on social religious, territorial and occupational distinctions. The main functions of these divisions are to regulate marriage alliance, indicate social status, ancestry and social control. They are aware of *varna* system. They have divisions like Brahmans, Kshatriya, and Vaishya and Sudra. Brahmans have divisions like Nambudries, Elayado, and Muthads. Kshatriyas at present have little difference with the Nairs. Kshatriyas were originally associated with ruling families while Nairs were a martial caste and formed the militia of the country. Their sub-castes are Kiriyam, Illam and Swarupi. Ambala vasis's traditional occupation was the performance of different services at temples. Their sub-divisions are Nambidis, Adikals, Chakiyars, Numbiyars, Thiyattunnis, Variyars and Marars, Sudras *i.e.* communities of lower order are Veluthandans (washermen), Vilakkithala Nairs (barber), Chaliyans (weavers) and Kadupattan (degraded Brahmans). They also have polluting castes like Kammalans, Ezhavas, and Valans. Ezhavas have gone up in the social ladder since Temple Entry Proclamation. In some areas their social status is higher than that of the Nairs. Their unity, by functioning as a well knit group through their caste organisation, the Sree Narayana Dharma Paripalan Sangha, and their numerical superiority have made them a powerful caste group in the south, and mainly in Kerala. The South-Indians originally had their surname at the beginning of their proper name. This surname indicates the father's name and place of origin. In case of Malayali subgroups, they use mother's name. But nowadays the South-Indians use the proper name of the head of the family as surname. viz. P. P. Damodaran's son and daughter use Damodaran as their surname and that also comes after their proper name. In some cases people use their caste name as surname e. g. Panikar, Pillai, Nainar, Menon, Rao etc.

In south India marriages are allowed only between persons belonging to two different exogamous group of an endogamous caste. Two important preferential marriages are highly prevalent, i.e. (1) maternal uncle-cross, niece marriage and (2) cross-cousin marriage - (a) mother's brother's daughter and father's sister's son and (b) father's sister's daughter and mother's brother's son. Marriages between *sapindas* and *sapravaras* are not permitted. Brahmans have endogamous sub-divisions which can not inter-marry within themselves. Marriage with same *gotra* is prohibited. Among Ranikkar no marriage within same clan is possible. In Kerala, the Kshatriyas follow hypergamy in some cases. In some parts of South India, the institution of domestic deity serves to define exogamous unit in the absence of known genealogical link. In the Christian community nuclear family is the exogamous unit. Marriage between cross-uncle and niece is forbidden among Nayars. They usually prefer adult marriage. Mate is acquired mainly through negotiation. But marriage by courtship and negotiation is also common in case of inter-community marriage. They usually follow monogamy. The marriage symbols of women are bangles, *thalli*, nose stud etc. The marriage symbol for Christian women is finger ring. They practise dowry system, which varies between various sub-groups. Dowry is paid both in cash and kind especially gold ornaments, silver and brass vessels, and costly dress. But in the Malayalese sub-groups, there is no dowry, particularly among castes which follow matrilineal inheritance. Among the non-Brahman communities in Kerala, the bride-groom is not supposed to take anything from the bride's family except ornaments. The rule of residence after marriage is patrilocal except in cases of some castes in Kerala where matrilocal residence is practised but now neolocal residence is becoming common. Either of the parties can divorce with judicial approval for adultery, maladjustment, chronic sickness, cruelty, insanity etc. Divorce compensation is to be given to the aggrieved party. Remarriage of widow, widower, male and female divorcees is permissible. The case of remarriage for widow and female divorcees, in case of Tamil, Telugu and Kannadis is not common. There is an increase in age at marriage. The rules of remarriage have been liberalised.

They have both nuclear and mixed extended type of family. The conflict and confrontation in the family is mainly due to the generation gap. The South-Indian community as a whole represents a complex rule of inheritance. Among Tamil, Telugu, Kanadis and some castes of Kerala, the male equigeniture is practised as the rule of inheritance. In other cases, where matrilineal inheritance is practised, there the situation is somewhat complex. In those cases the maternal uncle looks after the property on behalf of his nephew. So in that case the grandson is the main inheritor through his mother. In both the cases the eldest son succeeds his father as the head of the family. But in case of matrilineal inheritance, he becomes head of his sister's family. There is a rise in the formation of nuclear families. There are some changes in inheritance rule, like the daughters also get share of the property. Matrilocal residence and matrilineal inheritance are also becoming obsolete in case of South-Indians. South-Indian women have roles in economic activity and social function. Many women of this community are engaged in schools and offices, mainly as teachers, in secretarial jobs, as officers, clerks and creative artists. Women have equal status to men. They take decision in family and community matters. They contribute to family income and control family expenditure.

They observe pre-delivery rituals on the fifth, seventh and ninth months of pregnancy. Among Tamil sub-groups, in the sixth month, pregnant women wear new glass bangles in the mother's house. A ceremony is held in husband's place on the eighth month. In all the cases the delivery pollution is observed for 21 days in case of baby girl and for boy it is for 27 days. Now mother observes restriction for one month. She does not go to kitchen or do any household chores. *Namakarana* (naming) ceremony is observed on the tenth day. *Chaula (mundan* or head shaving) is an important occasion for South-Indian child. It is observed generally between the age of one to five years and in a temple. The Brahmans observe *upanayana* (thread-wearing) ceremony for boys. Among them marriage rituals are performed at bride's residence, but in Calcutta they prefer either community halls or temples. The feast is given by bride's parents. The consummation ceremony is performed at groom's residence. In case of South-Indian Christians, marriage is performed at the Church of the bride. The South-Indian Hindus cremate their dead body but Christians bury it. The Hindus observe 10 days' pollution period after the death of near relatives and observe ancestor worship. The Christians in some cases observe 40 days' mourning period. Some rituals mainly related to marriage and death has been curtailed. But marriage rituals have become very expensive.

The main occupation of South-Indians is service in government and private firms, restaurants, business houses etc. Nowadays some of them are also engaged in business and trade or are self-employed. Women of this community are also engaged in various services. They have direct link with daily market. The medium of exchange is cash. There is no child labour among them and the wages are paid in cash.

They have a few associations like Andhra Association, Mysore Society, Malayalam Samajam, and Tamil Association. Some of these associations have schools like Andhra Association School and National High School (Tamil). In these schools the medium of teaching is English but they also teach their respective mother tongue. These associations have halls for the performance of various functions. These associations arrange sports and cultural activities. They sometimes award stipends to good students.

They have two distinct religious groups, i.e. Hindu and Christians. Christians have sub-groups like Protestant, and Catholics. The Protestant are further sub-divided into the followers of the Church of South-Indian Baptists, Lutherans, Marthomites, Catholics have divisions like Romo-Syrian and Jacobites. Hindus have family and regional deities like Meenakshi, Subrahmaniam, Durga, Shiva, Balaji etc. Both Hindus and Christians have sacred specialists from the same community. The priest worship and perform birth, marriage, and death rites. Tamilians celebrate Pongal, Savitri-bratam, Adiperuku, Ameneabittam, and Vinayak Chaturithi. The Telugu community celebrates Ugadi, Rsam Navami, Gouri-Puja, and Ganesh Chaturthi. The Malayalam community celebrates Onam, New Year and Makar Sankranti and Kanada community celebrates New Year, Janmastami. All of them celebratc Dussersa and Diwali. The Christians celebrates Christmas, New Year, Good Friday and Easter. They have both traditional and classical dance and music. Their important instruments are *mridangam, panjobajom* etc.

The higher caste people do not accept water from lower caste people traditionally. But they do not follow the traditional relationship strictly. They have their own shrines. They participate in traditional festivals like Holi and Diwali. They have entrepreneurs like scholars, creative artists, teachers, administrators, doctors, etc., in their community.

The South-Indian boys and girls generally study up to college level and some of them receive higher education. After completion of study boys generally earn for family and girls either get married or earn for family. They avail themselves of modern medical facilities. Their attitude is favourable towards family planning. Couples prefer one or two children. They use modern methods of family planning. Drinking water from pipe lines is available within the locality. With the help of self-employment scheme they have started small-scale industry. They listen to radio, watch television and visit cinema. They have convenient connection of road and rail. They use electricity for domestic purpose. Kerosene oil and LPG are used as fuel for cooking. They enjoy ration distribution through fair price shops and have favourable attitude towards savings.

SMITA SENGUPTA

SUBARNABANIK

The Subarnabaniks are traders and bankers of Bengal. Risley (1891 : 261) mention that they claim to be the modern representatives of the ancient Vaishya. Bania, Banik, Sonarbene, Poddar are their synonyms. Roy, Mandal, Chowdhury, etc., are their titles. The word Subarnabanik is derived from the traders of gold. They are divided into four subgroups viz. i) Rarhi; ii) Saptagrami; iii) Dishi; and iv) Begampuri, Mitra (1953 : 34) has referred to *Brhaddharma Purana* which indicates that Subarnabanik and Swarnakara originated from Ambastha father and Vaishya mother. They claim that they came from Oudh and this has been mentioned by Risley also. They perceive their distribution at regional level. The studied areas are characterised by plains, warm and temperate climate, high humidity and medium rainfall. They speak and write in Bengali.

The somatometric information on the Subarnabaniks is available from the work of Majumdar and Rao (1960) and Mitra (unpublished), cited by Gupta and Dutta (1966). Available information are as follows : mean values of stature ranges from 1695.32 to 1725 mm. cephalic index ranges from 79.57 to 83.98, and nasal index varies from 66.06 to 72.44, facial index is 87.24.

The Subarnabaniks eat fish, meat of goat and fowls but not beef or pork. Rice is their staple cereals. Sometimes *roti* (hand-made wheat bread) is consumed at night. *Biri kalai* (black gram) is their favourite pulse dish. They use mustard oil as cooking medium. They consume all seasonal vegetables and fruits in a moderate way. *Alu-posta* (special preparation of potato and opium seeds) is their favourite dish. Most of them drink milk and tea. Some of their male members drink alcohol occasionally. They take milk product. Their male members smoke *bidis*, cigarettes or take snuff and both male and female members chew betel. They do not eat radish in the month of *Magha* (January February). Increase in the use of pulses is reported.

The community is divided into sub-castes subgroups and clans/ *gotras*. Differentiations of subgroups are territorially based, but they are not aware of hierarchy. Nagrishi, Moudgalya, Parashara, etc. are their names of *gotras*. Those differentiations (subgroups and *gotras*) regulate marriage alliances. *Gotras* indicate descent order also. Self-perception of the community vis-à-vis other communities in local social hierarchy is middle. They recognise themselves as Vaishya.

Endogamy at community level and exogamy at *gotra* level are their marriage rules. They negotiate marriage at the adult age of their sons and daughters. Monogamy is their general form. Vermilion and bangles of conch-shell and iron are marriage symbols of women. Dowry in cash and kind is practised. They live at patrilocal residence after marriage. Divorce due to adultery and maladjustment is permissible with judicial approval. Both parties can divorce and compensation or status of children depends on the decision of court. Remarriage of widow is not permissible. Female divorcee remarriages are accepted. Junior sororate is permissible only after the death of the first wife. Relaxation in endogamy at subgroup level, increase in age at marriage, decline in incidence of separation, introduction of divorce with judicial approval and social acceptance of some female divorcee remarriages are major changes in their society.

The Subarnabaniks mostly belong to nuclear families but extended families are not absent. Avoidance relationship is found in a family between *shashuri* and *jamai* (wife's mother and daughter's husband) and with *shvashur* and *bhasur* (husband's father and elder brother), whereas joking relationship exists with *shala* and *shali* (younger siblings of wife) and grandparents. Unequal sharing of property and of workload causes conflict in a family. Equigeniture is their rule of inheritance whereas the eldest son succeeds to father's responsibility. Inter-family linkages are established through different festive occasions and ritual observances. Increase in the formation of nuclear families and male equigeniture giving way to equigeniture (for all children) as the rules of inheritance are reported.

Now, the Subarnabanik women have the right to inherit their father's property. Besides household work many of them are engaged in different services. They perform significant role in ritual performances. The Subarnabanik women worship Lakshmi and make arrangements for worship of Mangalachandi, Satyanarayan, etc. Some of them are also involved in politics. Generally, family expenditures are controlled by the women. But they are not independent.

The Subarnabaniks observe a good number of rituals related to life cycle. They observe *panchamrita* in the fifth month and *sadh* in the ninth month of pregnancy of a woman. Shasthi puja is observed on the sixth or ninth or twenty-first day as post-delivery ritual. They observe post-delivery pollution for one month. *Annaprashan* (first rice feeding ceremony) is observed on the sixth month for a male child and on the seventh month for a female child. They bring *prasad* (food offered to a god) from a sacred centre and the *mama* (mother's brother) puts that *prasad* into the mouth of the child. Barber shaves the head of the child on that day. Some of them shave the head hair of the child on the eighteenth month at Tarakeswar (a sacred place for Hindus). When the boys and girls become adult their parents negotiate marriage. After completion of negotiation a marriage date is finalised and the bride's party go to the boy's home to bless him. *Gayehalud* (smearing of turmeric on the body), *nannimukh* (or *nandimukh*, i.e., ancestor worship) etc. are performed at both the houses of the bride and the bridegroom on the very day of main marriage ceremony. Main marriage ceremony is performed at bride's residence. *Sindurdan* (smearing of vermilion on the hair parting of the bride), *malabadal* (exchange of garland), etc. are essential rites to be observed on this occasion. Bride's father arranges a feast on that day. *Boubhat* ceremony is observed at bridegroom's residence on the second day of marriage. Bridegroom's father invites kin, relatives, neighbours and friends on the third day of marriage. Marriage is consummated at bridegroom's residence on that day. Some of them worship Bageshwari (goddess of learning) on the second day of marriage, *gachbera* (a kind of plant) on the day of marriage and Manasa from the day before marriage to *ashtamangala* (eighth day of marriage). The Subarnabaniks cremate dead body. They observe a pollution period for fifteen days and perform *ghat* rite on the fifteenth day and *sradhha* (propitiation of ancestors) on the sixteenth day. *Anshpanna* rite is observed on the seventeenth day. They invite their kin, relatives and neighbours on the day of *sradhha*, whereas some kin are invited on the occasion of *anshpanna* in a non-vegetarian feast. Some of the rituals have been curtailed, viz. puberty rites for females are not observed and pollution after death has been curtailed from thirty to fifteenth days. Observation of rituals is becoming more expensive.

Traditionally, the Subarnabaniks are traders in gold and gold ornaments. They also make gold ornaments. Now, many of them are engaged in the business of cloth, transport, etc. or are engaged in service. Most of them are owners of agricultural land. So, agriculture is their subsidiary occupation. They carry out their business either directly or through middlemen in exchange of cash. They pay their agricultural labourers both in cash and kind.

They have no caste panchayat, *Gram panchayat*, the statutory council plans and implements welfare and development activities along with other communities of the village.

A great majority of them belong to the Vaishnav sect of Hindus but they worship all the local deities. Lakshmi (who is in their view identical with Radha) and *tulsi* basil plant are propitiated at the family level, whereas Dharmaraj, Kali, etc. are their village deities. Dharmaraj, Manasa etc. are their regional deities also. The Brahman priest performs their different worship and rituals. Durga puja and Kali puja are recognised as their major festivals.

The women make *alpana* (floor painting) on different occasions related to worship or rituals performances. They also make beautiful designs on gold ornaments. Different myths about them are in vogue. One such myth is as follows: The Subarnabaniks say that their ancestors came from Oudh during the reign of Adisura. They were degraded by Ballal Sen, the king of Bengal. Once the king had to expiate for his illicit love with a low caste girl and the Subarnabaniks in a body refused to be present at the penance. This attitude of the caste enraged the king. Another offence of the community was the refusal of a leading Subarnabanik to lend Ballal Sen, large sums of money to carry on a war. The king degraded them to take the revenge for their behaviour. Such legends have also been referred to by Risley (1891 : 261-262) Their upgradation was made during the period of Chaitanya Mahaprabhu. Once in a Vaishnav conference, the Brahmans refused to take food as it was served by Uddharan Datta (a leading Subarnabanik of that time). At that time Nityananda Mahaprabhu accepted that food. Thus the community became upgraded.

Traditionally, the Brahmans would not take water from their hands. But now such rigidity is not maintained. They exchange food and water with the Aguri, Gandhabanik, etc., but do not exchange food and water with the Hari, Muchi, etc. Although a few inter-caste love matches are reported with the Tilli, the Tambuli, the Brahman, etc., it is not an accepted norm in their society. Putative kinship terms are not reported. Patron-client relationship exists with the Brahman, the Napit, etc. Members of other communities act as share-croppers or agricultural labourers. They have among them scholars, doctors, engineers, political leaders etc. whose efforts have established modern inter-community linkages also.

As a wealthy community their response towards literacy is favourable. Most of them avail themselves of the modern medical facilities. Some, however, avail themselves of the indigenous medicare also. Potable water is collected from tube wells. Some of them have taken bank loans to purchase trucks, to start grocery shops or garment shops etc. They listen to the radio, visit cinemas and watch television. With the development of transport, the urban areas and metropolis like Calcutta have become accessible. They often go to the urban areas and to the metropolitan city of Calcutta for their business. The Subarnabaniks use electricity for domestic consumption. Coal is the common fuel. Some of them also use cooking gas or *gobar* gas. Shallow tube wells and canal water are their common sources of irrigation. They use organic manure, chemical fertilisers, insecticides and pesticides for better crops. Their children do not avail themselves of the facility of midday meal. Members of the community avail themselves of the rationing facility. They use bank to deposit their money. It is a common character of the community that they are very proud of their wealth.

ARCHANA DATTA

SUNRI

According to Risley, Sunri, Saundika, Sundaka, Shaha are a large and widely diffused caste, found in most districts of Bengal and Bihar, whose original profession is believed to be the manufacture and sale of spirituous liquors. Many of its members have now taken to mercantile pursuits, call themselves by the title, Shaha, and disown all connections with those who still follow the characteristic occupation of the caste. Their striving for social advancement has as yet not been entirely successful, and in spite of their wealth and enterprise ancient associations still hold them down. The bond of tradition is hard to break. According to Hindu ideas distillers and sellers of strong drink rank among the most degraded castes, and a curious story in the Vaivarta Purana keeps alive the memory of their degradation. (Risley, 1891:II:275).

The present field investigations reveals no synonym as well as no segmentation of the caste into subgroups, Some of them, however, mention that they have two occupational divisions among them i.e. ordinary Saha who are engaged only in business and the other group known as "Modo Saha" (*mad* means wine), some of whom are still in their traditional occupation. According to Risley, the Saha caste of central and western Bengal was divided into four sub-castes, like Rarhi, Barendra, Banga, and Magi, which the present day respondents do not seem to be aware of. None of them is able to explain the etymology of the word Saha. Risley (*ibid*:276) mentioned that their only title was Saha or Shaha, but he also pointed out that "on becoming rich a merchant often adopts Das as a surname by way of concealing the fact that he is Sunri" (*ibid*:277). At present they mention only Saha as their caste name. There is a story about the origin of the Sunri caste in Risley's *The Tribes and Castes of Bengal*, "It is said that when Sani, the Hindu Saturn, failed to adapt an elephant's head to the mutilated trunk of Ganesa, who had been accidentally beheaded by Shiva, Viswakarma, the celestial artificer, was sent for, and by careful dissection and manipulation he fitted the incongruous parts together and made a man called Kedara Sena from the slices out off in fashioning his work. This Kedara Sena was ordered to fetch a drink of water for Bhagavati, weary and athirst. Finding on the river's bank a shell full of water he presented it to her without noticing that a few grains of rice left in it by a parrot had fermented and formed an intoxicating liquid. Bhagavati, as soon as she had drunk, became aware of the fact, and in her anger condemned the offender to the vile and servile occupation of making spirituous liquors for mankind" (*ibid* :275-276). According to their version many of their caste men have come from East Bengal and have settled in various parts of West Bengal after partition.

At present the Sunris are distributed all over West Bengal. Major concentration can be found in the districts like Bankura, Burdwan, Birbhum and the 24-Parganas. According to the members of the community studied in the 24-Parganas they perceive that they are distributed in the villages like Gopalpur, Basirhat, Makalgachhi, Pita, Saraupnagore, and Harikathi, and nearby villages in the district of 24-Parganas. The natural environment is that of lower Bengal, i.e. an environment which permits the growth of varieties of vegetables and crops, jungle wood and wild animals like deer and Royal Bengal Tiger etc. The total population of the Sunris was 2,52,331 in West Bengal (1981 census). The language, dialect and script of the community is Bengali in all respects. Their constitutional status is that of a scheduled caste.

The Sunris are a non-vegetarian group of people, but do not eat beef, pork or meat of buffalo. Their staple food is rice with vegetable curry, fish and pulses. Mustard oil is their cooking medium. They take varieties of vegetables as they grow it and can purchase it from the market. They also eat seasonal locally available fruits like mango, jackfruit, litchi, date palm fruits (as the area under study is very renowned for its date palm molasses), palm, black berry, guava, banana, cucumber etc. They take tea in morning and evening and as their economic condition is not so bad and many of them have cows, they can consume milk. They drink alcohol sometimes, purchasing it from the market, as they have to work in agricultural fields. They arrange special food item on different ceremonial occasions. Many of them do not like to take sea fish. They do not take radish after the month of *Paush* (December-January) and *dumur* (fig) and pumpkin in the month of *Bhadra* (August-September). There are some minor changes in the food habit of the Sunris.

It has already been mentioned that the Sunris now give their identity as Saha. In previous days the Sunris were of two categories i.e. one group was responsible for the selling of liquor and others were general businessmen. Even now these two divisions can be met with, but in actual sense, these divisions have no function. According to some of the Sunris, their only *gotras* is Gargarashi and marriage within the same *gotra* is allowed from past days. But according to some others, their *gotras* are Gargarashi, (Maudgalya), Kashyapa, Alman, Sandilya etc. and marriage within the same *gotra* is not allowed. According to the Sunris, the castes like Kahar, Muchi, Dhopa, and Napit are inferior to them and Kamar and Goala are superior to them in social hierarchy. According to the perception of other communities, the Sunris are a very low caste, as well as a scheduled caste, but as they have now improved their economic condition, their position has become high in society. The Sunris think that they belong to Vaishya group in the *varna* order, as their main occupation is business. At present *varna* order system has no significance or function in their society.

Endogamy is the marriage rule of the Sunris. Now their marriages are taking place at the age of fifteen to twenty years for girls and twenty-five to twenty-eight years for boys. Negotiation is the primary mode of acquiring mates. Monogamy is the form of marriage. The symbols of marriage for women are *sankha* (conch shell bangles), *sindur* (vermilion) and *loha* (iron bangle). Now dowry is paid both in cash and kind and the amount varies from Rs. 5000/- to Rs. 20,000/-, according to the economic condition of the family. They have to collect dowry money by selling their landed property. Rules of residence after marriage are patrilocal. Divorce is allowed but its occurrence is very rare. Remarriage is also permissible. The widow remarriage is called *nika*. The noticeable changes in the marriage pattern are the abolition of infant marriage and bride price.

Most of the families of the Sunris are vertically extended or may be described as of vertico-laterally extended type. Some nuclear type families can also be found. Families are bound by various types of interpersonal relationships like those of love, fear, avoidance, obligation etc. Rules of inheritance till now allow only the sons to share their parental properties. Succession to family headship is also through male line. Inter-family linkages are also found on social and religious ceremonies. Women of the Sunri families are found to play their usual roles in traditional Hindu joint family system. They are not so educated and they have no role outside their houses. They have roles in family management, such as picking up grains from harvested plants, preparing food for the family rituals etc. Still at present the daughters are married with heavy amount of dowry, so they are not getting father's property.

After birth the Sunris have to observe a pollution period of one month for female child and twenty-one days for male child. They become purified after three *kaman* rites (cutting of nails and taking of bath). The ninth day's *kaman* rite is called *natia* and on this day the mother and the new born baby along with all the family members are sprinkled by some holy water taken from the temple. The last *kaman* is done on the day of Sasti puja. *Annaprashan* is performed on *chhaychanda*, that means after six full moon days in case of a male child. The child is named at the time of Sasthipuja or *annaprashan*. Marriage of the Sunris starts with *ashirbad*, followed by other rites, like *gayehalud*, sending of *gayehalud tatta*, *abhhuti*, *aiburobhat*, *gangabaran*, *sampradan*, *basar*, *kalratri*, *baubhat* and completed by the marriage consummation rite *phulsajja*. Now the Sunris are following the pollution period of thirteen days after death instead of one month. On the thirteenth day they perform *ghat* rite i.e. a *kaman* rite is performed for sons and lineage members. On the fourteenth day, they perform *sradh* ceremony. On the sixteenth they perform *terodasa*. In *terodasa* function, they generally invite close relatives *(kutum* and *gnati)* to a non-vegetarian feast and from this day onward they are permitted to eat fish or meat. They have to perform also *bachharkria* and *swapindikaran*. The significant charges in the above mentioned aspects are shortening of pollution period after death, abolition of adolescence rite for the girls etc.

Land is the major economic resource of the Sunris. Besides landholding, many of them are businessmen, a very few are service holders. They till the land which they also own on the basis of individual proprietorship. Traditional occupation of the community is cultivation and making of liquor. Now agriculture is their primary occupation. They have grocer's shops, which is a secondary occupation for some persons. The Sunris neither give their land nor take other's land for sharecropping. They sometimes employ day labourers from the Muslim community, refugees, the Napits and Karmakars with a daily wage of Rs. 10/- to Rs. 12/- per day for eight hours' duty. They do not have bonded labour system, and do not employ child labourers.

In previous days they used to have *jati panchayat*, but at present there is no remnant of that panchayat. Now all the disputes are settled by the village elders or by the *gram panchayat* members or by the legal court.

Hinduism is the religion of the Sunris today. Many of them also have taken Vaishnav *mantras*. The Sunris observe various family rituals and worship many household deities. In the month of *Baisakh* (April-May) they have Bhagabati puja and Harish Mangalbar (only performed by married and widow women), *thara* (to hang a small pitcherful of water from the top of a basil plant) and a religious singing group sing Harinam songs throughout the month with '*harilut*' (throwing of *batasha*, a kind of sweet). In the month of *Jaistha* (May-June) they observe Jaymongal Chandi and *Ambubachi*. In the month of *Ashar* (June-July) they observe Ratha Jatra (car festival) of Lord Jagannath. In the month of *Bhadra* they have '*Ranna*' *Puja* and Biswakarma puja. Besides these, their women observe Itu or Ghat puja, Lakshmi, Kulimongal Chandi, Dhana Sudh bandhsa (feeding to paddy plant before harvest), Bauni Sankranti or Paus Parban, Durga Sasti, Durga Astami, Sital Sasti, Sibratri, Neel and Baupuja in the month of *Magh* (January-February). In *Chaitra* (March-April) they observe Charak festival and Holi. Their village deities are Manasa and Kali. Their regional deities are Durga, Kali, Saraswati, Basanti, Shiva, and Jagannath. Brahman priests are their sacred specialists. Barber's services are required for performing various rituals. Their major fair and festivals are Holi and the fair of Hazratala on the occasion of Charak. Their sacred places for pilgrimage are Gaya, Mathura, Brindaban, Tarapith, Dakshineswar, Kalighat etc.

The present community has traditional inter-community linkages with Brahmans and barbers who serve in their ceremonial occasions. There is no restriction on acceptance or exchange of water between various communities but when a priest has to eat in the home of a Sunri, he himself cooks his own meal. He never accepts cooked food from the houses of the Sunris. Some inter-caste marriages also have taken place. There is no system of putative kinship, but when they are disciples of a guru they are all considered as gurubhais irrespective of their caste status. They do not face any problem in sharing village temple or water source or crematorium. They have linkages with various communities as their children are going to schools and colleges, as they have to go to *anchal parisad* office and to the *gram panchayat* for agricultural equipments and participate in religious songs with various communities. The Sunris were involved in a caste movement in the early twentieth century for getting wider recognition of their new caste name as Saha. Today the movement seems to have lost its reason of existence as the Sunris now invariably mention only Saha to designate themselves, and the new name is also socially recognised.

Literacy level of the Sunris is not high. Only one student of first year B. Com. class is the highest qualified person among 150 people in a village studied during the present field investigation. Others have studied up to VIII to X standard. Men and women of the previous generations are found to have studied only up to III or IV standard. All the children of the present generation are going to school. For health and medical care they go to local dispensaries and for more serious cases they go to hospital. They are all accepting family planning measures after two or three children. Their drinking water is procured from their own tube wells. For employment they have to register their names in the Basirhat employment exchange. Their villages are connected by non-metalled road and the mode of communication to the nearest bus stop is rickshaw van. Everyone has radio set and some of them have also television set. Many of them are able to read newspaper in the village library. A very few of them are using electric light. Their conservation of energy resources are through the preparation of "gobar bari" two to four pieces of jute sticks two or to three feet long, are smeared with one inch depth cow-dung). They store it for the whole year's consumption. They irrigate their field with their own shallow tube well or hire it from others. They use chemical and insecticides. Under nutrition programme the children of primary classes sometimes get pieces of bread from their schools. They are availing themselves of the public distribution system, i.e. ration. Though there is a gramin bank, they usually keep their savings in village post offices. They can take loan from the Basirhat co-operative bank after mortgaging their land. It has been found that the Sahas are getting agricultural equipments from the *gram panchayat* after purchasing them by instalment. The Sunris houses are mostly made of concrete and only a few are mud built.

CHANDRIMA CHOWDHURY

SUTRADHAR

The Sutradhars having the synonyms of Chhutor/Chuthar is a carpenter caste. The name is derived "from the Sanskrit *sutra*, the thread, with which the course of the saw is marked" (Risley 1891 : 287). Some say that Kulin and Moulik are their two subgroups whereas some of them mention their subgroups as Rarhi and Barendra. The Sutradhars claim themselves to be descendants of Vishvakarma, whereas either Vishvakarma or Karna of the Mahabharata has been referred to in Risley's work (1891 ;287) as their first father. Mitra (1953 : 58) thinks, on the basis of the evidence of the *Brahmavaivarta Purana* that their first parents were Vishvakarman and Ghritachi. They think that their community members live in the districts of Burdwan, Medinipur, Nadia, Murshidabad, 24-Parganas, Howrah, Calcutta, etc. as well as in Rangpur district of Bangladesh. They live in the plains characterised by warm and temperate climate, high humidity and medium rainfall. The Sutradhars speak and write in Bengali.

Majumdar and Rao (1960), as cited by Gupta and Dutta (1966 : 326), gave following somatometric information on the Sutradhars : Mean values of stature-1616 mm (average), cephalic index - 76.76 (mesocephalic) and nasal index - 74.04 (mesorrhine)

The Sutradhars eat fish, egg, mutton, chicken, etc. but do not eat beef. Rice is their staple cereal, though some of them take roti (home made wheat bread) at night. *Moong* and *masur* (lentil) are their favourite pulses. Mustard oil is used as cooking medium. They consume all seasonal vegetables and fruits which are available in their locality. Consumption of vegetables and fruits are moderate. Tea is their universal hot drink. Milk and milk products are taken by them if they can afford. Their male members smoke *bidi* or cigarette and both males and females chew betel. The people of this community do not eat *boal* fish. They do not consume radish in the month of *Magh* (the tenth month of the Bengali calendar) and *lau* (bottle gourd) in *Bhadra* (the fifth month of the Bengali calendar). Decrease in the use of pulses and fruits and increase in the use of vegetables are remarkable changes in their food habit.

Subgroups and *gotras* indicate their social divisions. Kulin and Moulik, the two divisions are at social level whereas Rarhi and Barendra divisions are based on territorial distinction. No hierarchic differentiation exists among them and now those subgroups have no function also. They are divided into a number of *gotras* to regulate marriage alliances. Madhukulya, Kashyapa, Alamyan, etc. are their *gotras*. The Sutradhars think themselves to be equal to the Napit, Kumar, etc. and place themselves as Sudra, though some claim themselves to be Vaishya. The Napit, the Kumar, etc. on the other hand, place them at a lower status.

Endogamy at community level and exogamy at *gotra* level are their marriage rules. They negotiate marriage of their boys and girls at adult age. Monogamy is the form of marriage. Vermilion, iron and shell bangles are the marriage symbols of women. Dowry in cash and kind is prevalent among the Sutradhars. Their boys live in their father's residence after marriage. Divorce due to adultery and maladjustment is permissible with judicial approval. Remarriage of female divorce and widow is not permissible but recently there have been a few cases where their society has accepted such marriages. Remarriage of male divorcee and widower is permissible. Junior sororate is permissible only after the death of the first wife. Earlier they would not practise sub-group exogamy, but it has been accepted at present. Earlier they used to marry their daughters during their infancy, which has also been referred to by Risley (11891 : 289). Now, marriageable age has increased. Introduction of dowry instead of bride price, introduction of judicial separation and liberalisation of rules for remarriage are also reported.

The Sutradhars live mostly in nuclear families but vertically extended families are not unknown. Reciprocal duties, obligations and privileges exist within a family unit. *Jamai*, *shavashur* and *bhasur* (daughter's husband, husband's father and husband's elder brother respectively) are avoided by a woman. Joking relationship exists with *boudi* (elder brother's wife), with wife's younger siblings and with grandparents. Property, restrictions on the freedom of youngsters, unequal sharing of economic burden are the causes of conflict among the family members. All children inherit father's property equally. The eldest son generally succeeds father's responsibility. The Sutradhars maintain inter-family linkages through different ritual observances and festivals. Increase in the number of nuclear families with the declining trend of extended family system and acceptance of equigeniture in the place of male equigeniture are the significant changes in the family structure of the Sutradhars.

Nowadays, the Sutradhar women have right to inherit father's property. But most of their women do not claim their share. The Sutradhar women take care of domestic animals, bring potable water and have significant role in ritual performance. Generally, family expenditures are controlled by the male members and the status of their women is low.

The Sutradhars observe pre-delivery rituals in the fifth, seventh and ninth months of pregnancy. *Panchute*, the post-delivery ritual, is observed on the fifth day of child birth. Shashthi puja is performed on the ninth or thirteenth or on the twenty first day of child birth. The Brahman priest offers this *puja* in Shasthitala (sacred centre of the village). *Kaman* rite is observed on the thirteenth day. They clean their clothes and house and a barber pares the nails of the mother and the baby on that day. Pollution period for the other members of the family is over after Shashthi puja, whereas pollution period for the mother and the baby is over after thirty days. The new mother and the persons who have nursed her are required to take bath in the Ganga after thirty days for purification. Many restrictions are imposed on the women during pre- and post-delivery period, viz., she is not allowed to go out or go to the pond at night, cross the river after the eighth month or participate in any religious performance till she takes bath in the Ganga after completion of the post delivery pollution period etc. *Annaprashan* (first rice feeding ceremony) is observed on the sixth month for a male child and on the seventh month of the female child. *Nannimukh* (or *nandimukh)* or oblation to the ancestors is to be performed for the first male child in this occasion, otherwise they have to perform the same rite for each of the male child during their marriage. They offer *puja* to the family deity, and *mama* (mother's brother) gives the *prasad* into the mouth of the baby. When the boy or the girl reaches marriageable age the parents negotiate marriage. They follow orthodox Hindu rites to marry their sons and daughters. *Gayehalud*, *nandimukh*, etc. are common rituals which are performed at both the house of the bride and the bridegroom. The main marriage ceremony is performed at bride's residence. *Satpak* (carrying the bride seven times round the bridegroom), *shubha drishti* (exchange of glances), *sindur-dan* (smearing of vermilion on the hair parting of the bride), etc. are the obligatory items of the main marriage ceremony. A grand feast is given by the bride's father on that night. The relatives, neighbours and friends are invited in the feast. The bride goes with her husband to her father-in-law's house on the second day. The bridegroom's father gives a feast on the third day of the marriage. *Phulsajjya* (consummation ceremony) is observed on that day. Cremation is the mode of disposal of the dead body. They observe pollution for fifteen or thirty days, whereas *sradh* is performed on the sixteenth or the thirty-first day. The Sutradhars dispose of bones in the water of the Ganga. Discontinuation of observation of puberty rites for women and reduction of pollution period from thirty to fifteen days after death in some areas and increase in the expenses for rituals are reported.

The Sutradhars are mainly a landless community (except homestead land) and only a few have marginal agricultural land. Carpentry is their traditional as well as primary occupation. Now, many of them have shifted to other occupations like driving, business, making of images, ivory work, jewellery work, services, etc. They have direct link with daily and weekly markets. Medium of exchange is cash. Rise in number of daily wage casual labourers is reported. They pay to the labourers both in cash and kind.

Gram panchayat, the statutory council, plans and implements welfare and development programmes for the area as a whole. Previously, they had a caste leader known as *gramni*. Five villages of the Sutradhars were under his jurisdiction. He used to control different social problems of the people of the Sutradhars of those five villages. Now this post has been abolished.

The Sutradhars are Hindus. The great majority are followers of Vaishnavism but some are Saktas. Vishvakarma is their patron deity. Lakshmi is their family deity. Kali, Shani, etc. are propitiated as village deities. Dakshineswar, Tarakeswar, Puri, etc. are their pilgrimage centres. The degraded Brahman priests serve them to perform birth, marriage and death rites as well as different worships. Durga puja, Kali puja Charak, Vishvakarma puja, Pousparban, etc. are festivals of socio-religious and socio-economic significance.

Making of images and wooden, ivory or stone carving work indicate their traditional skill in art and crafts. They have a legend about their origin which goes like this: the Lord Vishvakarma had four sons — Sutradhar (carpenter) was one of them. All the sons had sacred threads, but once Sutradhar used these sacred threads to mark on timber by using black colour on it. Thus he was degraded and lost the sacred thread. As he used *suta* were known as Sutradhar.

The Brahmans do not accept water from them, whereas the Sutradhars accept and exchange water and food with the Kamar and the Kumor, but not with their neighbouring communities like the Bauri, the Chunari, etc. Inter-caste marriages with the Brahman and the Kayastha are reported but this is not the regular accepted norm of the community. *Sai* is their friendship term. They themselves arrange Vishvakarma puja and participate in Durga puja, Kali puja, etc., with other communities. Sometimes they make images of gods and goddesses. The Bauri make the total frame of their houses receiving wooden frames from them. Patron-client relationship exists with the Brahman priest, the Napit, etc. The Bagdi, the Dom etc. work in their agricultural fields as agricultural labourers. The Bauri, the Kamar, the Muslim, work as casual labourers at their shops of wooden works. Modern inter-community linkages have been established as they emerge as business men, creative artists, service holders, political leaders at village and national level.

Generally, their boys and girls read up to secondary level, but a few of them have gone beyond the college level also. They use both modern and traditional medicare. Their attitude is favourable towards family planning. Generally, women get sterilized after two to three children. The Sutradhars collect their potable water from tube wells or from the tap. Provisions for employment through IRDP, NREP, etc. exist in their locality but any help for them through those schemes has not yet been reported. They listen to the radio, visit cinemas and some of them watch television also. The cultivators get the advice of agricultural extension agency, whereas members of different political parties meet them during election. Their localities have the facility of roads, railways and post offices. The Sutradhars use electricity where it is available. Wood, cowdung cakes and coal are used as fuel. The cultivators of this community avail themselves of the canal water for irrigation and use organic manure, chemical fertilisers and pesticides for better return from agriculture. Their children do not avail themselves of the facility of mid day meal scheme or ICDS. The carpenters can not deposit their money with the bank due to their poor pecuniary condition, whereas the ivory workers are well to do and their attitude is favourable to savings. Some of the Sutradhars have to take loans from money-lenders and shop keepers for their craftwork.

ARCHANA DATTA

SWARNAKAR

The Swarnakars are the goldsmith caste of Bengal. Sankara is their synonym. Sinha and Chowdhury, are their titles. Their name seems to have been derived from gold. They can recognise only two subgroups, viz. Rarhi and Saptagrami. Mitra (1953 : 34) referred to *Brhaddharma Purana* which indicates that they have originated from an Ambastha father and a Vaishya mother. The Swarnakar claim that Vishvakarma is their forefather. They can locate their relatives at regional level. This small community lives mostly in the plains with warm and temperate climate, high humidity and medium rainfall. They speak and write in Bengali. They belong to the other backward classes category.

The Swarnakars are non vegetarian, but they do not eat beef and pork. Rice and sometimes wheat are their staple cereals. *Biri kalai* (black gram) and *masur* (lentil) are their favourite pulses. Mustard oil is used as cooking medium. They consume in moderation all seasonal vegetables and fruits available in the market. Most of them drink tea and milk regularly. A few persons drink alcohol occasionally and it is purchased from the market. Increase in the use of pulses and vegetables and decrease in fruit consumption are reported.

The two divisions or *thaks* viz. Rarhi and Saptagrami as referred by them are territorially based. They are also divided into a number of *gotras* which indicate ancestry. Both the social divisions had the function to regulate marriage alliances, but now it is not followed strictly. Changes in surnames from Shee to Sheel, Marik or Bag to Sarkar are reported. Their self perception vis-à-vis perception of other communities about them in local social hierarchy is middle. They recognise themselves as Vaishya.

Endogamy at community level as well as subgroup level and exogamy at *gotra* level are their rules of marriage. They negotiate marriage of their children after they are adult. Monogamy is the common form. Vermilion, iron and conch-shell bangles are the marriage symbols of women. Dowry in cash and kind is accepted. Their rule of residence after marriage is patrilocal. Divorce due to adultery and maladjustment is permissible with judicial approval. Both parties can seek divorce and compensation is given as per direction of the court. Divorce usually does not occur after child birth. Remarriage of females is not permissible. Junior sororate may take place after the death of the first wife. They do not follow sub-caste endogamy strictly as earlier. Increase in age at marriage, introduction of dowry instead of bride-price and introduction of divorce with judicial approval instead of social approval are reported.

The majority of the Swarnakars live in vertically extended families, but nuclear families are not uncommon. Avoidance relationship does not exist. Joking relationship exist with *boudi* (elder brother's wife), *jamaibabu* (elder sister's husband) and with grandparents. Property and unequal sharing of economic burden are major sources of conflict in a family. Equigeniture is their rule of inheritance. The eldest son succeeds to his father's position and takes up his responsibilities. Inter-family linkages are maintained through different ritual observations. Break in the family structure, introduction of equigeniture instead of male equigeniture are some of the recent changes in their family life.

The Swarnakar women are mostly engaged in household work. They take care of their domestic animals and birds. Lakshmi is worshipped everyday. A few of them are engaged as teachers and nurses or in other economic activities. They have significant roles in ritual and religious spheres. The Swarnakar women worship goddess Lakshmi every day. The women who earn money contribute to the family income. Some of them control family expenditure also, but they enjoy a low status vis-à-vis the men.

The Swarnakars observe a good number of rituals related to their life cycles. They observe *panchamrita* in the fifth month of pregnancy. The pregnant woman is to take five types of fruits and sweets and is to wear new clothes on this occasion. *Bhaja* is observed in the seventh month and the woman is to take seven types of fruits and sweets and is to wear new clothes. In the ninth month, they observe *sadh* and the pregnant lady is offered nine types of sweets, nine types of curries, *payesh* (sweet preparation of milk and rice) and a new *sari*. They invite their kin and relatives to a feast on that occasion and give the pregnant woman a gold ornament. The expecting woman does not cross the river after eighth month, does not go out at night or take any food at the time of lunar and solar eclipse. After child birth *panchute* is observed on the fifth day, *sentera* on the sixth day and Shashthi puja on the sixth or twenty-first day as post delivery rituals. The Napit pares the nails on those days and the *dai* (midwife) washes the clothes and other things on those days as well as offers Shashthi puja on the sixth or on the twenty first day. They observe a pollution period for thirty days. *Annaprashan* (first rice feeding ceremony) is observed when the male baby attains six or eight months and the female baby attains seven or nine months of age. The barber shaves the head of the child. *Nannimukh* (propitiation of ancestors) is observed only for the first male child of the eldest son in the family. Then *mama* (mother's brother) gives the *prasad* of *duar dhara thakur* (family deity) and rice into the mouth of the child. When the child reaches the marriageable age, the parents negotiate marriage. After completion of negotiation the family priest and elderly persons of the girl's party bless the boy. *Aiburobhat* (a feast held on the eve of one's marriage), *dadhimangal*, *gahehalud* (smearing of turmeric on the body) *briddhi* (ancestor worship) etc. are performed at both the houses of bride and bridegroom as marriage rituals. *Malabadal* (exchange of garland), *shubha drishti* (exchange of glances) etc. are observed at bride's residence as ritual parts of main marriage ceremony. *Boubhat* is observed at groom's residence on the second day of main marriage ceremony. They invite kin and relatives to a luncheon feast on this occasion. Marriage is consummated (*phulsajjya*) on the third day and kin, relatives, neighbours, friends, and invitees from the bride's residence are invited to a feast on this occasion. They perform *puja* of Satyanarayan and Subachandi on the eighth day at both the houses of bride and bridegroom. The bride goes with the groom to her father's home on that day (*astamangala*).

Cremation is the mode of disposal of dead body. They observe pollution for thirty or fifteen days. *Ghat* ceremony is performed on the thirtieth or fifteenth day. *Shraddh* (ancestor worship) is observed on the thirty first or the sixteenth day. The thirty-second or seventeenth day is demarcated as *anshpanna*. They invite their kin to a non vegetarian feast on that day. The Brahman priest serves them to perform different death rites. Reduction of death pollution period from thirty to fifteen days and increase in expenses on rituals are reported.

The Swarnakars are an artisan caste and are primarily dependant on metal work specially of gold and silver. Most of them own agricultural land. Agriculture is their secondary source of income. Making of ornaments is their traditional occupation but many of them are engaged in other businesses or in different services. They also act as money lenders. They purchase raw materials directly or through middleman. They have linkage with daily and weekly markets. Medium of exchange is money. Agricultural labourers are paid in cash and kind.

Gram panchayat, the statutory council plans and implements welfare and development activities for them as well as other communities. Earlier they had *moral* (leader), who had a control over their society.

The Swarnakars are Hindu and mostly belong to Vaishnav sect. Krishna, Tulsi, Lakshmi, etc. are their family deities. Gopinath, Kali etc. are their village deities. Srikhanda, Mathura, etc. are their pilgrimage centres. Brahman priests officiate in the rituals and ceremonies related to life cycle. Kali puja, Durga puja, etc. are their major socio-religious festivals whereas Vishvakarma puja is related to their religio-economic pursuit.

The jewellery of Bengal formed a distinctive school of art and craft from very ancient time and the Swarnakars are creators of this art and craft.

In general they have commensal relationship with the Teli, Tili, Kamar, etc. but not with the Handi, or Dom who are considered to be ritually unclean. The old people do not accept food and water from them. But the members of younger generations do not obey the norms of commensal relationship. A few inter-community love matches have occurred with the Kayastha, the Bagdi, etc. but it is not well accepted by their society. *Bhiksha ma*, *dharma ma*, etc. are their kinship terms. As an artisan caste of gold and due to universal demand of gold ornaments, they develop traditional inter-community relationship with others on the occasion of *annaprashan*, marriage, and other ritual performances. Patron client relationship with the Brahman priest, the Napit, etc. is in vogue. The Muchi, the Kora, etc. work as agricultural labourers in their agricultural fields. Their involvement in political sphere, as well as their modern occupational pattern has helped in the establishment of modern inter-community linkages.

Educationally, the Swarnakars are quite advanced. Most of their boys and girls read up to college level. They try their best to avail themselves of modern medical facilities, but the traditional way of treatment is not uncommon to them. Married couples have a good response to family planning. They collect potable water from tube wells. Some of them have taken loan from bank or co-operatives for agriculture or to start small business. The people of this community listen to radio, visit cinema and watch television. Their settlements are well connected by road and sometimes by rail also. They use electricity. Fuel wood, cowdung cakes, coal and kerosene oil are their fuel sources. The cultivators use irrigation water from shallow tube wells and canals. They use organic as well as chemical fertilisers, pesticides and insecticides for better return from agricultural land. They avail themselves of modified ration from the fair price ration shops. Some persons have surplus money to deposit with the bank.

ARCHANA DATTA

TAMANG

The Tamangs are a "Mongolian or semi-Mongolian caste (Risley : 1891 : 110) " of West Bengal having synonyms like Tamang Lama, Lama and the like. The etymology of the word shows that it has come from horse trading (in Tibetan language '*ta*' means 'horse' and '*mang*' means 'trader'.) They are locally called 'Nepali' as they originally migrated from Nepal to West Bengal. The Tamangs have a large number of *thars* or sub-castes which are found in their inhabited areas. The most important *thars* are Yangden, Moktan, Yonzone, Bonjan, Lopchan, Pakhrin, Bal, Titung, Kalden, Dong, Golay, Syangbo, Grandan, Ghising, Glan, Gyba, Yaba, Lo, Blon, Bozu, Singar, Singden, Theng, Thokar, Zimbas, Rumbha, Gomden and Nearga. Risley (*ibid.*) says, " About their origin little is known, nor do their own traditions throw much light upon the question; but their physical characteristics, and the fact that their exogamous divisions (*thars*) bear Tibetan names, seem to lend support to the opinion that they are descended from a Tibetan stock, modified more or less by intermixture with Nepalese races." This opinion is supported by a good number of Tamangs in West Bengal. The Tamangs are primarily distributed in different parts of Darjeeling and Jalpaiguri districts of West Bengal. They are not generally concentrated in large numbers in any village especially in the tea plantation areas. The climate of the inhabited areas varies from extreme cold to cold specially in the high altitude areas, hilly terrain and the like. Rainfall is found from high to medium. The major rivers that flow through their inhabited regions are the Rangit, Mahananda, and Tista etc. The Tamangs speak Nepali language while they communicate with one another among the members of their own community as well as other Nepali communities. They speak Hindi in relations to others. The Tamangs use Devanagari script. Male members wear *daura sura* (traditional male dress) *alpali dhaka tupi* (popularly known as Nepali *tupi*) and female members wear *chubandi chol* and *pharia* which are considered as their traditional dress. The Tamangs belong to the constitutional status of other backward class, depressed backward class.

The Tamangs are non-vegetarian, i.e., they eat meat, beef, buffalo meat, fish, and egg etc. A section of them inform that they do not eat garlic and park which are considered by them as taboo. They take rice as staple food and use mustard oil for cooking. Locally available food grains, roots, tubers, vegetables etc. are used as food items. Seasonal fruits especially orange, apple etc. are taken off and on. Those who can afford milk prefer it. Tea is their common drink. They prefer *nimkeen* tea (instead of sugar and milk they use salt) which is considered as medicated tea (for muscle pain and others). The community members indulge freely in drinking spirituous liquors which are prepared by themselves *(jhanr)* and purchased from the markets. Female members prepare several food items like *sinki* (prepared with radish), *kinema* (prepared with Soya bean), *gundruk* (prepared with small mustard herb) etc. on certain occasions especially when invited guests come. A significant change observed is that at present many of them take maize as staple food.

The major social divisions of the Tamangs are the *thar* which have already been mentioned above. Among these *thars* the Yangden and the Moktan seem to be considered as belonging to the same kin group and accordingly marriage between the members of one group and another is prohibited. Similarly the Yonzone and the Bonjan are regarded as same consanguineal kin group and marriage relation between the groups are not permitted. All groups are regarded equal by them except the Nearga who generally maintain their livelihood through unclean occupations. The Tamangs say that the basis of differentiation among the various groups is primarily based upon territorial divisions. These are intermarrying groups except those which have been described above. The sub-divisions or *thars* are used as surname by them. These divisions are also considered as clans though most of them are not aware of the meaning of each clan name. A few Tamangs especially those who follow Buddhism inform that they have a clan known as *lasa*. This name has come from a place and is used as clan mainly by those who have migrated from Lasa of Tibet. The Tamangs, especially those who follow Hinduism claim that they belong to both Kshatriya and Vaishya *varnas*. Due to their traditional occupation, i.e., horse trading, they come under the Vaishya and as they were admitted into the Kiranti regiments raised by Jang Bahadur in Nepal they say that they also belong to the *varna* order of Kshatriya. Many of them serve in the police/military and "Lama Murmis are enlisted as recruits by the 1st Gurkhas" (Risley 1891 : 113).

The Tamangs follow exogamous *(thar)* marriage rule. Risley (1881 : 111) mentions , "the form of exogamy observed is the simple one that a man may not marry a woman of his own *thar*. For the rest marriage is regulated by the standard formulas mamera, chachera, etc. calculated to seven generations in the descending line". The Tamangs practise adult marriage and they start negotiation when their daughters become fifteen or sixteen years, old and sons become twenty or twenty-one years old. Marriage by negotiation is the general custom. Risley (*ibid*) says "...sexual intercourse before marriage is tolerated, it being understood that if a girl becomes pregnant she will disclose the name of her lover, and he will come forward to marry her". They are monogamous though polygyny is permitted by them. A married woman is recognised by her *sindur* in the parting of hairs and *pottey mala* (necklace). Bride-price is their common custom but at present dowry has become more popular among them. After marriage the bride comes to live in the home of her in-laws and she becomes a member of her husband's family. Divorce is permitted on the ground of adultery or unsuitability of temper. Divorced woman may not marry again but become "concubines on the same terms as widows" (Risley : 1891 : 112). The practice however has been discontinued in recent years. Male members can remarry as a young widower or in the case when his first wife is barren or is without a male child. Following changes are found in the institution of marriage (i) age at marriage has increased (ii) a few instances of inter-community marriages are found (iii) dowry is given both in cash and kind and (iv) young widow and divorced women can remarry.

The Tamangs live both in nuclear and mixed extended families. Interpersonal relations within the family are very close and respectful. Relationship between husband and wife are maintained through love, respect and mutual cooperation. Parents and adult children maintain a relation of mutual affection and obligation. The grandparents and grandchildren relation is of love, affection and joking. This relation is also found between husband's younger brothers/sisters and elder brother's wife. Conventional avoidance relation is observed between husband's elder brother and younger brother's wife and between father-in-law and son's wife. Conflict and confrontation are not generally found in the nuclear families. It arises in joint families due to following reasons :-

i) Unequal distribution of parental properties; and ii) conflict between the daughter-in-law and her mother-in-law and sister-in-law, often leading to an unpleasant situation between father and son dissolving the joint family into nuclear families. Sons inherit parental property; in the absence of sons the daughters get equal shares. The widow inherits the property if she does not have any children. But she must be maintained by the persons who succeed to the property.

Succession is patrilineal. Inter-family linkages are close as well as competitive. Economic assistance, supply of labour in agricultural pursuits and construction of houses, participation in various ceremonies etc. are of common occurrence among the members of the different families.

The Tamangs do not provide any share of parental property to their daughters under normal circumstances after the demise of their father, though they are aware of daughter's legal claim over the parental property. The women play their economic role through collection of water and other domestic work. Their social role is confined to the specific activities while they have innumerable roles as wife, mother, mother-in-law and grandmother. They have their roles in life-cycle rituals. Religious role is performed through the observances of *brata* and *upas*. Except for a few most of the women are not actively involved in any political activity other than exercising their right of voting at the time of elections. Some of the Tamang women are employed in several government and non-government organisations and earn money which they contribute to run the family expenditure. In fact, there are hardly any specific prescribed rights for women, but their obligation in economic, social religious and other spheres of life are many and explicit.

After birth of a child, the Tamangs observe pollution for a period of twenty-two days. The mother of the newborn child is not allowed to move outside the room for twenty-one days. She is not allowed to do any household work also. Between three and eleven days they arrange *nauran* ceremony. On an auspicious day between these days all family members as well as lineage neighbouring members come together and observe a day for purification, except for the new mother and her baby. On that day they invite a *lama pandit* who gives a name to the child in consultation with the old family members. Between two and three years of birth of a male child, a day is fixed when the maternal uncle comes and ceremonially starts shaving the head of the child, which is completed by the Napit. On that day they arrange a feast where neighbours, friends and relatives are invited. On that day alcoholic drinks are also served. The Tamangs arrange *bhat khai* (first rice feeding) ceremony after five months of birth (both for male and female).

Being accepted as a *lama* (Buddhist priesthood) is an important occasion among the Tamang community. After five years of age any male member may be accepted as a *lama*. It is performed by a ceremony which is called *topche* and the ceremony is conducted by a '*loden*' i.e. the senior most *lama* and a younger *lama*. Hair of the child is first shaved by the *loden* ceremonially and it is followed by other *lama*. Smoking, drinking and taking meat are prohibited in this ceremony. All village members assemble and participate in the ceremony. The acceptance of *lamahood* is not compulsory for all. It depends on the willingness of the person concerned and members of the concerned family.

Marriage is an elaborate and long ceremony of ritual and the main wedding is performed at night in the house of the bride. Drinks, meats etc. are brought to the bride's house when groom and his party come to the house of the bride for marriage. Elder members of the family put a mixture of curd and rice paste on the forehead of the groom when he starts from the house to the bride's house for performing marriage ceremony. There is *hom* (fire) lit during the actual marriage ceremony. A *lama* or a *pandit* officiates as priest who smears the foreheads of the bride and the groom with a mixture of curd and rice. Vermilion is put on the forehead and in the parting of the hairs of the bride by the bridegroom and then *lama/pandit* brings their heads together so that their foreheads touch. It is rather a binding portion of the ceremony. Hindu Tamangs invite a barber who performs a ritual part of the ceremony. The next morning the bridegroom and bride come to the house of the bridegroom and on that night a feast is arranged in honour of the newlywed bride at the bridegroom's home. The Tamangs do not maintain any taboo for consummation of marriage. The dead are cremated and a formal mourning is observed for a period of thirteen days. A sacred lamp, a khukuri (dagger) and a looking glass are placed near the dead body. Risley mentioned "the rich burn their dead and preserve a piece of bone to be deposited in a private Gumpa. The ordinary practice is to bury, the body being laid in the grave with the head to the north and fire applied to the mouth" (1891:112). After cremation the head of the deceased's sons are shaved by an experienced member of the community or a *Napit*. Family members of the deceased do not east salt and oil with their food for three days. On the thirteenth day, they arrange a mourning ceremony which is called *ghewa*. On that day a propitiatory offering of meat, rice, plantains, sweetmeats etc. is presented to the soul of the deceased and a feast is given by the chief mourner. The final ceremony is performed by a *lama* or *pandit*. After one and half months of death the Buddhist Tamangs arrange a ceremony by offering prayer to the soul of the deceased for peace and happiness. A feast is arranged on that day also. The Tamangs arrange a funeral procession with the help of several instruments like *laboba, galin, dambran, dilbu, dhengur* etc. which last up to the end of cremation. Sacred flags numbering about one hundred and eight are flown at the crematorium after cremation.

The major economic resource of the community is land which lies in the hands of the owner. Ownership of land is controlled by individual proprietors. The community is mainly a landowning community. Traditional occupation of the community is horse trading. At present the primary occupation for this community is cultivation either as owner or as sharecropper and they have a number of subsidiary occupations. viz. service in police/defence or Government/non-Government organisations, tea plantation labour, animal husbandry, business, milk selling and the like. Their economic activities are mainly dependent on markets. There is no bonded labour among the Tamangs. The extent of landlessness, number of labourers working in agriculture, plantation, industry etc. are significantly low among the community. Children are often found to assist their parents in agriculture, business etc., but no one ever comes across a child labourer among them. Payment of wages for agricultural and tea plantation labourers is mainly made in cash. Those who work in the tea gardens collect tea leaves on contract basis. Generally female members are employed for this purpose. Due to contact with the outsiders, development of communication and other governmental activities, a good number of them have taken the advantage of trade, commerce and other vocations rather than cling to traditional occupation.

The Tamangs have a traditional caste council and regional association known as 'Tamang-Buddhist Association'. President is the head of the association who functions for five years or more as per wishes of the members of the association. Head of the traditional *jati* council is called '*mukhia*' who settled primary disputes of the community members. The above mentioned caste council of the Tamangs can punish a miscreant by imposing social boycott or fine or by admonishing the guilty person. The prevalent form of giving reward is to raise social status. The role of modern statutory councils is important. Without consulting these councils no development work can be undertaken. Besides, they consult council members for economic assistance, getting self employment schemes etc. Following changes have taken place after Independence : i) literate members of the community are becoming members of the statutory councils and participating in parliamentary democracy; and ii) traditional councils are gradually losing control over the members of community, while statutory councils are becoming more and more powerful.

Two types of religion viz., Buddhism and Hinduism are noticed among the Tamangs of West Bengal. Majority of them follow Buddhism. Risley pointed out that "the religion of the caste is not easy to define. We may discern in it a substratum of primitive animism overlaid by elements borrowed from Hinduism, and less freely, from Buddhism. Everything tends towards gradual adoption of the Nepalese form of Hinduism, and Buddhist usages are believed to be on the decline, though the Lama still serves as priest" (1891 : 112). Phupu, Guru, Changresi, Buddha, etc. are worshipped as family deities. Lakshmi, Saraswati, Kali, Krishna, Ram, etc. are village and regional deities. They worship Purbuja devata, a forest god who generally lives in as tree and is believed to visit with fever and other diseases those who neglect his worship. Sherkijho is a fetish of ill-defined attributes, while Gyong and Changreshi appear to be defined lamas. *Gumpa* (Buddhist monastery), and other major sacred centres and shrines are regarded by them as potential centres for pilgrimage *lama/pandit* is employed as sacred specialist in several religious ceremonies. Buddha Purnima mela, Chaso-moni mela, etc. are the major fairs in the Tamang inhabited region. Durga Puja, Kali Puja, Shiva puja, Bhagwan Srikrishna puja etc. are observed by them as general community festivals. The Tamangs organise socio-religious movement through 'Tamang Buddhist Association' from time to time for the establishment of their socio-religious identity in West Bengal. The change reported in the religious behaviour is as stated below: due to communication facilities and contact between India and Nepal many people visit religious centres of Nepal on several occasions. Besides a good number of them visit the Gumpa in Bhutan also on certain occasions which is also bordering country of the state.

A few Tamangs are specialised in Gumpa decoration. Those who engage in such profession are called '*khaiba*'. They do not have any special craft and handicraft. Oral traditions i.e. folk song, folklores, etc. are sung by the community members. A few of them participate in folk songs which are generally broadcast from the Radio station of Kurseong. Mrs. Aruna Lama is one of the popular radio artists of Kurseong All India Radio. Besides they inherit a number of folk songs which are sung by them in several ceremonies. One of the songs is quoted below :

"Amailey amailey amilejan khailala Aila maya, nailala, nala maiya khalche lala".

(It is generally sung at the time of marriage ritual. The song says that I (i.e. the groom) am considering you (i.e. to be my bride) and on compensatory ground accepting you as wife but who will save and compensate me?)

The Tamangs perform dance and music which are part of their social life. Some of them compose and set the tune to their songs. At the time of performing dance and music they use *dhamphu* and other instruments like *dal*, *narshing*, *sanai*, etc.

The Tamangs are considered as *jal-chal* group. Their social status in the Himalayan region is respectable. The Nepali Brahmans, Chettris, Gurungs, etc. take water and sweetmeats from their hands. They themselves eat with the Limbus, Khambus, Lepchas and Bhotias. The Tamangs do not receive water, *pucca* food etc. from the castes like the Kami, Damai, Sarki, etc. Connubial relations with others are not permitted by them. Risley says "in British territory a man who infringes them by marrying a woman within the forbidden degrees is punished by exclusion from the caste... In Nepal the penalties are said to be more severe. : the offender is denounced as har-phura, and is liable to be sold as a slave, or, according to some accounts to be punished capitally" (1891:111). Ritual based kinship is observed among them. There is no bar regarding access to wells and other water sources, facilities of roads, schools, temple, *panchayat ghar* etc. The Tamangs maintain a kind of patron-client relationship with the *lama/pandit* and sometimes with the Napit. The Tamangs have some representation in administration, teaching service, engineering, business and other statutory democratic councils. They actively participate in political activities and public functions at the local, *taluka* and district levels. From time to time the Tamangs launch an ethnic movement for enlisting their names as one of the scheduled tribes of West Bengal. The 'Tamang-Buddhist Association' plays an important role for this purpose. Landowning families employ *adhiar* (share-cropper) from their neighbouring communities and also employ labour from the neighbouring communities. Relationship between them is maintained through love, mutual help and co-operation. Besides, those who work in the tea estates in different areas of Darjeeling and Jalpaiguri maintain as good linkage with the employers.

Percentage of literacy is not poor though majority of them are not well educated. These who have become well-off, are endeavouring to get their children educated. They take care about their health and medical care. The Tamangs use both modern and traditional medicare. They take precaution for their family planning. Those who live in the hill-regions collect spring water for drinking and those who live in the plains, tube wells have solved the problem of drinking water. Employment and self-employment programmes have made little impact on them. Radio, television, local newspapers are their media of communication. Sometimes they collect information through extension agencies. The villagers avail themselves of the mechanical transport system. Electricity has reached some of the inhabited areas of the Tamang community. Environmental conservation is not anything that primarily concerns the members of the community. They use wood as fuel. Irrigation is not developed both for terrace and settled cultivation. Rain water is the only source of irrigation. Use of chemical fertilisers, insecticides, organic manures is in vogue among the landowning families. The Tamangs complain that nutrition programmes, i.e. mid-day meal, feeding programme at school etc. are irregular for school going children. They collect essential commodities i.e. wheat, rice, sugar, kerosene etc. from the nearest ration shop. The Tamangs show their positive attitude towards savings, investment and other banking facilities.

SUBHRENDU MAITI

TAMBULI

The Tambulis are a respectable trading caste. Tamuli and Tamli are the synonyms of the community. Singha, Chaudhury, etc. are their titles. The very name 'Tambuli' comes from the trading of *tambula* (betel leaf). Their original occupation is supposed to have been the selling of betel leaf, Sanskrit *tambula* (Risley 1891 : 292). Chauddagrami, Biallishgrami, Bardhamani, Ashtagrami, Saptagrami. Chaturthagrami and Rajhati are their seven subgroups (as reported by the informants). Risley referred to five sub-groups or sub-castes, viz., Saptagrami or Kusadayi, Ashtagrami or Kataki, Chauddagrami, Biallishgrami and Bardhamani. The Saptagrami came from northern India and their chief settlement was at Saptagram or Satgaon. A similar origin is claimed for the Biallishgrami. The Chauddagrami is said to owe its origin to one Sashthibar Singh, a member of the Biallisgrami group, who being turned out of his father's house for marrying the daughter of Srimanta Pal, a Tambuli of the Bardhamani sub-caste, took refuge with his father-in-law at Bainchi, in Hooghly and headed a faction of his own. Risley also states that the Tambuli are the descendants of a Vaishya father and a Brahman mother. (Risley 1891 : 292). Mitra (1953 : 50) referred to *Brahmavaivarta Purana*, which describes them as the descendant of Vaishya father and Brahman mother. The Tambulis agree to Risley's version on their origin and say that Sashthibar Singh resided at Adi Saptagram and he had the business of *tambul*. About Chatuthagrami and Rajhati they say that those two groups are found in Purulia, Bankura and Medinipur. According to the local people the Chouddagrami are mostly found in Burdwan, Hooghly Bankura, Medinipur, Murshidabad, Nadia, Malda and Howrah. The Biallishgrami are mostly found in Hooghly, Burdwan, Howrah, Darjeeling, Murshidabad, West Dinajpur, Bankura, Birbhum, Purulia and Nadia. The Bardhamanis are in Burdwan, Bankura, Birbhum etc. They can locate the Ashtagrami in Purulia, Calcutta, Allahabad and Benaras. The Tambulis live in the plains of West Bengal, where monsoon is the prevailing climatic type. They speak and write in Bengali. They belong to other backward class category.

The Tambulis are a non-vegetarian community. Their staple cereals are rice in day time and roti (bread) at night. *Mashkalai* (black gram), *mung*, *masur* (lentil) are their common pulses. They do not take *khesari*. Food restrictions of widows of the Biallishgrami and the

Choudagrami are almost similar to those among the Brahman. Widows of those groups do not take *masur*, onion, and non-vegetarian food. They observe fasting on the day of the *ekadashi* (eleventh day of the lunar fortnight). The Tambulis use mustard oil as cooking media and rapeseed oil is used occasionally. The Tambulis consume all seasonal vegetables and fruits available in the market. They are habituated in tea and most of them drink milk. Very few people take alcoholic drinks. Smoking of *bidi*, cigarettes and chewing of betel are also common and it is purchased from the market. They do not consume *chichinga* (snake gourd) and *boal* fish. They do not consume mango before *ambaruni* in the months of *Chaitra/Baisakh* (the last and the first months of the Bengali calendar respectively), *sim* (a kind of bean) during the month of *Chaitra* (the last month of the Bengali calendar) as well as on *ekadashi*, *lau* (bottle gourd) in the month of *Bhadra* (the fifth month of the Bengali calendar), radish in the month of *Magh* (the tenth month of the Bengali calendar), etc. Previously, the Tambulis did not take meat and egg of hen. Now this taboo no longer exists. *Roti* (hand made bread) at night as the staple food is the new addition in their food habit. Fruit consumption has decreased with its decreasing production in the village.

It has already been mentioned that the Tambulis have seven subdivisions locally known as *thak*. Among them Chouddagrami demand the first position in social hierarchy. Then the Biallisgrami, the Bardhamani, the Ashtagrami, the Saptagrami, the Chaturthagrami and the Rajhati are ranked in the above order. The hierarchy is based on socio-economic condition as well as territorial distribution of the community. The Chouddagrami generally do not marry their son or daughter with members of other subgroups, though at present they have arranged some marital negotiations with the Biallishgrami, the Bardhamani and the Ashtagrami. The Tambulis are divided into a number of *gotras* viz. Kapil Rishi, Bharadwaj, Byas Rishi, Kashyapa, Sandilya, Maudgalya, etc. Recently, many Tambulis have changed their title from Mandal to Dey. To-day, many people of the Tambuli community introduce themselves as Kayastha also. Dey, Datta, Kundu, etc. are their surnames. Except the Brahman whom they place in higher position, they think all other members of different clean caste Hindu communities of their locality as equal to them. They place all scheduled caste and scheduled tribes in lower position, whereas other higher caste people, except *nabasakha*, place them in subordinate status. The Tambulis identify their place in the *varna* system as Vaishya.

Clan exogamy and caste endogamy are the common marriage rules of the Tambuli community. The marriageable age of boys is around twenty-five years and for girls it is about twenty to twenty-five years, whereas Risley (1891 : 292-295) referred to the prevalence of the practice of child marriage. Generally, marriages are arranged by negotiation, self arranged inter-caste marriages are not unknown, though such type of marriage is rare in their society. Monogamous marriage is the common rule of the Tambuli community. A person can marry again in case of death of the first wife in young age. *Sindur* (vermilion), *shankha* (conch shell bangles) and *noa* (iron bangle) are the marriage symbols of the married woman. At present the Tambulis have to spend a large amount of money in cash and kind as dowry, whereas bride-price was prevalent among them at the time of Risley's study. Rule of residence after marriages is patrilocal. Divorce is very rare among the Tambulis and previously was not in vogue among them. At present a few cases of judicial separation due to maladjustment and adultery have been reported. Divorce compensation is given according to the decision of the court. Either party can seek divorce. Remarriage of widower and male divorcee is permissible in the Tambuli society. But remarriage of widow or female divorcee has not yet been accepted. The second marriage of a person is performed in a very simple way. Junior sororate is permissible only after the death of the first wife. Acceptance of sub-group exogamy in some cases, increase in the age at marriage, introduction of dowry and acceptance of judicial separation are the changes in their marriage customs. At present a father of a girl is to pay an exorbitant amount of dowry in the form of cash and kind. Previously after staying seven days or eight days in father-in-law's house after marriage, a girl used to stay for one year in her father's house. After one year she had to go to her father-in-law's house on an auspicious day. But this system has been abolished with the increasing age of marriage. Now the bride and the bridegroom go to any nearby house of a Brahman (which will be near the girl's father's house) on an auspicious day after marriage and come back on the same day. A relationship is established with that Brahman's wife as mother who is known as *dinkara ma*. At present, the girl does not stay one year in her father's house after marriage.

As long as the father is alive, a Tambuli family does not get a nuclear shape. But after the death of the father the break in the family types are found among the Tambuli. The eldest person is the head of the family. All the younger members of the family respect and obey him. Children are treated with a lot of affection. The relation between father and the adult sons is just like friends. The children generally, show much reverence to their parents. Avoidance relation is found between *bhasur* (husband's elder brother). Joking relation is found between *dadu/thakuma* (grandfather/grandmother) and *nati/natni* (grandchildren), and between *boudi* (elder brother's wife) and *deor* (husband's younger brother). Joking relation is also found between *shala/shali* (wife's younger brother/wife's younger sister) and *jamaibabu* (elder sister's husband) and between co-brothers of nearer age. The duty of the husband is to maintain the establishment whereas wife looks after the comfort of her husband and children as well as of other family members. Adult sons help the father by their earnings as well as sharing the work load with their father. Adult daughters help their mother in household work. Conflicts and confrontations between the brothers crop-up on the issue of sharing the property. Unequal workload as well as unequal economic share of the male members of a family are the major points of conflict between two married women. Property is inherited from father by son and daughter. Equigeniture is the present rule of inheritance of the Tambuli society. Sometimes, daughters do not claim the share of the property but they seek pecuniary help from their brothers during their daughter's marriage. Right of succession generally, goes from father to the son and it is normally the eldest one. Inter-family linkage within the community is generally maintained through the ceremonial occasions, different religious festivals and ritual performances. Need of consultation with the elders during problems also create a linkage between two families. Increase in the number of nuclear families, with decrease in that of the vertically extended families is a noticeable change in the Tambuli family structure. Some changes are also observed in the inter-personal relations. Previously, sons generally were afraid of their father. They did not use to talk with him directly. But now a relation of friendship is established between them as soon as a son becomes adult. The rigidity of avoidance relationship between *bhasur* and *bhadrabou* has loosened. Earlier, the *shashuri* (wife's mother) never used to take seat in the place where the *jamai* (daughter's husband) used to sit. She also used to draw a corner of her *sari* (*ghomta*) over her head as veil before her *jamai*. Such relations have become easier. Rule of inheritance has been changed from male equigeniture to equigeniture. Previously, relation between two neighbouring families of the Tambuli society was much closer. But such closeness does not exist now.

Women have equal right to inherit their father's property with their brothers. Most of the Tambuli women of Chouddagrami, Biallishgrami and Ashtagrami have no role in economic sphere. A few are engaged in banks or in other services. But the women of Saptagrami, Chaturthagrami, Rajhati work sometimes in the agricultural field. The Tambuli women attend *jatra*, theatre, etc. in the village, visit cinema in the nearby urban or semi urban centres. They also take initiatives to prepare *naibedya* (oblation) during different religious festivals of the village. The Tambuli women have a significant role in pre-delivery rituals as well as rituals related to the marriage ceremony. A few of them also participate in political activities. The women who have participation in economic activities contribute their income to their family. Although the Tambuli girls get equal opportunity with their brothers to acquire education, they possess a lower status than the male members.

The Tambulis observe a number of rituals on the occasion of birth, marriage and death. During pregnancy the Tambulis observe *kanchasadh* in the seventh month and *sadh* in the ninth month as pre-delivery rituals. A barber comes to pare the nails and to colour the feet of the pregnant woman with *alta* (lac dye), and he or she gets *sidha* and cash for the service. It is their custom to give gold and new *sari* to the carrying woman from the side of the father-in-law's family on the occasion of *kanchasadh*. The performance of *sadh* ceremony is the duty of bride groom's house. They present the girl a *dora* (striped) *sari* with red border. They only inform the date of *sadh* ceremony to the family of the girl's father but do not invite them on that occasion. They invite only the neighbouring women on that day. The pregnant girl has to observe a number of restriction after five months, e.g. she can not pare her nails in the *jora mash* (even months), she can not draw a line or cut anything during the time of eclipse, etc. The mother and the family members who had nurse the baby and its mother must have to take bath in the Ganga on any day after confinement period, for purification. After thirty days the new mother gets permission to enter into the kitchen. There is no name-giving ceremony among the Tambulis. They perform a rice-eating ceremony in the sixth month for the male child and in the seventh moth for the female child. They offer *pujas* to *panchadevatas* (five gods and goddesses) of the village and the *prasad* is given to the child by the *mama* (maternal uncle). After that he (*mama*) puts rice in the mouth of the baby. Barber comes to pare the nails of the baby and attends the baby at the time of bathing in the pond. They invite their relatives and neighbours to a luncheon feast. At present no restriction and rituals are observed during puberty, except that the girl takes a bath with soap on the fourth day of menstruation for purification.

The marriage ceremony is performed in the bride's house. The month of *Chaitra* (March-April), *Bhadra* (August-September), *Kartik* (October, November), and *Poush* (December-January) are avoided in fixing a marriage date. The family priest fixes the date and *ashirbad* (blessing) ceremony is observed first at the bridegroom's house on an auspicious day. The priest of the bride's family has the priority to bless the bride groom on the occasion. On another occasion the same is observed at bride's house. On the day of marriage, *briddhi* (ancestor's worship) is performed. Then *gayehalud* and other rituals are performed by women. The bridegroom arrives with his friends and relatives under the leadership of his father or any elderly person of the family to the bride's house. The main marriage ceremony is always performed in an open place of the house. The family barber brings the bridegroom from *barasar* to the fixed place known as *chhadnatala*. After that the married men of the family bring the girl on a *pinri* (low wooden seat) and move around bridegroom for seven times (*sat pak ghora*). The barber of the girl's family assists the bride and bridegroom in the *malabadal* (exchange of garlands) and *shubhadrishti* (exchange of garlands) by telling some rhymes. Father, generally, performs, the duty of *dan* (handing over). *Sindurdan* (smearing of vermilion) is an important aspect of the marriage. A grand feast is given by the father of the bride on that night to the *barjatri* (bridegroom's party), relatives and neighbours. On the second day morning the bridegroom comes back to his house with bride and the *boubhat* ceremony is observed in his house on that day. Bride serves rice to the elderly persons on the same day. *Phulsajjya* (consummation ceremony) is observed on the third day of the marriage. Father of the bridegroom invites the friends, relatives and neighbours to a feast on that night.

The deceased person is cremated. Fifteen days are observed as mourning period. They observe *ghat* ceremony (purification) on the last day of this period. The *sraddha* ceremony is performed on the sixteenth day. All the relatives and some of the neighbours are invited to a luncheon feast and are offered a vegetarian meal. The *anshdore* ceremony is observed on the eighteenth day when the kin are invited to a non-vegetarian feast. Various changes are found in the life cycle rituals of the Tambulis. Previously, the pregnant woman was not permitted to consume egg or to sew any cloth after five months; now nobody obeys the restrictions. Earlier, all the Tambuli families had to observe all the post-delivery rituals like *panchute*, *sentera*, *shashthipuja*, etc. but at present, all those ritual performances have disappeared from most of the families except *shashthipuja*. Previously, so many restrictions and rituals were observed by the Tambulis at the onset of menstruation of a girl. A girl would not see the face of males for four days during that period. She would not see her face in the mirror, would not use hair oil or would not comb her hair during those days. On the first day of menstruation a *nikhunt poati* (whose all children are alive) used to collect rice from five or seven families and used to cook that rice in a new *handi* (earthen pot). The girl would take the rice with unboiled milk keeping the plate on the leaf of a brinjal and *indurmati* (soil collected by rat). On the fifth day she would have to take bath in the pond before the sun rise and pick up *gugli* (water snail) from the bottom of the pond. After taking bath she would have to see her face in the mirror. Some of the married women from their relatives used to be invited to a feast on the same day. But with the increasing age of marriage such ritual performances have disappeared from their society. The Tambulis had to observe a mourning period for thirty days which has been reduced to fifteen days from the fifties of this century.

Though the Tambulis are a landowning community, the majority of them depend on business. Agriculture is their secondary source of income. A good number of people who used to depend on land, have left the major part of the agricultural land and begun to depend on service or business after the abolition of *zamindary* system and introduction of Operation Barga. The business of *tambul* was their traditional occupation. Today most of them are engaged in the trade of *ghee*, hardware, cloth, grocery, etc. and this is their primary occupation. Most of their business centres are at the urban or semi urban areas. Some Tambuli villagers have grocery shops in the rural areas also. All these people have to depend on the urban markets for collection of their trading commodities. They collect their business materials either directly or through middlemen. All the Tambulis who have land, cultivate it with the help of agricultural labourers. Labourers are paid in cash and kind. Generally, boys began to go to the trading centres after eighteen years. Occupation pattern of the community has changed from the traditional betel leaf trading to the trading of other commodities and this change had also been noticed by Hunter (1877 : 51), Risley, 1891 :292-295) and Bhattacharya and Sinha (1966 : 20)

To-day the Tambulis have no caste council, though they have a government registered regional association known as Tambuli Mahasammelan which mainly negotiates their marriages. This organisation also arranges annual general meeting, picnic and sports every year, where the community people get a chance to meet each other. They have executive committees with thirty five elected members. *Grampanchayat*, the statutory council, bears responsibilities of their welfare. Previously, the Tambulis had *moral* (leader) who used to control all the social problem of the village. Now, there is no existence of such *moral* among the Tambulis.

The religion of the Tambulis present no special feature. Most of them are Vaishnavs. A few are worshippers of Sakti and Shiva. Lakshmi, Narayan, Durga, etc. are their family deities; Shiva Dashabhuja, Kali, Gopal, Balaram, Dharmaraj, etc. are their village deities. Dharmaraj is their regional deity too. Shiva temple, Dashabhuja temple, Kali temple, temple of Gopal and Balaram, Pirtala, etc. are their local sacred centres. Being economically well-to-do, the aged persons visit different sacred centres of Hindus for pilgrimage. They employ the Brahman for religious and ceremonial purposes. Maker Sankranti mela (fair in the end of ninth month of Bengali calendar), fair at Shivtala in the month of *Jaishtha* (the second month of the Bengali calendar) are their major fairs, whereas Durga puja, Kali puja and Dolyatra are their major festivals.

The Tambuli women draw *alpana* (floor painting) during different *pujas*. They have folk tales about their origin referred to earlier.

Traditional form of *jajmani* system no longer exists between the Tambulis and other communities, but even to day the Brahman priest, barber, and *dai* (from the Hari community), Kumhar (potter) etc. are fixed for them. The Brahman priest serves them during religious and ceremonial occasions, the Napit and *dai* serve them during the rituals related to the life cycle and all of them are paid in cash and kind for their services. The Kumhar supply them earthen pots and they have a special duty to prepare *naibedya* (offering oblation) during the Durga puja of the Tambulis and do other works related to the *puja*. The Swarnakar serve the Tambulis by making gold ornaments during different ceremonial occasions related to birth and marriage. The Kora work as their agricultural labourers and they are essential to carry the idol of the goddess Durga during *bhasan* (immersion). The Muchi come to their religious festivals to bit the drum. Thus it is observed that inter-caste linkages have grown up through the life cycle rituals and religious festivals of the community. They often go to the Pirtala (religious place of Muslims) to offer *puja* through which an inter-community relationship has been established with the Muslims. The Tambulis at present accept invitations from the similar clean castes of the *navasakha* group, which was not prevalent earlier. In the past even one subgroup did not accept water from the other subgroups. But, to day such restrictions are not prevalent in their society. Traditionally, the Tambulis refrained from taking water from the scheduled castes; this system is also gradually waning. But the womenfolk retain the earlier conservatism to a great extent till now. Putative kinship like *bhiksha chhele* (kinship term) with the son of a Brahman during his thread wearing ceremony and *dinkarama* (another putative kinship referred to earlier) have increased the inter-community linkage. The Tambulis have offered to the society industrialists, scholars, service holders, teachers, engineers, doctors, etc. Modern inter-community linkages have been established in the socio-economic spheres of activities. They have sent their members to the *gram panchayat* and legislative assembly. A kind of political and economic inter-community linkage has been established by those people. As traders, they have to make contact with other people who may not exclusively belong to the Tambuli community; a kind of secular inter-community relationship has grown at the economic level. Agricultural labourers get help mostly in cash from their landlords during their necessity and repay it by their labour in the agricultural field. The increasing accessibility also has accelerated the development of inter-community linkage.

Development programmes did not have any special impact on the Tambuli society, rather they have shared the benefit with others. With advancement of our village society, the Tambuli boys and girls have made much progress in the sphere of education. Many of their boys and girls are generally taking education up to bachelor degree. At present, the community spontaneously avail themselves of the modern medical facilities. Sometimes they give *jalpara* (sacred water) to a child when he or she becomes ill. The Tambulis are also aware of family planning. Generally, women of the Tambuli society get sterilisation and it is sought for after two to three children. Potable and cooking water is drawn from tube wells installed either by the government or through self efforts. Water from wells is also used for cooking purpose. They have not received any type of loan from government or from bank. Radio is found in all the Tambuli houses, whereas television may be found in a few houses in the rural areas also. They visit the cinemas in the nearby urban areas. They often use the road and railway facilities for journey to the nearby towns and the city of Calcutta for their business purposes. Post offices exist in all the villages where the Tambulis live. Electricity is available in most of the Tambuli villages and most of them avail it. Coal, fuel wood and kerosene are the major fuel used by the Tambuli community. Canal water and shallow tube wells are their major sources of irrigation. They use chemical fertilisers, organic manures and insecticides for better crops. They have the facility of mid-day meal scheme, but, their children do not avail themselves of that facility due to inferior quality of food. The Tambuli villagers procure their ration from local fair price shops. They deposit their money in the bank.

With the cultural development, the freedom of women has also been increased. Previously, the women did not visit cinema, theatre etc. They used to attend *yatra* which was arranged within the compound of a house and they had to sit behind a *chik* (blind). In conclusion, it may be said that the Tambulis do not hold the plough even now as it is a taboo to them and cultivate their land with hired labour a practice which was observed also by Risley.

ARCHANA DATTA

TANTI

The Tantis are the weaver caste of Bengal. They are also known as the Tantubaya. The "Tantu" means natural fibre or *ansh*. "Tanti (Bengal) or Tantwa (Bihar), is the generic term for all weavers, but the Tantis in Bengal themselves form a separate caste, being one of the nine pure castes of Nabasakhas... whose social position is only next to the Kayasthas." (Mitra: 1953: 342). They have several *thaks* or sub groups like, Aswini Tanti, Balarami, Madhukari, and Purandari. Regarding their origin a mythological story related to Shiva has been reported. Rich ethnographic and historical accounts about the Tantis are also available in Risley's books, and in few other monographs and research publications on cotton fabrics of Bengal. The Tantis are distributed in almost all the districts of West Bengal. As per 1931 census, the Tantis had a population of 3,10,805 in the then undivided Bengal. They speak Bengali at home and speak Bengali and Hindi with others. They use Bengali script at home and use Bengali, Devanagari and Roman scripts with the outsiders. They hold the constitutional status of other backwards class.

Bio-anthropological information on the somatometric, character of the Tantis is available. According to D. N. Majumdar, and C. R. Rao, the stature is 1602 mm (average), the nasal index is 71.47 and the cephalic index is 76.80. It means that they have below mean stature, messorhine nose and mesocephalic head form.

The Tantis are non-vegetarian. They eat fish, egg and meat. Rice is their staple food. They take all kinds of vegetables which are available in the market. They take pulses like gram, *urad*, *moong*, *masur*, peas, beans etc. They use mustard oil as their cooking medium. They do not indulge in alcoholic drinks. They drink milk and tea. They also take milk products. They smoke *bidi* and cigarette. Fruit consumption is occasional.

The Tantis have four *thaks* (sub-groups), known as Aswini Tanti, Balarami, Madhukari, Purandari. Of the sub-groups, Aswini Tantis rank themselves higher than the others and the hierarchy is based on social differentiation. The Aswini Tantis *thak*, because of its relatively higher rank, had been claiming to be regarded as a separate caste in the early twentieth century. They had among them, four endogamous sub-divisions like Bardhamaner Aswini, Barnakul Aswini, Madhykul Aswini and Uttarkul Aswini. At present the rule of endogamy is not so rigidly observed as in the earlier days. The Tanti have several exogamous *gotras*, like, Sandilya, Kashyapa, Bharadwaj, Batsya, Parasar, Modgoula, Alamyan, Goutam, Kularishi, Sabarna, etc. They use various surnames like, Basak, Dey, Dutta, Mandal, Pal, Nandi, Sadhu, Guin, Sarkar, Kar, etc. They rank themselves among the *nabasakha* group of Bengal, others also consider them accordingly. They are aware of the *varna* order and rank themselves as clean Sudra.

The Tantis maintain community endogamy and sub-group endogamy. However, nowadays, they do not follow the endogamy rule rigidly at sub-group level. They practise *gotra* exogamy. They prefer adult marriage by negotiation. The prefer monogamy. The married women use *sankha* (conch-shell bangles) *sindur* (vermillion) and *noa* (iron bangles). They practise dowry in cash and kind. After marriage wife goes to live with her husband. Divorce is not recognized but nowadays a few divorce cases are reported. These are due to adultery and maladjustment. In case of such a divorce, children become the liability of either mother or father. Divorced men or women can marry again. Widow and widower can marry again. Junior sororate marriage is permissible. Increase in age of marriage and a higher incident of divorce are reported.

The Tantis prefer to live in nuclear families, though a few cases of mixed extended families can also be seen. The father is the head of the family. The relation between husband and wife is of love and respect and of co-operation. Avoidance relationship is found between daughter-in-law and father-in-law, between husband's elder brother and younger brother's wife. A joking relation is observed among the elder brother's wife and husband's younger brother. Conflict within the family arises on property matters. Parental property is equally shared by sons. Eldest son get the right of succession in other family matters. Inter-family linkages are observed during the social, ritual and religious, ceremonies.

Women do not inherit their parental property. They have various roles in collecting of fuel or in fetching drinking water from the wells or tube wells. They do the household jobs. They also have roles in ritual and religious ceremonies. They do not earn any money and so the question of contribution to the family finance does not arise. They do not control family expenditure. They do not participate in political activities. They have low status than the men.

The Tantis observe pre-delivery rituals like *sadh*, *panchamrita*, etc., as well as observe *janmashouch* (birth pollution) for a month after child birth. *Annaprashan* and *namkaran* (name giving ceremony) are observed when the baby is six or seven months old. Marriage rituals are arranged at bride's residence. The main rituals are, *kanyadan*, *sinduradan*, *malabadal*, *sat pak*, *homjogna*, etc. The Brahman does the job of the priest. A feast is given by the bride's parents to the relatives and neighbours. The nuptial ceremony is held at groom's house on the third day, after the marriage is over. They cremate their dead bodies. They observe thirteen days' pollution period after death. The Brahman officiates in the purificatory ceremony or *shraddha* ceremony. A feast is given to the relatives on such occasions.

The traditional and present occupation of the Tantis is textile weaving. However, nowadays many of the Aswini Tantis have given up weaving and have settled down as cultivations. Apart from the Aswini Tantis, a few others also depend on land. There are both landholding and landless people in the community. Other occupations which they pursue are, business in cloth, job in government and private sectors, teaching in schools, etc. They depend on daily or weekly market directly or through middlemen. They get their wages in cash. Due to landlessness, daily wager, agricultural labourer, etc. are increasing in number.

The Tantis have their own *jati* council at the state level known as 'Bangiya Tantubaya Samaj Samiti'. This council has representatives from each district of West Bengal. The main function of the council is to look after the welfare of the community and to save the great weaving tradition of Bengal from its present decadence, resulting from the competition with the mill woven textiles. Statutory panchayats are also present to look after the welfare and development programmes.

The Tantis profess Hinduism. The Aswini Tantis carry out *kulo puja* (tribute to family deity Lord Shiva) as their household deity worship. The Purandari Tantis worship Viswakarma as they consider themselves to be an artisan caste. They also worship Krishna, Durga, Kali, Manasa, Saraswati, etc. The Brahmans officiate as priests. They have festivals like Viswakarma puja, Dolyatra, Surya puja, Janmasthami, etc. They visit Kalighat, Tarakeswar, Puri, Kashi, etc., as their pilgrimage centres.

The Tantis have the traditional art of weaving cotton and silk textiles. Besides this the womenfolk are efficient in embroidery work. They have rich folktales, folklores, etc.

They have social, ritual, economic linkages with the neighbouring communities. The Brahmans take water from them. The Kayastha, the

Kamar, the Vaidya, etc., take water and food from them. The Tantis do not take water and food from the Hari, the Methor, the Dom, the Muchi, etc. They do not marry outside their community. They share wells, roads, schools, crematorium with others. Patron-client relationship, cultivator-labour relationship exists with the other communities. The community have businessmen, artists, teachers, doctors, political leaders, etc.

At present the Tantis are aware of the value of education. They use modern as well as traditional medicines. They use drinking water drawn from tube wells and wells. They use electricity. Transistor radios are very common. A few of them get benefits IRDP and other small loans from the bank. Wood, coal, cowdung cake are their main fuel. They use chemical fertilizer in their land (those who practise agricul-ture). The children get mid-day meal. They make use of banking facilities and ration system. They also depend on money lenders and shop keepers.

AMITABHA MITRA

TILI

The Tilis are an oil trading community of Bengal. The name has been derived from 'tula' or balance. The other view is that it has been derived from *tel* (oil) of *til* (sesamum). Ekadash, Dwadash, Peno and Panta are their four subgroups. Roy and Mandal are their titles. Risley (1891 : 307) mentioned that originally all oil men would belong to one group. In the long run those who become richer called themselves Tili and others were known as Teli. Mitra (1953 : 54) cited their origin from *Brhaddharma Purana* and *Jatimala*. *Brhaddharma Purana* referred to the Tailika as the descendant of a Vaishya mother and Brahman father whereas Jatimala referred to the Tailika as the descendant of a Barujivi father and Gopa mother. The Tili perceive of their distribution in Burdwan, Birbhum, Murshidabad, Nadia, Hooghly, Calcutta, Bankura, Medinipur, Howrah, etc. having monsoon climate. They speak and write in Bengali. They belong to other backward class category.

Somatometric information on the Tilis referred by Chanda (1916) and cited by Gupta and Datta (1966 : 331) are as follows : Mean values of Stature - 1624.24 mm (average), Cephalic index 77.65 (mesocephalic) and nasal index - 82.11 (mesorrhine).

The Tilis are non-vegetarian. They consume rice as their staple food twice a day and *muri* (puffed rice) as breakfast. But sometimes they take roti (wheat bread) also. *Biri kalai* (blackgram) is their favourite pulse dish. Beside this they also consume *moong*, *masur* (lentil) and *chhola* (gram). *Alu posta* (curry of potato with opium seed) is a very favourite dish of the Tilis. They eat radish and seasonal vegetables moderately. Mustard oil is used as the cooking medium. The Tilis drink tea. A few young men occasionally drink local alcohol purchased from the market. Most of the Tili families have cows and can take milk and milk products. Male members of this community smoke *bidi*s and cigarettes and both male sand female members chew betel. The Tilis eat all seasonal fruits like mango, banana, jackfruits, etc. which are available in the village or in the market, but their fruit consumption is moderate. They do not consume radish in the month of *Magh* (January-February), and *nim* leaves on Thursdays and Saturday. Introduction of meat and egg of hen and decrease in attraction for alcohol are the changes in their food habits.

Subgroups and *gotras* denote their social divisions. Differentiation with hierarchy exists among the subgroups but they are not aware of the basis of this differentiation. The Dwadash subgroup ranks first, followed by Ekadash, Peno and Patna. Sandilya, Madhukulya, Kashyapa, etc. are their *gotras*. The Tilis recognise themselves as Vaishya and place themselves lower than the Brahmans and the Kayastha, whereas the Aguri, the Sadgop and the Napit are equal in status to them. On the other hand the Vaishnav, the Kamar, the Subarnabanik, etc. think themselves equal to the Tilis. The Sadgop community on the other hand places the Tilis in subordinate status. The Tilis also belong to *nabasakha* group.

Clan exogamy and caste endogamy are the marriage rules of the Tilis. Junior sororate is permissible only after the death of the first wife. The marriageable age of boys is around twenty-five years and for girls it is twenty years. Normally, marriages are arranged by negotiation. Monogamous marriage is the common rule of the Tili community. One can marry again in case of barrenness or death of the first wife. *Sindur* (vermilion) *shankha* (conch-shell bangles) and *noa* (iron bangles) are the marriage symbols of the Tili women. Dowry in cash and kind is also prevalent among them. Rule of residence after marriage is patrilocal. As there is no report of divorce case the Tili villagers are not aware of the divorce rule. Widow remarriage does not yet exist among the Tilis. Remarriage of widowers is performed with a very simple ceremony.

Previously, marriage across the subgroups was strictly prohibited, but it takes place today. The marriageable age of the Tili boys and girls has increased and difference of age between bride and bridegroom has decreased. Previously, bride-price was not prevalent among the Tilis, yet sometimes the bridegroom's father would help the poor father of the bride with money at the time of marriage. Such cases are rare today. Today dowry has been introduced.

Though the number of nuclear families is increasing, joint families are still the Tilis' basic social unit. The youngsters always obey the head of the family as well as elderly persons. The elders show affection to the youngsters. Generally children are respectful to their parents. Avoidance relationship is found between *bhasur* (husband's elder brother), and *bhadra bou* (wife of younger brother), *shvashur* (husband's father) and *betar bou* (son's wife). Joking relationship is observed between wife's younger sister as well as younger brother and husband of elder sister, elder brother's wife and husband's younger brothers and sisters, grandparents and grandchildren, *nandai* (husband of sister-in-law) and *shaaj* (wife of wife's younger brother). Property and unequal sharing of economic burden are the main points of conflict within the Tili families. Generally sons equally inherit father's property. Though at present daughters also enjoy the right to inherit their paternal property, they do not claim the share. Succession to family headship generally goes from father to the eldest son. Inter-family linkages are renewed on various occasions like life cycle rituals or during festivals. Increase in number of nuclear families is the principal change in the family structure of the Tilis. According to the informants, because of increasing education the younger members of a family do not respect the elders as earlier. Avoidance relation between *bhasur* and *bhadra bou* has somewhat loosened. The terms of address also have been changed from *batthakur* to *barda*. Change in inheritance rule from the male equigeniture to equigeniture is also reported.

Though women have right to inherit the share of their father's property equally with their brothers, they do not claim it till now. In general, the women are engaged mainly in household work. But some of them are also engaged in rice processing. Some are also engaged as school teachers. Today the young girls participate in the cultural programmes of the village and draw *alpana* (floor painting) in the *puja mandap* (*puja* pandal). The aged women arrange all things which are necessary for worship. Very few of them are working actively in the political field. They also have an active role in different life cycle rituals; like pre-delivery rituals, rice eating ceremony, marriage, etc. But their women enjoy low status. Those who are engaged in different economic activities contribute to family income and share in the control of family expenditure with the male members.

A good number of rituals on the occasion of birth, marriage and death are observed by the Tili community. During pregnancy the Tilis observe *bhaja* in the seventh month and *sadh* in the ninth month. They invite their relatives and kin specially the married ladies from the bride's father's side on the occasion of *sadh* ceremony. The pregnant women have to observe a number of restrictions, e.g. they do not cross the river or canal, they do not go outside at night, they do not go to wash the fish in the pond, etc. Generally, at present, after child birth they offer *puja* to the goddess Ma Shashthi on the third day or on the seventh day when the mother of the new born baby comes back from the hospital and the ceremony is known as *sentera puja*. The *puja* is offered by a *dai* (from the Hari community) at Shashthitala (the common religious place of the village). They perform *kaman* (a post delivery ritual) on the twenty-first day. A barber pares the nail of the baby as well as its mother on the day of *sentera puja*, *kaman* and on the thirtieth day when the pollution period comes to an end. This pollution period is termed by them as *anandashouch*. The mother and other members who had nursed the mother and the new born baby are required to take bath in the river Ganga after the thirtieth day for purification. Otherwise, they are not considered to be fit for the performance of any religious activity. They do not observe any name-giving ceremony. They perform rice eating ceremony in the sixth month for a male child and in the seventh month for a female child. On the day of rice feeding ceremony they offer *puja* to Dharamaraj, Shankhani, Ma Shashthi, Didithakrun, etc. at the common religious places of the village and the *prasad* is given into the mouth of the child by the maternal uncle and in his absence by the grandfather. After that the same person feeds rice to the child. On the day of rice feeding ceremony a barber shaves the baby's head at a religious place of the village. They invite their neighbours and relatives to a luncheon feast on this occasion. At present no restriction and rituals are observed during puberty, except the girls being required to take a bath after using the juice of *keshut* leaves on the fourth day of menstruation for purification and they do the same in each menstruation period.

After negotiation for a marriage a date is fixed on an auspicious day and after *gaye halud* and *nandimukh* (propitiation of the ancestors) the *barjatri* (marriage party) reach the bride's house on the auspicious day accompanying the bride groom under the leadership of his father or any other elderly person of the family. A barber and a priest of their families accompany them to complete the marriage rituals. The marriage is always performed in an open place of the house, known as *chhadnatala*. Family barber of the bride's house assists the bride and the bride groom during *malabadal* (exchange of garlands). The barber of the bride groom's family assists the priest during *kusumdinga* (a marriage ritual). Generally, the father performs the duty of *dan* (literally, handing over the bride). Religious performances of the marriage are over within two to two and a half hour. The young ladies mostly *boudi*, sister-in-law, brother-in-law, friends and grandmother take initiative for other ritual performances. A grand feast is arranged by the father of the bride on the night of that day. The relatives, neighbours, and friends are invited to the feast. The second day is known as *kalratri* when the new husband and wife are not permitted to see the face of each other. *Boubhat* ceremony is observed on the second day of marriage, and the *phulsajjya* (consummation) ceremony is observed on the third day. Now many families are observing *boubhat* on the day of *phulsajjya*. *Boubhat* and *phulsajjya* ceremonies are observed in the house of the bridegroom. A luncheon feast is given by the bridegroom's father on the day of *boubhat*. Kin, relatives and neighbours are invited to that feast. On the day of *phulsajjya* the friends of the bridegroom are invited. Though, at present many families arrange only one grand feast in the night of *phulsajjya* and it is termed *pritibhoj*.

After death cremation is the mode of disposal of the body. Bones are disposed in the water of the Ganga. The eldest son and in his absence the youngest son puts fire in the mouth of the corpse. Fifteen days are observed as mourning period and on the sixteenth day *sraddha* ceremony is performed. On the seventeenth day all the relatives and some of the neighbours are invited for lunch and have a non-vegetarian feast.

Various changes are found in the life cycle rituals of the Tilis. Previously they used to perform a ritual known as *panchute* which was done on the fifth day of child birth. It is not observed now. Earlier, on the fourth day of first menstruation the girls had to take unboiled milk and *bhija bhat* (wet rice) after taking bath with applying of *keshut* juice in the hair. It is not observed at present. Previously, the *gayehalud* ceremony was observed on the day before the date of marriage. But, now, it is observed on the marriage day. Previously they used the garland of akanda flower during *malabadal*, but the modern system of using the garland of *rajanigandha* (tube rose) or *bel*, etc. has now replaced the old system. The Tilis had to observe a mourning period for thirty days which has been reduced to fifteen days now. Increase in expenses for observation of rituals has also been reported.

Cultivation and business are the principal sources of income of the Tilis. Most of the Tili families have land. Running the grocery shop, cloth shop, husking mill, etc. are main business of the community. The Tili villagers who are cultivators plough their land with their own hand. Many people are also engaged in service and this is their subsidiary source of income. Generally, *farias* (middleman) from other communities collect their produce to sell in the big urban markets. Barter or any other forms of direct exchange system are absent. They themselves purchase items of trade from the wholesale markets of Burdwan and Calcutta. At present landlessness of the community has decreased to a great extent. Generally, boys begin to go to the field or help the elders in business at the age of fifteen years. A small number of them work as agricultural labourers and they are paid in cash and kind. They pay to the agricultural labourers also in both cash and kind. Occupational pattern of the community has changed from the traditional oil trade to the trades of other commodities. The decrease in landlessness also indicates a shift from the community's complete dependence on the tertiary sector (business) of occupation to partial dependence on the primary sector (agriculture).

Now, the Tili community has no caste panchayat. The *gram panchayat* is their statutory council. They have sent their representatives to the *gram panchayat*. The *gram panchayat* plans and implements different welfare and development programmes for the entire local population including other communities. Previously, they had caste councils which were formed by respectable persons (*moral)* of a number of villages. They used to control all the social problems and prospects. But, today the descendants of *moral* are there with the title of Mandal but their control over the community no longer exists.

The Tilis are a Hindu community and mostly belong to the Vaishnavite sect. They profess all the religious attributes that are common in their localities. Lakshmi, Narayan, Tulsi, etc. are their family deities. There is one *Tulsi* plant in front of each of the Tili house and they worship it daily. This is due to their adherence to Vaishnavism. They also respect Shankhani Manasa, Dharmaraj, and Didithakrun which are deities of lower caste communities. Shiva temple, Shashthitala, Shankhanitala, Dharmaraj temple, temple of Didithakrun, etc. are their local sacred centres. Gaya, Kashi, Mathura, Vrindaban, Puri, etc. are their pilgrimage centres. The Tili take the services of a Brahman priest during worship and to perform marriage and death rites. Dharmarajer *gajan*, worship of Shankhani Manasa, worship of Didithakrun, *nabanna* etc. are their major festivals of socio-religious and socio-economic significance. Worship of Shankhani Manasa is to save the villagers from snake bite, whereas worship of Didithakrun is to prevent the villagers from the attack of cholera. The Tilis enjoy these festivals with other communities of the village. The significant change in the life of the community is observed in their religious organisation. The responsibilities of the caste council for these religious festivals have been transferred to the "Baroari committee" which consists of members from different communities of the village.

The Tili women are expert in floor painting. They have oral tradition and folk tales about their origin as referred to by Risley (1891 : 307).

The Tilis live in multiethnic villages, so inter-community linkages automatically grow up between the Tilis and other communities. The Brahman acts as their priest. The old Brahmans do not accept rice from them, but they take water and *sidha* food. Previously, they would not accept food from the Vaishnav, Kumar, Subarnabanik, Tanti, Aguri, Napit, etc. and other unclean Sudras. But at present the young generations do not obey the tradition. The old generations, however, do not take food in the houses of unclean Sudras till now. *Sai*, *Gangajal*, etc. are ceremonial friendship with other women and these are established during Shaokhani puja. But this type of kinship is gradually waning. Traditional *jajmani* system no longer exists between the Tili and other communities, but even today Brahman priest, barbers and *dai* (mid-wife from the community Hari) are fixed for every family, although they are paid in cash for their services. A Brahman serves them in worship of family deities and to perform marriage and death rites. The Napit attends them after child birth, during marriage and death rituals. Earlier, a *dai* from the Hari community used to come at the time of child birth but with the increasing availability of the hospital facilities now, she attends the new mother and her baby after their return from the hospital. She is paid in cash and kind for her service. The *dai* also attends the first rice eating ceremony of the baby and performs Shashthi puja on the day of marriage of that baby when he or she reaches marriageable age. The Muchi, Kotal, Dom, Muslims, etc. act as their agricultural labourers. They are paid in cash and kind. On the other hand, those economically depressed people take loan during the times of distress and they repay it by their labour. The Tilis also go to the Doms to purchase basket, broom-sticks, etc. against cash payment. As a business community they have established linkages with others at economic level. With their cultural development they have offered to the society teacher, engineer, doctor service holder, political leaders at *gram panchayat* level, etc.

The Tilis have shared the benefit of development programmes with other communities. Many of their boys study up to graduate level and girls up to secondary level. A few boys and girls have acquired post graduate degree also. A girl generally drops out after secondary level of education to avoid the problems of big amount of dowry for a suitable bridegroom for her. The Tilis are well aware of modern medicare, but they also go to the *ojhas* (exorcist) in case of snake bite, scabies and other diseases. The Tili spouses are also conscious of the necessity of family planning. Generally, a woman gets sterilised after two to three children. Potable and cooking water is drawn from tube wells installed either by the government or by themselves. Tank water also is used for cooking purposes. They take loan through IRDP to open grocery shops, potteries etc. and loan from co-operative to install shallow tube wells, to purchase bullock cart, etc. Radios are very common among them. Urban dwellers watch television. They visit cinema, get help from agricultural extension agency. Different political parties meet them during election. They avail themselves of road, railway and post office facilities. They use electricity for domestic consumption where it has reached. Coal, fuel wood and kerosene oil are used as fuel. A few have *gobar* (cowdung) gas plants. Canal water and shallow tube wells are their major sources of irrigation. The Tilis use chemical fertilisers, organic manure, insecticide and pesticide for agriculture. Their children avail themselves of the facility of mid-day meal scheme. They take their ration from fair price ration shop. The Tilis deposit money with the banks or in the post office. They prefer post offices to banks for this purpose. Sometimes they have to take loan from moneylenders or purchase business materials in credit from the whole-sellers.

It is observed that various Hindu communities have come closer to each other in terms of friendship (non formal, i.e. non-putative) or in other words there is increasing inter-community interaction due to laxity of the rigidity of caste hierarchy.

ARCHANA DATTA

TIYOR

The present day Tiyors do not mention any synonym for their caste, although Risley mentioned several, like Tiyar, Tiar, Tior, Rajbangshi, Machhua (Risley 1891 : II : 328). They are not aware of the etymology of the word Tiyor, but they claim to be Raj Kshatriya Jati, who have descended from the lineage of Ramchandra. According to them, their subgroups are Chasi Tiyor, Nale Tiyor and Jela Tiyor.

At present, as they perceive they are distributed in the villages like Barabankra, Chhota Bankra, Aturia, Kendo, Hasnabad, Jirakpore, Dhalkhanra, Mahanpur, Bhonkali, Gopalpur, Sangrampur in the district of North 24-Parganas. As for distant places, they cite places like Tangra, Ranaghat and Nadia.

Sufficient rainfall and fertile soil condition in the areas of their settlement permit the growth of various kinds of vegetables, crops, and fruit plants (mango, coconut, litchi, guava etc). The jungles of the Sunderbans have an abundance of wild animals like deer, snakes and Royal Bengal tiger. A number of rivers in the area are supplying plenty of fish to the region and elsewhere.

The total population of the Tiyors was 82,018 as per 1981 Census. Except Bankura, Calcutta and Purulia, the Tiyors are found in all the districts of West Bengal (1981 Census). Bengali is the language and script used by the Tiyors, both at home and with outsiders. The constitutional status of the Tiyors is that of a scheduled caste in West Bengal.

The Tiyors are a non-vegetarian group of people, but they do not eat beef, pork, and the meat of buffaloes. Egg is also taken by them. They consume fishes of and on. Their staple food is rice and they take two major meals a day. When there is scarcity of rice they also take *roti* or hand made bread. *Roti* is also taken by them in their breakfast. The pulses consumed by them are *musur* (lentil), *mung* or *moong* (green gram), *beauli* (*muskalai*) (black gram), *chholar dal* (gram) etc. The Tiyors take varieties of locally available seasonal vegetables. However, their vegetable consumption is moderate. They generally use mustard oil for their cooking. They also consume various kinds of locally available (sometimes available in their garden) seasonal fruits like guava, banana papaya (ripe), mango, lichi, *bel*, *sapeda*, jackfruit, cucumber, black berry, *jamrul*, coconut, water melon, *khejur* (date palm fruit), *tal* etc.. Some fruits which are not locally grown like *musumbi*, apple *bedana* (pomegranate) etc. are also eaten by them when the doctors advise them to do so. Many of the Tiyors can consume milk as many of them have own cows. Most of them drink tea in the morning and evening. Some of them drink alcohol purchasing it from local market, because of the hardship of their work in agricultural fields and weaving. They never consume pumpkin in the month of *Chaitra* (March-April), radish in the month of *Magh* (January-February) and fig in the month of *Bhadra* (August-September).

Tiyors have three sub-groups, but they are not aware of their hierarchical order. The basis of this group differentiation is occupational. But all these groups are inter-marrying groups, so there is no function of this group differentiation at present. They mention two of their clan names such as Kashyapa and Alman. Marriage within the same *gotra* was allowed among them from previous days. Their surnames are Sarkar, Hela, Hati, Moral (Mondal) and Sardar. According to the perception of the Tiyors about the local social hierarchy, the Brahman, Kayastha, Napit, Kapali, Chhator, are higher than them, on the other hand, the Kapali, Patni, Malo and Rajbanshi *Jele* regard them as a low caste as their caste status is that of a scheduled caste. According to the Tiyors themselves they perceive to be of Kshatriya *varna* as they descended from the lineage of Ramchandra. But according to the other castes like the Brahman, Malo, etc. they belong to the Sudra group in *varna* order.

The Tiyors follow caste endogamy in their marriage. Their marriages generally do not take place within the same village, Marriage within one's clan is allowed among them. Marriageable age for the Tiyor girls is sixteen or seventeen years and for boys it is twenty-five or thirty years. Negotiation is the primary mode of acquiring mates. Monogamy is the form of their marriage. *Sankha* (conch shell bangles), *sindur* (vermilion) and *loha* (iron bangle) are the marriage symbols of the Tiyor women. Dowry is paid both in cash and kind in their marriage. The amount dowry varies from Rs. 500 to 10,000, according to economic condition of the bride's family, as well as bridegroom's merit.

The rule of residence after marriage is patrilocal. Divorce is permitted and it is sought through the help of the court. There is no social rule regarding divorce. There are also one or two cases of desertion. Post-divorce maintenance depends on the decision of the court. Remarriage is allowed for male members only. If their women do remarry, they are cut off from all connections with their father's family. The significant changes that have occurred in their marriage pattern are the increase in marriageable age, increase in the amount of dowry and abolition of bride price system.

The Tiyors live in both vertically extended and nuclear type of families, Husband in a nuclear family or eldest person in a vertically extended family is the head of the family and everybody obeys his order with respect. Husband and wife are related to each other by love, respect and mutual cooperation. Children are treated with affection and care. Youngsters respect their elders. Some avoidance relationship is maintained between *bhasur* (husband's elder brother) and *bhadrabau* (younger brother's wife), between *mamasasur* (mother-in-law's brother) and *bhagna bau* (sister's son's wife). Son-in-law and mother-in-law relationship is like that between mother and son. Grandparents and grandchildren relationship is that of joking, as it is between *jamaibabu* (elder sister's husband) and *sali-sala* (wife's younger brother and sister). If conflict arises in the family, the elders settle the matter. Inter-family linkages are also found among the lineage members as well as neighbouring families in different social and ceremonial functions on such occasions as birth, marriage, *annaprashan*, *sraddha* etc. In their economic activities everybody help each other. The Tiyors are aware of the present rule of property inheritance, i.e., Hindu Code Bill, but their daughters are not exerting their right. The traditionally held office is succeeded from father to eldest son, while male children get the surname and *gotra* of their father, married women get the same of their husband.

The women now have the right of property inheritance, but none of them are claiming their shares. Most of them are housewives and family management is their sole responsibility. They cook food, serve it to each and every family member, cut grass or straw for their domestic animals, wash clothing, bring drinking water etc. They play a major role in performance of household rituals. They utilise their democratic right by casting vote. A certain percentage of them working outside their family and contributing in their family income.

After birth the Tiyors observe a pollution period of twenty-one days for male child and thirty days for female child. They become purified by performing three successive *kaman* rites (cutting of nails and taking of bath and holy water from the river Ganga or *santijal* (holy water) from a temple. The ninth day *kaman* rite is called *natta*. They become semi-purified after *natta*. Their final purificatory rite is *Sastipuja* on the twenty-first day or thirtieth day respectively for male and female child. As a pre- birth restriction a pregnant women does not cross any river or canal. The pregnant women also do not take any food prepared with rice flour. Name-giving ceremony is done during *annaprasan* ceremony of a child. *Annaprasan* is done on the sixth or eighth month of a male child and on the fifth or seventh month of a female child. The Tiyors in some villages perform a *panama* rite.

Pakadekha or *asirbad* is the first marriage rite of the Tiyors. At first the bridegroom is blessed by some relations of the bride and then the *asirbad* of the bride takes place. Bride's *asirbad* may also be done on the eve of the marriage. Both of them are blessed with paddy, *durba* grass, some coins or rupees or ornaments. *Aiburobhat* (last meal before marriage) rite is done on the previous day of the marriage in the respective houses of the bride and bridegroom. On the morning of the marriage day, a rite known as *dadhimongal* or *jolsoa* is performed by some married women in both the houses. This water is essential for *abhhutie* rite. *Gayehalud tatta* is sent from the bridegroom's house to the bride's house by a barber after smearing of turmeric paste on the body of the bridegroom. The same turmeric paste is also sent for smearing of the bride. Next, *abhhutie* is done in the respective houses by the father or *jyatha* (father's elder brother). *Sampradan* is also done by those elders. Next day of marriage they have *kusumdika* (sacrificial fire) rite. *Baubhat* is performed on the third day of marriage in bridegroom's house. The third day night is also called *phulsajjya* and it is their marriage consummation day. They have a system of *joreasha* (coming of bride and bridegroom together from bride's father-in-laws house to bride's father's house and this day is also called *ashtamangala*). *Boubhat* ceremony may be deferred for three or seven days due to necessity, i.e., shortage of fund etc.

They cremate their dead at a burning ghat. After the death of a person the Tiyors observe a pollution period of twelve days. On the twelfth day they go to the *ghat* for cutting of nails by all the family members and shaving of hair by the sons. On the thirteenth day they perform the *sraddha* rite in the presence of a priest. On the fourteenth day they observe a rite known as *terodasa*, in which *amish* (feast with fish, animal flesh or egg) is prepared and relatives known as *gnati* (lineage relatives) and *kutum* (relatives through marriage) are invited. This rite is also known as *niyombhanga* (breaking the rule of taking vegetarian or *niramish* food after death). They have annual death rite, known as *baccharkria*. The major change that has taken place in the life cycle ritual performances is the shortening of pollution period after death from one month to twelve days.

Land is the major economic resource of the Tiyors. They themselves exercise control over their lands. They are mainly a land owning community with individual ownership of land. Agriculture or cultivation of land is the occupation of the community. Agriculture is also their traditional as well as primary occupation of this community. As subsidiary occupation many of the Tiyor boys of twenty years onward, are engaged in weaving of ganjee cloth, taking raw material from the *mahajans* (middlemen). They also supply it to those *mahajans* after taking their wages or some of them do it as their own individual enterprise. They have to depend on market. They sell their excess production to the middle men in cash price. Some also grow and sell small mango plants which are grown by grafting. Very poor families have to depend on day labourers' jobs but they have no bonded labourers. They also do not employ their children in jobs. All kind of wages are paid in cash. The significant changes that are taking place according to them are the reduction in the size of individual land holding due to increase of population and their shift from secondary to tertiary occupations for filling the gap.

They once had union board for settling village disputes etc. Some elderly persons were the members of that board and severe punishment or fine was imposed for evil deeds. Final settlement of marriage was also done by those people. At present statutory bodies like gram panchayats help to settle disputes etc. if the dispute is not settled by the elderly members of the communities. The changes that have taken place in the mechanism of social control are that the *jati panchayat* or union board has become completely defunct and instead of those institutions, the modern *gram panchayat* have some functions towards settling disputes etc. For settling major disputes they have to go to court.

Hinduism is the religions of the Tiyors. Their family deities are Manasa, Bipadtarini, Itu, Sitala, Kulimangal Chandi etc. Besides these they have some other *pujas* or *bratas* like Bhagabati puja, Rama puja, Bastupuja, Jamaisasthi, Durga Sasti, and Astami, Neel and Asoka Sasti. They have Kali temple or Radhagobinder *mandir* and place of Bastu puja as their local sacred centres. Their regional deities are Durga, Kali Shiva, Lakshmi, Basanti, Narayan, Saraswati etc. According to them their sacred places for pilgrimage are Kamarpukur, Jayrambati, Tarakeswar, Kalighat, Belur Math, Dakshineswar, Mayapur, Nabadwip etc. Their major festivals are Charak, *Mahotsab* (arrangement for *kirtan* songs) in the month of *Baisakh* (April-May) and Durga puja festival. Brahman priest is the sacred specialist for all their religious rites and festivals. In comparison to what Risley (1891, II, 329) had observed, their religious behaviours has undergone a great change in course of the last century.

The Tiyors have traditional inter-community linkages with respect to social, ritual or occupational activities as they take service of the Brahman priest and barber. They do not ritually accept water from the hands of the Keora, Muchi, Dom, Methor and Muslim, but sometimes they have to take it when many of these caste people get together in their annual *mahotsab* in the village. They have to take *pucca* food also from the above mentioned castes in the *mahotsab* ceremony. Some inter-caste marriages also have taken place with the Kapali and Kaibarta. They have no kinship based friendship, but they may have *guru bhai* relationships with many other castes, because many of them are the disciples of Advaitya Acharya. They do not face any difficulty regarding sharing of water source, temple, road, school, crematorium etc. They establish modern inter-community linkages when many of them work as weavers of *ganjee* cloth under *mahajans* (middlemen), when they are in shops for selling *mudi* (grocer's articles) commodities, when many of their children go to schools and colleges, when they visit panchayat office for taking various kinds of loans and developmental advices etc. The Tiyors have no political participation, but they cast their votes. They have share-cropping system. They also cultivate their land themselves. They have to employ sometimes agricultural labourers at the wage rate of Rs. 15/- per day. Literacy level of the Tiyors of elder generation is not very high, i.e. many read up to class IV or V standard. Many boys and girls are however matriculate and even graduate. All the children of the present generation are going to school. For medical needs they generally go to hospitals. As a family welfare measure their women get sterilised usually after two or three children. For drinking, the Tiyors use tube well water. None of them are employed through IRDP or DRDA. Many of them are self-employed through loans taken from the bank. The Tiyors, as observed, are well connected by ferry, bus or train services. Many of them regularly listen to the radio regarding developmental programmes especially for agricultural development. Some of them have the habit of newspaper reading. The majority of them do not have electricity. They sometimes irrigate their agricultural fields by hiring shallow tube wells and sometimes they have their own shallow machines. For fuel, they use some environmental resources like cowdung and jute sticks. They use chemical fertilisers of various kinds i.e. urea, phosphate, sulphate, potash etc. They use organic manures like cowdung and mustard oil cake. They use various kinds of insecticides available in the market. The Tiyors inform that somc schools previously had the system of feeding their students by distributing ***khichuri*** (a food prepared by boiling rice with pulse), but this system is not in vogue now. Some of them avail of banking facilities.

CHANDRIMA CHOWDHURY

TOTO

Totopara, a small hilly village in the Madarihat *thana* of Alipurduar subdivision of Jalpaiguri district just on the border of Bhutan is the home of the Totos, a tiny sub-Himalayan Mongoloid tribe. They are living in their present habitat since the eighteenth century, after driving out the Rabhas. They moved to this area from western part of Dooars because of fatal diseases like kala-azar, malaria and to avoid the unfriendly and more powerful Bhutias. In the sixties of the nineteenth century the British had captured the village from Bhutan. Then the British policy was to keep Totopara exclusively reserved for the Totos. According to a survey conducted by the Anthropological Survey of India in 1990 their population is 924. The Toto language belongs to the Tibeto-Burman family of languages. They are conversant with Bengali and Nepali, and use the Bengali script. They are not only regarded as a scheduled tribe but are also recognised as a 'Primitive Tribal Group' (PTG).

The Totos have flat nose, small eyes, broad cheeks and thick lips. Chaudhuri *et al* (1964) reported that the Toto have lowest ever recorded frequency of blood group O (3 per cent) and very high heterozygous phenotype AB (15 per cent) in the Indian subcontinent for the ABO blood group system. This community is also reported to have very high percentage (47 per cent) of gene B. A_2 allele has been found to be significantly high (8 per cent). A significant feature in the MNS system is that both M and N have very little difference in their frequencies. S has an equal association with M and N. In the Rh blood group system they show a very high R_z (7 per cent) haplotypes with an absence of r and very high R (70 per cent), a trend closer to other Mongolian groups of north-east India.

They are non-vegetarian and eat fish, meat of cow, buffalo, pig, fowl, pigeon, deer, etc. Previously there was no check against eating the meat of dead animals. Carrion eating has not been abandoned even now. An attitude against carrion eating, however, seems to be growing at least among the young generation. Rice is their staple food. They eat potato, onion and garlic. Mustard oil is their medium of cooking. In preparation of curry, a very little amount of oil is used. It is mostly boiled with little salt and chilli. They prepare a non-alcoholic drink from the bark and branches of *khayer* (catechu) trees by boiling them in water. They drink this red water without sugar and milk though sometimes they add some salt. They drink a kind of country liquor *eu* almost daily. They are fond of taking liquor fermented from rice, maize, *mahua* and *kareni*. They chew betel leaf and betel nuts.

The Totos are divided into thirteen exogamous clans namely Damku Be, or Dam Be, Dantro Be, Mangkang Be, Nurekang Be, Bodu Be, Boudi Be, Pishu Cankaiji Be, Lengkaiji Be, Montro Be, Bomo Be, Mongku Be, Nube Be and Tring Koreku Be. Damku Be is accorded the highest status. The members of Boud Be or Boudi Be, Lengkaiji Be, Nurekang Be and Nube Be do not touch monkey or squirrel. They cannot take cooked food from any other community other than the Bhutia. There is no prescribed taboo for the members of Damku be, Mongku Be, Mangkang Be and Montro Be. Members of each clan or *gotra* used to live separately in separate groups.

They are a strictly endogamous group. If inter-community marriage happens, the person concerned is driven out of the village. Inter-clan marriage is prohibited. Marriage is also prohibited in mother's clan in her generation or in her mother's sister's husband's clan in one's own generation. Patrilineal cousins cannot marry. Marriage is however allowed if their fathers are not born of the same mother. Cross cousin marriage of both MBD (mother's sister's daughter) and FSD (father's sister's daughter) type is preferred. Junior sororate is allowed. One year after the death of a wife, the man can marry the younger sister of the wife. Widow remarriage is also allowed. Monogamy is the general rule but rare cases of polygyny are found. They prefer adult marriage but child marriage is not unknown. There are two types of marriage. The most respectable one is *deba behoyia* is which the whole village is to be fed with the sacrifice of a number of cows. In *jipeka behoyia* only two pigs or two cows are sacrificed. The main difference between *deba behoyia* and *jipeka behoyia* is that in the former case the bride is always older than the groom while in the latter the bridegroom is older than the bride. Hence *deba behoyia* and *jipeka behoyia* are also known as *bara behoyia* and *choto behoyia*, respectively. Now *deba behoyia* has almost disappeared. Patrilocal is their post-marital rule of residence. A widow, widower and divorced male and female can remarry. It is reported that divorce takes place. In the assembly of elders the husband announces the divorce. The wife is paid compensation. No compensation is paid in the opposite case.

The Toto live in nuclear or extended families. All sons inherit paternal property equally. Succession is held by the eldest son.

The women participate in agricultural operations but they do not till the soil. They also know the art of spinning and weaving. Homemade coarse cloth is exclusively used by the female folk. They contribute earnings to the family and share the economic burden with the husband in the family. They perform major household chores but do not have any inheritance or succession right under normal circumstances. In the political sphere they do not perform any major role except exercising their franchise at the time of election. They however perform some vital role in rituals associated with religion and life crises events.

Temporary arrangements are made for childbirth in the bedroom itself. No professional mid-wife is available. Some elderly woman comes to help in the delivery of the child. The sharp edge of a strip of bamboo is used to cut the umbilical cord. No special ceremony is attended with childbirth. On the seventh, ninth, eleventh or fifteenth day, some thread (spun and coloured with turmeric by the mother) is tied round the hand of the child. The village *chowkidar*, a government employee or the *mandal* comes to the house at dawn and gives the child a name. *Eu* (country liquor) is served. The child also must have a drop of liquor on its tongue. The name of the newborn baby is announced by the *chowkidar*, *mandal*, or priest. Usually the mane of the great grandfather is considered for the purpose. Where there is no issue, the couple may purchase and adopt a son. The adopted son gets the *gotra* of the adopting father. No religious ceremony is necessary. A simple community feast is enough.

In *jipeka behoyia* system, the father of the boy goes to the father of the girl with a pitcher of *eu* (country liquor) and a hen. If the girl's father accepts the gifts, it is to be presumed that the marriage is settled. After marriage, the girl goes to the house of her husband. On the third day of the arrival of the girl at the house of the bridegroom, a feast is held with members of both the families. The newly married couple is named anew. From that day onward they become known to the society in their new name. The main ceremony of marriage begins after the wife becomes pregnant. At this point, the marriage is socially complete. When the father of the bridegroom is informed of the news of pregnancy, he informs a member of Boudi Be or Bodu Be. The father of the bride is also informed. The date of the festival is fixed by the members of the Boudi Be and the father of the bridegroom. In the appointed day, invited guests come to the house of the bridegroom, dressed in special Toto dresses. Nearly eighty to one hundred pitchers of *eu* are required. The members of the bride's family are received in a befitting manner. Pigs are sacrificed. The front left leg of the pig and *eu* are sacrificed first to their deity Isla, by the members of the Boudi Be or Bodu Be. Then a feast begins which lasts for three days. In *deba behoyia* system, the festivals take place when the bride comes to the house of the bridegroom. In it, the social festival relating to pregnancy does not arise.

The Totos believe that death is due to disease caused by evil spirits. Pigs, fowls and pigeons are offered to get rid of evil spirits. Dead bodies are disposed of by burial. An arrow is placed by the side of the head of the deceased person. When a Toto dies, the villagers fell a *gambhari* tree from the nearby forest. A *bokui* (coffin) is made according to the length of the body. Six plantain leaves form the bed of the deceased. A grave is dug to cover the coffin with earth. Those who attend the burial are fed on the fifth or sixth day of burial. *Eu* is also served. The mourning continues for a year. During this period the husband of a deceased woman does not sleep with any other woman or in any other house. He does not take food in other's house. He does not cut his hair or nails. After the death of the husband, the same rituals are observed by the wife. After the mourning period of one year, the husband or wife may marry again. Sons observe mourning as above for six days when the father dies and for five days in case of the mother. At the end of the mourning period clothes are washed. Sons purify themselves by bathing. The house is purified by the priest who dips a flower in cow's urine and sprinkles it in the rooms. Thereafter normal food is allowed.

About two to three generations ago trading of orange was the main means of their livelihood. Orange was abundant in Totopara and adjacent area of Bhutan. About seventy or eighty years ago orange groves began to die out and today Totopara is devoid of any orange tree. In spite of that, the orange trade plays a vital role in their economic life. From the middle of October to the middle of November most of the Toto families earn a good amount of cash working as porters carrying orange from the garden of Bhutan to Totopara which is one of the centres for export of orange to outside market. A few affluent Toto purchase some oranges from Bhutan and sell it in the neighbouring markets. The Toto have learnt the art of agriculture from the Nepalese some seventy or eighty years ago. At present their primary occupation by and large veers around plough cultivation. A few however practise shifting cultivation. They mainly cultivate *maize*, *kaonia*, *marua*, and paddy. Fishing is one of their pastimes. They rear fowl, pig, bovine cattle and so on. During winter i.e., after harvesting of *marua* they earn their livelihood by working as agricultural and non-agricultural serf. Some get employment under contractors for road clearance in the reserve forest. They also sell their poultry products. Previously they had lac and *banga* (cotton) cultivation. These cultivations have dwindled into practically nothing due to the restrictions imposed by the forest department.

They have the traditional village council of their own. *Kaji* is their religious head, who in consultation with village elders settles any matter related to social norm and manner. *Mandal* is their secular head who settles village disputes, disputes pivoted around land in consultation with village elders. The main duty of the *panchayat* is to access *chowkidari,* tax and to realise it. The messengers carry *kaji's* and *mondals* summons to the village. The *chowkidar* performs his duty under the general supervision of the *panchayat*. The *deoshis* of the Toto conduct religious rites on behalf of the *kaji* or the chief village priest. A panel of *deoshis* is made in order of priority. Statutory *gram panchayat* performs welfare and development activities.

Ishpa is their highest deity. To the outsiders they describe their high deity as Mahakal. Omchu (Kaoni puja), Mayu (orange worship), Munkanin, etc., are their principal festivals. In July-August, on or about the fourteenth day after the new moon and in August-September on or about the fifteenth day after the new moon, all the Totos go to their Mahakali Bari. Mahakali Bari becomes a village. They stay there for five days in July-August and for nine days in August-September. Ten pairs of cocks and hens and one pair of pigs are offered as sacrifice. This is done for the *puja* of Kaleswar. Kaleswar is the other name of Mahakali, the powerful deity. There is no image. *Dhup* made of *tito* tree is burnt. Plantain leaves, rice, etc., are required in the *puja*. Animals of all sorts are killed. Pigs and cows are sacrificed. Recently sacrifice of cows has been stopped. A little flesh and liquor are offered to Mahakali by the *deoshi.* Then the entire meat is boiled and eaten with rice, salt, chillies and liquor. Songs are sung. Gorom *puja* is performed. A Garo priest conducts the *puja*. One duck, two pigs, three goats (one white, one black, and one reddish), fifteen pigeons, a number of cocks and hens and eggs of hens are sacrificed in Gorom *puja*. Ishpa or Mahakali is the most sacred deity enshrined in the great temple of Totopara. Mahakali is represented by two sacred drums kept hanging from the ceiling of the temple. Rice, meat and wine are offered to Mahakali. The devotees eat the offerings. During the *puja* none but the Totos are allowed. After the *puja,* the sacred drums are brought down by the big priests and the music begins. The priests and then the whole assembly join the music. The Totos worship road, sky, river, sun, moon, and star. It is said that the *puja* of Mahakali among the Totos has been derived from the Tibetan *tantrik* tradition. The Totos dance during the *puja*, males and females dance face to face. They do not dance together.

The Totos know basket making, spinning and weaving. They have a good number of folk songs. A song of the Totos collected by the present author is given below.

PE ... LA ... HO ... PE ... LA ... HO ... Zache Gonge Tepun Telay Chedo Mata Sasuing Ba Perlsa Ho

(Free translation: Lord Sun has arisen. Now there is no darkness. Seeing the Sun in the morning we have all become glad.) The Totos do not allow any non-Toto to hear their song. They do not even allow any non-Toto to know the exact meaning of the song.

The Totos maintain inter-community relationship with the Nepalis, Garos and Mechs. They take food and water from them. They have ceremonial friendship with the Nepalis. They maintain cultivator, labour, mortgagee-mortgager relationship with other communities.

The rate of literacy is very low among the Totos. They take indigenous medicines. They now take modern medical facilities from the hospital. They do not believe in family planning. They take spring water through pipes. The Totos have been covered by the new employment programme of the government. A Lutheran World Service Centre has come to their service. Four solar energy centres have been established. Irrigation facilities are not available. The Totos are covered by ICDS programme.

PABITRA KUMAR GUPTA

TURI

The community named Turi has no synonym in written records, but locally they are also called *Sardar* as other Bunos (mixture of many tribes), as their surname is *Sardar* like the Bunos. Their *para* (the neighbourhood where they reside) is also known as *sardar para*. The *gram panchayat pradhan* also knows them as Bunos, but some local people identify them as Turis, as one of their surnames is Turi. History available on this community in existing literature shows the Turis were a 'non-Aryan' caste of cultivators, workers in bamboo and basket makers in Chotanagpur. The physical types of the Turis, their language, their religion have resemblances with those of the Hinduised offshoot of the Mundas (Risley: 1891: II: 333). Present field investigation also reveals their close affinity with the Mundas in terms of the Mundari language, physical feature and in some of their religious practices i.e. sacrifice the cock or hen in their *goal puja* (worship of cattle shed). Their other religious practices are akin to the Hindu rituals. Regarding their migration, it can be said that a larger number of them had migrated to the 24-Parganas district between 1872 and 1881 (Risley: 1891: II: 333). The community perceives, they are at present distributed in the villages like Bhabanipur, Chimter Abad, Konanagore, Gosaba, Mollakhali, Amtali, Dhuchnikhali, Sayra, Nrityabera, Kalinagore, Najat, Ftararpur, Durga Mandap etc. in the district of 24-Parganas (N).

The Turis live in a natural environment of lower Bengal i.e. fertile land condition, sufficient rainfall and moderate temperature, usually they reside in places far away from the centre of the village itself or in the villages where only tribal people live or by the banks of the rivers. The area where the Turis live is a highly flood prone area and due to saline condition of the soil it is a monocrop area. But the area has plenty of fish supply from the surrounding rivers or *jalkars* (fish cultivation on paddy field, after storing of water from the river). The area is also not far from the jungle areas of Sunderban.

The total population of the Turis in West Bengal is 28,443, as per 1981 census.

The language of the Turis is Bengali with the outsiders, like the Bengali people, but they are also found to talk in broken form of Mundari with their neighbouring tribal communities as well as among themselves. As they are totally illiterate they have no script. The constitutional status of the community is that of scheduled caste in West Bengal.

The Turis are non-vegetarian but do not eat beef. They eat pork, meat, and the flesh of duck or chicken. They take meat very occasionally. Their staple food is rice and *panta* i.e. stale rice socked with water for a night and *amani* (water of the soaked rice). They usually take some vegetable curry or pulse with the rice but their vegetable consumption is not plenty. They eat various kinds of roots and tubers which they themselves collect. They consume fish and molluscs by collecting from the rivers or ponds. They use little quantity of mustard oil and spices in their cooking. Their fruit consumption is almost nil but their children consume palm fruits like *tal* and *khejur* when the seasons come, as the area has plenty of these kinds of trees. They have to drink alcohol bought from the market, as they have to do laborious work like earth digging. They do not take tea or milk. They also can not provide milk for their babies, due to their poverty-stricken condition. They do not eat pumpkin in the month of *Bhadra* (August-September), *ol* (a kind of tuber) in the month of *Kartik* (October-November) and *mulo* (radish) in the month of *Magh* (January-February). From observation, it can be concluded that some changes might have taken place in their food habits. They had sufficient land in the past and they never had to bother about food, but now they have to depend more on wheat instead of rice which is nowadays more expensive.

Their surname is usually Sardar though they also use Turi as surname. Their only clan is Kashyap. They place themselves higher than the surrounding tribal populations like Munda, Oraon, Bhumij, Bhuiya, etc. and those placed at the lowest among the Hindu scheduled caste groups like the Ghasi, Dom etc. They are not aware of their exact position in *varna* order, but the neighbouring Pods place them in the Sudra order.

Caste endogamy is the marriage rule of the Turis. Endogamy is also practised at clan level, but village exogamy is maintained. Marriageable age for a Turi girl is twelve or fourteen years. For boys it varies from sixteen to twenty-five years. Negotiation is the primary mode for acquiring one's mate. Monogamy is the form of marriage. *Sankha* (conch-shell bangle), *sindur* (vermilion) and *loha* (iron bangle) are the marriage symbols for a Turi married woman. Dowry is paid both in cash and kind in Turi marriages, the amount of dowry does not exceed Rs.200/- to Rs.800/-. Rules of residence after marriage are patrilocal. Divorce does not generally take place among the Turis, except on rare occasions. It must be settled in the presence of the headman of the *jati panchayat* as well as in the presence of *gramya moral* (who is a headman of a group of castes) and it is done after signing a paper (*chharpatra*). Divorce only takes place if the wife is barren. No compensation or post-divorce maintenance is given in the Turis. Remarriage is allowed both for men and women, and it is known as *nika*. Widows who have grown up children generally do not marry again. No significant change is noticeable in the above mentioned aspects, except abolition of an old custom of paying bride-price in marriage.

Most of the Turi families are of the nuclear type. A very few cases of vertically extended families can be met with. Inter-personal relations are very close and cordial. The relationship between the husband and wife are of love, respect and mutual cooperation. Children get affection from their parents. Some avoidance relationship is maintained between *bhasur* (husband's elder brother) and *bhadra bou* (younger brother's wife). Joking relationship is also found between grandparents and grandchildren. If conflict arises between the members of the family, it is resolved by the elderly members. Paternal property is inherited by the sons. Succession of *gotra*, surname etc. are follows the patriarchal rule. Inter-family linkages also exist among them and they become explicit during social ceremonies or any kind of crisis.

At present they have no property except *bastu* (homestead) land. Women do not get such land. Turi women have role in family management as well as work outside. In the family they cook food, collect fuel such as *harakata* (after harvesting the remaining portion of the paddy plant from the roots) and cowdung, fetch drinking water, look after their children etc.

Apart from looking after their families, they also go for day labourer's jobs i.e. cutting of earth on the paddy fields or *jalkars* or on the river banks which is lost every year by flood. There is no fixed wage rate for them. It varies from Rs. 3/- to Rs. 8/-.

After birth the Turis observe a pollution period of twenty-one days, irrespective of male or female child. Three successive *kamans* (cutting of hairs and taking of bath) are done after birth. One is done just after birth, the second *kaman* is done on the ninth day and the third *kaman* is done on the twenty-first day i.e. on the day of Shasthi puja. After Shasthi puja pollution period is over. A Brahman priest serves them in Shasthi puja and a barber is essential for the *kaman*. Sometimes the Brahman of the Paundra Kshatriya also serves them. They have *annaprasan*. The date for this rite is fixed by the Brahman priest and the maternal uncle puts the rice into the mouth of the new born.

Marriage starts with the *ashirbud* (blessing) rite. The bridegroom is blessed first by the father of the bride and then by other elderly relatives with some coins or clothing. Then the bride is blessed by the bridegroom's party. The marriage day is fixed by the priest, avoiding the month regarded as inauspicious for Bengali Hindu marriage. *Gayehalud* ceremony is done first in the bridegroom's house and then the rest of the turmeric paste along with some clothing and cosmetic articles or *gayehalud tatta* is sent to the bride's house through the barber. Then the bride is smeared with the turmeric paste, after which she takes a bath. *Abhhutic* rite is performed in both the houses. In the evening the *sampradan* (giving away of daughter in marriage) is done by the father or *jyatha* (father's elder brother) of the bride. Next day the married couple go to the house of the bridegroom's father. On the third day they perform the ceremony of *pakasparsa* or *bou bhat* in which the newly married bride serves cooked food to the relatives in a feast and from this day the married couple begin to stay as husband and wife. Marriage party always moves by boat or palanquin. The barber has another function in marriage that is in the morning of the marriage day he cuts nails of every married woman and puts *alta* (a red liquid) on their foot.

After death they cremate the dead body or the poverty-stricken Turis bury it in order to avoid the cost of cremation. This takes place by the side of the river. They go for a *ghat kaman* (cutting of nails and shaving of hair of the sons) on the tenth day. They perform *Sradh* on the thirteenth day. The sons of the deceased must cook their *habissi* in thirteen earthen pots, during this time. Before the *sradh*, the sons wear *uttario* and keep a piece of iron with them during the mourning period.

There is nothing much to be stated about the economic activity of the Turis, as they are a totally landless community. They only serve as day labourers. Their main occupation is cutting of earth and preparing ridges on the paddy fields or making river embankment etc. Their wage rate varies in different seasons or according to the availability of labour from Rs.6/- to Rs. 12/- per day. Their grown up children also go for day labourers job or for cattle herding. As they had sufficient quantity of land in the past, their traditional occupation was cultivation as well as *badakata* (clearing of jungle) for which they were brought to this region as other tribal people. Thus, some changes must have taken place as they are now a totally landless community.

The Turis have their own caste *(jati) panchayat*. The *moral* is the head of that *panchayat*. He is required for settling marriage or for solving cases of divorce etc. Then there is a head *moral* in the village who is recognised also by the other communities of the village. If a case is not settled by the *jati panchayat*, then it is referred to the head *moral* for further decision. The guilty persons are sometimes fined for their evil work. There is no direct role of the *gram panchayat* in social control, but the *gram panchayat* distributes free ration tokens to the Turis.

Hinduism is the religion of the Turis. Lakshmi is their family deity and it is worshipped every Thursday. Other household deities are Manasa and Tusu Lakshmi. Manasa is worshipped in the month of *Bhadra* (August-September) when the tribal people observe Karam festival. Tusu Lakshmi is worshipped on the day of *Paush Sankranti* (last day of the Bengali month *Paush* i.e., December-January) or it is also called *Bauni Sankranti*. The Turis have other household *bratas* and observances e.g. Goal puja, Hari puja, Bhagsaban puja, Jamaisasthi, Their village deities are Kali and Manasa. Their regional deities are Saraswati, Basanti, and Soni etc. The Brahman priest is the sacred specialist of the Turis in all social or religious ceremonies. They have no local fair, but they sometimes visit some in distant places. Their major festival is Dharma Charak in the month of *Baisakh* (April-May). The Turis have had no socio-religious movement but some changes might have taken place in their religious performances. This may be characterised as a shift from tribal religion towards Hindu religion, as evident from their tribal religious observances like cock or hen sacrifice in goal puja, which is prohibited in Hindu religious behaviour. The community have no art and craft, but they weave *château* (mat) or *petit* with dry date palm. This craft is not typically theirs, because many other communities also make such *château* or *petit*.

The Turis have traditional inter-community linkages at social, ritual or occupational levels, as they are served by the Brahman priest and barber. They have no restriction on taking water or cooked food from any community, except the Muslims, although they mix with the Muslims in social ceremonies. For social ceremonies they have to mix with their surrounding communities like the Pods, tribals (Munda, Oraon, Bhuiya, Bhumij etc.), and Muslims. They do not face any trouble in sharing well, tube well, ponds, school, temples etc. They inform that there are many Brahman priests in the surrounding locality whom they call at times of need. The Turis have minimum modern inter-community linkage, because very few of them are literate and only a limited number of their children are going to schools. They have only linkages through the present *gram panchayat* office which they visit of and on for collecting free ration token. In the economic sphere, they have linkages with the Pods and Muslims, whom they serve as day labourers. Cultivator-labour relationship is maintained through payment of wage in cash.

Education among the Turis of the previous generation has been nil, but at present a few of the boys appear to have studied up to class V standard and a few of their children are going to schools. There is no incidence female education.

In general the Turis never go to a hospital or health centre. They mostly depend on indigenous health practices or on medicines given by the neighbouring families. For serious cases, i.e. operations etc. they go to hospital. They are not following any family welfare measure. For drinking they use tube well water or water from the ponds. When the ponds become dry, they use tube well water. They are connected by ferry or bus service at a walking distance. They use no means of communication such as the radio, newspaper etc. except the *gram panchayat* which is the prime source of dissemination of news and information. Electricity is far beyond their reach. Their fuel is *nara* (remaining portion of the paddy plant after harvesting) or *gobar* (cowdung). Under the nutrition programme the Turi boys get a piece of bread once in a week.

CHANDRIMA CHOWDHURY

BIO-ANTHROPOLOGICAL INFORMATION

In this paper an attempt has been made to bring together all available information on the bio-anthropological studies of the people of West Bengal. The compilation of data for the present study is collected from various published materials (Gupta and Dutta 1966, Bhasin 1988, Chatterjee and Mukherjee, 1979, Reddy and Chopra, 1990 and others). The scope of this discourse is mostly confined to the fields of anthropometry, blood groups, dermatoglyphics, demography and other genetic markers.

The population of West Bengal comprises of a large number of endogamous caste populations including the upper castes, the artisans, the agricultural groups, scheduled castes besides a number of minority groups and tribal populations. The ethnic composition of the populations of West Bengal is mostly from the Indo-Aryan, Tibeto-Burman and Austro-Asiatic groups. The prominent tribal groups in this area are the Santal, Bhotia, Lepcha, Sherpa, Toto, Lodha and Bhumij and are mainly inhabited in the districts of Bankura, Purulia, Medinipur, Birbhum and Darjeeling. Among the castes the Brahman, Kayastha, Vaidya, Namasudra, Rajbanshi and Mahishya are predominant.

Anthropometry: The first anthropometric study of the population of Bengal was initiated by Risley in 1891, which was further pursued by Chanda (1916), Guha (1935), Chatterjee (1948), Raychaudhury (1952), Majumdar and Rao (1960), Basu (1969) and others. In this context the study of Bengal anthropometry by Majumdar and Rao (1960) is noteworthy. They have taken sixteen anthropometric measurements on 3681 populations from 29 districts. In this paper, the data on stature, cephalic index, nasal index and total facial index have been dealt with considering 91 samples drawn from 42 ethnic groups studied from West Bengal. Only four groups have been reported for both the sexes e.g. the Mahishya, Kora, Lodha, and Pahira. Some of the groups such as the Baidya, Brahman, Kayastha, Bagdi and Rajbanshi were studied repeatedly by different authors. In general the people of Bengal exhibit short to medium stature. The mean stature varies from 157 cm among the Lepcha (Risley 1915) to 169 cm among the Baidya of Calcutta (Chatterjee 1948). It is also observed that the tribal populations are relatively shorter than the higher caste populations of Bengal. The region is characterised by long to round headed people. The cephalic index ranges from 70.90 among the Vangaja Vaidya to 83.98 among the Subarna Banik.

The mesorrhine (60 per cent) is the predominant form of nose followed by leptorrhine (35 per cent). Only 4 per cent chamaerrhine nose are found mostly among the tribal groups. The average nasal index varies from 54.55 among the Kapali (Majumdar and Rao, 1960) and Keora (Dasgupta *et al.* 1981) to 85.50 among the Lodha (Bhowmick, 1956).

The data on facial measurements of some communities of this region are available. The mean total facial index varies from 82.98 among the Lodha to 91.68 among the Brahman.

Besides these somatometric studies, a good number of reports of growth and nutrition of the communities of West Bengal has been published by Roy and Roy (1969), Bharati (1983), Das (1985, 1986), Sen (1988), Bhowmick (1993), Bagchi (1994) indicating nutritional sex differences and inter-group variations in growth process.

Blood Groups: The serogenetic characteristics of the populations of Bengal have fairly been studied. Such studies were initiated by Macfarlane in 1938, followed by Sarkar *et al.* (1953), Sen (1954), Majumdar (1958), Bhattacharjee *et al.* (1977), Chakrabarti *et al.* (1986) and others. The distribution of blood groups among various populations of Bengal has been reviewed by Chatterjee and Mukherjee (1979). Altogether 77 samples comprising 22 ethnic groups were studied with regards to ABO blood group system (Singh *et al.* 1994). In general, the gene frequency of O blood is higher than that of the B and A genes, as revealed from other studies. In West Bengal the gene frequency of B varies from 15.50 per cent among the Kurmi Mahato (Basu *et al.* 1966) to 41.80 per cent among the Poundra Kshatriya (Roy and Das 1973), while the A gene ranges from 7.72 per cent among the Poundra Kshatriya to 37.0 per cent among the northern Pahariya (Basu *et al.* 1966). The average value of B gene in West Bengal appears to be higher than that in the Indian population and there is a tendency to increase of the B gene in successive samples of a few populations particularly among the Brahmans.

Only eight samples from different populations were studied from the A_2 blood group. The gene frequencies in the A_2 blood in the present series ranges from 0.27 per cent to 8.2 per cent among the Toto of Jalpaiguri (Chaudhuri *et al*. 1964). Some scholars suggested the high frequency of B gene and low O gene among the castes of lower social order resembling the local tribal population as compared to the communities belonging to the higher social order of Bengal (Macfarlane and Sarkar, 1941, Kumar 1957 and Sen 1960). The temporal trend of the declining of the O gene frequency and an increasing of the B gene in the successive Brahman population of this region has also been stressed upon by Chatterjee and Mukherjee (1979). However the materials so far available with regard to ABO blood groups are inadequate to focus a geographical cline and the ethnic diversities in different regions of Bengal.

Rh-blood groups. The characteristic features of the Rh-blood group distribution (based on five anti-sera) among the population of West Bengal indicates a high frequency of R1 (CDe) gene complex accompanied by low frequency of all other gene complex. The R1 (CDe) gene complex is highest among the Oraon of Jalpaiguri (86.83 per cent) studied by Piplai *et al* (1985), followed by two sub populations of the Bagdi (75 per cent) of Hooghly district (Kumar 1957). The Rarhi Brahman has a frequency (15.53 per cent) of r (cde) gene complex, followed by Tantulia Bagdi of Hooghly (12.11 per cent). Such a low value of r (cde) gene complex among the populations of West Bengal do not agree with the observation of Morunt *et al* (1958) which shows 24 per cent r genes in the upper caste people of eastern India. The complete absence of r (cde) gene is also reported from the Duley Bagdi of Hooghly (Kumar, 1957).

MNS Blood Groups. Only 23 samples comprising 20 ethnic groups have been studied for MN system of blood groups. In the present series the gene frequency of m is higher than n except the Oraon of Jalpaiguri (Piplai *et al.*, 1985). The frequency of m gene in this region varies from 35.71 per cent among the Oraon of Jalpaiguri to 70 per cent among the Rajbanshi of Cooch Bihar. The high frequency of m gene among the Rajbanshi suggests Mongoloid affinity. There is less reported work on MNS system, only four samples in this trait have so far been reported among the people of West Bengal. The general picture of MNS blood group system in this region is that M and s gene are more frequent than N and s genes.

Other Blood Groups. Among the other blood groups very few studies are so far reported from this region. The studies are mostly confined to the P blood group, Duffy, Diego, and Kell blood groups systems among the Brahman, Kayastha, Vaidya, Rajbanshi, Kaora and Toto. The P_2 gene is found to be higher than the P_2 in P blood group system. The Poundra Kshatriya of 24 Parganas has the highest frequency of P_2 gene (80.5 per cent) as reported by Roy and Das (1973) followed by Vaidya (71.9 per cent), Kayastha (70 per cent), and Brahman (68.9 per cent) (Sen, 1960). In West Bengal Duffy and Diego blood groups have been studied in three Rajbanshi samples only (Das *et al* 1967). The frequency of Fy^a gene ranges from 32 per cent among the Rajbanshi of Jalpaiguri to 48 per cent in Cooch Bihar with an average value of 38 per cent. In Diego blood group, the phenotypic frequency of Di (a+) is found to be 2 per cent in Medinipur to 6 per cent in Cooch Bihar among the three samples of Rajbanshi (Das *et al* 1967). With regard to Kell blood group, Chakraborty *et al* (1975) studied six communities from 24 Parganas and the gene frequency of K varies from 14.4 per cent among the Mahishya to 24.4 per cent among the Vaidya. Three upper caste populations of Bengal e.g. the Brahman, Kayastha, and Vaidya have also been studied from United Kingdom (Sen 1960). The K gene frequency ranges from one per cent among the Vaidya to 6.5 per cent among the Brahman.

ABH Secretion: There are 12 studies in ABH secretor status from this region. The secretor gene (Se) ranges from 22.54 per cent among the Vaidya of Calcutta to 52.25 per cent among the Rajbanshi.

Haemoglobin Variant: In West Bengal, the haemoglobin variants have been well studied. Among the various types of haemoglobin variants, the sickle cell trait (HbS) appear to be very low among the people of West Bengal. The HbS gene ranges from 0.49 per cent among the Oraon of Jalpaiguri to 0.60 per cent among the Santal of Medinipur. However, large numbers of HbE cases have been described from this region. Altogether 34 samples have so far been studied for HbE variant. The Deshi Koch population of West Bengal has a very high frequency of HbE gene (61.20 per cent) reported by Das *et al* 1990 followed by Poliya Koch (49.40 per cent) and Mech of Cooch Bihar (34.61 per cent) as reported by Kate *et al.* (1984).

Serum Proteins and Red Cell enzymes:

Haptoglobin:- In all 21 samples have so far been studied on Haptoglobin (Hp) out of which 13 samples belong to tribal populations. In West Bengal the occurrence of HP^2 is higher than HP^1 gene. The HP^2 gene varies from 75 per cent among the Rajbanshi of Cooch Bihar to 89.93 per cent among the Oraon of Jalpaiguri. The frequency of HP^1 is relatively higher among the tribal population of West Bengal except the Lodha of Medinipur in general and the tribes belonging to the Tibeto-Burman group in particular.

Transferrin:- The primary frequency of Tf^C allele is very high in this region which varies from 93.6 per cent among the Lepcha of Darjeeling to cent per cent in several populations. The Tf^D is relatively higher (6.34 per cent) among the Koch Poliya of Malda (Saha *et al* 1990) than the neighbouring populations. It is observed that the frequency of the Tf^D

is relatively higher among the tribal population than the caste groups in Bengal.

GC System: - Only five tribal groups have so far been reported in the Gc system. The frequency of Gc varies from 8.91 per cent among the Oraon of Jalpaiguri to 79.05 per cent among the Lepcha of Darjeeling (Saha *et al* 1987). The rare variant of Gc (Gc=0.40per cent) has also been reported among the Christian Lepcha.

PGM System: - Only 30 samples of PGM, system have so far been studied from West Bengal. The frequency of PGM allele varies from 59.10 per cent among the Rabha of Cooch Bihar (Chakraborty et al 1986) to 93 per cent among the Bagdi (Mukherjee *et al* 1982). The occurrence of PGM is relatively high among the caste populations of Bengal than that of the tribals.

Easterase – D: The Easterase – D system has also been reported on 16 samples from West Bengal. The gene frequency of ESD varies from 51.4 per cent among the Lodha of Medinipur to 78.5 per cent among the Vaidya of 24 Parganas (Chakraborty *et al.* 1986).

GLO System: Of the four samples so far studied in the GLO system; the Lepcha of Darjeeling has the highest frequency of GLO2 81.33 per cent as reported by Saha *et al.* (1987).

G-6PD: The G-6PD deficiency has been reported on six samples from West Bengal and it ranges from 1.7 per cent among the Bengali Hindu of Calcutta (Biswas, 1975) to 14.05 per cent among the Santal of Medinipur (Kate *et al.* 1978).

Other Genetic Markers: In other genetic markers, the phenylthiocarbamide (PTC) tasting ability and deficiencies of red-green colour vision of the people of West Bengal are well studied.

PTC: In West Bengal, 26 samples comprising 12 ethnic groups are so far reported in respect to the phenylthio-carbamide testing ability. The frequency of non-taster gene t varies from 33.25 per cent among the Rai Nepali of Darjeeling (Bhattacharjee and Chowdhury, 1976) to 70.71 per cent among the Ruhidas of Hooghly (De, 1967). It is interesting to point out that the caste populations of Bengal show a relatively higher frequency of non-taster gene than that of the tribal populations, where taster gene T is found to be higher.

Colour Blindness: In all three sample populations (23 male and 9 female) consisting of 18 groups mostly on the caste groups have so far been reported with regard to deficiency of red-green colour vision of people of West Bengal. The average incidence of colour blindness among the caste population of Bengalis is found to be high (4.47 per cent).

Dermatoglyphics: The dermatoglyphic study in West Bengal are mostly confined to finger prints and was initiated by Biswas (1939-40), followed by Chakrabartti, 1960; Sarkar, 1967, 1969, Chattopadhyay and Dash Sharma 1969; Banerjee and Banerjee 1975 and others.

Altogether 57 samples (44 males and 13 females) covering 22 populations have so far been reported from West Bengal. In dermatoglyphics, most of the caste populations of West Bengal are characterised by the high frequency of loop patterns (64.50 per cent) in Rarhi Brahman to 46.40 per cent in Bauri (scheduled caste) than that of the whorl pattern (54 per cent among the Buna to 61.80 per cent among the Rarhi Brahman). However, in tribal population majority of he samples show a reverse trend i.e., high frequency of whorl pattern (57.70 per cent among the Oraon of Bengal) than the loops, except among the Lodha and Mech. It is also reported that the Indo-Aryan and Austric speaking groups of West Bengal are in general having preponderance of loop patterns over the whorl. The occurrence of arch frequency in this region varies from 0.70 per cent among the Bagdi to 6.4 per cent among the Brahman (Banerjee 1970).

The pattern intensity index (PII) among the male sample varies from 1301among the Brahman of Burdwan to 15.6 among the Oraon of Bengal, while in the case of female it varies from 11.80 among the Brahman to 15.60 among the Oraon.

The data on total finger ridge counts (TFRC) are very few, the mean TFRC among the male series varies from 128.9 among the Vaidya of Barasat (Banerjee and Banerjee, 1975) to 147.3 among the Brahman (Banerjee 1970), while among the female it varies from 125 to 132.9 indicating sexual dimorphism with regard to Tpre

A few reports are available in palmer prints which are mostly confined to the main-line formula (Chakravartti 1960, Roy Choudhury 1962, Ghose *et al* 1973 and others). In general among the population of Bengal, the highest prevalence of main-line formula occurs in 11.9.7. - followed by 7.5.5 and 9.7.5.

Beside this ethnic variation, the genetic observation on traits of finger and palmar dermatoglyphics has also been reported by a few scholars (Mukherjee, 1967, Ghosh and Nanda, 1975, Sarkar, 2004 and others).

Demography: A good number of studies on demo-genetic aspects of various populations of West Bengal have been reported by different scholars (Basu, 1967, Talukdar, 1971, Barua, 1976, Gupta, 1980, Basu *et al* 1982, Chatterjee 2004 and others). These studies mostly deal with various problems such as consanguinity and inbreeding, incompatibility in matings in respect of ABO blood groups and fertility to understand the macro-evolution by estimating selection pressure and genetic drift etc. It reveals from all these studies that the mean live births in completed family size of 31 samples from West Bengal range between 4.7 of Varendra Kayasth (Talukdar, 1971) and 8.84 among the Muslim (Roy and Bharati, 1982). The total selection intensity (as measured following Crow's formula) varies from 0.275 among the Mahishya (Bharati, 1983) to 1.133 among the Northern Pahira (Basu, 1967). In general the fertility component of total selection is higher than mortality component of West Bengal.

Besides, the data collected from 18 locations of West Bengal under All India Bio-anthropological Survey of the Anthropological Survey of India suggests that the population distribution of West Bengal in the age group of 0-14 years, 15-44 years, and 45+ years are 38.67 per cent, 43.62 per cent, and 17.71 per cent respectively, indicating a progressive trend of population expansion. The sex ratio is estimated to be 108 which is more or less similar to all India average of 106. The child-woman ratio is estimated to be 55.63. The proportion of married male and female is 37.65 per cent. The average household size in West Bengal from 1-5 persons and 6-10 persons are 55.5 per cent and 40.06 per cent respectively. The literacy of the region is 58.24 per cent among the male and 47.84 per cent among the female which is relatively higher than the Indian average (Singh *et al.* 1994).

In recent years, the comprehensive study at the genomic level based on mitochondrial DNA, Y-chromosome, Short Tandem Repeat (STR) markers and human specific polymorphic insertion/deletion loci have been reported among the various castes and tribal populations namely the Brahmins, Bagdi, Mahishya, Lodha, Santal, Munda, Kayastha and others from West Bengal (Majumdar *et al.* 1999, Bhattacharya *et al.* 1999, Kashyap *et al.* 2003 and others.) It is observed that the level of heterozygosity among the studied population are very high than most of the global populations, except Africa.

Thus it is apparent from the foregoing presentation that the research on biological anthropology is mostly confined to only a few castes and tribes of West Bengal. A large number of populations are yet to be studied in order to understand the total biological variations in different ethnic and geographic areas of West Bengal.

B. N. SARKAR

GLOSSARY

abhyudaik - propitiating the ancestors

abou - grandfather

abur - grandmother

ada/odu - ginger

adap - etiquette

adhibas - a marriage ritual

adhibaser tatwa - bridal dress, costumes etc.

adhibeshan - meeting

adhikari - communal priest

adhiya - half

adravvun - a Parsee word for engagement

adreyang thongacho - naming ceremony

afika - naming ceremony

aghran, aghrayan - Eighth month of the Bengali calendar; falls in November-December

agit - Lepcha clan

Ahura Mazda - a Parsee word for God almighty

ai sari - grandmother's sari

aiburo khaono, aiburobhat - last eating ceremony of unmarried person, pre-marital feast

aina - mirror

ajiaur - father's mother

akad bandha - a principal ceremony of marriage without social and cultural paraphernalia

akanda - a kind of flower

akud naksha - relation of affection and joking

alga - free labour

alpana - floor painting

alu-posta - A preparation of potato and opium seed

alur chop - potato boiled and mixed with salt, spices and *besan* (powdered pulse) and then fried in oil

am - mango

aman chaul - late autumn crop of paddy

amil - representative of midwife
ana - one sixteenth of a rupee
anandashouch - post-delivery pollution
anga-mukut - a kind of ceremonial or ornamental dress
angua pechchua - middle-man
anjuman - assembly
annaprashan - first rice eating ceremony
antiya - blood relatives
apadevata - evil spirit
aratdar - whole seller
aru - a kind of potato available in the forest
asauch - pollution
ashar - third month of the Bengali calendar; falls in June-July
ashek - a marriage rite
ashirbad - blessing
astana - graveyard of a saint
at mangala - a marriage ritual observed on eighth day after marriage
ata - a kind of fruit
atvaja - a pre-delivery ritual
aulia - one who sings the praises of Allah
ayat - verse
azan/azaan - a summon to prayer
babla - Indian acacia tree
badal biha - marriage by exchange
badeh - country made liquor prepared from boiled rice
badeth - matchmaker
bagh - tiger
baghar - a kind of plant required as catalyst for fermenting of rice beer
baharain-jawa - marriage by elopement
bahun - Brahman
bairagya/vairagya - one who is free from human passion
baishakha - first month of the Bengali calendar; falls in April-May
baji - acrobatic work

bak dan - betrothal
bakhsin - woman possessed by evil spirit
bali phul - ritual friendship
bandha - the labourers who have received part payment before actual employment so that they are obliged to work for their masters
bandhak - mortgage
bandhu - friend
banna/bannya - flood
bansjhar - cluster of bamboos
bantarul - a kind of vegetable
bar dekha - to see bridegroom
bara bhag - larger share of property
baragaman - a marriage ritual, arrival of bridegroom
barasar - seat for the groom
barasu - naming ceremony of child
bargadar - sharecropper
bari-vasan - throwing away the debris in the marriage pandal
barmitzva - a Jewish word for son of commandment
baroa - a death rite
baromashya - a kind of folk song
bartani - a kind of reciprocity or exchange of services
barthakurer bar - Saturday, the day of Lord Sani
baryatry, barjatri - marriage party of bride grooms side
bashargriha - consummation ceremony
basi sraddha - ancestors worship
basia biha/basi biha - second day of marriage
basisraddha - The Vaishya observe ancestors worship of one year on the seventeenth day after death.
bati - lamp
batsarik sraddha - annual post-funeral ceremony
bayasham - breakfast
bedi - alter for the bride and bridegroom
behenra pata - a kind of medicinal plant

benja-pitra	-	cutting a mat of reed into several pieces
betar-bou	-	Sons wife
beti-jamai/biti-jamai	-	daughter and son-in-law
betkal	-	tender cane shoot
beuli/mashkalai	-	blackgram
beun	-	implement for weaving blanket
beyan	-	mother-in-law of a son or daughter
bhadra	-	fifth month of the Bengali calendar; falls in August-September
bhadralok	-	gentleman
Bhairav	-	God Mahesh
bhaisa/bhaish	-	buffalo
bhaj rakha	-	levirate
bhandari	-	barber
bhang	-	hemp
bhasur	-	Husband's elder brother
bhatua	-	a category of labour who are given meals as wage
bhayad	-	kin groups
bheja	-	donation
bhiksha jhuli	-	a bag for alms
bhiksha	-	alms
bhikshang dehi	-	give me alms
bhujno	-	first rice eating ceremony
bhute dhara	-	haunted by ghost
bichhatrisi	-	heterogeneous village council
bidhata-bidhuti	-	a birth rite
bidi	-	indigenous cigarette
binnar-jhad	-	a clump of elongated grass found in the boundaries of crop fields
biri kalai	-	black gram
bishma	-	a death rite of the Muslim
bishratri/kalratri	-	poison night/next day of marriage when bride and groom sleep separately
biye	-	marriage
biyerdin bandhiyeneoa	-	fixing of marriage date
boasin	-	younger brother's wife of a male member

bohonai - sister's husband
bohra - trader
bokhu - a female dress
bokul - coffin
boli - sacrifice
bongthing - sacred specialist
boroj or *baroj* - betel leaf vines
boubhat - a marriage ritual
boudi - elder brother's wife
boulat - interest-free loan
brata - vow
bwnanwi-lana - marriage by capture
byathum - coverlet
chacho chatiar/chaco chatiar - a puberty rite
chadi pecha - jungle owl
chaharam - a death rite of the Muslim
chai-daka - calling of spirits
chaitra/chait - last month of the Bengali calendar; falls in March-April
chakot - liquor
chalchitra - superstructure
challisha kaman - post-delivery purificatory ceremony
chamroy - leaf canopy
chang - a kind of musical instrument
char handi mad - four pitchers of liquor
charas - a kind of hemp
chas-bas - cultivation
chatti - naming ceremony
chaturtha - a death rite
cheeharlata - a kind of plant
chhadnatala - ear marked place, where main marriage ceremony is performed.
chhamu - a marriage rite
chhari/chara-chhari - divorce
chhata/chhatu - mushroom
chhatti - a post-delivery ritual
chhatu - mixture of ground gram, maize and jowar
chhaychanda - six full moon days
chhaymasi - a death rite

chhele	- son
chhenka	- engagement ceremony
chhi	- homebrewed alcoholic beverage
chhiri	- a birth ritual
chholar dal	- pulses of gram
chhollatala	- an open space
chhut/ chhutak	- pollution
chhutanum	- divorce
chhuter chul	- pollution hair of the newborn
chhutir raat	- a ritual signifying purified night
chhutok	- pollution
chi	- alcoholic drink of the Lepcha, prepared from millet
chiddhu samaj	- traditional Bhutia panchayat
ching ming	- A Chinese word for bright and clear
chira	- parched rice
chiri	- a birth rite
chiri	- ring
chirung	- a basketful of indigenous liquor
chiruni	- comb
chita	- funeral pyre
choddoana bhag	- fourteen out of sixteen parts
chohan jal	- a kind of fishing net
chopo	- ceremonial friend
chori biha	- marriage by courtship and elopement
choriya biya	- marriage by elopement
choukidari	- job of a watchman
chouthiary	- a marriage ritual
chua-chul	- hair at birth
chubondi	- a kind of female dress
chun	- lime
chung	- a popular drink (brewed alcohol) made from millet.
churakurun	- tonsure
chuti	- indigenous cheroot
cohen	- A Jewish priest
dade	- consanguineal kin
dahattar	- maternal grandparents property
dahin/daini	- witch

daidas - lineage members
dai-e-mutlaq - head and chief of socio-religious world of the Dawoodi Bohra.
daima - midwife
damu - conch shell
dan - handed over/gift
danda kata - cutting the evil teeth
dapatha - crossing
dar-chag - a prayer flag tied to the bamboo pole
dargah - Muslim sacred centre
dari-kata - shaving of beard
dasakarma - ten purificatory ceremonies
dash jan - ten important persons
dasha - a death rite
dashalaya bichar sabha - assembly of judges from the village
dashma - a death rite of the Muslim
dastur - a Parsee sacred specialist
daura sura - a kind of male dress
dekhasuna biha - marriage by negotiation
dena bibaha - ritual in which a daughter is offered to prospective bridegroom
denmohar/den-mehr - bride price
deor - husband's brother
deoshi - religious specialist of the Toto
deosi - sacred specialist
dhabal - leucoderma
dhaka tupi - a kind of Nepali cap
dhamsa - drum
dhan sudh bandhasa - fetching of paddy plant before harvesting
dhanushtankar - tetanus
dhar chhog - sacred flags
dhar - credit
dharam chacha - putative uncle
dharambhai/dharma-bhai - putative relation of brother
dhare biye - marriage is arranged and performed within a day.
dharma ma - god mother
dhatri - midwife

dhenki - husking pedal
dhibi - mound
dhokra - a kind of mat made from jute fibre
dhole/dholki/dhol - a kind of percussion instrument.
dhula paye lagan deoa - returning of bride and bridegroom to bride's house without wearing any footwear after marriage
dhumkuria - bachelors' dormitory
diara - current of the Ganga
din majdur/din majur - daily wage earner
diragaman - a marriage ritual
disum sendra - hunting festival
divo - light
doi-bhat - curd rice
dokhma - tower of silence
dokta - dry tobacco leaf
dol jatra - festival of colour
dopaira - junction of the paths
dosti - friendship
du handi mad - two pitchers of liquor
dua - private property
duana bhag - two out of sixteen parts
dudh-bhai - brothers who are given breast milk by the same mother
dudh-bon - sisters who are given breast milk by the same mother
dui supurir nimantran - invitation with two betel nuts
dulaga jal - a kind of fishing net
duor dharathakur - family deity
dupahra - lunch
dwnkhatnai - marriage by elopement
dyo - a kind of alcoholic drink
ejer - loose trouser
ek dupur - working for half a day
ek ghoro - excommunicated
ek supurir nimantran - invitation with one betel nut
ekatra parivar - joint family
ekusha/ekushar snan - a post-delivery ritual
enchor - green jack-fruit
fakir - saint

fariah - middleman
fate nagra - victory drum
fila - bullock's leg
fufi - father's sister
fulsajjya - consummation ceremony
gahwi-dwnnai - obtaining girls by service
gamcha - towel
ganga dewa - cremation on the bank of the river Ganga
gangajal - a friendship term
ganja - hemp
gaon ghar - a kind of reciprocity on the basis of village-level exchange of services
garba - a Gujarati folk dance
garh pratha - state system
garvadan - second marriage ritual when wife attains puberty
gayehalud - smearing of turmeric on the body
gembu - Bhutia panchayat
geruabastra - clothes of saffron colour
ghanta ghar - royal treasury
ghar ka mul - father's lineage
ghar nizar - those who have a house
ghar tarul - a kind of vegetable
ghara - earthen vessel
ghar-dekha - mutual visit to houses before finalization of marriage
ghar-jamai - one who lives at ones father-in-laws house
ghat - purificatory bath
ghatak - match-maker
ghate utha - ceremonial bath
ghee - clarified butter
gheedhali - offering of *ghee* in the fire
ghoptir - ancestor worship
ghot/ghat - earthen pot used for worship
ghuan jal - a kind of net
ghuni - fishing trap
ghunte / ghusi - cowdung cake
godak - squirrel

godet - messenger
gobal/goal - cow shed
gole-jal - round net
gompha/gumpha - monastery
goto - alcohol brewed from millet
gouridan - giving in marriage of the daughter before puberty or before the age of nine years
graha sankranta bidhi - ritual to ward of the evil effect of bad omen
gua - betel nuts
gua-vangni - exchange of betel nuts
gugli - small water snail
gunaguni - astrology
gur - molasses
guru dakshina - honorarium to a preceptor
gurubaba - Vaishnava preacher
guruman/gunin - indigenous medicine man/divinator
gushti/gusti - lineage
haba - a birth rite
habisanna - boiled sunned rice with *ghee* as a ritual food
haldat - turmeric
halud jal biha - marriage by negotiation
hans - goose
hansua - sickle
hanuman - monkey
har - bone
haram - sinful
hari paria - place of throwing earthen pot
haria/handia - home made rice beer
hashi-maja - joking
hatbain - blessing ceremony
hathi/hatho - elephant
hesped - special prayer
hila bria - mortuary rite
huji - priest cum medicine man
hukko - hubble bubble
hum chin pung - A Chinese dish of flour ball stuffed with meat.

husuk - Rabha clan or gotra
iddat - post-delivery maintenance
idli - a South Indian dish
ihab-sang - a religious purification ritual
ijjat - honour
illi - rice beer
imam - Muslim religious specialist/leader
indara - ring well
jagyaman - adult
jaistha - second month of the Bengali calendar; falls in May-June
jajmani - patron-client relationship
jal - water
jal/jaal - net
jal-ghati - mug of water
jalpara - a kind of indigenous treatment
jam - a kind of fruit
jamadar - sweeper
jamai - son-in-law
jamaibabu - sister's husband
jamat - people who perform prayer in the same mosque
jamrul - star apple
janaja namaj - prayer for the dead person
janpat - daily wage agricultural labourer
janr - alcohol brewed from cereals
jari - a kind of medicinal plant
jati-chhut - outcaste
jer lup - clothes used by the Lepcha
jesthangha - extra share of paternal property given to the eldest son
jhakris - oracle
jhal bhat - hot rice
jharfunk - a kind of indigenous treatment
jhinuk - oyster
jhora - spring
jhuntis - floor decoration
joutuk - gift, presentation
juin - a friendship term
kab-ni - white handloom shawl

kachim	- turtle
kachu	- arum
kado	- millet
ka-gyud	- Karnapa group
kaka	- father's younger brother
kalai-dal	- black gram pulse
kalo murgi chana	- black chicken
kalratri	- a marriage ritual
kaman	- post-delivery purificatory rite
kan phuka guru	- spiritual master who utters guru mantra in the ear
kanchasadh	- a pre-delivery ritual
kanga	- a kind of plant
kanjipani	- rice water that has been kept in an earthen pot for many days
kan-khoda/karna-chhed	- piercing of earlobes
kankra	- crab
kantha	- bedspread
kanya khuja	- searching for the bride
kanya sari	- sari for bride
kanya-dekha	- to see bride
kapad dhoa	- cleaning of clothes
kaphan-lephan	- clothes for burial
karam sari	- cloth given to the bride by her father-in-law during Karam festival
karanda saq	- a kind of vegetable leaf
karanik	- writer or scribe
karla	- a kind of vegetable
karsa bhanda/karsa banda	- burning the paddy stick with decorated pot
kartik	- seventh month of the Bengali calendar; falls in October-November
karzan hasanat	- to give loan without interest
kasi/kanshi	- a kind of percussion instrument
kantahar Brahman	- a category of degraded Brahman
kattas	- tobacco
keshut	- a kind of leaf
ketuba	- A Jewish word for marriage contact
ketuba	- marriage contract
kha-dang	- white coloured scarf

khai purano - parched paddy is given on the palms of the bride and both the bride and groom throw this in the sacred fire with the utterance of mantra
khalasi - manual labourer
khalian - paddy field
khalifa - Muslim tailor
khaloy - fishing basket
khan-chang - engagement
khara - drought
khari - a kind of reed
khartal - a kind of percussion instrument
khat phar - a marriage ritual
kha-thri - coloured handloom shawl
khatna - circumcision
khatsonnai - willingly going to the man's house
khenri - tonsure
khesari - a kind of pulse
kheya jal - casting net
khoraki - a mode of payment of wages mostly in terms of food
khorpose - compensation
khosal - headman
khoya-surki bhanga - making of stone chips
khunt katti - those who have cleared the virgin forest land for the purpose of cultivation.
khuppa - a Jewish word for alter
khuthben - a marriage ceremony
kind - a kind of fruit
kisani/krisani - a seasonal contract between labourer and landlord
kishan - daily wage agricultural labourer.
kodo - a kind of millet.
kolay biha - child marriage
kosher - a Jewish word for slaughter
krishi-karma - cultivation
kshir - dehydrated milk
kuanr bhat - a marriage ritual
kulo - winnowing fan

kulthi	- a kind of pulse
kumkum	- a kind of paste/vermilion
kunchra	- mahua seed
kundri	- a kind of vegetable
kure ghar	- hut
kusumdinga/kusumdika	- a marriage ritual
kut	- annual lease
kutor	- deer
kutum	- affinal relatives
kyi-du	- a regional body
kyidung	- community meeting
ladki ka mul	- wife's lineage
lagares	- labourer engaged on annual contract with liberty to serve others
lagto	- a marriage rite
lah	- umbilical cord
laja home	- a part of marriage rituals.
lakshmir-handi	- earthen pot denoting good luck
lal fita	- red ribbon
lal salu	- red cloth
lama	- Buddhist sacred specialist
landa	- messenger
lau	- bottle gourd
layek/bamre	- priest
li chun	- a Chinese word for spring
loha porano	- putting of iron bangles on wrist of the bride
loha, lohar kharu	- iron bangle
mach chash	- pisciculture
madal	- a kind of percussion instrument
madhyastha	- mediator
madrasa	- Islamic school
maduli/tabij	- talisman
magh	- tenth month of the Bengali calendar; falls in January-February
magni	- blessing
maha jal	- a kind of big fishing net
mahapa	- bier
mahato	- headman

mahendar	- a cowherd-cum-agricultural helping hand appointed on annual contract basis
mahi	- hot water with turmeric
mahua	- a kind of flower
majlis	- meeting of qualified members
makan	- wholesale centre
makha-ranga	- wall or floor design
makri	- earring
maktab	- Islamic educational centre
malabadal	- exchange of garlands
mali	- gardener
malini	- gardeners wife
malsa	- round earthen pot
mama	- maternal uncle
mama-shashur/mama-svashur	- maternal uncle-in-law
mami-shashuri/mami-svashuri	- maternal aunt-in-law
mang bara	- marriage by negotiation
mangal astak	- hymns
mangal sutra	- a special type of necklace used as marriage symbol
mangni biya	- marriage by negotiation
mangni	- engagement in marriage
mangni	- negotiation
mantra-data	- preceptor
marab sen	- traditional village council of the Rabha
marjholla	- starch of rice
mashem	- a kind of bean
masjid	- mosque
masur/musur	- lentil
mat mati saq	- a kind of vegetable leaf
math mongra	- first day of marriage
matsa-paras/matsa-mukhi	- eating of fish after the termination of pollution period
mayada	- flour
mazhar, majar	- Muslim sacred centre, graveyard of saint
mehendi	- red henna
mete sindur	- vermilion with dull reddish tone

methor - scavenger
misaq - a covenant
mita - friend
mit-baba - father of putative friend
miter sahin - religious friend
mit-ma - mother of putative friend
mo-kho - a kind of Drukpa female dress
moling - stump of a sal tree
momo - a snack, prepared from pork and wheat
moral - caste leader
mosem - a kind of pulse
moulavi - sacred specialist of the Muslim
mrigi - epilepsy
mug/moong - green gram
mujuthi - naming ceremony
mukhagni - to put fire on the mouth of the dead
mulo - radish
mum - sacred specialist
mundan/matha mundan - tonsure
munish - adult labourers
munish - daily wage agricultural labourer
murda-ghati - cremation ground
muri - puffed rice
murubbi - community elders
musalmani - circumcision or literally becoming a Muslim
myab - a school of thought
naba graha - nine planets
nabasakhas - nine artisan castes
naga - snake
nagare - contract labourer
naichched - cutting of the umbilical cord
naihar - mother-in-law
nakh-kata - trimming of nails
nakshi - bachelors' dormitory
nam dak nandi - a birth rite
namaj/namaz - prayer of the Muslim
na-majh - a special kind of food
namasi - a pre-delivery ritual

namkirtan - devotional song
namung sa-ajaong - dinner
nanad - husband's sister
nandimukh/nannimukh - ancestor worship
naniaur - mother's mother
nar-kata - cutting of umbilical cord
narolo - purification
naru/nadu - ball of sweetmeat
naryok palit - twin flute
nath - nose-stud
nati - grandson
natni - granddaughter
natta - a post-delivery ritual
natun jama - new garment
naya - priest
neem/nim - a kind of tree
neem-begun - frying of newly sprouted neem leaves with small pieces of brinjal.
nejra - a kind of plant
neoya-husuk - sub-clan of the Rabha community
nesh - umbilical cord
nichu - lower
nigar janr - liquor made from rice
nika/neka - agreement of *denmohar*
nikah - marriage
nikhunt-poati - woman whose all children are alive
nimki cha - salty tea
nitya seva - daily propitiation
niyam bhanga - break a vow specially after a fixed period
nong-chong - wedding
nuarmi - purification ceremony
nuarmi - purificatory ceremony after child birth
paikari - wholesale
paira - pigeon
pala - lac bangle
pamby lade - bowl and plates used by the Lepcha
pan - betel leaf/betel roll
panch faleati - a pre-delivery ritual

pancha devata - five gods and goddesses
panchagabbya - a preparation of cows milk, *ghee*, yoghurt, cowdung and urine of an ox.
panchagarva - a pre-delivery ritual
panchal - a pre-delivery ritual observed in the fifth month of pregnancy
panchamrita - a pre-delivery ritual on the fifth month of pregnancy
panch-bhagawan - caste-council
panchbhaja - a pre-delivery ritual
panchfal - a pre-delivery ritual
panchmasi - a pre-delivery ritual
panchute - a post-delivery ritual
pandhe - a female dress
pang-den - coloured apron
pan-gua - betel and nut
pani khet - wet land
pani - water
pani-ghati - metallic water pot
panjika/panji - Hindu almanac
pansbara - a post-delivery ritual
panta-bhoj - a feast with stale rice
para - residential area or zone
parab - festival
parganait - head of pargana, a cluster of some villages
parmani - deputy leader
patapanka - society
pater sak - leaf of jute
pati - mat
pati-hans - duck
pat-kathi - stem of jute plant
pat-kharga - iron sword
payesh - a sweet dish prepared by boiling of rice in sweetened milk
pet fola - abortion
pet jharano - miscarriage
pet-dega - a birth ritual
peyal - a kind of fruit

phalgun	- eleventh month of the Bengali calendar; falls in February-March
phandi jal	- a kind of net
phaphar	- buck wheat
phira	- walking round the sacred fire by the bride and groom at the time of marriage.
pho-kho	- a Drukpa male dress
phool	- a ceremonial friendship term
phool	- flower
phulasauch	- birth pollution
phylacteries	- special prayer
pidyon	- a birth rite
pinda/pindi	- mixture of raw rice, *ghee*, banana, etc., offer to the ancestors.
pir	- Muslim saint
pirer mela	- A fair
pirstan	- graveyard of a saint
pishima/pishi	- father's sister
pitha	- cake
pithi	- turmeric
piyaj	- onion
posto	- poppy seed
potemala	- bead necklace
poush	- ninth month of the Bengali calendar; falls in December-January
pradhan	- headman
prasad	- consecrated food
prayaschitta	- penance
pritibhoj	- feast given by the grooms father on the third day of marriage.
pryojon	- nuptial ceremony
puja	- worship
punjak bak	- veiling of women
punjak-bak	- yak
puntong palit	- flute
purha	- he-goat
puyati	- pregnant
raibar	- match maker
raibaysa	- middleman

raj mandal	-	village head
raji-khusi biha	-	love marriage
rakh panch	-	throwing of ash
rakhal	-	cowboy
rakhi	-	a piece of coloured thread worn round the wrist specially during Rakhi Purnima, i.e. full moon day in the month of Sravana (July-August)
rakhwal	-	one who rears
raobairati	-	group of five married women other than brides mother or aunt
rarh	-	widower
rarhi	-	widow
rasam	-	curry
rasun	-	garlic
ratha jatra	-	car festival
roja	-	fasting
rokshi	-	a kind of alcoholic drink
rokshi	-	alcoholic drink made from a kind of millet
roli	-	vermilion
rosh hashana	-	Jewish new year
ru	-	Sherpa clan
ruksati	-	the ceremony of sending the bride to her husband's house.
ruti	-	hand made bread
sada than	-	white dhoti without coloured border
sadh/sadhaury/	-	a pre-delivery ritual
sadhbhakshan/ sadhkhawa	-	a pre-delivery ritual in which a pregnant woman is given her desired food
sagai	-	engagement ceremony
sai	-	a ceremonial friendship term
saifi-rasam	-	mass marriage
saina saq	-	a kind of leafy vegetable
sajan ghot	-	nuptial feast
sakhi	-	a ceremonial friendship term
sakhi	-	friend
sali biha	-	sororate

sali - a measurement equivalent to approximately 18 to 20 kg of rice
samagotriya - those of the same clan or gotra
samaj - caste council
samajpati - council members
sambar - a kind of South Indian dish made from pulse and mixed vegetables
sanai/sehnai - a kind of wind instrument
sandha anhik - religious rituals observed daily at twilight
sanga - remarriage of a widow
sangat - a ceremonial kinship term
sanglion mat-gachio - a death rite
sank-alu - a kind of fruit
sankha - conch bangles
saptapadi/sat pak/ sat pakghora - a marriage ritual in which the bride moves around the groom for seven times
saq - leafy green
satmasi - a pre-delivery ritual observed in the seventh month
satvaja - a pre-delivery ritual observed in the seventh month
sauri ghar - delivery room
sawmati - mud and ash
sentera - a post-delivery ritual
serbum-komkat - one rupee coin
sevdat havraah - first meal eaten by the mourners on their return from the cemetery
shala - wife's brother
shali - wife's sister
shamuk - snail
shani shastayan - worship of gods and goddesses for mitigation of sufferings
shariat - tradition
shashthipuja - a post-delivery ritual
shashur - husband's or wife's father
shashuri/swash - husband's or wife's mother
shasthitala - a sacred place
shayabaybakoth - a marriage rite

shelyad	- a Jewish word for arm band
shi-due	- annual death rite
shitalpati	- a kind of fine mat
sho-rin	- bride price
shubhadrishti	- first exchange of glances between the bride and the bridegroom.
sika	- touching the left wrist with fire
siksha guru	- teacher
simal tarul	- a kind of vegetable
sindur ghasa/sindurdan	- putting of vermilion
sindur phonta	- mark of vermilion
sindur	- vermilion
sinkopangro	- divorce
sinni	- concentrated milk with wheat, sugar etc.
siphry torach	- sacred book
situ	- snail
smasanyatri	- participants in funeral procession
soa mahina	- one and a quarter month
sohagrat	- consummation ceremony
solo saguner biha	- sixteen auspicious marriage rituals
soloana	- village council
sonar gayana	- gold ornaments
songcharani	- token payments to the girls friends of the village
sraddha	- worship of the ancestors
sravaka	- a header
subodh pareni	- final birth purification
suji	- semolina
sujni	- bedcover
sukha khet	- dry land
sunnat	- circumcision
supari	- areca nut
sura	- chapter
surha/suor	- pig
sutanali	- shuttles for weaver
sutra	- thread
suya	- parrot
swasan ghat	- cremation ground
swngani	- marriage by negotiation

taga	-	bangle for upper arm
tai pao	-	a Chinese dish of pork ball in clear soup
tajia	-	representation in the memory of Hasan and Hussein
tal	-	palm
tama	-	copper
tana biha	-	marriage by elopement
tana jal	-	a kind of fishing net
tangdau	-	a kind of musical instrument
tari	-	fermented palm juice/toddy
tarpan	-	offering of water to the manes or to the gods
tauchi	-	egg
tel-machh	-	a death ritual
tephillin	-	forehead band
terodasa	-	a death rite
thak	-	subgroups
thakurda	-	father's father
thakurma	-	father's mother
thar	-	clan
thela jal	-	a kind of fishing net
thikuji	-	horoscope
thonga	-	paper bag
thor	-	inner stem of plantain tree
thukpa	-	a kind of meal prepared out of noodles
thumra-fat	-	end of pollution period
thunkpa	-	a dish made from wheat
thurva-khawano	-	wedding feast
thuvrha-bhat	-	a marriage ritual
tibu	-	bell
tika	-	a kind of ornament
tiki	-	tuft of hair on the head
tilapat sradh	-	a death ritual
tita-bhat	-	rice with curry of bitter taste usually made from leaves of *neem* or bitter gourd
tohra	-	Jewish sacred script
tukri	-	basket

tong-len	- farewell
toyan	- Lepcha family
tulsi-mandap	- sacred alter of holy basil plant
tumbu fat	- name giving ceremony for Lepcha child
tung-gang	- a marriage rite
ua	- kind of millet (barley)
ulki	- tattoo marks
ulu dhwani	- a marriage ritual
ulu-ulu	- auspicious oral sound
unchu	- higher
upajibika	- livelihood
upbas	- fasting
urad	- black gram
utan sa-ajaong	- breakfast
uvla	- a kind of cloth given to a ceremonial friend
vastu/bastu	- homestead
vela	- a kind of fruit
vihara	- Buddhist monastery
wari varan	- a pre-delivery ritual
woaz	- talk
yagya/hom yognu	- sacred fire
zabar catne	- ceremonial head hair shaving
zamindar	- landlord
zidang	- patron
zo mal lok	- agricultural dances performed by the Lepcha
zoman	- paddy

SELECT BIBLIOGRAPHY

Abraham, C. E., Rev., The rise and growth of Christianity in India. In *The Cultural Heritage of India.* Vol. 4, (ed.), H. Bhattacharya, The Ramakrishna Mission Institute of Culture, Calcutta, pp. 547-570, 1956.

Adhikary, A. K. and R. K. Bhattacharya, "The extremist–An appraisal of the Naxalite movement with special reference to its repercussion among tribes." In *Tribal Movements in India*. Vol. 2, (ed.) K. S. Singh, Manohar Book Service, New Delhi, pp. 119-1127, 1983.

Ali Yusuf, A., *The Holy Koran : Text, Translation and Commentary*. Three volumes edition. Shaik Muhammed Ashraf, Kashmiri Bazar, Lahore, n.d.

Anonymous, *West Bengal : An Analytical Study*, (Sponsored by the Bengal Chambers of Commerce and Industry), Oxford and IBH Publication, New Delhi, 1971.

Anthony, Frank, *Britain's Betrayal in India*. Allied Publishers, New Delhi, 1969.

Archer, M., The folk tales in Santal society. *Man in India*. Vol. 24, No. 4, pp. 226-232, 1944.

Archer, W. G., An anthology of marriage sermons of Santal. *Man in India*. Vol. 23, pp. 106-107, 1943.

——, More Santal songs. *Man in India*. Vol. 24, No. 3, pp. 141-144, 1944.

——, The illegitimate child in Santal Society. *Man in India*. Vol. 24, No. 3, pp. 154-169, 1944.

——, Santal rebellion songs. *Man in India*. Vol. 25, No. 4, pp. 201-207, 1945.

——, *The Hill of Flutes: Life, Love and Poetry in Tribal India – A Portrait of the Santals*. George Allen and Unwin Ltd., London, 1974.

——, Ritual friendship in Santal society. *Man in India*. Vol. 27, pp. 57-60, 1947.

——, The Santal treatment of witchcraft. *Man in India.* Vol. 27, No. 2, pp. 103-121, 1947.

Awasty, Indira, *Between Sikkim and Bhutan*. B. R. Publishing Corporation, Delhi, 1978.

Bag, D., *In the midst of the Santals*. Subarnarekha, Calcutta, 1987.

Bagchi, G. C. and S. Sinha, *Village Survey Monograph on Upper Pedong, Census of India 1961*. West Bengal and Sikkim. Manager of Publications, Delhi, 1972.

Bagchi, P.C., "Evolution of the Tantras". In *The Cultural Heritage of India*. Vol. 4, (ed.), H. Bhattacharya, pp. 211-226, The Ramakrishna Mission Institute of Culture, Calcutta, 1956,

Bagchi, T., *Profile of Some Indian Tribes : An Anthropo-nutritional Micro Study*. Punthi Pustak, Calcutta, 1994.

Bandhu, S., *Ugrakshatriya Parichiti* (in Bengali). Bijoyratan Prakashan, Bardhaman, 1392 BS

Bandopadhyay, B., Ceremonial friendship among the Bhumij of Manbhum. *Man in India*. Vol. 35, No. 4, pp. 274-286, 1955.

Bandopadhyay, S., *Caste, Protest and Identity in Colonial India : The Namasudra of Bengal*. Curzon Press, Surrey, 1977.

——, (ed.). *Bengal Rethinking History: Essays in Historiography*. Manohar, New Delhi, 2001.

——, Dalits Debates and Dynamics – A Socio-Economic Profile of Scavengers of Howrah and Calcutta. Socio-Economic Research Institute, Calcutta, 2001.

Banerjee, A. R. and D. K. Banerjee, Inter-caste distance in dermatoglyphics in some Bengalee caste groups. *Indian Journal of Physical Anthropology and Human Genetics*. Vol. 1, pp. 29-39, 1975.

Banerjee, B., Religious practices in Munda village. *Bulletin of the Cultural Research Institute*. West Bengal, Vol.8 , Nos.1 and 2, pp. 79-86, 1969.

Banerjee, D., Finger dermatoglyphics in some Bengalee caste groups, *Man in India*. Vol. 50, pp. 161-176, 1970.

——, Some songs of the Dom. *Indian Folklore*, Vol. 1, No. 1, pp. 14-16, 1958.

Banerjee, H. N., Clan ossuaries of the Bhumij of Barabhum. *The Eastern Anthropologist*, Vol. 15, No. 2, pp. 140-147, 1962.

——, A Santal marriage. *Bulletin of the Cultural Research Institute, West Bengal*. Vol. 2, No. 2, pp. 78-86, 1963.

Banerjee, H. N. and B. K. Dasgupta, The Santal of Madhupur, Purulia district. *Bulletin of the Department of Anthropology* Vol. 8, No. 2, pp. 55-62, 1959.

Banerjee, S. K., Marriage pattern among Lepcha community: Past and present. *Modern Review*. Vol. 101, No. 2, 1962.

Barua, S., Selection intensity among the consanguineous and non-consanguineous groups of a Muslim population of 24-Parganas, West Bengal. *Man in India*. Vol. 6, pp. 359-364, 1976.

Basil, A., *American Settlement in India from Earliest Time to Present Day*. American College, Calcutta, 1969.

Baske, D. N., *Pashimbanger Adibasi Samaj* (in Bengali). Vol. 1, Subarnarekha, Calcutta, 1993.

Basu, A., Selection intensities among Pahiras. *Eugenics Quarterly*. Vol. 41, pp. 241-242, 1967.

———, The Pahira: A population genetical study. *American Journal of Physical Anthropology*. Vol. 31, pp. 399-416, 1969.

———, Intrinsic rate of natural increase among Pahiras. *Social Biology*. Vol. 18, pp. 195-199, 1971.

Basu, A., J. Sarkar, B. Roy, P. Dasgupta, A. Sanyal and S. S. Sarkar, Anthropogenetic investigations in the Dalma and Ayodha Hills and neighbourhood. *Science and Culture*. Vol. 32, pp. 273-275, 1966.

Basu, A., R. Gupta and K. K. Bhattacharya, A demographic study of Mirpur : A village in coastal Medinipur district, West Bengal. *Journal of the Bio-Social Science*. Vol. 12, pp. 227-234, 1980.

Basu, K. P., Notes on Bhuiyas, Purans. *Man in India*. Vol. 1, No. 2, 1921.

Basu, L., *Amader Padabir Itihas* (in Bengali). Ananda Publisher Pvt. Ltd. Calcutta, 1981.

Basu, M. N., A Munda colony in Bengal. *Journal of the Department of Letters*. (University of Calcutta) Vol.27, pp.1-4, 1935

———, Bunas of Bengal. *Journal of the Department of Letters*, (University of Calcutta). Vol. 32, pp. 1-120, 1939.

———, The somatometry of the Chinese of Calcutta. *Calcutta Geographical Review*. Vol. 6, No. 3, 1944.

Bell, C. A., Ancestor worship among the Lepcha. *Journal of the Asiatic Society of Bengal*. Vol. 62 No. 3, 1903.

Beverley, H., *Report on the Census of Bengal, 1871*. Government Printing, Calcutta, 1872.

Bhaduri, B. N., Astronomy of the Mundas and their star myths. *Man in India*. Vol. 22, Nos. 1 & 2, pp. 69-77, 1942.

———, Some Munda religious ceremonies and their system of reckoning time. *Man in India*. Vol. 24, No. 3, pp. 148-153, 1944.

Bharati, P., *A Study on the Relationship between Socio-economic Condition, Nutrients and Health in a Mahishya Population Sample*. Ph.D Thesis, University of Calcutta, Calcutta, 1983.

Bhasin, M. K., *Biology of the Peoples of Indian Region : A Classified and Comprehensive Bibliography*. Kamala-Raj Enterprise, Delhi, 1988.

Bhatia, V. B., Technology of Asurs. *Vanyajati*. Vol. 7, 1959.

Bhattacharjee, B., *Cultural Oscillation (A Study of Patua Culture)*. Naya Prakash, Calcutta, 1980.

Bhattacharjee, P. N. and D. Chowdhury, Phenythiourea taste sensitivity among two populations of eastern Himalayas. *Man in India*. Vol. 56, pp. 269-275, 1976.

Bhattacharya, A. and S. Sinha., *Census of India, 1961 : West Bengal and Sikkim. Village Survey on Raibaghini*. Manager of Publications, Vol. 16, Part 6. Delhi, 1966.

Bhattacharya, J. N., *Hindu Castes and Sects*. Editions Indian, Calcutta, 1896. (reprinted in 1968).

Bhattacharya, P. N., S. Ghosh and N. Kumar, The Tamang : A case of hybridization. *Human Heredity*. Vol. 27, pp. 1-8, 1977.

Bhattacharya, R. K., Social and cultural constraints in agriculture in three villages (Hindu, Moslem and Tribal) of West Bengal. In *Science, Technology and Culture,* (ed.) S. Sinha. Research Council for Cultural Studies, New Delhi, 1970.

——, The concept and ideology of caste among the Moslems of rural Bengal. In *Caste and Social Stratification among the Muslims*, (ed.) Imtiaz Ahmed. Manohar Book Service, New Delhi, 1972.

——, Social and cultural organization of agriculture reappraisal and a plea for restudy. In *Agrarian Situation in India*, Vol. 1. (eds.) S. B. Chakraborty, B. R. Ghosh, and A. K. Danda. Anthropological Survey of India, Calcutta, pp. 115-117, 1984.

——, Kinship among the Sunni Sheik Moslem of Birbhum. West Bengal, *Journal of the Indian Anthropological Society*, Vol. 20, No. 2, pp. 99-110, 1985.

——, Marriage among the Sunni Sheik Moslem of Birbhum. West Bengal. *Human Science*, Vol. 35, No. 1, pp. 42-49, 1986.

——, *Moslems of Rural Bengal*. Subarnarekha, Calcutta, 1991

Bhattacharya, S., Reflection in the concept of regional history. In *Prospective on Indian Society and History : A Critique*, (ed.) H. Jha. pp. 81-90. Manohar, New Delhi, 2002,

Bhattacharya, S. N., *A History of Mughal North-East Frontier Policy*. Chakraborty, Chatterjee and Co., Calcutta, 1929.

Bhattacharya, T., *Pashimbanga Darshan, Purulia*. (in Bengali), Firma K.L.M. Pvt. Ltd., Calcutta, 1986.

——, *Purulia*. Firma K.L.M. Pvt. Ltd , Calcutta, 1988.

——, *Pashimbanga Darshan, Medinipur*. (in Bengali), Firma K.L.M. Pvt. Ltd, Calcutta, 1979.

Bhattacharyya H., A short note on the Dule Behera (Dulia Bagdi). *Folklore*. Vol. 3, pp. 187-188, 1961.

Bhattacharyya, N. P., P. Basu, M. Das, S. Paramanik, R. Banerjee, B. Roy, S. Roychowdhury and P. P. Majumdar, Negligible male gene flow across ethnic boundaries in India, revealed by analysis of Y-chromosomal DNA polymorphisms. *Genome Research*, Vol. 9, pp. 711-719, 1999.

Bhowmick, D. C., *A Cross-sectional Growth Study of the School Children of Medinipur*. Anthropological Survey of India, Calcutta, 1993.

Bhowmick, K. L., Bauris, a dominant scheduled caste of West Bengal. *Bulletin of the Cultural Research Institute, West Bengal*. Vol. 5, No. 1 and 2, pp. 35-47, 1966.

Bhowmick, P. K., Lodha marriage custom. *Man in India*. Vol. 34, No. 2, pp. 105-111, 1954.

——, Further notes on Lodha marriage. *Man in India*. Vol. 34, No. 4, pp. 301-314, 1954.

——, Savaras of Midnapur. *Vanyajati*. Vol. 3, pp. 60-64, 1955.

——, Social and religious officials of the Lodha caste. *Man in India*. Vol. 35, No. 2, pp. 127-139, 1955.

——, Treatment of disease among the Lodhas of West Bengal. *Man in India*. Vol. 35, No. 4, pp. 287-298. 1955.

——, The Lodhas of Midnapur (West Bengal). *Vanyajati*. Vol. 3, 1955.

——, Physical affinity of the Lodhas of Medinipur, *Man in India*. Vol. 36, pp. 110-131, 1956.

——, Annual festival of the Lodhas of West Bengal. *Man in India*. Vol. 37, No. 3, pp. 208-216. 1957.

——, The Lodhas and their folk-songs. *Vanyajati*. Vol. 5, No. 1, 1957.

——, Religions ideas of the Lodha (Midnapur). *Vanyajati*. Vol. 5, No. 4, 1957.

——, Kakmara : A nomadic community in West Bengal. *Man in India*. Vol. 39, No. 4, pp. 271-284, 1959.

——, Economic life of the Lodhas. *The Eastern Anthropologist*. Vol. 13, No. 3, pp. 105-120, 1959-60.

——, Some problems of the Lodhas : A denotified community of West Bengal. *Bulletin of the Cultural Research Institute, West Bengal*, Vol. 2, No. 2, pp. 64-69, 1963.

——, *The Lodhas of West Bengal : A Socio-economic Study*. Punthi Pustak, Calcutta, 1963.

——, *Socio-cultural Profile of Frontier Bengal. Punthi Pustak, Calcutta. 1976.*

——, *Some Aspects of Indian Anthropology*. Subarnarekha, Calcutta, 1980.

——, *Primitive Tribal Groups of Eastern India*. Gyan Publishing House, New Delhi, 1994.

Bhowmick, P. K., and B. Chaudhury, Some magico-religious rites of the Mundas of West Bengal. *Folklore.* Vol. 7, pp. 100-107, 1966.

Bhowmick, S. K., *Bangalir Jatitatwa o Krishijibi Sampradaya*, (in Bengali). Model Book Stores, Calcutta, 1986.

Bhowmick, S. N. *Padabir Utpatti o Krama Bikasher Itihas*, (in Bengali). Mitraloke, Calcutta, 1389 B.S.

Biswas, P. C., On the palmer prints of the Bengalis. *Journal of the Indian Anthropological Institute*. Vol. 2, pp. 31-46, 1939-40.

Biswas, S. K., Glucose-6-phosphate dehydrogenase deficiency in male sample of Bengalee Hindus. In *Bio-anthropological Research in India*. (ed.) H. K. Rakshit, Anthropological Survey of India, pp. 115-118, Calcutta, 1987.

Bodding, P. O., On taboos and customs connected therewith, amongst the Santals. *Journal of Royal Asiatic Society of Bengal*. Vol. 67, Part 3, No. 1, pp. 1-24, 1898.

Bose, N. K., Hindu Samajer Garan (in Bengali). Viswa Bharati Granthalaya, Calcutta, 1949.

——, (ed.) *Peasant life in India*. Calcutta Anthropological Survey of India. Memoir No. 8, Calcutta, 1967.

Bose, S. C., *Geography of West Bengal*. National Book Trust, New Delhi, 1968.

Bose, P. K., *Classes and Class Relations among Tribals of Bengal.* Ajanta Publications, New Delhi, 1985.

Campbell, A., Note on the Lepchas of Sikkim with a vocabulary of their language. *Journal of the Asiatic Society of Bengal*, Vol. 9, pp. 379-393, 1840.

Cavey, L. W., The Munda view of stars. *Man in India.* Vol. 26, No. 1, 1946.

Census of India, 1951. West Bengal District Census Handbook. Midnapur, Government Press, Calcutta, 1953.

Chakraborty, P. and K. Chatterjee, Some aspect of Toto ethnography, *Bulletin of the Cultural Research Institute, West Bengal*. Vol. 3, No. 2, P. 51, 1964.

Chakraborty, R., H. Walter, B. N. Mukherjee, K. C. Malhotra, P. Sarker, S. Banerjee and M. Roy, Gene differentiation among ten endogamous groups of West Bengal, India. *American Journal of Physical Anthropology*. Vol. 71, pp. 295-309, 1986.

Chakraborty, R., S. K. Das and M. Roy, Blood group genetics of some caste groups of southern 24-Parganas, West Bengal. *Human Heredity*. Vol. 25, pp. 218-225, 1975.

Chakravartti, M. R., Dermatoglyphics of the Santals of West Bengal. *Bulletin of the Anthropological Survey of India*. Vol. 9, pp. 41-52, 1960.

Chanda, R., *The Indo-Aryan Races: A Study of the Origin of Indo-Aryan People and Institutions*. Part-1, Barendra Research Society, Rajshahi, 1916.

Chandra, R. P., Gaur Rajmala. Barendra Research Society, Rajshahi, 1912.

——, *The Indo-Aryan Races : A Study of the Origin of Indo-Aryan People and Institution*. Indological Book Corporation. 1916, (reprinted in 1976).

Chari, R. B., *Census of India, 1971, Scheduled Caste and Scheduled Tribes*, Series-1, Paper 1 of 1975, Govt. of India Press, Delhi, 1975.

Chatterjee A. N., The variation of stature and cephalic index among Bengalee college students, Presidential Address, Section of Anthropology and Archaeology. *Proceedings of the 35th Session of Indian Science Congress*. Part-2, Indian Science Congress Association, pp. 153-176, Calcutta, 1948.

Chatterjee S. K., *Kirata-jana Kriti*. The Asiatic Society, Calcutta, 1951.

——, Adivasi language and literatures of India. In *The Cultural Heritage of India*, (ed.) S. K. Chatterjee. The Ramakrishna Mission Institute of Culture, Vol. 5, pp. 659-676, Calcutta, 1956 (reprinted in 1978).

Chatterjee Sikha, *The Paschatya Vaidik Brahmans of West Bengal : A Bio Anthropological Study*. Anthropological Survey of India, Memoir No 110, Calcutta, 2004.

Chatterjee, Sikha and D. P. Mukherjee, Distribution of ABO blood groups in the Bengali speaking population. *Journal of the Indian Anthropological Society*. Vol. 14, pp. 65-88, 1979.

Chattopadhyay, G., The festival 'Jatra' or *harmaghe* of the Hos. *Journal of the Asiatic Society of Bengal*. Vol. 22, pp. 15-19, 1956.

——, Kinship and marriage among the Hos. *Bulletin of the Cultural Research Institute, West Bengal*. Vol. 3, No. 2, West Bengal, 1964.

——, Hos. *Vanyajati*. Vol. 13, No. 3, pp.123-130, 1965.

Chattopadhyay, K. P., Changes in Santal economy. *Man in India*. Vol. 29, No. 2, pp. 71-75, 1949.

Chattopadhyay, P. K. and P. Dash Sharma, Finger dermatoglyphics of the Rarhi Brahmans of Bengal. *American Journal of Physical Anthropology*. Vol. 30, pp. 397-401, 1967.

Chattopadhyay, S. K., *The Origin and Development of Bengali Languages* (in three parts). George Allen and Unwin Ltd., 1926. (reprinted in 1970-71).

——, *Bangalir Samajik Itibaser Bhumika* (in Bengali). Sahitya Sansad. Calcutta, 1974.

Chattopadhyaya, A., *The People and Culture of Bengal*. Firma K. L. Mukhopadhyay, Kolkata, 2002.

Chattopadhyaya G., A short note on the Lepcha of Kalimpong sub-division of West Bengal. *Adibasi*. Vol. 3, No. 2, pp.17-21, 1958.

Chaudhary, R., Vedanta and Sufism : A comparative study (with special reference to Bengal). In *Religion and Society in Eastern India*, (eds.) G.C. Tripathi and H. Kulke. The Eschmann Memorial Fund, Bhubaneshwar, pp. 49-102, 1994.

Chaudhuri, A. D., *State Formation among Tribals : A Quest for Santal Identity*. Gyan Publishing House, New Delhi, 1993.

Chaudhuri, S., B. Mukherjee, J. Ghosh and A. K. Roy Choudhury, Blood groups of the Chinese in Calcutta. *Nature*. Vol. 213 (5082), London, 1967.

Chaudhuri, S., M. R. Chakravartti, B. Mukherjee, S. N. Sen, J. Ghosh and A. Mitra, Study of haematological factors, blood groups, anthropometric measurements and genetics of some of tribal and caste groups of 1. South India, Kerala, Nilgiri and Andhra Pradesh 2. North Eastern India (Indo Bhutan Border) – Totopara. *Bibl. Haemat.* Vol. 19, pp. 186-205, 1964.

Chaudhury, B., Bhumij. *Adibasi*. No. 3, pp.119-122. 1963-64.

——, Desua Bhumija. *Adibasi*. No. 3, pp.125-126. 1963-64.

——, Life in a Munda village. *Bulletin of the Cultural Research Institute, West Bengal*. Vol. 5, No. 1 and 2, pp.126-132. 1966.

——, The nature and extent of Munda-Hindu interactions. *Bulletin of the Cultural Research Institute, West Bengal.* Vol. 7, No. 1 and 2, 1968.

Choudhury, N. C., An aspect of contemporary Munda religion in Suderban area. *Bulletin of the Cultural Research Institute, West Bengal*. Vol. 1, No. 2, pp. 40-45, 1962.

——, Munda settlement in lower Bengal: A study in tribal migration. *Bulletin of the Cultural Research Institute, West Bengal*. Vol. 2, No. 2. pp. 23-32, 1953.

Choudhury, S, B. Mukherjee, J. Ghosh and A. K. Roychoudhury, Study of blood groups, ABH secretors and haemoglobin variants in three upper castes of West Bengal, India. *American Journal of Physical Anthropology*. Vol. 30, pp. 129-132, 1969.

Chowdhuri, Chandrima, A slum in Calcutta. *Bulletin of the Anthropological Survey of India*. Vol. 27, No. 3 & 4, pp.46-51, 1978.

Cormack, J. G., *Everyday Customs in China*. The Moray Press, London, 1935.

Coupland, H., *Bengal District Gazetteers, Manbhum*. Bengal Secretariat Book Depot, Calcutta, 1971.

Crissman, L., The segmentary structure of urban overseas Chinese communities. *Man*. Vol. 2, No. 2, pp. 185-204, 1967.

Crooke, W., *The Tribes and Castes of the North Western Provinces and Oudh*. Office of the Superintendent of Government Printing, India, Calcutta, 1896.

Dalton, E. T., *Descriptive Ethnology of Bengal*. Calcutta. 1872 (reprinted in 1960, Calcutta, Firma K. L. M.).

Danda, A. K., Tales of Bhutia religious dances. *Folklore*. Vol. 4, No. 6, pp. 196-198, 1963.

Das, A. C., *Vaisya Caste: The Gandhavaniks of Bengal*, A. K. Roy, Calcutta, 1903.

Das, A. K., Food habits and dietaries of the Oraon and their nutritional efficiency. *Vanyajati*. Vol. 7, No. 2, 1959.

——, *Report on the Lodha Ex-criminal Settlement at Dhalkut Pranab Palli*. Government of West Bengal, Calcutta, 1959.

——, A scheme of scientific analysis of the Oraon social system. *Vanyajati*. Vol. 9, No. 3, pp.115-123, 1961.

——, Study of socio-medical problems of a Sundarban village. *Science and Society*. Vol. 1, No. 2, 1962.

——, The Oraons of Sundarban. *Bulletin of the Cultural Research Institute, West Bengal*. Special series No. 3, Calcutta, 1963.

——, *The Koras and Some Little Known Communities of West Bengal*. Tribal Welfare Department, Government of West Bengal, Calcutta, 1964.

——, A systematic analysis of the social system of the Munda community. *Bulletin of the Cultural Research Institute, West Bengal*. Vol. 4, 1965.

——, *The Totos*, Scheduled Castes and Scheduled Tribes Welfare Department, Government of West Bengal, Special Series No. 11, Calcutta, 1969.

Das, A. K., B. Roychowdhury, and M. K. Raha, *The Malpaharias of West Bengal.* Cultural Research Institute, Calcutta, 1966.

Das, A. K., B. Roychowdhury, and M. K. Raha, *The Handbook on Scheduled Castes and Scheduled Tribes of West Bengal*, Cultural Research Institute, Calcutta, 1966.

Das, A. K. and M. K. Raha, The Rabhas or West Bengal. *Bulletin of the Cultural Research Institute, West Bengal*. Special Series No. 9, Calcutta, 1967.

Das, A. K. and S. K. Banerjee., *The Lepchas of Darjeeling District. Bulletin of the Cultural Research Institute, West Bengal*. Special Series No. 2, Calcutta. 1962.

Das, A. K., U. K. Roy and S. K. Basu, *To be with Santals*. Scheduled Castes and Tribes Welfare Department, Government of West Bengal, Calcutta, 1982.

Das, B. 'Introduction.' In *The Cultural Heritage of India*, Vol. 4, (ed.), H. Bhattacharya, The Ramakrishna Mission Institute of Culture, Calcutta, pp. 3-28, 1956.

Das, B. M., K. K. Agarwal, P. Gupta, B. Mukherjee, A. R. Banerjee and A. Bose, Blood group investigation in the 24-Parganas district, West Bengal. *Man in India*. Vol. 34, 1953.

Das, N., Karam festival in a Munda village. *Vanyajati*. Vol. 2, 1954,

——, Kora. *Adibasi*. No. 3, 1963-64.

Das, S. R., *Mixed Longitudinal Growth Data for 24 Measures : The Sarsuna Barisha Series, West Bengal, India*, Vol. 1, Boys. Anthropological Survey of India, Calcutta, 1985.

——, *Mixed Longitudinal Growth Data for 24 Measures : The Sarsuna Barisha Series, West Bengal, India*, Vol. 2, Girls. Anthropological Survey of India, Calcutta, 1986.

Das, S. R., D. P. Mukherjee and P. N. Bhattacharjee, Survey of blood groups and P. T. C. taste among the Rajbansi caste of West Bengal (ABO, MMS, Rh, Duffy and Diego). *Acta Genetica Statistica Medica*. Vol. 17, pp. 433-445, 1967.

Das T. C., *The Wild Kharias of Dhalbhum*. Anthropological Paper, University of Calcutta (N. S.), No. 3, Calcutta, 1931.

——, The modern trend of primitive culture on the borders of Bengal. *Calcutta Review*. Vol. 139, pp. 35-40, 1943.

Dasgupta, D., Linguistic observations on Kharia Thar and Mal Pahariya. *Journal of the Indian Anthropological Society*. Vol. 6, No. 1, pp. 29-33, 1971.

Dasgupta P., B. N. Mukherjee, S. K. Das, P. K. Das, K. Pakrashi and D. P. Mukherjee, A study of anthropometry and genetic markers amongst the Kaoras of West Bengal. *Indian Journal of Physical Anthropology and Human Genetics*. Vol. 7 pp.19-37, 1981.

Dasgupta, S., Religious concepts and ethics of Bagdi. *Bulletin of the Cultural Research Institute, West Bengal*. Vol. 2, No. 1, 1963.

——, Locality, groups among the Bagdis of Jai Nagar. *Bulletin of the Cultural Research Institute, West Bengal*. Vol. 2, No. 2, pp. 70-77, 1963.

——, Demographic aspects of marriage among the Dule Bagdis of Jai Nagar. *Bulletin of the Cultural Research Institute, West Bengal*. Vol. 3, No. 1, pp. 31-40, 1964.

——, Lineage and kinship structure among the Dule Bagdis of Jai Nagar, *Bulletin of the Cultural Research Institute, West Bengal*. Vol. 3, No. 3, 1964.

——, *Caste, Kinship and Communities : Social System of a Bengali Caste*. Universities Press (India) Pvt. Ltd., Madras, 1986.

Dash, A. J., *Bengal District Gazetteers, Darjeeling*. Bengal Government Press, Calcutta, 1947.

Datta, Archana and S. Datta, Ecology, demography and land use change in Darjeeling Himalaya. *Bulletin of the Anthropological Survey of India*. Vol. 29, No. 3 and 4, pp. 19-54, 1980.

Datta, B. N., Ethnological notes on some of the castes of West Bengal. *Man in India*. Vol. 15, No. 4, pp.196-224, 1935.

Datta Gupta, J., *Census of India, 1961*. Part VA (i), Tables on Scheduled Castes, Manager of Publications, Delhi, 1966.

Datta Majumdar, N., The economic organisation of the Bhotiya. *Man*. Vol. 30, No. 86, 1940.

De, B., A note on some genetic characters among Ruidas of Hooghly, West Bengal. *Bulletin of the Anthropological Survey of India*. Vol. 16, pp. 307-312, 1967.

Debnath, D., *Ecology and Rituals in Tribal Areas*, Sarup & Sons, New Delhi, 2003

Driver, W. H. P., Notes of the some Kolarian tribes (Asurs, Birjias, Birhors, Khariyas). *Jounal of the Asiatic Society of Bengal*. Vol. 58, No. 1, pp.7-18, 24-37, 1981.

Dube, S. C., Myths, religion and ritual of the Kamars. *The Eastern Anthropologist*. Vol. 1, No. 1, pp. 27-42, 1947.

——, The economic life of the Kamars. *Man in India*. Vol. 27, No.2, pp. 137-169, 1947.

Dubey, K. C., Bhunyias. *The Eastern Anthropologist*. Vol. 14, No. 1, pp. 48-55, 1961.

Dutta Majumdar, N., *The Santal: A Study in Culture Change*. The Manager of Publications, Government of India Press, Calcutta, 1956.

Eaton, R., *The Rise of Islam and Bengal Frontier*. University of California Press, Berkeley, 1993.

Elliot H. M., and J. Dowson, *History of India*. Vol. 6, Cosmopolitian Publishers, Aligarh, 1875.

Ezekiel, M., *History and Culture of the Bene-Israel in India*. Tara Print, Nadiad. 1948.

Foning, A. R., *Lepcha: My Vanishing Tribe*. Sterling Publications Pvt. Ltd., New Delhi, 1987.

Frazer J. G., Garo marriage. *Folklore*. Vol. 32, pp.202-209, 1921.

Fruzetti, Lina and A. Oster, *Kinship and Ritual in Bengal : Anthropological Essays*. South Asian Publishers, New Delhi, 1984.

Gai, G. S., *Introduction to Indian Epigraphy*, (With Special Reference to the Development of the Scripts and Languages). Central Institute of Indian Languages, Manasagangotri, Mysore, 1986.

Gaikwad, V. R., *The Anglo-Indians*. Asia Publishing House, Bombay, 1967.

Gait, E. A., *Census of India, 1901*, Vol. 6, The Lower Provinces of Bengal and Their Feudatories. Part -1, Report, Government Printing, Calcutta. 1902.

Ganguly, S. K., A few Munda and Oraon folk songs. *Indians Folklore*, Vol. 1, No. 4, pp. 18-21, 1958.

——, A Munda spring festival. *Folklore*, Vol. 3, No. 1, pp.23-29, 1962.

Garrets, J., *Bengal District Gazetteers*, Nadia. Bengal Secretariat Book Depot, Calcutta, 1910.

Ghosal, S., A frontier tribe and transformation into peasantry in a Himalayan state. *Man in India*. Vol. 63, No. 4, pp.363-369, 1983.

——, A transitional tribe of Sikkim with peasant life style and mode of production. In *Agrarian Situation in India*. Vol. 2, (eds.) S. B. Chakraborty, B. R. Ghosh and A. K. Danda, Anthropological Survey of India, pp.58-63, Calcutta, 1985.

——, Sexual division of labour in Lepcha subsistence economy. *Human Science*, Vol. 35, No.3, pp.226-231, 1986.

——, Polyandry among the Lepchas of Sikkim: A dead or dying institution. In *Polyandry in India*. (ed.) M. K. Raha, pp.356-363, Gian Publication, New Delhi, 1987.

——, Creole culture in Sikkim: A case of multiple acculturation. In *Acculturation and Social Chance in India: An Inter disciplinary*

Appraisal. (eds.) S. C. Panchbhai, and M. K. A. Siddiqui, Anthropological Survey of India, Calcutta, pp. 216-222, 1989.

Ghosh, A. K. and D. K. Nanda, A note on finger dermatoglyphics of the Lodha of Midnapur. *The Eastern Anthropologist*. Vol. 26, pp. 357-366, 1975.

Ghosh, A. K., Sudesh Kumari and D. K. Nanda, Palmer dermatoglyphics of the Lodha of Midnapur, The Eastern Anthropologist, Vol. 26, pp. 357-366, 1973.

Ghosh, M., Christan bibah (in Bengali). *Desh*, Vol. 55 years, No. 40, pp. 46-50, 1988.

Gist, N. P and A. G. Dworken, *Blending of races*. Wiley Inter Science, New York, 1972.

Gist, N. P. and R. D. Wright, *Marginality and Identity: Anglo-Indians as a Racially Mixed Minorities in India*, Leiden Publishers, Brill, 1973.

Goswami, K., Place names of Bengal. *Journal of the Development of Letters*. University of Calcutta, Vol. 33, 1943.

Greval, S. D. S. and S. N. Chandra, Blood groups of communities in Calcutta. *Indian Journal of Medical Research*, Vol. 27, pp. 1109-1116, 1940.

Guha, B. S., The racial affinities of the people of India. In *Census of India, 1931,* Vol. 1, Part 3A pp. i-lxxi and tables i-xxiv, (ed.) J. H. Hutton, Gyan Publishing House Delhi 1935 (reprinted in 1986).

——, (ed.), *Studies in Social Tension among the Refugees from East Pakistan*. Anthropological Survey of India, Calcutta, 1959.

Guha, Uma., Fine folktales of the Santals. *Folklores*. Vol. 2, No. 1, pp.33-45, 1957.

Gupta, P. and P. C. Dutta, *Anthropometry in India*. Anthropological Survey of India, Memoir No. 10, Calcutta, 1966.

——, A preliminary note on the Asura. *Man in India*. Vol. 43, pp.114-118, 1963.

Gupta, R., Selection intensity among the Sherpas. *Current Anthropology*. Vol. 21, pp. 136-137, 1980.

Gupta, R. K., Work among the Lodhas. *Police Journal*. Vol. 2, No. 2, Calcutta, 1954.

——, Lodhas revisited. *Man in India*. Vol. 39, No. 3, pp. 210-220, 1959.

Gupta, S. K., *Marriage among the Anglo Indians*. Ethnographic and Folk Culture Society, Lucknow, 1968.

Gurdon, P. R. T., Garo wedding chant. *Journal of the Asiatic Society of Bengal*. Vol. 72, No. 3, pp. 93-97, 1903.

Hahn, F., Notes on the religion and superstition of the Oraons. *Journal of Asiatic Society of Bengal*. Vol. 72, pp. 12-25, 1903.

Hodson, T. C., Garo marriages. *Folklore*. Vol. 32, pp. 133-135, 273, 1921.

——, The Garo and Khasi marriage systems contrasted. *Man in India*, Vol. 1, No. 2, pp.106-126, 1921.

Hoernle, R., Some problems of ancient Indian history. *Journal of the Royal Anthropological Society*. Vol. 35, pp. 1-14, 1905.

Hoffmann, J., Mundari poetry, music and dance. *Journal of the Royal Asiatic Society of Bengal*. Vol. 2, pp. 85-120, 1907.

——, Principles of succession and inheritance among the Mundas. *Man in India*. Vol. 41, No. 4, pp. 324-338. 1961.

Hoffmann, S. J., *Encyclopedia Mundarica*. Government Printing, Bihar, Patna, 1950.

Hosten, H., The twelve Bhuiyas or landlords of Bengal. *Journal of the Asiatic Society of Bengal*, N. S. Vol. 10, pp.437-449, 1913.

Hrach, H. G., The dialectics of Detribalization: The case of Santals. *Colloquies Internationaux du C. N. R. S.* No. 582, Asie du Sud Traditions et Changements, pp. 229-235, n.d.

——, From regulated anarchy to proto-nationalist: The case of Santals. In Aspects of Tribal Life in South Asia: Strategy and Survival. Berne, Switzerland, Studia Ethnologica Bernesia, 1978.

Hunter, W. N., *A Statistical account of Bengal*. (Reprint), D. K. Publishing House. Delhi, 1973.

Hunter, W. W., *A Statistical Account of Bengal*, Trubner and Company, London, 1877. (reprinted in 1973, D. K. Publishing House, New Delhi).

Ibbetson, D., *Landmarks in Indian Anthropology Punjab castes*. Vol. 17, Cosmo Publications, New Delhi, 1987.

Inden, R. B., *Marriage and Rank in Bengali Culture*. Vikas Publishing House, New Delhi, 1976.

Inden, R. B. and R. W. Nicholas. *Kinship in Bengali Culture*. University of Chicago Press, Chicago, 1977.

Jain, R. K., Features of kinship in an Asur village. *The Eastern Anthropologist*. Vol. 12, No. 1, pp.25-40, 141, 1958-59.

Kabir, H. Islam in India. In *The Cultural Heritage of India.*, Vol. 4, pp. 579-592. (ed.), H. Bhattacharya, The Ramakrishna Mission Institute of Culture, Calcutta, 1956.

Kabiraj, S., Jhum Cultivation of Garos and rain. *Folklore*. Vol. 3, No. 12, pp. 561-563, 1962.

Kashyap, V. K., N. Sarkar, Sanghamitra Sahoo, B. N. Sarkar and R. Trivedi, Genetic variation at fifteen microsatellite loci in human populations of India. *Current Science*. Vol. 85, No. 4, pp. 464-473, 2003.

Kate, S. L., B. N. Mukherjee, K. C. Malhotra, M. A. Phadke, G. S. Mutalik and G. S. Sainani, Red cell glucose-6-phosphate dehydrogenase deficiency and haemoglobin variants among ten endogamous groups of Maharashtra and West Bengal, *Human Genetics*. Vol. 44, pp. 339-343, 1978.

Kate, S. L., G. D. Mokashi, V. A. Khedkar and B. N. Mukherjee, Prevalence of haemoglobin–E in ten population groups of West Bengal. *Indian Journal of Haematology*. Vol. 11, pp. 221-223, 1984.

Kochar, V. K., Kinship terms and usages among the Santals of Bolpur area, Birbhum. *Bulletin of the Anthropological Survey of India*. Vol. 12, No. 1 and 2, pp. 47-56, 1963.

———, Socio-cultural denominators of domestic life in a Santal village. *The Eastern Anthropologist*. Vol. 16, No. 3, pp.167-179, 1963.

———, Tribal deities of the Santals. *Bharatiya Lokayan*. Vol. 3, No. 1 and 2, pp. 1-15, 1964.

———, Attributes of social status among the Santals. *Bulletin of the Cultural Research Institute, West Bengal*. Vol. 3, No. 3 and 4, pp 22-29, 1964.

———, More village *bongas* of the Santal. *Folklore*. Vol. 5, No. 12, pp. 448-453, 1964.

———, Nuclear units in the domestic groups of a Santal village. *The Eastern Anthropologist*. Vol. 18, No. 1, pp. 12-21, 1965.

Konow, S., Notes on the Munda family of speech in India. *Anthropos*. Vol. 3, pp.68-82, 1908.

Kumar, N., A genetic study among the Tentulia Bagdi and Duley of Hooghly district in West Bengal. *Bulletin of the Department of Anthropology, Government of India*. Vol. 6, No. 1, pp. 54-64, 1957.

Laha, B. N., Presidential Address: Bengal Gandhavaniks Mahasammilan. *Gandhavanik*. Vol. 11, 1979.

Lambat, A. I., Marriage among the Sunni Surti Bhoras of South Gujarat. In *Family, Kinship and Marriage among Muslims in India*. pp.44-81, (ed.) Imtiaz Ahmed, Monohar Book Service, New Delhi, 1976.

Leuva, K. K., *Asur*. Bhartiya Sewak Sangh, New Delhi, 1963.

Levi-Strauss, C., The Savage Mind, Chicago: The University of Chicago Press, 1966.

Macfarlane, E. W. E., Blood group distribution in India with special reference to Bengal. *Journal of Genetics*. Vol. 36, pp. 225-237, 1938.

Macfarlane, E. W. E., and S. S. Sarkar, Blood groups in India. *American Journal of Physical Anthropology*. Vol. 28, pp. 397-410, 1941.

Mahanty, Uma Charan, Traditional officials of Kisan Society. *Adibasi*, No.-1, pp. 56-60. 1963-64.

Mahar, R., *These are the Anglo-Indians*. Swallow Press, Calcutta, 1962.

Mahato, P. P., *Bharater Adibasi O Dalit Samaj*, (in Bengali). Sujan Publication, Kolkata, 1995.

——, *Sanskritization vs Nirbakization : Studies on Cultural Silence and Ethnic Memocide in Jharkhand*. Sujan Publication, Kolkata, 2000.

Mahato, V. C., *Souvenir of the Conference of Kurmi Mahasabha*. Kurmi Mahasabha, Ramgarh, 1985.

Maiterya, A. K., 'Preface' in *Gaur Rajmala*. (by) R. Chandra, Barendra Research Society, Rajshahi, 1912.

——, *Gaur Lekha Mala*. Barendra Research Society, Rajshahi, 1912.

Maiti, S., Changing concept of religion among the city youth. *Indian Folklore*. No. 1. 1976.

——, Naxalbari – A seed bed of agrarian revolution in West Bengal. *Man and Life*. Vol. 3, No. 1 and 2, 1977.

——, Agrarian unrest in West Bengal – A case study of the Naxalite movement in Debra. *Man and Life*. Vol. 3, No. 3 and 4, 1977.

——, Agrarian unrest in West Bengal: A case study in Midnapur. *Man and Life*. Vol. 4, No. 1 and 4, 1978.

——, Dichotomy of social and economic inequality – A case study. *Bulletin of the Cultural Research Institute, West Bengal*. Vol. 13, No. 1 and 2, 1978.

——, Marriage rituals among the Karans of Midnapur – A preliminary study. *Bulletin of the Cultural Research Institute, West Bengal*. Vol. 15. No. 1 and 2, 1980.

——, Concept of religion in a rural fringe. In *Current Anthropological Perspectives*, (ed.) K. L. Bhowmick. Inter-India Publication, New Delhi, 1986.

Majumdar, D. N., Some ethnographic notes on the Hos of Kolhan. *Man in India*. Vol. 5, No. 3 and 4, pp. 185-192, 1925.

——, The Pollas, Babupolias, Palias or Rajbanshi: An instance of the conversion of tribes into castes in Bengal. *Man in India*. Vol. 6, pp.155-173, 1926.

——, *The Fortunes of Primitive Tribes*. Universal Publication, Lucknow, 1944.

——, Religious life of the Ho. *Man in India*. Vol. 34, No. 4, 1954.

——, Blood groups of the tribes and castes of Bengal. *Sankhya*. Vol. 19, pp. 319-323, 1958.

Majumdar, D. N. and N. Kishen, Report on the serological survey of the United Provinces. *The Eastern Anthropologist*. Vol. 1, pp. 8-15, 1947.

Majumdar, D. N. and C. R. Rao, *Race Elements in Bengal: A Quantitative Study*, Indian Statistical Series-3, Asia Publishing House, Calcutta, 1960.

Majumdar, P. P., B. Roy, S. Banerjee, M. Chakraborty, B. Dey, N. Mukherjee, M. Roy, P. Guha-Thakurta, and S. K. Sil, Human-specific insertion/deletion polymorphisms in Indian populations and their possible evolutionary implications. *European Journal of Human Genetics*. Vol. 7, pp. 435-446, 1999.

Majumdar, P. P. and J. Roy, Distribution of ABO blood groups on the Indian Subcontinent: A cluster analytic approach. *Current Anthropology*. Vol. 23, No. 5, pp. 539-566, 1982.

Majumdar, S., Folklore of the Lepchas. *Folklore*. Vol. 2, No. 5, pp. 294-297, 1961.

Majumdar, R. C., Evolution of religio-philosophic cultures in India. In *The Cultural Heritage of India,* Vol. 4, pp. 31-62, (ed.), H. Bhattacharya. The Ramakrishna Mission Institute of Culture, Calcutta, 1956,

Malhotra, S. P., Birhor folk tales on their economic life. *Vanyajati*. Vol. 7, 1959.

Miller, R., High altitude mountaineering cash economy and the Sherpa. *Human Organisation*. Vol. 24, No. 3, pp. 244-249, 1965.

Mishra, S. C., *Muslim Communities in India*. Asia Publishing House, Bombay, 1964.

Mitra, A., Dhimal Samaj, Jeevan-O-Sanskriti (in Bengali). *Manab Bijnan Patrika Howrah*. Vol. 1, No. 1, pp. 34-36, 1988.

Mitra, A. K., Physical anthropology of the Muslims of Bengal. *Bulletin of the Department of Anthropology*. Govt. of India, Vol. 1, No. 2, pp. 79-104, 1952.

Mitra, Ashok, The Tribes and Castes of West Bengal, *Census of India, 1951*. Superintendent, Govt.Printing, Bengal Government Press, Alipore, Calcutta 1953.

Mitra, K., A Munda folktale. *Man in India*. Vol. 38, No. 2 and 3, pp. 153-162, 1938.

Mitra, V. and Main S., Bhadu ballads. *Indian Folklore*. Vol. 2, No. 2, pp. 64-71, 1957.

Mohanty, U. C., Traditional officials of Kisan Society. *Adibasi*. No. 1, pp. 56-60, 1963-64.

——, Kisan. *Adibasi*. No. 2, pp. 45-50, 1963-64.

——, Change in the leadership pattern in Kisan society. *Adibasi*. No. 2, pp. 52-60, 1963-64.

Morant, A. E., A. C. Koper and K Domanieswka Sobezak, *The ABO Blood Groups, Comprehensive Tables and Maps of World Distribution*, Blackwell Scientific Publications, Oxford, 1958.

Morris, C. J., *The Gurkhas: An Ethnology*. B. R. Publishing Corporation, Delhi, 1933. (reprinted in 1985).

Mukherjee, B. N., P. Sauber, H. Walter and K. C. Malhotra, Isoelectrofocusing in the detection of extended genetic polymorphism of PGM in ten endogamous groups of West Bengal and Orissa. In *Proceedings of the International Symposium of Recent Trends of Immunohaematology*. Indian Council of Medical Research, pp. 182-188, New Delhi, 1982.

Mukherjee, B., Rajbanshi kinship system. *Bulletin of the Anthropological Survey of India*. Vol 11, No. 1, pp. 47-56, 1962.

——, Socio-economic and religions organization of the Rajbanshi. *Bulletin of the Anthropological Survey of India.* Vol. 12, No. 1 and 2, pp. 65-80, 1963.

——, Santal in relation to Indian castes. *Man in India*, Vol. 40, No 4, pp. 300-306, 1960.

Mukherjee, C., The Santals. A Mukherjee & Co Pvt. Ltd., Calcutta, 1943 (revised edition in 1962).

Mukherjee, D. P., *Quantitative Genetics of Dermal Ridges with Special Reference to an Indian Population*. Ph. D Thesis, London University, London, 1970.

Mukherjee, Meera, *Metal Craftsmen of India*. Anthropological Survey of India, Calcutta 1978.

Mukherjee, P. N., The great migration of 1971. *Economic and Political Weekly.* Vol. 29, Nos. 9-11, 1971.

Mukherjee, S., The Oraons of North 24-Parganas. *Bulletin of the Cultural Research Institute, West Bengal.* 1965.

Mukhopadhyay, C., *Kharia : The Victim of Social Stigma*. K.P. Bagchi and Co., Calcutta, 1998.

Mukhopadhyay, S., *A Profile of Sundarban Tribes*. Firma KLM Pvt. Ltd., Calcutta, 1976.

Mukhopadhyay, T., A note on the Paliyas of West Dinajpur. *Man in India*. Vol. 45, No. 3, pp. 233-236, 1965.

Mundri, L. S., A comparative analysis of the economic aspects of the Munda culture. *Vanyajati*. Vol. 4, 1956.

Mundri, L. S., A Munda birth. *Man in India*. Vol. 36, No. 1, pp. 56-72, 1956.

Musleah, R. E. N., *On the Banks of the Ganga: The Sojourn of Jews in Calcutta*. The Christopher Publishing House, North Quiney, Massachusetts, U. S. A., 1975.

Nag, K., Brahmo Samaj. In *The Cultural Heritage of India*. Vol. 4, pp. 613-633, (ed.), H. Bhattacharya, The Ramakrishna Mission Institute of Culture, Calcutta, 1956.

Nakatani, T., Refugees. In *The Oxford Indian Companion to Sociology and Social Anthropology*. Vol. I, pp. 283-302 (ed), V. Das, Oxford University Press, New Delhi, 2003.

Nandi, (Basu), Arati., *Mundas in Transition: A Study in Cultural Geography*. Paritosh Nandi, Calcutta. 1993

Nandi, S. B., Cultural changes in an Oraon village. *Vanyajati*. Vol. 8, No. 1, pp. 12-20, 1960.

Narjinari, H. C., *In search of Identity* : *The Mech*. B. B. Prakashan, Calcutta. 1985.

Nath, R.G., A Survey of Caitanya Movement. In *The Cultural Heritage of India*. Vol. 4, pp. 186-200 (ed.), H. Bhattacharya, The Ramakrishna Mission Institute of Culture, Calcutta, 1956.

Nebesky-Wojwkowit and Renede. Hunting and fishing among the Lepchas. *Ethnos*. Vol. 18, pp. 18-30. 1953.

Nehru, Jawaharlal, Foreword. In *History of Bengali Literature*. pp. v-viii, Sahitya Academy, New Delhi, 1960.

O'Malley, L. S. S., *Bengal District Gazetteers*. Midnapur. Bengal Secretariat Book Depot, Calcutta, 1901.

——, *Bengal District Gazetteers*. Bankura. Bengal Secretariat Book Depot, Calcutta, 1908.

——, *Bengal District Gazetteers*. Birbhum. Bengal Secretariat Book Depot, Calcutta, 1910.

——, *Bengal District Gazetteers*. Hooghly district. Bengal Secretariat Book Depot, Calcutta, 1912.

——, *Census of India, 1911, Vol. 5. Bengal, Bihar and Orissa and Sikkim. Part-1, Report*. Bengal Secretariat Book Depot, Calcutta. 1913.

——, *Bengal District Gazetteers, Murshidabad*. Bengal Secretariat Book Depot, Calcutta, 1914.

O'Malley, L. S. S. and Chakravarty M., *Bengal District Gazetteers, Howrah*. Bengal Secretariat Book Depot, Calcutta, 1909.

Pal, M. K., *Crafts and Craftsmen in Traditional India*. Kanak Publications, New Delhi. 1978.

Panchbhai, S. C., The voluntary institution of the Marwaries in Calcutta–Some social psychological observations. In *Aspects of Society and Culture in Calcutta*. (ed.), M. K. A. Siddiqui, Anthropological Survey of India, Calcutta, 1982.

Paterson J. C. K., *Bengal District Gazetteers, Burdwan*. Bengal Secretariat Book Depot, Calcutta, 1910.

Patra, C., *Present Buddhist Tribals and Vihar in West Bengal*. Sarkar and Co., Calcutta, 1991.

Piplai Chumki, K. Vasantha, A. C. Gorakshaker, H. M. Bhatia and S. K. Bhattacharya, A note on ABO, MN, Rh and In(a) blood groups of the Tamang and Oraon tea labourer of the Jalpaiguri district. *Journal of the Indian Anthropological Society*. Vol. 20, pp. 66-70, 1985.

Planning Commission, Govt. of India, *National Human Development Report, 2001*, Oxford, New Delhi, 2002.

Porter A. E., *Census of India, 1931, Bengal and Sikkim*. Vol. 5, Part 1, Central Publication Branch, Calcutta, 1932.

——, *Census of India, 1931, Bengal and Sikkim*, Vol. 5, Part 1, Appendix 1, The Depress Classes, Central Publication Branch, Calcutta, pp. 494-513, 1933.

Pradhan, R. K., Ho. *Adibasi*. No. 3, pp. 167-170. 1963-64.

Pramanik, P., Marriage among the Buddhist Lepchas. *Vanyajati*. Vol. 5, 1957.

Prasad, N., *Land and People of Tribal Bihar*, Bihar Tribal Research Institute, Ranchi, 1961.

Raha, M. K., A note on the change in the magico-religious beliefs and practices of the Oraons. *Bulletin of the Cultural Research Institute, West Bengal*. Vol. 1, No. 2, pp. 9-12, 1962.

——, The Rabhas of West Bengal. *Bulletin of the Cultural Research Institute, West Bengal*. Vol. 1, No. 3, 1962.

——, Festivals of Oraons of Sunderban. *Folklore*. Vol. 5, No. 2, pp. 50-57, 1964.

——, The Khairas of Bankura. *Bulletin of the Cultural Research Institute, West Bengal*. Vol. 3, No. 1, pp. 41-46, 1964.

——, *Matriliny to Patriliny : A Study of the Rabha Society*, Gian Publishing House, New Delhi, 1989.

Raha, M. K., A. K. Das and S. K. Banerjee, Lepchader Lokhnritya O Oraonder Lokgeeti (in Bengali). *Lokyana*. Vol. 3, No. 1. 1957.

Ram, R., Bhangi : A study in magic in medicine. *Vanyajati*. Vol. 3, No. 2, pp.67-72, 1959.

——, The Nagesia. *Vanyajati*. Vol. 7, 1959.

Rana, K., A. Rafique and A. Sengupta, (with an Introduction by Amartya Sen), *The Pratichi Education Report*, Pratichi (India) Trust, Delhi, 2002.

Ray B., *Census of India, 1961, District Census Handbook, Twentyfour Parganas,* Government, West Bengal, Calcutta, 1961

Ray, G. S., and B. M. Das., An Oraon death ceremony. *Man in India*, Vol. 33, No. 3, 1953.

Ray, G. S., G. Chattopadhyay and B. Banerjee, Religious beliefs of the Hos. *Man-in-India*. Vol. 34, No. 4, pp. 288-299, 1954.

Ray, H. M., *Savara: The Snake Charmer*. Institute of Social Research and Applied Anthropology, Calcutta, 1986.

Ray, M. *The Bauls of Birbhum*. Firma KLM Pvt. Ltd., Calcutta, 1994.

Ray, Niharranjan, *History of the Bengali People (Ancient Period)*. Translated by John. W. Hood, Orient Longman, Calcutta, 1994 .

Raychoudhuri, T. C., The racial problem of Bengal, Presidential Address, Section of Anthropology and Archaeology. *Proceedings of the 39th Session of Indian Science Congress*. Part-II, pp. 169-188, Indian Science Congress Association, Calcutta 1952. (reprinted in 1952, *Man in India*, Vol. 32, No. 2, pp. 52-63)

Reddy, B. M., and V. P. Chopra, Opportunity for natural selection among the Indian populations. *American Journal of Physical Anthropology*. Vol. 83, No. 3, pp. 281-296, 1990.

Risley, H. H., *The Tribes and Castes of Bengal*. Vols. 1 and 2, Bengal Secretariat Press, Calcutta, 1891. (reprinted in 1981, Firma Mukhopadhyay, Calcutta.)

——, *The People of India*. Thacker, Spink & Co., Calcutta, 1915.

Roy, Annada Shankar, *Setubandhan*. (in Bengali) Ananda Publishers, Calcutta, 1996.

Roy, B. K., *Census of India, 1981, Regional Division of India : A Cartographic Analysis, Occasional Papers, Vol. 23, Series 1, West Bengal,* Registrar General and Census Commissioner, Delhi, 1989.

Roy, G. S., A study of the physical characteristics of Rajbanshis. *Journal of the Royal Asiatic Society of Bengal*, Letters. Vol. 12, pp. 31-42. 1946.

Roy, J., Economic and social customs of the Rajbanshis. *Modern Review*. Vol. 96, pp. 129-136. 1954.

Roy, J. K. and B. C. Roy, *Nutritional Background and Growth of Infants: A Major District of West Bengal*. Anthropological Survey of India, Calcutta 1969.

Roy, M. and S. R. Das Blood groups and genetic survey among the Poundra Kshatriya caste of 24-Parganas district of West Bengal. *Journal of the Indian Anthropological Society*. Vol. 8, pp. 83-86, 1973.

Roy, Manjushree, Leisure its utilisation in a Munda village. *Bulletin of the Cultural Research Institute, West Bengal*. Vol. 4, 1965.

Roy, Nihar Ranjan, *Bangalir Itihasa Adiparva* (in Bengali). Book Emporium, Calcutta. 1949-50.

Roy, P. C., *The Lodha and Their Spirit Possessed Men. A Psychological Study*. Anthropological Survey of India, Calcutta, 1965.

Roy, S. C., *The Mundas and Their Country*. Calcutta. City Book Society. 1912.

——, A note on totemism amongst the Asurs. *Journal of the Bihar and Orissa Research Society*. Vol. 4, pp. 307-321, 1918.

——, A new religious movement among the Oraons. *Man in India*, Vol. 1, No. 4, pp. 267-324, 1921.

——, The Gods of the Oraons. *Man in India*. Vol. 2, pp. 137-157, 1922.

——, The Asurs–ancient and modern, *Journal of the Bihar and Orissa Research Society*. Vol. 12, pp. 147-152, 1926.

Roy, S. C. and R. C. Roy, *The Hill Kharias. Man in India*. Ranchi, 1937.

Roy, U. K., A seminomadic tribe of West Bengal. *Bulletin of the Cultural Research Institute, West Bengal*. Vol. 12, No. 1 and 2, pp. 8-14, 1976.

Roy Burman, B. K., Drama of two drums. Mayu festival of the Totos. *Folklore*. Vol. 2, No. 1, pp. 16-31. 1957.

——, Structure of bridge and buffer communities in the border areas. *Man in India*. Vol. 46, No. 2, pp. 103-107, 1966.

Roy Chaudhary, B., *The Moon and the Net : Study of a Transient community of Fishermen at Jambudwip*. Anthropological Survey of India, Calcutta, 1980.

Roy Chaudhary, B. and B. Roy Chaudhary, *The Brahmans of Bengal : A Textual Study*. Anthropological Survey of India, Calcutta, 1981.

Roy Choudhury, D., Palmer dermatoglyphics of the Rajbanshis of Midnapur, West, Bengal. *Anthropologist*. Vol. 9, pp. 31-38, 1962.

Roychoudhuri, B. K., The Mahalis. *Bulletin of the Cultural Research Institute, West Bengal*. Vol. 1, No. 3, 1962.

Roychoudhuri, P. C., The Mahalis. *Modern Review*. Vol. 116 (Dec.), pp. 466-470. 1964.

Roychoudhury, B. K., The Birhors. *Bulletin of the Cultural Research Institute, West Bengal*. Vol. 3, No. 1, pp. 19-30, 1964.

Roychoudhury, B. K. and B. N. Chatterjee, A note of the progress of secondary education among the S. C. and S. T. of West Bengal. *Bulletin of the Cultural Research Institute, West Bengal*. Vol. 1, Nos. 1 and 2, Calcutta, 1966.

Russel, R. V. and Hiralal, *The Tribes and Castes of the Central Provinces of India*. Cosmo Publication, Delhi, 1916. (reprinted in 1975).

Saha, N., S. P. Bhattacharya, B. Mukhopadhyay, S. K. Bhattacharya, R. Gupta and A. Basu, A genetic study among the Lepchas of the Darjeeling area of eastern India. *Human Heredity*. Vol. 37, pp. 113-121, 1987.

Sahitya Akademi, *Contemporary Indian Literature*, Sahitya Akademi, New Delhi, 1997

Sahu, L. N., A Bhumija song. *Man in India*. Vol. 23, pp. 34-35, 1943.

——, Bhumija marriage. *Man in India*, Vol. 23, No. 2, pp. 173-174, 1943.

Sanyal, C. C., The Totos. *Man in India*, Vol. 27, pp. 174-176, 1947.

——, Notes on folklore of Rajbansis of Bengal. *Folklore*. Vol. 7, No. 1, pp. 50-51, 1956.

——, *The Rajbansis of North Bengal*. The Asiatic Society, Calcutta, 1965.

——, The Totos : A sub Himalayan tribe. *Journal of the Asiatic Society of Bengal*. Vol. 21, No. 1, pp. 57-126, 1979.

——, *The Mech and the Totos*, B. R. Publishing Corporation, New Delhi, 1979.

Sanyal, H. R., *Social Mobility in Bengal*, Papyrus, Calcutta, 1981.

Sapri, E., *Culture, Language and Personality: Selected Writings*. University of California, Berkley, 1962.

Sarkar, D., Dermatoglyphic study among three Bengali castes. *Man in India*. Vol. 49, pp. 80-92, 1969.

——, Finger dermatoglyphics of three populations from Nadia district, West Bengal. *Bulletin of the Anthropological Survey of India*. Vol. 16, pp. 139-153, 1967.

Sarkar, N. C., *Finger Ridge Minutiae: Classification, Distribution and Genetics*. Anthropological Survey of India. Memoir No. 111, Calcutta, 2004.

Sarkar, R. M., The religious activities of the Bauris and its modern trends. *Vanyajati*. Vol. 12, No. 1, pp. 32-40, 1964.

——, Further note on the Kakmaras. *Vanyajati*. Vol. 13, No. 4, pp. 161-164, 1965.

——, Bahubir sammelan : A case of social mobility movement. *The Eastern Anthropologist*, Vol. 19, pp. 225-229, 1966.

——, Profession of midwife and the Bauri women. *Vanyajati*. Vol. 15, No. 2, pp. 70-75, 1967.

Sarkar, S. S., B. M. Das and K. K. Agarwal, The Anglo-Indians of Calcutta. *Man in India*. Vol. 3, pp. 93-103, 1953.

Sen, B. K. and Jyoti Sen, Notes on the Birhors. *Man in India*, Vol. 35, No. 3, pp. 169-175, 1955.

Sen, D. C., *History of Bengali Language and Literature*. University of Calcutta, Calcutta, 1954.

Sen, D. K., Blood group distribution in India with special reference to Bengal. *Man in India*. Vol. 34, pp. 50-60, 1960.

——, Blood groups and haemoglobin variants in some upper castes of Bengal. *Journal of the Royal Anthropological Institute of Great Britain and Ireland*. Vol. 90, 1960.

——, Blood group investigation in the 24-Parganas district, West Bengal. *Man in India*. Vol. 34, 1954.

Sen, Jyoti, Anglo-Indians of Calcutta. *Human Science*. Vol. 32, No. 1, pp. 33-56, 1983.

Sen, Jyoti, and P. K. Dasgupta, *Ornaments in India*. Anthropological Survey of India. Memoir No. 22, Calcutta, 1973.

Sen, Tulika, *Growth and Development of Bengalee Girls*, Anthropological Survey of India, Calcutta, 1988.

Sen, Amartya, India Through its Calendars. *Proceedings of 62nd Indian History Congress*. pp. 9-18, Bhopal, 2001.

Sen, K., *Bangalir Sadhana* (in Bengali). Vishwa Bharati Granthalaya, Calcutta. 1352 B.S. (reprinted in 1360 B.S.).

Sen, S., The Natha Cult. In *The Cultural Heritage of India*. Vol.4, (ed.), H. Bhattacharya, The Ramakrishna Mission Institute of Culture, Calcutta, pp 280-290, 1956, (reprinted in 2001)

——, *History of Bengali Literature*. Sahitya Academi, New Delhi, 1960.

——, *The Santals : Crisis of Identity and Integration*. Ratna Publications, Calcutta, 1997.

Sengupta, A. K., Economic organisation of an Oraon village. *Vanyajati*. Vol. 13, No. 2, pp. 41-45, 1965.

Sengupta, S., *Bangalir Jibane Bibaha* (in Bengali). Indian Publications, Calcutta, 1974

Sengupta, Sadhan, Role of caste panchayat in an untouchable slum of Calcutta. *Journal of the Indian Anthropological Society*. Vol. 8, pp. 35-44, 1973,

——, The Hela caste in Calcutta. In *Aspects of Society and Culture in Calcutta*. (ed.) M. K. A. Siddiqui, Anthropological Survey of India, pp. 236-247, Calcutta, 1982,

Sengupta, S. C., *Census of India, 1961, Vol. 16, West Bengal, Part-6, Village Survey Monograph, Kodalia*. Supdt. of Census Operations, West Bengal and Sikkim, Calcutta, 1962.

Sengupta, S. K., *The Portrait of Mahali Economy in Midnapur*. Edition Indian, Calcutta, 1965.

——, Some aspects of life cycle of social contact of the Mahali of Midnapur. *Vanyajati*. Vol. 15, No. 2, pp. 56-61, 1967.

——, The Mahali clan organization. *Bulletin of the Cultural Research Institute, West Bengal*. Vol. 6, Nos. 1 and 2, pp. 19-28, 1967.

——, The structure and composition of the Mahali families. *Bulletin of the Cultural Research Institute, West Bengal*. Vol. 7, No. 1 and 2, 1968.

——, *The Social Profiles of the Mahalis*, Firma K. L. Mukhopadhayay, Calcutta, 1972.

Shasmal, K. C., Hindu religious ideas and beliefs as adopted by the Mundas of Sunderban. *Vanyajati*. Vol. 11, No. 2, pp. 75-79, 1963.

——, De-tribalisation of the Mundas of Sundarban. *Vanyajati*. Vol. 11, No. 4, pp. 164-168, 1963.

——, The worship of Bhadu and Barabhum among the Bauris of Hooghly district. *Folklore*. July, pp. 285-290, 1964.

——, Villages and demographic aspect of the Bauris of Hooghly district. *Vanyajati*. Vol. 13, No. 4, pp. 137-142, 1965.

——, Bauri : The role of artificial relationship towards growth of social solidarity. *Vanyajati*. Vol. 14, No. 1, pp. 3-7, 1966.

——, Economic condition of Bauri of West Bengal. *Khadi Gramodyog*. Vol. 13, No. 3, pp. 402-405, 1967.

——, *The Bauris of West Bengal*, Indian Publication, Calcutta, 1972.

Siddiqui, M. K. A., *Muslims of Calcutta*, Anthropological Survey of India, Calcutta, 1974.

Singh K. S., *The Dust, Storm and Hanging Mist : Story of Birsa Munda and Movement*. Firma K. L. M. Calcutta, 1966.

——, Ethnography old and new, *Journal of Anthropological Survey of India*. Vol. 40, pp. 1-9, 1991.

——, *People of India, Introduction* (Revised Edition), Anthropological Survey of India, Oxford University Press, 2002.

Singh, K. S., and P. P. Mahato, Mahato-Kurmi mobility movement: A preliminary appraisal. In *Tribal Movement in India*, Vol. 1, (ed.), K. S. Singh, Manohar Publications, Delhi, 1982.

Singh, K. S., V. Bhalla and V. Kaul, *The Biological Variation in Indian Population*. People of India, National Series, Volume-10, Oxford University Press, New Delhi, 1994.

Singh, R. L., *India : A Regional Geography*. National Geographical Society of India, Varanasi, 1991.

Sinha, D., *The Hill Kharias of Purulia–A Study on the Impact of Poverty on a Hunting and Gathering Tribe*. Anthropological Survey of India, Memoir No. 59, Calcutta, 1984.

Sinha, S., The media and nature of Hindu-Bhumij interaction. *Journal of the Asiatic Society, Letters and Science*. Vol. 23, No. 1, 1957.

——, Training of a Bhumij medicine man. *Man in India*. Vol. 38, No. 2, 1958.

——, Changes in the cycle of festivals in Bhumij village. *Journal of Social Research*. Vol. I, No.1, pp. 24-29, 1958

——, Bhumij Kshatriya movement in South Manbhum. *Bulletin of the Anthropological Survey of India*. Vol. 8, No.2. pp. 9 - 32, 1959,

——, (ed.) Agriculture, Craft and Weekly Market of South Manbhum, *Bulletin of the Anthropological Survey of India*. Vol. 10, No. 1. 1961.

——, State formation and Rajput myth in tribal central India. *Man In India*. Vol. 42, No. 1, pp. 36-80, 1962.

——, Tribe-caste and tribe-peasant continua in central India. *Man In India*. Vol. 45, No. 1, pp. 57-83, 1965.

——, Time space and ethnicity: Field study among the Bhuimij of Barabhum. In *Field Studies on the People of India: Methods and Perspectives*. (ed.), S. Sinha, Indian Anthropological Society, Calcutta, pp. 149-154, 1978.

——, *Tribes and Indian Civilization : Structure and Transformation*. N. K. Bose Memorial Foundation, Varanasi, 1981.

Sinha, S., and R. K. Bhattacharya, *Bhadralok* and *Chhotolok* in rural area of Bengal. *Sociological Bulletin*. Vol. 18, No. 1, pp. 50-56, 1969.

Srivastava, R. P., Rang-bang in the changing Bhotia life. *The Eastern Anthropologist*. Vol. 6, No. 3 and 4, pp. 190-203, 1952-53.

——, Marriage and divorce among the eastern Bhotia. *Anthropologist*. Vol. 4, pp. 34-43, 1957.

Stark, H. A., *Hostages to India*. The Calcutta Fine Art College, Calcutta. 1962.

Subba, T. B., *Dynamics of a Hills Society, (The Nepalese in Darjeeling and Sikkim Himalayas)*. Mittal Publication, Delhi, 1989.

Talukdar, (Poddar), Susmita, Selection intensity in two Bagdi groups of 24-Parganas, West Bengal. *Journal of the Indian Anthropological Society*. Vol. 6, pp. 131-133, 1971,

Thakur, K., *Matua Andolan O Banglar Anunnato Samaj* (in Bengali). Harichand Mission, Bamangachi, 1994.

Thompson, W. H., *Census of India, 1921, Bengal*. Vol. 5, Part-1, Bengal Secretariat Book Depot, Calcutta, 1923.

Timberg, J. A., The Jews of Calcutta. In *Jews in India*. (ed.) J.A. Timberg, Vikash Publishing House, New Delhi, 1986.

Upreti, H. C., Bhotia dormitory : A sociological analysis. *Bulletin of the Tribal Research and Training Institute*. Vol. 5, Nos. 1 and 2. Bhopal, 1965.

Vasu, N. N., The Castes and Sects of Bengal, Calcutta, 1936.

Verma, V. S., *Census of India. 1981. Regional Division of India–A Cartographic Analysis*. Vol. 23, Series-1, West Bengal. Registrar General and Census Commissioner, New Delhi. 1988.

Weber, Max, *Wirtschaft und Geselleschaft*, 1972

Wentz, W. Y. E., *The Tibetian Book of the Dead*. Oxford University Press. London. 1957.

Xaxa, V., Tribes in India. In *The Oxford Indian Companion to Sociology and Social Anthropology*. (ed.), V. Das, Vol. I, pp. 373-408, Oxford University Press, New Delhi, 2003,

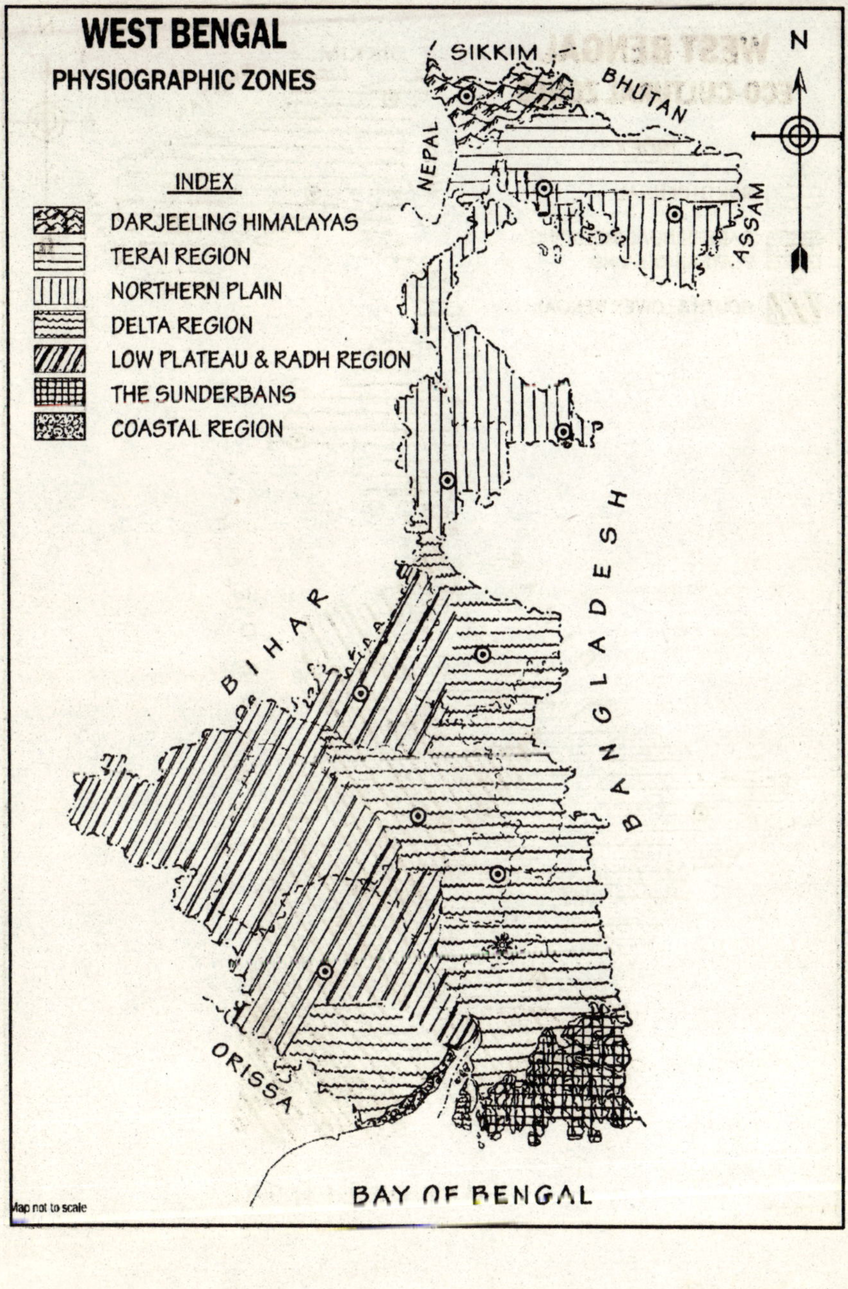
WEST BENGAL
PHYSIOGRAPHIC ZONES
INDEX
DARJEELING HIMALAYAS
TERAI REGION
NORTHERN PLAIN
DELTA REGION
LOW PLATEAU & RADH REGION
THE SUNDERBANS
COASTAL REGION
N
SIKKIM
BHUTAN
NEPAL
ASSAM
BANGLADESH
BIHAR
ORISSA
BAY OF BENGAL
Map not to scale

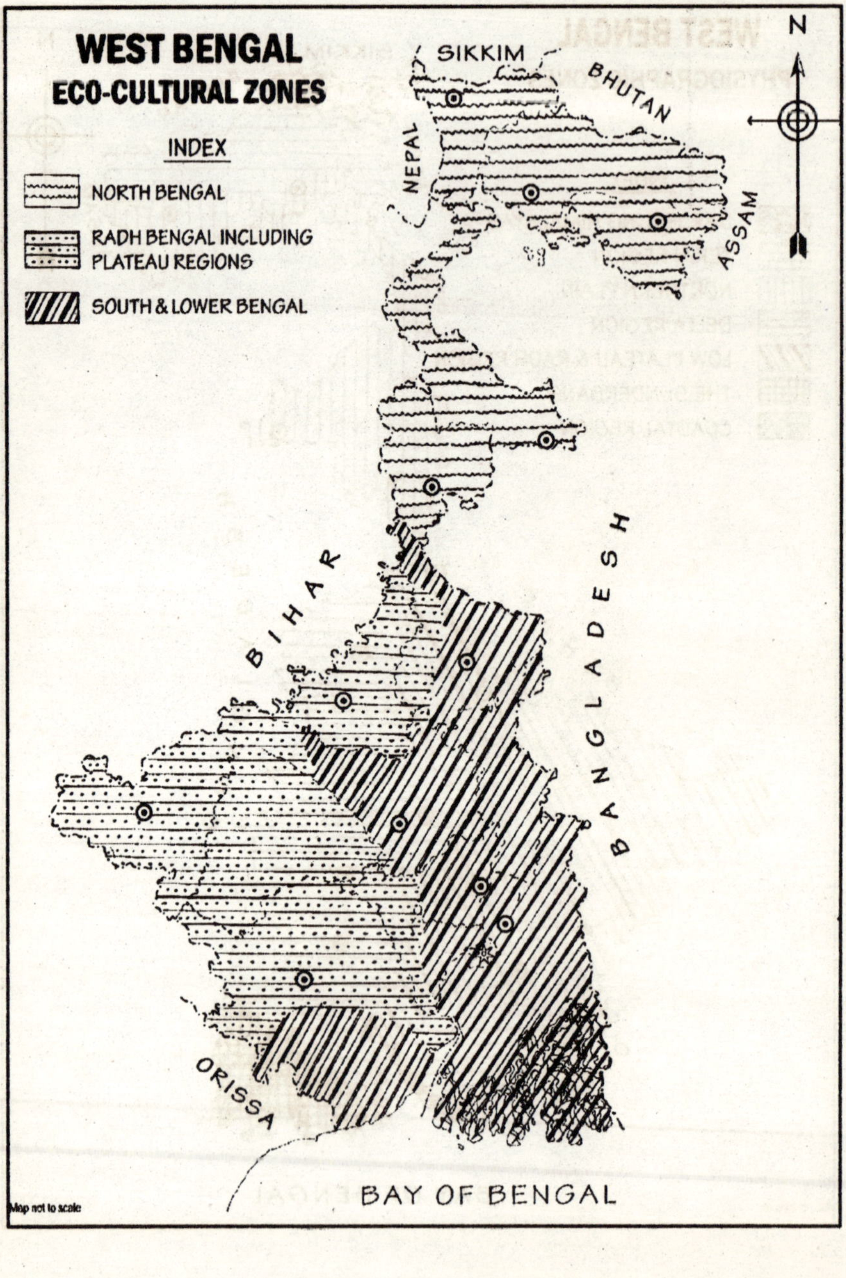
WEST BENGAL
ECO-CULTURAL ZONES
INDEX
NORTH BENGAL
RADH BENGAL INCLUDING PLATEAU REGIONS
SOUTH & LOWER BENGAL
N
SIKKIM
BHUTAN
NEPAL
ASSAM
BIHAR
BANGLADESH
ORISSA
BAY OF BENGAL
Map not to scale

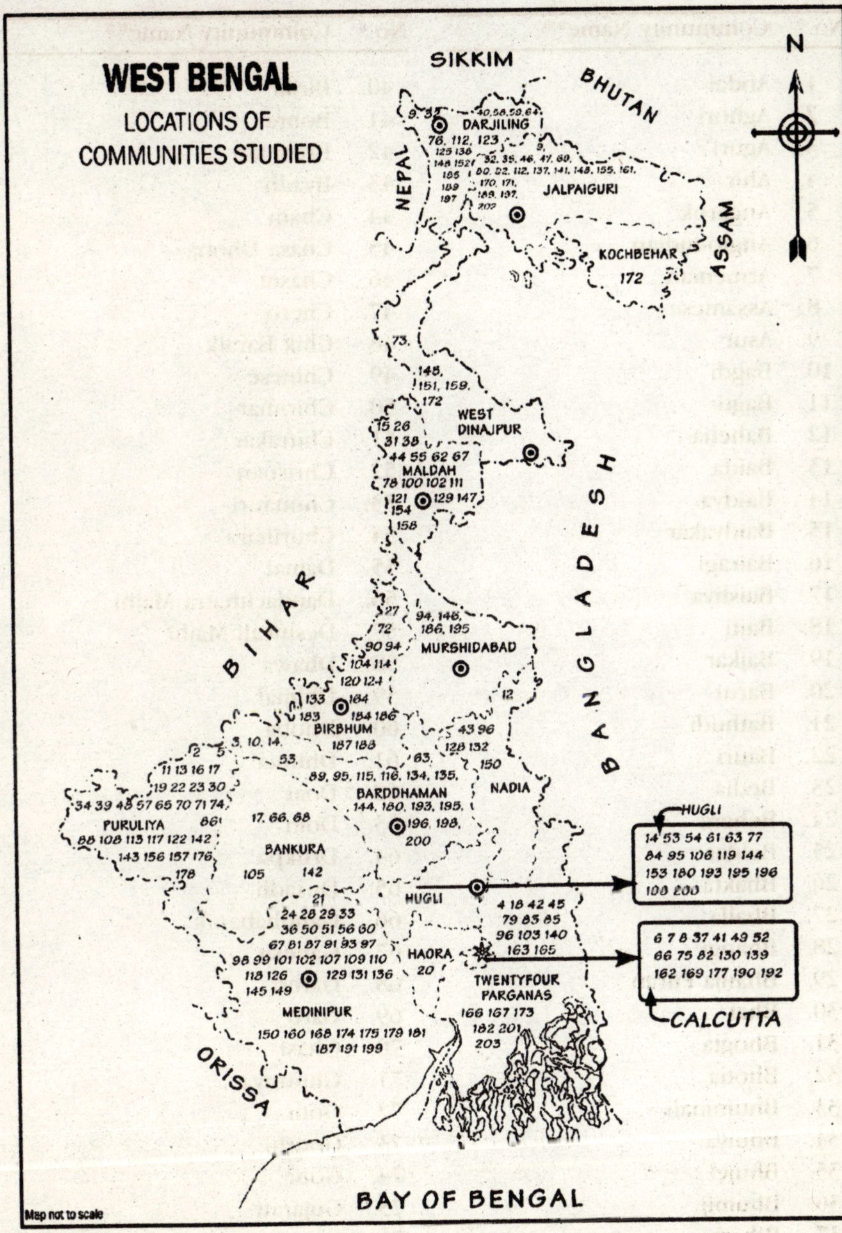
WEST BENGAL
LOCATIONS OF
COMMUNITIES STUDIED
N
SIKKIM
BHUTAN
NEPAL
DARJILING
JALPAIGURI
ASSAM
KOCHBEHAR
172
73
WEST
DINAJPUR
MALDAH
B I H A R
B A N G L A D E S H
MURSHIDABAD
BIRBHUM
BARDDHAMAN
NADIA
PURULIYA
BANKURA
HUGLI
14 53 54 61 63 77
84 95 106 119 144
153 180 193 195 196
198 200
HAORA
20
6 7 8 37 41 49 52
66 75 82 130 139
162 169 177 190 192
CALCUTTA
TWENTYFOUR
PARGANAS
166 167 173
182 201
203
MEDINIPUR
150 160 168 174 175 179 181
187 191 199
ORISSA
BAY OF BENGAL
Map not to scale

LIST OF COMMUNITIES

No.*	Community Name**
1.	Abdal
2.	Aghori
3.	Aguri
4.	Ahir
5.	Angarok
6.	Anglo-indian
7.	Armenian
8.	Assamese
9.	Asur
10.	Bagdi
11.	Bagti
12.	Bahelia
13.	Baida
14.	Baidya
15.	Baidyakar
16.	Bairagi
17.	Baishya
18.	Baiti
19.	Bajkar
20.	Barui
21.	Bathudi
22.	Bauri
23.	Bedia
24.	Behera
25.	Beldar
26.	Bhakta
27.	Bhalla
28.	Bhangi
29.	Bhanja Puran
30.	Bhat
31.	Bhogta
32.	Bhotia
33.	Bhuinmali
34.	Bhuiya
35.	Bhujel
36.	Bhumij
37.	Bihari
38.	Bin/Bind
39.	Birhor
40.	Birjia
41.	Bohra
42.	Brahman
43.	Byadh
44.	Chain
45.	Chasa Dhoba
46.	Chasot
47.	Chero
48.	Chik Baraik
49.	Chinese
50.	Chirimar
51.	Chitrakar
52.	Christian
53.	Chunauri
54.	Churihara
55.	Damai
56.	Dandachhatra Majhi
57.	Deshwali Majhi
58.	Dhawa
59.	Dhimal
60.	Dhoba
61.	Dhunia
62.	Doai
63.	Dom
64.	Drukpa
65.	Dusadh
66.	Gandhabanik
67.	Ganesh
68.	Gareri
69.	Garo
70.	Ghasi
71.	Ghunnya
72.	Gonr
73.	Gonrhi
74.	Gour
75.	Gujarati
76.	Gurung
77.	Hajjam
78.	Hari

No.*	Community Name**
79.	Hela
80.	Ho
81.	Jalia-kaibarta
82.	Jews
83.	Jhalo Malo
84.	Jola
85.	Jugi
86.	Kahar
87.	Kakmara
88.	Kalal
89.	Kalu
90.	Kalwar
91.	Kamar
92.	Kami
93.	Kandra
94.	Kandu (Kanu)
95.	Kansari
96.	Kapali
97.	Kapuria
98.	Karan
99.	Karanga
100.	Kawar
101.	Kayastha
102.	Kela
103.	Keora
104.	Keot
105.	Khaira
106.	Khalifa
107.	Khandait
108.	Kharia (Hill)
109.	Kharwar
110.	Khatik
111.	Khen
112.	Kisan
113.	Koeri
114.	Konai
115.	Kora
116.	Kotal
117.	Kudmi
118.	Kumhar
119.	Kunjra
120.	Kunui
121.	Kurol
122.	Lalbegi
123.	Lepcha
124.	Let
125.	Limbu
126.	Lodha
127.	Lohar
128.	Lohara
129.	Mahar
130.	Maharashtrian
131.	Mahishya
132.	Mahli
133.	Mal
134.	Malakar
135.	Malhar
136.	Mali
137.	Malpaharia
138.	Mangar
139.	Marwari
140.	Mayara
141.	Mech
142.	Mete
143.	Mirshikar
144.	Muchi
145.	Munda
146.	Musahar
147.	Nagar
148.	Nagesia
149.	Namasudra
150.	Napit
151.	Nat
152.	Newar
153.	Nikari
154.	Nuniya
155.	Oraon
156.	Oriya
157.	Pahariya
158.	Pakhimara
159.	Paliya
160.	Pan
161.	Parja/Porja
162.	Parsi

No.*	Community Name**
163.	Pasi
164.	Pathan
165.	Patikar
166.	Patni
167.	Pod
168.	Portuguese
169.	Punjabi
170.	Rabha
171.	Rai
172.	Rajbanshi
173.	Rajput
174.	Rajput Solanki
175.	Raju
176.	Rajwar
177.	Rangrez
178.	Rautia
179.	Sabar/Savara
180.	Sadgop
181.	Sahis
182.	Sankhakara
183.	Santal
184.	Sarak
185.	Sarki
186.	Sayyad
187.	Shah Or Shah Faqir
188.	Sheik
189.	Sherpa
190.	Sikh
191.	Siyalgir
192.	South Indian
193.	Subarnabanik
194.	Sunri
195.	Sutradhar
196.	Swarnakar
197.	Tamang
198.	Tambuli
199.	Tanti
200.	Tili
201.	Tiyor
202.	Toto
203.	Turi

*The numbers here correspond to the numbers in the map 'Locations of Communities Studied' (p. 1331). ** Community name as given in text.

INDEX